APPLIED REGRESSION ANALYSIS

FOR BUSINESS AND ECONOMICS

THIRD EDITION

Terry E. Dielman

M. J. Neeley School of Business
Texas Christian University

DUXBURY

™

THOMSON LEARNING

Australia • Canada • Mexico • Singapore • Spain • United Kingdom • United States

DUXBURY

THOMSON LEARNING

Sponsoring Editor: *Curt Hinrichs*
Marketing Manager: *Karin Sandberg*
Marketing Assistant: *Beth Kroenke*
Editorial Assistant: *Emily Davidson*
Marketing Communications: *Samantha Cabaluna*
Production Editor: *Kirk Bomont*
Production Service: *Forbes Mill Press*
Manuscript Editor: *Frank Hubert*

Permissions Editor: *Sue Ewing*
Interior Design: *Robin Gold*
Cover Design: *Denise Davidson*
Cover Photo: *Photodisc*
Print Buyer: *Jessica Reed*
Typesetting: *Forbes Mill Press*
Cover Printing: *Phoenix Color Corporation*
Printing and Binding: *R.R. Donnelley, Crawfordsville*

MINITAB is a trademark of Minitab, Inc., and is used herein with the owner's permission. Portions of MINITAB Statistical Software input and output contained in this book are printed with permission of Minitab, Inc. Microsoft is a registered trademark of Microsoft Corporation. SAS is a registered trademark of SAS Institute Inc. All products used herein are used for indentification purposes only and may be trademarks or registered trademarks of their respective owners.

For more information about this or any other Duxbury products, contact:
DUXBURY
511 Forest Lodge Road
Pacific Grove, CA 93950 USA
www.duxbury.com
1-800-423-0563 (Thomson Learning Academic Resource Center)

For permission to use material from this work, contact us by
www.thomsonrights.com
fax: 1-800-730-2215
phone: 1-800-730-2214

Printed in the United States of America

10 9 8 7 6 5 4 3 2 1

Library of Congress Cataloging-in-Publication Data
Dielman, Terry E.
  Applied regression analysis for business and economics / Terry E. Dielman.--3rd ed.
        p. cm.
  Includes bibliographical references and index.
  ISBN 0 534-37955-9 (text)
  1. Economics--Statistical methods. 2. Commercial statistics. 3. Regression analysis. I.
Title.

HB137.D54 2001   00-034618
330'.01'51936--dc21

Contents

III

Preface

*A*pplied Regression Analysis for Business and Economics is designed for a one-semester course in regression analysis for business and economics undergraduates and MBAs. The goal of the text is to present regression concepts and techniques in a way that avoids unnecessary mathematical rigor. The emphasis is on understanding the assumptions of the regression model, knowing how to validate a selected model for these assumptions, knowing when and how regression might be useful in a business setting, and understanding and interpreting output from statistical packages and spreadsheets. The text presents output from the statistical package MINITAB and the spreadsheet Microsoft® Excel. In the Using the Computer section at the end of each chapter, the MINITAB and Excel procedures used to perform the analyses shown in the chapter are presented. In addition, SAS commands for the procedures are shown, although SAS output is not included in the text. A brief general introduction to MINITAB, Excel, and SAS is presented in Appendix C. Other statistical packages and spreadsheets containing regression procedures can also be easily used with the text.

Level and Prerequisites

To use the text, little mathematical expertise beyond basic college algebra is necessary. No knowledge of linear algebra is assumed. Appendix D does provide a summary of matrices and matrix operations and a brief introduction to the use of matrices in presenting the least-squares method for the interested reader. An introductory (or first semester) course in statistics is assumed. Chapter 2 does, however, contain a brief review of most of the concepts covered in an introductory statistics course.

It is assumed throughout the text that students have access to a computer and statistical software. The text concentrates on using the computer to do the calculations, but the student is responsible for knowing what to do with the resulting computer output. Although the text could be used without computer access, the author believes that actually analyzing data is an important component of the learning process.

Real Data

Actual data drawn from various sources are used throughout the book in the examples and exercises. When data are simulated, an attempt has been made to provide realistic data and situations in which these data might occur. In this way, the relevance of the techniques being presented is highlighted for students.

Data sets for the exercises in this text can be accessed by going to the Web site www.duxbury.com and selecting "Data Library." Select this textbook, and then select the file format needed. Available file formats include Excel, MINITAB, SAS, and SPSS. Filename prefixes needed to read the data are shown with each exercise. The filename prefixes are the same regardless of the format. Only the filename suffixes differ. More information on accessing the data files is available on the endsheets of the text.

Organization and Coverage

Chapter 2 provides a quick review of most concepts covered in a first-semester statistics course. Chapters 3 through 8 provide the material on linear regression. Chapter 3 introduces simple linear regression, including MINITAB and Excel regression output. Chapter 4 provides the extension to multiple linear regression. Chapter 5 discusses the fitting of curves with regression. Chapter 6 discusses the implications of violations of assumptions of the regression model, presents ways to recognize possible violations, and suggests corrections for violations. Chapter 7 describes the use of indicator and interaction variables. Chapter 8 discusses several techniques used to aid in selecting explanatory variables for the regression.

Chapters 9 and 10 can be viewed as optional in a course on linear regression. Chapter 9 presents a brief introduction to analysis of variance. One-way analysis of variance and its relationship to regression with indicator variables are discussed. The chapter concludes with an examination of randomized block designs and two-way complete factorial designs. Chapter 10 introduces two procedures that can be used when qualitative dependent variables are encountered: discriminant analysis and logistic regression. The chapter concentrates on the two-group case.

Changes in the Third Edition

These are the major changes in the third edition:

- Most of the data sets in the text have been updated. Additional problems and examples involving real data have been added to the text. Some of these data sets come from actual business settings, while others are taken from journals and popular publications.

- Excel output is included in addition to MINITAB output.

- Chapter 5 of the second edition has been split into two parts. These two parts now make up Chapters 5 and 6. The new Chapter 5 discusses fitting curves with regression. The new Chapter 6 discusses the implications of violations of assumptions of the regression model, presents ways to recognize possible violations, and suggests corrections for violations. Reviews of the second edition of the text suggested that Chapter 5 was too long and was somewhat unwieldy for students. In addition, this new structure allows the instructor to present curve-fitting as part of multiple regression rather than as a response to violation of an assumption. Reviews of the second edition indicated this was a desired option for many instructors.

Acknowledgments

I would like to thank those who reviewed the manuscript at various stages of the revision: Sudhakar Deshmukh, Northwestern University; David E. Booth, Kent State University; Walter J. Mayer, University of Mississippi; Jamie Eng, San Francisco State University; Djeto Assane, University of Nevada, Las Vegas; Mark Haggerty, Clarion University; and Mack C. Shelley, II, Iowa State University.

I would also like to express my appreciation to the staff and associates of Duxbury, especially Curt Hinrichs, Emily Davidson, Karin Sandberg, Beth Kroenke, Samantha Cabaluna, Kirk Bomont, Robin Gold, Vernon Boes, Denise Davidson, Sue Ewing, and Jessica Reed.

Finally, thanks to my wife, Karen, for her support, patience, and input throughout this process.

Terry E. Dielman
Fort Worth

CHAPTER 1

An Introduction to Regression Analysis

Advances in technology including computers, scanners, and telecommunications equipment have buried present-day managers under a mountain of data. Although the purpose of these data is to assist managers in the decision-making process, corporate executives who face the task of juggling data on many variables may find themselves at a loss when attempting to make sense of such information. The decision-making process is further complicated by the dynamic elements in the business environment and the complex interrelationships among these elements.

This text has been prepared to give managers (and future managers) tools for examining possible relationships between two or more variables. For example, sales and advertising are two variables commonly thought to be related. When a soft drink company increases advertising expenditures by paying professional athletes millions of dollars to do its advertisements, it expects this outlay to increase sales. In general, when decisions on advertising expenditures of millions of dollars are involved, it is comforting to have some evidence that, in the past, increased advertising expenditures indeed led to increased sales.

Another example is the relationship between the selling price of a house and its square footage. When a new house is listed for sale, how should the price be determined? Is a 4000-square-foot house worth twice as much as a 2000-square-foot house? What other factors might be involved in the pricing of houses and how should these factors be included in the determination of the price?

In a study of absenteeism at a large manufacturing plant, management may feel that several variables have an impact. These variables might include job complexity, base pay, the number of years the worker has been with the plant, and the age of that worker. If absenteeism can cost the company thousands of dollars, then the importance of identifying its associated factors becomes clear.

Perhaps the most important analytic tool for examining the relationships between two or more variables is regression analysis. *Regression analysis* is a statistical technique for developing an equation describing the relationship between two or more variables. One variable is specified to be the *dependent variable,* or the variable to be explained. The other one or more variables are called the *independent* or *explanatory variables.* Using the previous examples, the soft drink firm would identify sales as the dependent variable and advertising expenditures as the explanatory variable. The real estate firm would choose selling price as the dependent variable and size as the explanatory variable to explain variations in selling price from house to house.

There are several reasons business researchers might want to know how certain variables are related. The retail firm may want to know how much advertising is necessary to achieve a certain level of sales. An equation expressing the relationship between sales and advertising is useful in answering this question. For the real estate firm, the relationship might be used in assigning prices to houses coming onto the market. To try to lower the absenteeism rate, the management of the manufacturing firm wants to know what variables are most highly related to absenteeism. Reasons for wanting to develop an equation relating two or more variables can be classified as follows: (a) to describe the relationship, (b) for control purposes (what value of the explanatory variable is needed to produce a certain level of the dependent variable), or (c) for prediction.

Much statistical analysis is a multistage process of trial and error. A good deal of exploratory work must be done to select appropriate variables for study and to determine the relationships between or among them. This requires that a variety of statistical tests and other procedures be performed and sound judgments be made before one arrives at satisfactory choices of dependent and explanatory variables. The emphasis in this text is on this multistage process rather than on the computations themselves or an in-depth study of the theory behind the techniques presented. In this sense, the text is directed at the applied researcher or the consumer of statistics.

Except for a few preparatory examples, it is assumed that a computer is available to the reader to perform the actual computations. The use of statistical software frees the user to concentrate on the multistage "model-building" process.

Most examples use illustrative computer output to present the results. The two software packages used are MINITAB™ (Version 12) and Microsoft® Excel 2000. MINITAB is included because it is widely used as a teaching tool in universities and is also used in industry. Excel is included because it is the prevalent spreadsheet available in businesses throughout the world. In a business environment, not all managers have access to a statistical package, but nearly all have access to a spreadsheet package, and that package is usually Excel. Knowing how to perform statistical routines with Excel enables the manager without a statistical package to conduct some statistical analyses. The output from MINITAB and Excel is fairly standard and easily understood. Many of the exercises are intended to be done with the aid of a computer. Most statistical software packages or spreadsheets could be used for this purpose. Some of the options available in MINITAB and Excel may not be present in other packages, but this should not create a problem in completing the exercises.

One note of caution at this point: Excel is a spreadsheet and was not created specifically for statistical analysis. It can be useful for many analyses, but it cannot take the place of a true statistical package such as MINITAB or SAS®. If you are involved in a substantial amount of data analysis, I recommend using a statistical package rather than a spreadsheet for this purpose. Throughout this text, there are many examples of regression analysis where Excel and MINITAB are used on the same data set. In all cases in this text, Excel produces the same answers as MINITAB. I have, however, heard that on certain types of analyses of some data sets, Excel may fail to produce correct answers. The data sets where this occurs are likely to be those that impose a severe computational burden on Excel. I have not seen this occur personally with Excel 2000, but the reader is cautioned to make sure the results of any analysis make sense. Results that are contrary to intuition should be called into question and verified with a statistical package. There are also procedures that are useful in more advanced analyses that are not available in Excel. These require the use of a package specifically designed for statistical analysis.

Data sets for the exercises in this text are available on a Web site. Instructions for downloading the data files are given in the preface and on the endsheets of this text. Data sets are provided in either MINITAB files or Excel spreadsheets. In addition, SAS and SPSS files are provided for users of these statistical packages, and ASCII files are provided for general use in other packages. In each problem where data sets are provided, the file names required to read the data are given. The filenames are the same regardless of the file format. Only the file name suffixes differ.

A section called Using the Computer is included at the end of each chapter. The procedures used in MINITAB, Excel, and SAS to produce the statistical analyses discussed in each chapter are presented there. SAS is often the package of choice in industry for statistical analysis. SAS output has not been included in this edition of the text, but the output from SAS is very similar to that of MINITAB, and the interpretation of SAS output should be easily accomplished by students. Appendix C provides a brief, general discussion of the use of MINITAB, Excel, and SAS. This book, however, is not intended to provide full information on the use of these software packages. For further information on MINITAB, Excel, and SAS, the interested reader is referred to one of the following references:

Berk, K., and Carey, P. *Data Analysis with Microsoft® Excel.* Pacific Grove, CA: Duxbury Press, 2000.

Carver, R. *Doing Data Analysis with MINITAB™ 12.* Pacific Grove, CA: Duxbury Press, 1999.

Freund, R., and Littell, R. *SAS® System for Regression* (2nd ed.). Cary, NC: SAS Institute, 1991.

Lehmann, M., and Zeitz, P. *Statistical Explorations with Microsoft® Excel.* Pacific Grove, CA: Duxbury Press, 1998.

McKenzie, J., and Goldman, R. *The Student Edition of MINITAB™.* Reading, MA.: Addison-Wesley, 1998.

MINITAB User's Guide, Release 12 for Windows®. State College, PA: MINITAB™, Inc., February 1998.

Neufeld, J. *Learning Business Statistics with Microsoft® Excel.* Upper Saddle River, NJ: Prentice Hall, 1997.

CHAPTER 2

Review of Basic Statistical Concepts

2.1 INTRODUCTION

This chapter summarizes and reviews many of the basic statistical concepts taught in an introductory statistics course. For the most part, introductory courses in statistics deal with three main areas of interest: descriptive statistics, probability, and statistical inference.

Typically, the problem in statistics is one of studying a particular population. A *population*, for purposes of this text, may be defined as the collection of all items of interest to a researcher. The researcher may want to study the sales figures for firms in a particular industry, the rates of return on public utility firms, or the lifetimes of a new brand of automobile tires. But because of time limitations, cost, or the destructive nature of testing, it is not always possible to examine all elements in a population. Instead, a subset of the population, called a *sample*, is chosen, and the characteristic of interest is determined for the items in the sample.

Descriptive statistics is that area of statistics that summarizes the information contained in a sample. This summary may be achieved by condensing the information and presenting it in tabular form. For example, frequency distributions are one way to summarize data in a table. Graphical methods of summarizing data also may be used. The types of graphs discussed in introductory statistics courses include histograms, pie charts, bar charts, and scatterplots.

Data also may be summarized by numerical values. For example, to describe the center of a data set, the mean or median is often suggested. To describe variability, the variance, standard deviation, or interquartile range might be used. Each of the numerical values is a single number computed from the data that describes a certain characteristic of a sample.

Describing the information contained in a sample is only a first step for most statistical studies. If the study of a population's characteristics is the researcher's goal, then he or she wants to use the information obtained from the sample to make statements about the population. The process of generalizing from characteristics of a sample to those of a population is called *statistical inference*. The bridge leading from descriptive measures computed for a sample to inferences made about population characteristics is the field of probability.

Statistical sampling is an additional topic discussed in introductory statistics. By choosing the elements of a sample in a particular manner, objective evaluations can be made of the quality of the inferences concerning population characteristics. Without proper choice of a sample, inferences can be made, but there is no way to evaluate these generalizations objectively. Thus, the manner in which the sample is chosen is important.

The most common type of sampling procedure discussed in introductory statistics is simple random sampling. Suppose a sample of *n* items is desired. To qualify as a *simple random sample* (SRS), the items in the sample are selected so that each possible sample of size *n* is equally likely to be chosen. In other words, each possible sample has an equal probability of being the one actually chosen. This is one of the pieces of the bridge that links descriptive statistics and statistical inference. Another piece of the bridge is a description of the behavior of certain numerical summaries that are computed as descriptive statistics.

Any numerical summary computed from a sample is called a *statistic*. A researcher may compute a single statistic from one sample chosen from the population of interest and use the numerical value of this statistic to make a statement about the value of some population characteristic. For example, suppose a particular brand of tires is to be studied to determine their average life. If the average life is known, the tire company might use this information to establish a warranty for its tires. An SRS of *n* tires is chosen, and each tire is tested to determine its individual lifetime. Then the sample average lifetime is computed. This sample average can be used as an estimate of the population average lifetime of these tires.

The statistic computed, however, is the sample average lifetime for one particular sample of tires chosen. If a different set of *n* tires had been chosen, a different sample average would have resulted because of individual variation in the tires' lifetimes. Thus, the sample means themselves vary depending on which set of *n* tires is chosen as the sample. If this variation in the sample means was without any pattern, then there is no way to relate the value of the sample mean obtained to the unknown value of the population mean. Fortunately, the behavior of the sample means (and other statistics) from random samples is not without a pattern. The behavior of statistics is described by a concept called a *sampling distribution*. Probability enters the picture because sampling distributions are simply probability distributions. Through knowledge of the sampling distribution of a statistic, procedures can be developed to objectively evaluate the quality of sample statistics used to approximate population characteristics.

In this chapter, many of the concepts mentioned previously are reviewed. These include descriptive statistics, random variables and probability distributions, sampling distributions, and statistical inference. Because most or all of these topics are covered in an introductory course in statistics, the coverage here is brief.

For detailed references on introductory statistics, the interested reader is referred to texts such as:

Albright, S., Winston, W., and Zappe, C. *Data Analysis and Decision Making with Microsoft® Excel.* Pacific Grove, CA: Duxbury Press, 1999.

Brightman, H. *Data Analysis in Plain English with Excel.* Pacific Grove, CA: Duxbury Press, 1999.

Hildebrand, D., and Ott, R. *Statistical Thinking for Managers* (4th ed.). Pacific Grove, CA: Duxbury Press, 1998.

Keller, G., and Warrack, B. *Statistics for Management and Economics* (5th ed.). Pacific Grove, CA: Duxbury Press, 2000.

 ## 2.2   DESCRIPTIVE STATISTICS

Table 2.1 shows the 5-year returns as of June 14, 1999, for a random sample of 60 mutual funds. Examining the 60 numbers in this list provides little useful information. Just looking at a list of numbers is confusing even when the sample size is only 60. For larger samples, the confusion becomes even greater.

The field of descriptive statistics provides ways to summarize the information in a data set. Summaries can be tabular, graphical, or numerical. One common tabular method of summarizing data is the frequency distribution. A *frequency distribution* is a table that is used to summarize quantitative data. The frequency distribution is set up by defining *bins* or *classes* that contain the data values. An examination of the returns in Table 2.1 shows that the largest 5-year rate of return is 40.9% and the smallest is −14.2%. We want to make sure that we include all the data in our frequency distribution, so the bins of the frequency distribution must begin at or below the smallest value and end at or above the largest. One example of how we might set up the frequency distribution is as follows: Start the first bin at −20.0%, end the last bin at 50.0%, and use a total of seven bins. The resulting frequency distribution is shown in Figure 2.1.

Note that the bins are set up in such a way that there is no confusion about where a data value should go. Each bin includes the lower limit, but excludes the upper limit. A 5-year return of 4% belongs in the third bin; a 20% return belongs in the fifth bin. Also note that each of the bins has the same width: 10%. Two guidelines for constructing an effective frequency distribution are (a) make sure each data value belongs in a unique bin and (b) if possible, make each bin width the same. Intervals covering the range of the data are constructed, and the number of observations in each interval is then tabulated and recorded.

TABLE 2.1   Five-Year Rates of Return for Mutual Funds

Mutual Fund	5-Year Return	Mutual Fund	5-Year Return
Accessor Small to Midcap	21.90	MAS Balanced Instl.	16.70
AIM Advisor Flex Fund C	16.20	Meridian Fund	12.70
Alliance Growth Investors A	15.60	MFS Research A	21.20
American Century Giftrust	9.50	Mutual Beacon Z	17.40
American Express IDS Growth A	24.70	Neuberger & Berman Focus	18.60
Ariel Fund	16.80	Northern Select Equity	24.30
BB&T Growth & Income A	20.10	One Group Diversified A	21.90
Brandywine Fund	15.70	Oppenheimer Quest Opportunity Value A	18.90
Chase Vista Equity Income A	20.70	Parkstone Small Cap A	13.00
Columbia Special	13.90	Phoenix-Goodwin Strategic Allocation A	9.70
DLJ Winthrop Small Company Value A	10.00	PIMCO StocksPlus Instl	26.40
Dreyfus Premier Aggressive Growth A	−8.00	Principal Balanced A	12.90
Dreyfus Small Company Value	18.80	Putnam Convertible Income Gro A	14.30
Enterprise Growth A	27.40	Rainier Investment Balanced	17.70
Excelsior Value & Restructuring	24.30	Rydex OTC	40.90
Fidelity Asset Manager Fund	13.40	Scudder Development	17.10
Fidelity Capital Appreciation	18.60	Sentinel Common Stock A	19.80
Fidelity Puritan	15.10	Smith Barney Concert Growth 1	21.30
Fidelity Select Home Finance	18.30	Standish Equity	19.30
First Investors Blue Chip A	19.80	STI Classic Capital Appreciation	20.60
Flag Investors Value Builder A	20.60	SunAmerica Balanced Assets B	16.30
Franklin Rising Dividends A	17.50	TIP Turner Growth Equity	23.80
Galaxy Equity Income A	18.40	T. Rowe Price Equity Income	20.70
Guardian Park Avenue A	22.40	United Continental Income A	12.30
Heartland Value	12.50	Van Eck Gold A	−14.20
Janus Enterprise	23.80	Vanguard Balanced Index	16.80
J.P. Morgan US Small Company	13.00	Vanguard Utilities Income	16.60
Kemper Worldwide 2004	9.00	Victory Special Value A	11.80
Lexington Strategic Investments	−11.50	Westcore Midco Growth	15.80
MainStay Cap Appreciation B	22.40	Zweig Strategy A	10.50

FIGURE 2.1   **Frequency Distribution for 5-Year Rates of Return**

5-Year Rates of Return	Number of Funds
−20% but less than −10%	2
−10% but less than 0%	1
0% but less than 10%	4
10% but less than 20%	34
20% but less than 30%	18
30% but less than 40%	0
40% but less than 50%	1

If the proportion or percentage of items in each class is noted rather than the number, the table is referred to as a *relative frequency distribution*. It is also possible to construct a *cumulative frequency distribution* in which the number of items at or below each class limit is noted.

A *histogram* is a graphical representation of a frequency distribution. The horizontal axis of the graph is marked off into classes or bins over the full range of the data, and the vertical axis represents the number or proportion (relative frequency) of observations in each of the classes. The bin limits for the horizontal axis are the limits established in the frequency distribution. Rectangles (bars) are drawn over the bin limits with the area of the bar proportional to the frequency in that particular bin. If the bin limits are all the same width, the height of the bars can be equal to the frequency in each bin. If the bin limits differ in width, adjustments must be made. It is recommended that bin widths be made the same whenever possible. The adjustments for unequal bin widths are not discussed here.

From the frequency distribution or the histogram, one can obtain a quick picture of certain characteristics of the data. For example, the center of the data and how much variability is present can be observed. The data have been summarized so that these characteristics are more obvious. When the frequency distribution in Figure 2.1 was constructed, we arbitrarily decided to use seven bins. In general, you do not want to have too few bins because the data will be oversummarized and it will be hard to see patterns in the data. Also, too many bins make the frequency distribution confusing and difficult to read. Various rules have been suggested concerning the appropriate number of bins. A good guideline is to use between 5 and 20 bins. As a rough idea of the number of bins to try, take the square root of the number of observations and start there. We have 60 five-year rates of return. The square root of 60 is between 7 and 8. There is no right or wrong number of bins. However, there are better and worse numbers—too few or too many bins are not good—and there are better choices than others (my choices are better than yours, for example, because I wrote this book), but constructing a frequency distribution is in large part a matter of preference. It may

FIGURE 2.2   Excel Frequency Distribution for 5-Year Rates of Return for Mutual Funds

Returns	Frequency
−10	2
0	1
10	4
20	34
30	18
40	0
50	1

take two or three tries to get the table the way you believe is most helpful in representing the data or clearest for presentation purposes.

Most statistical software packages and spreadsheets provide various tabular and graphical methods of summarizing data. Figure 2.2 shows the frequency distribution constructed by Excel for the mutual-fund-return data. Figures 2.3 and 2.4 show histograms constructed using Excel and MINITAB, respectively. The frequency distribution and histogram in Excel use the same bin limits as in Figure 2.1. The MINITAB histogram was allowed to choose its own limits.[1] Note that the numbers shown in the bin column of the Excel frequency distribution are the upper bin limits. Excel includes a final bin that is represented by the label More (indicating values more than the last bin limit shown). When constructing a frequency distribution or histogram in Excel, I prefer not to use the More class but to use numerical bin limits instead. I have eliminated the More class in the frequency distribution shown. On the Excel histogram, the numbers shown on the horizontal axis also represent the upper limits of the bin under which they are printed. Even though they are printed in the middle of the bin, they do not represent midpoints of the bins, but upper limits.

On the MINITAB histogram, the numbers shown on the horizontal axis are the midpoints of the bin intervals. For example, the four middle bins that are adjacent would have bin midpoints of 10, 15, 20, and 25. This would make the bin limits 7.5, 12.5, 17.5, 22.5, and 27.5, respectively. Each bin limit is halfway between two of the midpoints.

The idea of a graph such as a histogram is to summarize the data so that the viewer can get a quick picture of what is going on without masking too much of the information. Using too few classes on a histogram oversummarizes the data, whereas using too many does not summarize the data sufficiently. In either case, a histogram

---

[1] Excel can be allowed to choose its own bin limits as well. However, I find the limits chosen by Excel are often not to my liking. I prefer to set up the bin limits myself to make them easier to work with. This process is discussed in the Using the Computer section at the end of this chapter.

FIGURE **2.3**   **Excel Histogram for 5-Year Rates of Return for Mutual Funds**

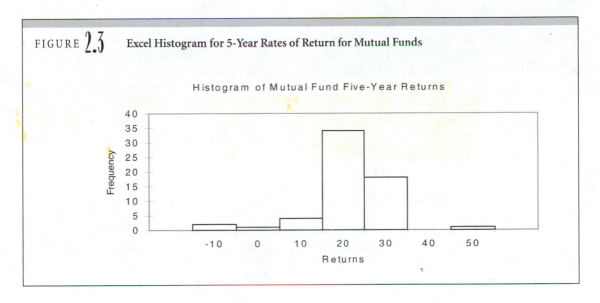

FIGURE **2.4**   **MINITAB Histogram for 5-Year Rates of Return for Mutual Funds**

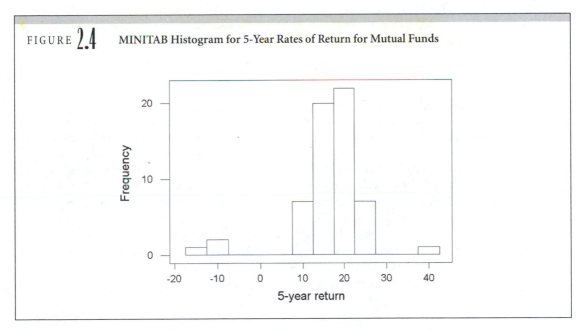

that is difficult to read is produced. Again, there is no right or wrong number of bins to use when constructing a histogram.

The histograms show that the returns for these funds vary from a low of about −17.5% (the lower boundary of the first interval is −17.5% on the MINITAB histogram and −20% on the Excel histogram) to a high of around 40% (50% is the upper boundary of the last interval on the Excel histogram; 42.5% is the upper limit of the last interval on the MINITAB histogram). Very high returns (above 30% or so) and very low returns (below 5% or so) are rare. Most returns cluster toward the center of the histogram (we might identify the center as around 15–20%).

Numerical summaries are single numbers computed from a sample to describe some characteristic of the data set. Some common numerical summaries are sample mean, sample median, sample variance, and sample standard deviation. The *sample mean* and *sample median* are measures of the center or central tendency of the data. The sample mean is the average of all the observations in the data set:

$$\bar{y} = \frac{\sum_{i=1}^{n} y_i}{n}$$

where y_i represents the ith observation in the data set. (See Appendix A for an explanation of summation notation.) The sample median is the midpoint of the data after they have been ordered. If n, the number of observations, is even, then the median is the average of the two middle observations after the observations have been ordered from smallest to largest. If n is odd, the unique middle value in the ordered data set is the median.

The *sample variance* and *sample standard deviation* are measures of variability. The sample variance is computed as

$$s^2 = \frac{\sum_{i=1}^{n} (y_i - \bar{y})^2}{n-1}$$

This is the average squared distance of each data point, y_i, from the center of the data $\bar{y}$. The divisor $n - 1$ is used, rather than n, to provide an unbiased estimator (one which neither consistently overestimates nor underestimates the true parameter) of the population variance. Because s^2 expresses variability in squared units, an intuitively more appealing measure is the sample standard deviation, s, which is simply the square root of s^2. Although many other numerical summaries exist, they are not discussed in this review.

Figure 2.5 shows the results of using MINITAB to compute several descriptive measures for the mutual-fund-return data, including the sample mean, sample median, sample variance, and sample standard deviation.

Figure 2.6 shows similar results using Excel.

FIGURE 2.5   MINITAB Numerical Summaries for the 5-Year Rates of Return[a]

Variable	N	Mean	Median	TrMean	StDev	SE Mean
5-year r	60	16.60	17.45	17.31	8.35	1.08

Variable	Minimum	Maximum	Q1	Q3
5-year r	−14.20	40.90	13.10	20.70

[a] The summaries computed include the number of observations (N), mean, median, 5% trimmed mean (TrMean), sample standard deviation (StDev), standard error of the mean (SEMean), minimum, maximum, first quartile (Q1), and third quartile (Q3).

FIGURE 2.6   Excel Numerical Summaries for the 5-Year Rates of Return[a]

5-Year Return	
Mean	16.600
Standard Error	1.078
Median	17.450
Mode	21.900
Standard Deviation	8.348
Sample Variance	69.687
Kurtosis	5.719
Skewness	−1.458
Range	55.100
Minimum	−14.200
Maximum	40.900
Sum	996.000
Count	60.000

[a] The summaries computed include the mean, standard error of the mean (Standard Error), median, mode, sample standard deviation (Standard Deviation), sample variance, kurtosis, skewness, range, minimum, maximum, the sum of all the data values (Sum), and the number of observations (Count).

EXERCISES

1 **Highway Mileages.** The highway mileages of 138 cars are shown in Table 2.2. These cars are 1999 models and were listed in the Road & Track '99 Car Buyer's Guide. Find the mean, standard deviation, and median for the mileages. Construct a histogram of the data.

All of the mileages are in one column in a file with the file name prefix CARS2.

2 **Graduation Rates.** The National Collegiate Athletic Association (NCAA) is concerned with the graduation rate of student athletes. Part of an effort to increase grad-

TABLE **2.2** Data for Highway Mileages Exercise

Car	HWY MPG	Car	HWY MPG	Car	HWY MPG
Acura 2.3 CL	31	Chevrolet Camaro Coupe	30	Ferrari 456M GT	14
Acura Integra LS Coupe	31	Chevrolet Cavalier Coupe	34	Ferrari 550 Maranello	15
Acura NSX	24	Chevrolet Corvette Coupe	25	Ford Contour LX	34
Acura 3.5RL	25	Chevrolet Lumina	29	Ford Crown Victoria	24
Acura TL	27	Chevrolet Malibu Sedan	32	Ford Escort LX Sedan	34
Aston Martin DB7 Coupe	21	Chevrolet Metro Coupe	44	Ford Escort ZX2 Cool	33
Audi A4 1.8T	32	Chevrolet Monte Carlo LS	29	Ford Mustang Coupe	30
Audi A6	28	Chevrolet Prizm Sedan	37	Ford Taurus LX Sedan	28
Audi A8 3.7	26	Chrysler Cirrus Lxi	29	Honda Accord DX Sedan	31
Bentley Arnage	18	Chrysler Concorde LX	30	Honda Civic CX Hatchback	37
BMW 318ti Coupe	31	Chrysler LHS	27	Honda Prelude	27
BMW 3 323i Sedan	29	Chrysler Sebring Convertible JX	30	Hyundai Accent L Coupe	36
BMW 528i	29	Chrysler Sebring LX	31	Hyundai Elantra Sedan	32
BMW 740i	24	Chrysler 300M	27	Hyundai Sonata	28
BMW Z3 2.3 Roadster	30	Daewoo Lanos S 3-door	36	Hyundai Tiburon	32
Buick Century Custom	29	Daewoo Leganza SE	29	Infiniti G20	31
Buick LeSabre Custom	30	Daewoo Nubira SX 4-door	31	Infiniti I30	28
Buick Park Avenue	28	Dodge Avenger	32	Infiniti Q45	23
Buick Regal LS	30	Dodge Intrepid	30	Jaguar XJ8	24
Buick Riviera	27	Dodge Neon Highline Coupe	40	Jaguar XK8 Coupe	25
Cadillac Catera	24	Dodge Stratus	37	KIA Sephia	31
Cadillac DeVille	26	Dodge Viper RT/10	21	Lamborghini Diablo Roadster VT	13
Cadillac Eldorado	26	Ferrari F355 Berlinetta	31	Lexus ES 300	22
Cadillac Seville SLS	26				

uation rates for student athletes involved implementing Proposition 48, beginning with the 1986–1987 school year. Proposition 48 mandated that student athletes obtain a 700 SAT or a 15 ACT test score to be eligible to play.

Table 2.3 shows the graduation rates (percentages) for several groups of students: all students entering freshman classes in 1983–1984 through 1985–1986 (as83) and student athletes from freshman classes entering in those same years (sa83); all students entering in 1986–1987 (as86) and student athletes entering in 1986–1987 (sa86); all students entering in 1987–1988 (as87) and student athletes entering in 1987–1988 (sa87); all students entering in 1988–1989 (as88) and student athletes entering in 1988–1989 (sa88); all students entering in 1989–1990 (as89) and student athletes entering in 1989–1990 (sa89); all students entering in 1990–1991 (as90) and

TABLE 2.2   (*continued*)

Car	HWY MPG	Car	HWY MPG	Car	HWY MPG
Lexus GS 300	25	Mitsubishi Diamante	26	Porsche Boxster	26
Lexus LS 400	25	Mitsubishi Eclipse RS	33	Rolls-Royce Silver Seraph	18
Lexus SC 300	24	Mitsubishi Galant DE	31	Saab 9-3 3-door	27
Lincoln Continental	24	Mitsubishi Mirage DE Sedan	40	Saab 9-5	28
Lincoln LS V6	25	Mitsubishi 3000GT	24	Saturn Coupe SC1	40
Lincoln Town Car Executive	25	Nissan Altima XE	31	Saturn SL Sedan	40
Lotus Esprit V8	23	Nissan Maxima GXE	27	Subaru Impreza L Coupe	29
Mazda Miata MX-5	29	Nissan Sentra XE	40	Subaru Legacy Brighton Wagon	29
Mazda Millenia	27	Oldsmobile Alero GX Sedan	29	Suzuki Esteem GL Sedan	37
Mazda Protégé DX	34	Oldsmobile Aurora	26	Suzuki Swift	43
Mazda 626 LX	33	Oldsmobile Cutlass GL	29	Toyota Avalon XL	31
Mercedes-Benz C230 Kompressor	29	Oldsmobile Eighty Eight	29	Toyota Camry CE	31
Mercedes-Benz CL500	22	Oldsmobile Intrigue GX	30	Toyota Camry Solara SE	32
Mercedes-Benz CLK320	29	Plymouth Breeze	37	Toyota Celica GT Liftback	28
Mercedes-Benz E300 Sedan	30	Plymouth Neon Coupe	38	Toyota Corolla VE	38
Mercedes-Benz S320	24	Plymouth Prowler	23	Toyota Tercel CE 2-door	39
Mercedes-Benz SL500	23	Pontiac Bonneville SE	29	Volkswagen Golf GL	31
Mercedes-Benz SLK320	30	Pontiac Firebird Coupe	28	Volkswagen Jetta GL	31
Mercury Cougar	34	Pontiac Grand Am SE Coupe	29	Volkswagen New Beetle GL	29
Mercury Grand Marquis GS	24	Pontiac Grand Prix SE Sedan	29	Volkswagen Passat GLS	32
Mercury Mystique GS	34	Pontiac Sunfire SE Coupe	34	Volvo C70 Coupe LPT	27
Mercury Sable GS Sedan	28	Porsche 911 Carrera Coupe	25	Volvo S70	28
Mercury Tracer GS Sedan	38			Volvo S80 2.9	27

From *Road & Track '99 Car Buyer's Guide.* Copyright 1999 by Hachette Filipacchi Magazines, Inc. Reprinted with permission.

TABLE 2.3   Data for Graduation Rates Exercise

Name of School	as83	sa83	as86	sa86	as87	sa87	as88	sa88	as89	sa89	as90	sa90	as91	sa91
Akron	42	63	41	58	40	49	39	47	36	41	34	53	37	43
Alabama	52	36	55	57	57	52	57	55	57	39	57	59	57	56
Alabama-Birmingham	36	28	31	33	32	47	31	45	33	32	31	37	31	34
Alabama State	18	29	16	22	14	21	20	39	20	23	21	50	18	26
American University	66	64	67	60	68	76	69	73	67	58	67	74	70	59
Appalachian State	54	55	59	58	64	60	66	59	61	71	64	60	62	44
Arizona	46	46	49	54	49	49	51	51	50	50	51	64	52	54
Arizona State	45	40	45	52	46	57	45	50	45	50	46	53	48	45
Arkansas	35	41	39	46	41	44	41	39	41	35	41	34	42	29
Arkansas State	30	27	29	37	26	26	31	32	30	38	31	49	27	33
Auburn	64	53	65	58	69	65	66	51	68	55	66	55	65	53
Austin Peay	29	31	32	29	29	34	25	35	33	39	35	50	29	40
Ball State	48	61	48	68	51	73	54	73	57	66	55	73	54	55
Baylor	69	63	71	66	71	53	71	55	70	61	69	60	70	66
Bethune-Cookman	37	32	36	57	38	50	23	67	36	71	30	44	38	23
Boise State	19	36	18	27	21	43	23	44	25	31	25	26	20	41
Boston College	85	86	88	94	87	92	91	87	87	84	86	90	85	71
Boston University	63	75	67	77	72	76	71	76	71	70	69	77	69	70
Bowling Green	54	54	63	61	60	56	65	59	64	67	62	71	60	69
Bradley	64	67	64	52	69	66	66	65	68	75	68	56	64	68
Brigham Young	39	41	48	42	51	55	52	50	56	56	58	59	67	40
Bucknell	90	93	94	97	89	85	95	92	92	91	92	96	89	87
Butler	58	72	66	80	66	77	65	61	66	73	62	80	60	63
California	73	67	77	61	76	71	79	76	79	57	80	64	81	57
Cal-Irvine	58	58	65	57	71	58	73	59	68	54	72	41	75	64
Cal-Santa Barbara	64	66	66	67	68	61	69	70	70	65	70	73	72	69
Cal State-Fullerton	41	29	45	38	45	38	45	31	44	35	42	24	40	18
Cal State-Sacramento	38	34	34	32	40	37	40	29	40	54	36	56	43	46
Canisius	55	58	59	76	58	56	66	84	55	82	55	64	54	63
Centenary	46	61	57	58	54	52	56	50	54	67	54	54	52	57
Central Florida	43	40	49	56	47	54	51	42	51	59	51	52	50	47
Central Michigan	53	63	56	60	61	57	57	65	53	58	51	63	54	63
Chicago State	11	20	8	25	20	38	22	18	23	39	16	27	12	31
Cincinnati	46	51	47	42	47	59	47	53	46	56	46	48	48	56
The Citadel	71	67	66	63	70	88	70	75	73	89	77	86	73	50
Clemson	70	50	70	47	71	64	72	53	72	53	70	41	70	50
Cleveland State	34	33	34	48	37	34	32	48	29	44	28	54	25	31
Coastal Carolina	31	47	34	62	30	62	32	46	35	56	31	43	34	32
Colgate	89	84	91	84	90	92	89	93	89	84	88	82	85	76
Colorado	60	56	66	58	64	43	66	51	66	54	66	51	65	49
Colorado State	55	60	57	55	58	58	55	58	56	45	56	33	58	61
Connecticut	68	55	68	70	72	71	68	55	70	58	68	70	68	62
Creighton	66	53	65	31	67	59	67	51	66	74	67	59	72	68
Davidson	88	81	91	66	87	57	88	50	92	100	89	79	89	73
Dayton	70	78	72	90	75	73	73	73	75	82	75	78	71	89
Delaware	69	61	71	57	73	75	73	64	72	67	71	63	70	82
Delaware State	30	41	26	38	26	31	22	26	29	44	30	52	30	50
DePaul	61	69	61	81	58	85	56	71	56	71	58	88	58	74
Detroit Mercy	47	49	54	68	48	37	53	42	49	67	37	68	40	51

TABLE **2.3** *(continued)*

Name of School	as83	sa83	as86	sa86	as87	sa87	as88	sa88	as89	sa89	as90	sa90	as91	sa91
Drake	55	56	60	56	62	45	62	67	71	57	61	60	68	61
Drexel	65	75	54	64	59	73	55	70	53	70	47	75	40	56
Duke	92	91	94	89	95	94	94	90	94	91	93	91	92	97
Duquesne	69	78	71	72	69	69	65	78	68	74	69	71	64	74
East Carolina	46	56	50	52	49	52	49	56	49	52	49	64	48	58
East Tennessee State	34	49	34	58	34	58	34	53	36	56	37	48	34	48
Eastern Illinois	54	59	61	53	62	63	63	58	65	57	69	63	70	61
Eastern Kentucky	33	43	30	61	31	61	30	54	28	59	25	47	27	48
Eastern Washington	35	39	38	42	39	31	40	35	41	28	44	46	45	32
Evansville	52	61	59	55	61	72	57	64	59	61	59	67	60	68
Fairfield	82	76	86	69	86	88	84	100	87	93	83	88	83	88
Fairleigh Dickinson	39	37	39	53	36	40	34	58	31	41	22	47	31	32
Florida	56	45	61	52	63	54	61	55	63	59	63	57	64	39
Florida A&M	35	28	33	41	36	31	42	37	43	29	42	48	45	35
Florida International	56	47	55	50	54	34	61	55	58	28	55	45	51	33
Florida State	53	43	50	50	61	51	63	73	65	55	64	68	65	61
Fordham	77	87	77	84	78	81	78	89	77	75	74	69	77	75
Furman	73	74	81	82	80	80	81	77	77	78	76	73	75	78
George Mason	41	54	46	63	51	60	50	55	53	67	48	62	49	59
George Washington	67	79	70	76	72	63	68	71	69	72	65	79	68	79
Georgetown	89	86	92	95	92	95	92	89	90	77	90	88	89	92
Georgia	59	43	61	58	59	47	61	61	62	55	60	51	62	55
Georgia Southern	38	48	36	45	36	50	40	52	41	75	40	47	36	51
Georgia State	32	31	40	52	36	33	41	49	39	44	41	54	25	43
Georgia Tech	66	60	68	57	69	60	68	53	69	59	67	68	68	57
Gonzaga	55	58	61	62	61	75	57	60	62	63	64	50	63	75
Grambling State	49	47	45	35	47	36	50	45	37	43	33	47	33	72
Hartford	56	80	51	65	54	65	50	62	53	70	50	68	53	76
Hawaii	81	75	78	78	80	79	78	77	73	73	72	71	55	62
Hofstra	57	59	58	55	57	45	57	71	57	58	61	53	62	69
Howard	41	41	45	49	50	41	44	49	47	41	47	51	54	83
Idaho	44	41	43	47	43	54	42	51	48	59	47	41	49	45
Idaho State	46	41	59	36	32	46	36	33	39	50	36	43	24	44
Illinois	78	66	78	74	80	64	80	73	79	74	78	76	77	64
Illinois-Chicago	33	48	32	55	36	58	35	51	38	58	34	74	32	58
Illinois State	49	49	53	62	55	60	59	56	53	57	54	67	53	64
Indiana	56	61	65	62	67	62	70	65	68	65	70	65	67	73
Indiana State	37	44	36	49	35	60	35	59	35	61	36	49	35	59
Iona	61	66	56	38	62	69	54	39	60	67	59	59	51	47
Iowa	60	63	59	63	62	67	61	72	61	66	63	68	62	72
Iowa State	60	51	64	67	63	58	64	63	62	59	60	62	60	59
Jackson State	19	37	34	43	28	43	33	41	34	39	33	47	29	24
Jacksonville University	39	41	50	56	42	42	52	25	36	37	41	44	41	46
James Madison	79	68	82	69	81	72	82	74	83	76	82	84	81	74
Kansas	54	48	55	56	56	49	58	64	57	52	56	56	54	56
Kansas State	48	46	48	66	54	57	48	48	45	52	48	48	45	43
Kent State	42	52	43	48	48	53	47	55	45	59	43	61	45	54
Kentucky	45	56	50	59	50	52	50	50	49	43	50	48	48	60
Lafayette	87	84	89	82	89	79	86	80	84	83	87	86	87	86

(continues)

TABLE **2.3** *(continued)*

Name of School	as83	sa83	as86	sa86	as87	sa87	as88	sa88	as89	sa89	as90	sa90	as91	sa91
Lamar	18	15	25	36	22	24	21	28	20	18	22	38	20	30
Lehigh	87	83	87	89	85	90	85	91	87	87	85	90	81	94
Liberty	26	48	35	49	37	54	36	48	37	47	37	49	39	52
Long Island University	32	43	28	44	27	41	24	70	28	45	27	73	20	64
Louisiana State	34	30	37	36	38	49	44	44	47	43	47	32	47	43
Louisiana Tech	39	41	36	59	41	55	40	46	38	38	39	35	38	51
Louisville	28	42	31	54	32	43	29	43	30	63	26	54	28	49
Loyola (IL)	59	87	63	77	65	73	63	61	62	88	66	83	63	81
Loyola (MD)	69	82	74	71	79	78	76	77	76	71	78	78	77	88
Loyola Marymount	67	42	68	68	71	64	72	56	79	44	74	75	71	72
Maine	49	53	56	59	57	56	53	63	52	53	54	43	53	60
Manhattan	70	83	70	100	72	93	71	87	66	86	71	93	73	96
Marist	60	50	63	67	62	100	61	50	66	60	61	54	64	63
Marquette	74	83	74	70	74	70	77	80	74	70	75	75	74	74
Marshall	39	39	39	51	39	43	38	46	35	47	41	41	32	39
Maryland	56	58	64	54	61	57	64	65	66	68	61	69	63	51
Maryland-Baltimore Co.	36	61	35	66	42	71	42	62	46	58	45	59	46	54
Maryland-Eastern Shore	19	23	21	25	22	33	30	43	27	48	30	50	32	5
Massachusetts	63	66	68	73	66	85	67	50	65	75	60	68	61	59
McNeese State	27	29	28	33	28	36	28	35	27	34	28	34	24	41
Memphis	34	37	33	64	26	59	35	58	34	51	34	59	32	30
Mercer	40	54	40	59	42	46	39	48	40	43	43	37	51	64
Miami (FL)	56	48	55	52	60	54	58	54	63	62	58	58	58	46
Miami (OH)	75	65	83	75	83	68	82	76	81	78	82	67	80	66
Michigan	82	65	85	79	85	76	85	71	85	80	84	71	82	68
Michigan State	66	64	69	62	72	52	70	74	69	51	66	74	66	67
Middle Tennessee State	33	31	36	44	36	48	36	40	38	46	38	31	33	47
Minnesota	34	47	42	53	49	52	51	46	48	62	52	56	52	48
Mississippi	48	48	49	57	51	59	49	58	48	55	47	60	49	50
Mississippi State	51	52	52	53	50	51	48	49	51	53	45	51	49	55
Mississippi Valley State	31	42	43	44	64	64	36	41	42	38	53	52	25	16
Missouri	55	53	55	54	58	51	60	55	60	53	57	58	58	63
Monmouth (NJ)	48	48	52	48	47	68	50	75	45	45	45	47	47	37
Montana	28	35	28	38	32	51	37	41	35	39	38	52	40	54
Morehead State	38	44	44	69	41	59	38	45	37	50	40	54	40	44
Morgan State	38	46	16	40	32	40	34	30	34	41	31	37	36	40
Mount St. Mary's	71	70	73	70	73	85	72	74	67	71	65	83	63	76
Murray State	39	47	43	40	46	68	41	48	49	55	46	43	39	33
Nebraska	48	48	50	64	53	58	48	59	48	60	49	61	46	57
Nevada-Las Vegas	27	34	27	40	34	38	33	23	35	43	35	37	37	36
New Hampshire	67	72	74	75	73	64	73	77	74	78	73	75	74	80
New Mexico	28	36	33	47	33	50	38	53	37	48	33	37	37	51
New Mexico State	37	41	38	51	40	43	38	50	41	40	40	45	39	58
New Orleans	18	25	19	21	20	34	20	56	24	44	26	37	24	27
Niagara	55	78	56	82	53	69	54	79	52	64	48	61	53	69
Nicholls State	18	28	22	35	20	44	22	31	20	31	19	38	23	33
North Carolina	78	74	82	67	83	75	85	76	84	74	82	63	84	66
North Carolina A&T	38	40	37	44	44	50	40	29	44	48	44	31	45	50
North Carolina-Asheville	34	43	35	47	42	65	43	70	42	42	41	32	45	100

TABLE 2.3   *(continued)*

Name of School	as83	sa83	as86	sa86	as87	sa87	as88	sa88	as89	sa89	as90	sa90	as91	sa91
North Carolina-Charlotte	49	50	49	64	53	54	61	57	58	61	53	51	51	41
North Carolina State	60	51	60	57	64	48	68	59	67	68	67	73	64	61
North Carolina-Wilmington	42	67	46	67	49	76	55	67	52	76	57	69	54	83
North Texas	32	29	34	42	36	15	36	48	38	33	35	41	35	45
Northeast Louisiana	27	36	32	43	27	36	31	46	34	39	30	32	28	36
Northeastern	47	67	46	60	43	67	42	64	39	64	40	67	42	56
Northern Illinois	52	52	52	57	54	63	57	65	55	52	51	50	50	60
Northern Iowa	56	61	62	58	62	64	60	71	62	74	59	70	60	69
Northwestern	87	82	89	77	89	84	88	82	89	82	91	93	90	85
Northwestern State	14	30	22	32	30	26	33	46	27	39	28	34	27	45
Notre Dame	92	83	94	84	95	82	93	85	94	86	93	93	93	88
Ohio State	52	60	54	69	59	59	61	61	60	67	55	49	57	54
Ohio University	53	69	61	70	65	59	66	76	70	76	58	66	66	69
Oklahoma	43	39	42	46	43	53	41	40	45	35	44	46	42	54
Oklahoma State	43	27	44	30	47	48	48	38	50	47	48	41	49	36
Old Dominion	47	44	45	38	47	38	47	57	45	50	40	44	41	68
Oregon	47	47	54	66	56	60	61	63	61	68	56	56	59	63
Oregon State	50	54	52	47	54	56	63	88	63	95	63	61	61	53
Pacific	62	65	62	63	63	64	56	81	58	46	59	70	62	53
Penn State	74	67	77	78	77	78	79	77	79	83	78	81	81	76
Pepperdine	59	42	68	50	64	48	65	50	63	54	69	79	72	80
Pittsburgh	61	55	62	56	62	75	65	65	65	59	62	49	61	64
Providence	83	84	95	93	87	100	92	98	57	84	93	86	83	82
Purdue	68	60	70	65	69	62	70	59	71	65	69	64	64	70
Radford	52	67	54	68	52	51	58	81	57	89	58	58	50	57
Rice	86	69	87	78	88	75	88	75	88	80	90	74	88	81
Richmond	82	75	81	73	79	76	82	68	77	87	83	83	83	79
Rider	62	60	63	74	61	64	63	63	60	68	55	74	54	57
Robert Morris	55	57	48	80	55	27	49	61	49	79	47	50	52	69
Rutgers	73	69	76	69	75	74	76	64	76	66	75	54	73	66
St. Bonaventure	68	76	70	83	73	63	72	73	65	50	72	80	76	76
St. Francis (NY)	34	57	34	27	44	67	40	70	45	45	39	53	39	66
St. Francis (PA)	55	61	64	80	53	53	55	58	52	56	53	62	55	65
St. John's	64	78	62	73	64	58	66	79	65	62	63	75	66	66
St. Joseph's	71	78	73	88	79	74	72	75	76	80	73	89	71	75
St. Louis U.	63	81	65	92	64	84	66	72	64	67	60	68	62	56
St. Mary's	65	63	66	100	64	68	65	86	64	69	68	68	62	68
St. Peter's	47	57	49	59	47	57	59	58	58	68	47	51	46	49
San Diego	53	72	60	81	67	59	68	88	70	90	67	70	65	75
San Diego State	37	31	41	40	39	39	41	39	36	37	34	40	36	31
San Francisco	56	61	58	100	63	71	58	62	56	62	61	68	61	92
San Jose State	30	33	39	36	39	38	36	38	35	56	39	46	34	47
Santa Clara	78	77	81	81	81	86	83	79	84	79	80	61	79	67
Seton Hall	59	59	61	71	65	64	64	73	65	72	65	70	64	71
Siena	79	67	81	75	82	83	79	100	81	100	81	83	84	88
South Alabama	25	33	23	48	36	63	32	47	30	42	30	42	30	39
South Carolina	59	56	61	49	61	67	62	63	62	64	63	73	56	62
South Carolina State	50	43	51	59	42	51	44	46	63	43	49	53	47	31
South Florida	38	46	46	54	42	58	43	45	47	64	46	39	47	50

TABLE 2.3 (continued)

Name of School	as83	sa83	as86	sa86	as87	sa87	as88	sa88	as89	sa89	as90	sa90	as91	sa91
Southeast Missouri State	34	33	34	48	35	41	36	49	34	52	37	53	36	47
Southeastern Louisiana	19	35	22	33	28	29	29	40	28	46	27	46	20	45
Southern California	64	51	66	69	67	53	67	56	65	71	67	57	69	53
Southern Illinois	43	56	20	61	43	62	44	69	43	58	39	57	35	55
SMU	69	48	68	71	73	69	69	84	71	80	72	72	70	84
Southern Mississippi	40	41	40	43	46	55	44	54	47	42	46	57	40	46
Southern University	24	26	25	30	27	44	28	38	27	45	22	41	21	30
Southwest Missouri State	37	52	43	62	42	62	41	53	41	49	39	45	40	42
Southwest Texas State	29	33	30	44	32	33	30	32	31	50	30	43	32	49
Southwestern Louisiana	29	24	30	39	28	47	27	40	27	39	27	41	24	39
Stanford	92	84	92	86	93	81	93	89	93	78	94	91	92	88
Stephen F. Austin	40	41	40	58	41	61	42	53	42	55	41	39	38	58
Stetson	58	59	58	48	63	60	61	48	66	56	64	58	63	64
Syracuse	62	61	64	69	67	65	71	77	71	61	70	65	69	65
Temple	44	56	43	57	42	46	47	55	43	68	49	53	37	59
Tennessee	52	48	50	49	51	55	56	52	55	47	55	44	56	37
Tennessee-Chatt.	28	38	33	33	33	47	40	30	42	31	38	50	42	43
Tennessee Tech	45	58	41	53	40	47	40	36	46	50	44	48	42	42
UT-Arlington	28	23	28	30	25	34	28	39	28	28	27	42	28	48
Texas	59	43	63	55	62	52	62	49	65	57	63	58	65	59
Texas A&M	67	38	66	53	66	53	67	47	68	58	68	53	69	52
TCU	61	54	62	57	61	60	59	62	60	60	59	39	63	66
UT-El Paso	25	23	26	38	25	36	23	32	24	21	24	32	22	28
UT-Pan Am	11	21	19	38	18	42	17	22	19	39	20	21	21	27
UT-San Antonio	21	32	22	26	23	22	23	30	23	22	24	32	24	39
Texas Southern	9	13	10	24	10	15	11	23	13	32	12	24	8	23
Texas Tech	41	35	40	45	39	47	40	54	38	57	40	51	44	43
Toledo	39	45	47	52	31	47	41	65	39	53	37	51	37	53
Tulane	68	57	70	62	74	72	73	66	73	74	72	75	74	71
Tulsa	47	49	44	51	45	68	53	55	54	56	59	57	56	61
UCLA	70	60	74	60	77	66	77	51	77	61	77	57	79	63
Utah	33	49	34	50	42	51	41	51	44	62	38	55	38	59
Utah State	47	33	46	32	46	46	54	53	56	38	50	41	36	50
Valparaiso	69	67	74	75	74	85	71	83	73	69	72	76	68	59
Vanderbilt	78	71	81	82	82	69	81	89	83	83	82	79	81	83
Vermont	76	79	77	79	76	74	76	86	73	79	72	77	68	75
Villanova	83	83	86	76	68	83	85	77	84	81	84	77	86	84
Virginia	80	81	92	88	92	80	91	84	93	90	91	83	92	80
Virginia Commonwealth	41	58	46	55	45	64	46	45	46	51	43	50	45	46
Virginia Military	65	61	66	67	65	55	66	83	62	77	67	50	56	60
Virginia Tech	71	46	72	55	73	70	74	70	73	64	73	62	74	70
Wagner	36	57	48	50	50	64	57	76	69	40	70	68	70	52
Wake Forest	78	62	84	71	88	69	86	72	87	71	85	71	85	76
Washington	60	53	63	61	65	52	67	57	70	68	69	57	70	64
Washington State	52	48	55	49	55	49	61	57	62	50	63	58	63	60
Weber State	20	27	43	31	38	40	31	33	33	42	40	38	39	40
West Virginia	54	62	55	66	55	62	55	67	56	64	56	52	54	54
Western Carolina	42	44	45	62	47	59	47	51	50	51	48	49	48	57
Western Illinois	40	52	43	58	46	55	44	58	49	68	46	60	45	41

TABLE **2.3**   *(continued)*

Name of School	as83	sa83	as86	sa86	as87	sa87	as88	sa88	as89	sa89	as90	sa90	as91	sa91
Western Kentucky	39	47	37	38	33	40	39	53	39	47	41	35	39	49
Western Michigan	46	50	54	49	51	46	55	63	52	57	52	47	52	48
Wichita State	45	27	44	33	32	57	31	41	28	44	27	50	24	46
William & Mary	84	83	89	85	92	87	90	84	92	87	91	73	89	90
Winthrop	51	44	50	49	48	52	50	45	51	51	57	70	51	54
Wisconsin	66	63	70	69	72	66	73	69	73	56	72	56	73	60
Wisconsin-Green Bay	32	53	37	67	40	60	40	70	39	60	41	53	42	70
Wright State	30	46	33	54	31	43	28	50	32	49	32	62	31	43
Wyoming	41	44	44	42	44	52	46	46	43	43	45	37	45	41
Xavier (OH)	66	78	65	77	64	92	66	83	66	71	69	83	67	100
Youngstown State	38	59	40	60	38	35	36	49	35	51	34	64	28	43

Reprinted courtesy of the *Fort Worth Star-Telegram.*

student athletes entering in 1990–1991 (sa90); all students entering in 1991–92 (as91) and student athletes entering in 1991–1992 (sa91). All Division I schools with complete data for all years are represented. [The data were obtained from the *Fort Worth Star-Telegram* (July 2, 1993; May 20, 1993; July 1, 1994; June 30, 1995; June 28, 1996; June 27, 1997; and November 9, 1998 issues).] Note that the 1983–1984 through 1985–1986 data provide graduation rates prior to the implementation of Proposition 48. All other years provide graduation rates after its implementation.

a Examine the 14 groups by finding the mean and median graduation rate for each. Construct a histogram for each set of graduation rates.

b U.S. District Judge Ronald Buckwalter invalidated the NCAA's academic eligibility standards for incoming freshmen athletes on March 8, 1999. The NCAA still believes in the standards and in the positive effect of Proposition 48 on graduation rates. To help support their position, the NCAA has asked for your input concerning the effect of Proposition 48 on graduation rates. Using any graphical or numerical summaries to support your position, what would you report to the NCAA based on the data you have been given?

These data are in a file with prefix GRADRAT2 in the following order: as83, sa83, as86, sa86, as87, sa87, as88, sa88, as89, sa89, as90, sa90, as91, sa91.

2.3   DISCRETE RANDOM VARIABLES AND PROBABILITY DISTRIBUTIONS

A *random variable* can be defined as a rule that assigns a number to every possible outcome of an experiment. A *discrete random variable* is one with a definite distance between each of its possible values. For example, consider the toss of a coin. The two possible outcomes are head (H) and tail (T). A random variable of interest could be defined as

$$X = \text{number of heads on a single coin toss}$$

Then X assigns the number 1 to the outcome H and the number 0 to outcome T.

As another example, suppose two cards are randomly drawn without replacement from a deck of 52 cards. Let

$$Y = \text{number of kings on two draws}$$

Then Y assigns the number 0, 1, or 2 to each possible outcome of the experiment.

In each of these examples, the outcome of the experiment is determined by chance. Probabilities can be assigned to the outcomes of the experiment and thus to the values of the random variables. A table listing the values of a random variable and the probabilities associated with each value is called a *probability distribution* for the random variable.

For the coin toss, the probability distribution of X is

x	$P(x)$
0	½
1	½

Here the notation $P(x)$ means "the probability that the random variable X has the value x" or $P(x) = P(X = x)$. The function $P(x)$ is called the *probability mass function* (pmf) of X.

For the card-drawing experiment, the probability distribution of Y is

y	$P(y)$
0	188/221
1	32/221
2	1/221

Note that probabilities must satisfy the following conditions:

1 They must be between 0 and 1. $0 \leq P(x) \leq 1$
2 They must sum to 1. $\sum P(x) = 1$

When we discussed a sample of observations drawn from a population in the previous section, certain characteristics were of interest, primarily center and variability. Numerical summaries were used to measure these characteristics. Describing the center and the variation in a probability distribution also is often useful. The measures most commonly used to do this are the mean and variance (or standard deviation) of the random variable.

As an example, consider two random variables X and Y, representing the profit from two different investments. Suppose the two probability distributions have been set up as follows:

x	$P(x)$	y	$P(y)$
−2000	.05	0	.40
−1000	.10	1000	.20
1000	.10	2000	.20
2000	.25	3000	.10
5000	.50	4000	.10

If only one of the investments can be chosen, some methods to compare the two would be useful. As can be seen, the chances of a loss are greater for investment X than for investment Y, although the chances for a large profit are also greater for investment X.

One way to compare the investments might be to use the expected value, or mean, of the random variables representing the outcomes of the investments. The expected value of a discrete random variable X is defined as the sum of each value of X times the probability associated with that value:

$$E(X) = \mu_X = \sum xP(x)$$

The subscript X on μ_X often is dropped if it is clear which random variable is being discussed. The computation of the expected values of X and Y is shown in Table 2.4. The expected value of X is greater than the expected value of Y. Thus, on the basis of maximizing expected values, investment X would be chosen.

The expected value of a random variable deserves some additional explanation. Consider again the coin-toss experiment with X equal to the "number of heads" and probability distribution

x	$P(x)$
0	½
1	½

Computing the expected value of X gives $E(X) = \dfrac{1}{2}$.

TABLE 2.4   Computation of $E(X)$ and $E(Y)$

x	$P(x)$	$xP(x)$	y	$P(y)$	$yP(y)$
−2000	0.05	−100	0	0.40	0
−1000	0.10	−100	1000	0.20	200
1000	0.10	100	2000	0.20	400
2000	0.25	500	3000	0.10	300
5000	0.50	2500	4000	0.10	400
	$E(X) = \sum xP(x) = 2900$			$E(Y) = \sum yP(y) = 1300$	

Obviously, if a coin is tossed once, either the outcome 0 (tail) or 1 (head) will appear. The expected value of X represents the average obtained over a large number of trials. If the coin is tossed a large number of times and zeros were recorded for tails and ones for heads, then the average of these zeros and ones is close to one-half. The same interpretation can be made for the case of the investments. The expected outcomes represent the averages obtained over a large number of trials rather than the outcome of a single trial. Thus, in the long run, investment X will provide a higher average profit than investment Y.

There are of course other criteria for choosing between investments than simply maximizing the expected returns. A measure of each investment's risk also might be important. The variability of the outcomes is sometimes used as a measure of such risk. One measure of a random variable's variation is the *variance*, defined for a discrete random variable, X, as

$$Var(X) = \sigma_X^2 = \sum (x - \mu)^2 P(x)$$

To compute $Var(X)$, the mean is subtracted from each possible value of X, and the differences are squared and then multiplied times the probability of the associated value of X. The resulting sum is the variance, which represents an average squared distance of each value of X to the center of the probability distribution. Note that no division is used in computing this "average." The division used to compute a sample variance has been replaced by the weighting of each outcome by its probability. An alternative formula for computing the variance of a discrete random variable is

$$\sigma_X^2 = \sum x^2 P(x) - \mu^2$$

This formula is sometimes preferred when doing computations on a calculator. Both formulas provide the same answer. The variances of X and Y are computed in Table 2.5.

The variances are

$$\sigma_X^2 = 5,490,000 \quad \text{and} \quad \sigma_Y^2 = 1,810,000$$

Obviously, investment X is more variable than investment Y. The variances are somewhat difficult to interpret, however, because they measure variability in squared units (squared dollars for the investments). To return to the original units of the problem, the square root of the variance, called the *standard deviation*, may be used:

$$\sigma_X = 2343.07 \quad \text{and} \quad \sigma_Y = 1345.36$$

The standard deviations are expressed in the original units of the problem (dollars for the investments).

All of the random variables discussed so far have been discrete random variables. A *continuous random variable* is one whose values are measured on a continuous scale. It is measured over a range of values with all numbers within that range as possible values (at least in theory). Examples of quantities that might be represented by continuous random variables are temperature, gas mileage, and stock prices. In the next section, a very useful continuous random variable in statistics, the normal random variable, is introduced.

TABLE **2.5**   Computation of σ_X^2 and σ_Y^2

x	$P(x)$	$xP(x)$	$x-\mu_x$	$(x-\mu_X)^2$	$(x-\mu_X)^2\,P(x)$
−2000	0.05	−100	−4900	24,010,000	1,200,500
−1000	0.10	−100	−3900	15,210,000	1,521,000
1000	0.10	100	−1900	3,610,000	361,000
2000	0.25	500	−900	810,000	202,500
5000	0.50	2500	2100	4,410,000	2,205,000
		$\mu_X=2900$			5,490,000

y	$P(y)$	$yP(y)$	$y-\mu_Y$	$(y-\mu_Y)^2$	$(y-\mu_Y)^2\,P(y)$
0	0.40	0	−1300	1,690,000	676,000
1000	0.20	200	−300	90,000	18,000
2000	0.20	400	700	490,000	98,000
3000	0.10	300	1700	2,890,000	289,000
4000	0.10	400	2700	7,290,000	729,000
		$\mu_Y=1300$			1,810,000

EXERCISES

3   Consider the roll of a single die. Construct the probability distribution of the random variable $X=$ number of dots showing on the die. Find the expected value and standard deviation of X. How would you interpret the number obtained for the expected value?

4   Let X be a random variable defined as

   $X = 1$ if an even number of dots appears on the roll of a single die
   $= 0$ if an odd number of dots appears on the roll of a single die

Construct the probability distribution of X. Find the expected value and standard deviation of X. How would you interpret the number obtained for the expected value?

5   Consider the roll of two dice. Let X be a random variable representing the sum of the number of dots appearing on each of the dice. The probabilities of each possible value of X are as follows:

x	$P(x)$
2	1/36
3	2/36
4	3/36
5	4/36
6	5/36
7	6/36
8	5/36
9	4/36
10	3/36
11	2/36
12	1/36

Determine the expected value and standard deviation of X.

6 The game of craps deals with rolling a pair of fair dice. In one version of the game, a field bet is a one-roll bet based on the outcome of the pair of dice. For every $1 bet, you lose $1 if the sum is 5, 6, 7, or 8; you win $1 if the sum is 3, 4, 9, 10, or 11; or you win $2 if the sum is 2 or 12.

a Using the probability distribution in Exercise 5, construct the probability distribution of the different outcomes available in a field bet.

b Determine the expected value of this probability distribution. How would you interpret this number?

7 A computer shop builds PCs from shipments of parts it receives from various suppliers. The number of defective hard drives per shipment is to be modeled as a random variable X. The random variable is assumed to have the following distribution:

x	$P(x)$
0	0.55
1	0.15
2	0.10
3	0.10
4	0.05
5	0.05

a What is the expected number of defective hard drives per shipment?

b If each defective drive costs the company $100 in rework costs, what is the expected rework cost per shipment?

c What is the probability that a shipment has more than two defective hard drives?

2.4   THE NORMAL DISTRIBUTION

A continuous random variable is a random variable that can take any value over a given range. An example that is important in statistical inference is the normal random variable. The probability distribution of the normal random variable, called the normal distribution, is often depicted as a bell-shaped symmetric curve as shown in Figure 2.7. The normal distribution is centered at the mean, μ. Variation in the distribution is described by the variance σ^2 or standard deviation σ.

Figure 2.8 shows two normal distributions with different means but equal standard deviations, and Figure 2.9 shows two distributions with the same mean but different standard deviations. The location of the distribution is determined by the mean; the spread of the distribution (how compressed or spread out it appears) is determined by the standard deviation.

For a continuous distribution such as the normal distribution, the probability that the random variable takes on a value within a certain range can be determined by computing the area under the curve that defines the probability distribution between the limits of the range. To determine the probability that a normal random variable is between 0 and 2, the area under the normal curve between these values must be computed. This computation is a fairly difficult task if done from scratch. Fortunately, a table of certain areas or probabilities under the normal curve is available to simplify these computations considerably.

Table B.1 in Appendix B lists probabilities between certain values of the standard normal distribution. The standard normal distribution has a mean of $\mu = 0$ and a standard deviation of $\sigma = 1$. Throughout this text, the standard normal random variable is

---

FIGURE **2.7**   The Normal Distribution with Mean μ and Standard Deviation σ

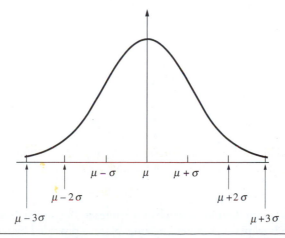

FIGURE 2.8   **Normal Distributions with Equal Standard Deviations but Different Means**

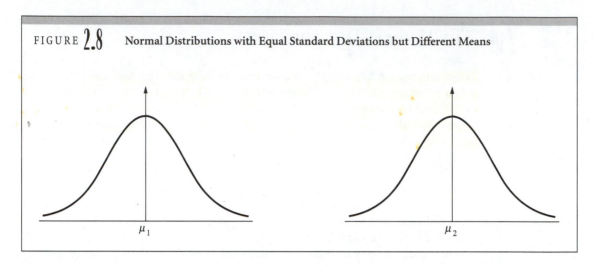

FIGURE 2.9   **Normal Distributions with Equal Means but Different Standard Deviations**

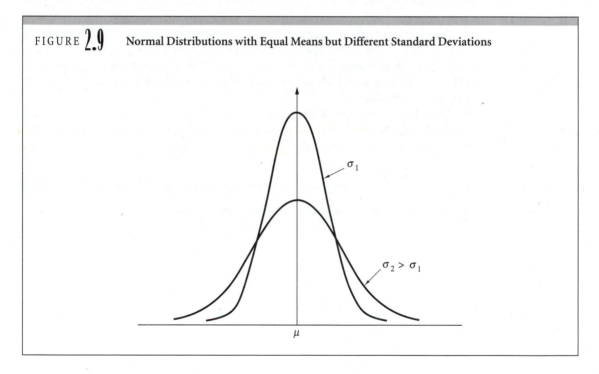

denoted by the letter Z. This table is set up to show the probability that the normal random variable is between 0 and some number z written

$$P(0 \leq Z \leq z)$$

The z numbers are given by the values in the far left-hand column of the table to one decimal place. A second decimal place is provided by using the values in the top

FIGURE **2.10**   **Area or Probability Under the Standard Normal Curve Between 0 and 1.0**

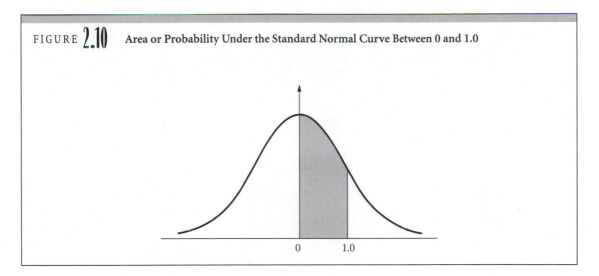

row of the table. For example, to find the probability that Z is between 0 and 1, the value 1.0 is located in the left-hand column and the probability is read from the .00 column of the table:

$$P(0 \leq Z \leq 1.0) = 0.3413$$

This area is illustrated by the shaded region in Figure 2.10.

Similarly, the probability between 0 and 2.3 is

$$P(0 \leq Z \leq 2.3) = 0.4893$$

To compute the probability between 0 and 1.96, first find 1.9 in the left-hand column. The probability is then read from the .06 column of the table as

$$P(0 \leq Z \leq 1.96) = 0.4750$$

Because the standard normal curve has a mean of 0, the numbers to the right of the mean are positive as illustrated in the examples thus far. The numbers to the left of the mean are negative. How is the table used to find the probability that Z is between, say, −1.0 and 1.0? There are no negative z values in the table. But the fact that the curve is symmetric can be used to determine the probabilities for numbers to the left of the mean.

The probability between 0 and 1.0 has been determined to be 0.3413. Because the curve is symmetric, the half of the curve to the left of the mean is a mirror image of the half to the right. Thus, in an interval between 0 and −1.0, there is exactly the same probability as in the interval between 0 and 1.0 because these regions are mirror images of each other. So,

$$P(-1.0 \leq Z \leq 1.0) = 0.3413 + 0.3413 = 0.6826$$

This probability is illustrated in Figure 2.11.

FIGURE **2.11**   Area or Probability Under the Standard Normal Curve Between −1.0 and 1.0

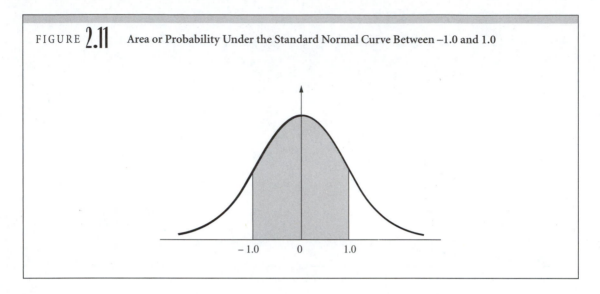

Now, consider finding the following probability

$$P(Z > 1.7)$$

The area between 0 and 1.7 can be found from Table B.1 in Appendix B as

$$P(0 \leq Z \leq 1.7) = 0.4554$$

The desired area is to the right of 1.7, however. Here, we use the facts that the total area under the curve must be 1.0 and that the curve is symmetric. The total area under the standard normal curve must be 1.0 because this area represents probability, and probability must sum to 1. Because the curve is symmetric, the area to the right of the mean (0) must be 0.5. In Figure 2.12, if the unshaded area between 0 and 1.7 is subtracted from the total area to the right of 0, the remainder is the area in the shaded region:

$$P(Z > 1.7) = 0.5 - 0.4554 = 0.0446$$

The probabilities in the standard normal table also can be used to find probabilities for normal distributions other than the standard normal distribution. For example, suppose X is a normal random variable with mean $\mu = 10$ and standard deviation $\sigma = 2$. Find the probability that X is between 10 and 12:

$$P(10 \leq X \leq 12)$$

The standard normal table cannot be used to find this probability as it is currently stated. But the problem can be solved by translating it into *standardized units*, or units of standard deviation away from the mean. Referring to Figure 2.13, first recognize that 10 is the mean of the normal distribution represented by X. Because $\sigma = 2$, 12 is one standard deviation above the mean $(10 + 2 = 12)$. Then, in standardized units, the problem becomes

$$P(10 \leq X \leq 12) = P(0 \leq Z \leq 1)$$

FIGURE 2.12   **Area or Probability Under the Standard Normal Curve Between 0 and 1.7 and Above 1.7**

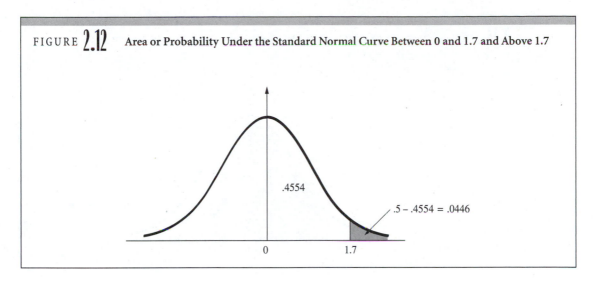

.4554

.5 − .4554 = .0446

0   1.7

FIGURE 2.13   **Finding $P(10 \leq X \leq 12)$ When X Is a Normal Random Variable with $\mu = 10$ and $\sigma = 2$**

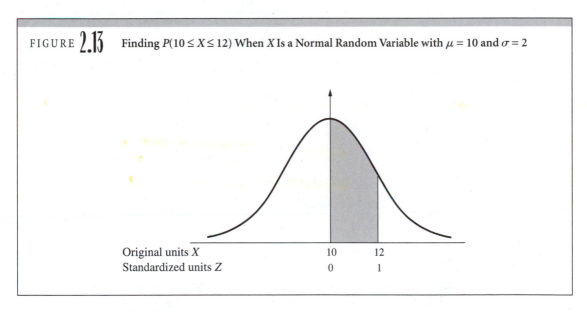

Original units X 10   12
Standardized units Z 0   1

The area between 10 and 12 under the normal curve with $\mu = 10$ and $\sigma = 2$ is the same as the area between 0 and 1 under the standard normal curve. By translating the original units into standardized units, any probability can be determined from the standard normal table. The general transformation is given by the formula

$$Z = \frac{x - \mu_X}{\sigma_X}$$

To translate a number, x, into standardized units, Z, simply subtract the mean and divide by the standard deviation. The following examples should help further illustrate.

FIGURE **2.14**

FIGURE **2.14**   Finding $P(30 \leq X \leq 60)$ When X Is a Normal Random Variable with $\mu = 50$ and $\sigma = 10$

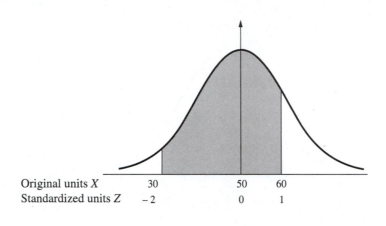

Original units X 30   50   60
Standardized units Z -2 0   1

EXAMPLE **2.1**

Suppose X is a normal random variable with $\mu = 50$ and $\sigma = 10$. What is $P(30 \leq X \leq 60)$?
Answer:

$$P(30 \leq X \leq 60) = P\left(\frac{30-50}{10} \leq Z \leq \frac{60-50}{10}\right)$$

$$= P(-2 \leq Z \leq 1) = 0.4772 + 0.3413 = 0.8185$$

The solution is illustrated in Figure 2.14.

EXAMPLE **2.2**

A large retail firm has accounts receivable that are assumed to be normally distributed with mean $\mu = \$281$ and standard deviation $\sigma = \$35$.

1   What proportion of accounts have balances greater than $316?
Answer:

$$P(X > 316) = P\left(Z > \frac{316-281}{35}\right)$$

$$= P(X > 1) = 0.5 - 0.3413 = 0.1587$$

Thus, 0.1587 or 15.87% of all accounts have balances greater than $316. The solution is illustrated in Figure 2.15.

FIGURE **2.15**   **Finding $P(X > 316)$ When X is a Normal Random Variable with $\mu = 281$ and $\sigma = 35$**

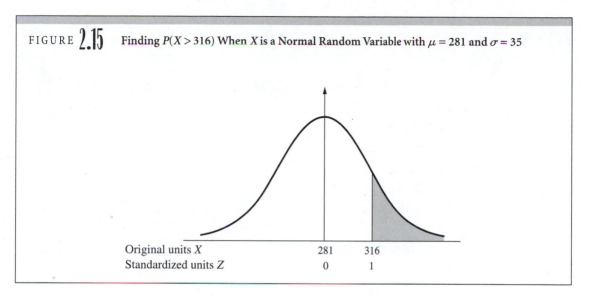

Original units X	281	316
Standardized units Z	0	1

FIGURE **2.16**   **Above What Value Do 13.57% of All Account Balances Lie When $\mu = 281$ and $\sigma = 35$?**

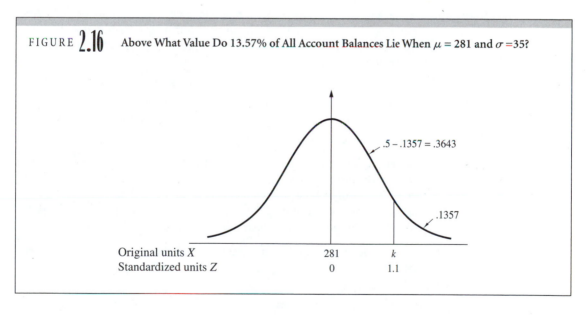

.5 − .1357 = .3643

.1357

Original units X	281	k
Standardized units Z	0	1.1

2   Above value what do 13.57% of all account balances lie?

Answer: Figure 2.16 illustrates the problem to be solved. Find an account balance, call it k, such that the probability above k is 0.1357. This means the probability between the mean and k must be 0.5 − 0.1357 = 0.3643. Looking up 0.3643 in the standard normal table, k has a z value of 1.1, so k is 1.1 standard deviations above the mean:

$$k = \mu + z\sigma = 281 + (1.1)(35) = \$319.50$$

EXERCISES

8 Calculate the following probabilities using the standard normal distribution:

a $P(0.0 \le Z \le 1.2)$

b $P(-0.9 \le Z \le 0.0)$

c $P(0.0 \le Z \le 1.45)$

d $P(0.3 \le Z \le 1.56)$

e $P(-2.03 \le Z \le -1.71)$

f $P(-0.02 \le Z \le 3.54)$

g $P(Z \ge 2.50)$

h $P(Z \le 1.66)$

i $P(Z \ge 5)$

j $P(Z \ge -6)$

9 All applicants at a large university are required to take a special entrance exam before they are admitted. The exam scores are known to be normally distributed with a mean of 800 and a standard deviation of 100. Applicants must score 700 or more on the exam before they are admitted.

a What proportion of all applicants taking the exam is granted admission?

b What proportion of all applicants will score 1000 or higher on the exam?

c For the coming academic year, 2500 applicants have registered to take the exam. How many do we expect to be qualified for admission to the university?

10 A manufacturer produces bearings, but because of variability in the production process, not all of the bearings have the same diameter. The diameters have a normal distribution with a mean of 1.2 centimeters (cm) and a standard deviation of 0.01 cm. The manufacturer has determined that diameters in the range of 1.18 to 1.22 cm are acceptable. What proportion of all bearings fall in the acceptable range?

11 Find the value of Z from the standard normal table such that the probability between Z and $-Z$ is

a 0.9544

b 0.9010

c 0.9802

d 0.9902

12 A large manufacturing plant uses light bulbs with lifetimes that are normally distributed with a mean of 1000 hours and a standard deviation of 50 hours. To minimize the number of bulbs that burn out during operating hours, all bulbs are replaced at once. How often should the bulbs be replaced so that no more than 1% burn out between replacement periods?

13 A company that produces an expensive stereo component is considering offering a warranty on the component. Suppose the population of lifetimes of the components is a normal distribution with a mean of 84 months and a standard deviation of 7 months. If the company wants no more than 2% of the components to wear out before they reach the warranty date, what number of months should be used for the warranty?

14 Periods of time that students use computers at a university computer center are known to be normally distributed with a mean of 36 minutes and a standard deviation of 5 minutes. Around 10,000 uses are recorded each week in the computer center. The computer center administrative committee has decided that, if more than 2000 uses of longer than 40 minutes at each sitting are recorded weekly, some new terminals must be purchased to meet usage needs. Should the computer center purchase the new computers?

2.5 POPULATIONS, SAMPLES, AND SAMPLING DISTRIBUTIONS

Statistics is concerned with the use of sample information to make generalizations or inferences about a *population,* which is simply the group to be studied. A population may consist of people, households, firms, automobile tires, and so on. A *sample* is a subset of a population. In other words, a sample is a group of items chosen from the population.

Typically, the study of every item in a population is not feasible. It may be too time-consuming or too expensive to examine every item. As an alternative, a few items are chosen from the population studied. From the information provided by this sample, we hope to make reliable generalizations about characteristics of the population.

In this section, we assume that the items of the sample are randomly chosen from the population. By choosing the sample in this way, it is possible to objectively evaluate the quality of the generalizations made about the population characteristics of interest.

As discussed in Section 2.1, many possible random samples can be chosen from a particular population. In practice, typically only one such sample is chosen and examined. (In some applications, such as statistical quality control, repeated samples may be used.) To understand the processes that govern how inferences should be made, it is necessary to imagine all possible random samples of a given sample size n chosen from a particular population. Suppose the characteristic of interest for this population is the mean, μ. To estimate the population mean, the statistic most often used is the sample mean, $\bar{y}$; each possible random sample has an associated value of $\bar{y}$. Thus, the sample mean acts just like a random variable: It assigns a number (the value of the sample mean for each sample) to each of the possible outcomes of an experiment. The experiment, in this instance, is the process of choosing samples of size n from the population. Because the samples are chosen randomly, each one has an equal probability of being chosen. Thus, each value of $\bar{y}$ has a probability associated with it.

Because the sample mean $\bar{y}$ can be viewed as a random variable, it has a probability distribution. This probability distribution is called the *sampling distribution of the sample mean.* In this section, some of the properties of the sampling distribution of the sample mean are reviewed. These are discussed in more detail in most introductory statistics courses. The sampling distribution of the sample mean is important because it allows us to make the link between population characteristics and sample values that make it possible to assess the quality of our inferences.

First, suppose the population of interest has a mean μ and variance σ^2. The mean of the sampling distribution of $\bar{y}$, written $\mu_{\bar{y}}$, is equal to the population mean:

$$\mu_{\bar{y}} = \mu$$

The variance of the sampling distribution of $\bar{y}$, written $\sigma_{\bar{y}}^2$, is

$$\sigma_{\bar{y}}^2 = \frac{\sigma^2}{n}$$

The standard deviation of the sampling distribution of $\bar{y}$, $\sigma_{\bar{y}}$, is the square root of the variance:

$$\sigma_{\bar{y}} = \frac{\sigma}{\sqrt{n}}$$

Thus, if all possible sample means for samples of size n could be collected, the average of the sample means would be the same as the average of all the individual population values. The sample mean values, however, would be less spread out than the individual population values because $\sigma_{\bar{y}}$ is always less than σ.

If the original population from which the samples were drawn is a normal distribution, then the sampling distribution of the sample mean is also a normal distribution for any sample size n. Thus, if μ and σ are known and the population to be sampled is normal, probability statements could be made about the sample mean $\bar{y}$. Consider the following example.

EXAMPLE **2.3**

In a certain manufacturing process, the diameter of a part produced is 40 centimeters (cm) on average, although it varies somewhat from part to part. This variation is thought to be well represented by a normal distribution with a standard deviation of 0.2 cm. If a random sample of 16 parts is chosen, what is the probability that the average diameter of the 16 parts is greater than 40.1 cm?

Answer: Because the population is normal, the sampling distribution of sample means is also is normal. The mean of the sampling distribution is $\mu_{\bar{y}} = 40$ and the standard deviation is:

$$\sigma_{\bar{y}} = \frac{0.2}{\sqrt{16}} = 0.05$$

Thus,

$$P(\bar{y} > 40.1) = P\left(Z > \frac{40.1 - 40}{0.05}\right) = P(Z > 2) = 0.5 - 0.4772 = 0.0228$$

Knowledge of the sampling distribution provides information about how sample means from a particular population should behave. But what if the population does not have a normal distribution, or what if the actual distribution of the population is unclear? In this case, there is an important result in statistics called the *central limit theorem* (CLT) that states

As long as the sample size is large, the sampling distribution of the sample mean is approximately normal, regardless of the population distribution.

The CLT states that probabilities still can be computed concerning sample means, even though the population does not have a normal distribution, as long as the sample size is large enough. How large is "large enough" varies somewhat from one population distribution to another, but a generally accepted rule is to treat a sample size of 30 or more as large.

The next example illustrates the use of the CLT.

EXAMPLE 2.4

A cereal manufacturer claims that boxes of its cereal weigh 20 ounces (oz) on average with a population standard deviation of 0.5 oz. The manufacturer does not know whether the population distribution is normal. A random sample of 100 boxes is selected. What is the probability that the sample mean is between 19.9 and 20.1 oz?

Answer: Because the sample size is large ($n = 100$), the sampling distribution is approximately normal even though the population distribution may be nonnormal. The mean and standard deviation of the sampling distribution are

$$\mu_{\bar{y}} = 20 \text{ and } \sigma_{\bar{y}} = \frac{0.5}{\sqrt{100}} = 0.05$$

Thus,

$$P(19.9 \le \bar{y} \le 20.1) = P\left(\frac{19.9 - 20}{0.05} \le Z \le \frac{20.1 - 20}{0.05}\right) = P(-2 \le Z \le 2)$$

$$= 0.4772 + 0.4772 = 0.9544$$

EXERCISES

15 The daily receipts of a fast-food franchise are normally distributed with a mean of $2200 per day and a standard deviation of $50. A random sample of 25 days' receipts is chosen for an audit.

a What is the probability that the sample mean is larger than $2220?

b What is the probability that the sample mean differs from the true population mean by more than ±$10?

16 The accounts receivable of a large department store are normally distributed with a mean of $250 and a standard deviation of $80. If a random sample of 225 accounts is chosen, what is the probability that the mean of the sample is between $232 and $268?

17 When a certain manufacturing process is correctly adjusted, the length of a machine part produced is a random variable with a mean of 200 cm and a standard deviation of 0.1 cm. The individual measurements are normally distributed.

a What is the probability that an individual part is longer than 200.2 cm?

b Suppose a sample of 25 parts is chosen randomly. What is the probability that the mean of the sample is bigger than 200.2 cm?

18 Suppose we have a large population of houses in a community. The average annual heating expense for each house is $400 with a population standard deviation of $25. A random sample of 25 houses had a sample mean of $380 and a sample standard deviation of $35.

a What is the mean of the sampling distribution of the sample mean for samples of size 25 chosen from the population of all houses?

b What is the standard deviation of the sampling distribution of the sample mean for samples of size 25 chosen from the population of all houses?

19 The average time to complete a certain production-line task is assumed to be normally distributed with a standard deviation of 5 minutes (min). A random sample of 16 workers' times is selected to estimate the average time taken to complete the task. What is the probability that the sample mean is within ±1 min of the population's true mean time?

20 The speed of automobiles on I-20 west of Fort Worth, Texas, is being investigated by the Texas Department of Public Safety (DPS). If the average speed of cars on the highway exceeds 80 miles per hour (mph), the DPS plans to add more patrol cars to the area. To decide what to do, they take a random sample of 150 cars and find the sample average speed to be 80.5 mph. Assuming that the population standard deviation is 8 mph, should the DPS add patrol cars to the area?

21 Suppose past evidence shows that the lifetimes of hard drives from a certain production line have a population standard deviation of 700 hours. But a modification has been made in the material used to manufacture the hard drives. The manufacturer wants to know if the average lifetime of the modified hard drives is longer than the previous average lifetime. It is believed that the modification does not affect the standard deviation of the lifetimes, just the average life. The previous average lifetime was 3250 hours. A random sample of 50 hard drives with the modification is taken and the drives are tested. The sample average lifetime for the drives from the new process is found to be 3575 hours. Should the manufacturer conclude that the new process produces hard drives with longer average lifetimes?

2.6   ESTIMATING A POPULATION MEAN

Two types of estimates can be constructed for any population parameter: point estimates and interval estimates. *Point estimates* are single numbers used as an estimate of a parameter. To estimate the population mean, μ, the sample mean $\bar{y}$, typically is used.

An *interval estimate* is a range of values used as an estimate of a population parameter. The width of the interval provides a sense of the accuracy of the point estimate. The interval tells us the likely values of the population mean.

Assuming the population standard deviation, σ, is known, a confidence interval for the population mean, μ, can be constructed as

$$\left(\bar{y} - z_{\alpha/2}\frac{\sigma}{\sqrt{n}}, \bar{y} + z_{\alpha/2}\frac{\sigma}{\sqrt{n}} \right)$$

where $z_{\alpha/2}$ is a standard normal value chosen so that the probability above $z_{\alpha/2}$ is $\alpha/2$. Thus, between $z_{\alpha/2}$ and $-z_{\alpha/2}$, there is a probability of $1-\alpha$ (see Figure 2.17). For this reason, the confidence interval written in its general form is referred to as a $(1-\alpha)100\%$ (read "one minus alpha times 100 percent") confidence interval estimate of μ. By replacing $z_{\alpha/2}$ by the appropriate standard normal value, the desired level of confidence can be achieved. For example, to achieve 95% confidence, use $z_{0.025} = 1.96$ because the probability under the standard normal curve between -1.96 and 1.96 is 0.95. Note that lowercase z's are used here to represent the specific values chosen from the standard normal distribution as opposed to uppercase Z's, which represent the standard normal random variable.

The term "95% confidence interval" means that, if repeated samples of size n are taken from the same population, and a confidence interval is constructed in the manner just described for each sample, 95% of those intervals contain the population mean.

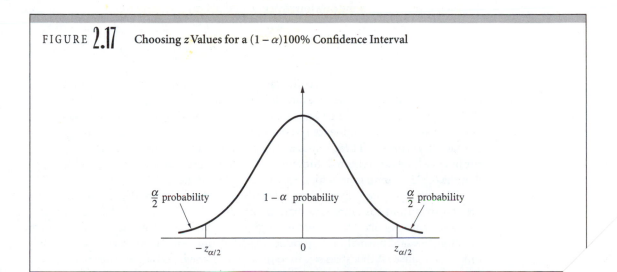

FIGURE 2.17   Choosing z Values for a $(1-\alpha)100\%$ Confidence Interval

$\frac{\alpha}{2}$ probability $1-\alpha$ probability $\frac{\alpha}{2}$ probability

$-z_{\alpha/2}$ 0 $z_{\alpha/2}$

The use of the interval assuming that σ is known is justified for any sample size if the population is normal. In this case, the sampling distribution of sample means is known to be normal, which is the basis for the construction of the interval. If the distribution of the population is unknown or if it is known to be nonnormal, the interval still can be used as long as the sample size is large (generally $n \geq 30$) because the CLT guarantees that the sampling distribution of sample means is approximately normal.

EXAMPLE **2.5**

Managers of Newman-Markups Department Store want a 90% confidence interval estimate of the current average balance of charge customers. With a random sample of 100 accounts, a sample mean of $245, and a population standard deviation of $45, what is the 90% interval estimate of the true average balance?

Answer:　The 90% confidence interval estimate of the true average balance is

$$\left(245 - 1.65\left(\frac{45}{\sqrt{100}}\right), \ 245 + 1.65\left(\frac{45}{\sqrt{100}}\right)\right)$$

or ($237.58, $252.43)

In Example 2.5, the population standard deviation σ was assumed to be known. In most instances, however, σ is unknown. In this case, σ can be estimated by the sample standard deviation:

$$s = \sqrt{\frac{\sum_{i=1}^{n}(y_i - \bar{y})^2}{n-1}}$$

Replacing σ by s in the previous interval and $z_{\alpha/2}$ by $t_{\alpha/2,\,n-1}$ gives

$$\left(\bar{y} - t_{\alpha/2,n-1}\frac{s}{\sqrt{n}}, \ \bar{y} + t_{\alpha/2,n-1}\frac{s}{\sqrt{n}}\right)$$

Changing $z_{\alpha/2}$ to $t_{\alpha/2,\,n-1}$ reflects the fact that s, an estimator of σ, is being used to construct a confidence interval estimate for μ. The value of $t_{\alpha/2,\,n-1}$ is chosen from Table B.2 in Appendix B. The t value chosen depends on the number of *degrees of freedom* (df) and on the confidence level desired. The number of degrees of freedom for estimating μ is $n - 1$. These values are listed on the left-hand side of the t table. The confidence levels are reflected through the upper-tail areas at the top of the table. Note that the 0.025 column is used for a 95% level of confidence ($\alpha/2 = 0.025$).

The shape of the t distribution depends on the number of degrees of freedom. The t distribution has fatter tails than the normal distribution and, thus, has greater probability in its tails. The t value for a given level of confidence is therefore larger than the standard normal value, producing wider confidence intervals (less precise estimates) because s rather than σ is used to construct the interval estimate.

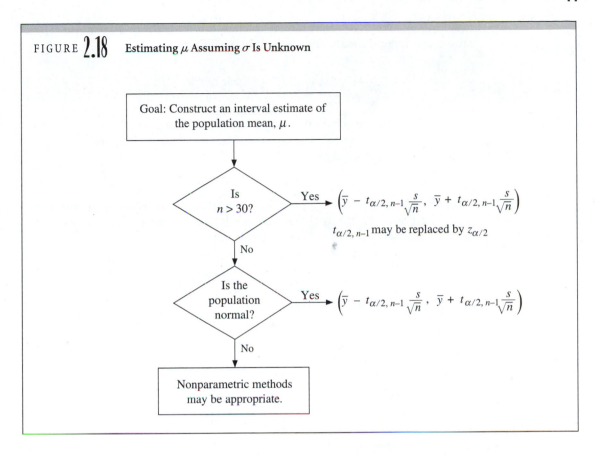

FIGURE **2.18**   **Estimating μ Assuming σ Is Unknown**

Also, as the number of degrees of freedom increases, the t distribution begins to look more like the normal distribution. In the last row of the t table, which is the ∞ degree of freedom row, the z values corresponding to the given upper-tail areas are shown. This indicates that, for a very large sample, the t and Z distributions are identical.

When the number of degrees of freedom is 30 or more, the t values are often replaced by z values because there is little difference between the two in these cases. Although using t values is more correct in all cases when σ is unknown, replacing the t values by z values for large degrees of freedom is often adopted simply for convenience. Note that MINITAB and Excel continue to use t values when σ is unknown, regardless of the sample size.

In small samples ($n < 30$), the population should be normal, or close to a normal distribution, before the interval is used. If the population is nonnormal and small samples are used, nonparametric methods may be appropriate. These methods are discussed in many introductory statistics texts (for example, see Chapter 19 of *Statistics for Management and Economics* by Mendenhall, Reinmuth, and Beaver[2]). When the sample size is large, the assumption of a normal population is not necessary. The

---

[2] See References for complete publication information.

flowchart in Figure 2.18 describes the interval choices when σ is unknown. The σ known case is not shown because it rarely occurs in practice.

EXAMPLE **2.6**

A manufacturer wants to estimate the average life of an expensive electrical component. Because the test to be used destroys the component, a small sample is desired. The lifetimes of five randomly selected components in hours are

$$92, 110, 115, 103, 98$$

What are a point estimate and a 95% confidence interval estimate of the population average lifetime of the components? The population of lifetimes is assumed to be normal.

Answer: Because σ is unknown, the interval to be used is

$$\left(\bar{y} - t_{0.025,4} \frac{s}{\sqrt{n}}, \bar{y} + t_{0.025,4} \frac{s}{\sqrt{n}} \right)$$

The quantities needed to construct the interval are

$$\bar{y} = \frac{\sum_{i=1}^{n} y_i}{n} = 103.6$$

$$s = \sqrt{\frac{\sum_{i=1}^{n} (y_i - \bar{y})^2}{n-1}} = 9.18$$

$$t_{0.025,4} = 2.776$$

The point estimate of μ is $\bar{y} = 103.6$.
The interval estimate of μ is

$$\left[103.6 - 2.776 \left(\frac{9.18}{\sqrt{5}} \right), 103.6 + 2.776 \left(\frac{9.18}{\sqrt{5}} \right) \right] \text{ or } (92.2, 115.0)$$

Computer packages such as MINITAB and Excel also can be used to construct confidence intervals. Figure 2.19 shows the MINITAB output for requests for 90%, 95%, and 99% confidence intervals using the data from Example 2.6.

FIGURE 2.19   **Using MINITAB to Construct Confidence Intervals**

T Confidence Intervals

Variable	N	Mean	StDev	SE Mean	90.0 % CI
lifetime	5	103.60	9.18	4.11	(94.85, 112.35)

T Confidence Intervals

Variable	N	Mean	StDev	SE Mean	95.0 % CI
lifetime	5	103.60	9.18	4.11	(92.20, 115.00)

T Confidence Intervals

Variable	N	Mean	StDev	SE Mean	99.0 % CI
lifetime	5	103.60	9.18	4.11	(84.70, 122.50)

EXERCISES

22   A local department store wants to determine the average age of the adults in its existing marketing area to help target its advertising. A random sample of 400 adults is selected. The sample mean age is found to be 35 years with a sample standard deviation of 5 years. Construct a 95% confidence interval estimate of the population average age of the adults in the area.

23   The management of a large manufacturing plant is studying the number of times employees in a large population of workers are absent. A random sample of 25 employees is chosen, and the average number of annual absences per employee in the sample is found to be six. The sample standard deviation is 0.6. Assuming the population of absences is normally distributed, construct a 99% confidence interval estimate of the population average number of absences.

24   A quality control inspector is concerned with the average amount of weight that can be held by a type of steel beam. A random sample of five beams is tested with the following amounts of weight added before the beams begin to show stress (in thousands of pounds):

9, 11, 10, 10, 8

Assuming that the population of weights is normally distributed, construct a 95% confidence interval estimate of the population average weight that can be held.

25   Table 2.2 shows the highway mileages for 138 different cars for 1999. Assume these cars represent a random sample of all new cars produced in 1999. Find a 95% confidence interval estimate for the population mean miles per gallon. See Exercise 1 for information on accessing the data.

26 The 1999 one-year returns for a random sample of 60 mutual funds are shown in Table 2.6. Find a 95% confidence interval estimate for the population mean rate of return. These data are in a single column in a file with the prefix FUND2.

TABLE **2.6** One-Year Rates of Return for Mutual Funds

Mutual Fund	1-Year Return	Mutual Fund	1-Year Return
Accessor Small to Midcap	7.70	MAS Balanced Instl.	14.10
AIM Advisor Flex Fund C	8.00	Meridian Fund	0.50
Alliance Growth Investors A	15.60	MFS Research A	10.70
American Century Giftrust	−6.20	Mutual Beacon Z	7.60
American Express IDS Growth A	22.30	Neuberger & Berman Focus	9.10
Ariel Fund	3.50	Northern Select Equity	24.20
BB&T Growth & Income A	12.20	One Group Diversified A	18.30
Brandywine Fund	6.90	Oppenheimer Quest Opportunity Value A	6.90
Chase Vista Equity Income A	11.10	Parkstone Small Cap A	−14.80
Columbia Special	8.50	Phoenix-Goodwin Strategic Allocation A	11.30
DLJ Winthrop Small Company Value A	−6.70	PIMCO StocksPlus Instl	19.70
Dreyfus Premier Aggressive Growth A	−15.50	Principal Balanced A	7.30
Dreyfus Small Company Value	0.80	Putnam Convertible Income Gro A	6.30
Enterprise Growth A	18.80	Rainier Investment Balanced	9.70
Excelsior Value & Restructuring	14.60	Rydex OTC	74.40
Fidelity Asset Manager Fund	11.90	Scudder Development	10.10
Fidelity Capital Appreciation	21.80	Sentinel Common Stock A	8.90
Fidelity Puritan	8.60	Smith Barney Concert Growth 1	18.50
Fidelity Select Home Finance	−21.70	Standish Equity	−3.70
First Investors Blue Chip A	13.00	STI Classic Capital Appreciation	17.30
Flag Investors Value Builder A	15.20	SunAmerica Balanced Assets B	14.80
Franklin Rising Dividends A	2.00	T. Rowe Price Equity Income	13.60
Galaxy Equity Income A	9.50	TIP Turner Growth Equity	27.60
Guardian Park Avenue A	9.90	United Continental Income A	5.20
Heartland Value	−8.80	Van Eck Gold A	−12.30
Janus Enterprise	48.40	Vanguard Balanced Index	11.30
J.P. Morgan US Small Company	−7.10	Vanguard Utilities Income	17.50
Kemper Worldwide 2004	0.90	Victory Special Value A	−11.10
Lexington Strategic Investments	11.00	Westcore Midco Growth	13.40
MainStay Cap Appreciation B	20.80	Zweig Strategy A	−6.80

2.7   HYPOTHESIS TESTS ABOUT A POPULATION MEAN

In Section 2.6, estimation of a population mean was discussed. Estimation was the first of our two main topics of statistical inference. In this section, we discuss the second topic: hypothesis tests. Again, the population mean is used to demonstrate tests of hypotheses.

The following definitions are useful in testing hypotheses:

Null Hypothesis, H_0:   The null hypothesis states a hypothesis to be tested.

Alternative Hypothesis, H_a: The alternative hypothesis includes possible values of the population parameter not included in the null hypothesis.

Test Statistic: A number computed from sample information.

Decision Rule: A rule used in conjunction with the test statistic to determine whether the null hypothesis should be accepted or rejected.

In setting up a hypothesis test, the null hypothesis is initially assumed to be true. Under this assumption, a decision rule is constructed based on the sampling distribution of the test statistic. The decision rule states a range of values for the test statistic that are plausible if H_0 is true and a range of values for the test statistic that seem implausible if H_0 is true. Depending on the test statistic value, a statistical decision is made either to accept H_0 (the test statistic falls in the plausible range) or to reject H_0 (the test statistic falls in the implausible range).

Because the decision is based on sample information, it is not possible to be certain that the correct decision has been made. A statistical decision does not prove or disprove the null hypothesis with certainty, although it does present support for one of the two hypotheses. In a business environment, decisions are typically made on the basis of limited information. Hypothesis-testing results provide support for alternative possible courses of action based on such limited (sample) information.

Two types of errors are possible in hypothesis testing. These are illustrated in Figure 2.20. On the left-hand side of the figure are the two possible states of nature: Either H_0 is true or H_0 is false. The statistical decisions, accept H_0 or reject H_0, are listed at the top of the figure. If H_0 is true and the sample information says to accept H_0, a correct decision has been made. Also, if H_0 is false and the sample information says to reject H_0, the decision is correct. If H_0 is true, however, and the sample information says to reject H_0, the decision is incorrect. Rejecting the null hypothesis when it is true is called a *Type I error*. A *Type II error* occurs if the null hypothesis is actually false but the sample information says to accept H_0.

Note that the decision made is always stated with reference to the null hypothesis: Either reject H_0 or accept H_0. Also note that, because only two possibilities are considered (either H_0 or H_a), rejecting H_0 implies agreement with H_a.

Some texts suggest using the expression "fail to reject H_0" or "do not reject H_0" rather than "accept H_0." When the data suggest that we should not reject H_0, this is not

FIGURE 2.20 The Risks of Hypothesis Testing

		Decision	
		Accept H_0	Reject H_0
State of Nature	H_0 True	Correct Decision	Type I Error
	H_0 False	Type II Error	Correct Decision

proof that H_0 is true. This is a statistical decision and may imply simply that we do not have enough evidence to reject H_0. The expression "accept H_0" is sometimes viewed as too strong in suggesting that H_0 has been proven true. In this text, "accept H_0" is used, but be sure to recognize that just because the null hypothesis is accepted, this is not proof of its truth. Our sample may simply not provide enough evidence to reject it.

When testing any hypothesis, it is desirable to keep the chances of an error occurring as small as possible. Typically, when setting up the test, a desired level for the probability of a Type I error is established. By specifying a small probability, control can be exercised over the chances of making such an error. The probability of a Type I error is called the *level of significance* (or *significance level*) of the test and is denoted α.

To illustrate, suppose the following hypotheses are to be tested:

$$H_0: \mu = 10$$

$$H_a: \mu \neq 10$$

Also assume that the population standard deviation is known to be 2. This assumption will be relaxed later. The sample to be drawn consists of 100 items, and the desired level of significance is $\alpha = .05$, or a 5% chance of making a Type I error.

The hypotheses have now been set up and a level of significance chosen. The next step is to establish the decision rule for the test. To do this, consider the sampling distribution of sample means as shown in Figure 2.21.

If the null hypothesis is true ($\mu = 10$), then a region can be determined in which 95% of all sample means will fall. The upper bound of this region is denoted C_1 and the lower bound C_2. Above and below these bounds, there is a combined probability of only .05 of obtaining a sample mean. The decision rule for the test can be set up as:

Reject H_0 if $\bar{y} > C_1$ or $\bar{y} < C_2$

Accept H_0 if $C_2 \leq \bar{y} \leq C_1$

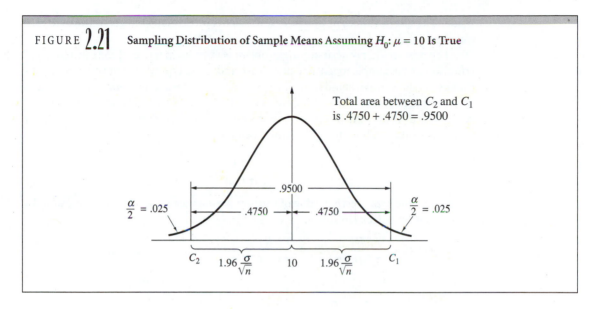

FIGURE 2.21 Sampling Distribution of Sample Means Assuming H_0: $\mu = 10$ Is True

If the null hypothesis is true, 95% of all sample means will fall between C_1 and C_2. So there is only a 5% chance of obtaining a sample mean that falls in the rejection region. In other words, there is a 5% chance of rejecting H_0 if H_0 is true. Thus, the desired level of significance for the test has been achieved.

The critical values C_1 and C_2 in the decision rule can be determined because the sampling distribution is normal (as guaranteed by the CLT because the sample size is large). Between C_1 and C_2, there is to be a probability of .95; the associated z value to produce this probability is 1.96. The upper critical value is

$$C_1 = 10 + 1.96 \frac{2}{\sqrt{100}} = 10.392$$

and the lower critical value is

$$C_2 = 10 - 1.96 \frac{2}{\sqrt{100}} = 9.608$$

The decision rule becomes:

Reject H_0 if $\bar{y} > 10.392$ or $\bar{y} < 9.608$

Accept H_0 if $9.608 \leq \bar{y} \leq 10.392$

Now suppose a sample of size 100 is randomly selected, and the sample mean computed is $\bar{y} = 11.2$. Based on this value of the sample mean, the null hypothesis is not supported. A sample mean of 11.2 is too extreme to believe that the individual values which produced it came from a population with mean $\mu = 10$. So the null hypothesis is rejected. Note that the null hypothesis has not been proved false. There is simply contradictory evidence, and so a statistical decision to reject was made. The alternative hypothesis, $\mu \neq 10$, seems more plausible given the evidence obtained.

The previous hypothesis-testing problem was set up in terms of the sampling distribution of the sample mean. An alternative and more typical way of performing hypothesis tests is with a standardized test statistic. The basic philosophy and structure of the test are the same. The only difference is that the test statistic is standardized and compared directly with the z value. For example, the standardized test statistic for testing hypotheses about the population mean is

$$z = \frac{\bar{y} - \mu_0}{\sigma / \sqrt{n}}$$

where μ_0 is the hypothesized value of the population mean. For the previous example, the standardized decision rule is

$$\text{Reject } H_0 \text{ if } \frac{\bar{y} - \mu_0}{\sigma / \sqrt{n}} > 1.96 \text{ or } \frac{\bar{y} - \mu_0}{\sigma / \sqrt{n}} < -1.96$$

$$\text{Accept } H_0 \text{ if } -1.96 \leq \frac{\bar{y} - \mu_0}{\sigma / \sqrt{n}} \leq 1.96$$

The standardized test statistic value is

$$\frac{\bar{y} - \mu_0}{\sigma / \sqrt{n}} = \frac{11.2 - 10}{2 / \sqrt{100}} = 6$$

Because the test statistic value falls in the rejection region ($6 > 1.96$), the null hypothesis is rejected.

Whether the standardized or unstandardized form of the test is used, the decision made (accept H_0 or reject H_0) will always be the same. Throughout this text, the standardized form is used unless otherwise noted.

If σ is unknown, the same adjustment is used as with confidence intervals. The unknown population standard deviation, σ, is replaced by an estimate, s, and the z value is replaced by the t value with $n-1$ degrees of freedom.

The hypothesis structure previously discussed is called a *two-tailed test* because rejection occurs in both the upper and lower tails of the sampling distribution. Two other hypothesis structures need to be considered: *upper-tailed* and *lower-tailed tests*. Both of these involve rejection in only one tail of the sampling distribution and are therefore referred to as *one-tailed tests*. The hypothesis structures, test statistic, and decision rules for the case when σ is unknown are shown in Table 2.7. The σ known case is omitted because it is rarely encountered in practice.

As was the case for confidence intervals, the t tests are constructed with the assumption that the sampling distribution is normally distributed. The population should be normal (or nearly so) before tests are used with small samples ($n < 30$), or nonparametric methods may be appropriate. Because the CLT guarantees that the sampling distribution is close to normal when n is large, the assumption of a normal population is unnecessary in cases with large sample sizes.

The following examples help illustrate hypothesis-testing techniques.

TABLE 2.7   Hypotheses, Test Statistics, and Decision Rules for Testing Hypotheses About Population Means (σ unknown)

Hypotheses	Test Statistic	Decision Rules
$H_0: \mu = \mu_0$ $H_a: \mu \neq \mu_0$	$t = \dfrac{\bar{y} - \mu_0}{s/\sqrt{n}}$	Reject H_0 if $t > t_{\alpha/2, n-1}$ or $t < -t > t_{\alpha/2, n-1}$ Accept H_0 if $-t_{\alpha/2, n-1} \leq t \leq t_{\alpha/2, n-1}$
$H_0: \mu \leq \mu_0$ $H_a: \mu > \mu_0$	$t = \dfrac{\bar{y} - \mu_0}{s/\sqrt{n}}$	Reject H_0 if $t > t_{\alpha, n-1}$ Accept H_0 if $t \leq t_{\alpha, n-1}$
$H_0: \mu \geq \mu_0$ $H_a: \mu < \mu_0$	$t = \dfrac{\bar{y} - \mu_0}{s/\sqrt{n}}$	Reject H_0 if $t < -t_{\alpha, n-1}$ Accept H_0 if $t \geq -t_{\alpha, n-1}$

EXAMPLE 2.7

Consider again the manufacturer of electrical components in Example 2.6. Suppose the manufacturer wishes to test whether the population average life of the components is 110 hours or more. If it is less than 110 hours, the components do not meet specifications, and the production process must be adjusted to raise the average lifetimes.

As in Example 2.6, five components are randomly selected, and the lifetimes in hours for these components are determined to be

$$92, 110, 115, 103, 98$$

Assume the population of lifetimes is known to be normally distributed. The hypotheses to be tested are

$$H_0: \mu \geq 110$$

$$H_a: \mu < 110$$

Using a 5% level of significance, the decision rule for the test is

$$\text{Reject } H_0 \text{ if } t < -t_{0.05, 4} = -2.132$$

$$\text{Accept } H_0 \text{ if } t \geq -t_{0.05, 4} = -2.132$$

The sample mean and standard deviation are

$$\bar{y} = 103.6, \; s = 9.18$$

and the standardized test statistic, t, is

$$t = \frac{\bar{y} - \mu_0}{s/\sqrt{n}} = \frac{103.6 - 110}{9.18/\sqrt{5}} = -1.56$$

resulting in a decision to accept the null hypothesis. Note that the sample mean of 103.6 hours is below the desired average lifetime of 110 hours. However, it is possible that the population mean could be 110 hours and our sample will produce a sample mean of 103.6 hours. We have not proved the null hypothesis is true, but there is not enough evidence in our small sample to reject it.

EXAMPLE 2.8

A company that manufactures rulers wants to ensure that the average length of its rulers is 12 inches (for obvious reasons). From each production run, a random sample of 25 rulers is selected and their lengths determined by very accurate measuring instruments. On one particular run, the average length of the 25 rulers is determined to be 12.02 inches with a sample standard deviation of 0.02 inch.

Using a 1% level of significance, is the average length of the rulers produced by this manufacturer equal to 12 inches?

Answer: The hypotheses to be tested are

$H_0: \mu = 12$

$H_a: \mu \neq 12$

Using a 1% level of significance, the decision rule for the test is

Reject H_0 if $t > t_{0.005, 24} = 2.797$ or if $t < -t_{0.005, 24} = -2.797$

Accept H_0 if $-2.797 \leq t \leq 2.797$

From the sample information, the standardized test statistic is

$$t = \frac{\bar{y} - \mu_0}{s/\sqrt{n}} = \frac{12.02 - 12}{0.02/\sqrt{25}} = 5.0$$

resulting in a decision to reject the null hypothesis. This decision suggests that the average length of rulers is not 12 inches. Some adjustment to the production process is necessary.

Most statistical software packages perform tests of hypotheses. Instead of reporting a reject or accept decision, however, the output often includes a number called a p value. By comparing the p value to the level of significance, α, an alternative decision rule can be constructed:

Reject H_0 if p value $< \alpha$

Accept H_0 if p value $\geq \alpha$

The p value is the computed area under the sampling distribution at or beyond the value of the standardized test statistic. That is, it is the probability of observing a t

FIGURE 2.22 Computation of *p* Value

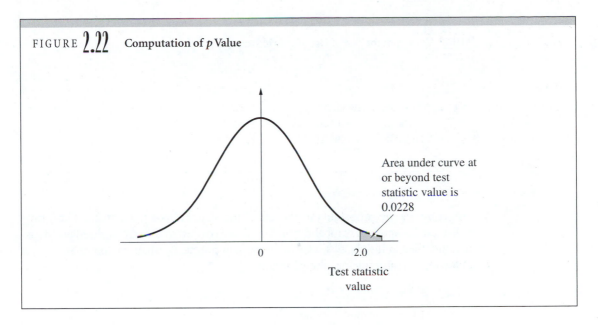

Area under curve at or beyond test statistic value is 0.0228

0   2.0

Test statistic value

value or *z* value as extreme as, or more extreme than, the sample test statistic. For example, suppose the hypotheses to be tested are

$H_0: \mu \leq 10$

$H_a: \mu > 10$

A sample size of 100 is to be used and σ is known to be 10 (for illustrative purposes, we assume σ is known; the process is similar when σ is unknown). From the random sample of 100 items, a sample mean of $\bar{y} = 12$ is obtained. The standardized test statistic is

$$z = \frac{12 - 10}{10/\sqrt{100}} = 2.0$$

In Figure 2.22, the standard normal distribution is shown, and the position of the test statistic has been located. The *p* value for this test is

$$p \text{ value} = P(Z \geq 2.0) = 0.5 - 0.4772 = 0.0228$$

If we require a 5% level of significance, our decision is to reject the null hypothesis because the *p* value of 0.0228 is less than 0.05.

Regardless of which approach to hypothesis testing is chosen (unstandardized or standardized test statistic or *p* value), the decision made is identical for a given level of significance.

The way *p* values are computed differs depending on whether the test is an upper-tailed, lower-tailed, or two-tailed test. In all three cases, the first step is to compute the standardized test statistic. For an upper-tailed test (as in the previous illustration), compute the probability to the right of the standardized test statistic. For a lower-tailed

FIGURE 2.23 MINITAB Output for Test of Hypothesis in Example 2.7

T-Test of the Mean

```
Test of mu = 110.00 vs mu < 110.00
Variable      N       Mean     StDev     SE Mean         T          P
lifetime      5      103.60      9.18        4.11     -1.56      0.097
```

test, compute the probability to the left of the standardized test statistic. For a two-tailed test, compute the probability in the tail area closest to the standardized test statistic, and then multiply this area by 2. By computing p values in this manner, the following decision rule can always be used:

Reject H_0 if p value $< \alpha$

Accept H_0 if p value $\geq \alpha$

EXAMPLE 2.9

Figure 2.23 shows the MINITAB output for testing the hypothesis discussed in Example 2.7. The output shows, $\bar{y} = 103.60, s = 9.18, s/\sqrt{n} = 4.11, t = -1.56$, and the p value $= 0.097$. Using the p value decision rule, note that the null hypothesis is accepted with levels of significance of 1% or 5% but is rejected at 10%. Reporting the p value is somewhat more informative in a case such as this than simply reporting a reject or accept decision.

EXERCISES

27 If a null hypothesis is rejected at the 5% level of significance, what decision would have been made at the 10% level? Why?

28 To investigate an alleged unfair trade practice, the Federal Trade Commission (FTC) takes a random sample of sixteen "5-ounce" candy bars from a large shipment. The mean of the sample weights is 4.85 ounces and the sample standard deviation is 0.1 ounce. Test the hypotheses

$H_0: \mu \geq 5$

$H_a: \mu < 5$

at the 5% level of significance. Assume the population of candy bar weights is approximately normally distributed. Based on the results of the test, does the FTC have grounds to proceed against the manufacturer for the unfair practice of short-weight selling? State the decision rule, the test statistic, and your decision.

29   A quality inspector is interested in the time spent replacing defective parts in one of the company's products. The average time spent should be at most 20 minutes (min) per day according to company standards. The following hypotheses are set up to examine whether the standards are being met:

$$H_0: \mu \leq 20$$

$$H_a: \mu > 20$$

where μ represents the population average time spent replacing defective parts. To conduct the test, a random sample of 16 employees is chosen. The average time spent replacing defective parts for the sample was 20.5 min with a sample standard deviation of 4 min. Perform the test at a 5% level of significance. Assume the population of service times is approximately normally distributed. State the decision rule, the test statistic, and your decision. Are company standards being met?

30   Consider again the mileage figures for 138 cars for 1999 shown in Table 2.2. Assume this is a random sample of cars produced in 1999. The corporate average fuel economy (CAFE) standards set by the government require that average fuel economy for cars is more than 27.5 miles per gallon. To examine whether the CAFE standard is being met, the following hypotheses are tested:

$$H_0: \mu \leq 27.5$$

$$H_a: \mu > 27.5$$

where μ is the population average gas mileage for all 1999 cars. Use a 5% level of significance. State the decision rule, the test statistic, and your decision. What is your conclusion regarding the average mileage of 1999 cars? (See Exercise 1 for information on accessing these data.)

31   The 1999 one-year returns for a random sample of 60 mutual funds are shown in Table 2.6. The return for the S&P 500 stock index for the same one-year time period was 19.9%. Test to see if there is evidence that the average 1999 one-year return for the population of funds is more than the return for the S&P 500 stock index.

Use a 5% level of significance. State the hypotheses to be tested, the decision rule, the test statistic, and your decision. What is your conclusion regarding the average 1999 one-year return for mutual funds? (See Exercise 26 for information on accessing these data.)

2.8 ESTIMATING THE DIFFERENCE BETWEEN TWO POPULATION MEANS

The comparison of two separate populations often is of more concern than the estimation of the parameters of a single population as discussed in Section 2.6. In many cases, the comparison is between the means of the two populations. In this section, point and interval estimates of the difference between two population means are discussed.

Throughout this section, we assume that two populations with parameters μ_1, σ_1 and μ_2, σ_2 are being studied. Random samples are drawn independently from the two populations. Summary statistics from the two samples are:

	Sample 1	Sample 2
Sample size	n_1	n_2
Sample mean	$\bar{x}_1$	$\bar{x}_2$
Sample standard deviation	s_1	s_2

A point estimate of the difference between the two population means, $\mu_1 - \mu_2$, is given by the difference between the two sample means, $\bar{y}_1 - \bar{y}_2$.

If σ_1 and σ_2 are known, the standard deviation of the sampling distribution of $\bar{y}_1 - \bar{y}_2$ is written as

$$\sqrt{\frac{\sigma_1^2}{n_1} + \frac{\sigma_2^2}{n_2}}$$

In addition, the sampling distribution of $\bar{y}_1 - \bar{y}_2$ can be shown to be normally distributed if each of the populations is normal. The sampling distribution is approximately normal if both sample sizes are large ($n_1 \geq 30$ and $n_2 \geq 30$) even if the populations are not normal. A $(1 - \alpha)100\%$ confidence interval for $\mu_1 - \mu_2$ would be

$$\bar{y}_1 - \bar{y}_2 \pm z_{\alpha/2} \sqrt{\frac{\sigma_1^2}{n_1} + \frac{\sigma_2^2}{n_2}}$$

As in the previous situations we discussed, it is unlikely that the population variances, σ_1^2 and σ_2^2, are known in practice. They must be estimated by the sample variances, s_1^2 and s_2^2. These estimates are substituted into the formula for the standard deviation of the sampling distribution of $\bar{y}_1 - \bar{y}_2$, which results in

$$\sqrt{\frac{s_1^2}{n_1} + \frac{s_2^2}{n_2}}$$

An approximate $(1 - \alpha)100\%$ confidence interval for $\mu_1 - \mu_2$ is then

$$\bar{y}_1 - \bar{y}_2 \pm t_{\alpha/2,\Delta} \sqrt{\frac{s_1^2}{n_1} + \frac{s_2^2}{n_2}}$$

The interval is approximate because the population variances may differ. When $\sigma_1^2 \neq \sigma_2^2$, an exact interval cannot be constructed. This interval is referred to as the *approximate* interval.

The approximate degrees of freedom for the sampling distribution of $\bar{y}_1 - \bar{y}_2$ are given by

$$\Delta = \frac{(s_1^2/n_1 + s_2^2/n_2)^2}{\left[(s_1^2/n_1)^2/(n_1-1)\right] + \left[(s_2^2/n_2)^2/(n_2-1)\right]}$$

If the population variances can be assumed equal, $\sigma_1^2 = \sigma_2^2$, then an exact interval can be constructed. Because $\sigma_1^2 = \sigma_2^2$, it is no longer necessary to provide separate estimates of the two variances. The information in both samples can be combined, or pooled, to estimate the common variance. The pooled estimator of the population variance is

$$s_p^2 = \frac{(n_1 - 1)s_1^2 + (n_2 - 1)s_2^2}{n_1 + n_2 - 2}$$

The $(1 - \alpha)100\%$ confidence interval is given by

$$\overline{y}_1 - \overline{y}_2 \pm t_{\alpha/2, n_1 + n_2 - 2} \sqrt{s_p^2 \left(\frac{1}{n_1} + \frac{1}{n_2} \right)}$$

This interval is referred to as the *exact* interval.

Which of these intervals, exact or approximate, should be used in practice? The answer depends on what we know about the population variances, σ_1^2 and σ_2^2. If σ_1^2 and σ_2^2 are known to be equal, choose the exact interval. If σ_1^2 and σ_2^2 are known to be unequal, choose the approximate interval. But what if we have no information on whether or not the variances are equal? In this case, current research recommends using the approximate interval.[3]

EXAMPLE 2.10

Table 2.8, panel A, lists the 5-year returns for a random sample of 33 load mutual funds. (Load funds require the payment of an up-front sales charge to invest in the fund.) Table 2.8, panel B, shows the return figures over the same 5-year period for a random sample of 27 no-load funds (no up-front sales charge is required).

Construct a 95% confidence interval estimate of the difference between the population average 5-year returns for no-load and load funds.

The MINITAB output shown in Figure 2.24 can be used to obtain the confidence interval. As is discussed in Section 2.9, this output also can be used to test hypotheses about the difference between the two population means.

In panel A of Figure 2.24, the results correspond to the approximate interval (assuming $\sigma_1^2 \neq \sigma_2^2$). Panel B shows the results for the exact interval (assuming $\sigma_1^2 = \sigma_2^2$).

Which interval is appropriate in this problem? Since we really have no information on the population variances, the approximate interval is probably the better choice. In this case, there is little difference between the two intervals, but sizable differences can occur that can produce misleading conclusions if the exact interval is used in an inappropriate situation. The approxi-

---

[3] We could test for equality of the variances and choose an approach based on the test result, but this procedure has been shown to be less powerful than simply using the approximate interval. See, for example, "Homogeneity of Variance in the Two-Sample Means Test" by Moser and Stevens in *The American Statistician* 46(1992): 19–21.

TABLE 2.8   5-Year Rates of Return

Panel A: Load Funds		Panel B: No-Load Funds	
Load Mutual Fund	5-Year Return	No-Load Mutual Fund	5-Year Return
AIM Advisor Flex Fund C	16.20	Accessor Small to Midcap	21.90
Alliance Growth Investors A	15.60	American Century Giftrust	9.50
American Express IDS Growth A	24.70	Ariel Fund	16.80
BB&T Growth & Income A	20.10	Brandywine Fund	15.70
Chase Vista Equity Income A	20.70	Columbia Special	13.90
DLJ Winthrop Small Company Value A	10.00	Excelsior Value & Restructuring	24.30
Dreyfus Premier Aggressive Growth A	−8.00	Fidelity Asset Manager Fund	13.40
Dreyfus Small Company Value	18.80	Fidelity Capital Appreciation	18.60
Enterprise Growth A	27.40	Fidelity Puritan	15.10
Fidelity Select Home Finance	18.30	Heartland Value	12.50
First Investors Blue Chip A	19.80	Janus Enterprise	23.80
Flag Investors Value Builder A	20.60	J.P. Morgan US Small Company	13.00
Franklin Rising Dividends A	17.50	MAS Balanced Instl.	16.70
Galaxy Equity Income A	18.40	Meridian Fund	12.70
Guardian Park Avenue A	22.40	Mutual Beacon Z	17.40
Kemper Worldwide 2004	9.00	Neuberger & Berman Focus	18.60
Lexington Strategic Investments	−11.50	Northern Select Equity	24.30
MainStay Cap Appreciation B	22.40	PIMCO StocksPlus Instl.	26.40
MFS Research A	21.20	Rainier Investment Balanced	17.70
One Group Diversified A	21.90	Rydex OTC	40.90
Oppenheimer Quest Opportunity Value A	18.90	Scudder Development	17.10
Parkstone Small Cap A	9.70	Standish Equity	19.30
Phoenix-Goodwin Strategic Allocation A	13.00	T. Rowe Price Equity Income	20.70
Principal Balanced A	12.90	TIP Turner Growth Equity	23.80
Putnam Convertible Income Gro A	14.30	Vanguard Balanced Index	16.80
Sentinel Common Stock A	19.80	Vanguard Utilities Income	16.60
Smith Barney Concert Growth 1	21.30	Westcore Midco Growth	15.80
STI Classic Capital Appreciation	20.60		
SunAmerica Balanced Assets B	16.30		
United Continental Income A	12.30		
Van Eck Gold A	−14.20		
Victory Special Value A	11.80		
Zweig Strategy A	10.50		

FIGURE 2.24   MINITAB Output for Examples 2.10 and 2.11

Panel A: Assumes Variances Are Unequal

```
Two sample T for 5-year return

load/no      N       Mean      StDev      SE Mean
0            27      18.64     6.12         1.2
1            33      14.93     9.57         1.7

95% CI for mu (0) - mu (1): (-0.4, 7.8)
T-Test mu (0) = mu (1) (vs not =): T = 1.82 P = 0.075 DF = 55
```

Panel B: Assumes Variances Are Equal

```
Two sample T for 5-year return

load/no      N       Mean      StDev      SE Mean
0            27      18.64     6.12         1.2
1            33      14.93     9.57         1.7

95% CI for mu (0) - mu (1): (-0.6, 8.0)
T-Test mu (0) = mu (1) (vs not =): T = 1.74 P = 0.087 DF = 58
Both use Pooled StDev = 8.21
```

mate interval provides a conservative result when the population variances are equal but also provides protection against the case when the variances are not equal.

The interval produced by the approximate method is (−0.4%, 7.8%). This result suggests that we can be 95% confident that the difference in population average 5- year returns for load and no-load funds ($\mu_{NoLoad} - \mu_{Load}$) is between −0.4% and 7.8%. What does this result suggest to you regarding the two types of funds?

EXERCISES

32 A graduate school of business is interested in estimating the difference between mean GMAT scores for applicants with and without work experience. Independent random samples of 50 applicants with and 50 applicants without work experience are chosen. The following results were obtained:

	With Work Experience	Without Work Experience
Sample size	50	50
Sample mean	545	510
Sample standard deviation	104	95

Construct a 95% confidence interval estimate of the difference between the mean GMAT scores for the two groups.

33 Two suppliers are being considered by a manufacturer. Independent random samples of ten parts from shipments from each supplier are selected, and the lifetime in hours for each part is determined for each sample. Use the following information to construct a 98% confidence interval estimate of the difference in the population average lifetimes. Assume that the population variances are equal and the populations are normally distributed.

	Supplier 1	Supplier 2
Sample size	10.0	10.0
Sample mean	15.0	11.0
Sample standard deviation	1.5	1.0

34 To help validate a new employee-rating form, a company administers it to independent random samples of employees in two different divisions. The following information is obtained from the scores on the forms:

	Division 1	Division 2
Sample size	15.0	15.0
Sample mean	82.0	78.0
Sample standard deviation	3.0	2.5

Use the information to construct a 95% confidence interval estimate of the difference in mean scores between the two divisions. Assume that the population variances are equal and the populations are normally distributed.

35 The 1999 one-year returns for a random sample of 33 load mutual funds and 27 no-load funds were obtained. The returns for the load funds are shown in Table 2.9, panel A, and for the no-load funds in Table 2.9, panel B. Construct a 95% confidence interval estimate of the difference between the population mean returns. Assume that the populations are approximately normally distributed.

These data are available in a file with prefix RETURNS2 in two columns. The first column contains the returns for the load funds and the second column contains the returns for the no-load funds.

36 Table 2.10 shows the city mileage and the type of transmission for a sample of cars. The transmissions variable is coded 1 for automatic and 0 for manual. Construct a 99% confidence interval estimate for the difference between population average city mileage for cars with manual and automatic transmissions.

TABLE 2.9   One-Year Rates of Return

Panel A: Load Funds		Panel B: No-Load Funds	
Load Mutual Fund	1-Year Return	No-Load Mutual Fund	1-Year Return
AIM Advisor Flex Fund C	8.00	Accessor Small to Midcap	7.70
Alliance Growth Investors A	15.60	American Century Giftrust	−6.20
American Express IDS Growth A	22.30	Ariel Fund	3.50
BB&T Growth & Income A	12.20	Brandywine Fund	6.90
Chase Vista Equity Income A	11.10	Columbia Special	8.50
DLJ Winthrop Small Company Value A	−6.70	Excelsior Value & Restructuring	14.60
Dreyfus Premier Aggressive Growth A	−15.50	Fidelity Asset Manager Fund	11.90
Dreyfus Small Company Value	0.80	Fidelity Capital Appreciation	21.80
Enterprise Growth A	18.80	Fidelity Puritan	8.60
Fidelity Select Home Finance	−21.70	Heartland Value	−8.80
First Investors Blue Chip A	13.00	Janus Enterprise	48.40
Flag Investors Value Builder A	15.20	J.P. Morgan US Small Company	−7.10
Franklin Rising Dividends A	2.00	MAS Balanced Instl.	14.10
Galaxy Equity Income A	9.50	Meridian Fund	0.50
Guardian Park Avenue A	9.90	Mutual Beacon Z	7.60
Kemper Worldwide 2004	0.90	Neuberger & Berman Focus	9.10
Lexington Strategic Investments	11.00	Northern Select Equity	24.20
MainStay Cap Appreciation B	20.80	PIMCO StocksPlus Instl.	19.70
MFS Research A	10.70	Rainier Investment Balanced	9.70
One Group Diversified A	18.30	Rydex OTC	74.40
Oppenheimer Quest Opportunity Value A	6.90	Scudder Development	10.10
Parkstone Small Cap A	−14.80	Standish Equity	−3.70
Phoenix-Goodwin Strategic Allocation A	11.30	T. Rowe Price Equity Income	13.60
Principal Balanced A	7.30	TIP Turner Growth Equity	27.60
Putnam Convertible Income Gro A	6.30	Vanguard Balanced Index	11.30
Sentinel Common Stock A	8.90	Vanguard Utilities Income	17.50
Smith Barney Concert Growth 1	18.50	Westcore Midco Growth	13.40
STI Classic Capital Appreciation	17.30		
SunAmerica Balanced Assets B	14.80		
United Continental Income A	5.20		
Van Eck Gold A	−12.30		
Victory Special Value A	−11.10		
Zweig Strategy A	−6.80		

TABLE **2.10** Data on City Mileage for Automatic (1) and Manual (0) Transmission Cars

Car	CITY MPG	TRANS	Car	CITY MPG	TRANS
Acura 2.3 CL	25	0	Chrysler Sebring LX	22	0
Acura Integra LS Coupe	25	0	Chrysler 300M	18	1
Acura NSX	17	0	Daewoo Lanos S 3-door	26	0
Acura 3.5RL	19	1	Daewoo Leganza SE	20	0
Acura TL	19	1	Daewoo Nubira SX 4-door	22	0
Aston Martin DB7Coupe	14	0	Dodge Avenger	22	0
Audi A4 1.8T	23	0	Dodge Intrepid	21	1
Audi A6	17	1	Dodge Neon Highline Coupe	27	0
Audi A8 3.7	17	1	Dodge Stratus	27	0
Bentley Arnage	12	1	Dodge Viper RT/10	12	0
BMW 318ti Coupe	23	0	Ferrari F355 Berlinetta	26	0
BMW 3 323i Sedan	20	0	Ferrari 456M GT	11	0
BMW 528i	20	0	Ferrari 550 Maranello	10	0
BMW 740i	17	1	Ford Contour LX	24	0
BMW Z3 2.3 Roadster	20	0	Ford Crown Victoria	17	1
Buick Century Custom	20	1	Ford Escort LX Sedan	25	0
Buick LeSabre Custom	19	1	Ford Escort ZX2 Cool	26	0
Buick Park Avenue	19	1	Ford Mustang Coupe	20	0
Buick Regal LS	19	1	Ford Taurus LX Sedan	19	1
Buick Riviera	18	1	Honda Accord DX Sedan	25	0
Cadillac Catera	18	1	Honda Civic CX Hatchback	32	0
Cadillac DeVille	17	1	Honda Prelude	23	0
Cadillac Eldorado	17	1	Hyundai Accent L Coupe	28	0
Cadillac Seville SLS	17	1	Hyundai Elantra Sedan	24	0
Chevrolet Camaro Coupe	19	0	Hyundai Sonata	21	0
Chevrolet Cavalier Coupe	24	0	Hyundai Tiburon	24	0
Chevrolet Corvette Coupe	17	1	Infiniti G20	23	0
Chevrolet Lumina	20	1	Infiniti I30	21	1
Chevrolet Malibu Sedan	23	1	Infiniti Q45	18	1
Chevrolet Metro Coupe	41	0	Jaguar XJ8	17	1
Chevrolet Monte Carlo LS	20	1	Jaguar XK8 Coupe	17	1
Chevrolet Prizm Sedan	31	0	KIA Sephia	24	0
Chrysler Cirrus Lxi	20	1	Lamborghini Diablo Roadster VT	9	0
Chrysler Concorde LX	21	1	Lexus ES 300	19	1
Chrysler LHS	18	1	Lexus GS 300	20	1
Chrysler Sebring Convertible JX	21	1	Lexus LS 400	19	1

TABLE **2.10**   *(continued)*

Car	CITY MPG	TRANS	Car	CITY MPG	TRANS
Lexus SC 300	19	1	Oldsmobile Intrigue GX	19	1
Lincoln Continental	17	1	Plymouth Breeze	26	0
Lincoln LS V6	17	0	Plymouth Neon Coupe	29	0
Lincoln Town Car Executive	17	1	Plymouth Prowler	17	1
Lotus Esprit V8	15	0	Pontiac Bonneville SE	19	1
Mazda Miata MX-5	25	0	Pontiac Firebird Coupe	19	0
Mazda Millenia	20	1	Pontiac Grand Am SE Coupe	21	1
Mazda Protégé DX	29	0	Pontiac Grand Prix SE Sedan	20	1
Mazda 626 LX	26	0	Pontiac Sunfire SE Coupe	24	0
Mercedes-Benz C230 Kompressor	21	1	Porsche 911 Carrera Coupe	17	0
Mercedes-Benz CL500	15	1	Porsche Boxster	19	0
Mercedes-Benz CLK320	21	1	Rolls-Royce Silver Seraph	12	1
Mercedes-Benz E300 Sedan	21	1	Saab 9-3 -door	21	0
Mercedes-Benz S320	17	1	Saab 9-5	21	0
Mercedes-Benz SL500	16	1	Saturn Coupe SC1	29	0
Mercedes-Benz SLK320	22	0	Saturn SL Sedan	29	0
Mercury Cougar	24	0	Subaru Impreza L Coupe	22	0
Mercury Grand Marquis GS	17	1	Subaru Legacy Brighton Wagon	22	0
Mercury Mystique GS	24	0	Suzuki Esteem GL Sedan	31	0
Mercury Sable GS Sedan	19	1	Suzuki Swift	39	0
Mercury Tracer GS Sedan	28	0	Toyota Avalon XL	21	1
Mitsubishi Diamante	18	1	Toyota Camry CE	23	0
Mitsubishi Eclipse RS	22	0	Toyota Camry Solara SE	23	0
Mitsubishi Galant DE	23	1	Toyota Celica GT Liftback	22	0
Mitsubishi Mirage DE Sedan	33	0	Toyota Corolla VE	31	0
Mitsubishi 3000GT	19	0	Toyota Tercel CE 2-door	32	0
Nissan Altima XE	24	0	Volkswagen Golf GL	24	0
Nissan Maxima GXE	22	0	Volkswagen Jetta GL	24	0
Nissan Sentra XE	30	0	Volkswagen New Beetle GL	23	0
Oldsmobile Alero GX Sedan	21	1	Volkswagen Passat GLS	23	0
Oldsmobile Aurora	17	1	Volvo C70 Coupe LPT	20	1
Oldsmobile Cutlass GL	20	1	Volvo S70	20	0
Oldsmobile Eighty Eight	19	1	Volvo S80 2.9	19	1

These data are available in a file with the prefix TRANS2 in two columns. The first column contains the mileages and the second column contains the transmissions variable. Note that the data for both samples is contained in the first column. The second column indicates to which sample (automatic = 1, manual = 0) each value in column 1 belongs.

2.9   HYPOTHESIS TESTS ABOUT THE DIFFERENCE BETWEEN TWO POPULATION MEANS

We may be interested in testing hypotheses about the difference between two population means rather than estimating that difference. The most common hypotheses tested in comparing two populations are

$$H_0: \mu_1 = \mu_2$$

$$H_a: \mu_1 \neq \mu_2$$

The null hypothesis states that the means of the two populations are equal, whereas the alternate states that the two population means differ. These hypotheses can be restated in terms of the difference between two means as

$$H_0: \mu_1 - \mu_2 = 0$$

$$H_a: \mu_1 - \mu_2 \neq 0$$

The decision rule for the test is

Reject H_0 if $t > t_{\alpha/2}$ or $t < - t_{\alpha/2}$

Accept H_0 if $- t_{\alpha/2} \leq t \leq t_{\alpha/2}$

The construction of the test statistic, t, depends on whether the population variances can be assumed equal. If $\sigma_1^2 = \sigma_2^2$, then

$$t = \frac{\overline{y}_1 - \overline{y}_2}{\sqrt{s_p^2 \left(\frac{1}{n_1} + \frac{1}{n_2} \right)}}$$

and the critical value, $t_{\alpha/2}$, is chosen with $n_1 + n_2 - 2$ degrees of freedom. The pooled estimate of the population variance s_p^2, is used in computing the standard deviation of the sampling distribution.

If $\sigma_1^2 \neq \sigma_2^2$, then

$$t = \frac{\overline{y}_1 - \overline{y}_2}{\sqrt{\frac{s_1^2}{n_1} + \frac{s_2^2}{n_2}}}$$

and the approximate critical value is chosen with

TABLE 2.11   Hypotheses, Test Statistics, and Decision Rules for Testing Hypotheses About Differences Between Population Means When $\sigma_1^2 = \sigma_2^2$

Hypotheses	Test Statistics	Decision Rules
$H_0: \mu_1 - \mu_2 = 0$ $H_a: \mu_1 - \mu_2 \neq 0$	$t = \dfrac{\bar{y}_1 - \bar{y}_2}{\sqrt{s_p^2\left(\dfrac{1}{n_1} + \dfrac{1}{n_2}\right)}}$	Reject H_0 if $t > t_{\alpha/2, n_1+n_2-2}$ or if $t < -t_{\alpha/2, n_1+n_2-2}$ Accept H_0 if $-t_{\alpha/2, n_1+n_2-2} \leq t \leq t_{\alpha/2, n_1+n_2-2}$
$H_0: \mu_1 - \mu_2 \geq 0$ $H_a: \mu_1 - \mu_2 < 0$	$t = \dfrac{\bar{y}_1 - \bar{y}_2}{\sqrt{s_p^2\left(\dfrac{1}{n_1} + \dfrac{1}{n_2}\right)}}$	Reject H_0 if $t < -t_{\alpha, n_1+n_2-2}$ Accept H_0 if $t \geq -t_{\alpha, n_1+n_2-2}$
$H_0: \mu_1 - \mu_2 \leq 0$ $H_a: \mu_1 - \mu_2 > 0$	$t = \dfrac{\bar{y}_1 - \bar{y}_2}{\sqrt{s_p^2\left(\dfrac{1}{n_1} + \dfrac{1}{n_2}\right)}}$	Reject H_0 if $t > t_{\alpha, n_1+n_2-2}$ Accept H_0 if $t \leq t_{\alpha, n_1+n_2-2}$

$$\Delta = \frac{(s_1^2/n_1 + s_2^2/n_2)^2}{\left[(s_1^2/n_1)^2/(n_1-1)\right] + \left[(s_2^2/n_2)^2/(n_2-1)\right]}$$

degrees of freedom.

The justification for using two different standard errors in constructing the test statistics is the same as that for constructing the confidence intervals in the previous section.

Table 2.11 shows the three possible hypothesis structures, the test statistic to be used, and the decision rules for the case when $\sigma_1^2 = \sigma_2^2$. Table 2.12 presents similar information for $\sigma_1^2 \neq \sigma_2^2$

EXAMPLE 2.11

Consider again the random sample of mutual funds examined in Example 2.10 of Section 2.8. The 5-year returns for 33 load funds and 27 no-load funds were shown in Table 2.8.

Let μ_L represent the population mean 5-year return for load funds and μ_N represent the population mean 5-year return for no-load funds. Then the hypotheses

$$H_0: \mu_N - \mu_L = 0$$

$$H_a: \mu_N - \mu_L \neq 0$$

TABLE 2.12   Hypotheses, Test Statistics, and Decision Rules for Testing Hypotheses About Differences Between Population Means When $\sigma_1^2 \neq \sigma_2^2$

Hypotheses	Test Statistics	Decision Rules
$H_0: \mu_1 - \mu_2 = 0$ $H_a: \mu_1 - \mu_2 \neq 0$	$t = \dfrac{\bar{y}_1 - \bar{y}_2}{\sqrt{\dfrac{s_1^2}{n_1} + \dfrac{s_2^2}{n_2}}}$	Reject H_0 if $t > t_{\alpha/2,\Delta}$ or if $t < -t_{\alpha/2,\Delta}$ Accept H_0 if $-t_{\alpha/2,\Delta} \leq t \leq t_{\alpha/2,\Delta}$
$H_0: \mu_1 - \mu_2 \geq 0$ $H_a: \mu_1 - \mu_2 < 0$	$t = \dfrac{\bar{y}_1 - \bar{y}_2}{\sqrt{\dfrac{s_1^2}{n_1} + \dfrac{s_2^2}{n_2}}}$	Reject H_0 if $t < -t_{\alpha,\Delta}$ Accept H_0 if $t \geq -t_{\alpha,\Delta}$
$H_0: \mu_1 - \mu_2 \leq 0$ $H_a: \mu_1 - \mu_2 > 0$	$t = \dfrac{\bar{y}_1 - \bar{y}_2}{\sqrt{\dfrac{s_1^2}{n_1} + \dfrac{s_2^2}{n_2}}}$	Reject H_0 if $t > t_{\alpha,\Delta}$ Accept H_0 if $t \leq t_{\alpha,\Delta}$

can be tested to determine if there is a difference between the average returns for these two groups.

Figure 2.24 shows the MINITAB output for testing the hypotheses; Figure 2.25 shows the Excel output. Assuming that the population variances are unequal (or that we have no information about the variances), the panel A output is appropriate in each figure. Using this output, the null hypothesis is accepted. The t statistic or the p value can be used to reach this decision. If the t statistic is used, the decision rule is:

Reject H_0 if $t > 1.96$ or $t < -1.96$

Accept H_0 if $-1.96 \leq t \leq 1.96$

There are 55 degrees of freedom for this test, so the z value of 1.96 was used as the critical value. Note that Excel provides the t value for 55 degrees of freedom for a two-tailed test: $t = 2.004$. This value could be used (and is in fact preferred) rather than the z value if it is available. The test statistic value is $t = 1.82$.

If the p value is used, the decision rule is

Reject H_0 if p value < 0.05

Accept H_0 if p value ≥ 0.05

where the p value is 0.075. As always, both procedures lead to the same decision.

The statistical decision is to accept the null hypothesis, so we conclude that there in no difference between the average 5-year returns for load and no-load mutual funds.

FIGURE 2.25   **Excel Output for Examples 2.10 and 2.11**

Panel A: Assumes Variances Are Unequal

t-Test: Two-Sample Assuming Unequal Variances

	Variable 1	Variable 2
Mean	18.641	14.930
Variance	37.513	91.617
Observations	27.000	33.000
Hypothesized Mean Difference	0.000	
df	55.000	
t Stat	1.818	
P(T<=t) one-tail	0.037	
t Critical one-tail	1.673	
P(T<=t) two-tail	0.075	
t Critical two-tail	2.004	

Panel B: Assumes Variances Are Equal

t-Test: Two-Sample Assuming Equal Variances

	Variable 1	Variable 2
Mean	18.641	14.930
Variance	37.513	91.617
Observations	27.000	33.000
Pooled Variance	67.364	
Hypothesized Mean Difference	0.000	
df	58.000	
t Stat	1.742	
P(T<=t) one-tail	0.043	
t Critical one-tail	1.672	
P(T<=t) two-tail	0.087	
t Critical two-tail	2.002	

EXERCISES

37 Consider again Exercise 32 in Section 2.8. Two independent random samples of applicants to business schools who had and did not have work experience were chosen. Each sample contained 50 applicants.

To determine whether there is a difference in the population average test scores, the following hypotheses should be tested:

$$H_0 : \mu_1 - \mu_2 = 0$$

$$H_a: \mu_1 - \mu_2 \neq 0$$

Use a 5% level of significance. State the decision rule, the test statistic, and your decision. What implication do these test results have for admissions officers in MBA programs?

38 Use the information in Exercise 33. Suppose that the manufacturer currently uses supplier 2. A change to supplier 1 will be made only if the average lifetime of parts for supplier 1 is greater than the average for supplier 2. Using a 1% level of significance, conduct the appropriate test. State the hypotheses to be tested, the decision rule, the test statistic, and your decision. Assume that the population variances are equal and the populations are normally distributed. On the basis of the test result, which supplier will the manufacturer choose?

39 Use the information in Exercise 34. Is there a difference in population mean rating scores for the two divisions? State the hypotheses to be tested, the decision rule, the test statistic, and your decision. Assume that the population variances are equal and the populations are normally distributed. Use a 5% level of significance.

40 The 1999 one-year returns for a random sample of 33 load mutual funds and 27 no-load funds were obtained. The returns for these funds were shown in Table 2.9. Test to see if there is any difference between the population average 1999 one-year returns for load and no-load funds. Assume that the populations are approximately normally distributed. Use a 5% level of significance. State the decision rule, the test statistic, and your decision. Is there a difference in the population averages? Based on the test results, what conclusions do you draw concerning investment in load versus no-load funds? (See Exercise 35 for information on reading the data.)

41 Use the data from Exercise 36 of Section 2.8. Let μ_0 = the population average city mileage for cars with manual transmissions and μ_1 = the population average for cars with automatic transmissions. Suppose that a claim is made that the cars with manual transmissions have better (higher) city gas mileage, on average, than cars with automatic transmissions. Examine the claim by testing the following hypotheses:

$$H_0 : \mu_0 - \mu_1 \leq 0$$

$$H_a: \mu_0 - \mu_1 > 0$$

Use a 5% level of significance. State the decision rule, the test statistic, and your decision. Is the claim supported? (See Exercise 36 for information on reading the data.)

2.10 USING THE COMPUTER

The Using the Computer section in each chapter describes how to perform the computer analyses in the chapter using MINITAB, Excel, and SAS. For further detail on MINITAB, Excel, and SAS, see Appendix C.

2.10.1 MINITAB

Note that Version 12 of MINITAB is fully menu driven. Commands can be used, however, and they are included for any interested users. The menu headings and subheadings used to perform the procedures are listed first, followed by commands in parentheses. For example, GRAPH: HISTOGRAM means to click on the Graph menu and then on HISTOGRAM. (HISTOGRAM C1 means to type in the command as shown.)

Descriptive Statistics

```
GRAPH: HISTOGRAM     (HISTOGRAM C1)
```

Creates a histogram. In the histogram dialog box (see Figure 2.26), fill in the variables to be graphed and click OK. There are a variety of options available which are described in the MINITAB Help facility.

FIGURE 2.26   **MINITAB Histogram Dialog Box**

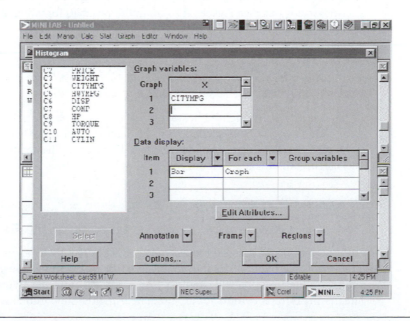

FIGURE **2.27** MINITAB Descriptive Statistics Dialog Box

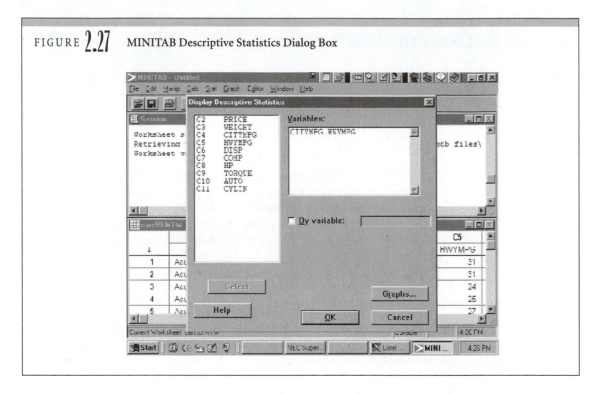

STAT: BASIC STATISTICS: DISPLAY DESCRIPTIVE STATISTICS (DESCRIBE C1)

Generates a variety of descriptive statistics (see Figure 2.5). In the Display Descriptive Statistics dialog box (see Figure 2.27), fill in the variables for which descriptive statistics are desired and click OK.

Confidence Interval Estimate of μ

STAT: BASIC STATISTICS: 1-SAMPLE T (TINT C1)

Constructs a 95% confidence interval estimate of the population mean, μ. Other levels of confidence can be requested. In the 1-Sample t dialog box (see Figure 2.28), fill in the variables for which a confidence interval is desired. The default confidence level is 95%. This can be changed if desired.

Hypotheses Tests About μ

STAT: BASIC STATISTICS: 1-SAMPLE T (TTEST OF MU = K C1)

Produces the output necessary to test the hypotheses H_0: $\mu = k$ versus H_a: $\mu \neq k$, where k represents the hypothesized value in the problem. An upper-tailed test can be requested in the 1-Sample t dialog box (see Figure 2.29) by specifying the alternative "greater than" (or if commands are used, by using the subcommand ALTERNATIVE

FIGURE 2.28 MINITAB 1-Sample t Dialog Box for Confidence Interval

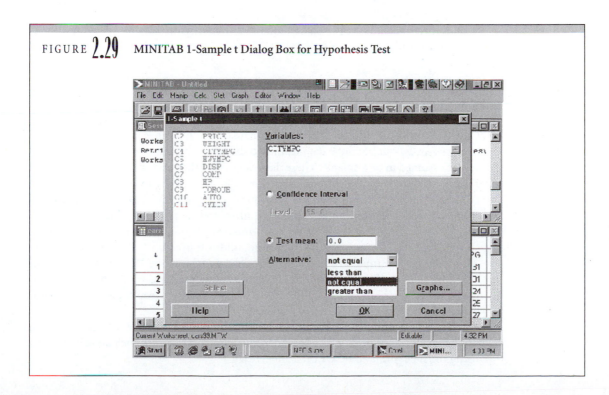

FIGURE 2.29 MINITAB 1-Sample t Dialog Box for Hypothesis Test

FIGURE 2.30   MINITAB 2-Sample t Screen

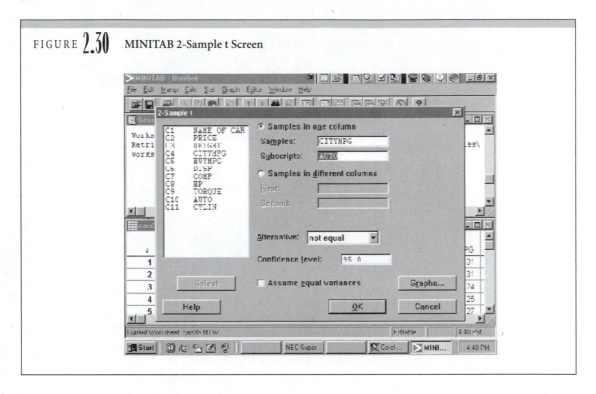

= 1). A lower-tailed test can also be requested by specifying the alternative "less than" (or by using the subcommand ALTERNATIVE = –1).

Confidence Interval Estimate of $\mu_1 - \mu_2$

`STAT: BASIC STATISTICS: 2-SAMPLE T (TWOSAMPLE C1 C2 or TWOT C1 C2)`

Constructs a 95% confidence interval estimate of the difference between two population means, $\mu_1 - \mu_2$. Sample data from two different populations with means μ_1 and μ_2 are assumed to be available. These data can be in either one or two columns. The 2-Sample t dialog box is illustrated in Figure 2.30. If the data from both samples are contained in one column, check the "Samples in one column" button. If you use this option, a second column must contain numbers indicating from which sample each data point came (number the items from the first sample 0 and the items from the second sample 1, for example.) (The command for this case is TWOT C1 C2.) If the data from each sample are in a different column, check the "Samples in different columns" button. Then indicate the two columns containing your data. (The command for this case is TWOSAMPLE C1 C2.) The choice between these two options is based purely on how your data are arranged.

The assumption that the population variances (or standard deviations) are equal can be included by checking the "Assume equal variances" box in the dialog box (or by using the subcommand POOLED).

Hypotheses Tests About $\mu_1 - \mu_2$

STAT: BASIC STATISTICS: 2-SAMPLE T (TWOSAMPLE C1 C2 or TWOT C1 C2)

Produces the output necessary to test H_0: $\mu_1 - \mu_2 = 0$ versus H_a: $\mu_1 - \mu_2 \neq 0$ (see Figure 2.30). The same dialog box is used for constructing a confidence interval for the difference between two means and testing hypotheses about the difference between two means. The form of the alternative hypothesis can be chosen. An upper-tailed test can be requested by specifying the alternative "greater than" (or if commands are used, by using the subcommand ALTERNATIVE = 1). A lower-tailed test can also be requested by specifying the alternative "less than" (or by using the subcommand ALTERNATIVE = −1). See the previous section for a description of how data should be arranged and how the equal variance option is handled.

2.10.2 Excel

Descriptive Statistics

TOOLS: DATA ANALYSIS: HISTOGRAM

Creates a histogram. In the histogram dialog box (see Figure 2.31), fill in the input range of the variable to be graphed. Fill in the range of the data you want included in your frequency distribution. In the language of worksheets, the range of the data indicates the cells in which the data are contained. For example, if you have 100 observations to be included in your frequency distribution and you have typed these 100 numbers into cells A1 through A100, you specify the range as A1:A100 in the Input Range box.

You can specify the bins you want Excel to use. If you enter nothing in this box, Excel picks the bin limits for your frequency distribution/histogram. To specify the bins for Excel to use, just put the numbers you want to use as bin limits in a column. Then indicate the range of this column in the Bin Range box.

If the first row of your column of data contains a label, check the Label box. The next three options determine where you want the frequency distribution to appear. If you click Output Range, you can tell Excel a specific spot in the spreadsheet to put your frequency distribution and histogram. For example, if you check the Output Range button and put C3 in this box, the frequency distribution starts in cell C3. Check the New Worksheet Ply button and Excel puts your frequency distribution on a new ply in this same workbook. You can name the worksheet ply if you want. Check New Workbook and Excel puts your frequency distribution in a completely new workbook.

The next three options determine exactly what kind of output you want from Excel. If you want only a frequency distribution, do not check any of these options. The Pareto option constructs a histogram with the bins arranged from biggest to smallest. This option is often not very useful when quantitative data are used. It is more useful when qualitative data are used and the order of importance of certain categories is of interest. A Pareto chart is often used in quality control situations. For example, if customer complaints are being monitored and the most frequent com-

FIGURE 2.31   Excel Histogram Dialog Box

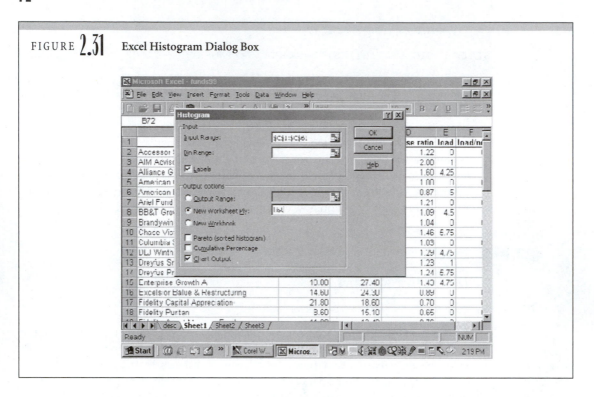

plaints are of primary interest, a Pareto chart emphasizes those complaints by listing them first. The Cumulative Percentage option constructs a histogram but superimposes a line on the histogram that represents the cumulative percentage (sometimes called an *ogive).* Chart Output requests Excel to construct a histogram in addition to a frequency distribution.

Once you have the options set as you want, click OK.

TOOLS: DATA ANALYSIS: DESCRIPTIVE STATISTICS

Generates a variety of descriptive statistics (see Figure 2.6). In the Descriptive Statistics dialog box (see Figure 2.32), fill in the input range for the variable for which descriptive statistics are desired. Typically, this variable is in a column, but the option is available to indicate whether it is in a column or row. Choose the output option and click Summary statistics. Click Confidence Level for Mean to produce a 95% error bound. (The 95% error bound is the default value and can be set at any desired level.) Click OK.

Confidence Interval Estimate of μ

The descriptive statistics option on the Data Analysis toolpack produces a value for the sample mean and a 95% (or any other desired) error bound which can be used to construct a confidence interval. See Descriptive Statistics and Figure 2.32 for informa-

FIGURE **2.32**   **Excel Descriptive Statistics Dialog Box**

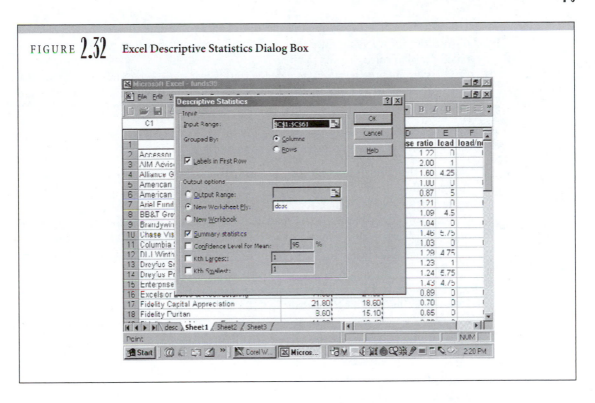

tion on this procedure. The confidence interval can be constructed as sample mean ± error bound.

Alternatively, a formula can be constructed to compute the upper and lower confidence interval bounds. For example, suppose we have data in cells A1 through A100 and want to construct a 95% confidence interval. The formulas for the upper (UCL) and lower (LCL) confidence interval limits are

UCL:	= average(A1:A100)+tinv(0.05,99)*stdev(A1:A100)/sqrt(100)
LCL:	= average(A1:A100)-tinv(0.05,99)*stdev(A1:A100)/sqrt(100)

Note that tinv(0.05,99)*stdev(A1:A100)/sqrt(100) is the 95% error bound produced by the descriptive statistics procedure. The function tinv(0.05,99) returns the t value that puts a combined probability of .05 in the upper and lower tails of the t distribution with 99 degrees of freedom.

Hypotheses Tests About μ

Suppose we want to test the hypotheses $H_0 : \mu = k$ versus $H_a: \mu \neq k$, where k represents the hypothesized value in the problem. Let's say the data are in cells A1 through A100. The t statistic for this test can be constructed using the formula

$$= (\text{average}(A1:A100) - k)/(\text{stdev}(A1:A100)/\text{sqrt}(100))$$

This value can be compared to the appropriate t critical value chosen with 99 degrees of freedom (or a z value since we have lots of degrees of freedom here) using a two-tailed decision rule.

To compute the p value associated with this test statistic requires use of the tdist function. Suppose we build the formula for the t statistic in cell C10. Then the p value is computed as

= tdist(abs(C10),99,2) or

= tdist(test statistic, degrees of freedom, number of tails)

Note that the number of tails is two because this is a two-tailed test. You have to make sure that the numeric value provided to the tdist function is positive, so the absolute value function is applied to C10.

For a one-tailed test, the test statistic is computed in exactly the same way, but a one-tailed decision rule is used. The computation of the p value is a little trickier.

Upper-tailed test: If the test statistic in C10 is positive, use = tdist(abs(C10),99,1)

If the test statistic in C10 is negative, use = 1 – tdist(abs(C10),99,1)

Lower-tailed test: If the test statistic in C10 is positive, use = 1 – tdist(abs(C10),99,1)

If the test statistic in C10 is negative, use = tdist(abs(C10),99,1)

Hypotheses Tests About $\mu_1 - \mu_2$

Confidence Interval Estimate of $\mu_1 - \mu_2$

To construct confidence intervals or test hypotheses about the difference between two population means, use either t-Test: Two-Sample Assuming Equal Variances or t-Test: Two-Sample Assuming Unequal Variances as shown in Figure 2.33. The t-Test: Paired Two Sample for Means option is used when samples are matched rather than independent. This procedure for matched-sample tests was not discussed in this book. The z-Test: Two Sample for Means option is used when the population standard deviations are known (a fairly unlikely situation). The dialog boxes for the test procedures assuming either equal or unequal variances are identical. The dialog box from the unequal variance option is shown in Figure 2.34. Fill in the Variable Range 1 and 2 boxes with the ranges of the two independent samples. The Hypothesized Mean Difference is typically set to zero. This is the case discussed in this text, although tests for nonzero differences can be performed if these make sense. The Alpha level should be adjusted to the level desired for your test. This is because Excel prints out the critical value to compare with the standardized test statistic and needs to know the level of significance to do this. Specify the output option and click OK.

FIGURE 2.33   Excel Data Analysis Dialog Box with Two-Sample Test Options

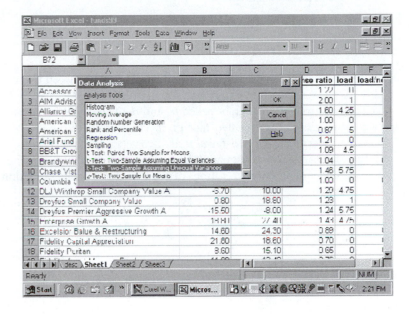

FIGURE 2.34   Excel Two-Sample Test Assuming Unequal Variances Dialog Box

2.10.3 SAS

Hypothesis Tests About $\mu_1 - \mu_2$

```
PROC TTEST;
CLASS V1;
VAR V2;
```

Produces output to conduct a test of the difference between two population means. V1 is a variable used to separate the observations of the variable V2 into two groups. The two group means can be called μ_1 and μ_2. The t statistic produced can be used to conduct either a one- or two-tailed test. The p values in the Prob |T| column are designed specifically for two-tailed tests. Two versions of the test statistic are produced: the variances-equal version and the variances-unequal version. The appropriate statistic depends on the assumptions deemed correct for the population variances.

ADDITIONAL EXERCISES

42 A university wants to examine starting monthly salaries for its finance and marketing graduates. Independent random samples of 12 finance graduates and 12 marketing graduates are selected from the files of last year's graduates. The following starting salaries are obtained from these people:

Finance	Marketing
1850	1675
2150	1275
1700	1800
1500	2100
2200	2200
1650	2250
2100	1950
2140	1850
1790	2000
1650	1800
2300	2100
2000	2150

Use these data to determine the following:

a Find the sample mean starting salaries for finance graduates and marketing graduates (separately).

b Construct a histogram for starting salaries in both finance and marketing.

c Construct a 95% confidence interval estimate of the population mean starting salary for finance majors. Do the same for marketing majors. Assume that the populations of starting salaries for both groups are normally distributed.

The data are available in two columns in the data file with the prefix SALARY2. Finance salaries are in the first column and marketing salaries are in the second.

43 Consider again the finance and marketing starting salaries in Exercise 42.

a Conduct a test to determine whether the population mean starting salaries for the two majors are equal. State the hypotheses to be tested, the decision rule, the test statistic, and your decision. Use a 5% level of significance.

b What conclusion can be drawn from the result in part a?

44 A telemarketing firm is considering two different sales approaches for selling magazine subscriptions over the phone. Two independent random samples of 20 salespeople each are selected to use either approach 1 or 2 for the sample period and for the same number of household contacts. The sales data (number of subscriptions sold per period) are given here.

Approach 1	Approach 2
12	8
15	10
28	24
14	14
18	10
10	20
15	20
20	15
5	0
4	7
12	10
10	16
24	17
16	20
13	12
14	4
18	12
22	18
6	3
12	16

a Is there a difference in average sales produced by the two approaches? Assume that the populations are normally distributed. State the hypotheses to be tested, the decision rule, the test statistic, and your decision. Use a 10% level of significance.

b What does the result in part a suggest to a sales division manager?

The data are available in two columns in the data file with the prefix SALES2. Sales for approach 1 are in the first column and sales for approach 2 are in the second.

45 Table 2.13 shows 1977 annual starting salary data for 93 employees of Harris Bank of Chicago. The column of data denoted MALE indicates whether the employees were MALE(1) or FEMALE(0). These data were obtained from a 1987 article by Daniel W. Schafer, "Measurement-Error Diagnostics and the Sex Discrimination Problem," which appeared in *Journal of Business and Economic Statistics* 5 (1987): 529–537.

These data are available in two columns in the data file with the prefix HARRIS2. The first column contains the salaries and the second column contains the classification variable (male = 1, female = 0).

Let μ_0 = average starting salary for females and μ_1 = average starting salary for males.

a Set up and test hypotheses to determine whether there is evidence of wage discrimination for the Harris Bank employees. Use a 5% level of significance. Set up the hypotheses assuming that discrimination is represented by an average wage for females that is less than the average wage for males.

TABLE 2.13   Starting Salaries for Harris Bank Employees

Salary	Male	Salary	Male	Salary	Male
3900	0	5220	0	5040	1
4020	0	5280	0	5100	1
4290	0	5280	0	5100	1
4380	0	5280	0	5220	1
4380	0	5400	0	5400	1
4380	0	5400	0	5400	1
4380	0	5400	0	5400	1
4380	0	5400	0	5400	1
4440	0	5400	0	5400	1
4500	0	5400	0	5700	1
4500	0	5400	0	6000	1
4620	0	5400	0	6000	1
4800	0	5400	0	6000	1
4800	0	5400	0	6000	1
4800	0	5400	0	6000	1
4800	0	5400	0	6000	1
4800	0	5520	0	6000	1
4800	0	5520	0	6000	1
4800	0	5580	0	6000	1
4800	0	5640	0	6000	1
4800	0	5700	0	6000	1
4800	0	5700	0	6000	1
4980	0	5700	0	6000	1
5100	0	5700	0	6300	1
5100	0	5700	0	6600	1
5100	0	6000	0	6600	1
5100	0	6000	0	6600	1
5100	0	6120	0	6840	1
5100	0	6300	0	6900	1
5160	0	6300	0	6900	1
5220	0	4620	1	8100	1

b   What implications do your test results have for Harris Bank?

c   Are there other factors that might need to be considered in this analysis? If so, state them and why you believe they are important.

46   Can expert stock analysts pick stocks that perform better than stocks chosen at random? Or better than a stock market index? There are no definitive answers to these questions, but people have lots of fun trying to find out. For example, in Fort Worth, TX, we have Rusty, a 1700-pound steer. At the start of each calendar year, Rusty is pitted against several of the state's top stock analysts. The analysts pick their portfolio of stocks and Rusty picks his. Rusty makes his picks in a special corral in Sundance Square in downtown Fort Worth with rectangles representing local companies. He lets the chips (as they say) fall where they may and his stocks are chosen accordingly. The results for 1997: Rusty's stocks gained 62.87% and the experts' stocks gained 37.09% (the S&P 500 gained 31% in 1997). Rusty beat the experts again in 1998.

In another comparison, *The Wall Street Journal* forms a panel of four experts each month and compares the performance of their four stock picks to four stocks chosen by throwing darts at stock tables. A 6-month holding period is used for the comparison. Table 2.14 shows the results of the first 106 contests along with the return for the Dow Jones Industrial Average for each time period.

a   Assume that the returns for the experts' portfolios and the dartboard portfolios represent two independent random samples of results. Test to see if there is a difference in the average returns for the experts and the average of the randomly chosen stocks.

b   Perform the same test to compare the experts' average performance with the average performance of the Dow Jones Industrial Average.

c   Based on the results of the tests in parts a and b, what do you conclude about the stock picking ability of the experts?

d   What problems might there be in comparing performance in this manner? What other comparisons might be useful in deciding whether expert stock analysts can pick stocks that perform better than stocks chosen at random or better than a stock market index?

The data are available in a data file with prefix DARTS2. The three columns of data represent returns for the pros, darts, and the Dow Jones Industrial Average, respectively.

TABLE 2.14 Returns for Experts (PROS), Dartboard Portfolio (DARTS), and Dow Jones Industrial Index (DJIA)

Contest	Period	PROS	DARTS	DJIA
1	January–June 1990	12.7	0.0	2.5
2	February–July 1990	26.4	1.8	11.5
3	March–August 1990	2.5	−14.3	−2.3
4	April–September 1990	−20.0	−7.2	−9.2
5	May–October 1990	−37.8	−16.3	−8.5
6	June–November 1990	−33.3	−27.4	−12.8
7	July–December 1990	−10.2	−22.5	−9.3
8	August 1990–January 1991	−20.3	−37.3	−0.8
9	September 1990–February 1991	38.9	−2.5	11.0
10	October 1990–March 1991	20.2	11.2	15.8
11	November 1990–April 1991	50.6	72.9	16.2
12	December 1990–May 1991	66.9	16.6	17.3
13	January–June 1991	7.5	28.7	17.7
14	February–July 1991	17.5	44.8	7.6
15	March–August 1991	39.6	71.3	4.4
16	April–September 1991	15.6	2.8	3.4
17	May–October 1991	12.4	38.0	4.4
18	June–November 1991	3.0	−23.2	−3.3
19	July–December 1991	12.3	4.1	6.6
20	August 1991–January 1992	39.3	−14.0	6.5
21	September 1991–February 1992	51.2	11.7	8.6
22	October 1991–March 1992	25.2	1.1	7.2
23	November 1991–April 1992	−3.3	−3.1	10.6
24	December 1991–May 1992	7.7	−1.4	17.6
25	January–June 1992	−21.0	7.7	3.6
26	February–July 1992	−13.0	15.4	4.2
27	March–August 1992	−2.5	3.6	−0.3
28	April–September 1992	−19.6	5.7	−0.1
29	May–October 1992	6.3	−5.7	−5.0
30	June–November 1992	−5.1	6.9	−2.8
31	July–December 1992	14.1	1.8	0.2
32	August 1992–January 1993	15.6	−13.9	−0.8
33	September 1992–February 1993	−26.7	15.6	2.5
34	October 1992–March 1993	25.2	18.7	9.0
35	November 1992–April 1993	−13.9	−3.6	5.8
36	December 1992–May 1993	27.9	6.6	6.7
37	January–June 1993	−6.6	4.7	7.7

(continues)

TABLE 2.14 (*continued*)

Contest	Period	PROS	DARTS	DJIA
38	February–July 1993	29.1	−43.0	3.7
39	March–August 1993	0.3	−5.6	7.3
40	April–September 1993	2.6	−17.7	5.2
41	May–October 1993	5.0	−4.9	5.7
42	June–November 1993	−7.4	−21.4	4.9
43	July–December 1993	2.2	42.2	8.0
44	August 1993–January 1994	27.8	18.5	11.2
45	September 1993–February 1994	3.7	1.5	5.5
46	October 1993–March 1994	4.7	−9.2	1.6
47	November 1993– April 1994	5.4	−10.5	0.5
48	December 1993–May 1994	−9.5	1.4	1.3
49	January–June 1994	−13.1	−8.7	−6.2
50	February–July 1994	−10.0	16.9	−5.3
51	March–August 1994	28.4	−4.3	1.5
52	April–September 1994	10.6	20.6	4.4
53	May–October 1994	27.2	10.3	6.9
54	June–November 1994	37.0	−6.8	−0.3
55	July–December 1994	−15.8	5.3	3.6
56	August 1994–January 1995	20.4	2.8	1.8
57	September 1994–February 1995	5.4	11.9	3.2
58	October 1994–March 1995	−14.8	3.8	7.3
59	November 1994–April 1995	12.1	1.4	12.8
60	December 1994–May 1995	10.8	9.0	19.5
61	January–June 1995	72.7	11.8	16.0
62	February–July 1995	30.5	16.5	19.6
63	March–August 1995	26.7	11.4	15.3
64	April–September 1995	75.0	3.3	14.0
65	May–October 1995	12.6	17.6	8.2
66	June–November 1995	31.0	23.8	13.1
67	July–December 1995	−11.0	18.7	9.3
68	August 1995–January 1996	28.1	−2.4	15.0
69	September 1995–February 1996	15.1	25.4	15.6
70	October 1995–March 1996	1.5	50.5	18.4
71	November 1995–April 1996	10.8	24.4	14.8
72	December 1995–May 1996	2.0	11.5	9.0
73	January–June 1996	−9.2	−5.3	10.2
74	February–July 1996	−8.6	2.6	1.3
75	March–August 1996	31.7	−5.7	0.6

TABLE 2.14 *(continued)*

Contest	Period	PROS	DARTS	DJIA
76	April–September 1996	8.7	7.8	5.8
77	May–October 1996	7.0	2.0	7.2
78	June–November 1996	5.1	6.2	15.1
79	July–December 1996	41.2	6.9	15.5
80	August 1996–January 1997	7.7	4.7	19.6
81	September 1996–February 1997	47.6	24.6	20.1
82	October 1996–March 1997	−10.0	−16.9	9.6
83	November 1996–April 1997	−13.6	−9.7	15.3
84	December 1996–May 1997	10.5	−21.4	13.3
85	January–June 1997	20.2	18.0	16.2
86	February–July 1997	29.3	−13.9	20.8
87	March–August 1997	20.7	0.1	8.3
88	April–September 1997	50.3	35.6	20.2
89	May–October 1997	38.4	20.7	3.0
90	June–November 1997	−3.5	6.5	3.8
91	July–December 1997	−14.1	6.5	−0.7
92	August 1997–January 1998	14.3	−9.0	−0.3
93	September 1997–February 1998	10.9	−3.3	10.7
94	October 1997–March 1998	5.5	13.3	7.6
95	November 1997–April 1998	17.4	−10.5	22.5
96	December 1997–May 1998	0.0	28.5	10.6
97	January–June 1998	24.4	3.2	15.0
98	February–July 1998	39.3	−10.1	7.1
99	March–August 1998	−18.8	−20.4	−13.1
100	April–September 1998	−20.1	−34.2	−11.8
101	May–October 1998	−23.6	−21.5	−6.2
102	June–November 1998	16.4	−19.0	1.6
103	July–December 1998	29.9	−20.0	0.1
104	August–January 1999	4.3	−16.7	9.5
105	September–February 1999	21.3	76.3	16.3
106	October–March 1999	33.3	24.6	26.4

47 The following is a relative frequency distribution that appeared in *The Wall Street Journal* (1/31/96 issue, reprinted courtesy of *The Wall Street Journal*). Use the distribution to help answer the questions that follow.

The Going Rate

Price distribution of homes sold through the Multiple Listing Service in Texas for the year ended October 1995.

Price of Home	% of Homes Sold
$29,999 or less	5.3
$30,000–39,999	5.1
$40,000–49,999	7.8
$50,000–59,999	10.0
$60,000–69,999	10.6
$70,000–79,999	9.9
$80,000–89,999	8.9
$90,000–99,999	6.4
$100,000–119,999	9.5
$120,000–139,999	7.4
$140,000–159,999	4.9
$160,000–179,999	3.5
$180,000–199,999	2.4
$200,000–299,999	5.2
$300,000–399,999	1.6
$400,000–499,999	0.7
$500,000 and more	0.8

a What percentage of homes sold for less than $50,000?

b What percentage of homes sold for $120,000 or more but less than $400,000?

c Can you determine what percentage of homes sold for more than $130,000?

d In what range of prices is the median price of the homes sold?

48 Our company produces metal parts that must have holes of a certain diameter punched for later use. As long as the center of each hole is within 1.5 centimeters (cm) of a particular spot on the metal part, the part will be acceptable to the buyer. The distance from the center of the hole punched to the desired center is called the error (errors can be positive or negative depending on their direction). Figure 2.35 shows a histogram of the errors for a sample of the last 50 parts to come off the punch line. Managers have decided that, as long as no more than 2 parts in a sample of 50 are in error by more than 1.5 cm, the punch machine is operating acceptably and no adjustments will be made.

a How many of the parts from the sample of 50 have an error of 1.5 cm or more?

b What percentage of parts in this sample has an error of 1.5 cm or more?

c Based on the histogram, what is management's decision?

FIGURE 2.35   Histogram of Punch Errors

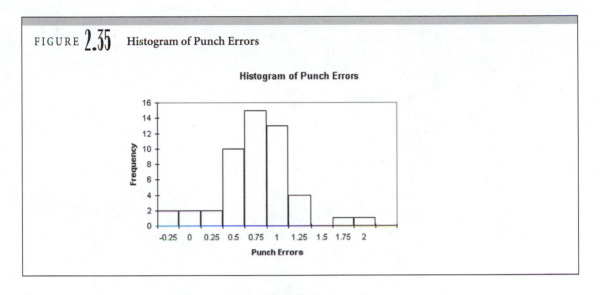

FIGURE 2.36   Time-Series Plot of Punch Errors

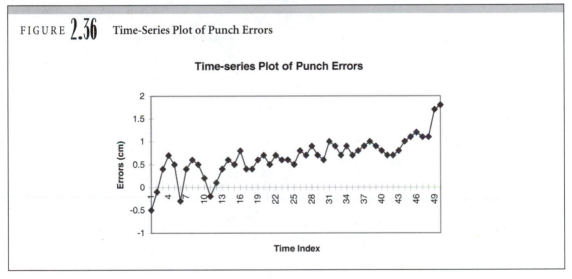

49 Figure 2.36 is a time-series plot of the errors for the 50 parts examined in problem 48. The errors are plotted in the order that the parts were handled by the punch machine. Based on the histogram in problem 48, management decided that the punch machine was operating correctly and needed no adjustment. After examining the time-series plot in addition to the histogram, do you agree or disagree with management's conclusion? Justify your answer.

CHAPTER 3

Simple Regression Analysis

3.1 USING SIMPLE REGRESSION TO DESCRIBE A LINEAR RELATIONSHIP

Regression analysis is a statistical technique used to describe relationships among variables. The simplest case to examine is one in which a variable y, referred to as the *dependent* variable, may be related to another variable x, called an *independent* or *explanatory* variable. If the relationship between y and x is believed linear, then the equation expressing this relationship is the equation for a line:

$$y = b_0 + b_1 x$$

If a graph of all the (x, y) pairs is constructed, then b_0 represents the *y intercept*, the point where the line crosses the vertical (y) axis, and b_1 represents the *slope* of the line.

Consider the data shown in Table 3.1. A graph of the (x, y) pairs would appear as shown in Figure 3.1. Regression analysis is not needed to obtain the equation expressing the relationship between these two variables. In equation form:

$$y = 1 + 2x$$

This is an exact or deterministic linear relationship. Exact linear relationships are sometimes encountered in business environments. For example, from accounting:

assets = liabilities + owner equity

total costs = fixed costs + variable costs

TABLE 3.1   Example Data

x	1	2	3	4	5	6
y	3	5	7	9	11	13

FIGURE 3.1   Graph of an Exact or Deterministic Linear Relationship (data in Table 3.1)

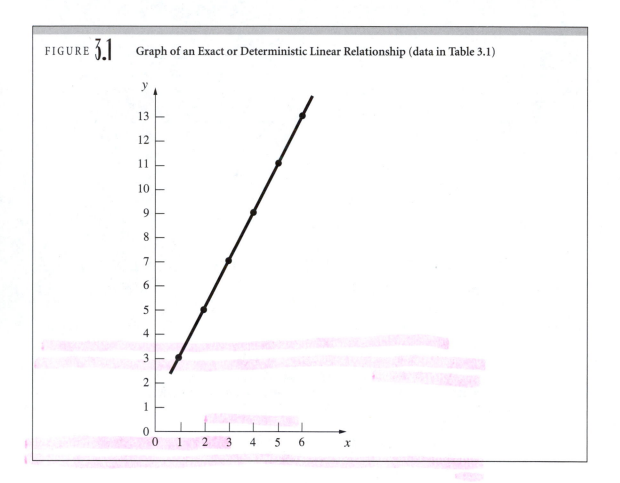

Other exact relationships may be encountered in various science courses (for example, physics or chemistry). In the social sciences (for example, psychology or sociology) and in business and economics, exact linear relationships are the exception rather than the rule. Data encountered in a business environment are more likely to appear as in Table 3.2. These data graph as shown in Figure 3.2.

It appears that x and y may be linearly related, but it is not an exact relationship. Still it may be desirable to describe the relationship in equation form. This can be done by drawing what appears to be the "best-fitting" line through the points and estimating (guessing) what the values of b_0 and b_1 are for this line. This has been done in Figure 3.2. For the line drawn, a good guess might be the following equation:

TABLE 3.2   **Example Data**

x	1	2	3	4	5	6
y	3	2	8	8	11	13

FIGURE 3.2   **Graph of a Relationship That Is Not Deterministic (data in Table 3.2)**

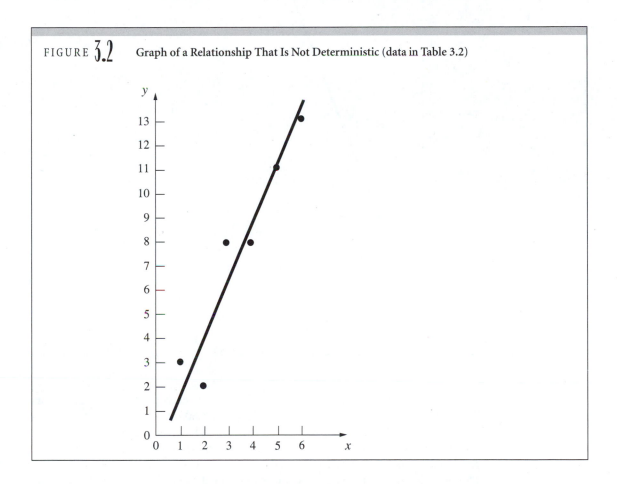

$$\hat{y} = -1 + 2.5x$$

The drawbacks to this method of fitting the line should be clear. For example, if the (x, y) pairs graphed in Figure 3.2 were given to two people, each would probably guess different values for the intercept and slope of the best-fitting line. Furthermore, there is no way to assess who would be more correct. To make line fitting more precise, a definition of what it means for a line to be the "best" is needed. The criterion for a best-fitting line that we will use might be called the "minimum sum of squared errors" criterion or, as it is more commonly known, the least-squares criterion.

FIGURE **3.3** Motivation for the Least-Squares Regression Line

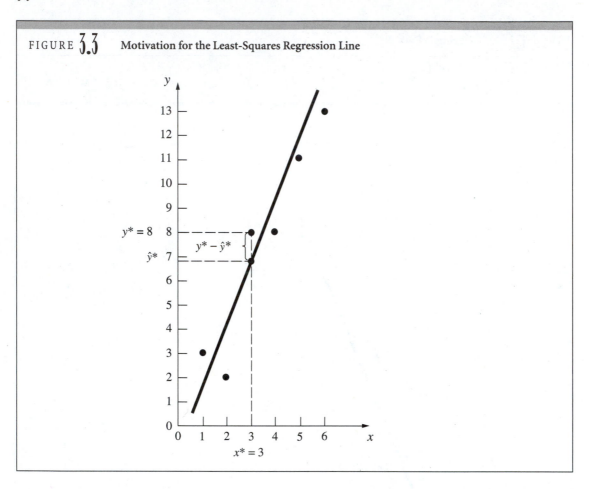

In Figure 3.3, the (x, y) pairs from Table 3.2 have been plotted and an arbitrary line drawn through the points. Consider the pair of values denoted (x^*, y^*). The actual y value is indicated as y^*; the value predicted to be associated with x^* if the line shown were used is indicated as $\hat{y}^*$. The difference between the actual y value and the predicted y value at the point x^* is called a *residual* and represents the "error" involved. This error is denoted $y^* - \hat{y}^*$. If the line is to fit the data points as accurately as possible, these errors should be minimized. This should be done not just for the single point (x^*, y^*), but for all the points on the graph. There are several possible ways to approach this task.

1 Use the line that minimizes the sum of the errors, $\sum_{i=1}^{n}(y_i - \hat{y}_i)$. The problem with this approach is that, for any line that passes through the point $(\bar{x}, \bar{y})$,

$$\sum_{i=1}^{n}(y_i - \hat{y}_i) = 0$$

FIGURE 3.4   Lines A and B Both Satisfy the Criterion $\sum_{i=1}^{n}(y_i - \hat{y}_i) = 0$

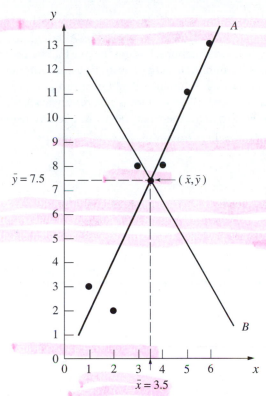

so there are an infinite number of lines satisfying this criterion, some of which obviously do not fit the data well. For example, in Figure 3.4, lines A and B have both been constructed so that

$$\sum_{i=1}^{n}(y_i - \hat{y}_i) = 0$$

But line A obviously fits the data better than line B; that is, it keeps the distances $y_i - \hat{y}_i$ small.

As mentioned previously, any line that passes through the point represented by the means of x and y, $(\bar{x}, \bar{y})$, has errors that sum to zero. The line passes through the points in such a way that positive and negative errors cancel each other out. Because a criterion that simply makes the errors small, regardless of whether they are positive or negative, is desired, some method of removing negative signs is required. One such method uses absolute values of the errors; another squares the errors. Each method provides another possible criterion.

2 Use the line that minimizes the sum of the absolute values of errors,

$$\sum_{i=1}^{n} |y_i - \hat{y}_i|$$

This is called the minimum sum of absolute errors criterion. The resulting line is called the *least absolute value* (LAV) regression line. Although use of this criterion is gaining popularity in many situations, it is not the one that we use in this text. Finding the line that satisfies the minimum sum of absolute errors criterion requires solving a fairly complex problem by a technique called linear programming. This is a difficult problem by hand, and the LAV procedure is not readily available in most statistical software packages. Furthermore, there may be no unique LAV regression line.

3 Use the line that minimizes the sum of the squared errors,

$$\sum_{i=1}^{n} (y_i - \hat{y}_i)^2$$

Applying the least-squares (LS) criterion results in a unique *least squares* regression line. Its advantages over the LAV line include computational simplicity and the wide availability of statistical packages that contain easily implemented least-squares regression routines.

Now that a criterion has been established, the next question is: Can convenient computational formulas for the values of b_0 and b_1 that minimize

$$\sum_{i=1}^{n} (y_i - \hat{y}_i)^2 \tag{3.1}$$

be developed? The answer is "yes" and the resulting equations are

$$b_1 = \frac{\sum_{i=1}^{n} (x_i - \bar{x})(y_i - \bar{y})}{\sum_{i=1}^{n} (x_i - \bar{x})^2} \tag{3.2}$$

$$b_0 = \bar{y} - b_1 \bar{x} \tag{3.3}$$

A computationally simpler form of Equation (3.2) is

$$b_1 = \frac{\sum_{i=1}^{n} x_i y_i - \frac{1}{n} \sum_{i=1}^{n} x_i \sum_{i=1}^{n} y_i}{\sum_{i=1}^{n} x_i^2 - \frac{1}{n} \left(\sum_{i=1}^{n} x_i \right)^2} \tag{3.4}$$

TABLE 3.3   **Computations for Finding b_0 and b_1**

i	x_i	y_i	$x_i y_i$	x_i^2
1	1	3	3	1
2	2	2	4	4
3	3	8	24	9
4	4	8	32	16
5	5	11	55	25
6	6	13	78	36
Sums	21	45	196	91

EXAMPLE 3.1

As an example of the use of these formulas, consider again the data in Table 3.2. The intermediate computations necessary for finding b_0 and b_1 are shown in Table 3.3. The slope, b_1, can now be computed using the formula in Equation (3.4):

$$b_1 = \frac{196 - \frac{1}{6}(21)(45)}{91 - \frac{1}{6}(21)^2} = \frac{38.5}{17.5} = 2.2$$

The intercept, b_0, is computed as in Equation (3.3):

$$b_0 = 7.5 - 2.2(3.5) = -0.2$$

because

$$\bar{x} = \frac{21}{6} = 3.5 \text{ and } \bar{y} = \frac{45}{6} = 7.5$$

The least-squares regression line for these data is

$$\hat{y} = -0.2 + 2.2x$$

There is no longer any guesswork associated with computing the best-fitting line once a criterion has been stated that defines "best." Using the criterion of minimum sum of squared errors, the regression line we computed provides the best description of the relationship between the variables x and y. Any other values used for b_0 and b_1 result in larger sum of squared errors. For example, Table 3.4(a) shows the computation of the sum of squared errors for the original "guessed" line $\hat{y} = -1 + 2.5x$, and Table 3.4(b) shows the same computation for the least-squares line $\hat{y} = -0.2 + 2.2x$.

TABLE **3.4**

(a) Computation of Sum of Squared Errors (line: $\hat{y} = 1 + 2.5x$)

x	y	$\hat{y}$	$y - \hat{y}$	$(y - \hat{y})^2$
1	3	1.5	1.5	2.25
2	2	4.0	−2.0	4.00
3	8	6.5	1.5	2.25
4	8	9.0	−1.0	1.00
5	11	11.5	−0.5	0.25
6	13	14.0	−1.0	1.00

$$\sum_{i=1}^{n} (y_i - \hat{y}_i)^2 = 10.75$$

(b) Computation of Sum of Squared Errors (line: $\hat{y} = -0.2 + 2.2x$)

x	y	$\hat{y}$	$y - \hat{y}$	$(y - \hat{y})^2$
1	3	2.0	1.0	1.00
2	2	4.2	−2.2	4.84
3	8	6.4	1.6	2.56
4	8	8.6	−0.6	0.36
5	11	10.8	0.2	0.04
6	13	13.0	0.0	0.00

$$\sum_{i=1}^{n} (y_i - \hat{y}_i)^2 = 8.8$$

EXERCISES

Exercises 1 and 2 should be done by hand.

1 **Flexible Budgeting.** A budget is an expression of management's expectations and goals concerning future revenues and costs. To increase their effectiveness, many budgets are flexible, including allowances for the effect of variation in uncontrolled variables. For example, the costs and revenues of many production plants are greatly affected by the number of units produced by the plant during the budget period, and this may be beyond a plant manager's control. Standard cost-accounting procedures can be used to adjust the direct-cost parts of the budget for the level of production, but it is often more difficult to handle overhead. In many cases, statistical methods are used to estimate the relationship between overhead (y) and the level of production (x) using historical data. As a simple example, consider the historical data for a certain plant:

Production (in 10,000) units:	5	6	7	8	9	10	11
Overhead costs (in $1000):	12	11.5	14	15	15.4	15.3	17.5

a   Construct a scatterplot of y versus x.

b   Find the least-squares line relating overhead costs to production.

c   Graph the regression line on the scatterplot.

2   **Central Company.** The Central Company manufactures a certain speciality item once a month in a batch production run. The number of items produced in each run varies from month to month as demand fluctuates. The company is interested in the relationship between the size of the production run (x) and the number of hours of labor (y) required for the run. The company has collected the following data for the ten most recent runs:

Number of items:	40	30	70	90	50	60	70	40	80	70
Labor (hours):	83	60	138	180	97	118	140	75	159	144

a   Construct a scatterplot of y versus x.

b   Find the least-squares line relating hours of labor to number of items produced.

c   Graph the regression line on the scatterplot.

3.2   EXAMPLES OF REGRESSION AS A DESCRIPTIVE TECHNIQUE

EXAMPLE 3.2   Estimating Residential Real Estate Values

The Tarrant County Appraisal District must appraise properties for all of the county. The appraisal district uses data such as square footage of the individual houses as well as location, depreciation, and physical condition of an entire neighborhood to derive individual appraisal values on each house. This avoids labor-intensive reinspection each year.

Regression can be used to establish the weight assigned to various factors used in assessing values. For example, Table 3.5 shows the value and size in square feet for a sample of 100 Tarrant County homes (these data are from 1990). A scatterplot of value (y) versus size (x) is shown in Figure 3.5.

Using a statistical package, the regression equation relating value to size can be determined as

$$VALUE = -50{,}035 + 72.8SIZE$$

If size were the only factor thought to be of importance in determining value, this equation could be used by the appraisal district. But obviously, other factors need to be considered. Developing an equation that includes more than one important factor (explanatory variable) is discussed in Chapter 4.

TABLE 3.5   VALUE and SIZE for Residential Real Estate Value Example

VALUE	SIZE	VALUE	SIZE	VALUE	SIZE
23,974	1442	12,001	783	21,536	1404
24,087	1426	37,650	1874	24,147	1676
16,781	1632	27,930	1242	17,867	1131
29,061	910	16,066	772	21,583	1397
37,982	972	20,411	908	15,482	888
29,433	912	23,672	1155	24,857	1448
33,624	1400	24,215	1004	17,716	1022
27,032	1087	22,020	958	224,182	2251
28,653	1139	52,863	1828	182,012	1126
33,075	1386	41,822	1146	201,597	2617
17,474	756	45,104	1368	49,683	966
33,852	1044	28,154	1392	60,647	1469
29,046	1032	20,943	1058	49,024	1322
20,715	720	17,851	1375	52,092	1509
19,461	734	16,616	648	55,645	1724
21,377	720	38,752	1313	51,919	1559
52,881	1635	44,377	1780	55,174	2133
43,889	1381	43,566	1148	48,760	1233
45,134	1372	38,950	1363	45,906	1323
47,655	1349	44,633	1262	52,013	1733
53,088	1599	12,372	840	56,612	1357
38,923	1171	12,148	840	69,197	1234
57,870	1966	19,852	839	84,416	1434
30,489	1504	20,012	852	60,962	1384
29,207	1296	20,314	852	47,359	995
44,919	1356	22,814	974	56,302	1372
48,090	1553	24,696	1135	88,285	1774
40,521	1142	23,443	1170	91,862	1903
43,403	1268	35,904	960	242,690	3581
38,112	1008	21,799	1052	296,251	4343
27,710	1120	28,212	1296	107,132	1861
27,621	960	27,553	1282	77,797	1542
22,258	920	15,826	916		
29,064	1259	18,660	864		

FIGURE 3.5   MINITAB Scatterplot of VALUE Versus SIZE for Residential Real Estate Value Example

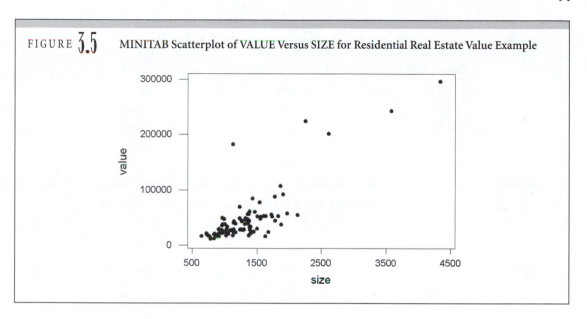

EXAMPLE 3.3   **Pricing Communications Nodes**

In recent years, the growth of data communications networks has been amazing. The convenience and capabilities afforded by such networks are appealing to businesses with locations scattered throughout the United States and the world. Using networks allows centralization of a main computer with access through personal computers at remote locations.

The cost of adding a new communications node at a location not currently included in the network was of concern for a major Fort Worth manufacturing company. To try to predict the price of new communications nodes, data were obtained on a sample of existing nodes. The installation cost and the number of ports available for access in each existing node were readily available information. These data are shown in Table 3.6 and a scatterplot of cost (y) versus number of ports (x) is shown in Figure 3.6.

Again, using a statistical package, the equation relating the price of the new communications node to the number of access ports to be included at the node is

$$COST = 16,594 + 650NUMPORTS$$

where NUMPORTS represents the number of ports. This equation could be used to help predict the cost of installing new communications nodes based on the number of access ports to be included.

TABLE 3.6   Cost and Number of Ports for Communications Node Example*

Cost	Number of Ports	Cost	Number of Ports	Cost	Number of Ports
52,388	68	57,088	56	24,269	12
51,761	52	54,475	56	53,479	52
50,221	44	33,969	28	33,543	20
36,095	32	31,309	24	33,056	24
27,500	16	23,444	24		

* Note: These data have been modified as requested by the company to provide confidentiality.

FIGURE 3.6   Excel Scatterplot of Cost Versus Number of Ports for the Communications Node Example

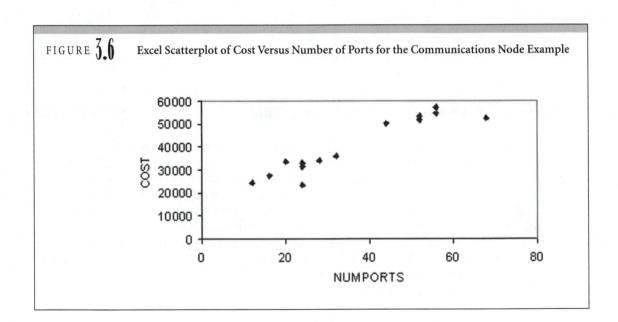

EXAMPLE 3.4   Forecasting Housing Starts

Forecasts of various economic measures are important to the U.S. government and to various industries throughout the United States. The construction industry is concerned with the number of housing starts in a given year. Accurate forecasts can help with plans for expansion or cutbacks within the industry.

Table 3.7 shows data on the number of housing starts for the years 1963 to 1996. Also shown are data on home mortgage rates for new home purchases (U.S. average) for the same years. These data were obtained from *Business Statistics of the United States, 1997 Edition.* A scatterplot of housing starts (y) versus mortgage rates (x) is shown in Figure 3.7. Note that the

TABLE 3.7   Annual Housing Starts and Mortgage Rates for 1963–1996

Year	Starts	Rates	Year	Starts	Rates	Year	Starts	Rates
1963	1603.2	5.80	1975	1160.4	9.04	1987	1620.5	10.20
1964	1528.8	5.75	1976	1537.5	8.87	1988	1488.1	10.34
1965	1472.8	5.74	1977	1987.1	8.84	1989	1376.1	10.32
1966	1164.9	6.14	1978	2020.3	9.64	1990	1192.7	10.13
1967	1291.6	6.33	1979	1745.1	11.19	1991	1013.9	9.25
1968	1507.6	6.83	1980	1292.2	13.77	1992	1199.7	8.40
1969	1466.8	7.66	1981	1084.2	16.63	1993	1287.6	7.33
1970	1433.6	8.27	1982	1062.2	16.08	1994	1457.0	8.36
1971	2052.2	7.59	1983	1703.0	13.23	1995	1354.1	7.95
1972	2356.6	7.38	1984	1749.5	13.87	1996	1476.8	7.80
1973	2045.3	8.04	1985	1741.8	12.42			
1974	1337.7	9.19	1986	1805.4	10.18			

FIGURE 3.7   MINITAB Scatterplot of Housing Starts Versus Mortgage Rates for Housing Starts Example

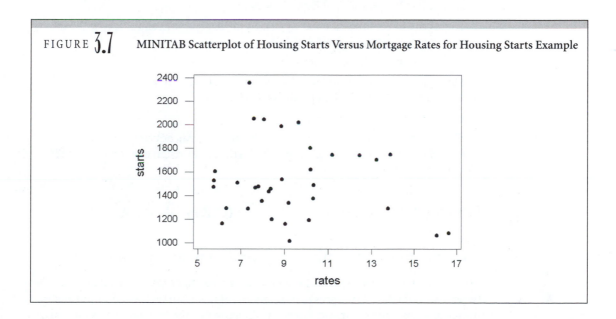

relationship appears to be considerably "weaker" than in the other scatterplots presented in this section. Intuitively, we might expect the relationship between housing starts and mortgage rates to be a strong one. But from the data, this does not appear to be the case. Perhaps there are other variables that might be more strongly related to housing starts that could be used to provide accurate forecasts for future years. From viewing the scatterplot, mortgage rates alone do not appear to be particularly helpful.

Cross-sectional data are gathered on a number of different individual units at approximately the same point in time. Examples 3.2 and 3.3 use cross-sectional data. The data examined in Example 3.4 are called *time-series data* because they are gathered over a time sequence (years in this case).

Most of the techniques discussed in this and subsequent chapters can be applied to either time-series or cross-sectional data. There are certain special techniques available when working with time-series data that may be helpful in developing forecasts. These techniques will be discussed throughout subsequent chapters where appropriate. When special techniques apply to only one type of data, this will be mentioned.

EXERCISES

3   For each of the data sets discussed in this section, use a computer to read the data, construct a scatterplot of *y* versus *x*, and produce the regression output relating *y* to *x*.

   a   Estimating Residential Real Estate Values

   There are two columns of data. Value is in the first column and size is in the second. The datafile prefix is REALEST3.

   b   Pricing Communications Nodes

   There are two columns of data. Cost is in the first column and the number of ports is in the second. The datafile prefix is COMNODE3.

   c   Forecasting Housing Starts

   There are three columns. The year is in the first column, housing starts is in the second column and mortgage rates is in the third. The datafile prefix is HSTARTS3.

3.3 INFERENCES FROM A SIMPLE REGRESSION ANALYSIS

3.3.1 Assumptions Concerning the Population Regression Line

Thus far, regression analysis has been viewed as a way to describe the relationship between two variables. The regression equation obtained can be viewed in this manner simply as a descriptive statistic. However, the power of the technique of least-squares regression is not in its use as a descriptive measure for one particular sample, but in its ability to draw inferences or generalizations about the relationship for the entire population of values for the variables *x* and *y*.

To draw inferences from a sample regression equation, we must make some assumptions about how *x* and *y* are related in the population. These initial assumptions describe an "ideal" situation. Later, each of these assumptions is relaxed and we demonstrate modifications to the basic least-squares approach that provide a model that is still suitable for statistical inference.

FIGURE 3.8   **Examples of Possible Population Regression Lines**

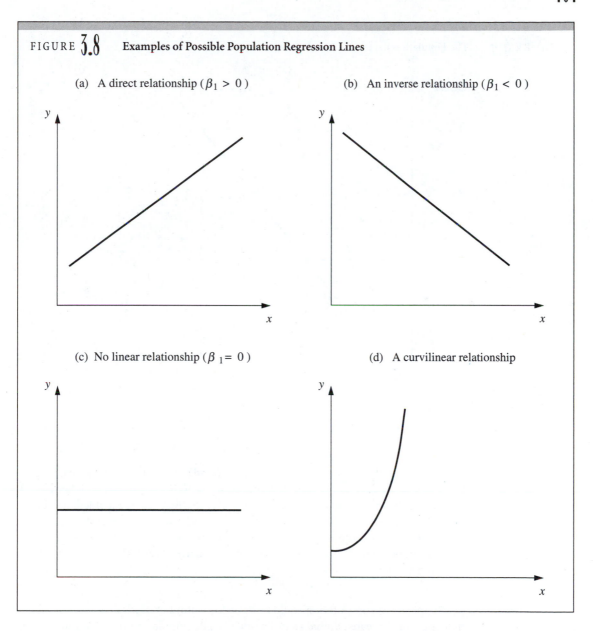

(a) A direct relationship ($\beta_1 > 0$)

(b) An inverse relationship ($\beta_1 < 0$)

(c) No linear relationship ($\beta_1 = 0$)

(d) A curvilinear relationship

Assume that the relationship between the variables x and y is represented by a population regression line. The equation of this line is written as

$$\mu_{y|x} = \beta_0 + \beta_1 x, \qquad (3.5)$$

where $\mu_{y|x}$ is the *conditional mean* of y given a value of x, β_0 is the y intercept for the population regression line, and β_1 is the slope of the population regression line. Examples of possible relationships are shown in Figure 3.8.

FIGURE **3.9** The Population Regression Line Passes Through the Conditional Means

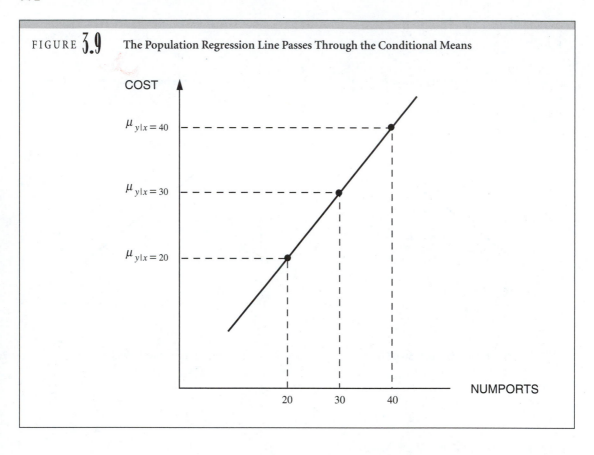

The use of $\mu_{y|x}$ requires some additional explanation. Suppose the y variable represents the cost of installing a new communications node as discussed in Example 3.3, and x represents the number of access ports (NUMPORTS) to be included. It is possible that these two variables are related. Now consider all possible communications nodes with 30 access ports. If the costs were known, the average value for all communications nodes with 30 access ports could be calculated. This is the conditional mean of y given $x = 30$:

$$\mu_{y|x=30}$$

Suppose this computation could be done for a number of x values and the resulting conditional means plotted as in Figure 3.9. The population regression line is the line passing through the conditional means. The relationship between y and x is linear if all of the conditional means lie on a straight line (or nearly so).

For a given number of ports (say, 30) costs vary; that is, not every communications node has a cost equal to the mean of y given $x = 30$. The actual cost is distributed around the point $\mu_{y|x=30}$, or around the regression line. Thus, in a sample of communications nodes with 30 ports, the costs are expected to differ from points on the population regression line (see Figure 3.10).

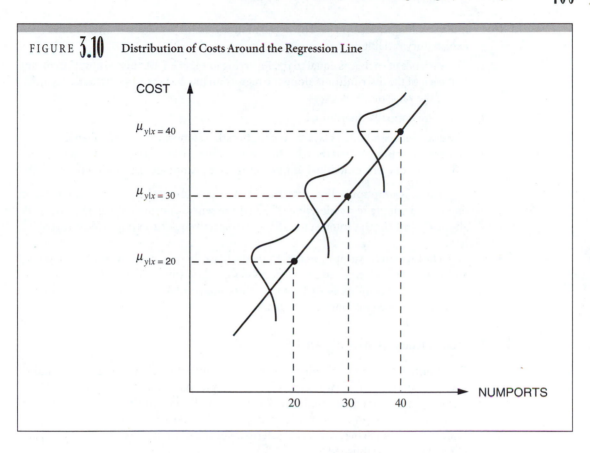

FIGURE **3.10**   **Distribution of Costs Around the Regression Line**

Because of this variation of the y values around the regression line, it is conven-ient to rewrite the equation representing an individual response as

$$y_i = \beta_0 + \beta_1 x_i + e_i \tag{3.6}$$

where β_0 and β_1 have the same interpretation as they did in Equation (3.5). The term e_i represents the difference between the true cost for communications node i and the conditional mean of all costs for nodes with that number of ports:

$$e_i = COST_i - \mu_{y|x} = y_i - (\beta_0 + \beta_1 x_i).$$

The e_i are called *disturbances*. These disturbances keep the relationship from being an exact one. If the e_i were all equal to zero, then there would be an exact linear relation-ship between COST and NUMPORTS. The effects of all factors other than the x vari-able which influence COST are included in the disturbances. To allow statistical inference from a sample to the population, some assumptions about the population regression line are necessary.

1   The expected value of the disturbances is zero: $E(e_i) = 0$. This implies that the regres-sion line passes through the conditional means of the x variable. For our purposes, we

interpret this assumption as: The population regression equation is linear in the explanatory variable.[1]

2 The variance of each e_i is equal to σ_e^2. Referring to Figure 3.10, this assumption means that each of the distributions along the regression line has the same variance regardless of the value of x.

3 The e_i are normally distributed.

4 The e_i are independent. This is an assumption that is most important when data are gathered over time. When the data are cross-sectional (i.e., gathered at the same point in time for different individual units), this is typically not an assumption of concern.

These assumptions allow inferences to be made about the population regression line from a sample regression line. The first inferences considered will be those made about β_0 and β_1, the intercept and slope, respectively, of the population regression line.

The previous assumptions define an ideal case for linear regression. In Chapters 3 and 4, we examine regression procedures designed for this ideal case. In Chapter 6, we examine how violations of each of the assumptions might be detected and how corrections for these violations can be made.

3.3.2 Inferences About β_0 and β_1

The point estimates of β_0 and β_1 were previously justified by saying that b_0 and b_1 minimize the sum of squared errors for the sample. With the assumptions made concerning the random disturbances of the model, additional justification for the use of b_0 and b_1 can be made by stating certain properties these estimators possess. To fully discuss these properties, some characteristics of the sampling distributions of b_0 and b_1 must first be established.

Recall that a statistic is any value calculated from a sample. Thus, b_0 and b_1 are statistics. Because statistics are random variables, they have probability distributions called sampling distributions. Some characteristics of the sampling distributions of b_0 and b_1 are given here:

Sampling Distribution of b_0

1 $E(b_0) = \beta_0$ $\hspace{6cm}$ (3.7)

2 $Var(b_0) = \sigma_e^2 \left(\dfrac{1}{n} + \dfrac{\overline{x}^2}{\sum\limits_{i=1}^{n}(x_i - \overline{x})^2} \right) = \sigma_e^2 \left(\dfrac{1}{n} + \dfrac{\overline{x}^2}{(n-1)s_x^2} \right)$ $\hspace{2cm}$ (3.8)

---

[1] Our assumption here is that the population regression equation is linear in the x variable. In Chapter 5, we relax this assumption and find that we can fit curves by allowing equations that are not linear in the x variables. Throughout this text, however, we always assume that the equations are linear in the parameters. This means that equations such as $y = \beta_0 + \beta_1^2 x + e$, for example, are not considered. These types of equations are beyond the scope of this text.

where $s_x^2 = \sum_{i=1}^{n}(x_i - \bar{x})^2 / (n-1)$ is the sample variance of the x values.

3   The sampling distribution of b_0 is normally distributed.

Sampling Distribution of b_1

1    $E(b_1) = \beta_1$ $\hfill (3.9)$

2    $Var(b_1) = \dfrac{\sigma_e^2}{\displaystyle\sum_{i=1}^{n}(x_i - \bar{x})^2} = \dfrac{\sigma_e^2}{(n-1)s_x^2}$ $\hfill (3.10)$

3   The sampling distribution of b_1 is normally distributed.

The sampling distributions of both b_0 and b_1 are centered at the true parameter values of β_0 and β_1, respectively. Because the means of the sampling distributions are equal to the parameter values to be estimated, b_0 and b_1 are called unbiased estimators of β_0 and β_1 [see Figure 3.11(a)]. The variances of the sampling distributions are given in Equations (3.8) and (3.10). The standard deviations of the sampling distributions are obtained by taking the square roots of the variances:

$$\sigma_{b_0} = \sigma_e \sqrt{\frac{1}{n} + \frac{\bar{x}^2}{(n-1)s_x^2}} \qquad (3.11)$$

$$\sigma_{b_1} = \sigma_e \sqrt{\frac{1}{(n-1)s_x^2}} \qquad (3.12)$$

With the assumption that the disturbances are normally distributed, the sampling distributions of b_0 and b_1 are also normally distributed regardless of the sample size.

The estimators b_0 and b_1 also possess certain other properties that make them desirable as estimators of β_0 and β_1. Although these properties do not have a direct bearing on the work in this text, they are stated here for completeness. Each is a consistent estimator of its population counterpart. Using b_1 as an example, this means that as sample size increases, the probability increases that b_1 is "close" to β_1. Another way to view this property is by considering the standard deviation of the sampling distribution of b_1. As the sample size increases, the standard deviation of the sampling distribution decreases (as it did for the sample mean when viewed as an estimator of the population mean in Chapter 2). When this happens, the probability under the curve representing the sampling distribution becomes more concentrated near the center, β_1, and less concentrated in the extreme tails [see Figure 3.11(b)].

A final property of b_0 and b_1 can be illustrated by considering all other possible estimators of β_0 and β_1 that are unbiased. The standard deviations of the sampling distributions of b_0 and b_1 are smaller than those of any of the other unbiased estimators. This minimum variance property can be restated by saying that b_0 and b_1 have smaller sampling errors than any other unbiased estimator. Of course, this says

FIGURE **3.11**   Properties of b_0 and b_1 as Estimators of β_0 and β_1 (illustrated for b_1)

(a) *Unbiased Estimators:* The mean of the sampling distribution is equal to the population parameter being estimated.

Sampling distribution of a biased estimator

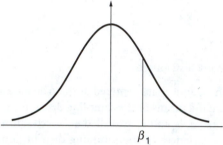

β_1

Sampling distribution of an unbiased estimator

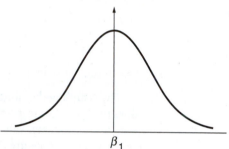

β_1

(b) *Consistent Estimators:* As n increases, the probability that the estimator will be close to the true parameter increases.

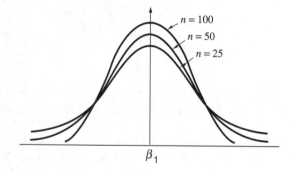

$n = 100$
$n = 50$
$n = 25$

β_1

(c) *Minimum Variance Estimators:* The varaiance of b_1 is smaller than the variance of any other linear unbiased estimator of β_1, say b_1^*.

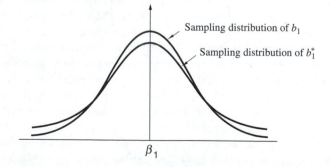

Sampling distribution of b_1

Sampling distribution of b_1^*

β_1

nothing about estimators that are biased. It does specify that the least squares estimators are best within a certain class of estimators [see Figure 3.11(c)].

Using the properties of the sampling distributions of b_0 and b_1, inferences about the population parameters β_0 and β_1 can be made. This is analogous to what was done in Chapter 2 when properties of the sampling distribution of the sample mean, $\bar{y}$, were used to make inferences about the population mean, μ.

First, however, an estimate of one other unknown parameter in the regression model is needed: an estimate of σ_e^2, the variance around the regression line. This estimate of σ_e^2 is given by

$$s_e^2 = \frac{\sum_{i=1}^{n}(y_i - \hat{y}_i)^2}{n-2} = \frac{SSE}{n-2} = MSE$$

where $\hat{y}_i = b_0 + b_1 x_i$. The term s_e^2 represents an estimate of the variance around the regression line. Recall that in Figure 3.3, $y_i - \hat{y}_i$ represented the distance from the ith sample y value to the point on the regression line associated with the ith sample x value. The sum of the squares of these distances (SSE) adjusted for (or divided by) degrees of freedom ($n-2$) is used as an estimator of the variance around the regression line. MSE stands for mean square error. A *mean square* is any sum of squares divided by its degrees of freedom. In any regression problem, the number of degrees of freedom is n (the sample size) minus the number of regression coefficients to be estimated. In simple regression, there are two regression coefficients, β_0 and β_1, so the degrees of freedom is $n-2$.

The square root of s_e^2, denoted s_e, is an estimate of the standard deviation around the regression line. It is often referred to as the *standard error of the regression*.

Now it is possible to discuss inferences about the population regression coefficients. Point estimates of β_0 and β_1 are simply the least-squares estimates b_0 and b_1. Point estimates are single numbers. Often it is more desirable to state a range of values in which the parameter is thought to lie rather than a single number. These ranges are called confidence interval estimates. They are less precise than point estimates because they cover a range of values rather than a single number. There is a trade-off, however, between the precision of an estimate and confidence in it.

Think back to Chapter 2 and the construction of estimates for the population mean, μ. A point estimate of μ was given by the sample mean, say, $\bar{y} = 40$. This is a very precise estimate, but the population mean does not equal 40. This value was obtained from one of a large number of possible samples, each of which has a different sample mean. The chances of one of these sample means being exactly equal to the population mean is so small that a 0% level of confidence is assigned to the possibility that μ is exactly 40. When constructing a confidence interval estimate of μ, however, the situation changes. For example, using the fact that the sampling distribution of $\bar{y}$ is normal (or approximately normal), 95% error bounds could be determined using a value from the standard normal table times the standard deviation of the sampling distribution. Putting these numbers into interval form, a 95% confidence interval for the population mean is

$$\left(\bar{y}-1.96\frac{\sigma}{\sqrt{n}}, \bar{y}+1.96\frac{\sigma}{\sqrt{n}} \right)$$

Although the interval estimate is less precise, confidence that the true population mean falls between the interval limits is considerably increased. In constructing interval estimates, a high level of confidence in the estimates is desired (90%, 95%, or 99% are commonly used), but the interval also should be precise enough to be practically useful. Telling the boss, "I'm 90% confident that our average monthly sales will be between $1000 and $1500" is probably better than, "I'm 100% confident that our average monthly sales will be between $0 and $100,000." These same considerations in constructing interval estimates of the population mean also apply to interval estimates of population regression coefficients.

To construct a confidence interval estimate for β_1, the slope of the regression line, an estimate of the standard deviation of the sampling distribution is needed. This estimate is obtained by substituting s_e for σ_e in Equation (3.12):

$$s_{b_1} = s_e\sqrt{\frac{1}{(n-1)s_x^2}}$$

When sample sizes are small (say, $n \leq 30$), the t distribution is used to construct the interval estimate. A $(1-\alpha)100\%$ confidence interval for β_1 is given by

$$(b_1 - t_{\alpha/2}s_{b_1}, b_1 + t_{\alpha/2}s_{b_1})$$

The value $t_{\alpha/2}$ is a number chosen from the t table to ensure the appropriate level of confidence. For example, for a 90% confidence interval estimate, $\alpha = .10$, so that $(1-\alpha)100\% = 90\%$, and a t value with $\alpha/2 = .05$ probability in each tail of the t distribution with $n-2$ degrees of freedom is used.

For β_0, the $(1-\alpha)100\%$ confidence interval is

$$(b_0 - t_{\alpha/2}s_{b_0}, b_0 + t_{\alpha/2}s_{b_0})$$

where

$$s_{b_0} = s_e\sqrt{\frac{1}{n} + \frac{\bar{x}^2}{(n-1)s_x^2}}$$

The estimated standard deviations of the sampling distribution of b_0 and b_1 are sometimes referred to as *standard errors of the coefficients* or estimated standard deviations of the coefficients. Thus, s_{b_0} is the standard error of b_0, and s_{b_1} is the standard error of b_1.

Hypothesis tests about β_0 and β_1 also can be performed. The most common hypothesis test in simple regression is

$H_0: \quad \beta_1 = 0$

$H_a: \quad \beta_1 \neq 0$

where H_0 represents the null hypothesis and H_a is the alternative hypothesis. The null hypothesis states that the slope of the population regression line is zero. This means that there is no linear relationship between y and x and that knowledge of x does not help explain the variation in y. The alternative hypothesis states that the slope of the population regression line is not equal to zero; that is, x and y are linearly related. Knowledge of the value of x does provide information concerning the associated value of y.

To test this hypothesis, a t statistic is used:

$$t = \frac{b_1}{s_{b_1}}$$

If the null hypothesis is true, then the t statistic has a t distribution with $n - 2$ degrees of freedom, and it should be small in absolute value. If the null hypothesis is false, then the t statistic should be large in absolute value.

To decide whether to accept or reject the null hypothesis, a level of significance, α, must first be chosen. The level of significance is the probability of a Type I error; that is, α is equal to the probability of rejecting the null hypothesis if the null hypothesis is really true. Typical α values are .01, .05, and .10. The decision rule for the test can be stated as:

Reject H_0 if $t > t_{\alpha/2}$ or $t < -t_{\alpha/2}$

Accept H_0 if $-t_{\alpha/2} \leq t \leq t_{\alpha/2}$

The value $t_{\alpha/2}$ is called a critical value and is chosen from the t table to ensure that the test is performed with the stated level of significance. A t value with probability $\alpha/2$ in each tail of the t distribution with $n - 2$ degrees of freedom is used.

Although the test of the null hypothesis $H_0: \beta_1 = 0$ is the most common and important test in simple regression analysis, tests of whether β_1 is equal to any value are possible. The general hypotheses can be stated as

H_0: $\beta_1 = \beta_1{}^*$

H_a: $\beta_1 \neq \beta_1{}^*$

where $\beta_1{}^*$ is any number chosen as the hypothesized value. The decision rule is

Reject H_0 if $t > t_{\alpha/2}$ or $t < -t_{\alpha/2}$

Accept H_0 if $-t_{\alpha/2} \leq t \leq t_{\alpha/2}$

and the test statistic is

$$t = \frac{b_1 - \beta_1{}^*}{s_{b_1}}$$

When the null hypothesis is true, t should be small in absolute value because b_1 (the estimate of β_1) should be close to $\beta_1{}^*$, making the numerator, $b_1 - \beta_1{}^*$, close to zero. When the null hypothesis is false, b_1 should be different in value from the hypothesized value, $\beta_1{}^*$, and the difference $b_1 - \beta_1{}^*$ should be large in absolute value, resulting in a large absolute value for the t statistic.

Tests for hypotheses about β_0 proceed in a similar fashion. To test

H_0: $\beta_0 = \beta_0{}^*$

H_a: $\beta_0 \neq \beta_0{}^*$

the test statistic is

$$t = \frac{b_0 - \beta_0^*}{s_{b_0}}$$

where β_0^* is any hypothesized value. The decision rule for the test is:

Reject H_0 if $t > t_{\alpha/2}$ or $t < -t_{\alpha/2}$

Accept H_0 if $-t_{\alpha/2} \leq t \leq t_{\alpha/2}$

Note that tests about β_0 do not provide information about the existence of a relationship between x and y. Testing whether the slope coefficient is equal to zero tells you if there is a relationship between x and y; testing whether the intercept is equal to zero does not.

An alternative method of reporting hypothesis-testing results also is available in many software packages. Consider again the hypotheses

H_0: $\beta_1 = 0$

H_a: $\beta_1 \neq 0$

The test statistic used is

$$t = \frac{b_1}{s_{b_1}}$$

Some computerized regression software routines perform this computation and then report the p value associated with the computed test statistic. The p value is the probability of obtaining a value of t at least as extreme as the actual computed value if the null hypothesis is true. Suppose a simple regression analysis is performed on a sample of 25 observations and the computed test statistic value is 2.50. The p value for the two-tailed test of H_0: $\beta_1 = 0$ is p value = $P(t > 2.5$ or $t < -2.5) = .02$ from the t table because there is a probability of .01 above 2.5 and .01 below -2.5 in the t distribution with $n - 2 = 23$ degrees of freedom.

The p value can be viewed as the minimum level of significance, α, that can be chosen for the test and result in rejection of the null hypothesis. Thus, a decision rule using p values can be stated as:

Reject H_0 if p value < α

Accept H_0 if p value ≥ α

For a given level of significance, the same decision results regardless of which test procedure is used.

Using the previous example, the decision is to reject H_0 if $\alpha = .05$, but to accept H_0 if $\alpha = .01$. Reporting p values associated with hypothesis tests provides additional information beyond simply reporting that the null hypothesis was rejected or accepted at a single level of significance. Readers then can make their own decisions about the strength of the relationship by comparing the p value to any desired significance level.

FIGURE 3.12   Illustration of MINITAB and Excel Regression Outputs

(a)   **MINITAB**

Predictor	Coef	Stdev	T	P
Constant	b_0	s_{b_0}	b_0/s_{b_0}	p-value
x1 variable name	b_1	s_{b_1}	b_1/s_{b_1}	p-value

(b)   **Excel**

Predictor	Coefficient	Standard Error	t stat	p value	Lower 95%	Upper 95%
Constant	b_0	s_{b_0}	b_0/s_{b_0}	p-value	$b_0 - t_{\alpha/2}s_{b_0}$	$b_0 + t_{\alpha/2}s_{b_0}$
x1 variable name	b_1	s_{b_1}	b_1/s_{b_1}	p-value	$b_1 - t_{\alpha/2}s_{b_1}$	$b_1 + t_{\alpha/2}s_{b_1}$

TABLE 3.8   Hypothesis Structures and Their Associated Decision Rules for Hypotheses About β_0 and β_1

Hypotheses		Decision Rules
$H_0: \beta_1 = \beta_1^*$ $\quad$ or $\quad$ $H_a: \beta_1 \neq \beta_1^*$	$H_0: \beta_0 = \beta_0^*$ $H_a: \beta_0 \neq \beta_0^*$	Reject H_0 if $t > t_{\alpha/2, n-2}$ or $t < -t_{\alpha/2, n-2}$ Accept if H_0 if $-t_{\alpha/2, n-2} \leq t \leq t_{\alpha/2, n-2}$
$H_0: \beta_1 \geq \beta_1^*$ $\quad$ or $\quad$ $H_a: \beta_1 < \beta_1^*$	$H_0: \beta_0 \geq \beta_0^*$ $H_a: \beta_0 < \beta_0^*$	Reject H_0 if $t < -t_{\alpha, n-2}$ Accept H_0 if $t \geq -t_{\alpha, n-2}$
$H_0: \beta_1 \leq \beta_1^*$ $\quad$ or $\quad$ $H_a: \beta_1 > \beta_1^*$	$H_0: \beta_0 \leq \beta_0^*$ $H_a: \beta_0 > \beta_0^*$	Reject H_0 if $t > t_{\alpha, n-2}$ Accept H_0 if $t \leq t_{\alpha, n-2}$

Figure 3.12(a) shows the structure of the initial portion of the MINITAB output for a regression analysis. The estimated regression coefficients b_0 and b_1 are given along with the standard errors of the coefficients, s_{b_0} and s_{b_1}, and the t ratios for testing either $H_0: \beta_0 = 0$ or $H_0: \beta_1 = 0$. The last column reports the p values associated with the two-tailed test of the hypotheses $H_0: \beta_0 = 0$ and $H_0: \beta_1 = 0$. Note that the t ratios can be used for performing either one- or two-tailed tests as long as the hypothesized value is zero. The one-tailed tests simply require an adjustment in the decision rules. These are shown in Table 3.8 for the more general hypothesis structures. The MINITAB t ratios are always appropriate when β_0^* and β_1^* (the hypothesized values) are zero.

Figure 3.12(b) shows the structure of the equivalent Excel output. Again, the coefficients, standard errors, t ratios, and p values are reported. Excel also prints out the 95% confidence interval estimates for both β_0 and β_1. In addition, Excel allows the user to request confidence intervals for levels of confidence other than 95%.

The p values for both MINITAB and Excel represent the appropriate values only for a two-tailed test. Both the MINITAB and Excel outputs are fully illustrated in Example 3.6.

EXAMPLE **3.5**

Consider the data in Table 3.2 and the computations required to obtain the least squares estimates in Table 3.3. To compute s_{b_0} and s_{b_1}, the following quantities are needed:

$$n = 6$$

$$\bar{x}^2 = \left(\frac{\sum x_i}{n}\right)^2 = \left(\frac{21}{6}\right)^2 = 12.25$$

and

$$(n-1)s_x^2 = \sum x_i^2 - \frac{1}{n}\left(\sum x_i\right)^2 = 91 - \frac{1}{6}(21)^2 = 17.5$$

which can be determined using the sums obtained in Table 3.3. In addition, the standard error of the regression must be computed:

$$s_e = \sqrt{\frac{\sum(y_i - \hat{y}_i)^2}{n-2}} = \sqrt{\frac{8.8}{4}} = 1.48$$

The error sum of squares $\sum(y_i - \hat{y}_i)^2$, was computed in Table 3.4.

Using this information:

$$s_{b_0} = s_e\sqrt{\frac{1}{n} + \frac{\bar{x}^2}{(n-1)s_x^2}} = 1.48\sqrt{\frac{1}{6} + \frac{12.25}{17.5}} = 1.38$$

and

$$s_{b_1} = s_e\sqrt{\frac{1}{(n-1)s_x^2}} = 1.48\sqrt{\frac{1}{17.5}} = 0.35$$

The 95% confidence interval estimates for β_0 and β_1 now can be constructed.

For β_0: $[-0.2 - 2.776(1.38), -0.2 + 2.776(1.38)]$

or $(-4.03, 3.63)$

For β_1: $[2.2 - 2.776(0.35), 2.2 + 2.776(0.35)]$

or $(1.23, 3.17)$

EXAMPLE 3.6   **Pricing Communications Nodes (continued)**

Table 3.6 shows the cost of installing a sample of communications nodes for a large manufacturing firm whose headquarters is based in Fort Worth, Texas, with branches throughout the United States. The number of access ports at each of the sampled nodes is also shown. The administrator of the network wants to develop an equation that is helpful in pricing the installation of new communications nodes on the network.

Figure 3.6 shows the Excel scatterplot of cost versus number of nodes. The MINITAB scatterplot is in Figure 3.14. The MINITAB and Excel regression results are shown in Figures 3.13 and 3.15, respectively. Use the outputs to answer the following questions:

1   What is the sample regression equation relating NUMPORTS to COST?

   Answer: COST = 16,594 + 650NUMPORTS

2   Is there sufficient evidence to conclude that a linear relationship exists between COST and NUMPORTS?

   Answer:

   (a)   To answer this question, the hypotheses

   H_0: $\beta_1 = 0$
   H_a: $\beta_1 \neq 0$

FIGURE 3.13   **MINITAB Regression Output for Communications Node Examples (3.3 and 3.6)**

```
The regression equation is
COST = 16594 + 650 NUMPORTS

Predictor        Coef        StDev          T        P
Constant        16594         2687       6.18    0.000
NUMPORTS       650.17        66.91       9.72    0.000

S = 4307        R-Sq = 88.7%       R-Sq(adj) = 87.8%

Analysis of Variance

Source          DF          SS          MS          F        P
Regression       1    1751268376  1751268376     94.41    0.000
Residual Error  12     222594146    18549512
Total           13    1973862521

Unusual Observations
Obs    NUMPORTS        COST        Fit    StDev Fit    Residual    St Resid
  1        68.0       52388      60805        2414       -8417      -2.36R
 10        24.0       23444      32198        1414       -8754      -2.15R

R denotes an observation with a large standardized residual
```

FIGURE 3.14

MINITAB Scatterplot of Cost Versus Number of Ports for Communications Node Examples (3.3 and 3.6)

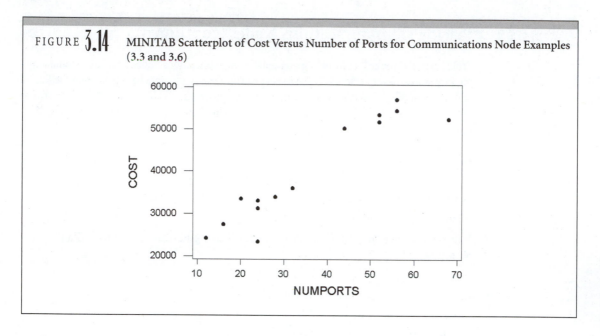

should be tested. Choosing a 5% level of significance, the decision rule for the test is

Reject H_0 if $t > 2.179$ or $t < -2.179$

Accept H_0 if $-2.179 \leq t \leq 2.179$

The test statistic from either Figure 3.13 or 3.15 is $t = 9.72$, so the decision is to reject H_0. There is sufficient evidence to conclude that a linear relationship between COST and NUMPORTS does exist.

(b) The p value also could be used to test the hypotheses. The decision rule is:

Reject H_0 if p value $< .05$

Accept H_0 if p value $\geq .05$

The p value is 0.000, so the decision is to reject H_0.

3 Find a 95% confidence interval estimate of β_1.

Answer: $650.17 \pm (2.179)(66.91)$ or 650.17 ± 145.80

Our point estimate of the change in cost, on average, for each additional port is $650.17. The confidence interval provides an error bound for this estimate, $145.80. We can now construct a range of values that can be used as an estimate of the average change in cost for each additional port. The range is 650.17 ± 145.80 or $504.37 to $795.97. We can be 95% confident that the true average change falls within this range. The upper and lower confidence limits provide an idea of the accuracy of our estimates of the cost of each additional port.

4 Test whether there is a direct (positive) relationship between COST and NUMPORTS.

Answer:

To answer this question, the hypotheses

FIGURE **3.15**   **Excel Regression Output for Communications Node Examples (3.3 and 3.6)**

SUMMARY OUTPUT

Regression Statistics

Multiple R	0.942
R Square	0.887
Adjusted R Square	0.878
Standard Error	4306.914
Observations	14.000

ANOVA

	df	SS	MS	F	Significance F
Regression	1	1751268375.709	1751268375.709	94.410	0.000
Residual	12	222594145.791	18549512.149		
Total	13	1973862521.500			

	Coefficients	Standard Error	t Stat	P-value	Lower 95%	Upper 95%
Intercept	16593.647	2687.050	6.175	0.000	10739.068	22448.226
NUMPORTS	650.169	66.914	9.717	0.000	504.376	795.962

$$H_0: \quad \beta_1 \leq 0$$
$$H_a: \quad \beta_1 > 0$$

should be tested. The null hypothesis states that the slope of the population regression line is either zero (no relationship) or negative (an inverse relationship). The alternate hypothesis states that the slope of the population regression line is positive (a direct relationship). Choosing a 5% level of significance, the decision rule for the test is:

Reject H_0 if $t > 1.782$

Accept H_0 if $t \leq 1.782$

The test statistic from either Figure 3.13 or 3.15 is $t = 9.72$, so the decision is to reject H_0. There is sufficient evidence to conclude that a direct (positive) linear relationship between COST and NUMPORTS does exist.

If the null hypothesis had been accepted, the conclusion is that either there is an inverse relationship or there is no relationship. The relationship is not direct, but acceptance does not imply that no linear relationship existed as in the case of the two-tailed test. Care must be taken in interpreting the results of one-tailed tests.

5   A claim is made that each new access port adds at least $1000 to the installation of a communications node. To examine this claim, we test the hypotheses

$$H_0: \quad \beta_1 \geq 1000$$
$$H_a: \quad \beta_1 < 1000$$

using a 5% level of significance.

Answer:

The decision rule is:

Reject H_0 if $t < -1.782$

Accept H_0 if $t \geq -1.782$

The test statistic is

$$t = \frac{b_1 - \beta_1^*}{s_{b_1}} = \frac{650.17 - 1000}{66.91} = -5.23$$

so the decision is to reject H_0. The slope of the line is not 1000 or more. In practical terms, there is no evidence to support the claim that each port adds at least $1000 to the cost of installing a new communications node.

The previous problems illustrate the aspects of greatest interest in the communications node example. Simply for illustrative purposes, here are two problems showing how the techniques discussed for the intercept term in the equation could be used.

6 Find a 95% confidence interval estimate of β_0.

Answer:

$16{,}594 \pm 2.179(2687)$ or $16{,}594 \pm 5854.97$

7 Test the hypotheses

H_0: $\beta_0 = 0$

H_a: $\beta_0 \neq 0$

using a 5% level of significance.

Answer:

(a) Decision rule:

Reject H_0 if $t > 2.179$ or $t < -2.179$

Accept H_0 if $-2.179 \leq t \leq 2.179$

Test statistic: $t = 6.18$

Decision: Reject H_0

Conclusion: The population intercept is not equal to zero.

Note: This test has no *practical* significance in this problem and is performed merely to illustrate tests for the intercept. Note that rejection of the null hypothesis H_0: $\beta_0 = 0$ does not indicate that x and y are related. It merely makes a statement about the intercept of the population regression line.

(b) Decision rule using p value:

Reject H_0 if p value $< .05$

Accept H_0 if p value $\geq .05$

Test statistic: p value $= 0.000$

Decision: Reject H_0

EXERCISES

Exercises 4 and 5 should be done by hand.

4 **Flexible Budgeting (continued)**   Refer to Exercise 1.

a Test the hypotheses $H_0: \beta_1 = 0$ versus $H_a: \beta_1 \neq 0$ at the 5% level of significance. State the decision rule, the test statistic value, and your decision.

b From the result in part a, are production and overhead costs linearly related?

c Test the hypotheses $H_0: \beta_1 = 1$ versus $H_a: \beta_1 \neq 1$ at the 5% level of significance. State the decision rule, the test statistic value, and your decision.

d From the result in part c, what can be concluded?

5 **Central Company (continued)**   Refer to Exercise 2.

a Test the hypotheses $H_0: \beta_1 = 0$ versus $H_a: \beta_1 \neq 0$ at the 5% level of significance. State the decision rule, the test statistic value, and your decision.

b From the result in part a, are hours of labor and number of items linearly related?

c Test the hypotheses $H_0: \beta_0 = 0$ versus $H_a: \beta_0 \neq 0$ at the 5% level of significance. State the decision rule, the test statistic value, and your decision.

d From the result in part c, what can be concluded?

6 **Dividends**   A random sample of 46 firms was chosen from the June 1998 *Standard and Poor's Security Owner's Stock Guide.*[1] The indicated dividend yield for May 1998 (DIVYIELD) and the earnings per share for the last 12 months (EPS) were recorded for these 46 firms.

Using DIVYIELD as the dependent variable and EPS as the independent variable, a regression was run. Use the output to answer the questions. The list of firms and the accompanying data are shown in Table 3.9. The MINITAB scatterplot and regression output are in Figures 3.16 and 3.17, respectively. The Excel regression output is in Figure 3.18.

a What is the sample regression equation relating dividends to EPS?

b Is there a linear relationship between dividend yield and EPS? Use $\alpha = .05$. State the hypotheses to be tested, the decision rule, the test statistic, and your decision.

c What conclusion can be drawn from the test result?

d Construct a 95% confidence interval estimate of β_1.

e Construct a 95% confidence interval estimate of β_0.

These data are arranged in columns with DIVYIELD first and EPS second in a datafile with prefix DIV3.

---

[1] *Standard and Poor's Security Owner's Stock Guide.* ©1998 Standard and Poor's, a division of McGraw-Hill Inc.

TABLE 3.9   Dividend Yield and EPS Data for Dividends Exercise

Company	Dividend Yield	EPS	Company	Dividend Yield	EPS
1 Bristol-Myers Squibb	1.56	3.35	24 Tandy	0.40	1.31
2 Intel	0.12	3.23	25 Betzdearborn Inc.	1.52	2.60
3 Waterlink Inc.	0.00	0.44	26 Owens & Minor	0.20	0.49
4 Schering-Plough	0.88	2.16	27 Wendy's International	0.24	0.89
5 Weyerhaeuser	1.60	1.83	28 General Signal	1.08	2.70
6 PNC Bank	1.56	3.44	29 Kansas City Southern Industries	0.16	0.24
7 Marion Capitol Holdings	0.88	1.29	30 New York Bancorp	0.60	2.34
8 Park Electrochemical	0.32	2.02	31 Ohio Casualty	1.76	3.37
9 United National Bank Holdings	0.60	1.68	32 Maytag Corp.	0.64	2.51
10 Burlington Resources	0.55	0.97	33 Tidewater	0.60	5.39
11 Consolidated Papers	0.88	1.45	34 Brookline Bancorp	0.00	0.39
12 AMRESCO Inc.	0.00	1.74	35 Stone & Webster	0.60	2.06
13 Consolidated Natural Gas	1.94	2.41	36 Wilmington Trust	1.56	3.20
14 Louisiana-Pacific	0.56	0.41	37 Idaho Power	1.86	2.32
15 Wheelabrator Technologies	0.12	0.57	38 PacifiCorp	1.08	1.57
16 Baker Hughes	0.46	0.83	39 Millipore	0.44	1.84
17 McGraw-Hill	1.56	3.09	40 Masco Corp.	0.44	1.29
18 Clorox	1.28	2.82	41 Central Maine Power	0.90	0.40
19 Nalco Chemical	1.00	2.17	42 Lance Inc.	0.96	1.01
20 Pioneer Hi-Bred International	0.40	1.09	43 Seagrams Co.	0.66	2.17
21 TJX	0.12	1.00	44 Health Management Associates	0.00	0.48
22 DPL	0.94	1.22	45 Jones Pharma Inc.	0.12	1.41
23 Johnson Controls	0.92	3.33	46 Diamond Offshore Drilling	0.50	2.40

From *Standard & Poor's Security Owner's Stock Guide.* Copyright 1988, Standard & Poor's, a division of McGraw-Hill, Inc.

FIGURE 3.16   MINITAB Scatterplot for Dividends Exercise

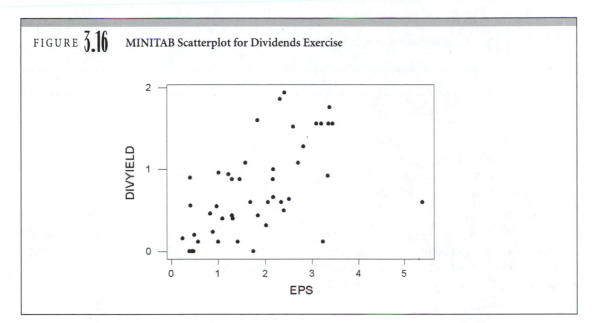

FIGURE 3.17   MINITAB Regression Output for Dividends Exercise

```
The regression equation is
DIVYIELD = 0.239 + 0.277 EPS

Predictor         Coef        StDev            T        P
Constant        0.2393       0.1382         1.73    0.090
EPS             0.27746      0.06457        4.30    0.000

S = 0.4743      R-Sq = 29.6%       R-Sq(adj) = 28.0%

Analysis of Variance

Source            DF          SS           MS        F        P
Regression         1       4.1550       4.1550    18.47    0.000
Residual Error    44       9.8998       0.2250
Total             45      14.0548

Unusual Observations
Obs       EPS    DIVYIELD         Fit    StDev Fit     Residual    St Resid
  2      3.23      0.1200      1.1355       0.1135      -1.0155       -2.20R
 13      2.41      1.9400      0.9080       0.0788       1.0320        2.21R
 33      5.39      0.6000      1.7348       0.2393      -1.1348       -2.77RX
 37      2.32      1.8600      0.8830       0.0763       0.9770        2.09R

R denotes an observation with a large standardized residual
X denotes an observation whose X value gives it large influence.
```

FIGURE 3.18   Excel Regression Output for Dividends Exercise

SUMMARY OUTPUT

Regression Statistics
Multiple R	0.5437
R Square	0.2956
Adjusted R Square	0.2796
Standard Error	0.4743
Observations	46.0000

ANOVA

	df	SS	MS	F	Significance F
Regression	1.000	4.1550	4.1550	18.4668	0.0001
Residual	44.000	9.8998	0.2250		
Total	45.000	14.0548			

	Coefficients	Standard Error	t Stat	P-value	Lower 95%	Upper 95%
Intercept	0.2393	0.1382	1.7316	0.0904	−0.0392	0.5178
EPS	0.2775	0.0646	4.2973	0.0001	0.1473	0.4076

7 **Sales/Advertising**   The vice-president of marketing for a large firm is concerned about the effect of advertising on sales of the firm's major product. To investigate the relationship between advertising and sales, data on the two variables were gathered from a random sample of 20 sales districts. The data are shown in Table 3.10. The MINITAB and Excel outputs for the regression of sales (SALES) on advertising (ADV) are shown in Figures 3.19 and 3.20, respectively. The scatterplot is in Figure 3.21. Using the outputs, answer the following questions:

a Is there a linear relationship between sales and advertising? Use $\alpha = .05$. State the hypotheses to be tested, the decision rule, the test statistic, and your decision.

b What implications does this test result have for the firm?

c What is the sample regression equation relating sales to advertising?

d Construct a 90% confidence interval estimate of β_0.

e Construct a 95% confidence interval estimate of β_1.

f Test the hypotheses

H_0: $\beta_1 = 20$
H_a: $\beta_1 \neq 20$

using a 5% level of significance. State the decision rule, the test statistic, and your decision.

TABLE 3.10   Sales and Advertising Data

District	Sales (in $100)	Advertising Expenditures (in $100)	District	Sales (in $100)	Advertising Expenditures (in $100)
1	4250	235	11	3200	200
2	3700	210	12	3500	210
3	2000	160	13	4000	230
4	5800	345	14	5175	210
5	6200	325	15	5450	300
6	6500	365	16	5900	325
7	7000	400	17	7110	390
8	4900	370	18	6500	375
9	6100	350	19	7400	415
10	2900	200	20	6600	380

FIGURE 3.19   MINITAB Regression Output for Sales and Advertising Exercise

```
The regression equation is
SALES = - 57 + 17.6 ADV


Predictor        Coef        StDev           T        P
Constant        -57.3        509.8       -0.11     0.912
ADV            17.570        1.642       10.70     0.000


S = 594.8       R-Sq = 86.4%      -Sq(adj) = 85.7%


Analysis of Variance


Source            DF          SS            MS           F          P
Regression         1      40523671      40523671     114.54     0.000
Residual Error    18       6368342        353797
Total             19      46892014


Unusual Observations
Obs       ADV       SALES        Fit    StDev Fit    Residual     St Resid
  8       370        4900       6444          176       -1544        -2.72R
 14       210        5175       3632          198        1543         2.75R


R denotes an observation with a large standardized residual
```

FIGURE **3.20**   **Excel Regression Output for Sales and Advertising Exercise**

SUMMARY OUTPUT

```
Regression Statistics
Multiple R              0.930
R Square                0.864
Adjusted R Square       0.857
Standard Error        594.808
Observations           20.000
```

ANOVA

	df	SS	MS	F	Significance F
Regression	1.000	40523671.367	40523671.367	114.539	0.0000
Residual	18.000	6368342.383	353796.799		
Total	19.000	46892013.750			

	Coefficients	Standard Error	t Stat	P-value	Lower 95%	Upper 95%
Intercept	−57.281	509.750	−0.112	0.9118	−1128.227	1013.666
ADV	17.570	1.642	10.702	0.0000	14.121	21.019

FIGURE **3.21**   **MINITAB Scatterplot for Sales and Advertising Exercise**

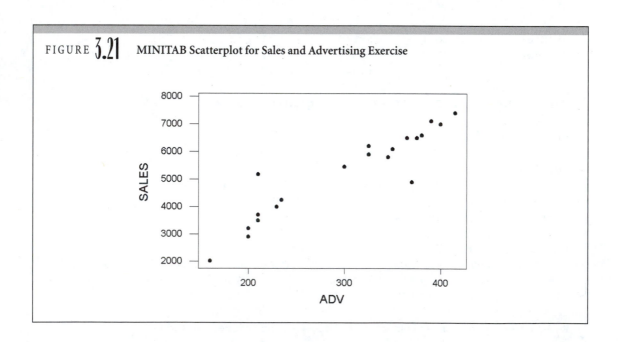

g   What conclusion can be drawn from the result of the test in part f?

These data are available in a file with prefix SALESAD3. The data file contains two columns of data: sales and advertising expenditures in that order.

3.4 ASSESSING THE FIT OF THE REGRESSION LINE

3.4.1   The ANOVA Table

In Example 3.6 (communications nodes), the goal might be to obtain the best possible prediction of the cost of a new node to be installed. Using a sample of n previously installed nodes, the sample mean of the n costs could be computed and used to predict the cost of any future node. But additional information on the number of access ports at each communications node might be used to obtain "better" predictions. When predicting, the goal in fitting a regression equation is to obtain a more accurate prediction of a node's cost. This improvement in accuracy can be measured in terms of how much better the predictions are using the regression line instead of simply the mean of the y variable. If there is a significant improvement in prediction accuracy, then it is worthwhile to utilize the additional information.

In Figure 3.22, suppose that x^* represents the number of access ports at a particular communications node and y^* is the true cost of that node. If $\bar{y}$ is used to predict the cost of this node, then the prediction error is

$$y^* - \bar{y}$$

But if the regression equation is used, the error is

$$y^* - \hat{y}$$

thus reducing the error by

$$\hat{y} - \bar{y}$$

Note that the error in using the sample mean to predict $y^* - \bar{y}$, is equal to the error produced by using the regression line, $y^* - \hat{y}$, plus the improvement over using the mean, $\hat{y} - \bar{y}$:

$$y^* - \bar{y} = (y^* - \hat{y}) + (\hat{y} - \bar{y}) \tag{3.13}$$

Squaring both sides of Equation (3.13) gives

$$(y^* - \bar{y})^2 = [(y^* - \hat{y}) + (\hat{y} - \bar{y})]^2$$

or expanding the right-hand side,

$$(y^* - \bar{y})^2 = (y^* - \hat{y})^2 + 2(\hat{y} - \bar{y})(y^* - \hat{y}) + (\hat{y} - \bar{y})^2 \tag{3.14}$$

The terms on either side of Equation (3.14) can be summed for all the individuals in the sample to obtain

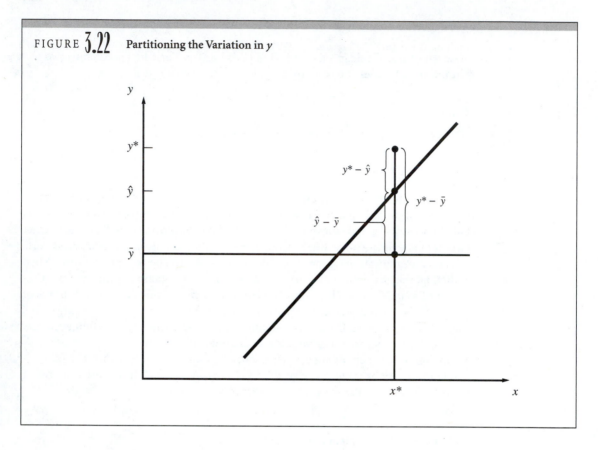

FIGURE 3.22 Partitioning the Variation in y

$$\sum_{i=1}^{n}(y_i - \overline{y})^2 = \sum_{i=1}^{n}(y_i - \hat{y}_i)^2 + 2\sum_{i=1}^{n}(\hat{y}_i - \overline{y})(y_i - \hat{y}_i) + \sum_{i=1}^{n}(\hat{y}_i - \overline{y})^2$$

The term $\sum_{i=1}^{n}(\hat{y}_i - \overline{y})(y_i - \hat{y}_i)$ can be shown to equal zero so that

$$\sum_{i=1}^{n}(y_i - \overline{y})^2 = \sum_{i=1}^{n}(y_i - \hat{y}_i)^2 + \sum_{i=1}^{n}(\hat{y}_i - \overline{y})^2 \qquad (3.15)$$

Each term in Equation (3.15) is a sum of squares and has a special interpretation in regression analysis. The term on the left-hand side of the equality,

$$SST = \sum_{i=1}^{n}(y_i - \overline{y})^2$$

is called the *total sum of squares (SST)*. This is the numerator of the fraction used to compute the sample variance of y and is interpreted as the total variation in y.

On the right-hand side of the equation are two additional sums of squares:

$$SSE = \sum_{i=1}^{n}(y_i - \hat{y}_i)^2$$

FIGURE 3.23   Analysis of Variance Tables from MINITAB and Excel Regressions

(a) MINITAB

Source	DF	SS	MS	F	p
Regression	1	SSR	$MSR = SSR/1$	$F = MSR/MSE$	p value
Residual Error	$n-2$	SSE	$MSE = SSE/(n-2)$		
Total	$n-1$	SST			

(b) Excel

	df	SS	MS	F	Significance F
Regression	1	SSR	$MSR = SSR/1$	$F = MSR/MSE$	p value
Residual	$n-2$	SSE	$MSE = SSE/(n-2)$		
Total	$n-1$	SST			

---

called the *error sum of squares (SSE)*, and

$$SSR = \sum_{i=1}^{n} (\hat{y}_i - \bar{y})^2$$

called the *regression sum of squares (SSR)*.

The terms in SSE, $y_i - \hat{y}_i$, are the prediction errors for the sample—that is, the differences between the true y values and the values predicted by using the regression line. *SSE* is often referred to as the "unexplained" sum of squares or as a measure of "unexplained" variation in y.

The terms in SSR, $\hat{y}_i - \bar{y}$, are measures of the improvement in using the regression line rather than the sample mean to predict. *SSR* often is referred to as the "explained" sum of squares or as a measure of "explained" variation in y. The "explaining" is done through the use of the variable x.

The terms *explained* and *unexplained* should be interpreted with some caution. Explained does not necessarily mean that x causes y. It means that the variation in y around the regression line is smaller than the variation around the sample mean, $\bar{y}$. This caveat is explored in more detail in Section 3.7.

Figure 3.23 shows how MINITAB and Excel report certain of the quantities discussed in this section. The tables shown are called *analysis of variance* (ANOVA) tables. This name refers to the partitioning of the total variation in the dependent variable into the regression and error sums of squares. These tables are typical of ANOVA tables presented in most statistical packages.

In the MINITAB ANOVA table in Figure 3.23(a), the three sources of variation in y are denoted Regression, Residual Error, and Total. In the Excel ANOVA table in Figure 3.23(b), the name Residual rather than Residual Error is used. The quantities *SSR*, *SSE*, and *SST* are found in the SS column in both MINITAB and Excel. In addition, the DF column reports the degrees of freedom associated with each of these sums of squares. *SSR* has 1 degree of freedom, *SSE* has $n-2$ degrees of freedom, and *SST* has $n-1$ degrees of freedom. Just as $SSR + SSE = SST$, it is also true that the regression and residual degrees of freedom always add up to the total degrees of freedom:

$$1 + (n-2) = n - 1$$

Mean squares are shown in the MS column. The mean squares are sums of squares divided by their degrees of freedom:

$$MSR = \frac{SSR}{1}$$

$$MSE = \frac{SSE}{n-2}$$

MSR is referred to as the *mean square due to regression*, and *MSE* is the *mean square due to error* (or more simply, "mean square regression" and "mean square error"). Note that *MSR* always equals *SSR* because the divisor is 1. This holds true in the case of simple regression, but will differ when multiple regression is discussed in the next chapter. *MSE* was used earlier in this chapter and was denoted s_e^2 to represent an estimate of the variance around the regression line. The square root of *MSE*, denoted s_e, was called the standard deviation around the regression line or the standard error of the regression.

The remaining columns in the ANOVA tables and further uses of *MSR* and *MSE* are discussed in the next section.

3.4.2 The Coefficient of Determination and the Correlation Coefficient

In an exact or deterministic relationship, $SSR = SST$ and $SSE = 0$. A line could be drawn that passed through every sample point. But this is not the case in most practical business situations. A measure of how well the regression line fits the data is needed. In other words, "What proportion of the total variation has been explained?" This measure is provided through a statistic called the *coefficient of determination*, denoted R^2 (this is read "R squared"):

$$R^2 = \frac{SSR}{SST}$$

R^2 is computed by dividing the explained sum of squares by the total sum of squares. The result is the proportion of variation in y explained by the regression. R^2 falls between 0 and 1. The closer to 1 the value of R^2 is, the better the "fit" of the regression line to the data. An alternative formula for computing R^2 is to compute the proportion of variation unexplained by the regression and subtract this proportion from 1:

$$R^2 = 1 - \frac{SSE}{SST}$$

Most computerized regression routines report R^2, and some also report another quantity called the *correlation coefficient*, which is the square root of R^2 with an appropriate sign attached:

$$R = \pm\sqrt{R^2}$$

Note that this relationship holds in the case of simple regression, but not for multiple regression (discussed in Chapter 4).

The sign of R is positive if the relationship is direct ($b_1 > 0$, or an upward-sloping line) and negative if the relationship is inverse ($b_1 < 0$, or a downward-sloping line). R ranges between -1 and 1.

Note that R^2 is referred to as a measure of fit of the regression line. It is not interpreted as a measure of the predictive quality of the regression equation even though the ANOVA decomposition was motivated using the concept of improved predictions. R^2 generally overstates the regression equation's predictive ability. This fact is discussed further in Section 3.5, and an alternative measure of the regression's predictive ability is suggested. R^2 will continue to be referred to as a measure of fit.

3.4.3 The *F* Statistic

An additional measure of how well the regression line fits the data is provided by the F statistic, which tests whether the equation $\hat{y} = b_0 + b_1 x$ provides a better fit to the data than the equation $\hat{y} = \bar{y}$. The F statistic is computed as

$$F = \frac{MSR}{MSE}$$

MSR is the mean square due to the regression, or the regression sum of squares divided by its degrees of freedom. MSE is the mean square due to error, or the error sum of squares divided by its degrees of freedom, so $MSE = SSE/(n-2)$. If the regression line fits the data well (that is, if the variation around the regression line is small relative to the variation around the sample mean $\bar{y}$), then MSR should be large relative to MSE. If the regression line does not fit well, then MSR is small relative to MSE. Thus, large values of F support the use of the regression line, whereas small values suggest that x is of little use in explaining the variation in y.

To formalize the use of the F statistic, consider again the hypotheses

$$H_0: \beta_1 = 0$$
$$H_a: \beta_1 \neq 0$$

The F statistic can be used to perform this test. The decision rule is:

Reject H_0 if $F > F(\alpha; 1, n-2)$

Accept H_0 if $F \leq F(\alpha; 1, n-2)$

where $F(\alpha; 1, n-2)$ is a critical value chosen from the F table for level of significance α. The F statistic has degrees of freedom associated with both the numerator and denominator sums of squares used in its computation. For a simple regression, there is 1 numerator degree of freedom and $n-2$ denominator degrees of freedom. These are

---

FIGURE 3.24 Additional Statistics Provided on MINITAB and Excel Regression Outputs

(a) MINITAB

$s = s_e$ R-sq $= R^2$ R-sq(adj) $= R^2_{adj}$

(b) Excel

Regression Statistics
Multiple R $= R$
R Square $= R^2$
Adjusted R Square $= R^2_{adj}$
Standard Error $= s_e$
Observations $= n$

---

the degrees of freedom associated with *SSR* and *SSE*, respectively. *F* tables are provided in Appendix B.

If the null hypothesis $H_0: \beta_1 = 0$ is rejected, then the conclusion is that *x* and *y* are linearly related. In other words, the line $\hat{y} = b_0 + b_1 x$ provides a better fit to the data than $\hat{y} = \bar{y}$.

The hypotheses tested by the *F* statistic also can be tested using the *t* test previously discussed. The decision made using either test is exactly the same. This is because the *F* statistic is equal to the square of the *t* statistic. Also, the $F(\alpha; 1, n-2)$ critical value is the square of the $t_{\alpha/2}$ critical value for the *t* distribution with $n-2$ degrees of freedom:

$$F = \frac{MSR}{MSE} = t^2$$

and

$$F(\alpha; 1, n-2) = t^2_{\alpha/2, n-2}$$

Because the two test procedures yield exactly the same decision, it does not matter which is used when testing $H_0: \beta_1 = 0$ versus $H_a: \beta_1 \neq 0$, (when testing $H_0: \beta_1 \leq 0$, vs. $H_a: \beta_1 > 0$, or $H_0: \beta_1 \geq 0$ vs. $H_a: \beta_1 < 0$ or any tests where $\beta_1^* \neq 0$, the *t* test should be used). The importance of the *F* statistic in multiple regression, however, makes it necessary to learn how to use this test. When there are two or more explanatory variables, the *F* test can be used to test hypotheses that cannot be tested using the *t* test.

Figure 3.24 shows the additional statistics provided by both MINITAB [3.24(a)] and Excel [3.24(b)]. In MINITAB, these statistics appear as shown directly above the ANOVA table. In Excel, the statistics appear as shown as the first entries in the regression output. Figure 3.25 shows a representation of the complete MINITAB and Excel outputs. The bracketed sections are discussed in later chapters.

In the MINITAB output, *s* is the standard deviation around the regression line or standard error of the regression. This was denoted s_e in the text. Also, *R-sq* is the R^2

FIGURE 3.25   Complete Regression Outputs for MINITAB and Excel

(a) MINITAB

The regression equation is

$y = b_0 + b_1 x$

Predictor	Coef	StDev	T	P
Constant	b_0	s_{b_0}	b_0 / s_{b_0}	p-value
x1 variable name	b_1	s_{b_1}	b_1 / s_{b_1}	p-value

$s = s_e$ R-sq $= R^2$ R-sq(adj) $= R^2_{adj}$

Analysis of Variance

Source	DF	SS	MS	F	p
Regression	1	SSR	MSR $=$ SSR/1	$F =$ MSR/MSE	p value
Residual Error	$n-2$	SSE	MSE $=$ SSE/$(n-2)$		
Total	$n-1$	SST			

Unusual Observations						
Obs	X	Y	Fit	StDev Fit	Residual	St Resid
Obs. No.	Value of X	Value of y	$\hat{y}$	s_m	$y - \hat{y}$	—

R denotes an observation with a large standardized residual
X denotes an observation whose X value gives it large influence

(b) Excel

Regression Statistics

Multiple R	$= R$
R Square	$= R^2$
Adjusted R Square	$= R^2_{adj}$
Standard Error	$= s_e$
Observations	$= n$

Predictor	Coefficient	Standard Error	t stat	P-value	Lower 95%	Upper 95%
Constant	b_0	s_{b_0}	b_0 / s_{b_0}	p-value	$b_0 - t_{\alpha/2} s_{b_0}$	$b_0 + t_{\alpha/2} s_{b_0}$
x1 variable name	b_1	s_{b_1}	b_1 / s_{b_1}	p-value	$b_1 - t_{\alpha/2} s_{b_1}$	$b_1 + t_{\alpha/2} s_{b_1}$

ANOVA

	df	SS	MS	F	Significance F
Regression	1	SSR	MSR $=$ SSR/1	$F =$ MSR/MSE	p value
Residual	$n-2$	SSE	MSE $=$ SSE/$(n-2)$		
Total	$n-1$	SST			

value. The Excel output labels s_e as *Standard Error* and R^2 as *R Square*. In addition, Excel shows the *Multiple R,* which is the positive square root of R^2, and the number of observations *(Observations).* Both outputs also show the *Adjusted R Square* [*R-sq(adj)* in MINITAB]. This quantity is discussed in Chapter 4.

EXAMPLE 3.7

To compute the R^2 for the data in Table 3.2, the quantities *SSE* and *SST* must be computed.

$$R^2 = 1 - \frac{SSE}{SST} = 1 - \frac{\sum (y_i - \hat{y}_i)^2}{\sum (y_i - \bar{y})^2}$$

SSE was computed in Table 3.4 as *SSE* = 8.8. *SST* can be computed by the formula

$$\sum y_i^2 - \frac{1}{n}\left(\sum y_i\right)^2 = 431 - \frac{1}{6}(45)^2 = 93.5$$

The coefficient of determination or R^2 is

$$1 - \frac{8.8}{93.5} = 0.91$$

so 91% of the variation in *y* has been explained by the regression.

Note that the formula

$$R^2 = \frac{SSR}{SST}$$

could have been used here. But because *SSE* already had been computed and *SSR* had not, the alternative formula was used. If it were desired to compute *SSR,* this could be done by recalling that $SSR = SST - SSE = 93.5 - 8.8 = 84.7$.

The *F* statistic is computed as

$$F = \frac{MSR}{MSE} = \frac{SSR/1}{SSE/(n-2)} = \frac{84.7}{8.8/4} = 38.5$$

The hypotheses

$H_0: \quad \beta_1 = 0$

$H_a: \quad \beta_1 \neq 0$

can be tested using the *F* statistic. Using a 5% level of significance, the decision rule is:

Reject H_0 if $F > F(.05; 1,4) = 7.71$

Accept H_0 if $F \leq F(.05; 1,4) = 7.71$

The test statistic was computed as $F = 38.5$, which results in a decision to reject H_0. In this case, the conclusion is that β_1 is not equal to zero and that the two variables *x* and *y* are linearly related.

EXAMPLE **3.8**   **Pricing Communications Nodes (continued)**

Refer to Example 3.6 to complete the following problems using the regression output in Figure 3.13 or 3.15.

1   What percentage of the variation in COST is explained by the regression?

Answer: Using the R^2 value, 88.7% of the variation in COST has been explained by the regression.

2   Use the F test and a 5% level of significance to test the hypotheses

$$H_0: \quad \beta_1 = 0$$
$$H_a: \quad \beta_1 \neq 0$$

Answer:

(a)   Decision rule:

Reject H_0 if $F > 4.75$

Accept H_0 if $F \leq 4.75$

Test Statistic: $F = 94.41$
Decision: Reject H_0

Conclusion: There is evidence to conclude that COST and NUMPORTS are linearly related.

(b)   Decision rule:

Reject H_0 if p value $< .05$

Accept H_0 if p value $\geq .05$

Test Statistic: p value $= 0.000$
Decision: Reject H_0

EXERCISES

Exercises 8 and 9 should be done by hand.

8   **Flexible Budgeting (continued)** Refer to Exercise 1.

a   Compute the coefficient of determination (R^2) for the regression of overhead costs on production.

b   What percentage of the variation in overhead costs has been explained by the regression?

c   Use the F test to test the hypotheses $H_0: \beta_1 = 0$ versus $H_a: \beta_1 \neq 0$ at the 5% level of significance. Be sure to state the decision rule, the test statistic value, and your decision.

d   From the result in part c, are production and overhead costs linearly related?

9   **Central Company (continued)** Refer to Exercise 2.

a   Compute the coefficient of determination (R^2) for the regression of the number of labor hours on number of items produced.

b What percentage of the variation in hours of labor has been explained by the regression?

c Use the F test to test the hypotheses $H_0: \beta_1 = 0$ versus $H_a: \beta_1 \neq 0$ at the 5% level of significance. Be sure to state the decision rule, the test statistic value, and your decision.

d From the result in part c, are hours of labor and number of items produced linearly related?

10 **Dividends (continued)** Use the output in Figure 3.17 or 3.18 to help answer the questions.

a What percentage of the variation in dividend yield has been explained by the regression?

b Use the F test to test the hypotheses $H_0: \beta_1 = 0$ versus $H_a: \beta_1 \neq 0$ at the 5% level of significance. Be sure to state the decision rule, the test statistic value, and your decision.

11 **Sales/Advertising (continued)** Use the output in Figure 3.19 or 3.20 to help solve these problems.

a What percentage of the variation in sales has been explained by the regression?

b Use the F test to test the hypotheses $H_0: \beta_1 = 0$ versus $H_a: \beta_1 \neq 0$ at the 5% level of significance. Be sure to state the decision rule, the test statistic value, and your decision.

3.5 PREDICTION OR FORECASTING WITH A SIMPLE LINEAR REGRESSION EQUATION

One of the possible goals for fitting a regression line to data is to be able to use the regression equation to predict or forecast values of the dependent variable y. Given that a value of x has been observed, what is the best prediction of the response value, y? To discuss how to best predict y and how to make inferences using predictions based on a random sample, two cases that may arise in practice are considered.

3.5.1 Estimating the Conditional Mean of y Given x

In Example 3.6, suppose that the network administrator wants to consider all possible nodes with 40 communications ports. The question to be answered is, "What will the cost be, on average, for nodes with 40 ports?"

The average cost of all nodes with 40 communications ports is to be estimated. Thus, an estimate of the conditional mean cost given $x = 40$, or an estimate of $\mu_{y|x=40}$ is required (see Figure 3.26). If a relationship between y and x does exist, the best estimate of this point on the population regression line is given by

$$\hat{y}_m = b_0 + b_1 x_m$$

FIGURE 3.26   Estimating a Conditional Mean $\mu_{y|x=x_m}$

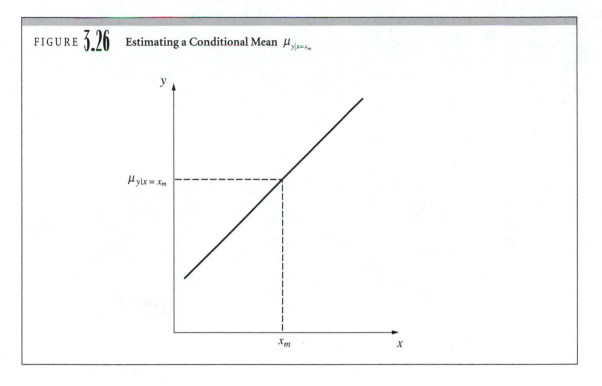

where b_0 and b_1 are the least-squares estimates of β_0 and β_1, x_m is the number of ports for which an estimate is desired, and $\hat{y}_m$ is the estimate of the conditional mean cost. In this case, $\hat{y}_m$ represents the estimate of the point on the regression line corresponding to (or conditional on) $x = x_m$. Thus, it is the estimate of a population mean. The variance of this estimate can be shown to equal

$$\sigma_m^2 = \sigma_e^2 \left(\frac{1}{n} + \frac{(x_m - \bar{x})^2}{(n-1)s_x^2} \right) \tag{3.16}$$

Because σ_e^2 is unknown, s_e^2 is substituted to obtain an estimate of σ_m^2:

$$s_m^2 = s_e^2 \left(\frac{1}{n} + \frac{(x_m - \bar{x})^2}{(n-1)s_x^2} \right) \tag{3.17}$$

The standard deviation or standard error of the estimate, s_m, is simply the square root of s_m^2.

The standard error of the estimate of the point on the regression line is affected by the distance of the value x_m from the sample mean $\bar{x}$. The closer the value of x_m to the mean of all the sample x values, the closer the term $(x_m - \bar{x})^2$ is to zero. If $x_m = \bar{x}$, the term $(x_m - \bar{x})^2/(n-1)s_x^2$ equals zero, and the standard error equals $s_e / \sqrt{n}$. Thus, the closer the value x_m is to the sample mean, $\bar{x}$, the smaller the standard error is or the more accurate the estimate is expected to be.

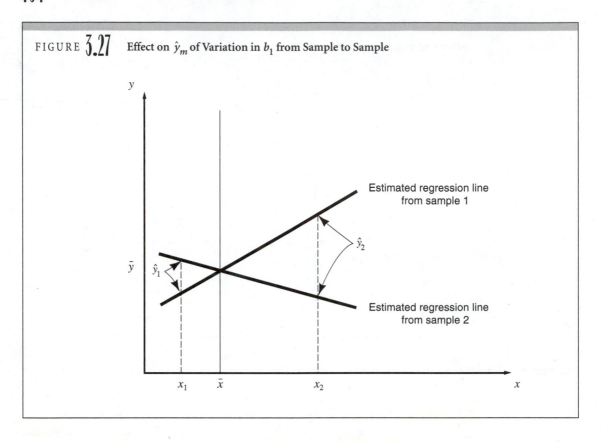

FIGURE **3.27**   **Effect on $\hat{y}_m$ of Variation in b_1 from Sample to Sample**

The reason is illustrated in Figure 3.27. Because all least-squares lines pass through the point $(\bar{x}, \bar{y})$, two least-squares lines have been drawn intersecting at the point $(\bar{x}, \bar{y})$. The two lines could represent least-squares lines fitted to two independent random samples taken from the same population. It is assumed that the two samples have means $\bar{x}$ and $\bar{y}$. Even though both lines pass through a common point, the slopes of the two estimated lines could be quite different, as illustrated. Thus, there is more certainty as to the value of a point on the regression line near the value $\bar{x}$ than at the extreme values of x. When estimating a point on the regression line for an extreme value of x, the greater uncertainty is reflected through a larger standard error.

It was previously stated that when the term $(x_m - \bar{x})^2 / (n-1)s_x^2$ is zero, the standard error is $s_m = s_e/\sqrt{n}$. This happens when $x_m = \bar{x}$. The quantity $s_e/\sqrt{n}$ is very much like the standard error associated with the sample mean $\bar{y}$, when it is used to estimate the (unconditional) population mean of the y values. A population mean is being estimated in the case of regression, so this is to be expected. The difference is that the mean in regression, $\mu_{y|x}$, is conditional on the value of x, rather than being unconditional.

Confidence intervals can be constructed for estimates of a conditional mean using

$$(\hat{y}_m - t_{\alpha/2}s_m, \hat{y}_m + t_{\alpha/2}s_m) \qquad (3.18)$$

where $\hat{y}_m$ is the point estimate and $t_{\alpha/2}$ is chosen from the t distribution with $n-2$ degrees of freedom in the usual fashion.

Hypothesis tests also can be conducted. To test

$$H_0 : \mu_{y|x_m} = \mu^*_{y|x_m}$$
$$H_a : \mu_{y|x_m} \neq \mu^*_{y|x_m}$$

where $\mu^*_{y|x_m}$ is a hypothesized value for the point on the population regression line, the decision rule is

Reject H_0 if $t > t_{\alpha/2}$ or $t < -t_{\alpha/2}$
Accept H_0 if $-t_{\alpha/2} \leq t \leq t_{\alpha/2}$

The test statistic, t, is computed as

$$t = \frac{\hat{y}_m - \mu^*_{y|x_m}}{s_m}$$

and it has a t distribution with $n-2$ degrees of freedom when H_0 is true.

One-tailed tests also can be performed provided the usual modifications are made in constructing the decision rule.

3.5.2   Predicting an Individual Value of *y* Given *x*

Now suppose the network administrator is interested in a single communications node in a plant in Kansas City, Missouri, which will have 40 access ports. Predict the cost of installation for this particular node.

With $x_p = 40$ access ports, the best prediction of the cost of this node is

$$\hat{y}_p = b_0 + b_1 x_p$$

which is exactly the same number that would be used to estimate the average cost for all nodes with 40 access ports. One can do no better in predicting cost for an individual node than to use the estimate of average cost for all nodes with the same number of access ports. This is because there is no additional information used in the regression that distinguishes this one node from all the others (see Figure 3.28).

The prediction for an individual value, however, is not as accurate as the estimate of a population mean for all individuals in a certain category. The variance of the prediction for an individual is

$$\sigma_p^2 = \sigma_e^2 \left(1 + \frac{1}{n} + \frac{(x_p - \bar{x})^2}{(n-1)s_x^2}\right) \qquad (3.19)$$

which can be estimated by replacing σ_e^2 by s_e^2:

FIGURE **3.28** Predicting an Individual y Value

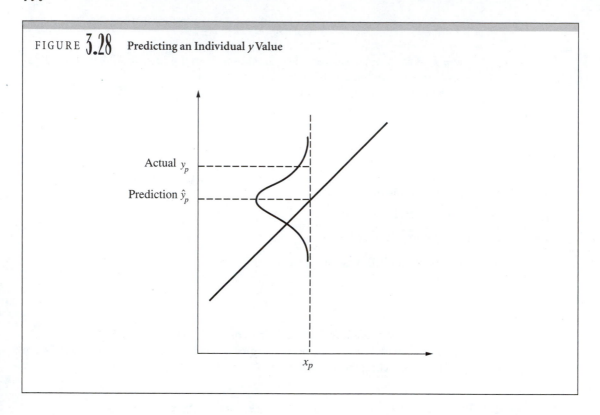

$$s_p^2 = s_e^2 \left(1 + \frac{1}{n} + \frac{(x_p - \bar{x})^2}{(n-1)s_x^2} \right) \tag{3.20}$$

To compare s_p^2 to the variance of the estimate of a conditional mean, write the prediction variance as

$$s_p^2 = s_e^2 + s_m^2$$

The variance of the prediction for an individual value is equal to the variance from estimating the point on the regression line for $x = x_p$, s_m^2, plus the estimate of the variation of the individual y values around the regression line, s_e^2. Even if the exact position of $\mu_{y|x_p}$ were known, y_p still would not be known. The individual y values are distributed around $\mu_{y|x_p}$ with standard deviation σ_e. Because $\mu_{y|x_p}$ is actually unknown, there is uncertainty associated with the estimation of this value (reflected in s_m or s_m^2) plus the uncertainty in predicting an individual value (reflected in s_e or s_e^2).

Interval estimation of y_p is accomplished by constructing prediction intervals. The term *prediction interval* is used rather than confidence interval because a population parameter is not being estimated in this case; instead, the response or performance of a single individual in the population is being predicted.

A $(1 - \alpha)100\%$ prediction interval for y_p is

FIGURE 3.29   Confidence Interval Limits Versus Prediction Interval Limits

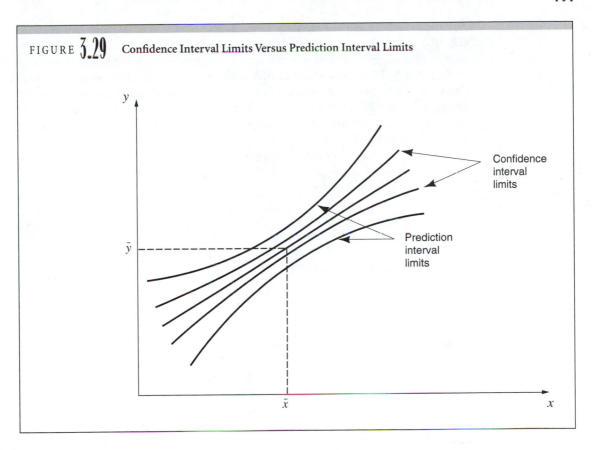

$$(\hat{y}_p - t_{\alpha/2}s_p, \hat{y}_p + t_{\alpha/2}s_p)$$ (3.21)

where $\hat{y}_p$ is the predicted value and $t_{\alpha/2}$ is chosen from the t distribution with $n-2$ degrees of freedom.

Figure 3.29 illustrates the difference between the confidence interval estimate of $\mu_{y|x}$ and the prediction interval for an individual. Both the confidence interval in Equation (3.18) and the prediction interval in Equation (3.21) are narrower, more precise, near $x = \bar{x}$, and wider at the extreme values of x. The prediction interval is always wider than the confidence interval because of the added uncertainty involved in predicting an individual response.

3.5.3   Assessing Quality of Prediction

As noted in Section 3.4, the R^2 of the regression is a measure of the fit of the regression to the sample data. It is not generally considered an adequate measure of the regression equation's ability to estimate $\mu_{y|x}$ or to predict new responses. The standard R^2 overestimates the quality of future (or out-of-sample) predictions.

Two possible means of assessing prediction quality are presented in this section. The first is called *data splitting*. In this method, partition the data set into two groups. One group of n_1 data points is used to estimate or fit possible equations used for forecasting. The second group of n_2 data points, called a *holdout sample* or *validation sample,* is used to assess predictive ability of the models estimated using the fitting sample. Any models that are considered possible candidates are estimated using the fitting sample. Predictions, $\hat{y}_i$, are then computed for these models using the explanatory variable values in the validation sample. For each candidate model, prediction errors, $y_i - \hat{y}_i$, are computed for all n_2 observations in the validation sample. A measure of forecast accuracy based on the forecast errors can then be computed. For example, the *mean square forecast error*

$$\frac{\sum_{i=1}^{n_2}(y_i - \hat{y}_i)^2}{n_2}$$

and the *mean absolute forecast error*

$$\frac{\sum_{i=1}^{n_2}|y_i - \hat{y}_i|}{n_2}$$

are two commonly computed measures.

Models with smaller mean square forecast errors or mean absolute forecast errors are better for prediction purposes. The advantage of using this approach is that the models are tested on data that were not used in the fitting or model estimation process. This provides an independent assessment of the models' predictive ability.

After an appropriate model has been chosen, the entire data set can be used to estimate the model parameters. This model is then used to produce future predictions.

A second means of assessing prediction quality is to use the *PRESS* statistic. *PRESS* stands for prediction sum of squares and is defined as

$$PRESS = \sum_{i=1}^{n}(y_i - \hat{y}_{i,-1})^2$$

In this formula $\hat{y}_{i,-1}$, represents the prediction obtained from a model estimated with one of the sample observations deleted. If there are n observations in the sample, there are n different predictions, $\hat{y}_{i,-1}$. The prediction, $\hat{y}_{i,-1}$ is obtained by evaluating the regression equation at x_i, but the data point (x_i, y_i) is not used in obtaining the estimated regression equation. Thus, as with the use of a validation sample, predictions are obtained from data that are not used to fit the model.

The quantities $y_i - \hat{y}_{i,-1}$ often are called *PRESS* residuals because they are similar to the actual regression residuals, $y_i - \hat{y}_i$. The prediction sum of squares also is similar to the error sum of squares, *SSE*. This suggests construction of an R^2-like statistic that might be called the prediction R^2:

$$R^2_{PRED} = 1 - \frac{PRESS}{SST}$$

Larger values of R^2_{PRED} (or smaller values of *PRESS*) suggest models of greater predictive ability.

EXAMPLE 3.9

1   Again, refer to the data in Table 3.2. Find an estimate of the conditional mean of y when $x = 6$ and find the standard deviation of this estimate.

Answer: Using the least-squares regression equation $\hat{y} = -0.2 + 2.2x$, an estimate of the point on the regression line when $x = 6$ is $\hat{y} = -0.2 + 2.2(6) = 13$
The standard deviation of the estimate of the point on the regression line is

$$s_m = s_e\sqrt{\frac{1}{n} + \frac{(x_m - \bar{x})^2}{(n-1)s_x^2}} = 1.48\sqrt{\frac{1}{6} + \frac{(6-3.5)^2}{17.5}} = 1.07$$

[For computation of s_e, $\bar{x}$, and $(n-1)s_x^2$, see Example 3.5.]

2   Find a prediction of the y value when $x = 6$ and find the standard deviation of the prediction.
Answer: Using the least-squares regression equation $\hat{y} = -0.2 + 2.2x$, the prediction of y when $x = 6$ is $\hat{y} = -0.2 + 2.2(6) = 13$.
The standard deviation of the prediction is

$$s_p = s_e\sqrt{1 + \frac{1}{n} + \frac{(x_p - \bar{x})^2}{(n-1)s_x^2}} = 1.48\sqrt{1 + \frac{1}{6} + \frac{(6-3.5)^2}{17.5}} = 1.83$$

3   Find a 95% confidence interval and 95% prediction interval when $x = 6$.

Answer: The 95% confidence and prediction intervals are, respectively,

$[13 - 2.776(1.07), 13 + 2.776(1.07)]$ or $(10.03, 15.97)$

and

$[13 - 2.776(1.83), 13 + 2.776(1.83)]$ or $(7.92, 18.08)$

EXAMPLE 3.10   **Pricing Communication Nodes (continued)**

1   On average, how much do we expect communication nodes to cost if there are to be 40 access ports.
Answer: Figure 3.30 shows the MINITAB regression output using the PREDICT option with 40 as the value of the x variable. The resulting output (following the regression results) can be used to answer the question. A point estimate of cost for all nodes with 40 access ports is $42,600. A 95% confidence interval estimate is given by ($40,035, $45,166). Thus, we can say with 95% confidence, that the average cost of all nodes with 40 access ports is expected to be between $40,035 and $45,166.

2   For an individual node with 40 access ports, find a prediction of cost.
Answer: The point prediction is again $42,600. A 95% prediction interval for the individual node is ($32,872, $52,329). Note that the prediction interval is considerably wider than the confidence interval, reflecting the additional uncertainty of predicting for an individual as opposed to estimating an average.

FIGURE **3.30**   MINITAB Regression Output Requesting a Prediction for Example 3.10

```
The regression equation is
COST = 16594 + 650 NUMPORTS


Predictor          Coef        StDev            T        P
Constant          16594         2687         6.18    0.000
NUMPORTS         650.17        66.91         9.72    0.000


S = 4307          R-Sq = 88.7%        R-Sq(adj) = 87.8%

Analysis of Variance

Source             DF           SS            MS          F          P
Regression          1   1751268376   1751268376      94.41      0.000
Residual Error     12    222594146     18549512
Total              13   1973862521


Unusual Observations
Obs    NUMPORTS         COST         Fit    StDev Fit     Residual     St Resid
  1        68.0        52388       60805         2414        -8417        -2.36R
 10        24.0        23444       32198         1414        -8754        -2.15R

R denotes an observation with a large standardized residual

Predicted Values

    Fit   StDev Fit         95.0% CI            95.0% PI
  42600        1178    (   40035,    45166)   (   32872,    52329)
```

EXERCISES

Exercises 12 and 13 should be done by hand.

12 Flexible Budgeting (continued)   Refer to Exercise 1.

a Find a point estimate of the overhead costs, on average, for production runs of 80,000 units.

b Find a 95% confidence interval estimate of overhead costs, on average, for production runs of 80,000 units.

c Find a point prediction of the overhead costs for a single production run of 80,000 units.

d Find a 95% prediction interval for overhead costs for a single production run of 80,000 units.

e State why the prediction interval is wider than the confidence interval.

13 Central Company (continued)   Refer to Exercise 2.

a Find a point estimate for the number of hours of labor required, on average, when 60 units are produced.

b Find a 95% confidence interval estimate of hours of labor required, on average, when 60 units are produced.

c Find a point prediction of the number of hours of labor required for one run producing 60 units.

d Find a 95% prediction interval for the number of hours of labor required for one run producing 60 units.

14 Dividends (continued)   Consider the dividend-yield problem in Exercise 6 and the associated computer output in either Figure 3.17 or 3.18. An analyst wants an estimate of dividend yield for all firms with earnings per share of $3. Does the equation developed provide a more accurate estimate than simply using the sample mean dividend yield for all 46 firms examined? State why or why not.

15 Sales/Advertising (continued)   Use the output in Figure 3.31 or 3.32 to help solve these problems.

a Find an estimate of average sales for all sales districts with advertising expenditures of $25,000. Find a point estimate and a 95% confidence interval estimate. The output in Figure 3.31 was obtained from MINITAB requesting a prediction with $x = 250$ (representing $25,000).

b Predict sales for individual districts having advertising expenditures of $20,000, $25,000, $30,000, and $35,000. Find point predictions as well as 95% prediction intervals. The output in Figure 3.32 was obtained from MINITAB requesting predictions for $x = 200, 250, 300,$ and 350, respectively (representing $20,000, $25,000, $30,000, and $35,000).

FIGURE 3.31 MINITAB Regression Output for Exercise 15(a)

```
The regression equation is
SALES = - 57 + 17.6 ADV


Predictor          Coef        StDev           T         P
Constant          -57.3        509.8       -0.11     0.912
ADV              17.570        1.642       10.70     0.000


S = 594.8        R-Sq = 86.4%       R-Sq(adj) = 85.7%

Analysis of Variance

Source            DF          SS          MS         F         P
Regression         1    40523671    40523671    114.54     0.000
Residual Error    18     6368342      353797
Total             19    46892014

Unusual Observations
Obs        ADV       SALES        Fit   StDev Fit     Residual    St Resid
  8        370        4900       6444         176        -1544       -2.72R
 14        210        5175       3632         198         1543        2.75R

R denotes an observation with a large standardized residual

Predicted Values


    Fit  StDev Fit         95.0% CI             95.0% PI
   4335        156    (    4007,     4663)  (    3043,     5627)
```

FIGURE 3.32 MINITAB Regression Output for Exercise 15(b)

```
The regression equation is
SALES = - 57 + 17.6 ADV


Predictor        Coef       StDev          T        P
Constant        -57.3       509.8      -0.11    0.912
ADV            17.570       1.642      10.70    0.000


S = 594.8       R-Sq = 86.4%      R-Sq(adj) = 85.7%

Analysis of Variance

Source            DF         SS         MS         F        P
Regression         1   40523671   40523671    114.54    0.000
Residual Error    18    6368342     353797
Total             19   46892014


Unusual Observations
Obs        ADV       SALES        Fit   StDev Fit      Residual    St Resid
  8        370        4900       6444         176         -1544       -2.72R
 14        210        5175       3632         198          1543        2.75R

R denotes an observation with a large standardized residual

Predicted Values

    Fit   StDev Fit        95.0% CI              95.0% PI
   3457        211    (   3013,    3900)  (   2131,    4783)
   4335        156    (   4007,    4663)  (   3043,    5627)
   5214        133    (   4934,    5493)  (   3933,    6494)
   6092        157    (   5763,    6421)  (   4800,    7384)
```

3.6 FITTING A LINEAR TREND TO TIME-SERIES DATA

Data gathered on individuals at the same point in time are called *cross-sectional data. Time-series data* are data gathered on a single individual (person, firm, and so on) over a sequence of time periods, which may be days, weeks, months, quarters, years, or virtually any other measure of time. In a given problem, however, it is be assumed that the data are gathered over only one interval of time (daily and weekly data are not combined, for example).

When dealing with time-series data, the primary goal often is to be able to produce forecasts of the dependent variable for future time periods. Two separate approaches to this problem can be identified. On the one hand, a researcher may identify variables that are related to the dependent variable in a causal manner and use these in developing a *causal regression model*. For example, when trying to forecast sales for a particular product, causal variables might include advertising expenditures and competitors' market share. Changes in these variables are felt to produce or cause changes in sales. Thus, the term causal regression model is used.

The researcher may, on the other hand, identify patterns of movement in past values of the dependent variable and extrapolate these patterns into the future using an *extrapolative regression model*. An extrapolative model uses explanatory variables, although they are not related to the dependent variable in a causal manner. They simply describe the past movements of the dependent variable so that these movements can be extended into future time periods. Variables that represent trend and seasonal components often are included in extrapolative models.

Both causal and extrapolative models have their benefits and drawbacks. Causal models require the identification of variables that are related to the dependent variable in a causal manner. Then data must be gathered on these explanatory variables to use the model. Furthermore, when forecasting for future time periods, the values of the explanatory variables in these periods must be known. In extrapolative models, only past values of the dependent variable are required, and thus variable selection and data gathering are simpler processes.

Whether a causal or extrapolative model performs better is determined to some extent by how far into the future the forecast refers. Forecasts often are classified as short-term (0 to 3 months), medium-term (3 months to 2 years), or long-term (2 years and longer). Extrapolative models tend to perform best in the short term, but they can be reasonably accurate for medium-term forecasts. Causal models often outperform extrapolative models when long-term forecasts are desired. In addition to being just as effective as causal models in the short term and often in the medium term, extrapolative models tend to be easier to develop and use.

The success of extrapolative models depends on the stability of the behavior of the time series. If past time-series patterns are expected to continue into the future, then an extrapolative model should be relatively successful in making accurate forecasts. If these past patterns are altered for some reason, and future movements differ in general from past movements, then extrapolative models do not perform well.

Thus, an assumption when using an extrapolative model for forecasting is that past patterns of data movement are reflective of future patterns.

Causal models can respond, to some extent, to more drastic changes in patterns. Changes in the explanatory variables caused by changes in economic or market conditions should produce relatively accurate forecasts of changes in the dependent variable. Of course, this assumes that the changes in the explanatory variables will be known for future time periods. In addition, if the model itself changes (that is, if the way the variables are related changes in the future), the causal model is not capable of making accurate forecasts.

In this section, the use of a *linear trend model* for time-series data is examined. The linear trend model is a type of extrapolative model that may be useful in certain time-series applications. In subsequent chapters, other techniques useful in building extrapolative time-series models are examined.

A *trend* in time-series data is a tendency for the series to move upward or downward over many time periods. This movement may follow a straight line or a curvilinear pattern. Regression analysis can be used to model certain trends and to extrapolate these trends into future time periods.

The simplest form of a trend over time is a linear trend. The linear trend model can be written

$$y_i = \beta_0 + \beta_1 t + e_i$$

The explanatory variable simply indicates the time period ($x_i = t$). Usually, the variable t is constructed by using the integers, $1, 2, 3, \ldots$ to indicate the time period. This is preferred to using the actual years ($1980, 1981, 1982, \ldots$) because it reduces computational problems.

Forecasts are simple to compute when the linear trend model is used. Simply insert the appropriate value for the time period to be forecast into the regression equation. The time period T forecast can be written as

$$\hat{y}_T = b_0 + b_1 T$$

Many other types of trends can be modeled using regression. Some examples, including the linear trend, are shown in Figure 3.33. Note that the other types of trends are represented by curves. Equations to represent curvilinear trends are discussed in Chapter 5.

FIGURE 3.33   Examples of Types of Trends

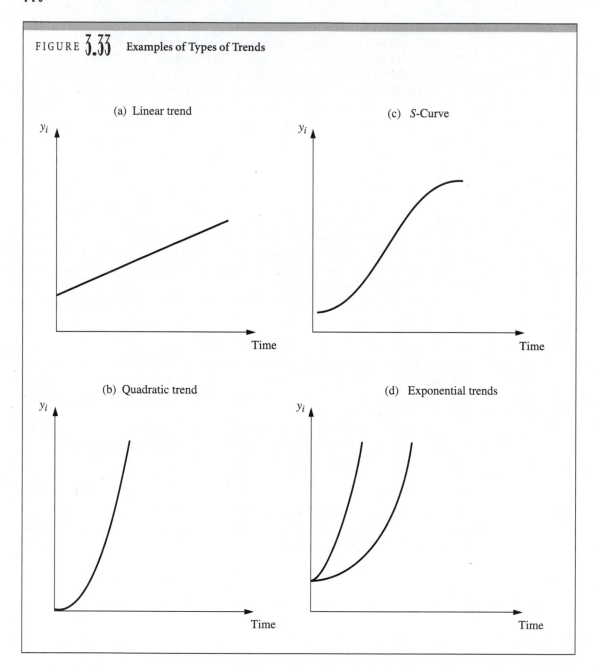

TABLE 3.11   Data for ABX Company Sales Example

Year.Qtr	Sales	Time	Year.Qtr	Sales	Time	Year.Qtr	Sales	Time
1990.1	221.0	1	1993.3	230.0	15	1997.1	296.0	29
1990.2	203.5	2	1993.4	254.5	16	1997.2	260.0	30
1990.3	190.0	3	1994.1	257.0	17	1997.3	271.5	31
1990.4	225.5	4	1994.2	238.0	18	1997.4	299.5	32
1991.1	223.0	5	1994.3	228.0	19	1998.1	297.0	33
1991.2	190.0	6	1994.4	255.0	20	1998.2	271.0	34
1991.3	206.0	7	1995.1	260.5	21	1998.3	270.0	35
1991.4	226.5	8	1995.2	244.0	22	1998.4	300.0	36
1992.1	236.0	9	1995.3	256.0	23	1999.1	306.5	37
1992.2	214.0	10	1995.4	276.5	24	1999.2	283.5	38
1992.3	210.5	11	1996.1	291.0	25	1999.3	283.5	39
1992.4	237.0	12	1996.2	255.5	26	1999.4	307.5	40
1993.1	245.5	13	1996.3	244.0	27			
1993.2	201.0	14	1996.4	291.0	28			

EXAMPLE 3.11   **ABX Company Sales**

The ABX Company sells winter sports merchandise including skis, ice skates, sleds, and so on. Quarterly sales (in thousands of dollars) for the ABX Company are shown in Table 3.11. The time period represented starts in the first quarter of 1990 and ends in the fourth quarter of 1999.

A MINITAB time-series plot of the sales figures is shown in Figure 3.34. The time-series plot suggests a strong linear trend in the sales figures. The regression with the linear trend variable (labeled TIME) was estimated and the resulting output is shown in Figure 3.35 for MINITAB and Figure 3.36 for Excel. The linear trend model estimated is

$$y_i = \beta_0 + \beta_1 t + e_i$$

To test whether the linear trend component is useful in explaining the variation in sales, the following hypotheses should be tested:

H_0: $\beta_1 = 0$

H_a: $\beta_1 \neq 0$

Using a 5% level of significance, the decision rule is:

Reject H_0 if $t > 1.96$ or $t < -1.96$

Accept H_0 if $-1.96 \leq t \leq 1.96$

FIGURE 3.34   MINITAB Time-Series Plot of ABX Company Sales

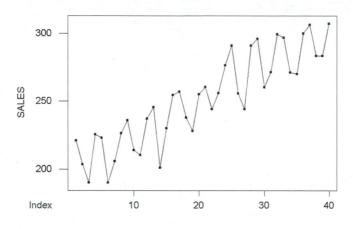

FIGURE 3.35   MINITAB Regression Output for ABX Company Sales Exercise

```
The regression equation is
SALES = 199 + 2.56 TIME

Predictor        Coef        StDev           T         P
Constant       199.017       5.128       38.81     0.000
TIME             2.5559      0.2180       11.73     0.000

S = 15.91        R-Sq = 78.3%        R-Sq(adj) = 77.8%

Analysis of Variance

Source           DF          SS           MS         F         P
Regression        1        34818        34818     137.50     0.000
Residual Error   38         9622          253
Total            39        44440

Unusual Observations
Obs      TIME       SALES          Fit    StDev Fit     Residual      St Resid
 14      14.0      201.00       234.80         2.89       -33.80        -2.16R

R denotes an observation with a large standardized residual
```

FIGURE 3.36 Excel Regression Output for ABX Company Sales Exercise

SUMMARY OUTPUT

Regression Statistics
Multiple R   0.885
R Square   0.783
Adjusted R Square   0.778
Standard Error   15.913
Observations   40.000

ANOVA

	df	SS	MS	F	Significance F
Regression	1.000	34817.883	34817.883	137.505	0.000
Residual	38.000	9622.061	253.212		
Total	39.000	44439.944			

	Coefficients	Standard Error	t Stat	P-value	Lower 95%	Upper 95%
Intercept	199.017	5.128	38.811	0.000	188.636	209.398
TIME	2.556	0.218	11.726	0.000	2.115	2.997

The z value of 1.96 is used as a critical value because the number of degrees of freedom is large (38).

When using time-series data for forecasting, it is generally true that prediction intervals are more appropriate than confidence intervals for representing the uncertainty in predictions for future time periods. Figure 3.37 shows the MINITAB output for the next four periods' forecasts. Using the linear trend equation estimated by MINITAB, the point forecasts are determined by substituting values of the trend variable for the appropriate time period into the equation:

2000.1 sales = 199.017 + 2.5559(41) = 303.81

2000.2 sales = 199.017 + 2.5559(42) = 306.36

2000.3 sales = 199.017 + 2.5559(43) = 308.92

2000.4 sales = 199.017 + 2.5559(44) = 311.48.

The prediction intervals in the output would be used as our interval predictions of sales in each of the four quarters. Thus, our interval prediction for sales in the first quarter of 2000 is $269,960 to $337,650.

If you look closely again at the time-series plot of sales in Figure 3.34, you may notice a pattern other than the trend. Note that the sales figures for the first and fourth quarters tend to be higher than the figures for the second and third quarters. This systematic variation among time periods from year to year is called *seasonal variation*. In Chapter 7, methods to account for seasonal variation are discussed.

FIGURE 3.37 MINITAB Regression Output to Obtain the Next Four Periods' Forecasts

```
The regression equation is
SALES = 199 + 2.56 TIME

Predictor        Coef       StDev          T        P
Constant      199.017       5.128      38.81    0.000
TIME           2.5559      0.2180      11.73    0.000

S = 15.91      R-Sq = 78.3%      R-Sq(adj) = 77.8%

Analysis of Variance

Source             DF          SS         MS        F        P
Regression          1       34818      34818   137.50    0.000
Residual Error     38        9622        253
Total              39       44440

Unusual Observations
Obs      TIME       SALES        Fit   StDev Fit    Residual    St Resid
 14      14.0      201.00     234.80        2.89      -33.80       -2.16R

R denotes an observation with a large standardized residual

Predicted Values

   Fit  StDev Fit         95.0% CI              95.0% PI
303.81       5.13   ( 293.43,  314.19)   ( 269.96,  337.65)
306.36       5.32   ( 295.60,  317.13)   ( 272.40,  340.33)
308.92       5.51   ( 297.76,  320.08)   ( 274.83,  343.01)
311.48       5.71   ( 299.92,  323.03)   ( 277.25,  345.70)
```

EXERCISES

16 **Fort Worth Water Department** In 1990, the city of Fort Worth, Texas, conducted a study examining the level of water purity. One aspect helpful in maintaining water purity is monitoring the quality of water at storm drains that pour into the Trinity River. This river supplies drinking water for Fort Worth. Even though water from the river is filtered later, preventing contaminants from entering the river from storm

TABLE 3.12   Data for Fort Worth Water Department Exercise

Odor	Color	Scum	Sheen	Bacteria	Odor	Color	Scum	Sheen	Bacteria
11	9	8	7	2	3	5	3	5	4
12	5	4	6	3	1	6	2	3	2
9	2	6	6	3	3	2	1	10	2
9	3	2	5	4	6	1	5	1	2
8	6	6	3	1	3	1	3	2	1
10	4	2	5	4	2	3	3	3	0
8	1	5	7	2	2	1	6	4	0
7	6	4	6	2	2	1	4	1	0
6	2	5	4	1	1	0	5	3	1
7	4	3	6	1	0	2	2	5	0
4	2	6	5	1	0	2	4	3	0
8	6	2	10	2	0	1	4	1	0
5	3	4	4	3	3	4	4	2	0
7	4	4	4	2	1	1	5	3	1
2	2	6	3	2	2	0	7	0	0
6	7	9	3	1	2	1	7	1	1
4	7	2	5	3	1	0	6	1	0
5	0	3	3	0	3	0	4	0	1
7	4	6	4	2	1	0	5	1	0
3	7	4	6	3	1	0	6	0	1
2	4	4	6	3	1	0	9	0	0
3	4	4	9	2	1	0	2	1	1
4	0	1	7	2	4	1	1	0	1
2	2	3	7	2	2	0	6	0	1

drains is helpful in maintaining purity. Table 3.12 shows five of the variables the city monitored to test purity of water entering the river from storm drains. These are monthly data from January 1986 through December 1989. In all cases, lower numbers are better. The variables are

odor: determined by a sensory test

color: no color is best—determined by comparison to a standard water sample

scum: floatable solids

hydrocarbon sheen: hydrocarbon (oil) sheen on surface of water

sewage bacteria: filamentous sewage bacteria

Your job is to use time-series plots and linear trend regression to examine the performance of the city's water department in improving the quality of storm drain water entering the Trinity River. Which of the variables show a significant decrease?

Are there areas where the city might concentrate their efforts to achieve future improvements? Use a 5% level of significance in any tests.

These data are in the file with prefix WATER3 in five columns in the following order: ODOR, COLOR, SCUM, SHEEN, and BACTERIA.

3.7 SOME CAUTIONS IN INTERPRETING REGRESSION RESULTS

3.7.1 Association versus Causality

A common mistake made when using regression analysis is to assume that a strong fit (high R^2) of a regression of y on x automatically means that "x causes y." This is not necessarily true. Some alternative explanations for the good fit include:

1 The reverse is true; y causes x. Linear regression computations pay no attention to the direction of causality. If x and y are highly correlated, a high R^2 value results even if the causal order of the variables is reversed.

2 There may be a third variable related to both x and y. It may be that neither x causes y nor y causes x. Both variables may be related to some third common cause. As an example, consider the price and gasoline mileage of automobiles. These two variables are inversely related. As mileage rises, price goes down (on average). But it is not the rise in mileage that "causes" the price to drop. A third variable, size of car, may be influencing both of the other two variables. As size increases, price increases and mileage drops.

To infer that x causes y requires that additional conditions be satisfied. A high R^2 for a regression of y on x might be considered supporting evidence for causality, but on its own, this is not enough to ensure that x causes y.

Note that the absence of causality is not necessarily a drawback in regression analysis. An equation showing a relationship between x and y can be important and useful even if it is recognized that x does not cause y.

3.7.2 Forecasting Outside the Range of the Explanatory Variable

When using an estimated regression equation to construct estimates of $\mu_{y|x}$ or to predict individual values of the dependent variable, some caution must be used if forecasts are outside the range of the x variable. Consider the communications nodes example. The explanatory variable was NUMPORTS, the number of access ports. The sample values ranged from 12 to 68. The estimated regression model can be expected to be reliable over this range of the x variable. If, however, a node is to be installed with 100 ports, there is some question as to how reliable the model will be. The relationship that holds over the range from 12 to 68 may differ from the relationship outside this range. Estimates of $\mu_{y|x}$ or predictions outside the range of the x variable require some caution for this reason.

There are often occasions where forecasts outside the range of the x variable must be made. One common example is when time-series data are used and forecasts for future time periods are desired. It may be that the values of the explanatory variables in future time periods are outside the range observed in the past as, for example, when the linear trend model is used. In such cases, it must be recognized that the quality of the forecasts depends on whether the estimated relationship still holds for values of the explanatory variables that are outside the observed range.

EXERCISES

17 **Sales/Advertising (continued)** Use the output in Figure 3.19 or 3.20 to help answer the following questions.

a Find a point estimate of average sales for all sales districts with advertising expenditures of $60,000. Are there any cautions that should be exercised regarding this estimate?

b A district sales manager examines the model developed. The manager points out that $0 advertising expenditure results in sales of –$5700, which is impossible. She suggests that this means the model is of no use. Do you agree or disagree with her assessment? Explain why.

3.8 USING THE COMPUTER

The Using the Computer section in each chapter describes how to perform the computer analyses in the chapter using MINITAB, Excel, and SAS. For further detail on MINITAB, Excel, and SAS, see Appendix C.

3.8.1 MINITAB

Note that Version 12 of MINITAB is fully menu driven. Commands can be used, however, and they are included for any interested users. The menu headings and subheadings used to perform the procedures are listed first, followed by commands in parentheses. For example, GRAPH: PLOT means to click on the GRAPH menu and then on PLOT. (Plot C1*C2 means to type in the command as shown.)

Plotting Data

`GRAPH: PLOT (PLOT C1*C2)`

See the Plot dialog box in Figure 3.38. Fill in the *Y* and *X* variable requests and click OK. Plots the Y-data on the vertical axis and the X-data on the horizontal axis to create a scatterplot.

FIGURE **3.38** MINITAB Plot Dialog Box

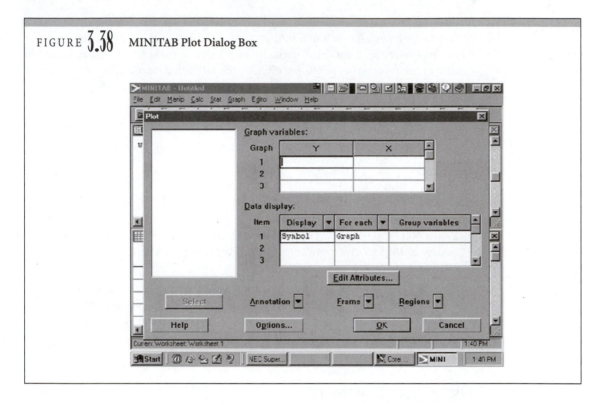

GRAPH: TIME SERIES PLOT   (TSPLOT [K] C1)

See the Time Series Plot dialog box in Figure 3.39. Fill in the variable(s) to be graphed as Y and MINITAB plots the Y-data in time sequence. MINITAB assumes the data are entered in a column with the most recent time period as the last entry in the column. The use of month, quarter, and so on is chosen using the Time Scale—Calendar option and appropriate numbering appears on the horizontal axis. (If the TSPLOT command is used, the optional K indicates the period of the data: K = 4 for quarterly; K = 12 for monthly; and so on.)

Regression

STAT: REGRESSION: REGRESSION   (REGR C1 1 C2)

See the Regression dialog box in Figure 3.40. Fill in the response (Y) and predictor (X) variable and click OK. (When using the REGR command, the dependent, *y*, variable data values are listed in the first column shown and the independent, *x*, variable data values are listed in the second. The 1 in the command tells MINITAB that just one independent variable is to be used.)

FIGURE **3.39**   MINITAB Time Series Plot Dialog Box

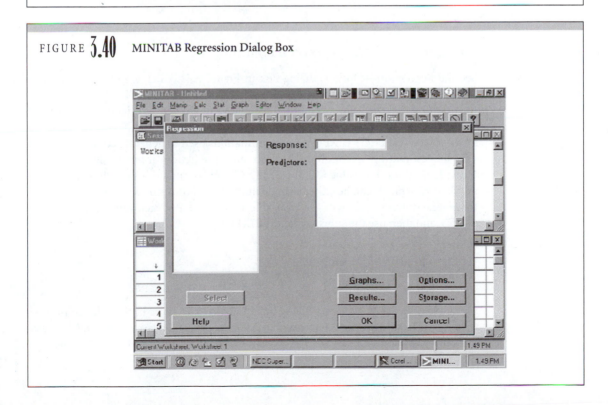

FIGURE **3.40**   MINITAB Regression Dialog Box

FIGURE 3.41   **MINITAB Regression-Options Dialog Box**

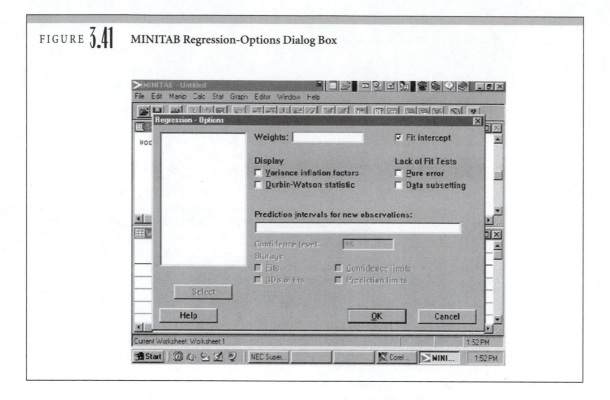

Forecasting with the Regression Equation

See the Regression—Options dialog box in Figure 3.41. Click OPTIONS in the Regression dialog box (Figure 3.40) to get to this screen. Fill in the "Prediction intervals for new observations" line with either a single value for the x variable or a column if predictions for more than one value are desired. [If using the REGR command for regression, the PREDICT (PRED K) subcommand is used to generate confidence intervals for estimating a conditional mean and prediction intervals for predicting individual values. The value K in the PREDICT subcommand is the value of the independent variable. K can be either a single number or a column of numbers if forecasts for several different values of the x variable are desired. Put each value into a column, say, C3, and then use the subcommand PRED C3.]

Creating a Trend Variable

`CALC: MAKE PATTERNED DATA: SIMPLE SET OF NUMBERS`

See the Simple Set of Numbers dialog box in Figure 3.42. Type in the column number to store the trend variable. Then enter a first value of 1 and a last value of n (the number of time periods) in steps of 1. Make sure "List each value" and "List the whole sequence" are set at 1. Then click OK.

FIGURE 3.42   **MINITAB Dialog Box to Create a Trend Variable**

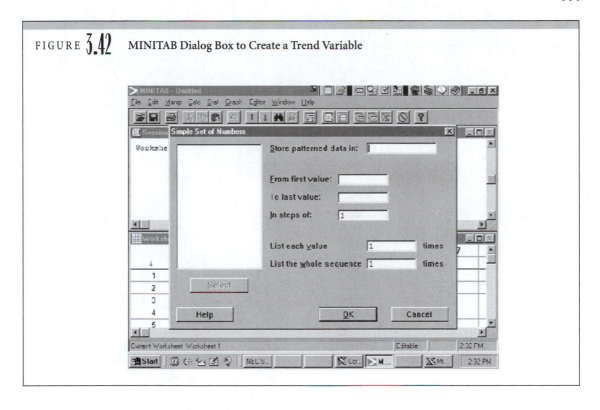

(Using commands: SET IN C1

1:n

END.)

3.8.2 Excel

Plotting Data

Use the Chart Wizard to create a scatterplot (or XY plot). Click on the Chart Wizard button. A window opens showing chart types. Click on XY (Scatter), pick the type of scatterplot you want (see Figure 3.43), click Next> and follow the directions to create the scatterplot.

Regression

`TOOLS: DATA ANALYSIS: REGRESSION`

To perform a simple regression in Excel, use the Regression procedure on the Data Analysis menu. The Regression dialog box is shown in Figure 3.44. Fill in the Input Y Range and Input X Range with the cells containing the Y variable and X variable, respectively. Choose the desired Output option and click OK.

FIGURE **3.43**   **Chart Wizard Dialog Box Showing Excel Chart Types**

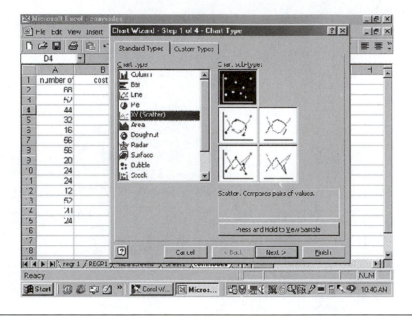

FIGURE **3.44**   **Excel Regression Dialog Box**

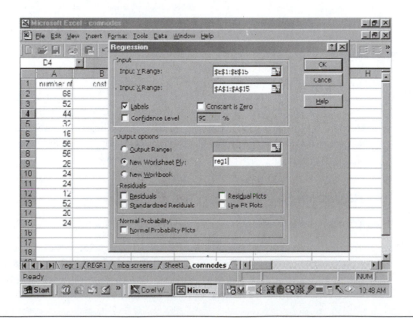

Creating a Trend Variable

To put the numbers 1 through *n* in column B (for example), type 1 in B1, 2 in B2, then select these two cells, put the cursor on the rectangle at the bottom right-hand corner of cell B2, and drag through cell *n*.

3.8.3 SAS

Plotting Data

Plots in SAS are generated using the following command sequence:

```
PROC PLOT;
    PLOT COST*NUMPORTS;
```

The variable to be plotted on the vertical axis (COST) is listed first, with the variable to be plotted on the horizontal axis (NUMPORTS) second.

Regression

The following command sequence produces a regression with COST as the dependent variable and NUMPORTS as the independent variable

```
PROC REG;
    MODEL COST=NUMPORTS;
```

Forecasting with the Regression Equation

Forecasts in SAS are generated using an "appended" data set. To the values of the independent variable in the original data set, add the values for which predictions are desired. Then to the values of the dependent variable add "." (SAS for missing data), because we do not know those values. Now rerun the regression as follows:

```
PROC REG;
    MODEL COST=NUMPORTS/P CLM CLI;
```

The option P requests forecasts (or predicted values), CLM requests upper and lower confidence interval limits for the estimate of the conditional mean, and CLI requests upper and lower prediction interval limits for an individual prediction.

Creating a Trend Variable

In the data input phase in SAS, use the command

```
TREND=_N_;
```

to create a trend variable. The command TREND=_N_ sets the variable TREND equal to the integers 1 through N, where N is the total number of observations in the data set. To do a time-series plot of a dependent variable SALES, use the commands

```
PROC PLOT;
    PLOT SALES*TREND;
```

To fit the linear trend model, use the commands

```
PROC REG;
    MODEL SALES=TREND;
```

ADDITIONAL EXERCISES

18 Indicate whether the following statements are true or false.

a If the hypothesis $H_0: \beta_1 = 0$ is rejected, then it can be safely concluded that x causes y.

b Suppose a regression of y on x is run and the t statistic for testing $H_0: \beta_1 = 0$ versus $H_a: \beta_1 \neq 0$ has a p value of 0.0295 associated with it. Using a 5% level of significance, the null hypothesis should be rejected.

c If the correlation between y and x is 0.9, then the R^2 value for a regression of y on x is 90%.

d As long as the R^2 value is high for an estimated regression equation, it is safe to use the equation to predict for any value of x.

e If the R^2 value for a regression of y on x is 75%, then the R^2 value for a regression of x on y is also 75%.

19 Suppose a regression analysis provides the following results;

$$b_0 = 1, \qquad b_1 = 2, \qquad s_{b_0} = 0.5$$
$$s_{b_1} = 0.25, \qquad SST = 117.2873, \qquad SSE = 30.0$$

and $n = 24$. Use this information to solve the following problems:

a Test the hypotheses

$$H_0: \quad \beta_1 = 0$$
$$H_a: \quad \beta_1 \neq 0$$

using a 5% level of significance. State the decision rule, the test statistic, and your decision. Use a t test.

b Perform the same test as in part a using an F test. Use a 10% level of significance.

c Compute the R^2 for the regression.

20 Suppose a regression analysis provides the following results:

$$b_0 = 4.0, \qquad b_1 = 10.0, \qquad s_{b_0} = 1.0$$
$$s_{b_1} = 4.0, \qquad SST = 67.36, \qquad SSE = 50.0$$

and $n = 20$. Use this information to solve the following problems:

a Test the hypotheses

$$H_0: \quad \beta_0 = 0$$
$$H_a: \quad \beta_0 \neq 0$$

TABLE 3.13   Data for Salary and Education Exercise

SALARY	EDUC	SALARY	EDUC	SALARY	EDUC	SALARY	EDUC
3900	12	5100	8	5520	12	5400	15
4020	10	5100	12	5520	12	5700	25
4290	12	5100	12	5580	12	6000	8
4380	8	5100	15	5640	12	6000	12
4380	8	5100	15	5700	12	6000	12
4380	12	5100	16	5700	12	6000	12
4380	12	5160	12	5700	15	6000	12
4380	12	5220	8	5700	15	6000	12
4440	15	5220	12	5700	15	6000	12
4500	8	5280	8	6000	12	6000	15
4500	12	5280	8	6000	15	6000	15
4620	12	5280	12	6120	12	6000	15
4800	8	5400	8	6300	12	6000	15
4800	12	5400	8	6300	15	6000	15
4800	12	5400	12	4620	12	6000	16
4800	12	5400	12	5040	15	6300	15
4800	12	5400	12	5100	12	6600	15
4800	12	5400	12	5100	12	6600	15
4800	12	5400	12	5220	12	6600	15
4800	12	5400	12	5400	12	6840	15
4800	12	5400	15	5400	12	6900	12
4800	16	5400	15	5400	12	6900	15
4980	8	5400	15	5400	15	8100	16

using a 5% level of significance. State the decision rule, the test statistic, and your decision.

b Test the hypotheses

$$H_0: \quad \beta_1 \leq 0,$$
$$H_a: \quad \beta_1 > 0,$$

using a 5% level of significance. State the decision rule, the test statistic, and your decision. What conclusion can be drawn from the test result?

c Compute the R^2 for the regression.

21 **Salary/Education**   Data on beginning salary (y) and years of education (x) for 93 employees of Harris Bank Chicago in 1977 are shown in Table 3.13. These data were taken from an article by Daniel W. Schafer, "Measurement-Error Diagnostics and the Sex Discrimination Problem," *Journal of Business and Economic Statistics*, 5: 529–537, 1987.

The MINITAB scatterplot and regression output for a regression of salary on education are shown in Figures 3.45 and 3.46, respectively. The Excel regression output is shown in Figure 3.47. Use the output to answer the following questions:

a Is there a linear relationship between salary and education? State the hypotheses to be tested, the decision rule, the test statistic, and your decision. Use a 10% level of significance.

b What percentage of the variation in salary has been explained by the regression?

c For an individual with 12 years of education, find a point prediction of beginning salary.

d For all individuals with 12 years of education, find a point estimate of the conditional mean beginning salary.

e What other factors, in addition to education, might be useful in helping to estimate beginning salary?

These data are available in a file with prefix SALED3 in two columns: SALARY and EDUC.

22 **Income/Consumption**   The following data are annual disposable income and total annual consumption for 12 families selected at random from a large metropolitan area. Regard annual disposable income as the explanatory variable and total annual consumption as the dependent variable. From the regression of y on x, answer the questions that follow.

Annual Disposable Income ($)	Total Annual Consumption ($)
16,000	14,000
30,000	24,545
43,000	36,776
70,000	63,254
56,000	40,176
50,000	49,548
16,000	16,000
26,000	22,386
14,000	16,032
12,000	12,000
24,000	20,768
30,000	34,780

a What is the estimated regression equation relating y to x?

b What percentage of the variation in y has been explained by the regression?

c Construct a 90% confidence interval estimate of β_1.

d Use a t test to test the hypotheses $H_0: \beta_1 = 0$ versus $H_a: \beta_1 \neq 0$ at the .05 level of significance. State the decision rule, the test statistic, and your decision. What conclusion can be drawn from the result of the test?

e Use an F test to test the hypotheses $H_0: \beta_1 = 0$ versus $H_a: \beta_1 \neq 0$ at the .05 level of significance. State the decision rule, the test statistic, and your decision.

FIGURE 3.45   MINITAB Scatterplot for Salary and Education Exercise

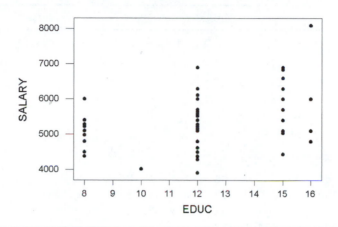

FIGURE 3.46   MINITAB Regression Output for Salary and Education Exercise

```
The regression equation is
SALARY = 3819 + 128 EDUC

Predictor          Coef        StDev           T          P
Constant         3818.6        377.4       10.12      0.000
EDUC             128.09        29.70        4.31      0.000

S = 650.1       R-Sq = 17.0%       R-Sq(adj) = 16.1%

Analysis of Variance

Source             DF           SS           MS          F          P
Regression          1      7862534      7862534      18.60      0.000
Residual Error     91     38460756       422646
Total              92     46323290

Unusual Observations
Obs      EDUC      SALARY          Fit    StDev Fit     Residual    St Resid
  1      12.0      3900.0       5355.6         69.1      -1455.6       -2.25R
  9      15.0      4440.0       5739.8        100.2      -1299.8       -2.02R
 91      12.0      6900.0       5355.6         69.1       1544.4        2.39R
 93      16.0      8100.0       5867.9        123.8       2232.1        3.50R

R denotes an observation with a large standardized residual
```

FIGURE 3.47   Excel Regression Output for Salary and Education Exercise

SUMMARY OUTPUT

Regression Statistics

Multiple R	0.412
R Square	0.170
Adjusted R Square	0.161
Standard Error	650.112
Observations	93.000

ANOVA

	df	SS	MS	F	Significance F
Regression	1.000	7862534.292	7862534.292	18.603	0.0000
Residual	91.000	38460756.031	422645.671		
Total	92.000	46323290.323			

	Coefficients	Standard Error	t Stat	P-value	Lower 95%	Upper 95%
Intercept	3818.560	377.438	10.117	0.0000	3068.826	4568.293
EDUC	128.086	29.697	4.313	0.0000	69.097	187.075

f   Can the F test be used to test the hypotheses $H_0: \beta_1 \leq 0$ versus $H_a: \beta_1 > 0$?

g   Test the hypotheses $H_0:$ $\beta_1 = 1$ versus $H_a: \beta_1 \neq 1$ at the .05 level of significance. State the decision rule, the test statistic, and your decision. What conclusion can be drawn from the result of the test?

These data are in a file with prefix INCONS3 in two columns: INCOME and CONS.

23   **Apex Corporation**   The Apex Corporation produces corrugated paper. It has collected monthly data on the following two variables:

   y, total manufacturing cost per month (in thousands of dollars)

   x, total machine hours used per month

   The data are shown in Table 3.14. These time-series data refer to the period January 1998 through March 2000. Perform any analyses necessary to answer the following questions:

   a   What is the estimated regression equation relating y to x?

   b   What percentage of the variation in y has been explained by the regression?

   c   Are y and x linearly related? Conduct a hypothesis test to answer this question and use a 5% level of significance. State the hypotheses to be tested, the decision rule, the test statistic, and your decision. What conclusion can be drawn from the result of the test?

TABLE 3.14   Data for APEX Exercise

	Cost	Machine			Cost	Machine
1/98	1102	218		3/99	1287	259
2/98	1008	199		4/99	1451	286
3/98	1227	249		5/99	1828	389
4/98	1395	277		6/99	1903	404
5/98	1710	363		7/99	1997	430
6/98	1881	399		8/99	1363	271
7/98	1924	411		9/99	1421	286
8/98	1246	248		10/99	1543	317
9/98	1255	259		11/99	1774	376
10/98	1314	266		12/99	1929	415
11/98	1557	334		1/00	1317	260
12/98	1887	401		2/00	1302	255
1/99	1204	238		3/00	1388	281
2/99	1211	246				

d Use the equation developed to estimate the average manufacturing cost in a month with 350 machine hours. Find a point estimate and a 95% confidence interval estimate. How reliable do you believe this forecast to be?

e Use the equation developed to estimate the average manufacturing cost in a month with 550 machine hours. Find a point estimate and a 95% confidence interval estimate. How reliable do you believe this forecast might be?

These data are available in a file with prefix APEX3 in two columns: COST and MACHINE.

24 **Wheat Exports**   The relationship between exchange rates and agricultural exports is of interest to agricultural economists. One such export of interest is wheat. Table 3.15 lists data on the following variables:

y, U.S. wheat export shipments

x, the real index of weighted-average exchange rates for the U.S. dollar

These time-series data were observed monthly from January 1974 through March 1985. Perform any analyses necessary to answer the following questions:

a What is the estimated regression equation relating y to x?

b Are y and x linearly related? Conduct a hypothesis test to answer this question and use a 5% level of significance. State the hypotheses to be tested, the decision rule, the test statistic, and your decision. What conclusion can be drawn from the result of the test?

c What percentage of the variation in y has been explained by the regression?

TABLE 3.15   Data for Wheat Export Exercise

Shipment	Exchange Rate	Shipment	Exchange Rate	Shipment	Exchange Rate	Shipment	Exchange Rate
2264	104.142	1478	108.894	3528	87.483	3209	119.634
1983	101.705	1561	108.600	4056	88.498	3383	120.571
1787	97.857	1346	108.949	2963	88.730	3565	122.312
1519	97.813	1572	108.992	3127	86.734	2681	124.902
1500	96.250	1433	108.737	2250	86.010	2575	126.268
1556	97.757	1911	108.593	2436	86.687	2407	121.503
2256	98.164	1810	108.539	2578	90.213	3896	120.526
2503	99.703	2098	108.313	2676	91.175	3990	122.656
2346	100.450	2277	106.419	2411	86.894	3569	123.793
2495	99.725	2543	107.189	2618	84.960	3060	125.055
2676	101.497	3011	108.054	3364	84.693	2619	125.394
2247	96.896	1881	106.701	3849	86.025	3087	128.639
2951	95.162	1567	104.882	3737	85.473	3176	130.112
1957	93.528	2378	102.368	3183	86.470	2388	133.188
1774	92.920	1764	100.715	3054	89.057	3246	133.413
2099	94.951	2576	100.118	3594	90.491	3125	131.639
1778	94.723	2870	98.637	3537	91.082	2800	134.792
2111	94.600	2811	98.386	3386	95.509	3508	137.699
2721	98.184	3268	100.022	3504	95.911	3221	140.244
3033	101.109	2965	97.929	3474	98.784	3024	137.112
3428	102.870	2888	95.475	2124	103.492	3231	133.865
3368	102.639	3590	92.913	3389	106.459	2644	136.153
3228	102.567	3255	92.346	3760	109.238	3070	140.147
2516	103.561	3144	88.609	3958	111.529	2867	140.467
2506	104.059	2514	91.297	5284	107.243	3627	145.506
1974	104.547	2450	90.805	4273	106.059	3979	145.425
2105	106.535	1916	90.001	3470	104.473	6605	151.073
2099	108.225	1826	90.129	3749	105.432	3736	153.787
1845	108.547	2056	90.069	3379	107.414	2648	151.330
1818	108.955	2096	91.132	3775	110.954	3591	155.922
2330	108.707	2131	91.706	4329	113.599	1897	160.254
3081	108.143	2847	90.650	4033	115.587	2327	166.005
3004	107.990	3627	88.004	3170	112.341	1576	165.932
2736	108.605	3206	87.986	4270	117.854		

TABLE 3.16   Total Payroll and Number of Wins for MLB Teams in 1998

Team	Payroll	Wins	Team	Payroll	Wins
Baltimore	73995921	79	Seattle	44735014	76
NY Yankees	73813698	114	Chicago White Sox	37830000	80
Texas	62155368	88	Toronto	37268500	88
Atlanta	61740254	106	Milwaukee	36854036	74
Los Angeles	60731667	83	Kansas City	35610000	72
Boston	59347000	92	Arizona	32814500	65
NY Mets	58660665	88	Philadelphia	29922500	75
Cleveland	56643441	89	Tampa Bay	27620000	63
Anaheim	54189000	85	Detroit	23318980	65
San Diego	52996166	98	Minnesota	22027500	70
Chicago Cubs	50686000	90	Cincinnati	20707333	77
Houston	48294000	102	Florida	19141000	54
San Francisco	47914715	89	Oakland	18585114	74
Colorado	47884648	77	Pittsburgh	13695000	69
St. Louis	47608948	83	Montreal	8317500	65

Reprinted courtesy of the *Fort Worth Star-Telegram*.

d Construct a 95% confidence interval estimate of β_1.

These data are available in a file with prefix WHEAT3 in two columns: SHIPMENT and EXCHRATE. These data were obtained from D.A. Besseler and R.A. Babubla, "Forecasting Wheat Exports: Do Exchange Rates Really Matter?" *Journal of Business and Economic Statistics* 5 (1987): 397–406.

25 **Major League Baseball Salaries**   The owners of Major League Baseball (MLB) teams are concerned with rising salaries (as are owners of all professional sports teams). Table 3.16 provides the total payrolls of the 30 MLB teams for the 1998 season. Also provided is the number of wins for each team during the 1998 season. Is there evidence that teams with higher total payrolls tend to be more successful? Justify your answer.

These data are available in a file with prefix BBALL3 in two columns: PAYROLL and WINS.

26 **Work Orders**   During the construction phase of a nuclear plant, the number of corrective work orders open should gradually decline until reaching a steady state that would be present during the operational phase. The Nuclear Regulatory Commission has licensing requirements that the number of work orders open at licensing and for operational plants be less than 1000. (This was, of course, back in the days when nuclear plants were still being constructed in the United States.) This number is

TABLE 3.17   Data for Work Orders Exercise

Day	Work Orders	Day	Work Orders	Day	Work Orders	Day	Work Orders
1	3332	31	3209	61	2827	91	2396
2	3348	32	3192	62	2827	92	2333
3	3348	33	3184	63	2828	93	2301
4	3387	34	3178	64	2823	94	2267
5	3391	35	3201	65	2827	95	2253
6	3421	36	3209	66	2828	96	2266
7	3400	37	3183	67	2801	97	2270
8	3408	38	3176	68	2806	98	2236
9	3420	39	3132	69	2761	99	2231
10	3431	40	3104	70	2763	100	2219
11	3425	41	3118	71	2764	101	2205
12	3416	42	3106	72	2734	102	2211
13	3407	43	3075	73	2700	103	2217
14	3395	44	3047	74	2660	104	2204
15	3377	45	3018	75	2618	105	2197
16	3363	46	3014	76	2608	106	2210
17	3335	47	3019	77	2603	107	2202
18	3315	48	2982	78	2603	108	2181
19	3307	49	2977	79	2576	109	2197
20	3292	50	2985	80	2566	110	2230
21	3304	51	3000	81	2545	111	2218
22	3275	52	2980	82	2553	112	2210
23	3242	53	2984	83	2534	113	2198
24	3217	54	3001	84	2541	114	2177
25	3179	55	3000	85	2545	115	2162
26	3220	56	3021	86	2527	116	2136
27	3205	57	3004	87	2470	117	2091
28	3206	58	2955	88	2442	118	2111
29	3198	59	2893	89	2424	119	2123
30	3197	60	2843	90	2398	120	2149

set to provide a goal indicating operational readiness. Table 3.17 shows the number of work orders for a consecutive 120-working-day period during the construction phase of a nuclear plant.

As a consultant to the plant, you have been asked to estimate how many days it will take to reach the operational level of 1000 work orders. In determining the number of days, state any assumptions you make and any caveats that might be in order.

These data are available in a file with prefix WKORDER3 in one column.

27 **Fanfare**   Fanfare International, Inc. designs, distributes and markets ceiling fans and lighting fixtures. The company's product line includes 120 basic models of ceiling fans and 138 compatible fan light kits and table lamps. These products are marketed to over 1000 lighting showrooms and electrical wholesalers that supply the remodeling and new construction markets. The product line is distributed by a sales organization of 58 independent sales representatives.

In the summer of 1994, Fanfare decided they needed to develop forecasts of future sales to help determine future sales force needs, capital expenditures, and so on. Table 3.18 provides monthly sales data and data on three additional variables for the period July 1990 through May 1994. The variables are defined as follows:

sales = total monthly sales in thousands of dollars

ad ex = advertising expense in thousands of dollars

mtg rate = mortgage rate for 30-year loans (%)

hs starts = housing starts in thousands of units

As a consultant to Fanfare, your job is to find the best single variable to forecast future sales. Try each of the three variables in a simple regression and decide which is the best to create a forecasting model for Fanfare. Justify your choice. What problems do you see with using each of the three possible variables to help forecast sales?

The data are available in a file with prefix FAN3. There are four variables as shown, each in a separate column, plus columns for year and month.

28 **College Graduation Rates**   Each fall, *U.S. News and World Report* publishes its college guide entitled *America's Best Colleges*. The 1999 issue contains rankings of the best national universities as determined by *U.S. News*. The data are shown at the end of Chapter 4 in Table 4.11. Only schools with complete information on all the categories listed are included. The variables are defined as follows:

Grad. Rate	1997 graduation rate (expressed as a percentage)
Fresh. Ret.	freshman retention rate: percentage of freshmen who return for their sophomore year
% ≤ 20	percentage of classes with 20 or fewer students
% ≥ 50	percentage of classes with 50 or more students
SAT 75	the 75th percentile of the SAT scores of students admitted
Top 10%	percentage of freshmen in top 10% of high school class
Accept. Rate	percentage of applicants who were accepted
Alumni Giving	alumni giving rate: percentage of alumni who contribute money

Using the 1997 graduation rate as the dependent variable, examine simple regressions using your choice of independent variable. Which variable appears to do the best job of explaining graduation rate? How might you go about determining which of the possible variables used in a simple regression provides the best equation for predicting graduation rates?

This information is included in a file with prefix COLLEGE4 for 173 schools.

TABLE 3.18   Data for Fanfare Exercise*

Date	sales	ad ex	mtg rate	hs starts	Date	sales	ad ex	mtg rate	hs starts
7/90	1538	14	10.04	111.2	7/92	1965	156	8.13	106.2
8/90	1360	14	10.10	102.8	8/92	1855	158	7.98	109.9
9/90	1202	68	10.18	93.1	9/92	1911	168	7.92	106.0
10/90	1243	35	10.18	94.2	10/92	1754	174	8.09	111.8
11/90	1076	35	10.01	81.4	11/92	1559	321	8.31	84.5
12/90	691	32	9.67	57.4	12/92	1333	206	8.22	78.6
1/91	1036	94	9.64	52.5	1/93	1675	224	8.02	70.5
2/91	891	75	9.37	59.1	2/93	1360	183	7.68	74.6
3/91	1120	76	9.50	73.8	3/93	1667	281	7.50	95.5
4/91	1490	73	9.49	99.7	4/93	1889	255	7.47	117.8
5/91	1672	71	9.47	97.7	5/93	1906	318	7.47	120.9
6/91	1517	209	9.62	103.4	6/93	2246	235	7.42	128.5
7/91	1866	95	9.58	103.5	7/93	2232	169	7.21	115.3
8/91	1588	59	9.24	94.7	8/93	2300	250	7.11	121.8
9/91	1430	77	9.01	86.6	9/93	2097	231	6.92	118.5
10/91	1636	94	8.86	101.8	10/93	2008	222	6.83	123.2
11/91	1225	168	8.71	75.6	11/93	1931	184	7.16	102.3
12/91	1027	149	8.50	65.6	12/93	1720	177	7.17	98.7
1/92	1323	100	8.43	71.6	1/94	1936	363	7.06	76.2
2/92	1257	128	8.76	78.8	2/94	1847	268	7.15	83.5
3/92	1915	88	8.94	111.6	3/94	2399	229	7.68	134.3
4/92	1422	124	8.85	107.6	4/94	2176	287	8.32	137.6
5/92	1697	103	8.67	115.2	5/94	2463	294	8.60	148.8
6/92	2053	89	8.51	117.8					

*The sales data have been transformed to provide confidentiality.

CHAPTER 4

Multiple Regression Analysis

USING MULTIPLE REGRESSION TO DESCRIBE A LINEAR RELATIONSHIP

In Chapter 3, the method of least squares was used to develop the equation of a line that best described the relationship between a dependent variable y and an explanatory variable x. In business and economic applications, however, there may be more than one explanatory variable that is useful in explaining variation in the dependent variable y or obtaining better predictions of y. An equation of the form

$$\hat{y} = b_0 + b_1 x_1 + b_2 x_2$$

where x_1 and x_2 are the explanatory variables and b_1 and b_2 are estimates of the population regression coefficients may be desired. The relationship is still "linear"; each term on the right-hand side of the equation is additive, and the regression coefficients do not enter the equation in a nonlinear manner (such as $b_1^2 x_1$). The graph of the relationship is no longer a line, however, because there are three variables involved.

Graphing the equation thus requires the use of three dimensions rather than two, and the equation graphs as a plane passing through the three-dimensional space. Figure 4.1 shows how this graph might appear. The x_1 axis and y axis are drawn as before; the x_2 axis can be thought of as moving toward you to imitate the three-dimensional space. Because of the difficulty of drawing graphs in more than two dimensions on paper, the usefulness of graphical methods such as scatterplots is somewhat limited.

Still, when two or more explanatory variables are involved, two-dimensional scatterplots between the dependent variable and each explanatory variable can provide an

FIGURE 4.1   Graph Showing Regression "Plane"

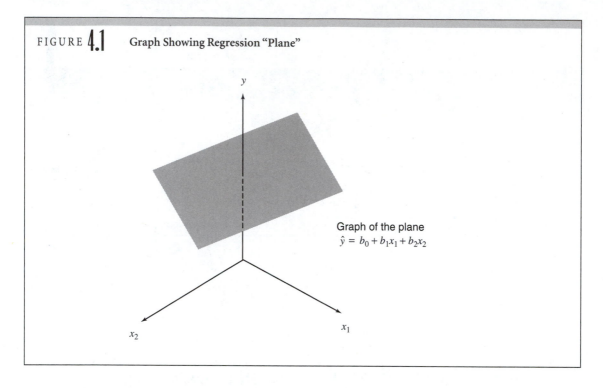

Graph of the plane
$\hat{y} = b_0 + b_1x_1 + b_2x_2$

initial indication of the relationships present. The relationship involving more than one explanatory variable may differ, however, from that involving each explanatory variable individually. The least-squares method can still be used to develop regression equations involving more than one explanatory variable. These equations are referred to as multiple regression equations. As discussed, the equations no longer graph as lines, but the terms "linear regression" and even regression "line" (when perhaps regression "surface" might be more appropriate) still are used.

As the number of explanatory variables increases, the formulas for computing the estimates of the regression coefficients become increasingly complex. The availability of computerized regression routines precludes the need for hand computation of the estimates. The equations for the two or more explanatory variable cases are not presented in this text. There is a convenient method for writing the equations for the least–squares estimates for any number of explanatory variables, but it requires using matrices and matrix algebra. Because this text attempts to avoid as much mathematical detail as possible and concentrate on the use of computer regression output, the matrix presentation has been avoided; however, Appendix D does contain a brief introduction to the topic. A more advanced treatment of multiple regression that utilizes the matrix presentation is found, for example, in *Classical and Modern Regression with Applications* by R. Myers and in *Regression Analysis: Concepts and Applications* by F. Graybill and H. Iyer.[1]

---

[1] See References for complete publication information.

The concepts involved in producing least–squares coefficient estimates for a multiple regression equation are very similar to those for simple regression. An equation that "best" describes the relationship between a dependent variable y and K explanatory variables $x_1, x_2, \ldots x_K$ can be written

$$\hat{y} = b_0 + b_1 x_1 + b_2 x_2 + \cdots + b_K x_K$$

where $b_0, b_1, b_2, \ldots, b_K$ are the least-squares coefficients. The case $K = 1$ is simple regression. The criterion for "best" is the same as it was for a simple regression; the difference between the true values of y and the values predicted by the multiple regression equation $\hat{y}$, should be as small as possible. As before, this is accomplished by choosing $b_0, b_1, b_2, \ldots, b_K$ so that the sum of squares of the differences between the y and $\hat{y}$ values, $\sum_{i=1}^{n} (y_i - \hat{y}_i)^2$, is minimized. The optimizing values, $b_0, b_1, b_2, \ldots b_K$, are the least-squares coefficients printed out by regression routines such as those available in MINITAB and Excel.

EXAMPLE 4.1

Meddicorp Sales

Meddicorp Company sells medical supplies to hospitals, clinics, and doctors' offices. The company currently markets in three regions of the United States: the South, the West, and the Midwest. These regions are each divided into many smaller sales territories.

Meddicorp's management is concerned with the effectiveness of a new bonus program. This program is overseen by regional sales managers and provides bonuses to salespeople based on performance. Management wants to know if the bonuses paid in 1999 were related to sales. (Obviously, if there is a relationship here, the managers expect it to be a direct—positive—one.) In determining whether this relationship exists, they also want to take into account the effects of advertising. The variables to be used in the study include:

y, Meddicorp's sales (in thousands of dollars) in each territory for 1999 (SALES)

x_1, the amount Meddicorp spent on advertising in each territory (in hundreds of dollars) in 1999 (ADV)

x_2, the total amount of bonuses paid in each territory (in hundreds of dollars) in 1999 (BONUS)

Data for a random sample of 25 of Meddicorp's sales territories are shown in Table 4.1.

Figure 4.2 shows the MINITAB regression obtained relating SALES(y) to ADV(x_1) and BONUS(x_2). Figure 4.3 shows the regression output using Excel.

After rounding, the multiple regression equation describing the relationship between sales and the two explanatory variables may be written

$$\hat{y} = -516.4 + 2.47x_1 + 1.86x_2$$

or

$$\text{SALES} = -516.4 + 2.47\text{ADV} + 1.86\text{BONUS}$$

This equation can be interpreted as providing an estimate of mean sales for a given level of advertising and bonus payment. Moreover, if advertising is held fixed, the equation shows that mean sales tends to rise by \$1860 (1.86 thousands of dollars) for each unit increase in

TABLE 4.1　　　Data for Meddicorp Example

Territory	SALES (in thousand $)	ADV (in hundred $)	BONUS (in hundred $)	Territory	SALES (in thousand $)	ADV (in hundred $)	BONUS (in hundred $)
1	963.50	374.27	230.98	14	1045.25	440.86	249.68
2	893.00	408.50	236.28	15	1102.25	487.79	232.99
3	1057.25	414.31	271.57	16	1225.25	537.67	272.20
4	1183.25	448.42	291.20	17	1508.00	612.21	266.64
5	1419.50	517.88	282.17	18	1564.25	601.46	277.44
6	1547.75	637.60	321.16	19	1634.75	585.10	312.25
7	1580.00	635.72	294.32	20	1159.25	524.56	292.87
8	1071.50	446.86	305.69	21	1202.75	535.17	268.27
9	1078.25	489.59	238.41	22	1294.25	486.03	309.85
10	1122.50	500.56	271.38	23	1467.50	540.17	291.03
11	1304.75	484.18	332.64	24	1583.75	583.85	289.29
12	1552.25	618.07	261.80	25	1124.75	499.15	272.55
13	1040.00	453.39	235.63				

FIGURE 4.2　　　MINITAB Output for Regression of SALES on ADV and BONUS for Meddicorp Example

```
The regression equation is
SALES = - 516 + 2.47 ADV + 1.86 BONUS


Predictor          Coef        StDev           T        P
Constant         -516.4        189.9       -2.72    0.013
ADV              2.4732       0.2753        8.98    0.000
BONUS            1.8562       0.7157        2.59    0.017


S = 90.75        R-Sq = 85.5%        R-Sq(adj) = 84.2%


Analysis of Variance

Source            DF           SS           MS        F        P
Regression         2      1067797       533899    64.83    0.000
Residual Error    22       181176         8235
Total             24      1248974


Source         DF       Seq SS
ADV             1      1012408
BONUS           1        55389
```

FIGURE **4.3**   **Excel Output for Regression of SALES on ADV and BONUS for Meddicorp Example**

SUMMARY OUTPUT					

Regression Statistics

Multiple R	0.925				
R Square	0.855				
Adjusted R Square	0.842				
Standard Error	90.749				
Observations	25.000				

ANOVA

	df	SS	MS	F	Significance F
Regression	2.000	1067797.321	533898.660	64.831	0.0000
Residual	22.000	181176.419	8235.292		
Total	24.000	1248973.740			

	Coefficients	Standard Error	t Stat	P-value	Lower 95%	Upper 95%
Intercept	-516.444	189.876	-2.720	0.0125	-910.223	-122.666
ADV	2.473	0.275	8.983	0.0000	1.902	3.044
BONUS	1.856	0.716	2.593	0.0166	0.372	3.341

BONUS. Also, if bonus payment is held fixed, it shows that mean sales tends to rise by $2470 (2.47 thousands of dollars) for each unit increase in ADV. (Note that a "unit" increase in either BONUS or ADV represents a $100 increase.) Clearly, such information provides a useful summary of the data.

4.2 INFERENCES FROM A MULTIPLE REGRESSION ANALYSIS

4.2.1 Assumptions Concerning the Population Regression Line

In general, a population regression equation involving K explanatory variables can be written as

$$\mu_{y|x_1, x_2, \ldots, x_K} = \beta_0 + \beta_1 x_1 + \beta_2 x_2 + \cdots + \beta_K x_K$$

This equation says that the conditional mean of y given $x_1, x_2, \ldots x_K$ is a point on the regression surface described by the terms on the right-hand side of the equation.

An alternative way of writing the relationship is

$$y_i = \beta_0 + \beta_1 x_{1i} + \beta_2 x_{2i} + \cdots + \beta_K x_{Ki} + e_i$$

where i denotes the ith observation and e_i is a random error or disturbance. Thus, y_i is related to the explanatory variables $x_1, x_2, \ldots x_K$, although the relationship is not an exact one. The random error e_i shows that, given the same values for $x_1, x_2, \ldots x_K$, each point y_i will not be exactly on the regression surface. Rather, the individual y_i values are distributed around the regression surface in the manner discussed for a simple regression line in Chapter 3. The following assumptions about e_i are made:

1   The expected value of the disturbances is zero: $E(e_i) = 0$. This implies that the regression line passes through the conditional means of the y variable for each set of x variables. For our purposes, we interpret this assumption as: The population regression equation is linear in the explanatory variables.[2]

2   The variance of each e_i is equal to σ_e^2. This assumption means that each of the distributions along the regression line has the same variance regardless of the value of x.

3   The e_i are normally distributed.

4   The e_i are independent. This is an assumption that is most important when data are gathered over time. When the data are cross-sectional (that is, gathered at the same point in time for different individual units), this is typically not an assumption of concern.

These assumptions allow inferences to be made about the population multiple regression line from a sample multiple regression line. The first inferences to be considered are those made about the individual population regression coefficients, $\beta_0, \beta_1, \beta_2, \ldots, \beta_K$.

The effects of violations of the assumptions are considered in Chapter 6. In this chapter, each assumption is assumed to hold so that an ideal situation exists for the use of least-squares inference procedures.

4.2.2   Inferences About the Population Regression Coefficients

This section considers estimates of the population regression coefficients and tests of hypotheses about the population coefficients. Much of the information required to construct estimates and perform tests of hypotheses can be found in standard multiple regression output. For example, Figure 4.4 shows, in general, what information is provided by the multiple regression output for MINITAB and Excel.

---

[2] As pointed out in Chapter 3, the assumption here is that the population regression equation is linear in the x variables. In Chapter 5, we relax this assumption and find that we can fit curves by allowing equations that are not linear in the x variables. Throughout this text, however, we always assume that the equations are linear in the parameters. This means that equations such as $y = \beta_0 + \beta_1^2 x_1 + e$, for example, are not considered. These types of equations are beyond the scope of this text.

The least-squares estimates $b_0, b_1, b_2, \ldots b_K$ are unbiased estimators of the corresponding population regression coefficients. A $(1 - \alpha)100\%$ confidence interval estimate of the population regression coefficient, β_k, is

$$b_k \pm t_{\alpha/2} s_{b_k}$$

Here, k refers to the kth regression coefficient, $k = 0, 1, \ldots , K$. The value $t_{\alpha/2}$ is a number chosen from the t table to ensure the appropriate level of confidence, and s_{b_k} is the standard deviation of the sampling distribution of b_k. The number of degrees of freedom used in determining the t value is $n - (K + 1)$, where $K + 1$ is the number of regression coefficients to be estimated (K coefficients corresponding to the K explanatory variables and one intercept or constant). Note that $n - (K + 1)$ can be (and sometimes is) written as $n - K - 1$.

Hypothesis tests about the individual β_k also can be performed. The general form of two-tailed hypotheses about the individual β_k is as follows:

$$H_0: \quad \beta_k = \beta_k^*$$
$$H_a: \quad \beta_k \neq \beta_k^*$$

where β_k^* is any number chosen as the hypothesized value of the kth regression coefficient.

The decision rule for this test is

Reject H_0 if $t > t_{\alpha/2}$ or $t < - t_{\alpha/2}$

Accept H_0 if $-t_{\alpha/2} \leq t \leq t_{\alpha/2}$

where α is the probability of a Type I error.

The standardized test statistic is

$$t = \frac{b_k - \beta_k^*}{s_{b_k}}$$

When the null hypothesis is true, the standardized test statistic, t, should be small in absolute value because the estimate, b_k, is close to the hypothesized value β_k^*, making the numerator $b_k - \beta_k^*$, close to zero. When the null hypothesis is false, the difference between b_k and β_k^* is large in absolute value leading to a large absolute value of the test statistic and resulting in the decision to reject H_0.

The most common hypothesis test encountered in multiple regression analysis is

$$H_0: \quad \beta_k = 0$$
$$H_a: \quad \beta_k \neq 0$$

as in simple regression. This test is typically most important when β_k refers to the coefficient of the explanatory variable x_k rather than the constant.

If the null hypothesis $H_0: \beta_k = 0$ is accepted, then it can be concluded that, once the effects of all other variables in the multiple regression are included, x_k is not linearly related to y. In other words, adding x_k to the regression equation is of no help in explaining any additional variation in y left unexplained by the other explanatory variables.

FIGURE 4.4   Illustration of MINITAB and Excel Multiple Regression Output

(a)   MINITAB

The regression equation is
$$y = b_0 + b_1 x_1 + b_2 x_2 + \cdots + b_K x_K$$

Predictor	Coef	StDev	T	P
Constant	b_0	s_{b_0}	b_0 / s_{b_0}	p value
x1 variable name	b_1	s_{b_1}	b_1 / s_{b_1}	p value
x2 variable name	b_2	s_{b_2}	b_2 / s_{b_2}	p value
.	.	.	.	.
.	.	.	.	.
.	.	.	.	.
xK variable name	b_K	s_{b_K}	b_K / s_{b_K}	p value

$s = s_e$ R-sq $= R^2$ R-sq(adj) $= R^2_{adj}$

Analysis of Variance

Source	DF	SS	MS	F	P
Regression	K	SSR	$MSR = SSR/K$	$F = MSR/MSE$	p value
Residual Error	$n - K - 1$	SSE	$MSE = SSE/(n - K - 1)$		
Total	$n - 1$	SST			

Unusual Observations

Obs.	X1	Y	Fit	StDev Fit	Residual	St Resid
Obs. No.	Value of X1	Value of y	$\hat{y}$	s_m	$y - \hat{y}$	—

R denotes an observation with a large standardized residual
X denotes an observation whose X value gives it large influence

(b)   Excel

Regression Statistics

Multiple R	$= R$
R Square	$= R^2$
Adjusted R Square	$= R^2_{adj}$
Standard Error	$= s_e$
Observations	$= n$

Predictor	Coefficient	Standard Error	t stat	P value	Lower 95%	Upper 95%
Constant	b_0	s_{b_0}	b_0 / s_{b_0}	p value	$b_0 - t_{\alpha/2} s_{b_0}$	$b_0 + t_{\alpha/2} s_{b_0}$
x1 variable name	b_1	s_{b_1}	b_1 / s_{b_1}	p value	$b_1 - t_{\alpha/2} s_{b_1}$	$b_1 + t_{\alpha/2} s_{b_1}$
x2 variable name	b_2	s_{b_2}	b_2 / s_{b_2}	p value	$b_2 - t_{\alpha/2} s_{b_2}$	$b_2 + t_{\alpha/2} s_{b_2}$
.	.	.	.	.	.	.
.	.	.	.	.	.	.
.	.	.	.	.	.	.
xK variable name	b_K	s_{b_K}	b_K / s_{b_K}	p value	$b_K - t_{\alpha/2} s_{b_K}$	$b_K + t_{\alpha/2} s_{b_K}$

ANOVA	df	SS	MS	F	Significance F
Regression	K	SSR	$MSR = SSR/1$	$F = MSR/MSE$	p value
Residual	$n - K - 1$	SSE	$MSE = SSE/(n - K - 1)$		
Total	$n - 1$	SST			

On the other hand, if the null hypothesis is rejected, then there is evidence that y and x_k are linearly related and that x_k does help explain some of the variation in y not accounted for by the other explanatory variables.

In Figure 4.4, it can be seen that the test statistic used for testing

$$H_0: \quad \beta_k = 0$$

is printed out on the regression output. The test statistic is

$$t = \frac{b_k}{s_{b_k}}$$

and is found in the column labeled "T" for MINITAB and the column labeled "t stat" for Excel. Also note that the p values for testing whether each population regression coefficient is equal to zero are found in the column labeled "P" in MINITAB and the column labeled "P value" in Excel.

EXAMPLE 4.2   ## Meddicorp (continued)

Refer again to the MINITAB output in Figure 4.2 or the Excel output in Figure 4.3.

1. Use the regression output to test the following hypotheses:

$$H_0: \quad \beta_1 = 0$$
$$H_a: \quad \beta_1 \neq 0$$

where β_1 is the coefficient of ADV. Use a 5% level of significance. What conclusion can be drawn from the result of the test?

Answer 1:   Decision Rule: Reject H_0 if $t > 2.074$ or $t < -2.074$

Accept H_0 if $-2.074 \leq t \leq 2.074$.

Note: The t value with 22 degrees of freedom is 2.074 when a two-tailed test with a 5% level of significance is required.

Test Statistic: 8.98

Decision: Reject H_0

Conclusion: ADV is related to SALES (even when the effect of BONUS is taken into account).

Answer 2:   Using the p value from the output:

Decision Rule: Reject H_0 if p value $< \alpha$

Accept H_0 if p value $\geq \alpha$

Test Statistic: p value $= 0.000$

Decision: Reject H_0

2   Use the regression output to test the following hypotheses:

$$H_0: \quad \beta_2 = 0$$
$$H_a: \quad \beta_2 \neq 0$$

where β_2 is the coefficient of BONUS. Use a 5% level of significance. What conclusion can be drawn from the result of the test?

Answer 1: Decision Rule: Reject H_0 if $t > 2.074$ or $t < -2.074$

Accept H_0 if $-2.074 \le t \le 2.074$

Test Statistic: 2.59

Decision: Reject H_0

Conclusion: BONUS is related to SALES (even when the effect of ADV is taken into account).

Answer 2: Using the p value from the output:

Decision Rule: Reject H_0 if p value $< \alpha$

Accept H_0 if p value $\ge \alpha$

Test Statistic: p value $= 0.017$

Decision: Reject H_0

3 Use the regression output to test the following hypotheses:

$$H_0: \quad \beta_2 \le 0$$

$$H_a: \quad \beta_2 > 0$$

where β_2 is the coefficient of BONUS. Use a 5% level of significance. What conclusion can be drawn from the result of the test?

Answer: Decision Rule: Reject H_0 if $t > 1.717$

Accept H_0 if $t \le 1.717$

Note: The t value with 22 degrees of freedom is 1.717 when a one-tailed test with a 5% level of significance is required.

Test Statistic: $t = 8.98$

Decision: Reject H_0

Conclusion: BONUS is directly related to SALES (even when the effect of ADV is taken into account).

Construct a 95% confidence interval estimate of β_1, the coefficient of ADV.

Answer: $(2.4732 - (2.074 * .2753), 2.4732 + (2.074 * .2753))$
or $(1.9022, 3.0442)$

4.3 ASSESSING THE FIT OF THE REGRESSION LINE

4.3.1 The ANOVA Table, the Coefficient of Determination and the Multiple Correlation Coefficient

As with simple regression, the variation in the dependent variable y in a multiple regression can be written as follows:

$$SST = SSE + SSR$$

The total variation in y is given by the total sum of squares:

$$SST = \sum_{i=1}^{n}(y_i - \overline{y})^2$$

The error sum of squares represents the variation in y left "unexplained" by the regression:

$$SST = \sum_{i=1}^{n}(y_i - \hat{y}_i)^2$$

The regression sum of squares represents the variation in y "explained" by the regression:

$$SST = \sum_{i=1}^{n}(\hat{y}_i - \overline{y})^2$$

In SSE and SSR, the $\hat{y}_i$ values are the predicted or fitted values from the multiple regression equation. These three sums of squares can be interpreted as in a simple regression context.

The values of each of the three sums of squares are listed in the analysis of variance (ANOVA) table as shown in Figure 4.5. Also listed in the ANOVA table are the number of degrees of freedom associated with each of the sums of squares. For SSR, the number of degrees of freedom is equal to the number of explanatory variables, K. For SSE, the number of degrees of freedom is $n - (K + 1)$ or, equivalently, $n - K - 1$. As in the simple regression ANOVA table, the mean squares are also shown. These are computed by dividing the sums of squares by the appropriate number of degrees of freedom.

SST, SSR, and SSE can be used to evaluate how well the regression equation is explaining the variation in y. One measure of the goodness of fit of the regression is the coefficient of determination, R^2. The R^2 value, as for a simple regression, is computed by dividing SSR by SST:

$$R^2 = \frac{SSR}{SST}$$

Thus R^2 represents the proportion of the variation in y explained by the regression. As before, R^2 ranges between 0 and 1. The closer to 1 the value of R^2 is, the better the fit of the regression equation to the data. If R^2 is multiplied by 100, it represents the percentage of the variation in y explained by the regression.

FIGURE 4.5   Analysis of Variance Tables from MINITAB and Excel Multiple Regressions

(a)   MINITAB

Analysis of Variance

Source	DF	SS	MS	F	p
Regression	K	SSR	$MSR = SSR/K$	$F = MSR/MSE$	p value
Residual Error	$n - K - 1$	SSE	$MSE = SSE/(n - K - 1)$		
Total	$n - 1$	SST			

(b)   Excel

ANOVA

	df	SS	MS	F	Significance F
Regression	K	SSR	$MSR = SSR/K$	$F = MSR/MSE$	p value
Residual	$n - K - 1$	SSE	$MSE = SSE/(n - K - 1)$		
Total	$n - 1$	SST			

Although R^2 has a nice interpretation, there is a drawback to its use in multiple regression. As more explanatory variables are added to the regression model, the value of R^2 will never decrease, even if the additional variables are explaining an insignificant proportion of the variation in y. The addition of these unnecessary explanatory variables is not desirable. An alternative measure of the goodness of fit that is useful in multiple regression is R^2 adjusted for degrees of freedom (or simply, adjusted R^2). Recall that another way of writing R^2 is as:

$$R^2 = 1 - \frac{SSE}{SST}$$

SSE/SST can be interpreted as the unexplained proportion of the total variation in y. Since the addition of explanatory variables to the model causes SSE to decrease, R^2 gets increasingly closer to 1. This happens even if the added explanatory variables have little significant relationship to y.

The adjusted R^2 does not suffer from this limitation. The adjusted R^2 is denoted as R^2_{adj}. It is computed by

$$R^2_{adj} = 1 - \frac{SSE/(n - K - 1)}{SST/(n - 1)}$$

Note that the sums of squares have been divided by (adjusted by) their degrees of freedom before they are used in computing R^2_{adj}. Now, suppose an explanatory variable is added to the regression model that produces only a very small decrease in SSE. The divisor, $n - K - 1$, also decreases because the number of explanatory variables, K, has been incremented by 1. It is possible that $SSE/(n-K-1)$ may increase if the decrease in SSE from the addition of an explanatory variable is very small, because there is also a decrease in the size of the divisor. Thus, R^2_{adj} may decrease when the added explanatory variable adds little to the ability of the model to explain the variation in y. (It is also possible that negative R^2_{adj} values may occur. This is not a mistake, but a result of a model that fits the data very poorly. In MINITAB, when negative R^2_{adj} values occur, they are simply printed as 0.0.)

R^2_{adj} no longer represents the proportion of variation in y explained by the regression, but it can be useful when comparing two regressions with different numbers of explanatory variables (say, a two-variable model with a three- or more variable model). A decrease in R^2_{adj} from the addition of one or more explanatory variables signals that the added variable(s) was of little importance in the regression equation. R^2_{adj} is purely a descriptive measure, however. The t test discussed previously can be used to compare two regressions which differ by just one variable. Comparing two regressions which differ by more than one variable will be discussed in more detail in Section 4.4.

MINITAB and Excel both print out the R^2 value for the regression and the value of R^2_{adj}. For regression routines that do not print out R^2_{adj}, it can be computed using the equation

$$R^2_{adj} = 1 - \frac{SSE/(n-K-1)}{SST/(n-1)}$$

or by using the relationship

$$R^2_{adj} = 1 + \frac{(n-1)}{(n-K-1)}(R^2-1)$$

Excel also prints a measure called the multiple correlation coefficient, R, which is the positive square root of R^2. The multiple correlation coefficient is equal to the simple correlation between the predicted y values, $\hat{y}$ and the true y values. Thus, it represents a measure of how closely associated the true values of y are with the points on the regression line. R^2 may be a preferable measure of goodness of fit because of its interpretation as percentage of variance explained.

4.3.2 The F Statistic

Another measure of how well the multiple regression equation fits the data is the F statistic:

$$F = \frac{MSR}{MSE}$$

MSR is the mean square due to the regression, or the regression sum of squares divided by its degrees of freedom:

$$MSR = \frac{SSR}{K}$$

Note that the degrees of freedom associated with SSR is K, the number of explanatory variables in the model. MSE is the mean square due to error, or the error sum of squares divided by its degrees of freedom:

$$MSE = \frac{SSE}{n - K - 1}$$

The degrees of freedom associated with the error sum of squares is equal to $n - K - 1$.

The F statistic is used to test the hypotheses

H_0: $\beta_1 = \beta_2 = \cdots = \beta_K = 0$

H_a: At least one coefficient is not equal to zero

The decision rule for the test is:

Reject H_0 if $F > F(\alpha; K, n - K - 1)$

Accept H_0 if $F \leq F(\alpha; K, n - K - 1)$

where $F(\alpha; K, n - K - 1)$ is a value chosen from the F table for the appropriate level of significance, α. The critical value depends on the number of degrees of freedom associated with the numerator of the F statistic, K, and the number of degrees of freedom associated with the denominator, $n - K - 1$.

Acceptance of the null hypothesis implies that the explanatory variables in the regression equation are of little or no use in explaining the variation in the dependent variable, y. Rejection of the null hypothesis implies that *at least one* of the explanatory variables helps explain the variation in y. Rejection does not mean that all the population regression coefficients are different from zero (although this *may* be the case). Rejection does mean that the regression equation is useful, however.

If the hypothesis that all the population regression coefficients are zero is rejected, the t test discussed previously can be used to determine which of the individual variables are significant contributors to the model's ability to explain the variation in y. If the null hypothesis is accepted, there is no need to perform the individual t tests. The F test can be thought of as a global test designed to assess the overall fit of the regression.

The information necessary to perform F tests is typically included in computer regression output in the ANOVA table. The Excel and MINITAB outputs provide the computed value of the F statistic and the p value associated with the statistic (as shown in Figure 4.5).

EXAMPLE 4.3 Meddicorp (continued)

Refer again to the MINITAB output in Figure 4.2 or the Excel output in Figure 4.3.

1 What percentage of the variation in sales has been explained by the regression?

   Answer: 0.855 or 85.5%

2 What is the adjusted R^2?

   Answer: 0.842 or 84.2%

3 Conduct the F test for overall fit of the regression. Use a 5% level of significance.

   H_0: $\beta_1 = \beta_2 = 0$

   H_a: At least one of the coefficients is not equal to zero

Answer: (a) Decision Rule: Reject H_0 if $F > F(.05;2,22) = 3.44$

Accept H_0 if $F \le F(.05;2,22) = 3.44$

Test Statistic: $F = 64.83$.

Decision: Reject H_0

Answer: **(b)** Decision Rule: Reject H_0 if p value $< \alpha$

Accept H_0 if p value $\ge \alpha$

Test Statistic: p value $= 0.000$

Decision: Reject H_0

4   What conclusion can be drawn from the result of the F test for overall fit?

Answer: At least one of the coefficients (β_1, β_2) is not equal to zero. In other words, at least one of the variables (x_1, x_2) is important in explaining the variation in y.

EXERCISES

1   **Cost Control**   Ms. Karen Ainsworth is an employee of a well-known accounting firm's management services division. She is currently on a consulting assignment to the Apex Corporation, a firm that produces corrugated paper for use in making boxes and other packing materials. Apex called in consulting help to improve its cost control program, and Ms. Ainsworth is analyzing manufacturing costs to understand more fully the important influences on these costs. She has assembled monthly data on a group of variables, and she is using regression analysis to help assess how these variables are related to total manufacturing cost. The variables Ms. Ainsworth has selected to study are:

y, total manufacturing cost per month in thousands of dollars (COST)

x_1, total production of paper per month in tons (PAPER)

x_2, total machine hours used per month (MACHINE)

x_3, total variable overhead costs per month in thousands of dollars (OVERHEAD)

x_4, total direct labor hours used each month (LABOR)

The data shown in Table 4.2 refer to the period January 1997 through March 1999. Use the MINITAB regression output in Figure 4.6 or the Excel output in Figure 4.7 to answer the following questions:

a   If Ms. Ainsworth wants to use a cost function developed by means of regression analysis, what is the equation that is empirically determined using all four explanatory variables?

TABLE **4.2** Data for Cost Control Exercise

COST	PAPER	MACHINE	OVERHEAD	LABOR	COST	PAPER	MACHINE	OVERHEAD	LABOR
1102	550	218	112	325	1287	646	259	127	387
1008	502	199	99	301	1451	732	286	155	433
1227	616	249	126	376	1828	891	389	208	878
1395	701	277	143	419	1903	932	404	216	660
1710	838	363	191	682	1997	964	430	233	694
1881	919	399	210	751	1363	680	271	129	405
1924	939	411	216	813	1421	723	286	146	426
1246	622	248	124	371	1543	784	317	158	478
1255	626	259	127	383	1774	841	376	199	601
1314	659	266	135	402	1929	922	415	228	679
1557	740	334	181	546	1317	647	260	126	378
1887	901	401	216	655	1302	656	255	117	380
1204	610	238	117	351	1388	704	281	142	429
1211	598	246	124	370					

Source: These data were created by Dr. Roger L. Wright, RLW Analytics, Inc., Sonoma, CA, and are used (with modification) with his permission.

b Conduct the F test for overall fit of the regression. State the hypotheses to be tested, the decision rule, the test statistic, and your decision. Use a 5% level of significance. What conclusion can be drawn from the result of the test?

c In the cost accounting literature, the sample regression coefficient corresponding to x_k is regarded as an estimate of the true marginal cost of output associated with the variable x_k. Find a point estimate of the true marginal cost associated with total machine hours per month. Also, find a 95% confidence interval estimate of the true marginal cost associated with total machine hours.

d Test the hypothesis that the true marginal cost of output associated with total production of paper is 1.0. Use a 5% level of significance and a two-tailed test procedure. State the hypotheses to be tested, the decision rule, the test statistic, and your decision. What conclusion can be drawn from the result of the test?

e What percentage of the variation in y has been explained by the regression?

f What is the adjusted R^2 for this regression?

g Based on the regression equation, what actions might be taken to control costs?

These data are available in a file with prefix COST4 in five columns in the following order: COST, PAPER, MACHINE, OVERHEAD, and LABOR.

FIGURE **4.6**   MINITAB Regression Output for Cost Control Exercise

```
The regression equation is
COST = 51.7 + 0.948 PAPER + 2.47 MACHINE + 0.048 OVERHEAD - 0.0506 LABOR

Predictor          Coef        StDev          T        P
Constant          51.72        21.70       2.38    0.026
PAPER            0.9479       0.1200       7.90    0.000
MACHINE          2.4710       0.4656       5.31    0.000
OVERHEAD         0.0483       0.5250       0.09    0.927
LABOR           -0.05058      0.04030     -1.26    0.223

S = 11.08        R-Sq = 99.9%        R-Sq(adj) = 99.9%

Analysis of Variance

Source               DF           SS           MS          F        P
Regression            4      2271423       567856    4629.17    0.000
Residual Error       22         2699          123
Total                26      2274122

Source         DF       Seq SS
PAPER           1      2255666
MACHINE         1        15561
OVERHEAD        1            3
LABOR           1          193

Unusual Observations
Obs      PAPER        COST        Fit    StDev Fit     Residual     St Resid
 17        891     1828.00    1823.22        8.68         4.78       0.69 X
 25        647     1317.00    1294.48        3.58        22.52       2.15R

R denotes an observation with a large standardized residual
X denotes an observation whose X value gives it large influence.
```

FIGURE **4.7**   Excel Regression Output for Cost Control Exercise

SUMMARY OUTPUT

Regression Statistics

Multiple R	0.999
R Square	0.999
Adjusted R Square	0.999
Standard Error	11.076
Observations	27.000

ANOVA

	df	SS	MS	F	Significance F
Regression	4.000	2271423.354	567855.838	4629.168	0.0000
Residual	22.000	2698.720	122.669		
Total	26.000	2274122.074			

	Coefficients	Standard Error	t Stat	P-value	Lower 95%	Upper 95%
Intercept	51.723	21.704	2.383	0.0262	6.712	96.734
PAPER	0.948	0.120	7.898	0.0000	0.699	1.197
MACHINE	2.471	0.466	5.308	0.0000	1.506	3.437
OVERHEAD	0.048	0.525	0.092	0.9275	−1.040	1.137
LABOR	−0.051	0.040	−1.255	0.2226	−0.134	0.033

2   **Salaries**   The data in Table 4.3 show the values of the following variables for 93 employees of Harris Bank Chicago in 1977:

y, beginning salary in dollars (SALARY)

x_1, years of schooling at the time of hire (EDUC)

x_2, number of months of previous work experience (EXPER)

x_3, number of months after January 1, 1969, that the individual was hired (TIME)

The MINITAB output for the regression of SALARY on the three explanatory variables is shown in Figure 4.8. The Excel output is in Figure 4.9. Use the outputs to answer the following questions:

a   What is the estimated regression equation relating salary to education, experience, and time?

b   Conduct the F test for overall fit of the regression. Use a 5% level of significance. State the hypotheses to be tested, the decision rule, the test statistic, and your decision. What conclusion can be drawn from the result of the test?

c   Is education linearly related to beginning salary (after taking into account the effect of experience and time)? Perform the hypothesis test necessary to answer

TABLE **4.3**   Data for the Salaries Exercise

SALARY	EDUC	EXPER	TIME	SALARY	EDUC	EXPER	TIME	SALARY	EDUC	EXPER	TIME
3900	12	0.0	1	5220	12	127.0	29	5040	15	14.0	3
4020	10	44.0	7	5280	8	90.0	11	5100	12	180.0	15
4290	12	5.0	30	5280	8	190.0	1	5100	12	315.0	2
4380	8	6.2	7	5280	12	107.0	11	5220	12	29.0	14
4380	8	7.5	6	5400	8	173.0	34	5400	12	7.0	21
4380	12	0.0	7	5400	8	228.0	33	5400	12	38.0	11
4380	12	0.0	10	5400	12	26.0	11	5400	12	113.0	3
4380	12	4.5	6	5400	12	36.0	33	5400	15	17.5	8
4440	15	75.0	2	5400	12	38.0	22	5400	15	359.0	11
4500	8	52.0	3	5400	12	82.0	29	5700	15	36.0	5
4500	12	8.0	19	5400	12	169.0	27	6000	8	320.0	21
4620	12	52.0	3	5400	12	244.0	1	6000	12	24.0	2
4800	8	70.0	20	5400	15	24.0	13	6000	12	32.0	17
4800	12	6.0	23	5400	15	49.0	27	6000	12	49.0	8
4800	12	11.0	12	5400	15	51.0	21	6000	12	56.0	33
4800	12	11.0	17	5400	15	122.0	33	6000	12	252.0	11
4800	12	63.0	22	5520	12	97.0	17	6000	12	272.0	19
4800	12	144.0	24	5520	12	196.0	32	6000	15	25.0	13
4800	12	163.0	12	5580	12	132.5	30	6000	15	35.5	32
4800	12	228.0	26	5640	12	55.0	9	6000	15	56.0	12
4800	12	381.0	1	5700	12	90.0	23	6000	15	64.0	33
4800	16	214.0	15	5700	12	116.5	25	6000	15	108.0	16
4980	8	318.0	25	5700	15	51.0	17	6000	16	45.5	3
5100	8	96.0	33	5700	15	61.0	11	6300	15	72.0	17
5100	12	36.0	15	5700	15	241.0	34	6600	15	64.0	16
5100	12	59.0	14	6000	12	121.0	30	6600	15	84.0	33
5100	15	115.0	1	6000	15	78.5	13	6600	15	215.5	16
5100	15	165.0	4	6120	12	208.5	21	6840	15	41.5	7
5100	16	123.0	12	6300	12	86.5	33	6900	12	175.0	10
5160	12	18.0	12	6300	15	231.0	15	6900	15	132.0	24
5220	8	102.0	29	4620	12	11.5	22	8100	16	54.5	33

Source: These data were obtained from D. Schafer, "Measurement-Error Diagnostics and the Sex Discrimination Problem," *Journal of Business and Economic Statistics* 5 (1987): 529–537. Copyright © 1987 American Statistical Assn.

FIGURE 4.8   MINITAB Regression Output for Salaries Exercise

```
The regression equation is
SALARY = 3180 + 140 EDUC + 1.48 EXPER + 20.6 TIME

Predictor         Coef        StDev          T        P
Constant        3179.7        383.5       8.29    0.000
EDUC            139.62        27.72       5.04    0.000
EXPER           1.4807       0.6970       2.12    0.036
TIME            20.633        6.155       3.35    0.001

S = 602.8      R-Sq = 30.2%      R-Sq(adj) = 27.8%

Analysis of Variance

Source           DF           SS          MS        F        P
Regression        3     13984437     4661479    12.83    0.000
Residual Error   89     32338854      363358
Total            92     46323290

Source      DF      Seq SS
EDUC         1     7862534
EXPER        1     2038491
TIME         1     4083411

Unusual Observations
Obs     EDUC      SALARY        Fit    StDev Fit     Residual     St Resid
  3     12.0      4290.0     5481.6        126.9      -1191.6       -2.02R
 21     12.0      4800.0     5439.9        232.0       -639.9       -1.15 X
 22     16.0      4800.0     6040.0        145.2      -1240.0       -2.12R
 90     15.0      6840.0     5479.9        112.4       1360.1        2.30R
 91     12.0      6900.0     5320.6         93.2       1579.4        2.65R
 93     16.0      8100.0     6175.2        158.9       1924.8        3.31R

R denotes an observation with a large standardized residual
X denotes an observation whose X value gives it large influence.
```

this question. State the hypotheses to be tested, the decision rule, the test statistic, and your decision. Use a 5% level of significance.

d   What percentage of the variation in salary has been explained by the regression?

These data are available in a file with prefix HARRIS4 in the following order: SALARY, EDUC, EXPER and TIME.

FIGURE 4.9   **Excel Regression Output for Salaries Exercise**

SUMMARY OUTPUT

Regression Statistics

Multiple R	0.549
R Square	0.302
Adjusted R Square	0.278
Standard Error	602.792
Observations	93.000

ANOVA

	df	SS	MS	F	Significance F
Regression	3.000	13984436.814	4661478.938	12.829	0.0000
Residual	89.000	32338853.508	363357.905		
Total	92.000	46323290.323			

	Coefficients	Standard Error	Stat	P-value	Lower 95%	Upper 95%
Intercept	3179.744	383.485	8.292	0.0000	2417.769	3941.719
EDUC	139.618	27.716	5.037	0.0000	84.546	194.690
EXPER	1.481	0.697	2.124	0.0364	0.096	2.866
TIME	20.633	6.155	3.352	0.0012	8.404	32.863

4.4 COMPARING TWO REGRESSION MODELS

4.4.1 Full and Reduced Model Comparisons Using Separate Regressions

Thus far, two types of hypothesis tests for multiple regression models have been considered:

1 a test of the overall fit of the regression.

H_0: $\beta_1 = \beta_2 = \cdots = \beta_K = 0$

H_a: At least one coefficient is not equal to zero

2 a test of the significance of each individual regression coefficient

H_0: $\beta_k = 0$

H_a: $\beta_k \neq 0$

In multiple regression models, it also may be useful to test whether subsets of coefficients are equal to zero. In this section, a *partial F* test to test whether any subset of coefficients in a multiple regression equals zero is considered.

To set up this hypothesis test, consider the following regression model:

$$y = \beta_0 + \beta_1 x_1 + \cdots + \beta_L x_L + \beta_{L+1} x_{L+1} + \cdots + \beta_K x_K + e$$

Testing whether the variables $x_{L+1}, \ldots, x_K$ are useful in explaining any variation in y after taking account of the variation already explained by $x_1, \ldots, x_L$ can be viewed as a comparison of two regression models to determine whether it is worthwhile to include the additional variables. The two models for comparison are called the *full* and *reduced* models.

Full Model

$$y = \beta_0 + \beta_1 x_1 + \cdots + \beta_L x_L + \beta_{L+1} x_{L+1} + \cdots + \beta_K x_K + e$$

This is called the full model because all K explanatory variables of interest are included.

Reduced Model

$$y = \beta_0 + \beta_1 x_1 + \cdots + \beta_L x_L + e$$

This is called the reduced model because the variables $x_{L+1}, \ldots, x_K$ have been removed.

The question to be answered is, "Is the full model significantly better than the reduced model at explaining the variation in y?" This question can be formalized by setting up the following null and alternative hypotheses:

H_0: $\beta_{L+1} = \cdots = \beta_K = 0$

H_a: At least one of the coefficients $\beta_{L+1}, \ldots, \beta_K$ is not equal to zero

If the null hypothesis is accepted, choose the reduced model; if the null hypothesis is rejected, at least one of $x_{L+1}, \ldots, x_K$ is contributing to the explanation of the variation in y, and the full model is chosen as superior to the reduced.

To test the hypotheses (that is, to compare the full and reduced models), an F statistic is used. The F statistic can be written:

$$F = \frac{(SSE_R - SSE_F)/(K - L)}{SSE_F /(n - K - 1)}$$

where the subscript F stands for full model, and the subscript R stands for reduced model.

Now consider what is being computed in the F statistic. If the full and reduced models are estimated, the regression output includes the error sum of squares for each of these regressions. In the F statistic, SSE_F refers to the error sum of squares from the full model output using all K explanatory variables. SSE_R refers to the error sum of squares from the reduced model output using only L explanatory variables. Recall that the error sum of squares represents the variation in y unexplained by the regression. Also, the reduced model error sum of squares can never be less than the full model error sum of squares, so the difference

$$SSE_R - SSE_F$$

is always greater than or equal to zero. This difference represents the additional amount of the variation in y explained by adding $x_{L+1}, \ldots, x_K$ to the regression model. This measure of improvement is then divided by the number of additional variables to be added to the model, $K - L$. The numerator thus represents the additional variation in y explained per additional variable used. Note that the numerator degrees of freedom, $K - L$, is equal to the number of coefficients included in the null hypothesis or, equivalently, to the difference in the number of explanatory variables in the full and reduced models.

The mean square error for the full regression model is used in the denominator:

$$MSE_F = \frac{SSE_F}{n - K - 1}$$

If the measure of improvement is large relative to the mean square error for the full model, then the F statistic is large. If the improvement measure is small relative to MSE_F, then the value of the F statistic is small. The decision rule for the test is:

Reject H_0 if $F > F(\alpha; K - L, n - K - 1)$

Accept H_0 if $F \leq F(\alpha; K - L, n - K - 1)$

Here, α is the probability of a Type I error, and $F(\alpha; K - L, n - K - 1)$ is a value chosen from the F table for level of significance α, $K - L$ numerator degrees of freedom and $n - K - 1$ denominator degrees of freedom. This test is referred to as a partial F test and can be performed with any statistical package by running both the full and reduced model regressions.

EXAMPLE 4.4 **Meddicorp (continued)**

Management of Meddicorp believes that, in addition to advertising and bonus, two other explanatory variables may be important in explaining the variation in sales. These variables are

x_3, market share currently held by Meddicorp in each territory (MKTSHARE)

x_4, largest competitor's sales in each territory (COMPET)

These two additional variables are shown in Table 4.4 for each territory.

The MINITAB regression of SALES on ADV, BONUS, MKTSHARE, and COMPET is shown in Figure 4.10. The Excel regression is shown in Figure 4.11.

The hypothesized population regression model is

$$y = \beta_0 + \beta_1 x_1 + \beta_2 x_2 + \beta_3 x_3 + \beta_4 x_4 + e$$

TABLE 4.4   Additional Data for Meddicorp Example

TERRITORY	MKTSHARE (percentage)	COMPET (in thousand $)	TERRITORY	MKTSHARE (percentage)	COMPET (in thousand $)
1	33	202.22	14	28	333.66
2	29	252.77	15	28	232.55
3	34	293.22	16	30	273.00
4	24	202.22	17	29	323.55
5	32	303.33	18	32	404.44
6	29	353.88	19	36	283.11
7	28	374.11	20	34	222.44
8	31	404.44	21	31	283.11
9	20	394.33	22	32	242.66
10	30	303.33	23	28	333.66
11	25	333.66	24	27	313.44
12	34	353.88	25	26	374.11
13	42	262.88			

Consider the test of the hypotheses

H_0: $\beta_3 = \beta_4 = 0$

H_a: At least one of the coefficients (β_3, β_4) is not equal to zero

The full model output is shown in Figures 4.10 and 4.11, and the reduced model output is in Figures 4.2 and 4.3. The F statistic can be computed as

$$F = \frac{(181,176 - 175,855)/2}{175,855/20} = 0.303$$

(Note that $K = 4$ and $L = 2$, so $K - L = 2$.) If a 5% level of significance is used, the decision rule is

Reject H_0 if $F > 3.49$

Accept H_0 if $F \leq 3.49$

where 3.49 is the 5% F critical value with 2 numerator and 20 denominator degrees of freedom.

The decision is to accept H_0 and conclude that both coefficients β_3 and β_4 are equal to zero. Thus, the variables x_3 and x_4 are not useful in explaining any of the remaining variation in y.

FIGURE 4.10   MINITAB Output for the Regression of SALES on ADV, BONUS, MKTSHARE, and COMPET

```
The regression equation is
SALES = - 594 + 2.51 ADV + 1.91 BONUS + 2.65 MKTSHARE - 0.121 COMPET

Predictor          Coef        StDev          T          P
Constant         -593.5        259.2      -2.29      0.033
ADV              2.5131       0.3143       8.00      0.000
BONUS            1.9059       0.7424       2.57      0.018
MKTSHARE          2.651        4.636       0.57      0.574
COMPET          -0.1207       0.3718      -0.32      0.749

S = 93.77       R-Sq = 85.9%       R-Sq(adj) = 83.1%

Analysis of Variance

Source            DF           SS          MS         F         P
Regression         4      1073119      268280     30.51     0.000
Residual Error    20       175855        8793
Total             24      1248974

Source        DF      Seq SS
ADV            1     1012408
BONUS          1       55389
MKTSHARE       1        4394
COMPET         1         927

Unusual Observations
Obs       ADV       SALES        Fit    StDev Fit     Residual      St Resid
 20       525      1159.2     1346.2        39.4       -187.0        -2.20R

R denotes an observation with a large standardized residual
```

FIGURE 4.11   Excel Output for the Regression of SALES on ADV, BONUS, MKTSHR and COMPET

SUMMARY OUTPUT

Regression Statistics

Multiple R	0.927
R Square	0.859
Adjusted R Square	0.831
Standard Error	93.770
Observations	25.000

ANOVA

	df	SS	MS	F	Significance F
Regression	4.000	1073118.542	268279.635	30.511	0.0000
Residual	20.000	175855.198	8792.760		
Total	24.000	1248973.740			

	Coefficients	Standard Error	t Stat	P-value	Lower 95%	Upper 95%
Intercept	−593.537	259.196	−2.290	0.0330	−1134.210	−52.865
ADV	2.513	0.314	7.997	0.0000	1.858	3.169
BONUS	1.906	0.742	2.567	0.0184	0.357	3.455
MKTSHARE	2.651	4.636	0.572	0.5738	−7.019	12.321
COMPET	−0.121	0.372	−0.325	0.7488	−0.896	0.655

4.4.2 Full and Reduced Model Comparisons Using Conditional Sums of Squares[3]

Another way to view partial F tests is through the use of conditional or sequential sums of squares. For a regression model with two explanatory variables,

$$\hat{y} = b_0 + b_1 x_1 + b_2 x_2$$

the standard ANOVA table appears as in Figure 4.12(a). In Figure 4.12(b), an alternative ANOVA table is presented. In this figure, the regression sum of squares has been decomposed into two parts. The first, $SSR(x_1)$, is the sum of squares explained by x_1 if it were the only explanatory variable. The second $SSR(x_2|x_1)$, is called a *conditional* or *sequential sum of squares*. It represents the sum of squares explained by x_2 in addition to that explained by x_1. That is, given that x_1 has explained a certain amount of variation in y, $SSR(x_2|x_1)$ shows how much of the remaining variation x_2 explains. Note that

$$SSR = SSR(x_1) + SSR(x_2|x_1)$$

---

[3] Optional section.

FIGURE 4.12   ANOVA Tables for Two Explanatory Variable Regressions

(a)   Standard ANOVA Table

Source of Variation	DF	SS
Regression	2	SSR
Error	$n-3$	SSE
Total	$n-1$	SST

(b)   ANOVA with Conditional Sums of Squares Explained by Each Explanatory Variable

Source of Variation	DF	SS
Regression		
x_1	1	$SSR(x_1)$
$x_2 \mid x_1$	1	$SSR(x_2 \mid x_1)$
Error	$n-3$	SSE
Total	$n-1$	SST

Here, SSR is the variation explained by both x_1 and x_2.

To test the hypotheses

$$H_0: \quad \beta_2 = 0$$

$$H_a: \quad \beta_2 \neq 0$$

an F statistic can be constructed using the conditional sum of squares.

$$F = \frac{SSR(x_2 \mid x_1)/1}{SSE/(n-3)}$$

The numerator of F is the conditional sum of squares for x_2, given that x_1 is in the model, divided by its degrees of freedom. The conditional sum of squares has 1 degree of freedom because it represents the sum of squares explained by only one variable. The denominator is the error sum of squares for the full model, the model with both x_1 and x_2, divided by its degrees of freedom. If x_2 explains little of the additional unexplained variation in y, then $SSR(x_2 \mid x_1)$ is small as is the F statistic. The more variation explained by x_2, the bigger the F statistic is. The decision rule for the test is

Reject H_0 if $F > F(\alpha; 1, n-3)$

Accept H_0 if $F \leq F(\alpha; 1, n-3)$

where $F(\alpha; 1, n-3)$ is chosen from an F table for level of significance α, 1 numerator degree of freedom, and $n-3$ denominator degrees of freedom.

Of course, this hypothesis could be tested with a two-tailed t test as described in Section 4.2 because it involves only one coefficient. It can be shown that an F statistic with 1 numerator degree of freedom is equal to the square of a t statistic and that the F

critical value equals the square of a t critical value for appropriately chosen levels of significance and degrees of freedom denoted df:

$$F(\alpha;\ 1,\ df) = t^2_{\alpha/2, df}$$

Therefore, the decision made is the same regardless of which test is used. Since t statistics routinely appear on regression output, the t test is typically used when testing hypotheses about individual coefficients. The t test has additional advantages over the F test. The t test can be used to perform one-tailed hypothesis tests, while the F is restricted to the two-tailed test. It is also easier to test whether a coefficient is equal to some value other than zero using a t test than it is using an F test.

The F test gains its advantage when testing whether a subset of coefficients are all equal to zero—for example, to test

H_0: $\beta_{L+1} = \cdots = \beta_K = 0$

H_a: At least one of $\beta_{L+1}, \ldots, \beta_K$ is not equal to zero

for the general model presented earlier. In this case, the t test cannot be used. Even performing individual t tests on each coefficient may not provide as much information as performing the F test on the coefficients as a group.

To test whether $\beta_{L+1}, \ldots, \beta_K$ are all zero, the following F statistic is used:

$$F = \frac{SSR(x_{L+1}, \ldots, x_K \,|\, x_1, x_2, \ldots, x_L)/(K - L)}{SSE/(n - K - 1)}$$

$SSR(x_{L+1}, \ldots, x_K | x_1, x_2, \ldots, x_L)$ is the additional variation in y explained by $x_{L+1}, \ldots, x_K$, given that $x_1, \ldots, x_L$ are already in the model. The number of degrees of freedom associated with this conditional sum of squares is $K - L$, the number of coefficients to be included in the test. SSE is the error sum of squares from the model with all the variables included and is divided by its degrees of freedom, $n - K - 1$. The conditional sum of squares can be computed as

$$SSR(x_{L+1}, \ldots, x_K \,|\, x_1, x_2, \ldots, x_K) =$$

$$SSR(x_{L+1} \,|\, x_1, x_2, \ldots, x_L) + SSR(x_{L+2} \,|\, x_1, x_2, \ldots, x_{L+1})$$

$$+ \cdots + SSR(x_K \,|\, x_1, x_2, \ldots, x_{K-1})$$

The regression output from certain statistical packages contains the necessary information to compute the conditional sums of squares. For example, in MINITAB, an additional sum of squares breakdown is provided as in Figure 4.13. The table provides the conditional sums of squares for each of the variables individually, given that the previous variables are in the model. By adding these sums of squares for appropriate individual variables, the conditional sum of squares for x_{L+1} through x_K is obtained. In the MINITAB output, the conditional sums of squares are denoted SEQ SS for sequential sums of squares. This term is used to indicate that the sums of squares explained by each of the x variables when entered sequentially are represented.

FIGURE 4.13   **Breakdown of SSR into Its Conditional Components as Provided by MINITAB Regression Output**

SOURCE	DF	SEQ SS
x_1	1	$SSR(x_1)$
x_2	1	$SSR(x_2|x_1)$
.	.	.
.	.	.
.	.	.
x_{L-1}	1	$SSR(x_{L-1}|x_1,\ldots,x_{L-2})$
x_L	1	$SSR(x_L|x_1,\ldots,x_{L-1})$
x_{L+1}	1	$SSR(x_{L+1}|x_1,\ldots,x_L)$
.	.	.
.	.	.
.	.	.
x_K	1	$SSR(x_K|x_1,\ldots,x_{K-1})$

The order in which the variables enter the regression is very important when using the conditional sums of squares to construct a partial F statistic. In MINITAB, for example, the explanatory variables whose coefficients are included in the null hypothesis must be the last ones in the list of variables in the regression dialog box (see Using the Computer at the end of this chapter). This ensures that the conditional sums of squares are computed appropriately for the hypothesis to be tested.

A more extensive look at the use of these conditional sums of square is provided in the following example.

EXAMPLE 4.5 **Meddicorp (continued)**

Consider again the problem posed in Example 4.4. In addition to BONUS and ADV, Meddicorp wants to consider the possibility that MKTSHARE and COMPET are important in explaining the variation in sales. The MINITAB regression of SALES on ADV, BONUS, MKTSHARE, and COMPET is shown in Figure 4.10.

The hypothesized population regression model is

$$y = \beta_0 + \beta_1 x_1 + \beta_2 x_2 + \beta_3 x_3 + \beta_4 x_4 + e$$

Consider the test of the hypotheses

H_0: $\beta_3 = \beta_4 = 0$

H_a: At least one of the coefficients (β_3, β_4) is not equal to zero

The MINITAB regression output gives the conditional sums of squares explained by each variable. The regression sum of squares for the full regression is $SSR = 1,073,119$. The conditional sums of squares are as follows:

$$SSR(x_1) = 1,012,408$$

$$SSR(x_2|x_1) = 55,389$$

$$SSR(x_3|x_1, x_2) = 4394$$

$$SSR(x_4|x_1, x_2, x_3) = 927$$

The decision rule for the test is

Reject H_0 if $F > 3.49$

Accept H_0 if $F \leq 3.49$

where 3.49 is the F critical value using a 5% level of significance with 2 and 20 degrees of freedom. The test statistic, F, is

$$F = \frac{SSR(x_3, x_4|x_1, x_2)/2}{SSE/20}$$

$$\frac{\left[SSR(x_4|x_1, x_2, x_3) + SSR(x_3|x_1, x_2)\right]/2}{SSE/20}$$

$$= \frac{(927 + 4394)/2}{175,855/20} = 0.303$$

The null hypothesis is accepted. The variables x_3 and x_4 do not significantly improve the model's ability to explain sales.

EXERCISES

3   **Cost Control (continued)**   Consider again the cost data from Exercise 4.1 and the regression output in either Figure 4.6 or Figure 4.7. Consider this output to be for the full model

$$y = \beta_0 + \beta_1 x_1 + \beta_2 x_2 + \beta_3 x_3 + \beta_4 x_4 + e$$

where y, x_1, x_2, x_3, and x_4 were defined in the first exercise.
Now consider the reduced model

$$y = \beta_0 + \beta_1 x_1 + \beta_2 x_2 + e$$

FIGURE **4.14**   **MINITAB Regression Output for Cost-Control Exercise**

```
The regression equation is
COST = 59.4 + 0.949 PAPER + 2.39 MACHINE


Predictor          Coef         StDev            T         P
Constant          59.43         19.64         3.03     0.006
PAPER            0.9489        0.1101         8.62     0.000
MACHINE          2.3864        0.2101        11.36     0.000


S = 10.98        R-Sq = 99.9%       -Sq(adj) = 99.9%


Analysis of Variance


Source              DF            SS           MS         F         P
Regression           2       2271227      1135613   9413.48     0.000
Residual Error      24          2895          121
Total               26       2274122


Source          DF      Seq SS
PAPER            1     2255666
MACHINE          1       15561


Unusual Observations
Obs       PAPER         COST          Fit    StDev Fit     Residual     St Resid
 25         647      1317.00      1293.83        2.59        23.17        2.17R


R denotes an observation with a large standardized residual
```

Conduct the test to compare these two models. State the hypotheses to be tested, the decision rule, the test statistic, and your decision. What conclusion can be drawn from the result of the test? The MINITAB and Excel regression output for the reduced model can be found in Figures 4.14 and 4.15, respectively. Use a 5% level of significance.

4   **Salaries (continued)**   Consider again the salary data from Exercise 4.2 and the regression output in either Figure 4.8 or Figure 4.9. Consider this output to be for the full model

$$y = \beta_0 + \beta_1 x_1 + \beta_2 x_2 + \beta_3 x_3 + e$$

where y, x_1, x_2, and x_3 were defined in Exercise 4.2.

FIGURE 4.15   Excel Regression Output for Cost-Control Exercise

SUMMARY OUTPUT

Regression Statistics
Multiple R   0.999
R Square   0.999
Adjusted R Square   0.999
Standard Error   10.983
Observations   27.000

ANOVA

	df	SS	MS	F	Significance F
Regression	2.000	2271226.787	1135613.394	9413.479	0.0000
Residual	24.000	2895.287	120.637		
Total	26.000	2274122.074			

	Coefficients	Standard Error	t Stat	P-value	Lower 95%	Upper 95%
Intercept	59.432	19.639	3.026	0.0058	18.899	99.964
PAPER 0.949	0.110	8.622	0.0000	0.722	1.176	
MACHINE 2.386	0.210	11.357	0.0000	1.953	2.820	

Now consider the reduced model

$$y = \beta_0 + \beta_1 x_1 + e$$

Conduct the test to compare these two models. State the hypotheses to be tested, the decision rule, the test statistic, and your decision. What conclusion can be drawn from the result of the test? The MINITAB and Excel regression output for the reduced model can be found in Figures 4.16 and 4.17, respectively. Use a 5% level of significance.

FIGURE 4.16   MINITAB Output for Salaries Exercise

```
The regression equation is
SALARY = 3819 + 128 EDUC

Predictor        Coef        StDev           T         P
Constant        3818.6       377.4       10.12     0.000
EDUC            128.09       29.70        4.31     0.000

S = 650.1       R-Sq = 17.0%        R-Sq(adj) = 16.1%

Analysis of Variance

Source           DF           SS           MS         F         P
Regression        1       7862534      7862534     18.60     0.000
Residual Error   91      38460756       422646
Total            92      46323290

Unusual Observations
Obs      EDUC      SALARY         Fit   StDev Fit      Residual    St Resid
  1      12.0      3900.0      5355.6        69.1       -1455.6      -2.25R
  9      15.0      4440.0      5739.8       100.2       -1299.8      -2.02R
 91      12.0      6900.0      5355.6        69.1        1544.4       2.39R
 93      16.0      8100.0      5867.9       123.8        2232.1       3.50R

R denotes an observation with a large standardized residual
```

FIGURE 4.17 Excel Output for Salaries Exercise

SUMMARY OUTPUT

Regression Statistics
Multiple R	0.412
R Square	0.170
Adjusted R Square	0.161
Standard Error	650.112
Observations	93.000

ANOVA

	df	SS	MS	F	Significance F
Regression	1.000	7862534.292	7862534.292	18.603	0.0000
Residual	91.000	38460756.031	422645.671		
Total	92.000	46323290.323			

	Coefficients	Standard Error	t Stat	P-value	Lower 95%	Upper 95%
Intercept	3818.560	377.438	10.117	0.0000	3068.826	4568.293
EDUC	128.086	29.697	4.313	0.0000	69.097	187.075

4.5 PREDICTION WITH A MULTIPLE REGRESSION EQUATION

As with simple regression, one of the possible goals of fitting a multiple regression equation is using it to predict values of the dependent variable. The two cases considered here are the same as in simple regression.

4.5.1 Estimating the Conditional Mean of y Given $x_1, x_2, \ldots, x_K$

In this case, the goal is to estimate the point on the regression surface for specific values of the explanatory variables. For example, in the Meddicorp example (Example 4.1), consider the population regression equation

$$\mu_{y|x_1,x_2} = \beta_0 + \beta_1 x_1 + \beta_2 x_2$$

where x_1 is ADV and x_2 is BONUS. The estimated regression equation from Figure 4.2 or 4.3 is

$$\hat{y} = -516.4 + 2.47 x_1 + 1.86 x_2$$

FIGURE 4.18   Prediction in the Meddicorp Example Using MINITAB

```
The regression equation is
SALES = - 516 + 2.47 ADV + 1.86 BONUS

Predictor          Coef        StDev           T        P
Constant         -516.4        189.9       -2.72    0.013
ADV             2.4732        0.2753        8.98    0.000
BONUS           1.8562        0.7157        2.59    0.017

S = 90.75       R-Sq = 85.5%       -Sq(adj) = 84.2%

Analysis of Variance

Source              DF          SS          MS          F        P
Regression           2     1067797      533899      64.83    0.000
Residual Error      22      181176        8235
Total               24     1248974

Source       DF      Seq SS
ADV           1     1012408
BONUS         1       55389

Predicted Values

    Fit  StDev Fit           95.0% CI              95.0% PI
 1184.2       25.2   ( 1131.8,  1236.6)  (  988.8,  1379.5)
```

A point estimate of the conditional mean of y given x_1 and x_2 can be written as

$$\hat{y}_m = b_0 + b_1 x_1 + b_2 x_2$$

In the Meddicorp problem, the point estimate of the conditional mean of y given $x_1 = 500$ and $x_2 = 250$ is

$$\hat{y}_m = -516.4 + 2.47(500) + 1.86(250) = 1183.6$$

This is an estimate of average sales for *all* territories with advertising 500 and bonus 250. Confidence interval estimates can also be constructed. The formula for the standard deviation of $\hat{y}_m$, s_m is omitted here due to its complexity.

Figure 4.18 shows the MINITAB output for this example. Here $\hat{y}_m$ = Fit, s_m = Stdev.Fit, and 95% C.I. shows the limits of the 95% confidence interval. (The difference in $\hat{y}_m$ computed by MINITAB and by hand is due to rounding. The MINITAB forecast, 1184.2, is more accurate and therefore is preferred.)

4.5.2 Predicting an Individual Value of y Given $x_1, x_2, \ldots, x_K$

Write the population regression equation for a single individual as

$$y_i = \beta_0 + \beta_1 x_{1i} + \beta_2 x_{2i} + e_i$$

where e_i is the random disturbance. Denote the predicted value of y for an individual as $\hat{y}_p$. To predict the value of a dependent variable for a single individual, the point on the regression surface is used:

$$\hat{y}_p = b_0 + b_1 x_1 + b_2 x_2$$

As in simple regression, the point estimate of $\mu_{y|x_1, x_2, \ldots, x_K}$, and the point prediction for an individual are the same. However, the standard error of the prediction, s_p, is larger than the standard error of the forecast, s_m. Thus, the prediction interval is wider than the confidence interval, reflecting the greater uncertainty in predicting for individuals than in estimating a conditional mean.

MINITAB produces a 95% prediction interval as shown in Figure 4.18. Note that the forecast standard error, s_m, also is printed. If the prediction standard error is desired, it can be computed using the relationship $s_p^2 = s_m^2 + s_e^2$, where s_e^2 is the *MSE* of the regression.

4.6 LAGGED VARIABLES AS EXPLANATORY VARIABLES IN TIME-SERIES REGRESSION

When using time-series data, it is possible to relate values of the dependent variable in the current time period to explanatory variable values in the current time period. For example, sales for a firm in the current month can be related to advertising expenditures in the current month. It may be, however, that sales in the current month are not affected as much by advertising expenditures in the current month as by advertising expenditures from the previous month or from 2 months ago. This fact can be incorporated into a time-series regression. To illustrate, let y_i represent sales in time period i, x_i represent advertising expenditures in time period i, x_{i-1} represent advertising expenditures in time period $i-1$, and so on. Then a possible model for sales could be written

$$y_i = \beta_0 + \beta_1 x_i + \beta_2 x_{i-1} + \beta_3 x_{i-2} + e_i$$

Here sales are modeled as a function of advertising expenditures in the current month and the 2 previous months.

The variables x_{i-1} and x_{i-2} are called lagged variables. Any lags felt to be appropriate may be used. Here the one- and two-period lags are used. Some caution must be exercised, however, because including several such lagged variables may result in multicollinearity problems (discussed in Chapter 6).

When lagged variables are used, a certain number of data points in the initial time periods are lost. This is illustrated in Table 4.5. Note that no value can be computed for x_{i-1} in time period 1. No prior time period exists from which to take this value. For the same reason, no value for the first or second time period can be

TABLE **4.5**   Creation of Lagged Values of the Explanatory Variables

i	x_i	x_{i-1}	x_{i-2}
1	4	*	*
2	7	4	*
3	8	7	4
4	10	8	7
5	11	10	8
6	9	11	10
7	15	9	11
8	16	15	9

* Indicates a missing value

TABLE **4.6**   Creation of Lagged Values of the Dependent Variable

i	y_i	y_{i-1}
1	22	*
2	24	22
3	27	24
4	35	27
5	38	35
6	42	38
7	47	42
8	50	47

* Indicates a missing value

computed for x_{i-2}. These time periods have to be omitted from the analysis, reducing the effective sample size from eight to six in the example.

Lagged values of the dependent variable also can be used as explanatory variables. Consider again the sales example. Now, however, assume that no information on advertising is available. Sales in the current month are modeled simply as a function of sales in the previous month:

$$y_i = \beta_0 + \beta_1 y_{i-1} + e_i$$

The data are illustrated in Table 4.6. Of course, further lags can be used if desired. One observation is lost for each lag.

Note that the model with the lagged value of the dependent variable as an explanatory variable may be viewed as an extrapolative time-series model (introduced in Chapter 3). We are using only past information from the series itself to help describe the behavior of the series and to forecast future values.

It should be noted, however, that regressions that include lagged dependent variable values are still sometimes interpreted as causal relationships. For example, the one-period lagged value of sales might be included along with the current and lagged values of advertising:

$$y_i = \beta_0 + \beta_1 y_{i-1} + \beta_2 x_i + \beta_3 x_{i-1} + e_i$$

If it is believed that last month's sales might help to generate new sales in the current month or to maintain sales, then this model could be justified as causal.

In the economics literature, a model with lagged values of the dependent variable (and possible lagged values of other explanatory variables) might be called an adaptive expectations model or a partial adjustment model (see, for example, G. Judge et al., *The Theory and Practice of Econometrics,* pp. 379–380). For alternatives to regression analysis useful in analyzing time-series data, see B. Bowerman and R. O'Connel, *Forecasting and Time Series: An Applied Approach.*[4]

EXAMPLE **4.6** ## Unemployment Rate

Table 4.7 lists the monthly unemployment rates from January 1981 until December 1998. (These data can be found on the Web page economagic.com/em-cgi/data.exe/fedstl/unrate+2 and were obtained from the St. Louis Federal Reserve Bank.) The data in Table 4.7 have been seasonally adjusted.

In Figure 4.19, the MINITAB time-series plot of unemployment rate is shown. The horizontal axis in this plot is an index that numbers each month from 1 to 216.

In Figure 4.20, the MINITAB regression of unemployment rate on the one-period lagged unemployment rate is shown. The regression for Excel is shown in Figure 4.21.

FIGURE **4.19**   MINITAB Time-Series Plot of Unemployment Rates

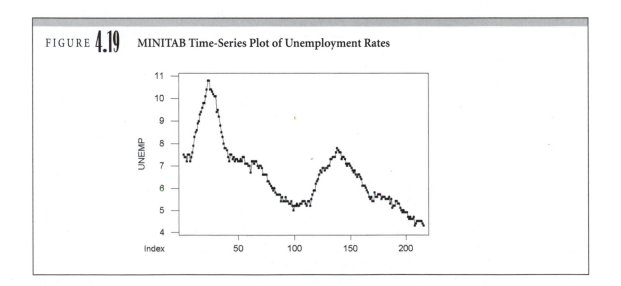

---

[4] See References for complete publication information.

TABLE 4.7   Data for Unemployment Rate Example

1/81	7.5	1/84	8.0	1/87	6.6	1/90	5.4	1/93	7.3	1/96	5.6
2/81	7.4	2/84	7.8	2/87	6.6	2/90	5.3	2/93	7.1	2/96	5.5
3/81	7.4	3/84	7.8	3/87	6.6	3/90	5.2	3/93	7.0	3/96	5.5
4/81	7.2	4/84	7.7	4/87	6.3	4/90	5.4	4/93	7.1	4/96	5.5
5/81	7.5	5/84	7.4	5/87	6.3	5/90	5.4	5/93	7.1	5/96	5.6
6/81	7.5	6/84	7.2	6/87	6.2	6/90	5.2	6/93	7.0	6/96	5.3
7/81	7.2	7/84	7.5	7/87	6.1	7/90	5.5	7/93	6.9	7/96	5.5
8/81	7.4	8/84	7.5	8/87	6.0	8/90	5.7	8/93	6.8	8/96	5.1
9/81	7.6	9/84	7.3	9/87	5.9	9/90	5.9	9/93	6.7	9/96	5.2
10/81	7.9	10/84	7.4	10/87	6.0	10/90	5.9	10/93	6.8	10/96	5.2
11/81	8.3	11/84	7.2	11/87	5.8	11/90	6.2	11/93	6.6	11/96	5.4
12/81	8.5	12/84	7.3	12/87	5.7	12/90	6.3	12/93	6.5	12/96	5.4
1/82	8.6	1/85	7.3	1/88	5.7	1/91	6.4	1/94	6.6	1/97	5.3
2/82	8.9	2/85	7.2	2/88	5.7	2/91	6.6	2/94	6.6	2/97	5.3
3/82	9.0	3/85	7.2	3/88	5.7	3/91	6.8	3/94	6.5	3/97	5.1
4/82	9.3	4/85	7.3	4/88	5.4	4/91	6.7	4/94	6.4	4/97	5.0
5/82	9.4	5/85	7.2	5/88	5.6	5/91	6.9	5/94	6.1	5/97	4.9
6/82	9.6	6/85	7.4	6/88	5.4	6/91	6.9	6/94	6.1	6/97	5.0
7/82	9.8	7/85	7.4	7/88	5.4	7/91	6.8	7/94	6.1	7/97	4.9
8/82	9.8	8/85	7.1	8/88	5.6	8/91	6.9	8/94	6.0	8/97	4.9
9/82	10.1	9/85	7.1	9/88	5.4	9/91	6.9	9/94	5.9	9/97	4.9
10/82	10.4	10/85	7.1	10/88	5.4	10/91	7.0	10/94	5.8	10/97	4.7
11/82	10.8	11/85	7.0	11/88	5.3	11/91	7.0	11/94	5.6	11/97	4.6
12/82	10.8	12/85	7.0	12/88	5.3	12/91	7.3	12/94	5.5	12/97	4.7
1/83	10.4	1/86	6.7	1/89	5.4	1/92	7.3	1/95	5.6	1/98	4.6
2/83	10.4	2/86	7.2	2/89	5.2	2/92	7.4	2/95	5.4	2/98	4.6
3/83	10.3	3/86	7.2	3/89	5.0	3/92	7.4	3/95	5.4	3/98	4.7
4/83	10.2	4/86	7.1	4/89	5.2	4/92	7.4	4/95	5.8	4/98	4.3
5/83	10.1	5/86	7.2	5/89	5.2	5/92	7.6	5/95	5.6	5/98	4.4
6/83	10.1	6/86	7.2	6/89	5.3	6/92	7.8	6/95	5.6	6/98	4.5
7/83	9.4	7/86	7.0	7/89	5.2	7/92	7.7	7/95	5.7	7/98	4.5
8/83	9.5	8/86	6.9	8/89	5.2	8/92	7.6	8/95	5.7	8/98	4.5
9/83	9.2	9/86	7.0	9/89	5.3	9/92	7.6	9/95	5.7	9/98	4.5
10/83	8.8	10/86	7.0	10/89	5.3	10/92	7.3	10/95	5.5	10/98	4.5
11/83	8.5	11/86	6.9	11/89	5.4	11/92	7.4	11/95	5.6	11/98	4.4
12/83	8.3	12/86	6.6	12/89	5.4	12/92	7.4	12/95	5.6	12/98	4.3

FIGURE **4.20**   MINITAB Output for Regression of Unemployment on One-Period Lagged Unemployment

```
The regression equation is
UNEMP = - 0.0022 + 0.998 UNEMPL1


215 cases used 1 cases contain missing values

Predictor          Coef        StDev           T         P
Constant       -0.00223      0.05479       -0.04     0.968
UNEMPL1        0.998088      0.008088      123.41     0.000


S = 0.1716       R-Sq = 98.6%       R-Sq(adj) = 98.6%

Analysis of Variance

Source            DF          SS          MS        F         P
Regression         1      448.37      448.37  15229.82     0.000
Residual Error   213        6.27        0.03
Total            214      454.64


Unusual Observations
Obs     UNEMPL1       UNEMP         Fit   StDev Fit     Residual    St Resid
 11         7.9      8.3000      7.8827      0.0156       0.4173       2.44R
 22        10.1     10.4000     10.0785      0.0305       0.3215       1.90 X
 23        10.4     10.8000     10.3779      0.0327       0.4221       2.51RX
 24        10.8     10.8000     10.7771      0.0358       0.0229       0.14 X
 25        10.8     10.4000     10.7771      0.0358      -0.3771      -2.25RX
 26        10.4     10.4000     10.3779      0.0327       0.0221       0.13 X
 27        10.4     10.3000     10.3779      0.0327      -0.0779      -0.46 X
 28        10.3     10.2000     10.2781      0.0320      -0.0781      -0.46 X
 29        10.2     10.1000     10.1783      0.0312      -0.0783      -0.46 X
 30        10.1     10.1000     10.0785      0.0305       0.0215       0.13 X
 31        10.1      9.4000     10.0785      0.0305      -0.6785      -4.02RX
 34         9.2      8.8000      9.1802      0.0239      -0.3802      -2.24R
 62         6.7      7.2000      6.6850      0.0117       0.5150       3.01R
172         5.4      5.8000      5.3874      0.0153       0.4126       2.41R
188         5.5      5.1000      5.4873      0.0148      -0.3873      -2.27R
208         4.7      4.3000      4.6888      0.0194      -0.3888      -2.28R

R denotes an observation with a large standardized residual
X denotes an observation whose X value gives it large influence.
```

FIGURE 4.21   **Excel Output for Regression of Unemployment on One-Period Lagged Unemployment**

```
                              SUMMARY OUTPUT

Regression Statistics
Multiple R              0.9931
R Square                0.9862
Adjusted R Square       0.9861
Standard Error          0.1716
Observations          215.0000


ANOVA
                    df           SS          MS          F      Significance F
Regression       1.000      448.3663    448.3663   15229.8163       0.0000
Residual       213.000        6.2707      0.0294
Total          214.000      454.6370

                             Standard
               Coefficients    Error    t Stat   P-value   Lower 95%   Upper 95%
Intercept        -0.0022      0.0548   -0.0407    0.9676    -0.1102      0.1058
UNEMPL1           0.9981      0.0081  123.4091    0.0000     0.9821      1.0140
```

The one-period lagged variable has been called UNEMPL1. Note that the first entry in the column for this variable is missing (see Figure 4.20, line 3) as discussed in the creation of Table 4.6. In any subsequent analyses involving UNEMPL1, there is one less observation than the total time-series length because missing cases are not used.

The regression of the monthly unemployment rate on the previous month's rate obviously produces a good fit. The t value for UMEMPL1 is 123.41 (p value = 0.000), resulting in rejection of the hypothesis H_0: $\beta_1 = 0$. Also, 98.6% of the variation in unemployment rate has been explained by the regression.

Now consider adding a two-period lagged variable, UNEMPL2, to the equation. The MINITAB regression of unemployment on UNEMPL1 and UNEMPL2 is shown in Figure 4.22, with the Excel regression in Figure 4.23. The regression model can now be written

$$y_i = \beta_0 + \beta_1 y_{i-1} + \beta_2 y_{i-2} + e_i$$

To test whether the two-period lag is of any importance in the model, the following hypotheses should be tested:

$$H_0: \quad \beta_2 = 0$$
$$H_a: \quad \beta_2 \neq 0$$

FIGURE **4.22** MINITAB Output for Regression of Unemployment on One- and Two-Period Lagged Unemployment

```
The regression equation is
UNEMP = 0.0029 + 1.06 UNEMPL1 - 0.0635 UNEMPL2

214 cases used 2 cases contain missing values

Predictor        Coef       StDev          T       P
Constant       0.00287     0.05529       0.05    0.959
UNEMPL1        1.06105     0.06871      15.44    0.000
UNEMPL2       -0.06353     0.06903      -0.92    0.358

S = 0.1720      R-Sq = 98.6%      R-Sq(adj) = 98.6%

Analysis of Variance

Source            DF          SS          MS         F        P
Regression         2      447.76      223.88   7571.93    0.000
Residual Error   211        6.24        0.03
Total            213      454.00

Source       DF      Seq SS
UNEMPL1       1      447.74
UNEMPL2       1        0.03

Unusual Observations
Obs     UNEMPL1       UNEMP         Fit    StDev Fit    Residual     St Resid
 11         7.9      8.3000      7.9023      0.0260      0.3977        2.34R
 22        10.1     10.4000     10.0968      0.0360      0.3032        1.80 X
 23        10.4     10.8000     10.3961      0.0378      0.4039        2.41RX
 24        10.8     10.8000     10.8014      0.0439     -0.0014       -0.01 X
 25        10.8     10.4000     10.7760      0.0360     -0.3760       -2.24RX
 26        10.4     10.4000     10.3516      0.0443      0.0484        0.29 X
 31        10.1      9.4000     10.0778      0.0307     -0.6778       -4.01R
 32         9.4      9.5000      9.3350      0.0557      0.1650        1.01 X
 34         9.2      8.8000      9.1609      0.0324     -0.3609       -2.14R
 35         8.8      8.5000      8.7556      0.0355     -0.2556       -1.52 X
 62         6.7      7.2000      6.6672      0.0230      0.5328        3.13R
 63         7.2      7.2000      7.2167      0.0373     -0.0167       -0.10 X
172         5.4      5.8000      5.3895      0.0155      0.4105        2.40R
188         5.5      5.1000      5.5019      0.0216     -0.4019       -2.36R
208         4.7      4.3000      4.6975      0.0216     -0.3975       -2.33R

R denotes an observation with a large standardized residual
X denotes an observation whose X value gives it large influence.
```

FIGURE 4.23   **Excel Output for Regression of Unemployment on One- and Two-Period Lagged Unemployment**

SUMMARY OUTPUT

Regression Statistics

Multiple R	0.9931
R Square	0.9863
Adjusted R Square	0.9861
Standard Error	0.1720
Observations	214.000

ANOVA

	df	SS	MS	F	Significance F
Regression	2.000	447.7613	223.8807	7571.9305	0.0000
Residual	211.000	6.2387	0.0296		
Total	213.000	454.0000			

	Coefficients	Standard Error	t Stat	P-value	Lower 95%	Upper 95%
Intercept	0.0029	0.0553	0.0519	0.9587	−0.1061	0.1119
UNEMPL1	1.0611	0.0687	15.4422	0.0000	0.9256	1.1965
UNEMPL2	−0.0635	0.0690	−0.9204	0.3584	−0.1996	0.0725

The test statistic value is −0.92 (p value = 0.358). At a 5% level of significance, the decision rule for the test is

Reject H_0 if $t > 1.96$ or $t < -1.96$

Accept H_0 if $-1.96 \leq t \leq 1.96$

The z value of 1.96 is used since a large number of degrees of freedom are available (211). The null hypothesis is accepted, suggesting that the two-period lagged variable is not useful in explaining any of the additional variation in unemployment rates.

A three-period lagged variable was created and included in the regressions shown in Figures 4.24 and 4.25. The three-period lagged variable is significant at the 5% level. You can conduct the hypothesis test to verify this using either the t value or the associated p value. Note that although the three-period lagged variable is significant, the resulting increase in R^2 is relatively small (from 98.6% to 98.7%, or only 0.1%).

Obviously, this process of lagging the dependent variable can be continued for additional lags if desired. However, the use of continued lagged variables as explanatory variables is questionable in this problem. The increases in R^2 due to the addition of variables is very small after the first lag. A regression using the one- and three-period lagged variables might be the best model choice among the alternatives examined (or for the sake of simplicity, perhaps using only the one-period lagged variable).

FIGURE 4.24   MINITAB Output for Regression of Unemployment on One- and Three-Period Lagged
Unemployment

```
The regression equation is
UNEMP = 0.0173 + 1.10 UNEMPL1 - 0.108 UNEMPL3

213 cases used 3 cases contain missing values

Predictor         Coef        StDev          T        P
Constant       0.01731      0.05521        0.31     0.754
UNEMPL1        1.10409      0.04685       23.57     0.000
UNEMPL3       -0.10845      0.04728       -2.29     0.023

S = 0.1706      R-Sq = 98.7%       R-Sq(adj) = 98.6%

Analysis of Variance

Source            DF          SS          MS         F         P
Regression         2      447.25      223.62   7685.43     0.000
Residual Error   210        6.11        0.03
Total            212      453.36

Source           DF      Seq SS
UNEMPL1           1      447.09
UNEMPL3           1        0.15

Unusual Observations
Obs     UNEMPL1       UNEMP        Fit    StDev Fit     Residual    St Resid
 11         7.9      8.3000     7.9371       0.0282       0.3629        2.16R
 12         8.3      8.5000     8.3571       0.0371       0.1429        0.86 X
 23        10.4     10.8000    10.4371       0.0414       0.3629        2.19RX
 24        10.8     10.8000    10.8462       0.0464      -0.0462       -0.28 X
 25        10.8     10.4000    10.8136       0.0389      -0.4136       -2.49RX
 26        10.4     10.4000    10.3286       0.0393       0.0714        0.43 X
 27        10.4     10.3000    10.3286       0.0393      -0.0286       -0.17 X
 31        10.1      9.4000    10.0625       0.0313      -0.6625       -3.95R
 32         9.4      9.5000     9.3004       0.0431       0.1996        1.21 X
 33         9.5      9.2000     9.4108       0.0399      -0.2108       -1.27 X
 34         9.2      8.8000     9.1555       0.0263      -0.3555       -2.11R
 35         8.8      8.5000     8.7030       0.0402      -0.2030       -1.22 X
 36         8.5      8.3000     8.4044       0.0389      -0.1044       -0.63 X
 43         7.2      7.5000     7.1317       0.0262       0.3683        2.19R
 62         6.7      7.2000     6.6556       0.0175       0.5444        3.21R
172         5.4      5.8000     5.3721       0.0167       0.4279        2.52R
188         5.5      5.1000     5.4825       0.0149      -0.3825       -2.25R
208         4.7      4.3000     4.7077       0.0210      -0.4077       -2.41R

R denotes an observation with a large standardized residual
X denotes an observation whose X value gives it large influence.
```

FIGURE 4.25   Excel Output for Regression of Unemployment on One- and Three-Period Lagged Unemployment

SUMMARY OUTPUT

Regression Statistics
Multiple R	0.9932
R Square	0.9865
Adjusted R Square	0.9864
Standard Error	0.1706
Observations	213.0000

ANOVA

	df	SS	MS	F	Significance F
Regression	2.000	447.2466	223.6233	7685.4349	0.0000
Residual	210.000	6.1104	0.0291		
Total	212.000	453.3570			

	Coefficients	Standard Error	t Stat	P-value	Lower 95%	Upper 95%
Intercept	0.0173	0.0552	0.3135	0.7542	−0.0915	0.1261
UNEMPL1	1.1041	0.0469	23.5659	0.0000	1.0117	1.1965
UNEMPL3	−0.1085	0.047	−2.2938	0.0228	−0.2017	−0.0152

If additional lags are examined, problems can arise. For example, the lagged variables are highly correlated among themselves, which could result in multicollinearity problems (discussed in Chapter 6). Also, for each additional lag used, one data point is lost. Since there were originally 216 monthly observations on unemployment, this loss is not a substantial part of the data set. However, in smaller data sets, the loss could be significant.

EXERCISES

5   **Mortgage Rates**   Table 4.8 shows monthly 30-year conventional mortgage rates from January 1981 to December 1998. (These figures are found on the Web page economagic.com/em-cgi/data.exe/fedbog/cm and are obtained from the Federal Home Mortgage Corporation.) Figure 4.26 provides the MINITAB time-series plot of the rates. The following model is to be used to forecast mortgage rates:

$$y_i = \beta_0 + \beta_1 y_{i-1} + e_i$$

TABLE 4.8   Data for Mortgage Rates Example

Date	Mortgage Rate	Date	Mortgage Rate	Date	Mortgage Rate	Date	Mortgage Rate
1/81	14.90	3/84	13.39	5/87	10.60	7/90	10.04
2/81	15.13	4/84	13.65	6/87	10.54	8/90	10.10
3/81	15.40	5/84	13.94	7/87	10.28	9/90	10.18
4/81	15.58	6/84	14.42	8/87	10.33	10/90	10.18
5/81	16.40	7/84	14.67	9/87	10.89	11/90	10.01
6/81	16.70	8/84	14.47	10/87	11.26	12/90	9.67
7/81	16.83	9/84	14.35	11/87	10.65	1/91	9.64
8/81	17.29	10/84	14.13	12/87	10.65	2/91	9.37
9/81	18.16	11/84	13.64	1/88	10.43	3/91	9.50
10/81	18.45	12/84	13.18	2/88	9.89	4/91	9.49
11/81	17.83	1/85	13.08	3/88	9.93	5/91	9.47
12/81	16.92	2/85	12.92	4/88	10.20	6/91	9.62
1/82	17.40	3/85	13.17	5/88	10.46	7/91	9.58
2/82	17.60	4/85	13.20	6/88	10.46	8/91	9.24
3/82	17.16	5/85	12.91	7/88	10.43	9/91	9.01
4/82	16.89	6/85	12.22	8/88	10.60	10/91	8.86
5/82	16.68	7/85	12.03	9/88	10.48	11/91	8.71
6/82	16.70	8/85	12.19	10/88	10.30	12/91	8.50
7/82	16.82	9/85	12.19	11/88	10.27	1/92	8.43
8/82	16.27	10/85	12.14	12/88	10.61	2/92	8.76
9/82	15.43	11/85	11.78	1/89	10.73	3/92	8.94
10/82	14.61	12/85	11.26	2/89	10.65	4/92	8.85
11/82	13.83	1/86	10.88	3/89	11.03	5/92	8.67
12/82	13.62	2/86	10.71	4/89	11.05	6/92	8.51
1/83	13.25	3/86	10.08	5/89	10.77	7/92	8.13
2/83	13.04	4/86	9.94	6/89	10.20	8/92	7.98
3/83	12.80	5/86	10.14	7/89	9.88	9/92	7.92
4/83	12.78	6/86	10.68	8/89	9.99	10/92	8.09
5/83	12.63	7/86	10.51	9/89	10.13	11/92	8.31
6/83	12.87	8/86	10.20	10/89	9.95	12/92	8.22
7/83	13.42	9/86	10.01	11/89	9.77	1/93	8.02
8/83	13.81	10/86	9.97	12/89	9.74	2/93	7.68
9/83	13.73	11/86	9.70	1/90	9.90	3/93	7.50
10/83	13.54	12/86	9.31	2/90	10.20	4/93	7.47
11/83	13.44	1/87	9.20	3/90	10.27	5/93	7.47
12/83	13.42	2/87	9.08	4/90	10.37	6/93	7.42
1/84	13.37	3/87	9.04	5/90	10.48	7/93	7.21
2/84	13.23	4/87	9.83	6/90	10.16	8/93	7.11

TABLE 4.8   (*continued*)

Date	Mortgage Rate	Date	Mortgage Rate	Date	Mortgage Rate	Date	Mortgage Rate
9/93	6.92	1/95	9.15	5/96	8.07	9/97	7.43
10/93	6.83	2/95	8.83	6/96	8.32	10/97	7.29
11/93	7.16	3/95	8.46	7/96	8.25	11/97	7.21
12/93	7.17	4/95	8.32	8/96	8.00	12/97	7.10
1/94	7.06	5/95	7.96	9/96	8.23	1/98	6.99
2/94	7.15	6/95	7.57	10/96	7.92	2/98	7.04
3/94	7.68	7/95	7.61	11/96	7.62	3/98	7.13
4/94	8.32	8/95	7.86	12/96	7.60	4/98	7.14
5/94	8.60	9/95	7.64	1/97	7.82	5/98	7.14
6/94	8.40	10/95	7.48	2/97	7.65	6/98	7.00
7/94	8.61	11/95	7.38	3/97	7.90	7/98	6.95
8/94	8.51	12/95	7.20	4/97	8.14	8/98	6.92
9/94	8.64	1/96	7.03	5/97	7.94	9/98	6.72
10/94	8.93	2/96	7.08	6/97	7.69	10/98	6.71
11/94	9.17	3/96	7.62	7/97	7.50	11/98	6.87
12/94	9.20	4/96	7.93	8/97	7.48	12/98	6.72

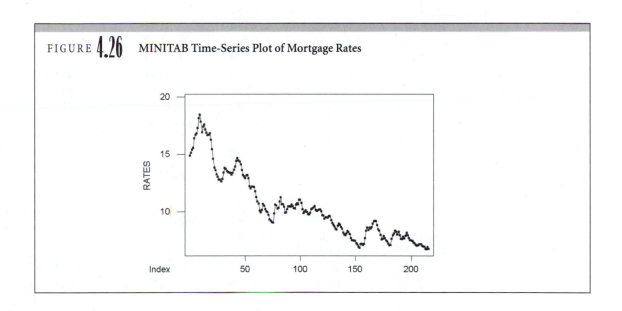

FIGURE 4.26   MINITAB Time-Series Plot of Mortgage Rates

FIGURE **4.27**   MINITAB Regression Output for Mortgage Rates Exercise

```
The regression equation is
RATES = 0.0342 + 0.993 RATESL1

215 cases used 1 cases contain missing values

Predictor        Coef        StDev          T        P
Constant       0.03424     0.07430       0.46     0.645
RATESL1        0.993055    0.006875     144.45     0.000


S = 0.2936      R-Sq = 99.0%      R-Sq(adj) = 99.0%

Analysis of Variance

Source            DF          SS          MS         F         P
Regression         1       1798.7      1798.7   20864.70     0.000
Residual Error   213         18.4         0.1
Total            214       1817.1

Unusual Observations
Obs    RATESL1      RATES       Fit    StDev Fit     Residual    St Resid
  5       15.6    16.4000   15.5060      0.0408       0.8940       3.07R
  9       17.3    18.1600   17.2042      0.0514       0.9558       3.31RX
 10       18.2    18.4500   18.0681      0.0569       0.3819       1.33 X
 11       18.5    17.8300   18.3561      0.0588      -0.5261      -1.83 X
 12       17.8    16.9200   17.7404      0.0548      -0.8204      -2.84RX
 14       17.4    17.6000   17.3134      0.0521       0.2866       0.99 X
 15       17.6    17.1600   17.5120      0.0533      -0.3520      -1.22 X
 16       17.2    16.8900   17.0751      0.0506      -0.1851      -0.64 X
 21       16.3    15.4300   16.1912      0.0450      -0.7612      -2.62R
 22       15.4    14.6100   15.3571      0.0399      -0.7471      -2.57R
 23       14.6    13.8300   14.5428      0.0351      -0.7128      -2.45R
 31       12.9    13.4200   12.8149      0.0262       0.6051       2.07R
 54       12.9    12.2200   12.8546      0.0264      -0.6346      -2.17R
 63       10.7    10.0800   10.6699      0.0201      -0.5899      -2.01R
 76        9.0     9.8300    9.0115      0.0221       0.8185       2.80R
 77        9.8    10.6000    9.7960      0.0204       0.8040       2.75R
 81       10.3    10.8900   10.2925      0.0200       0.5975       2.04R
160        7.7     8.3200    7.6609      0.0274       0.6591       2.25R

R denotes an observation with a large standardized residual
X denotes an observation whose X value gives it large influence.
```

FIGURE 4.28   Excel Regression Output for Mortgage Rates Exercise

SUMMARY OUTPUT

Regression Statistics

Multiple R	0.9949
R Square	0.9899
Adjusted R Square	0.9898
Standard Error	0.2936
Observations	215.0000

ANOVA

	df	SS	MS	F	Significance F
Regression	1.000	1798.7140	1798.7140	20864.6987	0.0000
Residual	213.000	18.3624	0.0862		
Total	214.000	1817.0764			

	Coefficients	Standard Error	t Stat	P-value	Lower 95%	Upper 95%
Intercept	0.0342	0.0743	0.4608	0.6454	−0.1122	0.1807
RATESL1	0.9931	0.0069	144.4462	0.0000	0.9795	1.0066

where y_i is the mortgage rate at time i and y_{i-1} is the rate at time $i - 1$. The MINITAB regression output is shown in Figure 4.27 and the Excel output is in Figure 4.28. Note that RATESL1 in the output represents the one-period lagged variable, y_{i-1}. Use the output to answer the following questions:

a What is the estimated regression equation?

b Is there a relationship between current and previous period mortgage rates? State the hypotheses to be tested, the decision rule, the test statistic, and your decision. Use a 5% level of significance.

c What percentage of the variation in mortgage rates has been explained by the regression?

d Use the estimated equation to produce a forecast of the mortgage rate in January 1999. Find out what the actual rate was and compare it to the forecast. How well did the equation do? Repeat this process for the remainder of 1999. Discuss any difficulties you encounter in forecasting more than 1 month ahead.

e Test whether the intercept of the equation is equal to zero. State the hypotheses to be tested, the decision rule, the test statistic, and your decision. Use a 5% level of significance.

f   Test whether the slope of the equation is equal to one. State the hypotheses to be tested, the decision rule, the test statistic, and your decision. Use a 5% level of significance.

g   Does the regression equation for this problem suggest to you any simpler way of forecasting one-period ahead mortgage rates?

These data are available in a file with prefix MRATES4 for any further analysis desired. There is only one column of data containing mortgage rates. You need to create the lagged variable to be used in the analysis.

4.7 USING THE COMPUTER

The Using the Computer section in each chapter describes how to perform the computer analyses in the chapter using MINITAB, Excel, and SAS. For further detail on MINITAB, Excel, and SAS, see Appendix C.

4.7.1   MINITAB

Note that Version 12 of MINITAB is fully menu driven. Commands can be used, however, and they are included for any interested users. The menu headings and subheadings used to perform the procedures are listed first, followed by commands in parentheses. For example, STAT:REGRESSION:REGRESSION means to click on the STAT menu, then on Regression, and then on Regression on the subsequent menu. (REGR Y in C1 on 2 PRED in C2 C3 shows a command sequence to be typed in.)

Multiple Regression

`STAT:REGRESSION:REGRESSION`   `(REGR Y in C1 on 2 PRED in C2 C3)`

To do a multiple regression in MINITAB, click on the Stat menu and the Regression option. Then click on the regression option on the subsequent menu. The Regression dialog box is shown in Figure 4.29. Fill in the Response variable and the Predictor variables. Then click OK.

Forecasting with a Multiple Regression Equation

`STAT: REGRESSION: REGRESSION: OPTIONS`

Click on Stat, then choose Regression from the Stat menu, and choose Regression again from the next menu. In the Regression dialog box (see Figure 4.29), click Options. The Regression—Options dialog box is shown in Figure 4.30. Fill in "Prediction intervals for new observations:" with the values of the independent variables for which predictions are desired. These values can be single numbers or columns with numbers. The number of entries on this line must be the same as the number of independent variables in the regression equation—one entry for each variable. (If using

FIGURE **4.29**   MINITAB Regression Dialog Box

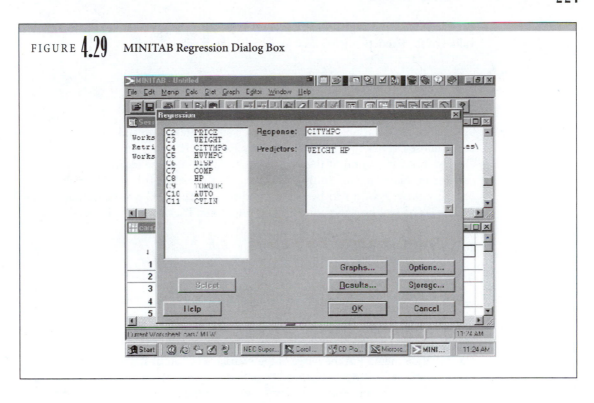

FIGURE **4.30**   MINITAB Regression—Options Dialog Box

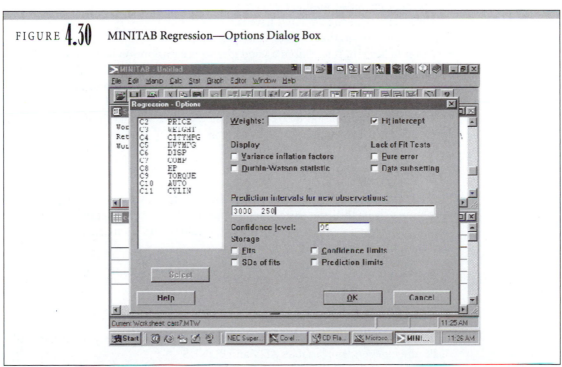

commands, use the subcommand PREDICT E1,E2, . . . EK where E1, E2, . . . EK are values of the K independent variables or columns of values.)

Creating a Lagged Variable

```
STAT: TIME SERIES:LAG      (LAG 1 C1,C2)
```

To create a lagged variable in MINITAB, click on the Stat menu and then on Time Series. Choose Lag from the available options. Figure 4.31 shows the Lag dialog box. In "Series," put the column of the variable to be lagged. Put the location of the lagged variable in "Store lags in." In the "Lag" box, put the order of the lag desired: 1 for a one-period lag, 2 for a two-period lag, and so on. (The LAG command can also be used to lag one column and put the result in another. The desired lag is specified.)

4.7.2 Excel

Multiple Regression

```
TOOLS: DATA ANALYSIS: REGRESSION
```

Figure 4.32 shows the Excel Regression dialog box. Regression is accessed in Excel by clicking on Tools and then Data Analysis. The Regression option is chosen from the Data Analysis menu. Put the range of the y variable in "Input Y Range." Put the range of the x variables in "Input X Range." Note that all x variables to be used in a multiple regression must be in adjacent columns. To accommodate this restriction, variables often must be moved around.

Click "Labels" if the variables have labels in the first row. Typically, "Constant is Zero" is not an option that is used. This option forces the constant or y intercept in a regression to be zero. It is seldom a good idea to use this option and can make interpretation of the regression results difficult. Excel produces 95% confidence interval estimates of the population regression coefficients by default. If another level is required, click the "Confidence Level" box and insert the desired level.

Click the output option desired. The Residuals and Normal Probability options are discussed in a later chapter.

Creating a Lagged Variable

One way to create a lagged variable in Excel is simply to copy the necessary portion of the column to be lagged and paste it in the appropriate position. Figure 4.33 shows an example. Once the column is copied, the initial values with no matches are not used when running any regressions.

4.7.3 SAS

Multiple Regression

The following command sequence produces a regression with dependent variable SALES and independent variables ADV and BONUS:

FIGURE **4.31**   **MINITAB Lag Dialog Box**

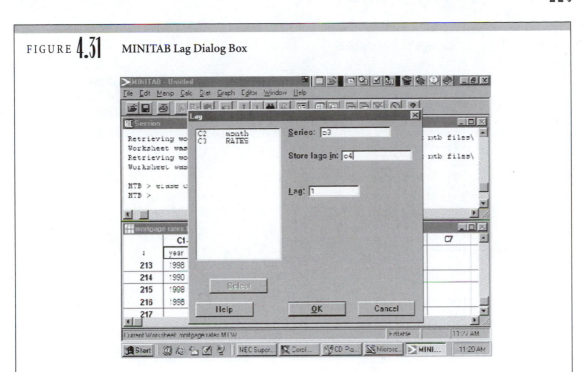

FIGURE **4.32**   **Excel Regression Screen**

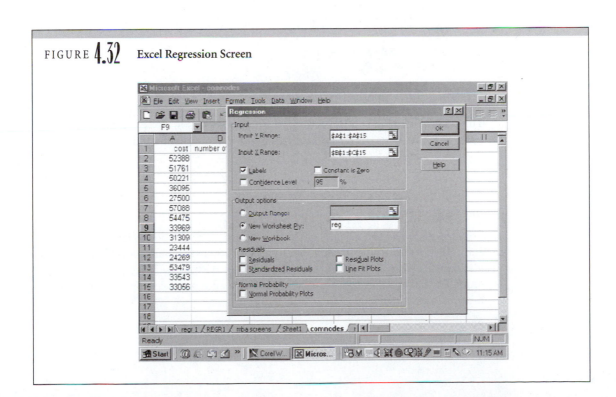

FIGURE 4.33 Creating a Lagged Variable

```
PROC REG;
    MODEL SALES=ADV BONUS;
```

Partial F Tests in Multiple Regression

The TEST command in SAS produces the partial F statistic for testing whether several coefficients are equal to zero. The following command sequence illustrates the use of the TEST command:

```
PROC REG;
    MODEL SALES=ADV BONUS MKTSHR COMPET;
    TEST MKTSHR COMPET;
```

This sequence produces the F statistic to test whether the coefficients of MKTSHR and COMPET are equal to zero. When the SAS TEST command is used, the explanatory variables in the MODEL command do not have to be listed in any particular order. For example, the following command sequence produces the same test result as the previous sequence:

```
PROC REG;
    MODEL SALES=ADV MKTSHR BONUS COMPET;
    TEST MKTSHR COMPET;
```

Forecasting with the Multiple Regression Equation

Forecasts in SAS for multiple regression are generated using an "appended" data set just as with simple regression. To the values of the independent variables in the original data set add the values for which predictions are desired. Then to the values of dependent variables add "." (SAS for missing data) because we do not know those values. Now rerun the regression as follows:

```
PROC REG;
    MODEL SALES=ADV BONUS/P CLM CLI;
```

The option P requests forecasts (or predicted values), CLM requests upper and lower confidence interval limits for the estimate of the conditional mean, and CLI requests upper and lower prediction interval limits for an individual prediction.

Creating a Lagged Variable

In the data input phase in SAS, use the LAG_ command to create lagged variables. For example, to create a one-period lagged variable for the unemployment variable in Example 4.6, use

```
UNEMPL1=LAG1(UNEMP);
```

For a two-period lagged variable, use

```
UNEMPL2=LAG2(UNEMP);
```

ADDITIONAL EXERCISES

6   **Wheat Exports**   The relationship between exchange rates, prices, and agricultural exports is of interest to agricultural economists. One such export of interest is wheat. Table 4.9 lists data on the following variables:

y, U.S. wheat export shipments (SHIPMENT)

x_1, the real index of weighted-average exchange rates of the U.S. dollar (EXCHRATE)

x_2, the per-bushel real price of no. 1 red winter wheat (PRICE)

The dependent variable is U.S. wheat export shipments. The explanatory variables are exchange rate and price. The data are observed monthly from January 1974 through March 1985. The MINITAB and Excel regression outputs are shown in Figures 4.34 and 4.35, respectively. Use the output to answer the following questions:

a   What is the estimated regression equation relating SHIPMENT to EXCHRATE and PRICE?

b   Test the overall fit of the regression. State the hypotheses to be tested, the decision rule, the test statistic, and your decision. Use a 5% level of significance. What conclusion can be drawn from the result of the test?

TABLE **4.9**   Data for Wheat Export Exercise

SHIPMENT	EXCHRATE	PRICE	SHIPMENT	EXCHRATE	PRICE	SHIPMENT	EXCHRATE	PRICE
2264	104.142	0.675969	1881	106.701	0.246300	3760	109.238	0.267277
1983	101.705	0.684394	1567	104.882	0.264202	3958	111.529	0.268925
1787	97.857	0.593693	2378	102.368	0.270112	5284	107.243	0.267571
1519	97.813	0.479903	1764	100.715	0.266093	4273	106.059	0.264126
1500	96.250	0.421644	2576	100.118	0.269372	3470	104.473	0.278931
1556	97.757	0.463543	2870	98.637	0.285304	3749	105.432	0.278236
2256	98.164	0.499162	2811	98.386	0.297034	3379	107.414	0.268141
2503	99.703	0.488550	3268	100.022	0.279991	3775	110.954	0.263977
2346	100.450	0.491222	2965	97.929	0.282057	4329	113.599	0.261508
2495	99.725	0.548979	2888	95.475	0.282499	4033	115.587	0.246816
2676	101.497	0.530823	3590	92.913	0.282695	3170	112.341	0.256175
2247	96.896	0.522932	3255	92.346	0.287967	4270	117.854	0.235281
2951	95.162	0.459886	3144	88.609	0.298474	3209	119.634	0.227856
1957	93.528	0.426019	2514	91.297	0.299235	3383	120.571	0.227389
1774	92.920	0.407098	2450	90.805	0.292863	3565	122.312	0.228175
2099	94.951	0.394918	1916	90.001	0.294996	2681	124.902	0.218801
1778	94.723	0.361930	1826	90.129	0.295454	2575	126.268	0.231150
2111	94.600	0.346000	2056	90.069	0.292349	2407	121.503	0.239250
2721	98.184	0.390863	2096	91.132	0.288898	3896	120.526	0.246865
3033	101.109	0.437014	2131	91.706	0.291523	3990	122.656	0.246697
3428	102.870	0.441748	2847	90.650	0.338378	3569	123.793	0.247752
3368	102.639	0.424429	3627	88.004	0.348430	3060	125.055	0.247244
3228	102.567	0.387923	3206	87.986	0.333526	2619	125.394	0.235778
2516	103.561	0.374701	3528	87.483	0.340297	3087	128.639	0.223716
2506	104.059	0.376692	4056	88.498	0.344550	3176	130.112	0.217042
1974	104.547	0.399818	2963	88.730	0.341522	2388	133.188	0.221998
2105	106.535	0.397904	3127	86.734	0.342148	3246	133.413	0.227979
2099	108.225	0.378107	2250	86.010	0.329736	3125	131.639	0.221738
1845	108.547	0.366381	2436	86.687	0.319842	2800	134.792	0.220599
1818	108.955	0.374828	2578	90.213	0.298573	3508	137.699	0.221591
2330	108.707	0.362312	2676	91.175	0.281348	3221	140.244	0.220712
3081	108.143	0.323255	2411	86.894	0.286996	3024	137.112	0.216040
3004	107.990	0.304265	2618	84.960	0.278684	3231	133.865	0.221864
2736	108.605	0.279868	3364	84.693	0.297887	2644	136.153	0.225505
1478	108.894	0.268899	3849	86.025	0.299195	3070	140.147	0.220339
1561	108.600	0.265363	3737	85.473	0.312402	2867	140.467	0.215567
1346	108.949	0.272095	3183	86.470	0.323602	3627	145.506	0.212044
1572	108.992	0.273863	3054	89.057	0.332600	3979	145.425	0.216859
1433	108.737	0.262259	3594	90.491	0.307294	6605	151.073	0.219725
1911	108.593	0.248590	3537	91.082	0.312945	3736	153.787	0.215539
1810	108.539	0.230318	3386	95.509	0.301696	2648	151.330	0.214202
2098	108.313	0.223497	3504	95.911	0.288256	3591	155.922	0.209881
2277	106.419	0.232193	3474	98.784	0.294955	1897	160.254	0.208585
2543	107.189	0.228678	2124	103.492	0.279304	2327	166.005	0.206186
3011	108.054	0.237409	3389	106.459	0.272203	1576	165.932	0.202214

Source: Data from D. A. Bessler and R. A. Babubla, "Forecasting Wheat Exports: do Exchange Rates Really Matter?," *Journal of Business and Economic Statistics,* 5 (1987): 397–406.

FIGURE 4.34 MINITAB Regression Output for Wheat Export Exercise

```
The regression equation is
SHIPMENT = 3362 + 1.87 EXCHRATE - 2414 PRICE

Predictor          Coef        StDev            T          P
Constant         3361.9        633.2         5.31      0.000
EXCHRATE          1.869        4.223         0.44      0.659
PRICE           -2413.8        846.5        -2.85      0.005

S = 798.3        R-Sq = 8.8%        R-Sq(adj) = 7.4%

Analysis of Variance

Source              DF           SS           MS          F          P
Regression           2      8117338      4058669       6.37      0.002
Residual Error     132     84112922       637219
Total              134     92230260

Source         DF       Seq SS
EXCHRATE        1      2935648
PRICE           1      5181690

Unusual Observations
Obs    EXCHRATE    SHIPMENT         Fit    StDev Fit     Residual     St Resid
  1         104      2264.0      1924.9        310.7        339.1        0.46 X
  2         102      1983.0      1900.0        313.2         83.0        0.11 X
  3          98      1787.0      2111.8        233.5       -324.8       -0.43 X
 93         107      5284.0      2916.5         77.9       2367.5        2.98R
129         151      6605.0      3113.9        171.4       3491.1        4.48R
134         166      2327.0      3174.5        224.7       -847.5       -1.11 X
135         166      1576.0      3184.0        223.9      -1608.0       -2.10RX

R denotes an observation with a large standardized residual
X denotes an observation whose X value gives it large influence.
```

c After taking account of the effect of PRICE, are SHIPMENT and EXCHRATE related? Conduct a hypothesis test to answer this question and use a 5% level of significance. State the hypotheses to be tested, the decision rule, the test statistic and your decision. What conclusion can be drawn from the result of the test?

d What percentage of the variation in the dependent variable has been explained by the regression?

FIGURE 4.35   Excel Regression Output for Wheat Export Exercise

```
Regression Statistics
Multiple R          0.2967
R Square            0.0880
Adjusted R Square   0.0742
Standard Error    798.2601
Observations      135.0000
```

ANOVA

	df	SS	MS	F	Significance F
Regression	2.000	8117337.71	4058668.86	6.3693	0.0023
Residual	132.000	84112922.44	637219.11		
Total	134.000	92230260.15			

	Coefficients	Standard Error	t Stat	P-value	Lower 95%	Upper 95%
Intercept	3361.9317	633.1943	5.3095	0.0000	2109.4124	4614.4510
EXCHRATE	1.8692	4.2230	0.4426	0.6588	−6.4844	10.2227
PRICE	−2413.8367	846.4798	−2.8516	0.0051	−4088.2554	−739.4181

e Construct a 95% confidence interval estimate for the population regression coefficient of PRICE.

f What is the value of the R^2 adjusted for degrees of freedom? What, if any, is the advantage of this number over the coefficient of determination?

These data are available in a file with prefix WHEAT4. There are three columns of data: SHIPMENT, EXCHRATE, and PRICE.

7 **Dividends**   A random sample of 46 firms was chosen from the June 1998 *Standard and Poor's Security Owner's Stock Guide.*[5] The indicated dividend yield (DIVYIELD), the earnings per share (EPS), and the stock price (PRICE) were recorded for these 46 firms. A regression was run using DIVYIELD as the dependent variable and EPS and PRICE as the independent variables. The list of firms and the accompanying data are shown in Table 4.10. The MINITAB and Excel regression outputs are shown in Figures 4.36 and 4.37, respectively. Use the outputs to answer the following questions:

a What is the sample regression equation relating DIVYIELD to PRICE and EPS?

b What percentage of the variation of DIVYIELD has been explained by the regression?

---

[5] Source: Reprinted by permission of Standard and Poor's, a division of the McGraw-Hill Inc. Companies.

TABLE 4.10   Dividend Yield, EPS and Price Data for Dividends Exercise

#	Company Name	DIVYIELD	EPS	PRICE	#	Company Name	DIVYIELD	EPS	PRICE
1	Bristol-Myers Squibb	1.56	3.35	102	24	Tandy	0.40	1.31	57
2	Intel	0.12	3.23	88	25	Betzdearborn Inc.	1.52	2.60	67
3	Waterlink Inc.	0.00	0.44	8	26	Owens & Minor	0.20	0.49	12
4	Schering-Plough	0.88	2.16	97	27	Wendy's International	0.24	0.89	22
5	Weyerhaeuser	1.60	1.83	42	28	General Signal	1.08	2.70	40
6	PNC Bank	1.56	3.44	54	29	Kansas City Southern Industries	0.16	0.24	49
7	Marion Capitol Holdings	0.88	1.29	25	30	New York Bancorp	0.60	2.34	46
8	Park Electrochemical	0.32	2.02	19	31	Ohio Casualty	1.76	3.37	43
9	United National Bank Holdings	0.60	1.68	30	32	Maytag Corp.	0.64	2.51	44
10	Burlington Resources	0.55	0.97	36	33	Tidewater	0.60	5.39	29
11	Consolidated Papers	0.88	1.45	29	34	Brookline Bancorp	0.00	0.39	14
12	AMRESCO Inc.	0.00	1.74	29	35	Stone & Webster	0.60	2.06	36
13	Consolidated Natural Gas	1.94	2.41	52	36	Wilmington Trust	1.56	3.20	59
14	Louisiana-Pacific	0.56	0.41	20	37	Idaho Power	1.86	2.32	30
15	Wheelabrator Technologies	0.12	0.57	16	38	PacifiCorp	1.08	1.57	21
16	Baker Hughes	0.46	0.83	25	39	Millipore	0.44	1.84	24
17	McGraw-Hill	1.56	3.09	82	40	Masco Corp.	0.44	1.29	29
18	Clorox	1.28	2.82	103	41	Central Maine Power	0.90	0.40	19
19	Nalco Chemical	1.00	2.17	34	42	Lance Inc.	0.96	1.01	19
20	Pioneer Hi-Bred International	0.40	1.09	32	43	Seagrams Co.	0.66	2.17	37
21	TJX	0.12	1.00	24	44	Health Management Associates	0.00	0.48	24
22	DPL	0.94	1.22	17	45	Jones Pharma Inc.	0.12	1.41	32
23	Johnson Controls	0.92	3.33	52	46	Diamond Offshore Drilling	0.50	2.40	33

FIGURE **4.36**   MINITAB Regression Output for Dividend Yield Exercise

```
The regression equation is
DIVYIELD = 0.157 + 0.216 EPS + 0.00501 PRICE

Predictor        Coef        StDev          T        P
Constant       0.1572       0.1489       1.06    0.297
EPS            0.21566      0.07779      2.77    0.008
PRICE          0.005007     0.003596     1.39    0.171

S = 0.4694      R-Sq = 32.6%       R-Sq(adj) = 29.5%

Analysis of Variance

Source             DF          SS          MS        F        P
Regression          2      4.5822      2.2911    10.40    0.000
Residual Error     43      9.4726      0.2203
Total              45     14.0548

Source      DF      Seq SS
EPS          1      4.1550
PRICE        1      0.4273

Unusual Observations
Obs       EPS    DIVYIELD       Fit    StDev Fit      Residual    St Resid
  2      3.23     0.1200     1.2945      0.1601       -1.1745       -2.66R
 13      2.41     1.9400     0.9374      0.0808        1.0026        2.17R
 18      2.82     1.2800     1.2812      0.2082       -0.0012       -0.00 X
 33      5.39     0.6000     1.4649      0.3060       -0.8649       -2.43RX
 37      2.32     1.8600     0.8078      0.0929        1.0522        2.29R

R denotes an observation with a large standardized residual
X denotes an observation whose X value gives it large influence.
```

c   Test the overall fit of the regression. Use a 10% level of significance. State the hypotheses to be tested, the decision rule, the test statistic, and your decision.

d   What conclusion can be drawn from the test result?

These data are available in a file with prefix DIV4 in three columns in the order: DIVYIELD, EPS, and PRICE.

FIGURE 4.37 Excel Regression Output for Dividend Yield Exercise

```
                            SUMMARY OUTPUT

Regression Statistics
Multiple R              0.5710
R Square                0.3260
Adjusted R Square       0.2947
Standard Error          0.4694
Observations           46.0000
```

ANOVA

	df	SS	MS	F	Significance F
Regression	2.000	4.5822	2.2911	10.4004	0.0002
Residual	43.000	9.4726	0.2203		
Total	45.000	14.0548			

	Coefficients	Standard Error	t Stat	P-value	Lower 95%	Upper 95%
Intercept	0.1572	0.1489	1.0559	0.2969	−0.1431	0.4575
EPS	0.2157	0.0778	2.7725	0.0082	0.0588	0.3725
PRICE	0.0050	0.0036	1.3927	0.1709	−0.0022	0.0123

8 Graduation Rates   Each fall, *U.S. News and World Report* publishes its college guide entitled *America's Best Colleges*. The 1999 issue contains rankings of the best national universities as determined by *U.S. News*. This information is included in a file with prefix COLLEGE4 for 173 schools. The data are shown in Table 4.11. Only schools with complete information on all categories listed are included. The variables are defined as follows:

Grad. Rate	1997 graduation rate (expressed as a percentage)
Fresh. Ret.	freshman retention rate: percentage of freshmen who return for their sophomore year
% <= 20	percentage of classes with 20 or fewer students
% >= 50	percentage of classes with 50 or more students
SAT 75	the 75th percentile of the SAT scores of students admitted
Top 10%	percentage of freshmen in top 10% of high school class
Accept. Rate	percentage of applicants who were accepted
Alumni Giving	alumni giving rate: percentage of alumni who contribute money

TABLE 4.11   Data for Graduation Rates Exercise

	Grad. Rate	Fresh. Ret.	% <=20	% >=50	SAT 75	Top 10%	Accept. Rate	Alumni Giving
Harvard University	97.0%	96.0%	69.0%	11.0%	1580	90.0%	13.0%	46.0%
Princeton University	96.0%	98.0%	68.0%	12.0%	1530	93.0%	13.0%	66.0%
Yale University	96.0%	98.0%	77.0%	8.0%	1530	95.0%	18.0%	50.0%
MIT	89.0%	97.0%	69.0%	6.0%	1560	93.0%	25.0%	44.0%
Stanford University	92.0%	97.0%	70.0%	12.0%	1540	87.0%	15.0%	34.0%
Cornell University	90.0%	95.0%	74.0%	10.0%	1440	82.0%	34.0%	35.0%
Duke University	92.0%	97.0%	69.0%	7.0%	1480	87.0%	30.0%	37.0%
University of Pennsylvania	90.0%	95.0%	59.0%	11.0%	1460	88.0%	31.0%	41.0%
California Institute of Technology	83.0%	92.0%	71.0%	7.0%	1570	99.0%	23.0%	46.0%
Brown University	92.0%	96.0%	59.0%	13.0%	1480	88.0%	18.0%	42.0%
Columbia University	90.0%	96.0%	59.0%	10.0%	1470	85.0%	17.0%	30.0%
Dartmouth College	94.0%	96.0%	57.0%	10.0%	1520	88.0%	22.0%	54.0%
Northwestern University	90.0%	96.0%	64.0%	9.0%	1450	87.0%	29.0%	31.0%
Johns Hopkins University	90.0%	95.0%	60.0%	14.0%	1460	76.0%	41.0%	27.0%
University of Chicago	83.0%	93.0%	63.0%	5.0%	1460	76.0%	62.0%	39.0%
Emory University	83.0%	92.0%	67.0%	6.0%	1430	86.0%	46.0%	34.0%
Washington University (St. Louis)	86.0%	95.0%	74.0%	8.0%	1390	70.0%	40.0%	30.0%
Rice University	88.0%	95.0%	60.0%	9.0%	1530	88.0%	27.0%	41.0%
University of Notre Dame	93.0%	97.0%	52.0%	12.0%	1410	82.0%	40.0%	50.0%
Georgetown University	89.0%	95.0%	54.0%	12.0%	1440	82.0%	21.0%	28.0%
Vanderbilt University	81.0%	91.0%	66.0%	5.0%	1370	63.0%	58.0%	32.0%
University of California—Berkeley	81.0%	94.0%	56.0%	16.0%	1440	95.0%	31.0%	18.0%
University of Virginia	92.0%	97.0%	45.0%	15.0%	1410	80.0%	36.0%	29.0%
University of No. Carolina—Chapel Hill	84.0%	94.0%	41.0%	13.0%	1330	67.0%	37.0%	27.0%
Carnegie Mellon University	72.0%	91.0%	66.0%	9.0%	1460	69.0%	43.0%	31.0%
Tufts University	86.0%	95.0%	66.0%	7.0%	1410	62.0%	32.0%	30.0%
University of California—Los Angeles	79.0%	95.0%	44.0%	26.0%	1360	97.0%	36.0%	15.0%
University of Michigan	82.0%	94.0%	48.0%	15.0%	1333	59.0%	69.0%	13.0%
University of Rochester	77.0%	93.0%	81.0%	5.0%	1380	66.0%	54.0%	23.0%
Wake Forest University	85.0%	93.0%	59.0%	4.0%	1390	66.0%	44.0%	39.0%
Brandeis University	82.0%	90.0%	62.0%	10.0%	1400	62.0%	54.0%	31.0%
University of California—San Diego	79.0%	93.0%	48.0%	28.0%	1340	95.0%	53.0%	11.0%
College of William and Mary	89.0%	94.0%	45.0%	7.0%	1390	71.0%	46.0%	28.0%
Case Western Reserve University	75.0%	91.0%	50.0%	16.0%	1410	66.0%	79.0%	31.0%
New York University	71.0%	88.0%	61.0%	9.0%	1390	60.0%	40.0%	13.0%
Boston College	85.0%	94.0%	41.0%	9.0%	1370	64.0%	39.0%	23.0%
Lehigh University	81.0%	92.0%	45.0%	10.0%	1323	52.0%	54.0%	48.0%
Tulane University	73.0%	86.0%	52.0%	8.0%	1370	54.0%	76.0%	24.0%
University of California—Irvine	75.0%	91.0%	44.0%	20.0%	1220	90.0%	66.0%	8.0%

TABLE 4.11 (*continued*)

	Grad. Rate	Fresh. Ret.	% <=20	% >=50	SAT 75	Top 10%	Accept. Rate	Alumni Giving
University of Wisconsin—Madison	73.0%	91.0%	39.0%	19.0%	1289	44.0%	68.0%	14.0%
University of Southern California	69.0%	90.0%	51.0%	17.0%	1330	52.0%	46.0%	22.0%
University of Illinois	79.0%	91.0%	31.0%	19.0%	1333	53.0%	68.0%	11.0%
Pennsylvania State University	81.0%	93.0%	33.0%	21.0%	1300	48.0%	53.0%	21.0%
University of California—Davis	75.0%	91.0%	30.0%	28.0%	1280	95.0%	70.0%	7.0%
Syracuse University	69.0%	89.0%	65.0%	7.0%	1270	33.0%	60.0%	21.0%
University of California—Santa Barbara	72.0%	86.0%	46.0%	19.0%	1260	95.0%	72.0%	10.0%
George Washington University	68.0%	89.0%	51.0%	10.0%	1330	45.0%	49.0%	19.0%
American University	70.0%	85.0%	42.0%	3.0%	1290	28.0%	79.0%	12.0%
Auburn University	65.0%	80.0%	40.0%	8.0%	1200	24.0%	86.0%	24.0%
Brigham Young University	67.0%	87.0%	34.0%	17.0%	1289	53.0%	71.0%	20.0%
Catholic University of America	72.0%	84.0%	63.0%	4.0%	1280	36.0%	82.0%	11.0%
Clarkson University	64.0%	85.0%	31.0%	19.0%	1290	39.0%	81.0%	29.0%
Clark University	68.0%	84.0%	65.0%	7.0%	1240	31.0%	77.0%	25.0%
Clemson University	70.0%	84.0%	39.0%	8.0%	1240	32.0%	74.0%	18.0%
Colorado School of Mines	59.0%	84.0%	41.0%	9.0%	1289	55.0%	80.0%	24.0%
Duquesne University	64.0%	90.0%	55.0%	8.0%	1200	51.0%	82.0%	18.0%
Florida State University	65.0%	84.0%	34.0%	13.0%	1230	43.0%	72.0%	24.0%
Fordham University	77.0%	87.0%	54.0%	0.2%	1230	26.0%	69.0%	14.0%
Indiana University	67.0%	86.0%	36.0%	17.0%	1230	23.0%	83.0%	21.0%
Iowa State University	60.0%	82.0%	28.0%	18.0%	1200	26.0%	91.0%	15.0%
Loyola University—Chicago	63.0%	83.0%	50.0%	4.0%	1200	27.0%	89.0%	16.0%
Miami (OH) University	80.0%	89.0%	25.0%	9.0%	1244	36.0%	77.0%	19.0%
Michigan Technological University	61.0%	84.0%	44.0%	11.0%	1244	35.0%	97.0%	20.0%
North Carolina State University	64.0%	88.0%	32.0%	14.0%	1260	31.0%	75.0%	19.0%
Ohio State University	57.0%	78.0%	41.0%	17.0%	1200	26.0%	79.0%	15.0%
Pepperdine University	72.0%	83.0%	68.0%	1.0%	1260	54.0%	54.0%	16.0%
Purdue University	64.0%	86.0%	23.0%	21.0%	1220	27.0%	89.0%	15.0%
Rutgers—Newark	51.0%	87.0%	40.0%	13.0%	1110	24.0%	55.0%	10.0%
Rutgers—New Brunswick	73.0%	90.0%	30.0%	24.0%	1280	31.0%	64.0%	17.0%
Southern Methodist University	70.0%	85.0%	57.0%	8.0%	1260	34.0%	88.0%	21.0%
Stevens Institute of Technology	70.0%	83.0%	36.0%	10.0%	1450	59.0%	67.0%	31.0%
St. Louis University	61.0%	84.0%	48.0%	7.0%	1289	34.0%	71.0%	18.0%
State University of New York—Albany	66.0%	83.0%	39.0%	19.0%	1230	14.0%	61.0%	31.0%
State Univ. of New York—Binghamton	79.0%	91.0%	39.0%	16.0%	1310	54.0%	42.0%	14.0%
State Univ. of New York—Buffalo	59.0%	84.0%	49.0%	13.0%	1230	22.0%	72.0%	9.0%
State Univ. of New York—Stony Brook	50.0%	82.0%	37.0%	24.0%	1200	25.0%	57.0%	4.0%
Texas A&M University	69.0%	87.0%	33.0%	17.0%	1270	47.0%	73.0%	22.0%
Texas Christian University	63.0%	80.0%	46.0%	7.0%	1230	29.0%	79.0%	26.0%

Continues

TABLE 4.11 (*continued*)

	Grad. Rate	Fresh. Ret.	% <=20	% >=50	SAT 75	Top 10%	Accept. Rate	Alumni Giving
University of Arizona	52.0%	76.0%	33.0%	16.0%	1210	33.0%	82.0%	7.0%
University of California—Riverside	68.0%	86.0%	39.0%	21.0%	1200	90.0%	84.0%	9.0%
University of California—Santa Cruz	65.0%	82.0%	40.0%	19.0%	1260	94.0%	83.0%	11.0%
University of Colorado	65.0%	81.0%	48.0%	15.0%	1260	25.0%	83.0%	15.0%
University of Delaware	70.0%	86.0%	41.0%	14.0%	1220	23.0%	65.0%	18.0%
University of Denver	68.0%	83.0%	71.0%	4.0%	1220	29.0%	84.0%	26.0%
University of Florida	64.0%	90.0%	30.0%	22.0%	1310	60.0%	67.0%	20.0%
University of Hawaii	56.0%	80.0%	54.0%	9.0%	1170	30.0%	69.0%	10.0%
University of Kansas	54.0%	77.0%	43.0%	10.0%	1244	26.0%	61.0%	17.0%
University of Maryland	63.0%	86.0%	33.0%	14.0%	1320	40.0%	65.0%	10.0%
University of Massachusetts	61.0%	79.0%	40.0%	15.0%	1220	16.0%	73.0%	14.0%
University of Miami (FL)	58.0%	80.0%	50.0%	7.0%	1260	44.0%	57.0%	18.0%
University of Minnesota	56.0%	83.0%	57.0%	14.0%	1200	27.0%	80.0%	9.0%
University of Missouri	58.0%	83.0%	25.0%	22.0%	1289	34.0%	80.0%	17.0%
University of Missouri—Rolla	52.0%	77.0%	36.0%	9.0%	1378	50.0%	97.0%	24.0%
University of New Hampshire	74.0%	83.0%	52.0%	9.0%	1220	24.0%	76.0%	14.0%
University of Oklahoma	54.0%	81.0%	30.0%	17.0%	1244	32.0%	87.0%	17.0%
University of Pittsburgh	61.0%	82.0%	32.0%	17.0%	1220	22.0%	78.0%	13.0%
University of San Diego	65.0%	89.0%	47.0%	0.4%	1230	34.0%	70.0%	20.0%
University of Tennessee	56.0%	77.0%	36.0%	9.0%	1156	24.0%	76.0%	22.0%
University of Texas	65.0%	87.0%	38.0%	18.0%	1300	37.0%	78.0%	13.0%
University of Vermont	68.0%	82.0%	54.0%	9.0%	1220	17.0%	85.0%	24.0%
Virginia Tech	74.0%	89.0%	23.0%	18.0%	1270	33.0%	69.0%	20.0%
Washington State University	63.0%	84.0%	33.0%	27.0%	1170	40.0%	88.0%	21.0%
Worcester Polytechnic Institute	75.0%	88.0%	70.0%	9.0%	1380	47.0%	78.0%	26.0%
Arizona State University	48.0%	71.0%	28.0%	18.0%	1210	25.0%	79.0%	6.0%
Bowling Green State University	60.0%	76.0%	49.0%	5.0%	1022	14.0%	86.0%	16.0%
Colorado State University	58.0%	82.0%	17.0%	30.0%	1156	23.0%	78.0%	10.0%
DePaul University	58.0%	82.0%	40.0%	3.0%	1200	22.0%	81.0%	11.0%
Drexel University	50.0%	79.0%	52.0%	2.0%	1220	22.0%	68.0%	15.0%
Florida Institute of Technology	53.0%	74.0%	55.0%	6.0%	1250	26.0%	85.0%	6.0%
Hofstra University	63.0%	80.0%	42.0%	5.0%	1170	18.0%	83.0%	11.0%
Indiana University of Pennsylvania	53.0%	75.0%	39.0%	6.0%	1140	26.0%	63.0%	17.0%
Indiana/Purdue—Indianapolis	22.0%	49.0%	43.0%	8.0%	1060	6.0%	94.0%	13.0%
Louisiana State University	47.0%	80.0%	31.0%	14.0%	1156	27.0%	79.0%	30.0%
Mississippi State University	49.0%	77.0%	41.0%	11.0%	1200	45.0%	78.0%	18.0%
New Jersey Institute of Technology	37.0%	82.0%	45.0%	3.0%	1210	23.0%	66.0%	11.0%
Northeastern University	41.0%	75.0%	43.0%	12.0%	1190	18.0%	70.0%	17.0%
Oklahoma State University	49.0%	77.0%	25.0%	19.0%	1244	30.0%	88.0%	12.0%

TABLE **4.11**   (*continued*)

	Grad. Rate	Fresh. Ret.	% <=20	% >=50	SAT 75	Top 10%	Accept. Rate	Alumni Giving
Oregon State University	68.0%	77.0%	42.0%	22.0%	1230	86.0%	97.0%	25.0%
Seton Hall University	64.0%	83.0%	56.0%	2.0%	1140	13.0%	79.0%	20.0%
St. John's University	64.0%	83.0%	39.0%	11.0%	1080	13.0%	86.0%	10.0%
University of Alabama	57.0%	81.0%	42.0%	12.0%	1200	22.0%	81.0%	34.0%
University of Alabama—Huntsville	33.0%	64.0%	55.0%	4.0%	1200	39.0%	85.0%	7.0%
University of Arkansas	42.0%	81.0%	42.0%	10.0%	1156	28.0%	91.0%	22.0%
University of Idaho	49.0%	76.0%	53.0%	12.0%	1156	22.0%	71.0%	15.0%
University of Illinois—Chicago	32.0%	71.0%	34.0%	17.0%	1067	26.0%	62.0%	7.0%
University of Kentucky	48.0%	78.0%	38.0%	10.0%	1200	23.0%	78.0%	15.0%
University of Maine	53.0%	78.0%	44.0%	13.0%	1200	21.0%	75.0%	17.0%
University of Maryland—Baltimore Co.	46.0%	85.0%	41.0%	13.0%	1300	33.0%	65.0%	10.0%
University of Mississippi	49.0%	74.0%	34.0%	18.0%	1200	37.0%	78.0%	13.0%
University of Missouri—Kansas City	37.0%	72.0%	60.0%	6.0%	1244	36.0%	61.0%	6.0%
University of Nebraska	46.0%	75.0%	37.0%	14.0%	1200	25.0%	81.0%	14.0%
University of New Mexico	37.0%	71.0%	45.0%	13.0%	1111	21.0%	69.0%	9.0%
University of North Dakota	47.0%	76.0%	42.0%	9.0%	1156	22.0%	68.0%	19.0%
University of Rhode Island	64.0%	76.0%	28.0%	9.0%	1180	15.0%	79.0%	18.0%
University of San Francisco	61.0%	84.0%	55.0%	2.0%	1200	26.0%	76.0%	14.0%
University of South Carolina	56.0%	79.0%	40.0%	16.0%	1200	28.0%	77.0%	10.0%
University of Southern Mississippi	40.0%	74.0%	50.0%	9.0%	1067	33.0%	67.0%	26.0%
University of Texas—Dallas	38.0%	75.0%	39.0%	19.0%	1324	35.0%	65.0%	8.0%
University of the Pacific	62.0%	82.0%	50.0%	3.0%	1240	39.0%	84.0%	12.0%
University of Tulsa	56.0%	79.0%	55.0%	3.0%	1244	38.0%	83.0%	10.0%
University of Utah	38.0%	59.0%	43.0%	12.0%	1200	21.0%	91.0%	9.0%
University of Wyoming	45.0%	73.0%	42.0%	8.0%	1200	22.0%	94.0%	15.0%
Virginia Commonwealth University	45.0%	77.0%	47.0%	7.0%	1130	13.0%	80.0%	9.0%
West Virginia University	54.0%	78.0%	37.0%	17.0%	1130	23.0%	93.0%	11.0%
Andrews University	47.0%	66.0%	68.0%	4.0%	1200	14.0%	65.0%	18.0%
Ball State University	54.0%	70.0%	35.0%	9.0%	1100	10.0%	92.0%	29.0%
Florida International University	40.0%	86.0%	31.0%	16.0%	1200	42.0%	75.0%	22.0%
Illinois State University	53.0%	74.0%	28.0%	12.0%	1067	11.0%	79.0%	9.0%
Indiana State University	35.0%	65.0%	40.0%	8.0%	1050	8.0%	88.0%	12.0%
Louisiana Tech University	38.0%	74.0%	54.0%	7.0%	1111	24.0%	98.0%	10.0%
Middle Tennessee State University	40.0%	74.0%	38.0%	3.0%	1111	18.0%	74.0%	10.0%
Montana State University	44.0%	69.0%	37.0%	21.0%	1111	15.0%	84.0%	12.0%
Northern Arizona University	41.0%	71.0%	36.0%	12.0%	1170	20.0%	81.0%	13.0%
Northern Illinois University	50.0%	76.0%	44.0%	10.0%	1111	12.0%	52.0%	8.0%
Nova Southeastern University	20.0%	69.0%	75.0%	1.0%	1180	26.0%	78.0%	1.0%
Portland State University	33.0%	57.0%	55.0%	8.0%	1160	13.0%	81.0%	9.0%

Continues

TABLE 4.11 (continued)

	Grad. Rate	Fresh. Ret.	% <=20	% >=50	SAT 75	Top 10%	Accept. Rate	Alumni Giving
Southern Illinois University	35.0%	66.0%	41.0%	11.0%	1067	10.0%	73.0%	8.0%
Texas Tech University	44.0%	75.0%	20.0%	21.0%	1170	26.0%	72.0%	23.0%
University of Akron	37.0%	71.0%	46.0%	4.0%	1022	11.0%	100.0%	14.0%
University of Central Florida	50.0%	72.0%	26.0%	19.0%	1220	29.0%	65.0%	17.0%
University of Colorado—Denver	31.0%	73.0%	37.0%	11.0%	1111	20.0%	76.0%	7.0%
University of Detroit—Mercy	42.0%	80.0%	42.0%	2.0%	1156	23.0%	75.0%	12.0%
University of Houston	36.0%	74.0%	23.0%	20.0%	1160	22.0%	70.0%	6.0%
University of Louisville	29.0%	74.0%	35.0%	8.0%	1067	19.0%	67.0%	18.0%
University of Missouri—St. Louis	31.0%	64.0%	51.0%	7.0%	1111	17.0%	66.0%	0.8%
University of Montana	37.0%	66.0%	41.0%	11.0%	1111	14.0%	85.0%	20.0%
University of NCarolina—Greensboro	50.0%	74.0%	37.0%	11.0%	1130	13.0%	76.0%	13.0%
University of Northern Colorado	41.0%	67.0%	29.0%	16.0%	1067	14.0%	81.0%	8.0%
University of North Texas	35.0%	70.0%	21.0%	17.0%	1200	22.0%	74.0%	5.0%
University of South Florida	47.0%	76.0%	26.0%	13.0%	1200	25.0%	66.0%	11.0%
University of Toledo	37.0%	71.0%	42.0%	12.0%	1067	15.0%	95.0%	10.0%
University of Wisconsin—Milwaukee	35.0%	68.0%	38.0%	13.0%	1067	8.0%	84.0%	7.0%
Western Michigan University	52.0%	78.0%	21.0%	18.0%	1111	19.0%	83.0%	10.0%

U.S. News is interested in determining a "value added" measure to help in establishing their rankings. Researchers have long sought ways to measure the educational value added by individual colleges. *U.S. News* has defined such a measure as the difference between the actual graduation rate and the predicted graduation rate. They use this difference to determine which schools produce higher and lower than expected graduation rates and from this derive the "value added" measure.

The bottom line is that *U.S. News* needs to predict graduation rates. They have hired you to come up with these predictions. Use the data provided to develop a regression equation for predicting graduation rates. The 1997 graduation rate is the dependent variable. Determine what variables should and should not be included in the regression. Assess how well your regression does with the predictions.

Write a report with your results to Robert J. Morse, Special Editor, *U.S. News College Guide.* Your report should consist of a letter/executive summary to Morse and a technical section with a description and justification of your regression equation. Also include a section with your graduation rate predictions for the included schools. This is important because it is the whole point of the project, and Morse needs these predictions immediately.

9 National Football League   The following data were obtained from *Jim Feist's Professional Football Annual (1999 Preview)* and refer to the 1998 National Football League (NFL) season:

wins (WINS)
net yards rushing (RUSH)
net yards passing (PASS)
passes attempted (PATT)
passes completed (PCOMP)
passes intercepted (PINT)
fumbles lost (FUMBLE)
fumbles by opponents (FUMBOPP)
net rushing yards allowed (RUSHOPP)
net passing yards allowed (PASSOPP)
passes attempted by opponents (PATTOPP)
passes completed by opponents (PCOMPOPP)
passes intercepted by opponents (PIOPP)

The dependent variable is the number of wins (WINS) for the season. The other variables are to be considered possible explanatory variables. The data for the 30 NFL teams are shown in Table 4.12.

Your NFL team is interested in what makes a winning season. You have gathered the data in Table 4.12 on various offensive and defensive statistics. Your job is to try to determine which combination of the variables provides the best explanation of what makes a winning team. Once you have determined your choice of the best equation, use your results to answer the following questions:

a What is the estimated regression equation relating WINS to your set of explanatory variables?

b Test the overall fit of the regression. Use a 5% level of significance. State the hypotheses to be tested, the decision rule, the test statistic, and your decision.

c What percentage of the variation in WINS is explained by the regression?

d Why did you omit certain variables? Why did you decide to keep others in the regression? Justify your choice of variables.

e What do your results tell you about winning teams?

These data are available in a file with prefix NFL4 in 13 columns in the order shown.

10 Prime Rate   Table 4.13 shows monthly prime rates during the time period from January 1986 through December 1998. (These data were found on the Web page economagic.com/em-cgi/data.exe/fedstl/mprime+2 and are from the Federal Reserve Bank of St. Louis.) Develop an extrapolative model to forecast the prime rate for each month in 1999.

Find the actual rates for each month in 1999 and compare them to your forecasts. How well did your model do?

These data are available in one column in a file with prefix PRIME4.

TABLE 4.12   Data for National Football League (NFL) Exercise

Name	WINS	RUSH	PASS	PATT	PCOMP	PINT	FUMBLE
NY Jets	12	1879	3836	532	318	21	11
Miami	10	1535	3395	546	316	29	12
Buffalo	10	2161	3380	461	269	18	6
New England	9	1480	3660	525	281	23	7
Indianapolis	3	1486	3630	576	326	8	5
Jacksonville	11	2102	3112	463	269	13	8
Tennessee	8	1970	3291	519	305	12	9
Pittsburgh	7	2034	2552	489	274	16	12
Baltimore	6	1629	2869	477	272	17	15
Cincinnati	3	1639	3185	521	307	28	10
Denver	14	2468	3624	491	290	19	6
Oakland	8	1727	3088	519	282	21	18
Seattle	8	1626	3000	480	273	24	16
Kansas City	7	1548	3260	543	305	13	14
San Diego	5	1728	2864	566	261	20	17
Dallas	10	2014	3436	474	279	14	7
Arizona	9	1627	3482	552	326	20	16
NY Giants	8	1889	2566	507	265	19	9
Washington	6	1685	3325	565	304	13	15
Philadelphia	3	1775	2413	534	282	9	8
Minnesota	15	1936	4328	533	327	19	4
Green Bay	11	1526	4110	575	361	13	11
Tampa Bay	8	2148	2606	449	234	12	13
Detroit	5	1955	3130	489	274	12	12
Chicago	4	1713	3053	494	284	14	21
Atlanta	14	2101	3386	424	237	19	9
San Francisco	12	2544	4256	556	347	21	15
New Orleans	6	1325	3138	534	278	21	14
Carolina	4	1458	3322	507	292	19	17
St. Louis	4	1385	3087	556	314	16	15

Source: From *Jim Feist's Professional Football Annual.* Copyright © 1999 National Sports Services, Inc. Reprinted with permission.

FUMBOPP	RUSHOPP	PASSOPP	PATTOPP	PCOMPOPP	PIOPP
9	1659	3040	544	285	13
7	1511	2924	504	252	16
13	1493	3198	531	294	14
7	1547	3635	539	318	17
11	2570	3266	461	275	28
17	2000	3559	577	325	12
7	1610	3511	511	319	10
13	1642	3321	482	268	20
6	1705	3592	539	316	15
7	2612	3151	406	233	53
11	1287	3648	596	345	14
14	1674	2876	497	291	25
18	1999	3690	597	343	18
20	1869	2985	479	259	18
7	1140	3068	530	271	34
12	1619	3545	553	290	8
19	1989	3276	518	299	20
7	2004	3167	521	282	15
8	2436	2918	493	281	14
8	2416	2720	449	249	18
15	1614	3452	555	320	16
10	1442	3065	540	296	23
14	1583	3762	473	274	18
9	2102	3015	474	284	13
14	1875	3228	456	292	13
25	1203	3531	551	311	15
12	1610	3733	566	294	15
11	1700	3968	539	328	19
14	2133	3709	501	298	18
7	2049	2831	475	256	18

TABLE **4.13**   Data for Prime Rate Exercise

Date	Prime Rate	Date	Prime Rate	Date	Prime Rate	Date	Prime Rate
1/86	9.50	4/89	11.50	7/92	6.02	10/95	8.75
2/86	9.50	5/89	11.50	8/92	6.00	11/95	8.75
3/86	9.10	6/89	11.07	9/92	6.00	12/95	8.65
4/86	8.83	7/89	10.98	10/92	6.00	1/96	8.50
5/86	8.50	8/89	10.50	11/92	6.00	2/96	8.25
6/86	8.50	9/89	10.50	12/92	6.00	3/96	8.25
7/86	8.16	10/89	10.50	1/93	6.00	4/96	8.25
8/86	7.90	11/89	10.50	2/93	6.00	5/96	8.25
9/86	7.50	12/89	10.50	3/93	6.00	6/96	8.25
10/86	7.50	1/90	10.11	4/93	6.00	7/96	8.25
11/86	7.50	2/90	10.00	5/93	6.00	8/96	8.25
12/86	7.50	3/90	10.00	6/93	6.00	9/96	8.25
1/87	7.50	4/90	10.00	7/93	6.00	10/96	8.25
2/87	7.50	5/90	10.00	8/93	6.00	11/96	8.25
3/87	7.50	6/90	10.00	9/93	6.00	12/96	8.25
4/87	7.75	7/90	10.00	10/93	6.00	1/97	8.25
5/87	8.14	8/90	10.00	11/93	6.00	2/97	8.25
6/87	8.25	9/90	10.00	12/93	6.00	3/97	8.30
7/87	8.25	10/90	10.00	1/94	6.00	4/97	8.50
8/87	8.25	11/90	10.00	2/94	6.00	5/97	8.50
9/87	8.70	12/90	10.00	3/94	6.06	6/97	8.50
10/87	9.07	1/91	9.52	4/94	6.45	7/97	8.50
11/87	8.78	2/91	9.05	5/94	6.99	8/97	8.50
12/87	8.75	3/91	9.00	6/94	7.25	9/97	8.50
1/88	8.75	4/91	9.00	7/94	7.25	10/97	8.50
2/88	8.51	5/91	8.50	8/94	7.51	11/97	8.50
3/88	8.50	6/91	8.50	9/94	7.75	12/97	8.50
4/88	8.50	7/91	8.50	10/94	7.75	1/98	8.50
5/88	8.84	8/91	8.50	11/94	8.15	2/98	8.50
6/88	9.00	9/91	8.20	12/94	8.50	3/98	8.50
7/88	9.29	10/91	8.00	1/95	8.50	4/98	8.50
8/88	9.84	11/91	7.58	2/95	9.00	5/98	8.50
9/88	10.00	12/91	7.21	3/95	9.00	6/98	8.50
10/88	10.00	1/92	6.50	4/95	9.00	7/98	8.50
11/88	10.05	2/92	6.50	5/95	9.00	8/98	8.50
12/88	10.50	3/92	6.50	6/95	9.00	9/98	8.49
1/89	10.50	4/92	6.50	7/95	8.80	10/98	8.12
2/89	10.93	5/92	6.50	8/95	8.75	11/98	7.89
3/89	11.50	6/92	6.50	9/95	8.75	12/98	7.75

TABLE **4.14**   Absenteeism Study Variables

	Variable	Description
1.	Absenteeism (ABSENT)	The number of distinct occasions that the worker was absent during 1999. Each occasion consists of one or more consecutive days of absence.
2.	Job Classification (JOBCLAS)	An integer identifying the 29 different jobs included in the study: 1 = Foundry Molder 2 = Automatic Screw Machine Operator 3 = Aluminum Extrusion Inspector 4 = Warehouse Order Picker 5 = Heavy Hydraulic Press Operator etc.
3.	Job Complexity (COMPLX)	An index ranging from 0 to 100.
4.	Base Pay (PAY)	Base hourly pay rate in dollars.
5.	Supervisor Satisfaction (SATIS)	Determined by employee response to the question: "How satisfied are you with your supervisor?" 1 = Very dissatisfied 2 = Somewhat dissatisfied 3 = Neither satisfied or dissatisfied 4 = Fairly well satisfied 5 = Very satisfied
6.	Seniority (SENIOR)	Number of complete years with the company on December 31, 1999.
7.	Age (AGE)	Employee's age on December 31, 1999.
8.	Number of Dependents (DEPEND)	Determined by employee response to the question: "How many individuals other than yourself depend on you for most of their financial support?"

11   **Absenteeism**   The ABX Company is interested in conducting a study of the factors that affect absenteeism among its production employees. After reviewing the literature on absenteeism and interviewing several production supervisors and a number of employees, the researcher in charge of the project defined the variables shown in Table 4.14. Then a sample of 77 employees was randomly selected, and the data shown in Table 4.15 were collected. The dependent variable is absenteeism. The other seven variables are considered possible explanatory variables.

Use the procedures discussed in Chapters 3 and 4 to identify factors that may be related to absenteeism. Write down your final model and justify your choice of variables in the model. Check to see if your choice of variables and the coefficient estimates make intuitive sense. How much variation in absenteeism has been explained? What does this tell you? Does your model give you some sense of which employees might be absent most often? If so, which ones? What might be done to reduce absenteeism?

These data are available in a file with preifx ABSENT4 in the following order: ABSENT, JOBCLAS, COMPLX, PAY, SATIS, SENIOR, AGE, and DEPEND.

TABLE 4.15 Data for Absenteeism Exercise

Absenteeism	Job Classification	Job Complexity	Base Pay	Supervisor Satisfaction	Seniority	Age	Number of Dependents
0	14	45	5.86	4	3	28	2
1	22	76	7.74	4	10	42	1
0	21	56	5.08	1	9	40	5
2	22	76	7.74	3	7	34	2
0	9	70	7.92	3	14	39	2
1	7	69	6.31	3	9	44	0
1	21	56	5.78	4	3	40	1
1	21	56	4.70	4	1	35	0
2	19	43	6.99	1	9	32	0
1	22	76	5.63	3	1	41	1
3	11	30	5.02	2	1	27	1
2	15	50	6.88	4	9	40	0
1	17	10	4.80	4	1	30	1
3	7	69	6.48	2	4	35	0
2	12	67	7.61	3	3	33	1
0	7	69	6.44	1	4	32	1
4	9	70	7.34	2	8	37	1
7	1	13	6.17	2	1	26	2
3	25	16	7.87	3	3	36	2
2	8	52	7.39	1	5	28	2
2	8	52	6.87	1	16	40	1
4	24	3	6.04	2	2	26	0
2	18	6	5.38	3	4	38	2
0	12	67	8.42	3	6	33	1
3	17	10	4.66	3	1	26	0
3	6	89	9.51	3	18	48	0
3	23	21	4.83	2	2	34	1
0	28	34	6.27	3	4	26	1
2	4	12	8.46	4	6	40	2
3	9	70	6.71	2	2	34	2
1	7	69	6.39	3	11	49	2
4	1	13	5.77	2	1	35	1
2	11	30	6.38	4	13	51	5
1	19	43	5.19	2	1	25	1
3	5	8	6.40	2	2	29	0
2	3	69	7.03	2	2	34	2
4	11	30	4.84	4	1	36	2
4	16	23	4.81	2	1	31	2
4	25	16	6.57	4	1	28	2
3	26	11	5.64	3	1	32	2

TABLE 4.15 *(continued)*

Absenteeism	Job Classification	Job Complexity	Base Pay	Supervisor Satisfaction	Seniority	Age	Number of Dependents
2	25	16	5.89	3	1	30	2
6	15	50	6.24	1	2	30	2
3	15	50	5.61	3	2	28	0
1	3	69	6.79	3	4	31	4
2	17	10	5.53	3	2	34	1
1	19	43	6.86	3	26	54	1
1	4	12	5.93	4	1	28	0
3	22	76	7.20	2	5	28	2
2	21	56	5.22	3	2	35	2
0	18	6	5.88	3	8	43	4
0	5	8	6.78	5	3	29	4
1	14	45	5.37	4	2	32	3
3	19	43	5.84	3	5	31	3
6	16	23	4.64	3	1	26	1
3	27	1	7.18	5	7	46	1
2	10	82	7.58	3	1	23	1
2	27	1	5.94	3	1	20	0
4	27	1	5.84	5	1	35	3
3	9	70	7.80	3	4	32	2
0	22	76	7.00	3	6	34	0
0	10	82	9.47	3	7	38	0
1	15	50	6.21	3	9	33	2
1	9	70	8.56	3	8	45	1
1	2	81	6.60	3	5	27	1
2	9	70	7.61	3	9	33	4
3	27	1	7.35	4	2	30	3
2	5	8	5.51	5	1	32	2
2	16	23	5.27	4	2	24	3
2	23	21	5.67	4	12	47	4
2	20	82	8.54	3	7	33	5
1	12	67	8.82	4	28	54	3
0	2	81	7.00	3	18	45	2
1	19	43	7.50	3	6	40	0
4	18	6	5.58	3	3	21	1
3	1	13	7.44	2	8	29	4
2	8	52	7.24	1	7	31	1
3	8	52	5.26	3	1	27	1

Source: These data were created by Dr. Roger L. Wright, RLW Analytics, Inc., Sonoma, CA, and are used (with modification) with his permission.

TABLE **4.16**   Data for Pricing Communications Nodes Exercise

Cost	Number of Ports	Bandwidth	Port Speed
52,388	68	58	653
51,761	52	179	499
50,221	44	123	422
36,095	32	38	307
27,500	16	29	154
57,088	56	141	538
54,475	56	141	538
33,969	28	48	269
31,309	24	29	230
23,444	24	10	230
24,269	12	56	115
53,479	52	131	499
33,543	20	38	192
33,056	24	29	230

Note: These data have been modified as requested by the company to provide confidentiality.

12   Pricing Communications Nodes   Refer to Chapter 3, Examples 3.3 and 3.6, on communications nodes. The cost of adding a new communications node at a location not currently included on the network was of concern to a major Fort Worth manufacturing company. To try to predict the price of new communications nodes, data were obtained on a sample of existing nodes. The installation cost and the number of ports available for access in each existing node were readily available. Data on two additional characteristics of communications nodes were also obtained: bandwidth and port speed. These data are shown in Table 4.16.

The network administrator wants to develop a method of estimating the cost of new nodes in a quick and fairly accurate manner. You have been asked to help in this project. Using the data available, develop an equation to help in the pricing of new communications nodes. Justify your choice of equation.

The data are available in a file with prefix COMNODE4 in four columns: COST, NUMPORTS, BANWIDTH, and PORTSPEED.

13   Fanfare   Fanfare International, Inc. designs, distributes, and markets ceiling fans and lighting fixtures. The company's product line includes 120 basic models of ceiling fans and 138 compatible fan light kits and table lamps. These products are marketed to over 1000 lighting showrooms and electrical wholesalers that supply the remodeling and new construction markets. The product line is distributed by a sales organization of 58 independent sales representatives.

In the summer of 1994, Fanfare decided they needed to develop forecasts of future sales to help determine future sales force needs, capital expenditures, and so on. In Chapter 3, Table 3.18 provided the monthly sales data and data on three additional variables for the period July 1990 through May 1994. The variables are defined as follows:

sales = total monthly sales in thousands of dollars

ad ex = advertising expense in thousands of dollars

mtg rate = mortgage rate for 30-year loans (%)

hs starts = housing starts in thousands of units

As a consultant to Fanfare, your job is to find a causal regression model to forecast future sales. Use the techniques discussed in Chapters 3 and 4 to help you decide which variables you should include in the equation and which should be omitted. Justify your choices. How well do you believe the equation you developed will do at forecasting future sales? What additional analyses might you use to examine forecasting ability?

Now use the techniques discussed in Chapters 3 and 4 to build an extrapolative model to forecast sales. Generate forecasts from both the causal model and the extrapolative model. What are the benefits and drawbacks of each of the models? How could you compare the forecasting ability of the two models?

The data are in a file with prefix FAN4 in this order: sales, ad ex, mtg rate, hs starts.

CHAPTER 5

Fitting Curves to Data

5.1 INTRODUCTION

In Chapter 4, the multiple linear regression model was presented as

$$y = \beta_0 + \beta_1 x_1 + \beta_2 x_2 + \cdots + \beta_K x_K + e \tag{5.1}$$

There we assumed that the true relationship was linear in the x variables. In this chapter, we find that this assumption need not be true to fit a regression equation to the data. We can fit *curvilinear* as well as linear relationships. This is accomplished through transformations of the variables in the model. The equation $y = \beta_0 + \beta_1 x + e$ represents a straight-line relationship between y and x. But the equation $y = \beta_0 + \beta_1 x + \beta_2 x^2 + e$ represents a curve (a parabola). The same x variable is involved in the equation; the fitting of the curve is accomplished through the transformation of the x variable to x^2. There are many possible transformations that produce some type of curvilinear relationship. The most commonly used transformations in business and economic applications are discussed in this chapter.

TABLE **5.1**   Data for Telemarketing Example

Months of Employment	Calls Placed per Day	Months of Employment	Calls Placed per Day
10	18	22	33
10	19	22	32
11	22	24	31
14	23	25	32
15	25	25	32
17	28	25	33
18	29	25	31
20	29	28	33
20	29	29	33
21	31	30	34

5.2 FITTING A CURVILINEAR RELATIONSHIP

EXAMPLE **5.1**   Telemarketing

A company that sells transportation services uses a telemarketing division to help sell its services. The division manager is interested in the time spent on the phone by the telemarketers in the division. Data on the number of months of employment and the number of calls placed per day (an average for 20 working days) is recorded for 20 employees. These data are shown in Table 5.1.

The average number of calls for all 20 employees is 28.95. The division manager, however, suspects that there may be a relationship between time on the job and number of calls. As time on the job increases, the employee becomes more familiar with the calling system and the correct procedures to use on the phone and also begins to acquire more regular clients. Thus, the longer the time on the job, the greater the number of calls per day. The scatterplot of CALLS (y) versus MONTHS (x) is shown in Figure 5.1. Looking at this scatterplot helps to verify that the relationship may not be linear. As the number of months on the job increases, the number of calls also increases. But the rate of increase begins to slow over time, thus resulting in a pattern that may be better modeled by a curve than a straight line.

In Figure 5.2, the plot of y versus x has been reproduced with a curve approximating the relationship between the two variables drawn in.

FIGURE **5.1** MINITAB Scatterplot of CALLS versus MONTHS

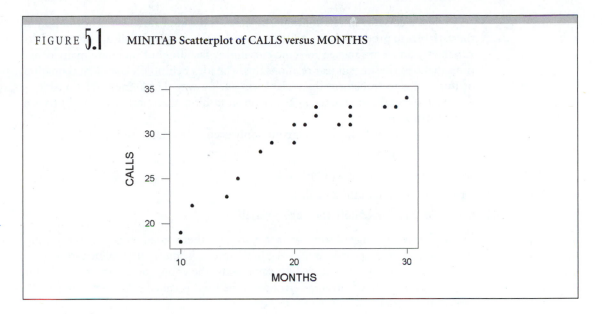

FIGURE **5.2** Scatterplot for Telemarketing Example with Curve Drawn to Represent the Relationship Between CALLS and MONTHS

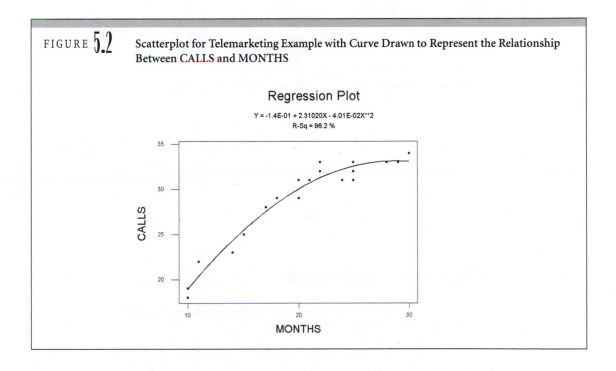

Regression Plot

$Y = -1.4E\text{-}01 + 2.31020X - 4.01E\text{-}02X^{**}2$

R-Sq = 96.2 %

When a curvilinear relationship is suspected, the appropriate transformation of the variables to produce the best-fitting curve for the data is not always obvious. The variables y and x are related in some curvilinear fashion, but there are many equations that describe curvilinear relationships. The idea behind the use of any equation of this sort is to transform the variables in such a way that a linear relationship is achieved. If x and y are related in a curvilinear fashion, then perhaps x^2 and y have a linear relationship.

In this text, the following four commonly used corrections are considered:

1 polynomial regression

2 reciprocal transformation of the x variable

3 log transformation of the x variable

4 log transformation of both the x and y variables

In this chapter, we suggest some ways to assess whether a good choice of transformations was used to fit a curve to the data. In Chapter 6, some additional methods of assessing the choice are considered. In some texts, the choice of linear or curvilinear model and the type of curvilinear model to be used is called selection of *functional form* of the model.

5.2.1 Polynomial Regression

A common correction when the linearity assumption is violated is to add powers of the explanatory variable that is viewed as the curvilinear component of the model. This type of model is called a *polynomial regression*. The *order* of the model is the highest power used for the explanatory variable. For example, a second-order polynomial regression in one variable is written as

$$y = \beta_0 + \beta_1 x + \beta_2 x^2 + e$$

Higher-order polynomial models may be developed by adding higher powers of x. A Kth-order polynomial regression model in one variable, x, is written as

$$y = \beta_0 + \beta_1 x + \beta_2 x^2 + \cdots + \beta_K x^K + e$$

In practice, the second-order model is often sufficient to describe curvilinear relationships encountered.

EXAMPLE 5.2 **Telemarketing (continued)**

To model the curvilinear relationship in the telemarketing data, a second-order polynomial regression can be tried. The model can be written

$$\text{CALLS} = \beta_0 + \beta_1 \text{MONTHS} + \beta_2 \text{XSQR} + e$$

where XSQR is a variable created by squaring each value of the MONTHS variable.

For comparison purposes, the MINITAB and Excel linear regressions using CALLS as the dependent variable and MONTHS as the explanatory variable are shown in Figures 5.3 and 5.4,

FIGURE 5.3   MINITAB Regression Output for Telemarketing Example Using Only MONTHS as an Explanatory Variable

```
The regression equation is
CALLS = 13.7 + 0.744 MONTHS

Predictor        Coef        StDev           T         P
Constant       13.671        1.427        9.58     0.000
MONTHS        0.74351      0.06666       11.15     0.000

S = 1.787       R-Sq = 87.4%       R-Sq(adj) = 86.7%

Analysis of Variance

Source            DF          SS          MS         F         P
Regression         1       397.45      397.45    124.41     0.000
Residual Error    18        57.50        3.19
Total             19       454.95
```

FIGURE 5.4   Excel Regression Output for Telemarketing Example Using Only MONTHS as an Explanatory Variable

```
                          SUMMARY OUTPUT

Regression Statistics
Multiple R            0.935
R Square              0.874
Adjusted R Square     0.867
Standard Error        1.787
Observations         20.000

ANOVA
                    df            SS           MS         F     Significance F
Regression       1.000       397.446      397.446   124.409           0.0000
Residual        18.000        57.504        3.195
Total           19.000       454.950

                                 Standard
                  Coefficients      Error   t Stat   P-value   Lower 95%   Upper 95%
Intercept           13.671         1.427    9.580    0.0000      10.673      16.669
MONTHS               0.744         0.067   11.154    0.0000       0.603       0.884
```

FIGURE 5.5   MINITAB Regression Output for Telemarketing Example with Second-Order Term Added

```
The regression equation is
CALLS = - 0.14 + 2.31 MONTHS - 0.0401 XSQR

Predictor          Coef        StDev            T        P
Constant         -0.140        2.323        -0.06    0.952
MONTHS           2.3102        0.2501         9.24    0.000
XSQR          -0.040118        0.006333      -6.33    0.000

S = 1.003        R-Sq = 96.2%        R-Sq(adj) = 95.8%

Analysis of Variance

Source               DF            SS           MS          F        P
Regression            2        437.84       218.92     217.50    0.000
Residual Error       17         17.11         1.01
Total                19        454.95

Source        DF        Seq SS
MONTHS         1        397.45
XSQR           1         40.39
```

respectively. Figures 5.5 and 5.6 show the MINITAB and Excel regression estimates of the second-order model. The estimated regression is

$$CALLS = -0.14 + 2.31 MONTHS - 0.04 XSQR$$

The primary check that should be made at this point to determine whether the second-order model is preferred to the original linear model is to test whether the coefficient of the second-order term is significantly different from zero.

To determine whether the x^2 variable has significantly improved the fit of the regression, the following hypotheses can be tested:

H_0: $\beta_2 = 0$

H_a: $\beta_2 \neq 0$

where β_2 is the coefficient of x^2. The t test discussed in Chapter 4 for multiple regression can be used to conduct the test. For $\alpha = 0.05$, the decision rule is:

Reject H_0 if $t > 2.11$ or $t < -2.11$

Accept H_0 if $-2.11 \leq t \leq 2.11$

FIGURE 5.6   **Excel Regression Output for Telemarketing Example with Second-Order Term Added**

SUMMARY OUTPUT

Regression Statistics
Multiple R	0.981
R Square	0.962
Adjusted R Square	0.958
Standard Error	1.003
Observations	20.000

ANOVA

	df	SS	MS	F	Significance F
Regression	2.000	437.839	218.920	217.503	0.0000
Residual	17.000	17.111	1.007		
Total	19.000	454.950			

	Coefficients	Standard Error	t Stat	P-value	Lower 95%	Upper 95%
Intercept	−0.140	2.323	−0.060	0.9525	−5.041	4.760
MONTHS	2.310	0.250	9.236	0.0000	1.782	2.838
XSQR	−0.040	0.006	−6.335	0.0000	−0.053	−0.027

The test statistic value is (see Figure 5.5 or 5.6)

$$t = -6.33.$$

The null hypothesis is rejected. The x^2 term adds significantly to the ability of the regression to explain the variation in y. Thus, the term should remain in the equation. Note that the p value could also have been used to conduct this test (p value $= 0.000 < 0.05$, so reject H_0).

Once a decision is made to keep the second-order term in the model, the lower-order term is typically kept in the model regardless of the t test result on its coefficient. There are good statistical reasons for keeping lower-order terms in a polynomial regression when the higher-order terms are judged important (see "A Property of Well-Formulated Polynomial Regression Models," by J.L. Peixoto).[1] Other indicators that the regression has been improved by adding the x^2 term include the reduction in the standard error of the regression from 1.787 to 1.003 and the increase in adjusted R^2 from 86.7% to 95.8%.

In our example, the second-order model is an improvement over the first-order model. Higher-order terms could be added to the model to see whether additional improvements are possible. Figure 5.7 shows the MINITAB estimate of a third-order model. The explanatory variables are MONTHS, XSQR, the square of the MONTHS variable, and X^3, the cube (third power)

---

[1] See References for complete publication information.

FIGURE 5.7   MINITAB Regression Output for Telemarketing Example with Second-Order and Third-Order Terms Added

```
The regression equation is
CALLS = - 5.58 + 3.26 MONTHS - 0.0907 XSQR + 0.00085 X^3

Predictor          Coef        StDev          T          P
Constant         -5.580        8.387      -0.67      0.515
MONTHS            3.258        1.425       2.29      0.036
XSQR           -0.09075      0.07518      -1.21      0.245
X^3            0.000847     0.001253       0.68      0.509

S = 1.020       R-Sq = 96.3%       R-Sq(adj) = 95.7%

Analysis of Variance

Source               DF          SS         MS         F          P
Regression            3      438.31     146.10     140.52      0.000
Residual Error       16       16.64       1.04
Total                19      454.95

Source          DF      Seq SS
MONTHS           1      397.45
XSQR             1       40.39
X^3              1        0.47
```

of the MONTHS variable. Note that the coefficient of the X^3 variable is not significant at the 0.05 level suggesting that the addition of this term is of little additional help in explaining the variation in CALLS. The third-order term is unnecessary in the model.

Table 5.2 summarizes the different measures that may be useful in determining the best model to use. The p values suggest that the second-order term is useful, but the third-order term is not. The R^2 increases from 86.7% for the linear model to 95.8% for the second-order model. The increase for the third-order model is very small, however. If R^2_{adj} is used, there is actually a decrease from the second-order to the third-order model. This is further verification that the third-order term is unnecessary. This is also reflected in the standard error, which decreases from 1.787 for the linear model to 1.003 for the second-order model but increases to 1.020 for the third-order model. (Recall that we want increases in R^2 and R^2_{adj}, but decreases in the standard error.)

TABLE 5.2   Summary Measures for Linear, Second-Order, and Third-Order Models
for Telemarketing Example

Model	p Value for Highest-Order Term	R^2	R^2_{adj}	s_e
Linear Model	0.000	87.4%	86.7%	1.787
Second-Order Model	**0.000**	96.2%	**95.8%**	**1.003**
Third-Order Model	0.509	96.3%	95.7%	1.020

One caution should be observed in using higher-order polynomial regression models. Correlations between powers of a variable can cause computational problems for least-squares. These correlations result in a problem called *multicollinearity*, which we discuss in more detail in Chapter 6. To reduce the possibility of computational difficulties, the use of explanatory variables which have been centered often is recommended. For example, instead of using the explanatory variables, x, x^2, x^3, use instead

$$x - \bar{x}, (x - \bar{x})^2, \text{ and } (x - \bar{x})^3$$

where $\bar{x}$ is the sample mean of the variable values. Using the centered variables helps avoid multicollinearity problems in polynomial regressions to some extent.

Choosing which curvilinear model to use in a particular case is not always a simple matter. In the telemarketing example, I chose to use a second-order polynomial regression as my starting point. Why not use the logarithm of the x variable instead? This is another of the transformations to be discussed in this chapter. Familiarity with the look of certain curves can be helpful in choosing the right curvilinear model. The curve shown in Figure 5.2 is similar to a parabola (or half of a parabola, at any rate), and this led me to make the second-order model my first choice (since the second-order equation is the equation of a parabola). If you are not sure about what type of transformation is best, you can always try different ones and check the summary measures used in the example to help make the choice. Chapter 6 also presents some additional methods of assessing the validity of a curvilinear model and choosing the best transformation.

5.2.2 Reciprocal Transformation of the x Variable

Other transformations may produce a linear relationship. A fairly common example is the reciprocal transformation:

$$y = \beta_0 + \beta_1 \left(\frac{1}{x} \right) + e$$

In this equation, x and y are inversely related, but the inverse relationship is not a linear one. (Note that this transformation is not defined when $x = 0$.)

EXAMPLE **5.3** **MPG Versus WEIGHT**

A scatterplot of a possible curvilinear inverse relationship is shown in Figure 5.8. The variables are CITYMPG (y), which is the number of miles per gallon obtained by a car in city driving, and WEIGHT (x), the weight of the car in pounds. This information is available for 138 cars listed in *Road and Track's The Complete '99 Car Buyer's Guide.* (The complete data set is listed in Table 8.3.)

As WEIGHT increases, the mileage decreases, as would be expected. However, it appears that the rate of decrease may be slower as the cars get heavier. The MINITAB regression output for the linear regression of CITYMPG on WEIGHT is shown in Figure 5.9 and the Excel output is in Figure 5.10. Can we find a curvilinear model that better describes the relationship between these two variables? The scatterplot suggests that the following curvilinear inverse relationship might be appropriate:

$$\text{CITYMPG} = \beta_0 + \beta_1 \left(\frac{1}{\text{WEIGHT}} \right) + e$$

An inverse relationship is one where y decreases as x increases. In a linear model, an inverse relationship results in a negative slope coefficient. If a relationship is expected to be inverse but curvilinear, then the reciprocal transformation of the x variable is often useful in representing this relationship.

Figure 5.11 shows the scatterplot of CITYMPG versus the transformed explanatory variable 1/WEIGHT (named WTINV).[2] This scatterplot appears linear. The regression output for the regression of CITYMPG on WTINV is shown in Figure 5.12 for MINITAB and in Figure 5.13 for Excel.

FIGURE **5.8** **MINITAB Scatterplot of CITYMPG Versus WEIGHT**

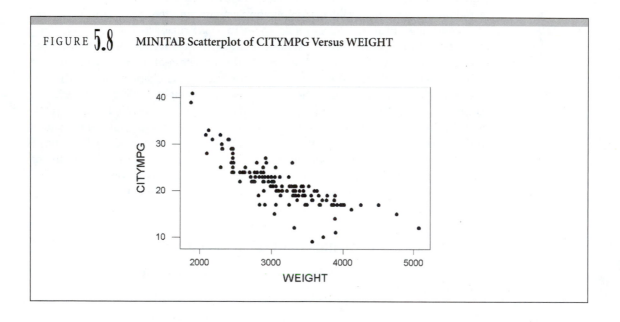

---

[2] A graphical method to see if a transformation might be effective in modeling a curvilinear relationship is to plot the dependent variable versus the transformed x variable, as was done in this example. If the resulting graph looks linear, the transformation likely gives a good result. Note that this was not done in the first example using the second-order model. Since this model has two terms (x and x^2), examining the transformation graphically is more difficult.

FIGURE **5.9**   **MINITAB Output for Regression of CITYMPG on WEIGHT**

```
The regression equation is
CITYMPG = 43.5 - 0.00700 WEIGHT


Predictor          Coef        StDev           T          P
Constant         43.505        1.327       32.78      0.000
WEIGHT       -0.0070044    0.0004124      -16.99      0.000


S = 2.852        R-Sq = 68.0%        R-Sq(adj) = 67.7%

Analysis of Variance


Source              DF           SS           MS          F          P
Regression           1       2346.8       2346.8     288.51      0.000
Residual Error     136       1106.2          8.1
Total              137       3453.0


Unusual Observations
Obs      WEIGHT    CITYMPG          Fit    StDev Fit      Residual     St Resid
 10        5070     12.000        7.992        0.822         4.008       1.47 X
 30        1895     41.000       30.231        0.577        10.769       3.86R
 46        3319     12.000       20.257        0.251        -8.257      -2.91R
 49        3725     10.000       17.413        0.335        -7.413      -2.62R
 69        3575      9.000       18.464        0.296        -9.464      -3.34R
 77        3043     15.000       22.190        0.248        -7.190      -2.53R
 83        4760     15.000       10.164        0.701         4.836       1.75 X
 86        4506     17.000       11.943        0.604         5.057       1.81 X
109        2838     17.000       23.626        0.278        -6.626      -2.33R
115        2910     17.000       23.122        0.264        -6.122      -2.16R
117        5075     12.000        7.957        0.824         4.043       1.48 X
125        1878     39.000       30.351        0.583         8.649       3.10R


R denotes an observation with a large standardized residual
X denotes an observation whose X value gives it large influence.
```

FIGURE **5.10**   Excel Output for Regression of CITYMPG on WEIGHT

SUMMARY OUTPUT

Regression Statistics

Multiple R	0.8244
R Square	0.6796
Adjusted R Square	0.6773
Standard Error	2.8520
Observations	138.000

ANOVA

	df	SS	MS	F	Significance F
Regression	1.000	2346.7606	2346.7606	288.5103	0.0000
Residual	136.000	1106.2322	8.1341		
Total	137.000	3452.9928			

	Coefficients	Standard Error	t Stat	P-value	Lower 95%	Upper 95%
Intercept	43.5049	1.3273	32.7774	0.0000	40.8801	46.1297
WEIGHT	−0.0070	0.000	−16.9856	0.0000	−0.0078	−0.0062

FIGURE **5.11**   MINITAB Scatterplot of CITYMPG Versus WTINV = 1./WEIGHT

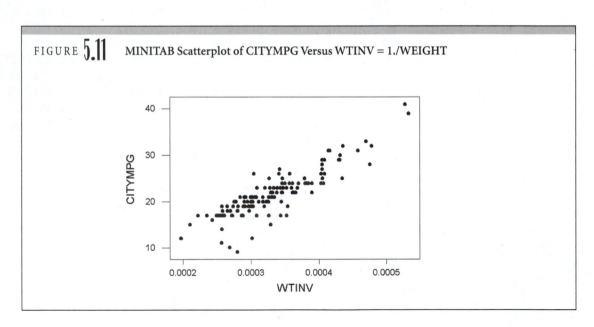

FIGURE **5.12**   MINITAB Output for Regression of CITYMPG on WTINV = 1./WEIGHT

```
The regression equation is
CITYMPG = - 1.62 + 70147 WTINV

Predictor         Coef       StDev          T         P
Constant        -1.616       1.087      -1.49     0.139
WTINV            70147        3262       21.51     0.000

S = 2.402       R-Sq = 77.3%        R-Sq(adj) = 77.1%

Analysis of Variance

Source            DF          SS          MS         F         P
Regression         1       2668.4      2668.4    462.55     0.000
Residual Error   136        784.6         5.8
Total            137       3453.0

Unusual Observations
Obs      WTINV     CITYMPG        Fit   StDev Fit     Residual      St Resid
 30   0.000528      41.000     35.401      0.685        5.599        2.43RX
 46   0.000301      12.000     19.519      0.221       -7.519       -3.14R
 47   0.000304      26.000     19.705      0.218        6.295        2.63R
 48   0.000256      11.000     16.370      0.309       -5.370       -2.25R
 49   0.000268      10.000     17.215      0.280       -7.215       -3.02R
 59   0.000476      28.000     31.771      0.526       -3.771       -1.61 X
 69   0.000280       9.000     18.005      0.257       -9.005       -3.77R
 77   0.000329      15.000     21.436      0.205       -6.436       -2.69R
 97   0.000470      33.000     31.363      0.509        1.637        0.70 X
109   0.000352      17.000     23.101      0.220       -6.101       -2.55R
115   0.000344      17.000     22.489      0.211       -5.489       -2.29R
125   0.000532      39.000     35.736      0.700        3.264        1.42 X
131   0.000478      32.000     31.947      0.534        0.053        0.02 X

R denotes an observation with a large standardized residual
X denotes an observation whose X value gives it large influence.
```

FIGURE 5.13   **Excel Output for Regression of CITYMPG on WTINV = 1./WEIGHT**

```
                            SUMMARY OUTPUT

Regression Statistics
Multiple R              0.8791
R Square                0.7728
Adjusted R Square       0.7711
Standard Error          2.4019
Observations          138.000


ANOVA
                df          SS           MS          F       Significance F
Regression    1.000     2668.4129    2668.4129   462.5458        0.0000
Residual    136.000      784.5799       5.7690
Total       137.000     3452.9928


                         Standard
            Coefficients   Error    t Stat   P-value    Lower 95%   Upper 95%
Intercep      -1.6164     1.0868   -1.4872   0.1393      -3.7656     0.5329
WTINV      70147.2366  3261.6186   21.5069   0.0000   63697.1907  76597.2825
```

TABLE 5.3   **Summary Measures for the Linear Model and the Model Using the Reciprocal of Weight for MPG Versus WEIGHT Example**

Model	p Value for Highest-Order Term	R^2	R^2_{adj}	s_e
Linear Model	0.000	68.0%	67.7%	2.852
Reciprocal Model	0.000	**77.3%**	**77.1%**	**2.402**

The R^2 value has increased from 68.0% for the linear model to 77.3% for the model with the transformed x variable. The standard error of the regression has decreased from 2.852 to 2.402. Both of these facts support the use of the curvilinear model. Table 5.3 summarizes the statistics for the two models.

5.2.3 Log Transformation of the x Variable

Another useful curvilinear equation is

$$y = \beta_0 + \beta_1 \ln(x) + e$$

where $\ln(x)$ is the natural logarithm of x. It is assumed here that the x values are positive, because $\ln(x)$ is not defined for $x \leq 0$.

EXAMPLE 5.4   **Fuel Consumption**

Table 5.4 shows the fuel consumption (FUELCON) in gallons per capita for each of the 50 states and Washington, DC. The following variables are also shown: the population of the state (POP), the area of the state in square miles (AREA), and the population density (DENSITY) defined as population/area. The object is to develop a regression equation to predict fuel consumption based on the population density. FUELCON is the dependent variable and DENSITY is the explanatory variable. The MINITAB scatterplot of FUELCON versus DENSITY is shown in Figure 5.14. Looking at the scatterplot of FUELCON versus DENSITY, it is clear that this is not a linear relationship. One thing to note about this plot is how the values spread out on the x axis. At the left-hand side of the x axis, the values are clumped together. Moving from left to right, the values become progressively more spread out. This suggests the use of a log transformation of DENSITY. The log transformation puts values on a different scale which compresses large distances so that they are more comparable to smaller distances. Table 5.5 shows the effect of applying the log to the base 10 to a series of numbers. (If we let q represent the log to the base 10 of a number x, then q is defined as the value that makes the following equation true: $10^q = x$. If we use log to the base 2, then the defining equation becomes $2^q = x$.) Note that the values of x in the table are successively more and more spread out; the distances between the values are becoming greater. The $\log_{10}(x)$ values do not exhibit this tendency. The log transformation evens out the successively larger distances between the values.

The scatterplot of FUELCON versus the log of DENSITY (LOGDENS) is shown in Figure 5.15. The natural log of DENSITY is used. The natural log uses the number called e (e is approximately equal to 2.717) as its base. It is common in business and economic applications to use natural logarithms, although the base used is usually not important. The relationship in Figure 5.15 appears to be linear. Fitting a line to the values in Figure 5.15 makes much more sense than trying to fit a line to the values in Figure 5.14. The log transformation is a good choice.

Figures 5.16 and 5.17 show, respectively, the MINITAB and Excel linear regression results for the regression of FUELCON on DENSITY. These are used for comparison purposes. The regressions using the natural log of DENSITY as the explanatory variable are shown in Figures 5.18 and 5.19. The regression results indicate that using LOGDENS as the explanatory variable produces a much better model fit than the regression using DENSITY. Table 5.6 provides summary statistics for the two models.

TABLE 5.4   Data for Fuel Consumption Example

STATE	FUELCON	POP	AREA	DENSITY	STATE	FUELCON	POP	AREA	DENSITY
Alabama	515.86	4136000	50750	81.50	Nebraska	470.74	1606000	76878	20.89
Alaska	422.15	587000	570374	1.03	Nevada	506.41	1327000	109806	12.08
Arizona	455.95	3832000	113642	33.72	New Hampshire	457.43	1111000	8969	123.87
Arkansas	514.71	2399000	52075	46.07	New Jersey	413.58	7789000	7419	1049.87
California	429.57	30867000	155973	197.90	New Mexico	515.37	1581000	121364	13.03
Colorado	433.31	3470000	103729	33.45	New York	299.26	18119000	47224	383.68
Connecticut	417.31	3281000	4845	677.19	North Carolina	473.83	6843000	48718	140.46
Delaware	499.86	689000	1955	352.43	North Dakota	541.51	636000	68994	9.22
Florida	445.91	13488000	53997	249.79	Ohio	421.88	11016000	40953	268.99
Georgia	521.97	6751000	57919	116.56	Oklahoma	521.73	3212000	68679	46.77
Hawaii	322.24	1160000	6423	180.60	Oregon	450.05	2977000	96002	31.01
Idaho	468.42	1067000	82751	12.89	Pennsylvania	375.62	12009000	44820	267.94
Illinois	383.85	11631000	55593	209.22	Rhode Island	367.76	1005000	1045	961.72
Indiana	459.91	5662000	35870	157.85	South Carolina	502.42	3603000	30111	119.66
Iowa	473.47	2812000	55875	50.33	South Dakota	549.37	711000	75896	9.37
Kansas	462.78	2523000	81823	30.83	Tennessee	489.89	5024000	41219	121.89
Kentucky	495.50	3755000	39732	94.51	Texas	477.42	17656000	261914	67.41
Louisiana	441.85	4287000	43566	98.40	Utah	414.67	1813000	82168	22.06
Maine	479.51	1235000	30865	40.01	Vermont	508.42	570000	9249	61.63
Maryland	420.17	4908000	9775	502.10	Virginia	471.57	6377000	39598	161.04
Massachusetts	387.93	5998000	7838	765.25	Washington	451.40	5136000	66581	77.14
Michigan	451.29	9437000	56809	166.12	West Virginia	461.26	1812000	24087	75.23
Minnesota	465.94	4480000	79617	56.27	Wisconsin	421.93	5007000	54314	92.19
Mississippi	490.05	2614000	46914	55.72	Wyoming	666.95	466000	97105	4.80
Missouri	528.13	5193000	68898	75.37	Washington, D.C.	285.23	589000	61	9655.74
Montana	545.39	824000	145556	5.66					

Source: Federal Highway Administration: Office of Highway Information Management.

TABLE 5.5   Effect of Applying Log to the Base 10 to a Set of Numbers

x	10	100	1000	10000
$\log_{10}(x)$	1	2	3	4

FIGURE **5.14**   MINITAB Scatterplot of FUELCON Versus DENSITY

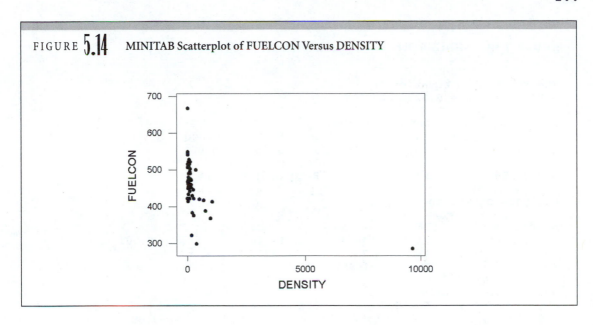

FIGURE **5.15**   MINITAB Scatterplot of FUELCON Versus LOGDENS

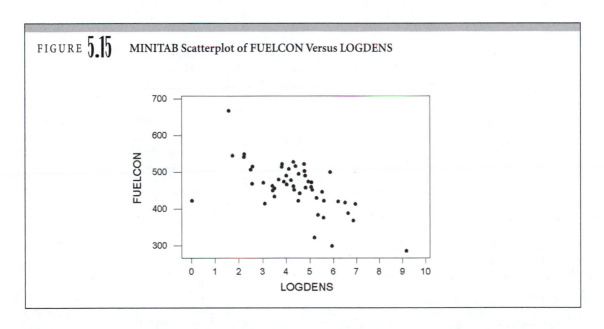

FIGURE 5.16 MINITAB Output for Regression of FUELCON on DENSITY

```
The regression equation is
FUELCON = 468 - 0.0222 DENSITY

Predictor          Coef       StDev           T        P
Constant        467.636       8.542       54.75    0.000
DENSITY       -0.022153    0.006181       -3.58    0.001

S = 58.96       R-Sq = 20.8%       R-Sq(adj) = 19.2%

Analysis of Variance

Source             DF          SS          MS        F        P
Regression          1       44646       44646       84    0.001
Residual Error     49      170312        3476
Total              50      214957

Unusual Observations
Obs     DENSITY     FUELCON        Fit   StDev Fit    Residual    St Resid
 30         384      299.26     459.14        8.27     -159.88      -2.74R
 48           5      666.95     467.53        8.53      199.42       3.42R
 49        9656      285.23     253.73       58.03       31.50       3.11RX
 50         181      322.24     463.64        8.33     -141.40      -2.42R

R denotes an observation with a large standardized residual
X denotes an observation whose X value gives it large influence.
```

FIGURE 5.17 Excel Output for Regression of FUELCON on DENSITY

```
                        SUMMARY OUTPUT

Regression Statistics
Multiple R             0.456
R Square               0.208
Adjusted R Square      0.192
Standard Error        58.955
Observations          51.000

ANOVA
                    df           SS           MS         F    Significance F
Regression       1.000    44645.897    44645.897    12.845            0.001
Residual        49.000   170311.549     3475.746
Total           50.000   214957.446

                                Standard
                  Coefficients     Error    t Stat   P-value   Lower 95%   Upper 95%
Intercept           467.636        8.542    54.748     0.000     450.471     484.801
DENSITY              -0.022        0.006    -3.584     0.001      -0.035      -0.010
```

FIGURE **5.18**   MINITAB Output for Regression of FUELCON on LOGDENS

```
The regression equation is
FUELCON = 576 - 26.3 LOGDENS

Predictor        Coef       StDev          T       P
Constant        575.59      21.43       26.86    0.000
LOGDENS         -26.339      4.593       -5.73    0.000

S = 51.24        R-Sq = 40.2%      R-Sq(adj) = 38.9%

Analysis of Variance

Source            DF          SS          MS        F        P
Regression         1        86325       86325     32.88    0.000
Residual Error    49       128632        2625
Total             50       214957

Unusual Observations
Obs    LOGDENS    FUELCON        Fit    StDev Fit    Residual    St Resid
  2       0.03     422.15     574.81       21.30     -152.66      -3.28RX
 31       5.95     299.26     418.88       10.12     -119.62      -2.38R
 49       1.57     666.95     534.27       14.84      132.68       2.71R
 50       9.18     285.23     333.92       23.09      -48.69      -1.06 X
 51       5.20     322.24     438.72        8.06     -116.48      -2.30R

R denotes an observation with a large standardized residual
X denotes an observation whose X value gives it large influence.
```

FIGURE **5.19**   Excel Output for Regression of FUELCON on LOGDENS

SUMMARY OUTPUT

```
Regression Statistics
Multiple R              0.634
R Square                0.402
Adjusted R Square       0.389
Standard Error         51.236
Observations           51.000
```

ANOVA

	df	SS	MS	F	Significance F
Regression	1.000	86325.392	86325.392	32.884	0.000
Residual	49.000	128632.054	2625.144		
Total	50.000	214957.446			

	Coefficients	Standard Error	t Stat	P-value	Lower 95%	Upper 95%
Intercept	575.587	21.432	26.857	0.000	532.518	618.655
LOGDENS	-26.339	4.593	-5.734	0.000	-35.569	17.109

TABLE 5.6   **Summary Measures for the Linear Model and the Model Using LOGDENS for Fuel Consumption Example**

Model	p Value for Highest-Order Term	R^2	R^2_{adj}	s_e
Linear Model	0.001	20.8%	19.2%	58.96
Log x Model	0.000	**40.2%**	**38.9%**	**51.24**

5.2.4   Log Transformation of Both the x and y Variables

It is also possible to transform the y variable in attempting to achieve a linear relationship. The natural logarithm of y is often used as the dependent variable with the natural logarithm of x as the explanatory variable:

$$\ln(y) = \beta_0 + \beta_1 \ln(x) + e$$

Some caution must be exercised if this model is chosen. First, all x and y values must be positive for the natural log transformation to be defined. Second, because $\ln(y)$ is used as the dependent variable, it becomes more difficult to compare this regression to any model using y as the dependent variable. The R^2 values of the two regressions cannot be compared, for example, because two different units of measurement are used for the dependent variable. (This applies as well to adjusted R-square and the standard error.) Thus, increases in R^2 when the natural logarithm transformation is applied to y do not necessarily suggest an improved model. (Note that transformations of the explanatory variables do not create this type of problem. It is only when the y variable is transformed that comparison becomes more difficult.)

EXAMPLE 5.5   **Imports and GDP**

The gross domestic product (GDP) and dollar amount of total imports (IMPORTS), both in billions of dollars for 25 countries are shown in Table 5.7. These data were obtained from The World Fact Book 1998 at www.odci.gov/cia/publications/factbook/index.html. The objective is to find an equation showing the relationship between IMPORTS (y) and GDP (x). The scatterplot of IMPORTS versus GDP in Figure 5.20 shows that this is not a linear relationship. One thing to note about this plot is how the values spread out on the x and y axes. At the left-hand side of the x axis and the bottom of the y axis, the values are clumped together. Moving from left to right on the x axis, the values become more spread out. The same thing happens when moving up the y axis. The values become progressively more spread out. This suggests the use of a log transformation for both the x and y variables. The motivation for using the log transformation is the same as in the Fuel Consumption Example, but the transformation needs to be applied to both the x and y variables.

TABLE 5.7   Data for Imports and GDP Example

Country	IMPORTS	GDP	Country	IMPORTS	GDP
Argentina	30.30	348.20	Israel	28.60	96.70
Australia	67.00	394.00	Jamaica	2.90	9.50
Bolivia	1.70	23.10	Japan	339.00	3080.00
Brazil	61.40	1040.00	Liberia	5.80	2.60
Canada	194.40	658.00	Malaysia	78.40	227.00
Cuba	3.20	16.90	Mauritius	2.20	11.70
Denmark	43.20	122.50	Netherlands	1791.00	343.90
Egypt	15.50	267.10	Nigeria	8.00	132.70
Finland	29.30	102.10	Panama	2.95	18.00
France	256.00	1320.00	Samoa	0.10	0.45
Greece	27.00	137.40	United Kingdom	283.50	1242.00
Haiti	0.67	7.10	United States	822.00	8083.00
India	39.70	1534.00			

FIGURE 5.20   MINITAB Scatterplot of IMPORTS Versus GDP

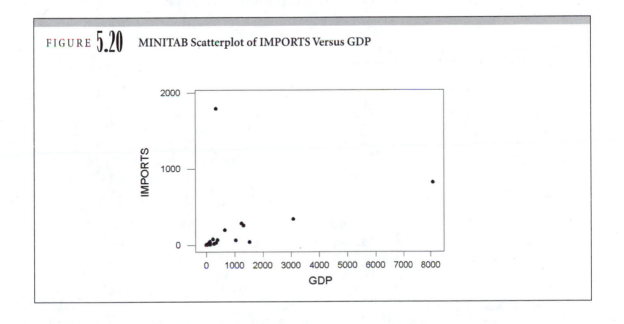

FIGURE **5.21** MINITAB Scatterplot of Log IMPORTS Versus Log GDP

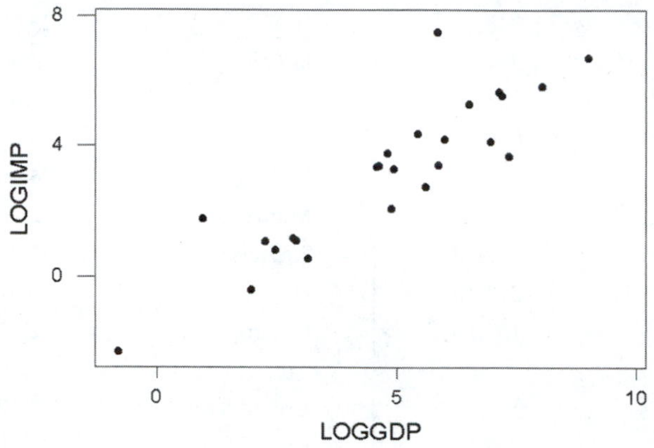

FIGURE **5.22** MINITAB Output for Regression of Log IMPORTS on Log GDP

```
The regression equation is
LOGIMP = - 1.07 + 0.875 LOGGDP

Predictor         Coef        StDev            T          P
Constant        -1.0701       0.5025        -2.13      0.044
LOGGDP           0.87540      0.09409        9.30      0.000

S = 1.090       R-Sq = 79.0%       R-Sq(adj) = 78.1%

Analysis of Variance

Source            DF           SS           MS          F         P
Regression         1        102.84       102.84      86.56     0.000
Residual Error    23         27.33         1.19
Total             24        130.17

Unusual Observations
Obs     LOGGDP      LOGIMP         Fit    StDev Fit     Residual    St Resid
 20       5.84       7.491       4.043       0.239        3.448        3.24R
 23      -0.80      -2.303      -1.769       0.571       -0.534       -0.57 X

R denotes an observation with a large standardized residual
X denotes an observation whose X value gives it large influence.
```

FIGURE 5.23   **Excel Output for Regression of Log IMPORTS on Log GDP**

SUMMARY OUTPUT

Regression Statistics

Multiple R	0.889
R Square	0.790
Adjusted R Square	0.781
Standard Error	1.090
Observations	25.000

ANOVA

	df	SS	MS	F	Significance F
Regression	1.000	102.840	102.840	86.559	0.000
Residual	23.000	27.326	1.188		
Total	24.000	130.167			

	Coefficients	Standard Error	t Stat	P-value	Lower 95%	Upper 95%
Intercept	−1.070	0.503	−2.129	0.044	−2.110	−0.031
LOGGDP	0.875	0.094	9.304	0.000	0.681	1.070

Figure 5.21 shows the scatterplot of the natural logarithm of imports (LOGIMP) versus the natural logarithm of GDP (LOGGDP). The relationship appears much closer to linear than in Figure 5.20. Figure 5.22 is the MINITAB output for the regression of LOGIMP on LOGGDP, and Figure 5.23 is the Excel output for the same regression. The regression of imports on GDP is not shown for comparison purposes as in previous examples. As noted, since the dependent variable has been transformed, the usual comparisons are not valid. In Chapter 6, we find alternative methods for judging which of the functional forms of the model appears better. At this stage, the scatterplot strongly supports the use of the log transformation.

It is important to keep in mind that the type of transformation to correct for curvilinearity is not always obvious. If y and x are related in a curvilinear manner, the goal is to transform the variables in some manner to achieve a linear relationship. Different transformations may be tried (including transformations not discussed in this section) and the one which appears to do the best job chosen.

In deciding what type of transformation to use, look at the scatterplot showing the relationship between y and x. This may help identify the form of the relationship between the two variables. In Chapter 6, we discuss other methods of recognizing when a linear model is not the best choice, when a curvilinear model may be more appropriate, and which curvilinear model provides an improvement.

5.2.5 Fitting Curvilinear Trends

In Chapter 3, the linear trend model was presented:

$$y_i = \beta_0 + \beta_1 t + e_i$$

where t is simply a variable indicating time sequence, $t = 1, 2, \ldots, n$. Just as curvilinear patterns can be observed with regard to x variables as discussed in this chapter, so can curvilinear trends occur. It is possible to model certain curvilinear trends using regression. This is done in a very similar manner to the fitting of curves to data just discussed. A few basic curvilinear trend models are presented here.

A *quadratic trend* equation can be written

$$y_i = \beta_0 + \beta_1 t + \beta_2 t^2 + e_i$$

Examples of the linear and quadratic trends are shown in Figures 5.24(a) and 5.24(b), respectively.

The equation for a curve called an *S-curve* is given by

$$y_i = \exp\left(\beta_0 + \beta_1 \left(\frac{1}{t}\right) + e_i \right)$$

where exp denotes the exponential operator: the value $e = 2.717$ (approximately) is raised to the power

$$\beta_0 + \beta_1 \left(\frac{1}{t}\right) + e_i$$

The S-curve is shown in Figure 5.24(c). This type of trend might be used to model demand for certain products over their lifetime. Demand is slow initially until the product becomes better known. Then demand picks up until a saturation point is reached. At that time, demand levels off.

The S-curve equation cannot be estimated directly using least-squares. By taking natural logarithms of both sides of the equation, however, a new equation is obtained that can be estimated. Because $\ln(\exp(x)) = x$ for any x, taking natural logarithms of both sides of the equation produces

$$\ln(y_i) = \beta_0 + \beta_1 \left(\frac{1}{t}\right) + e_i$$

Regressing $\ln(y_i)$ on $1/t$ produces estimates of β_0 and β_1. When forecasting with this model, care should be taken. For example, write $y_i' = \ln(y_i)$ and $t' = \frac{1}{t}$, and write the estimated regression equation as

$$\hat{y}_i' = b_0 + b_1 t'$$

The estimated equation provides the forecast for time period T:

$$\hat{y}_T' = b_0 + b_1 \left(\frac{1}{T}\right)$$

Note that this is a forecast of y_T' or the natural logarithm of y_T. To obtain a forecast of the original dependent variable, y_T, the conversion back to the original units from logarithmic units must be made:

$$\exp(\hat{y}_T') = \hat{y}_T$$

FIGURE **5.24**   **Examples of Types of Trends**

(a) Linear trend

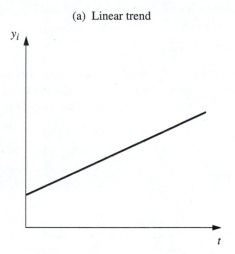

(c) S-curve

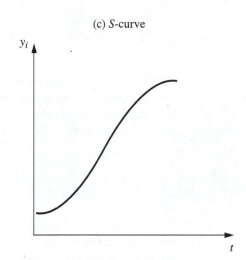

(b) Quadratic trend

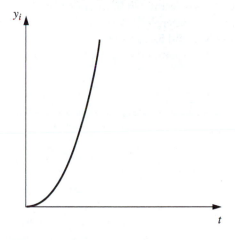

(b) Exponential trend ($\beta_0 = 0.0$)

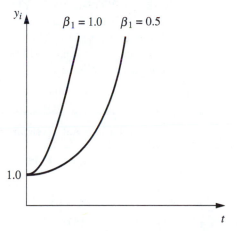

Exponential trends also are used in time-series applications. The equation for an exponential trend is

$$y_i = \exp(\beta_0 + \beta_1 t + e_i)$$

Again, to estimate β_0 and β_1, the equation is transformed using natural logarithms. Writing $y_i' = \ln(y_i)$, the transformed equation is

$$y_i' = \beta_0 + \beta_1 t + e_i$$

Regressing $\ln(y_i) = y_i'$ on t produces estimates of β_0 and β_1. As with the S-curve, exercise caution when using this equation for forecasting. The natural logarithm of $\hat{y}_i'$ must be transformed back to its original units to obtain the desired forecast. Examples of exponential trends are shown in Figure 5.24(d).

EXERCISES

1 **Research and Development** A company is interested in the relationship between profit on a number of projects and two explanatory variables. These variables are the expenditure on research and development for the project (RD) and a measure of risk assigned at the outset of the project (RISK). Table 5.8 shows the data on the three variables PROFIT, RISK, and RD. PROFIT is measured in thousands of dollars and RD is measured in hundreds of dollars. The scatterplots of PROFIT versus RISK and PROFIT versus RD are shown in Figures 5.25 and 5.26, respectively. The MINITAB and Excel regressions of PROFIT on the two explanatory variables RISK and RD are in Figures 5.27 and 5.28.

TABLE 5.8   Data for Research and Development Exercise

RD	RISK	PROFIT	RD	RISK	PROFIT
132.580	8.5	396	74.816	7.5	102
81.928	7.5	130	108.752	6.0	214
145.992	10.0	508	92.372	8.5	200
90.020	8.0	172	92.260	7.0	158
114.408	7.0	256	60.732	6.5	32
53.704	7.5	32	78.120	7.5	116
76.244	7.0	102	90.000	5.5	120
71.680	8.0	102	105.532	9.0	270
151.592	9.5	536	111.832	8.0	270

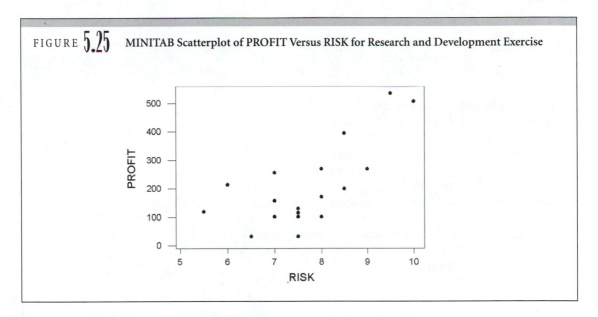

FIGURE **5.25**   MINITAB Scatterplot of PROFIT Versus RISK for Research and Development Exercise

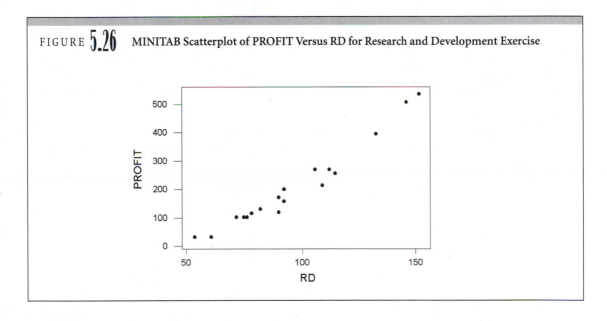

FIGURE **5.26**   MINITAB Scatterplot of PROFIT Versus RD for Research and Development Exercise

FIGURE 5.27 MINITAB Output for Regression of PROFIT on RISK and RD for Research and Development Exercise

```
The regression equation is
PROFIT = - 453 + 29.3 RISK + 4.51 RD

Predictor        Coef       StDev           T         P
Constant      -453.18       23.51      -19.28     0.000
RISK           29.309        3.669        7.99     0.000
RD             4.5100       0.1538       29.33     0.000

S = 14.34      R-Sq = 99.2%      R-Sq(adj) = 99.0%

Analysis of Variance

Source             DF          SS          MS         F         P
Regression          2      361639      180820    879.08     0.000
Residual Error     15        3085         206
Total              17      364724

Source        DF      Seq SS
RISK           1      184652
RD             1      176987

Unusual Observations
Obs      RISK      PROFIT         Fit   StDev Fit      Residual      St Resid
  9       9.5      536.00      508.94        7.98         27.06         2.27R

R denotes an observation with a large standardized residual
```

FIGURE **5.28**   **Excel Output for Regression of PROFIT on RISK and RD for Research and Development Exercise**

SUMMARY OUTPUT

Regression Statistics

Multiple R	0.996
R Square	0.992
Adjusted R Square	0.990
Standard Error	14.342
Observations	18.000

ANOVA

	df	SS	MS	F	Significance F
Regression	2.000	361639.057	180819.528	879.077	0.000
Residual	15.000	3085.388	205.693		
Total	17.000	364724.444			

	Coefficients	Standard Error	t Stat	P-value	Lower 95%	Upper 95%
Intercept	−453.176	23.506	−19.279	0.000	−503.279	−403.074
RISK	29.309	3.669	7.989	0.000	21.490	37.128
RD	4.510	0.154	29.333	0.000	4.182	4.838

Figures 5.29 and 5.30 show the MINITAB and Excel regressions, respectively, using PROFIT as the dependent variable with RISK, RD, and RDSQR (the square of the RD variable) as explanatory variables. Choose the model you prefer for PROFIT and provide a justification for your choice.

These data are available in a file with prefix RD5 in three columns: RD, RISK and PROFIT.

FIGURE 5.29   MINITAB Output for Regression of PROFIT on RISK and First- and Second-Order Terms
for RD for Research and Development Exercise

```
The regression equation is
PROFIT = - 245 + 23.2 RISK + 1.01 RD + 0.0176 RDSQR

Predictor        Coef       StDev            T        P
Constant      -245.37       14.81       -16.57    0.000
RISK          23.2492      0.9884        23.52    0.000
RD             1.0143      0.2324         4.36    0.001
RDSQR        0.017567    0.001152        15.25    0.000

S = 3.538       R-Sq = 100.0%      R-Sq(adj) = 99.9%

Analysis of Variance

Source            DF          SS          MS        F        P
Regression         3      364549      121516   9707.86    0.000
Residual Error    14         175          13
Total             17      364724

Source       DF      Seq SS
RISK          1      184652
RD            1      176987
RDSQR         1        2910

Unusual Observations
Obs     RISK     PROFIT         Fit   StDev Fit    Residual    St Resid
  5      7.0    256.000     263.357       1.466      -7.357      -2.28R

R denotes an observation with a large standardized residual
```

FIGURE 5.30   Excel Output for Regression of PROFIT on RISK and First- and Second-Order Terms for RD for Research and Development Exercise

SUMMARY OUTPUT

Regression Statistics

Multiple R	1.000
R Square	1.000
Adjusted R Square	0.999
Standard Error	3.538
Observations	18.000

ANOVA

	df	SS	MS	F	Significance F
Regression	3.000	364549.191	121516.397	9707.261	0.000
Residual	14.000	175.253	12.518		
Total	17.000	364724.444			

	Coefficients	Standard Error	t Stat	P-value	Lower 95%	Upper 95%
Intercept	-245.369	14.812	-16.566	0.000	-277.137	-213.601
RISK	23.249	0.988	23.521	0.000	21.129	25.369
RD	1.014	0.232	4.365	0.001	0.516	1.513
RDSQR	0.018	0.001	15.247	0.000	0.015	0.020

2   **Kentucky Derby**   On the first Saturday in May, the granddaddy of horse races—the Kentucky Derby—is run at Churchill Downs in Louisville, Kentucky. The amount of money bet, in millions of dollars, on this race is given in Table 5.9 for the 66-year period from 1927 through 1992. Figure 5.31 shows the MINITAB time-series plot of the amounts bet. Figures 5.32 and 5.33 show the MINITAB and Excel linear trend regressions using the amount bet as the dependent variable. Figures 5.34 and 5.35 show, the MINITAB and Excel quadratic trend regressions using the amount bet as the dependent variable. Choose the model you prefer for the amount bet and provide a justification for your choice. Once you have chosen your preferred model, use it to forecast the amount bet in 1993 and 1994.

The data are in a file with prefix DERBY5 in a single column.

TABLE 5.9   Data for Kentucky Derby Example

Year	Bets	Year	Bets	Year	Bets	Year	Bets
1927	0.68	1944	0.65	1961	1.48	1978	4.43
1928	0.62	1945	0.78	1962	1.55	1979	4.01
1929	0.68	1946	1.20	1963	1.82	1980	4.16
1930	0.58	1947	1.25	1964	2.14	1981	4.57
1931	0.50	1948	0.67	1965	2.23	1982	5.01
1932	0.28	1949	1.03	1966	2.13	1983	5.55
1933	0.23	1950	1.25	1967	1.93	1984	5.42
1934	0.38	1951	1.29	1968	2.35	1985	5.77
1935	0.31	1952	1.57	1969	2.63	1986	6.17
1936	0.37	1953	1.53	1970	2.38	1987	6.36
1937	0.59	1954	1.54	1971	2.65	1988	7.35
1938	0.53	1955	1.68	1972	2.89	1989	6.75
1939	0.58	1956	1.67	1973	3.28	1990	6.95
1940	0.46	1957	1.40	1974	3.44	1991	6.74
1941	0.65	1958	1.64	1975	3.37	1992	6.47
1942	0.63	1959	1.50	1976	3.45		
1943	0.59	1960	1.49	1977	3.67		

Source: "How the Betting Went," Louisvill *Courier-Journal*, May 3, 1992. Copyright 1992, Louisville *Courier-Journal*. Reprinted with permission.

FIGURE 5.31   MINITAB Time-Series Plot of Kentucky Derby Bets

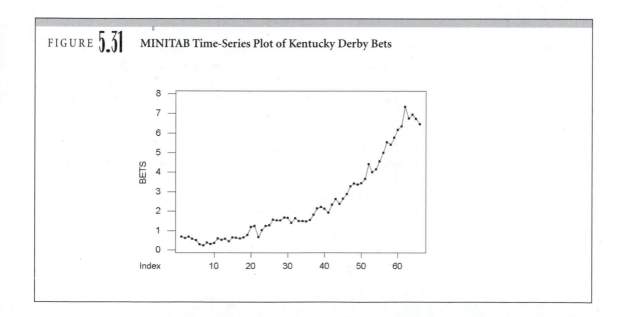

FIGURE **5.32**   MINITAB Regression Output for Linear Trend Model for Kentucky Derby Bets

```
The regression equation is
BETS = - 0.877 + 0.0985 TIME


Predictor       Coef       StDev          T         P
Constant      -0.8768     0.1977       -4.43     0.000
TIME         0.098493    0.005131      19.20     0.000


S = 0.7941      R-Sq = 85.2%      R-Sq(adj) = 85.0%


Analysis of Variance


Source          DF        SS          MS         F         P
Regression       1      232.36      232.36     368.52    0.000
Residual Error  64       40.35        0.63
Total           65      272.71


Unusual Observations
Obs     TIME       BETS       Fit    StDev Fit    Residual    St Resid
 62     62.0      7.3500    5.2298    0.1759      2.1202       2.74R


R denotes an observation with a large standardized residual
```

FIGURE **5.33**   Excel Regression Output for Linear Trend Model for Kentucky Derby Bets

SUMMARY OUTPUT

```
Regression Statistics
Multiple R            0.92
R Square              0.85
Adjusted R Square     0.85
Standard Error        0.79
Observations         66.00
```

ANOVA

	df	SS	MS	F	Significance F
Regression	1.000	232.359	232.359	368.516	0.000
Residual	64.000	40.354	0.631		
Total	65.000	272.713			

	Coefficients	Standard Error	t Stat	P-value	Lower 95%	Upper 95%
Intercept	−0.877	0.198	−4.434	0.000	−1.272	−0.482
TIME	0.098	0.005	19.197	0.000	0.088	0.109

FIGURE 5.34   MINITAB Regression Output for Quadratic Trend Model for Kentucky Derby Bets

```
The regression equation is
BETS = 0.795 - 0.0490 TIME + 0.00220 TIMESQR

Predictor        Coef        StDev           T        P
Constant       0.7947       0.1240        6.41    0.000
TIME         -0.048991     0.008539       -5.74    0.000
TIMESQR       0.0022012    0.0001235      17.82    0.000


S = 0.3256      R-Sq = 97.6%      R-Sq(adj) = 97.5%

Analysis of Variance

Source              DF          SS          MS          F        P
Regression           2      266.03      133.02    1254.44    0.000
Residual Error      63        6.68        0.11
Total               65      272.71

Source       DF      Seq SS
TIME          1      232.36
TIMESQR       1       33.67

Unusual Observations
Obs      TIME        BETS         Fit    StDev Fit     Residual     St Resid
 62      62.0      7.3500      6.2189       0.0910       1.1311         3.62R
 66      66.0      6.4700      7.1499       0.1167      -0.6799        -2.24R

R denotes an observation with a large standardized residual
```

FIGURE 5.35   Excel Regression Output for Quadratic Trend Model for Kentucky Derby Bets

SUMMARY OUTPUT

Regression Statistics
Multiple R	0.988
R Square	0.976
Adjusted R Square	0.975
Standard Error	0.326
Observations	66.000

ANOVA

	df	SS	MS	F	Significance F
Regression	2.000	266.033	133.016	1254.437	0.000
Residual	63.000	6.680	0.106		
Total	65.000	272.713			

	Coefficients	Standard Error	t Stat	P-value	Lower 95%	Upper 95%
Intercept	0.795	0.124	6.410	0.000	0.547	1.042
TIME	−0.049	0.009	−5.737	0.000	−0.066	−0.032
TIMESQR	0.002	0.000	17.820	0.000	0.002	0.002

5.3 USING THE COMPUTER

The Using the Computer section in each chapter describes how to perform the computer analyses in the chapter using MINITAB, Excel, and SAS. For further detail on MINITAB, Excel, and SAS, see Appendix C.

5.3.1 MINITAB

Note that Version 12 of MINITAB is fully menu driven. Commands can be used, however, and they are included for any interested users. The menu headings and subheadings used to perform the procedures are listed first, followed by commands in parentheses. For example CALC: CALCULATOR means to click on the CALC menu and then on CALCULATOR. (Let C3=C1*C2 means to type in the command as shown.)

Variable Transformations

```
CALC: CALCULATOR    (LET C3=C1*C1)
```

FIGURE **5.36**   MINITAB Dialog Box for Calculator

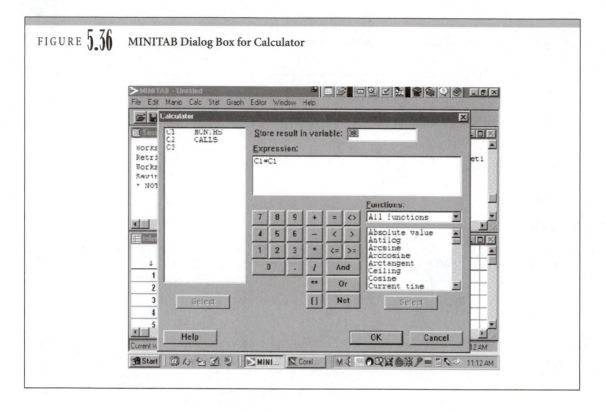

The CALCULATOR dialog box is shown in Figure 5.36. Any variable transformations can be performed using the calculator. As shown, the calculator is set up to multiply the numbers in column 1 by themselves (C1*C1) and place the result in C3. Thus, C3 will contain the square of the numbers in C1. Other transformations can be performed in similar fashion. Placing LOGE(C1) in the Expression box produces the natural logarithm of C1. Placing SQRT(C1) in the expression box produces the square root of C1. If you are not sure of the form of the function (LOGE, SQRT, and so on) , just double click on the desired function to the right of the keyboard and the appropriate expression appears in the Expression box. (The LET command can also be used to transform variables. For example, LET C3=C1*C1 multiplies C1 by C1 and puts the resulting values in C3. LET C3=LOGE(C1) puts the natural logarithms of the values in C1 into C3.)

5.3.2 Excel

Variable Transformations

Variable transformations in Excel are accomplished through the use of formulas. Consider the screen shown in Figure 5.37. We want to create a new column containing the square of the numbers in column A. To do this, we create a formula in cell C2. Multiply the value in cell A2 by itself (=A2*A2). To do this for each entry in column C,

FIGURE 5.37   **Excel Screen Showing Formula Creation for Variable Transformation**

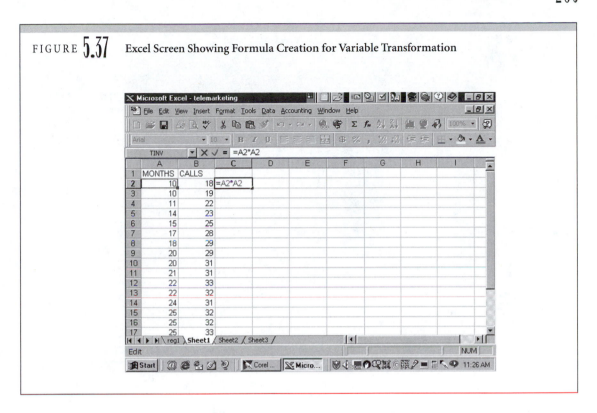

place the cursor on the lower right-hand corner of cell C2 and drag this cell to the last entry in column A (see Figure 5.38). Other transformations are created in a similar manner. If you are not sure of the form of a certain transformation, click on the f_x button. Figure 5.39 shows an example using the natural log function. Most functions used to transform variables can be found in the Math & Trig category.

5.3.3   SAS

Variable Transformations

In SAS, variable transformations are performed during the data input phase. Here are some typical examples:

Create the square of the variable MONTHS and call it XSQR:

```
XSQR = MONTHS**2;
```

Create the natural log of the variable MONTHS and call it LOGMONTH:

```
LOGMONTH = LOG(MONTH);
```

These transformed variables can then be used in PROC REG, PROC PLOT, and so on.

FIGURE **5.38**   Excel Screen Showing Formula Creation for Variable Transformation

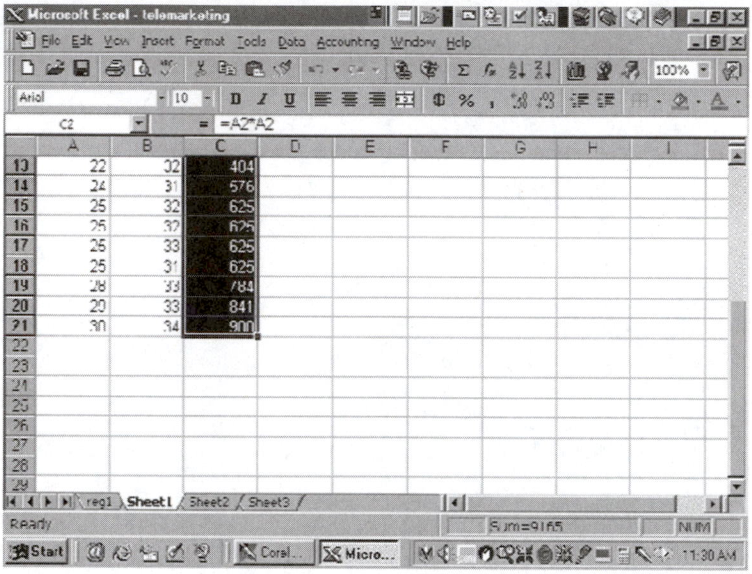

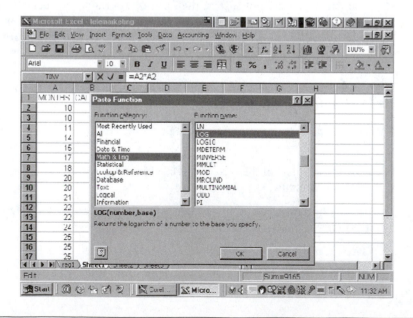

FIGURE **5.39**   Excel Screen Showing How to Access Functions

ADDITIONAL EXERCISES

3 Piston Corporation (Part A) Reginald Jackson was employed as a cost accountant by the Piston Corporation, a medium-size auto parts company located in the outskirts of Detroit. Kelly Jones, the controller for Piston, decided that she needed an assistant. Jackson was selected to fill that position. As part of his training program, Jackson was sent to night school to study quantitative applications in cost accounting.

Because the Piston Corporation's products were replacement parts, its sales were, fortunately, not as volatile as the new car market's. Piston had experienced a rather stable growth in sales in recent years and had been required to increase its capacity regularly. It appeared to be time for another expansion, but with an uncertain stock market prevailing and uncertainty concerning interest rates, Jones was worried about obtaining funds at a reasonable cost. On the other hand, Piston's production manager had been complaining, more than usual, about various personnel, material handling, and scheduling bottlenecks that arose from the high level of output demanded of his present facilities.

The executive officers had been asked by Piston's directors to formulate a proposal for expansion and price adjustments. Jones asked Jackson what he could determine statistically about the effect of inflation and the level of production on unit costs.

By looking at old budgets, Jackson was able to obtain quarterly data on manufacturing costs per unit, production level (a percentage of the total capacity), and the index of direct material and direct labor costs for a 5-year period (see Table 5.10). He immediately went to the computer and ran a regression of unit cost on production volume (PROD) and the cost index (INDEX). He began to wonder about the validity of modeling unit costs as a linear function of production level and the cost index.

The scatterplots of the dependent variable (COST) versus each explanatory variable are shown in Figures 5.40 and 5.41. The MINITAB regression output is in Figure 5.42 and the Excel output in Figure 5.43.

After spending several days trying to improve his model, Jackson had several new solutions but was still unsure which one was best. That night after his quantitative accounting class, he asked his professor for advice. The professor suggested that Jackson first derive a theoretically plausible solution and then see if the data satisfied this relationship.

Jackson knew that the basic relationship with which he was dealing was:

$$\text{total cost} = \text{variable cost per unit} \times \text{volume} + \text{fixed cost}$$

He also theorized that variable cost per unit was composed of a constant multiple of the index of direct materials and labor (x_2) and that fixed cost was simply the current capacity of the company times some constant.

Jackson realized that the basic equation could be rewritten as

$$\text{total cost} = \beta_1 \times \text{capacity} + \beta_2 \times x_2 \times \text{volume}$$

TABLE 5.10   Data for Piston Exercise

Quarter	Average Mfg. Cost Per Unit (y) (COST)	Production Level as a Fraction of Rated Capacity (x_1) (PROD)	Direct Material and Labor Costs (x_2) (INDEX)
1	3.65	.85	80
2	4.22	.78	93
3	4.29	.82	107
4	5.43	.64	115
5	6.42	.50	130
6	5.71	.62	128
7	5.39	.70	116
8	3.99	.90	92
9	4.08	.94	94
10	4.38	1.00	110
11	4.28	1.04	115
12	4.42	.82	117
13	5.11	.75	128
14	4.88	.84	134
15	4.99	.86	135
16	4.57	.90	135
17	4.84	.94	139
18	5.16	.80	142
19	5.67	.72	147
20	6.26	.60	150

Then it dawned on him that he actually wanted cost per unit. The preceeding equation could be divided by volume to get

$$\text{total cost/volume} = \beta_1 \times \text{capacity/volume} + \beta_2 \times x_2$$

Capacity/volume, however, is simply the reciprocal of production level, so the new equation becomes

$$y = \beta_1 \left(\frac{1}{x_1} \right) + \beta_2 x_2$$

where y is total cost/volume (or cost per unit), x_1 is production level and x_2 is cost index. Allowing for random error and allowing the equation to have an intercept term produces:

$$y = \beta_0 + \beta_1 \left(\frac{1}{x_1} \right) + \beta_2 x_2 + e$$

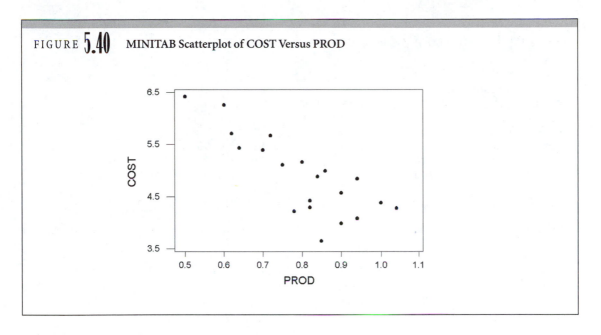

FIGURE 5.40 MINITAB Scatterplot of COST Versus PROD

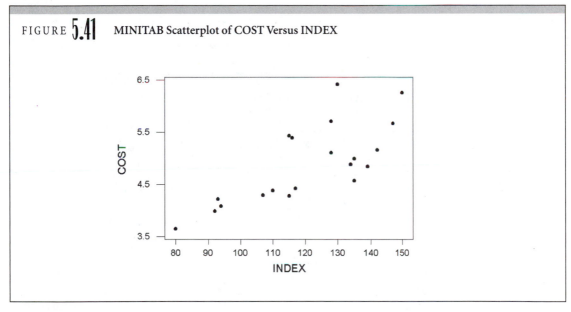

FIGURE 5.41 MINITAB Scatterplot of COST Versus INDEX

FIGURE 5.42   MINITAB Regression of COST on PROD and INDEX

```
The regression equation is
COST = 5.18 - 3.45 PROD + 0.0205 INDEX

Predictor        Coef        StDev           T        P
Constant       5.1829       0.5364        9.66    0.000
PROD          -3.4482       0.3961       -8.70    0.000
INDEX        0.020492     0.002796        7.33    0.000

S = 0.2280      R-Sq = 91.9%      R-Sq(adj) = 91.0%

Analysis of Variance

Source           DF          SS          MS          F        P
Regression        2     10.0586      5.0293      96.78    0.000
Residual Error   17      0.8834      0.0520
Total            19     10.9420

Source       DF      Seq SS
PROD          1      7.2677
INDEX         1      2.7909
```

FIGURE 5.43   Excel Regression of COST on PROD and INDEX

```
                        SUMMARY OUTPUT

Regression Statistics
Multiple R              0.959
R Square                0.919
Adjusted R Square       0.910
Standard Error          0.228
Observations           20.000

ANOVA
                   df           SS          MS          F    Significance F
Regression      2.000       10.059      5.029     96.784           0.000
Residual       17.000        0.883      0.052
Total          19.000       10.942

                        Standard
              Coefficients    Error    t Stat   P-value   Lower 95%   Upper 95%
Intercept           5.183     0.536     9.662     0.000       4.051       6.315
PROD               -3.448     0.396    -8.704     0.000      -4.284      -2.612
INDEX               0.020     0.003     7.329     0.000       0.015       0.026
```

Try Jackson's new model. How does this model compare with the original regression? In answering this question, use the R^2 values, the standard error of the regression, and any other information you feel might be useful in the comparisons. Which model do you prefer?

These data are in a file with prefix PISTON5 in three columns: COST, PROD, and INDEX.

4 **Piston Corporation (Part B)** Use the model developed in Part A to answer the following questions:

a A three-point rise in the cost index will cause what change in unit costs (assuming production level remains constant)?

b What is the marginal unit cost of a rise in production volume from 0.94 to 0.95 of capacity (marginal cost implies all other variables remain constant)?

c If forecasts of production level of 0.87 and cost index of 120 are obtained, find a prediction of the manufacturing cost per unit (use a point prediction).

d Construct a 95% prediction interval for manufacturing cost per unit under the conditions described in part c.

5 **Computer Repair** A computer repair service is examining the time taken on service calls to repair computers. Data are obtained for 30 service calls. The data are shown in Table 5.11. Information obtained includes

x_1 = number of machines to be repaired (NUMBER)

x_2 = years of experience of service person (EXPER)

y = time taken (in minutes) to provide service (TIME)

TABLE 5.11

Data for Computer Repair Exercise

NUMBER	EXPER	TIME	NUMBER	EXPER	TIME
1	9	66	16	11	383
1	11	74	17	10	383
3	11	88	20	9	515
4	8	99	19	9	474
6	9	134	20	9	495
6	9	120	22	9	628
7	10	178	22	9	636
8	9	139	23	10	660
9	8	187	24	10	731
11	10	227	25	11	752
11	10	225	26	8	800
12	7	270	27	10	863
13	9	265	28	9	918
14	9	301	29	9	976
15	10	343	30	10	1027

Develop a polynomial regression model to predict average time on the service calls using EXPER and NUMBER as explanatory variables. Justify your model choice including transformations of any variables.

These data are in a file with prefix COMPREP5 in three columns: NUMBER, EXPER, and TIME.

6 **Criminal Justice Expenditures**   Table 5.12 shows the following data for each of the 50 states:

total expenditures on a state's criminal justice system (in millions of dollars) (EXPEND)

total number of police employed in the state (POLICE)

State governments must try to project spending in many areas. Expenditure on the criminal justice system is one area of continually rising cost. Your job is to build a model that can be used to forecast spending on a state's criminal justice system. Once your model is complete, predict expenditures for a state that plans to hire 10,000 police personnel. Find a point prediction and a 95% prediction interval.

The data are in a file with prefix CRIMSPN5 in two columns: EXPEND and POLICE.

TABLE **5.12**   Data for Criminal Justice Expenditures Exercise

State	EXPEND	POLICE	State	EXPEND	POLICE	State	EXPEND	POLICE
Alabama	561	10312	Louisiana	748	13349	Ohio	1809	23780
Alaska	283	1928	Maine	169	2914	Oklahoma	442	7593
Arizona	962	10315	Maryland	1091	13351	Oregon	593	6221
Arkansas	233	4875	Massachusetts	1449	18475	Pennsylvania	1919	26199
California	8940	75043	Michigan	2132	22873	Rhode Island	194	2838
Colorado	701	9141	Minnesota	735	8798	South Carolina	553	8641
Connecticut	692	9282	Mississippi	263	5616	South Dakota	83	1569
Delaware	158	1841	Missouri	829	14037	Tennessee	756	12205
Florida	2810	39853	Montana	104	1799	Texas	2939	43745
Georgia	1187	18118	Nebraska	216	3696	Utah	282	3793
Hawaii	271	3122	Nevada	332	3379	Vermont	84	1254
Idaho	133	2305	New Hampshire	170	2978	Virginia	1195	15500
Illinois	2340	36925	New Jersey	2118	29049	Washington	887	10398
Indiana	688	12072	New Mexico	290	4520	West Virginia	168	3352
Iowa	354	5631	New York	7145	77571	Wisconsin	864	12905
Kansas	404	6506	North Carolina	1042	16259	Wyoming	98	1598
Kentucky	496	7234	North Dakota	71	1280			

Source: These data were obtained from the 1990 *Sourcebook of Criminal Justice Statistics*.

CHAPTER 6

Assessing the Assumptions of the Regression Model

6.1 INTRODUCTION

In Chapter 4, the multiple linear regression model was presented as

$$y_i = \beta_0 + \beta_1 x_{1i} + \beta_2 x_{2i} + \cdots + \beta_K x_{Ki} + e_i \tag{6.1}$$

Certain assumptions were made concerning the disturbances, e_i, of this model. The e_i represent the differences between the true values of the dependent variable and the corresponding points on the population regression line. Because the true disturbances cannot be observed, they are modeled as realizations of a random variable about which certain assumptions are made. Under a set of ideal assumptions, the method of least squares provides the best possible estimates of the population regression coefficients. Certain assumptions are necessary for inference procedures (confidence interval estimates and hypothesis tests) to perform as expected. In this chapter, we consider the problems with estimation and inference that may arise if any of these assumptions are violated. Methods of assessing the validity of the assumptions also are discussed. Graphical procedures such as scatterplots and residual plots may be used to examine certain assumptions, and statistical tests are available for a more formal examination. Finally, we discuss appropriate techniques to correct for violated assumptions.

6.2 ASSUMPTIONS OF THE MULTIPLE LINEAR REGRESSION MODEL

The "ideal" conditions for estimation and inference in the multiple regression model are as follows:

a The expected value of the disturbances is zero: $E(e_i) = 0$. This implies that the regression line passes through the conditional means of the y variable. For our purposes, we interpret this assumption as: The relationship is linear in the explanatory variables.

b The disturbances in Equation (6.1), e_i, have constant variance σ_e^2.

c The disturbances are normally distributed.

d The disturbances are independent.

An additional condition is added to this list that applies only to the explanatory variables in the equation:

e The explanatory variables are not highly interrelated.

The effects of violations of each of these assumptions on the least-squares estimates of the regression coefficients are examined in subsequent sections. Methods of assessing the validity of the assumptions are discussed and possible corrections for violations are offered. Because many of the methods of assessing assumption validity depend on the use of the residuals (the sample counterpart of the disturbances), the next section is devoted to a brief discussion of the computation and properties of the residuals.

6.3 THE REGRESSION RESIDUALS

The regression equation estimated from the sample data may be written

$$\hat{y}_i = b_0 + b_1 x_{1i} + b_2 x_{2i} + \cdots + b_K x_{Ki} \tag{6.2}$$

By substituting in the sample values for each explanatory variable, the predicted or fitted y value for each data point in the sample is obtained. The fitted y values are denoted as $\hat{y}_i$. The y values for each point in the sample are also available and are referred to as y_i. The differences between the true and fitted y values for the points in the sample are called the *residuals*. The residuals are denoted by $\hat{e}_i$:

$$\hat{e}_i = y_i - \hat{y}_i$$

They represent the distance that each dependent variable value is from the estimated regression line or the portion of the variation in y that cannot be "explained" with the data available. Because these "sample disturbances" approximate the population disturbances, they can be used to examine assumptions concerning the population disturbances.

After estimating a sample regression equation, it is highly recommended that some sort of analysis be conducted to assess the model assumptions. No regression analysis can be considered complete without such further examination. The residuals can be used to conduct such analyses through graphical techniques called *residual plots*. Often, violations of assumptions can be detected through the use of residual plots in combination with scatterplots without the use of statistical tests. The use of graphical techniques, however, is not an exact science. It might, in fact, be considered an "art." It takes some experience at examining plots to become adept at determining which, if any, assumptions may be violated. Several examples are presented later to illustrate this art and to aid in mastering residual analysis.

First, consider some properties of the residuals.

Property 1:   The average of the residuals is equal to zero. This property holds regardless of whether the assumptions are true or not and is a direct result of the way the least-squares method works. Least squares "forces" the mean of the residuals to be zero when it chooses the estimates of the regression coefficients.

Property 2:   If assumptions a through c of Section 6.2 are true, then the residuals should be randomly distributed about their mean (zero). There should be no systematic pattern in a residual plot.

Property 3:   If assumptions a through c are true and the disturbances are also normally distributed (assumption d), then the residuals should look like random numbers chosen from a normal distribution.

The residuals can be thought of as representing the variation in *y* that cannot be explained using the proposed regression model. Think of the process we are following as building a model for the data. We can write DATA = MODEL + ERROR. We have some DATA that we want to explain. We build a MODEL that we believe helps to explain patterns in the data. Any patterns in the DATA not included in the MODEL are accounted for in the ERROR term. These errors are represented by the residuals. Thus, if an assumption is violated, an indication of this violation appears as some type of pattern in the residuals. Identification of such patterns is a first step in correcting for the violation.

In a residual analysis, it is suggested that the following plots be used:

1   Plot the residuals versus each explanatory variable.

2   Plot the residuals versus the predicted or fitted values.

3   If the data are measured over time, plot the residuals versus some variable representing the time sequence.

As is shown in subsequent sections, each of these three types of plots plays a part in identifying violations of the basic assumptions.

If no assumptions are violated, then the residuals should be randomly distributed around their mean of zero and should look like numbers drawn randomly from a normal distribution. Figure 6.1 shows how a residual plot might appear when assumptions a through d are all true. There is no pattern visible in the scatter of residuals. For comparison, Figure 6.2 shows a residual plot with an obvious pattern to the residuals. Compare this to the random scatter of the residuals in Figure 6.1. A residual

FIGURE **6.1** MINITAB Residual Plot Assuming No Violation of Assumptions a Through d of Section 6.2

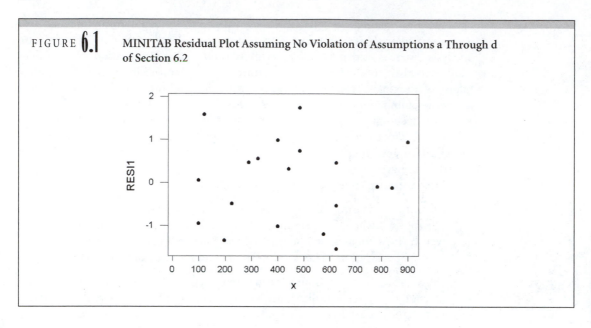

FIGURE **6.2** MINITAB Residual Plot Indicating That at Least One of Assumptions a Through d of Section 6.2 Has Been Violated

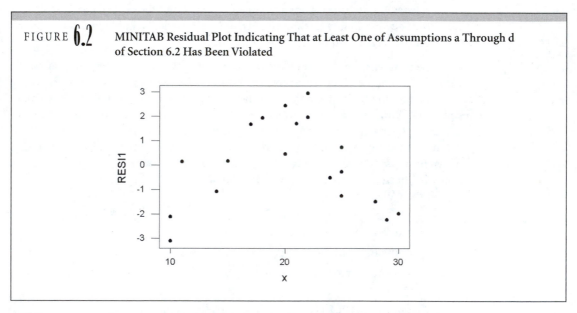

plot such as Figure 6.2 indicates that some assumption had been violated. (There are other patterns that could suggest violations, as is seen throughout this chapter.)

In certain regression software packages (Excel and MINITAB, for example), residual plots are easily constructed after a regression analysis has been performed. These plots may be constructed using the actual residuals, $\hat{e}_i$, or the standardized residuals. The *standardized residuals* are simply the residuals divided by their standard

FIGURE **6.3**   MINITAB Plot of the Residuals from Figure 6.1 After Standardizing

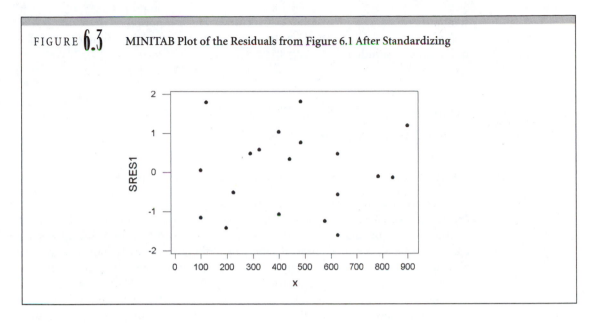

FIGURE **6.4**   MINITAB Plot of the Residuals from Figure 6.2 After Standardizing

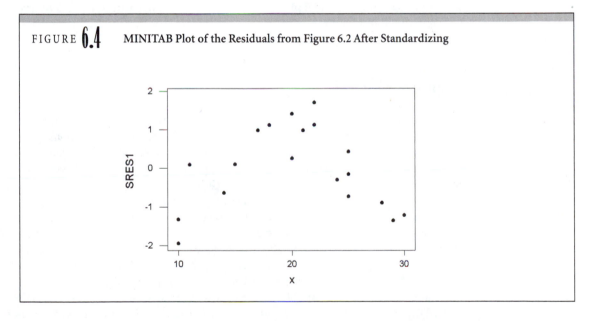

deviation. There is very little difference in the way residual plots with actual residuals or those with standardized residuals are used. To illustrate the difference in the two types of plots, compare Figure 6.1, a plot of actual residuals, to Figure 6.3, a plot of the same residuals after standardization. The residuals plotted in Figure 6.2 also have been standardized and plotted in Figure 6.4. The patterns in the actual and standardized plots are identical; only the scale has been changed. One advantage of using the standardized plots becomes more evident when the assumption of normality is discussed in Section 6.6. In this text, the residual plots shown are standardized plots unless otherwise indicated.

6.4 ASSESSING THE ASSUMPTION THAT THE RELATIONSHIP IS LINEAR

6.4.1 Using Plots to Assess the Linearity Assumption

The first assumption given in Section 6.2 was that the regression was linear in the explanatory variables. In Chapter 5, we saw that we can fit curvilinear as well as linear relationships using regression. In that chapter, we assumed that we could tell when a curvilinear relationship was needed simply by looking at the scatterplot. The scatterplots of y versus each of the explanatory variables may give an indication of whether the linearity assumption is an appropriate one, but this is not always the case. After performing a regression, this assumption can be checked visually through residual plots. Small deviations from linearity that are not evident in the scatterplots may show up clearly in the residual plots. The following example illustrates a violation of the linearity assumption.

EXAMPLE 6.1 **Telemarketing**

Consider again the telemarketing data from Example 5.1. A company that sells transportation services uses a telemarketing division to help sell its services. The division manager is interested in the time spent on the phone by the telemarketers in the division. Data on the number of months of employment and the number of calls placed per day (an average for 20 working days) are recorded for 20 employees. These data were shown in Table 5.1.

The average number of calls for all 20 employees is 28.95. The division manager, however, suspects that there may be a relationship between time on the job and number of calls. As time on the job increases, the employee becomes more familiar with the calling system and the correct procedures to use on the phone and also begins to acquire more regular clients. Thus, the longer the time on the job, the greater the number of calls per day. The MINITAB regression output relating CALLS to MONTHS is shown in Figure 6.5 and the Excel output is in Figure 6.6.

Plots of the standardized residuals versus the fitted values are shown in Figures 6.7 and 6.9 for MINITAB and Excel, respectively. Figures 6.8 and 6.10 show plots of the standardized residuals versus the explanatory variable values. The standardized residuals have been labeled SRES1 in the MINITAB plots. In the Excel plots, they are labeled Standardized Residuals. The fitted values are labeled FITS1 in the MINITAB plot and Fitted Values in the Excel plot.

A systematic pattern can be observed in both of the residual plots. The standardized residuals plot in a curvilinear pattern, suggesting a curvilinear component may be omitted from the equation expressing the relationship between CALLS and MONTHS. The plots of the standardized residuals versus the fitted values and MONTHS show identical patterns in this case. The plot

FIGURE **6.5**   MINITAB Regression Output for Telemarketing Example

```
The regression equation is
CALLS = 13.7 + 0.744 MONTHS

Predictor      Coef      StDev          T          P
Constant     13.671      1.427       9.58      0.000
MONTHS      0.74351    0.06666      11.15      0.000

S = 1.787        R-Sq = 87.4%       R-Sq(adj) = 86.7%

Analysis of Variance

Source           DF          SS         MS          F          P
Regression        1      397.45     397.45     124.41      0.000
Residual Error   18       57.50       3.19
Total            19      454.95
```

FIGURE **6.6**   Excel Regression Output for Telemarketing Example

```
                        SUMMARY OUTPUT

Regression Statistics
Multiple R           0.935
R Square             0.874
Adjusted R Square    0.867
Standard Error       1.787
Observations        20.000

ANOVA
                 df          SS          MS         F     Significance F
Regression    1.000     397.446     397.446   124.409         0.0000
Residual     18.000      57.504       3.195
Total        19.000     454.950

                    Standard
          Coefficients     Error    t Stat   P-value   Lower 95%   Upper 95%
Intercept       13.671     1.427     9.580    0.0000      10.673      16.669
MONTHS           0.744     0.067    11.154    0.0000       0.603       0.884
```

FIGURE **6.7**   MINITAB Plot of Standardized Residuals Versus Fitted Values
for Telemarketing Example

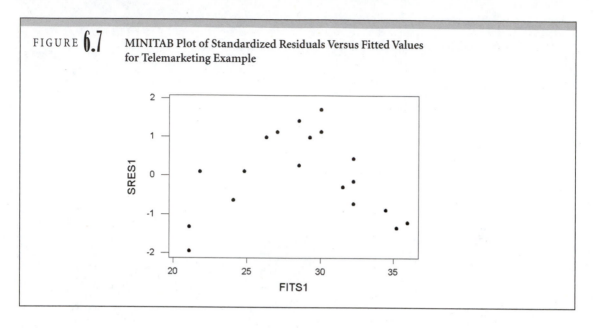

FIGURE **6.8**   MINITAB Plot of Standardized Residuals Versus Explanatory Variable MONTHS
for Telemarketing Example

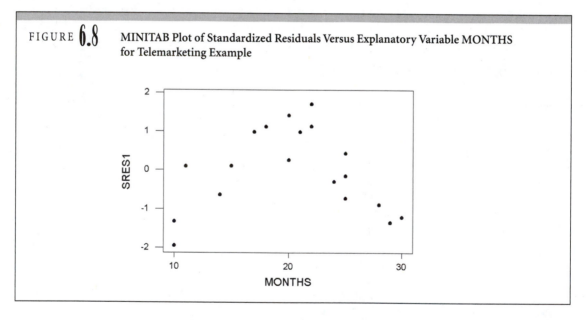

versus the fitted values may differ from the plot versus one of the explanatory variables, especially in a multiple regression. The fitted values combine the effects of all the explanatory variables used in the regression. In a multiple regression, the plot of the standardized residuals versus the fitted values provides an overall picture, while the plots of the standardized residuals versus each explanatory variable may help identify any violations specifically related to an individual explanatory variable.

FIGURE 6.9 Excel Plot of Standardized Residuals Versus Fitted Values
for Telemarketing Example

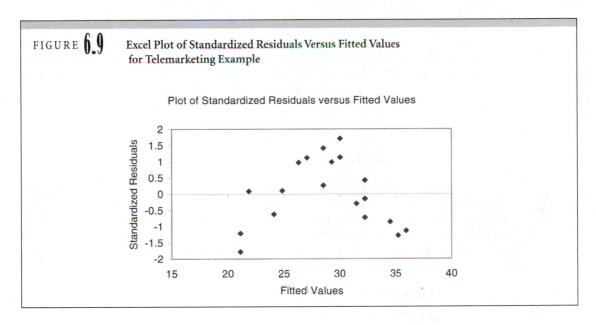

FIGURE 6.10 Excel Plot of Standardized Residuals Versus Explanatory Variable MONTHS
for Telemarketing Example

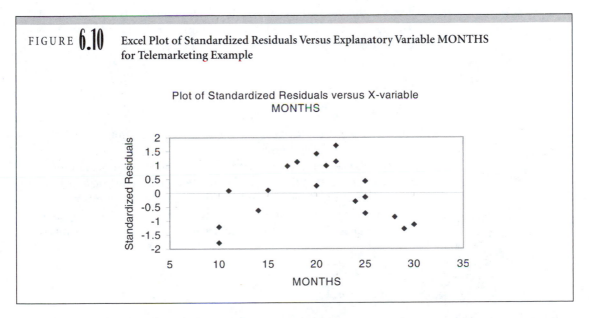

The systematic pattern observed in the residual plots suggests a violation of the linearity assumption. Looking back at the scatterplot of CALLS (y) versus MONTHS (x) helps verify that the relationship may not be linear. (The scatterplot is shown in Figure 5.1.) As the number of months on the job increases, the number of calls also increases. But the rate of increase begins to slow over time, thus resulting in a pattern that may be better modeled by a curve than a straight line (see also Figure 5.2).

Note that the residual plots were used to determine whether the linearity assumption had been violated, although this violation might have been suspected from looking at only the scatterplot of CALLS versus MONTHS. In many cases, the violation of an assumption is not obvious from a scatterplot. The residual plot, however, is intended to magnify the consequences of any possible violation. Thus, the residual plot should be depended on to identify the violation.

6.4.2 Tests for Lack of Fit[1]

MINITAB provides two tests to determine whether a curvilinear model might fit the data better than a linear model. These tests are referred to as *tests for lack of fit*. The first test is called the *pure error lack-of-fit test*. To perform this test, the error sum of squares is decomposed into two parts: the pure error component and the lack-of-fit component. These two components are used to construct an F statistic to test the hypotheses

H_0:   The relationship is linear

H_a: The relationship is not linear

If H_0 is accepted, the linear regression model is appropriate. If H_0 is rejected, the linear model does not fit the data well, and some other function may provide a better fit, although the test does not specify what that function is.

To conduct the F test, the decision rule is:

Reject H_0 if $F > F(\alpha; c - K - 1, n - c)$

Accept H_0 if $F \leq F(\alpha; c - K - 1, n - c)$

where K is the number of explanatory variables and n is the sample size. The value c requires some additional explanation.

The pure error lack-of-fit test requires that there be repeated observations (replications) for at least one level of the x variables. In the telemarketing data in Table 5.1, there are replicates for $x = 10, 20, 22,$ and 25. The value c is the number of distinct levels of x. In the telemarketing example, there are 14 levels of (or distinct values of) the explanatory variable. The decision rule to perform this test on the telemarketing data is:

Reject H_0 if $F > F(\alpha; 12, 6)$

Accept H_0 if $F \leq F(\alpha; 12, 6)$

(because $c = 14$, $K = 1$, and $n = 20$). The results are shown in Figure 6.11. From the output, the F statistic value is seen to be 5.25. If a 5% level of significance is used, the critical value for the test is $F(.05; 12, 6) = 4.00$, and the decision is to reject H_0 and conclude that a curvilinear model may fit the data better than the linear model. Also, the p value (.026) can be used in the usual manner to perform this test.

---

[1] This section refers specifically to MINITAB output, but the tests could be performed with other software.

FIGURE **6.11**   **MINITAB Output Showing Use of Pure Error Lack-of-Fit Test for Telemarketing Example**

```
The regression equation is
CALLS = 13.7 + 0.744 MONTHS

Predictor      Coef      StDev         T          P
Constant     13.671      1.427      9.58      0.000
MONTHS      0.74351    0.06666     11.15      0.000

S = 1.787        R-Sq = 87.4%       R-Sq(adj) = 86.7%

Analysis of Variance

Source              DF         SS         MS         F          P
Regression           1     397.45     397.45     124.41     0.000
Residual Error      18      57.50       3.19
  Lack of Fit       12      52.50       4.38       5.25     0.026
  Pure Error         6       5.00       0.83
Total               19     454.95

10 rows with no replicates
```

Note that this test cannot be performed unless there are replicates for at least one level of x. MINITAB does provide another test for lack of fit that does not require replicates. The *data subsetting test* actually involves a series of tests, and the results of several of these tests may be printed out on the output. For example, in Figure 6.12, results of tests examining curvilinearity in the variable MONTHS, lack of fit at the outer x values, and overall lack of fit are reported. These results are reported in terms of the p values, so the p value decision rule can be applied.

Reject H_0 if p value $< \alpha$

Accept H_0 if p value $\geq \alpha$

For $\alpha = 0.05$, the test result indicates possible curvature in the variable MONTHS and an overall lack of fit.

6.4.3   Corrections for Violations of the Linearity Assumption

When the linearity assumption is violated, the appropriate correction is not always obvious. The violation of this assumption implies that y and x are related in some curvilinear fashion, but there are many equations that describe curvilinear relationships. The idea behind the use of any equation of this sort is to transform the variables

FIGURE **6.12**   MINITAB Output Showing Data Subsetting Test for Telemarketing Example

```
The regression equation is
CALLS = 13.7 + 0.744 MONTHS


Predictor      Coef       StDev         T           P
Constant     13.671       1.427       9.58       0.000
MONTHS      0.74351     0.06666      11.15       0.000


S = 1.787        R-Sq = 87.4%      R-Sq(adj) = 86.7%


Analysis of Variance

Source             DF         SS          MS          F          P
Regression          1      397.45      397.45      124.41      0.000
Residual Error     18       57.50        3.19
Total              19      454.95


Lack of fit test
Possible curvature in variable MONTHS (P-Value = 0.000)
Possible lack of fit at outer X-values      (P-Value = 0.097)
Overall lack of fit test is significant at P = 0.000
```

in such a way that a linear relationship is achieved. If x and y are related in a curvilinear fashion, then perhaps x^2 and y have a linear relationship.

The violation of the linearity assumption was originally noted in the residual plots. If we have corrected for the violation, we should not see the same patterns in the residual plots from the corrected model. The residuals from a properly corrected model should be randomly scattered.

In Chapter 5, the following four commonly used corrections were considered:

1 polynomial regression
2 reciprocal transformation of the x variable
3 log transformation of the x variable
4 log transformation of both the x and y variables

After trying one of these transformations, check the new residual plots to see if the violation was effectively corrected. If not, try one of the other corrections. Refer to Chapter 5 for examples of the use of curvilinear models. The four corrections just listed are described in greater detail in Chapter 5 as well.

FIGURE **6.13**   **MINITAB Regression Output for Telemarketing Example with Second-Order Term Added**

```
The regression equation is
CALLS = -0.14 + 2.31 MONTHS - 0.0401 XSQR

Predictor       Coef       StDev          T          P
Constant      -0.140       2.323      -0.06      0.952
MONTHS        2.3102      0.2501       9.24      0.000
XSQR       -0.040118    0.006333      -6.33      0.000

S = 1.003        R-Sq = 96.2%      R-Sq(adj) = 95.8%

Analysis of Variance

Source           DF          SS         MS          F          P
Regression        2      437.84     218.92     217.92      0.000
Residual Error   17       17.11       1.01
Total            19      454.95

Source           DF      Seq SS
MONTHS            1      397.45
XSQR              1       40.39
```

EXAMPLE **6.2**   ## Telemarketing (continued)

In Chapter 5, a second-order polynomial regression was used to model the telemarketing data. The model can be written

$$CALLS = \beta_0 + \beta_1 \text{ MONTHS} + \beta_2 \text{XSQR} + e$$

where XSQR is a variable created by squaring each value of the MONTHS variable.

Figures 6.13 and 6.17 show, respectively, the MINITAB and Excel regression estimates of the second-order model. The estimated regression is

$$CALLS = -0.14 + 2.31\text{MONTHS} - 0.0401\text{XSQR}$$

Two checks should be made at this point to determine whether the second-order model is preferred to the original linear model: (a) test to see whether the coefficient of the second-order term is significantly different from zero and (b) check to see whether the new residual plots indicate an improved model. The t test was used in Chapter 5 to examine the significance of the second-order term. The coefficient was found to be significant. Next, we should examine the new residual plots.

FIGURE **6.14** MINITAB Plot of Standardized Residuals Versus Fitted Values for Second-Order Model

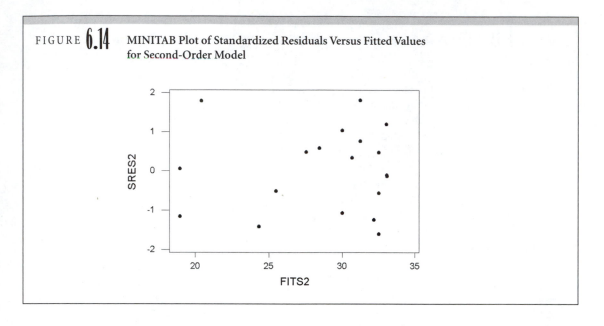

FIGURE **6.15** MINITAB Plot of Standardized Residuals Versus Explanatory Variable MONTHS for Second-Order Model

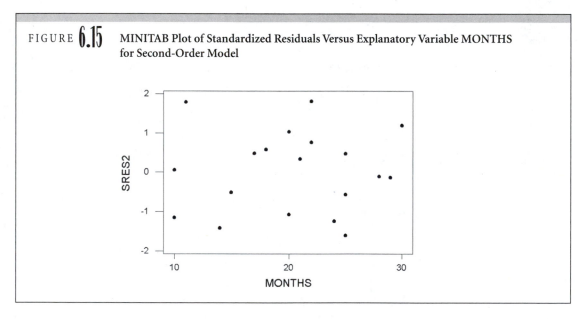

The test result on the second-order term by itself is not sufficient evidence to judge this model to be adequate. The goal in adding the second-order term was to correct for the curvilinear patterns noted in the original residual plots. To see if this has been accomplished, the residual plots from the new equation must be examined. The MINITAB residual plots of the standardized residuals versus the fitted values, the MONTHS variable, and the XSQR variable are shown in Figures 6.14, 6.15, and 6.16, respectively. The equivalent Excel plots are shown in Figures 6.18, 6.19, and 6.20.

FIGURE **6.16**   MINITAB Plot of Standardized Residuals Versus Explanatory Variable XSQR for Second-Order Model

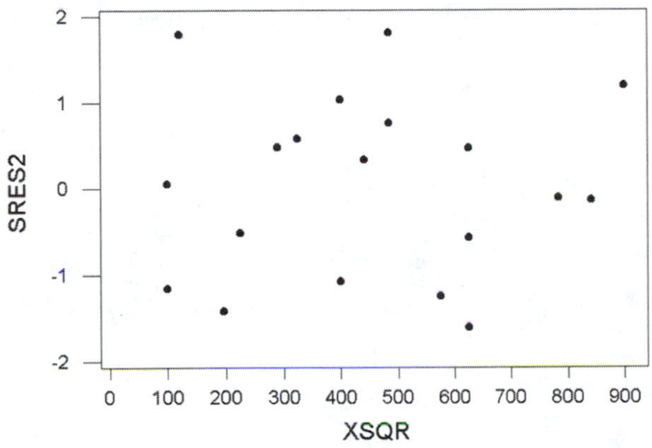

FIGURE **6.17**   Excel Regression Output for Telemarketing Example with Second-Order Term Added

SUMMARY OUTPUT

Regression Statistics

Multiple R	0.981
R Square	0.962
Adjusted R Square	0.958
Standard Error	1.003
Observations	20.000

ANOVA

	df	SS	MS	F	Significance F
Regression	2.000	437.839	218.920	217.503	0.0000
Residual	17.000	17.111	1.007		
Total	19.000	454.950			

	Coefficients	Standard Error	t Stat	P-value	Lower 95%	Upper 95%
Intercept	−0.140	2.323	−0.060	0.9525	−5.041	4.760
MONTHS	2.310	0.250	9.236	0.0000	1.782	2.838
XSQR	−0.040	0.006	−6.335	0.0000	−0.053	−0.027

FIGURE **6.18**   Excel Plot of Standardized Residuals Versus Fitted Values
for Second-Order Model

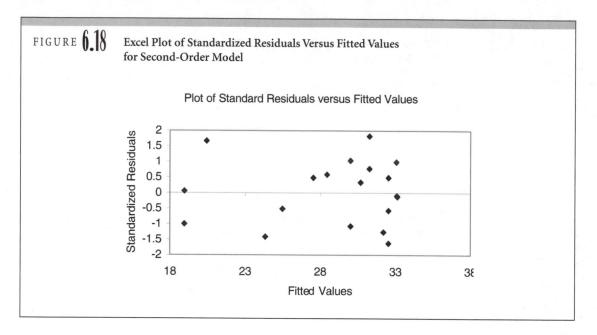

FIGURE **6.19**   Excel Plot of Standardized Residuals Versus Explanatory Variable MONTHS
for Second-Order Model

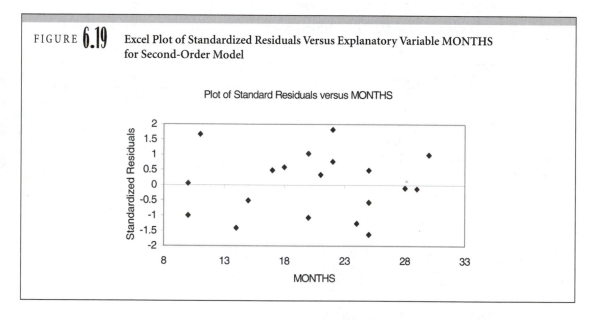

Looking at the residual plots, no distinct patterns can be seen. Contrast this with the obvious patterns of Figures 6.7 and 6.8 or 6.9 and 6.10. The addition of the x^2 variable appears to have corrected for the curvilinearity. The second-order model is an improvement over the first-order model, and the regression assumptions appear to be satisfied.

Higher-order terms could be added to the model, but there appears to be little justification in doing so from looking at the second-order model regression output and residual plots.

FIGURE **6.20**   **Excel Plot of Standardized Residuals Versus Explanatory Variable XSQR for Second-Order Model**

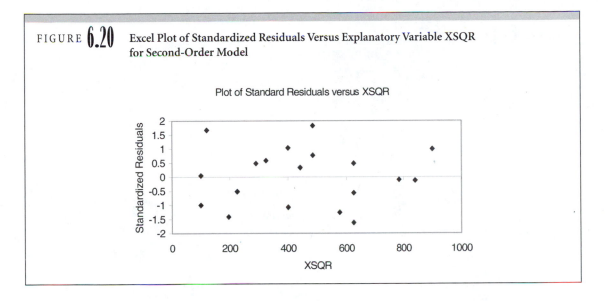

Other indicators that the regression has been improved by adding the x^2 term (as discussed in Chapter 5) include the reduction in the standard error of the regression from 1.787 to 1.003 and the increase in adjusted R^2 from 86.7% to 95.8%.

When curvilinear patterns appear in residuals plots, it is typically a sign that a linear model has been fit when a curvilinear model is more appropriate (or that an incorrect curvilinear model was fit). When this happens, a choice of the type of curvilinear model must be made. Some of the more common types of curvilinear models were discussed in Chapter 5, and that discussion is not repeated again here in Chapter 6. The reader should be sure to review these models. When one of the models is chosen as a possible improvement, be sure to recheck the residual plots. A random scatter in the residual plots indicates that the correct model was fit to the data. If patterns in the residual plots persist, try a different correction.

EXERCISES

1 **Parabola**   Consider the following data:

y	16	4	1	9	1	25	16	4	0	9	25
x	−4	−2	1	3	−1	−5	4	2	0	−3	5

Regard x as the explanatory variable and y as the dependent variable. Figure 6.21 shows the scatterplot of y versus x. Figure 6.22 shows the MINITAB regression output.

FIGURE 6.21   MINITAB Scatterplot of *y* Versus *x* for Parabola Exercise

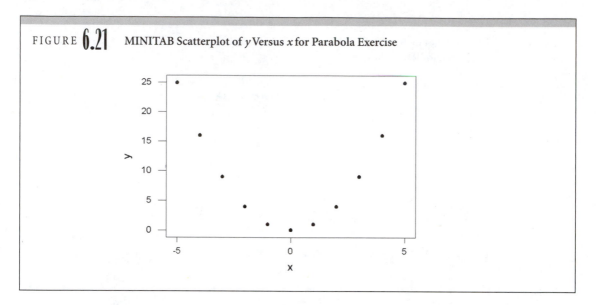

FIGURE 6.22   MINITAB Output for Regression of *y* Versus *x* for Parabola Exercise

```
The regression equation is
y = 10.0 - 0.000 x

Predictor      Coef       StDev          T            P
Constant     10.000       2.944        3.40        0.008
x           -0.0000      0.9309       -0.00        1.000

S = 9.764        R-Sq = 0.0%        R-Sq(adj) = 0.0%

Analysis of Variance

Source            DF         SS           MS          F           P
Regression         1       0.00         0.00       0.00       1.000
Residual Error     9     858.00        95.33
Total             10     858.00
```

a   Examine the scatterplot of *y* versus *x*. Does there appear to be a relationship between *y* and *x*?

b   What is the estimated linear regression equation relating *y* to *x*?

c   Test the hypothesis $H_0: \beta_1 = 0$ against the alternate $H_a: \beta_1 \neq 0$ at the 1% level of significance. What conclusion can drawn from the result of the test?

FIGURE **6.23**   MINITAB Plot of Standardized Residuals Versus Fitted Values for Research and Development Exercise

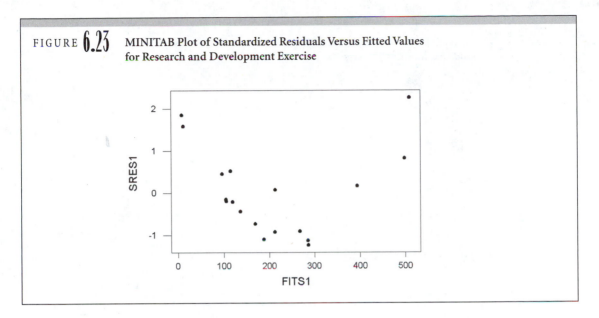

d   Despite the outcome of the test in part c, does there appear to be a "strong" or "weak" association between x and y? Express this association in the form of an equation.

2   **Research and Development**   In this problem, you will be asked to refer back to exercise 1 in Chapter 5 and to use the graphs and regression output provided there to help answer the questions. A company is interested in the relationship between profit on a number of projects and two explanatory variables. These variables are the expenditure on research and development for the project (RD) and a measure of risk assigned at the outset of the project (RISK). Table 5.8 shows the data on the three variables PROFIT, RISK, and RD. PROFIT is measured in thousands of dollars and RD is measured in hundreds of dollars. The scatterplots of PROFIT versus RISK and PROFIT versus RD are shown in Figures 5.25 and 5.26, respectively. The MINITAB and Excel regressions are in Figures 5.27 and 5.28. The MINITAB residual plots of the standardized residuals versus the fitted values, RISK, and RD are shown in Figures 6.23, 6.24, and 6.25, respectively. The corresponding Excel plots are in Figures 6.26, 6.27, and 6.28.

Using any of the given outputs, does the linearity assumption appear to be violated? Justify your answer. If you answered yes, state how the violation might be corrected. Then try your correction using a computer regression routine. Does your model appear to be an improvement over the original model? Justify your answer.

These data are available in a file with prefix RD6 in three columns: RD, RISK, and PROFIT.

FIGURE **6.24** MINITAB Plot of Standardized Residuals Versus RISK for Research and Development Exercise

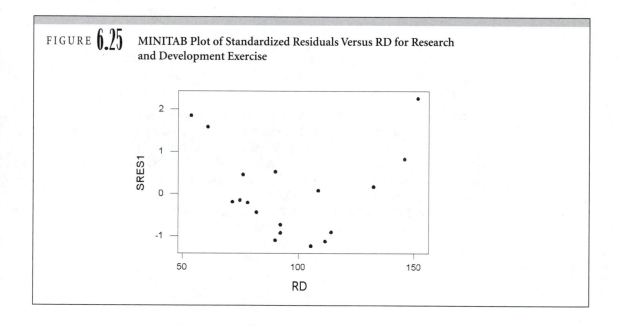

FIGURE **6.25** MINITAB Plot of Standardized Residuals Versus RD for Research and Development Exercise

FIGURE **6.26**   **Excel Plot of Standardized Residuals Versus Fitted Values for Research and Development Exercise**

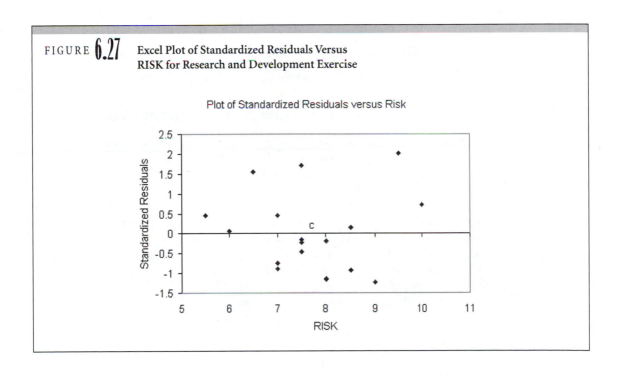

FIGURE **6.28** Excel Plot of Standardized Residuals Versus RD for Research and Development Exercise

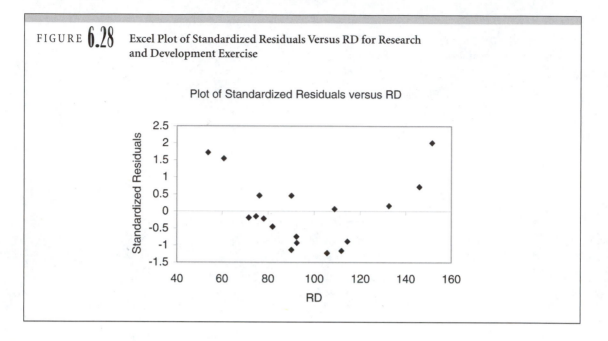

6.5 ASSESSING THE ASSUMPTION THAT THE VARIANCE AROUND THE REGRESSION LINE IS CONSTANT

6.5.1 Using Plots to Assess the Assumption of Constant Variance

Assumption b of Section 6.2 states that the disturbances in the population regression equation, e_i, have constant variance σ_e^2. In a residual plot of $\hat{e}_i$ versus an explanatory variable x, the residuals should appear scattered randomly about the zero line with no differences in the amount of variation in the residuals regardless of the value of x. If there appears to be a difference in variation (for example, if the residuals are more spread out for large values of x than for small values), then the assumption of constant variance may be violated. In a residual plot, nonconstant variance is often identified by a "cone-shaped" pattern as shown in Figure 6.29. Again, the violation is indicated by a systematic pattern in the residuals. In many texts, the term *heteroskedasticity* is used in place of "nonconstant variance." Example 6.3 illustrates the use of plots to assess the constant variance assumption.

FIGURE **6.29**   Cone-Shaped Pattern in Residual Plot Suggesting Nonconstant Variance

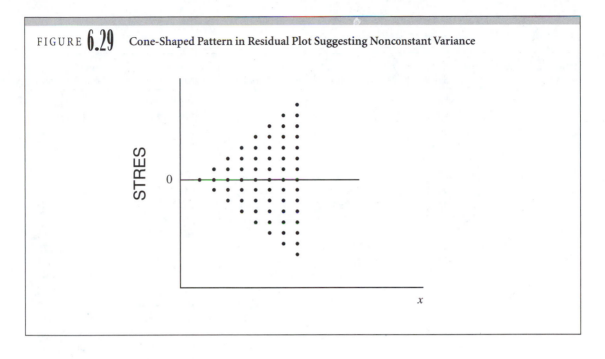

EXAMPLE **6.3**   **FOC Sales**

Techcore is a high-tech company located in Fort Worth, Texas. The company produces a part called a fibre-optic connector (FOC) and wants to generate reasonably accurate but simple forecasts of the sales of FOCs over time. They have weekly sales data for the past 265 weeks. These data are shown in Table 6.1. (The data have been disguised to provide confidentiality.) The time-series plot of FOC sales is shown in Figure 6.30. The MINITAB regression of FOC sales using a linear trend variable as the independent variable is shown in Figure 6.31 and the Excel output is in Figure 6.34. The MINITAB plots of the standardized residuals versus the fitted values and the standardized residuals versus the trend variable are shown in Figures 6.32 and 6.33, respectively (with the equivalent Excel plots in Figures 6.35 and 6.36). In both of these plots, the cone-shaped pattern of residuals is observed. Note that the variability of the residuals increases over time. This pattern also can be seen in the time-series plot of FOC sales. Such violations of assumptions, however, are typically magnified in the residual plots, as in this case.

When the disturbance variance is not constant, the use of the least-squares method has two major drawbacks:

1   The estimates of the regression coefficients are no longer minimum variance estimates.

2   The estimates of the standard errors of the coefficients are biased.

TABLE 6.1   Data for FOC Sales Example

Time Period	Sales	Time Period	Sales	Time Period	Sales	Time Period	Sales	Time Period	Sales	Time Period	Sales
1	2425	46	7631	90	9577	134	17947	178	20956	222	25054
2	6742	47	9892	91	8871	135	15886	179	12589	223	15754
3	5708	48	2688	92	12558	136	14299	180	19564	224	17766
4	5354	49	7394	93	10570	137	16727	181	16406	225	19075
5	6099	50	4836	94	12688	138	17251	182	15861	226	21718
6	5574	51	12655	95	13078	139	17063	183	17291	227	19815
7	7148	52	9114	96	10032	140	15195	184	11632	228	21979
8	6112	53	4399	97	8893	141	11866	185	13842	229	22063
9	5682	54	8529	98	13590	142	18312	186	19804	230	28064
10	5545	55	12080	99	15818	143	17634	187	24103	231	14462
11	5957	56	9011	100	8480	144	18414	188	15016	232	29676
12	5664	57	7127	101	16157	145	16071	189	15809	233	21617
13	6011	58	10917	102	11433	146	18727	190	15879	234	19068
14	5954	59	8525	103	13828	147	20121	191	23434	235	22706
15	5415	60	6834	104	11664	148	21417	192	16196	236	13779
16	5048	61	8660	105	4425	149	15016	193	17041	237	14576
17	6650	62	8377	106	6856	150	15511	194	17658	238	23166
18	6082	63	9435	107	10422	151	16290	195	23447	239	28113
19	6348	64	10633	108	11959	152	20031	196	30010	240	22449
20	6566	65	7965	109	13098	153	9258	197	18307	241	25389
21	7159	66	12965	110	10228	154	15293	198	23636	242	24570
22	5374	67	9443	111	11967	155	18773	199	24844	243	39514
23	4967	68	6185	112	10337	156	14069	200	29739	244	14004
24	7122	69	11846	113	12970	157	9712	201	20720	245	28502
25	7359	70	10620	114	12186	158	12623	202	21575	246	19945
26	8126	71	8906	115	12283	159	11030	203	20466	247	24518
27	7868	72	9787	116	15702	160	12156	204	24650	248	34138
28	4917	73	9446	117	16675	161	18692	205	12509	249	21071
29	6791	74	8901	118	11764	162	15535	206	25198	250	23312
30	9494	75	7025	119	9566	163	18926	207	20084	251	20894
31	8959	76	11133	120	14276	164	18529	208	20877	252	37976
32	9767	77	8122	121	12954	165	15930	209	10080	253	17546
33	9471	78	10113	122	15769	166	13528	210	5571	254	35900
34	7142	79	12531	123	10427	167	19739	211	14443	255	26701
35	6702	80	8302	124	14089	168	16451	212	16831	256	29392
36	7611	81	10725	125	10723	169	17785	213	24679	257	9574
37	6012	82	14100	126	14525	170	16298	214	14537	258	16205
38	8463	83	13198	127	10841	171	14799	215	13951	259	40481
39	6717	84	10097	128	16282	172	16557	216	17114	260	28947
40	7575	85	11046	129	14603	173	16391	217	26375	261	31091
41	10818	86	10756	130	16673	174	18792	218	13525	262	7456
42	7802	87	12432	131	13721	175	12734	219	20938	263	17953
43	7322	88	9813	132	11548	176	17173	220	13773	264	16302
44	6407	89	10058	133	15127	177	13516	221	21644	265	19521
45	8325										

FIGURE **6.30** MINITAB Time-Series Plot of FOC Sales

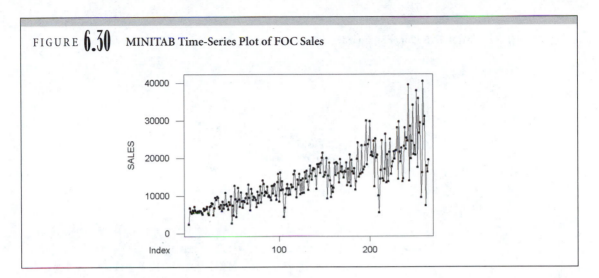

FIGURE **6.31** MINITAB Regression Output for FOC Sales Example

```
The regression equation is
SALES = 4704 + 72.5 TIME

Predictor      Coef      StDev         T         P
Constant     4703.8      512.5      9.18     0.000
TIME         72.459      3.340     21.69     0.000

S = 4159        R-Sq = 64.2%      R-Sq(adj) = 64.0%

Analysis of Variance

Source            DF          SS          MS         F         P
Regression         1   8142042913  8142042913    470.62     0.000
Residual Error   263   4550042800    17300543
Total            264  12692085712

Unusual Observations
Obs      TIME      SALES       Fit    StDev Fit     Residual    St Resid
196       196      30010     18906         331        11104       2.68R
200       200      29739     19196         340        10543       2.54R
209       209      10080     19848         360        -9768      -2.36R
210       210       5571     19920         363       -14349      -3.46R
243       243      39514     22311         448        17203       4.16R
244       244      14004     22384         450        -8380      -2.03R
248       248      34138     22674         461        11464       2.77R
252       252      37976     22963         473        15013       3.63R
254       254      35900     23108         478        12792       3.10R
257       257       9574     23326         487       -13752      -3.33R
259       259      40481     23471         492        17010       4.12R
262       262       7456     23688         501       -16232      -3.93R

R denotes an observation with a large standardized residual
```

FIGURE 6.32 MINITAB Plot of Standardized Residuals Versus Fitted Values for FOC Sales Example

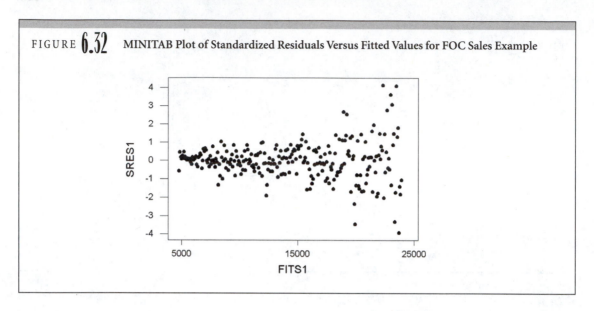

FIGURE 6.33 MINITAB Plot of Standardized Residuals Versus TIME for FOC Sales Example

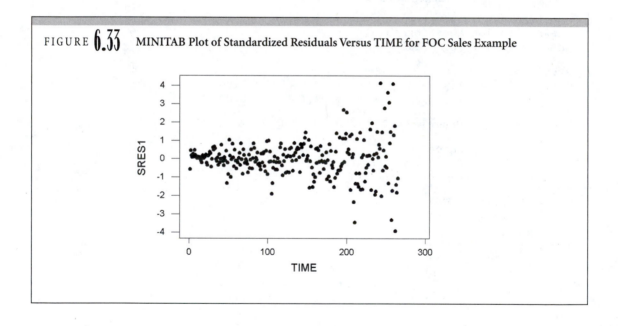

FIGURE **6.34**   Excel Regression Output for FOC Sales Example

SUMMARY OUTPUT

Regression Statistics

Multiple R	0.801
R Square	0.642
Adjusted R Square	0.640
Standard Error	4159.392
Observations	265.000

ANOVA

	df	SS	MS	F	Significance F
Regression	1.000	8142042913	8142042912.548	470.624	0.0000
Residual	263.000	4550042800	17300542.965		
Total	264.000	12692085712			

	Coefficients	Standard Error	t Stat	P-value	Lower 95%	Upper 95%
Intercept	4703.769	512.469	9.179	0.000	3694.706	5712.832
TIME	72.459	3.340	21.694	0.000	65.882	79.036

FIGURE **6.35**   Excel Plot of Standardized Residuals Versus Fitted Values for FOC Sales Example

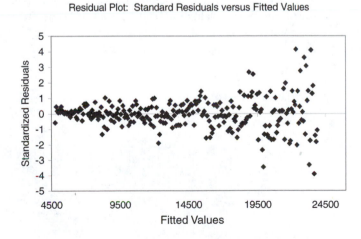

Residual Plot: Standard Residuals versus Fitted Values

FIGURE 6.36 Excel Plot for Standardized Residuals Versus TIME for FOC Sales Example

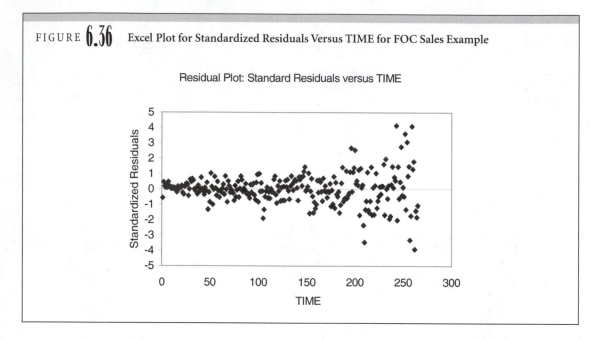

The first drawback suggests that estimates of the coefficients with smaller sampling variability may exist. Because of the second drawback, hypothesis tests about the population regression parameters may provide misleading results.

6.5.2 A Test for Nonconstant Variance

Several tests are available for nonconstant variance, although a study by Griffiths and Surekha ("A Monte Carlo Evaluation of the Power of Some Tests for Heteroscedasticity"[2]) demonstrated that a test from J. Szroeter tends to be better at detecting nonconstant variance. The hypotheses to be tested are:

H_0: Variance is constant

H_a: Variance is not constant.

Szroeter's test statistic is

$$Q = \left(\frac{6n}{n^2 - 1} \right)^{1/2} \left(h - \frac{n+1}{2} \right)$$

where n is the sample size,

---

[2] See References for complete publication information.

$$h = \frac{\sum\limits_{i=1}^{n} i\hat{e}_i^2}{\sum\limits_{i=1}^{n} \hat{e}_i^2}$$

and $\hat{e}_i$, is the residual from the ith observation in the regression equation. The decision rule for the test is

Reject H_0 if $Q > z_\alpha$

Accept H_0 if $Q \le z_\alpha$

where α is the level of significance for the test and z_α is chosen from the standard normal table with upper-tail area α.

Szroeter's test assumes that all the observations can be arranged in order of increasing variance. Typically, it is assumed that the variance increases as the value of one of the explanatory variables increases. Thus, the data need to be arranged according to the values of this explanatory variable. As a simple example, suppose the values of x and y in a simple regression are as follows:

x	3	2	7	9	4
y	6	4	16	15	8

Arranging the values of x in ascending order and maintaining the associated values of y results in the following arrangement of the data:

x	2	3	4	7	9
y	4	6	8	16	15

After reordering the data in this way, a regression is run and the residuals, $\hat{e}_i$, are saved and used to compute h. The value for h is then substituted into the equation to compute the test statistic Q.

6.5.3   Corrections for Nonconstant Variance

There are a number of possible corrections for nonconstant variance. All require a transformation of the dependent variable. This often makes comparison of the new regression equation with the old equation difficult. Some commonly used corrections for nonconstant variance are as follows:

1   In place of the dependent variable y, use the natural logarithm of y, $\ln(y)$. The natural logarithms of the y values are less variable than the original y values and may stabilize the variance. For example, consider the numbers in Table 6.2. Note the difference in variation between the original y values and their natural logarithms. Note also that the natural logarithm transformation is only defined for positive numbers.

The natural logarithm transformation is the appropriate transformation when the error standard deviation is proportional to the mean of the dependent variable.

TABLE 6.2   Example of Using the Natural Logarithm Transformation to Reduce Variability

y	1	2	5	10	50
$\ln(y)$	0	0.69	1.61	2.30	3.91

2   In place of the dependent variable y, use the square root of y, $\sqrt{y}$. The square roots of the y values are less variable than the original y values and may stabilize the variance. Note that the square root transformation is not defined for negative numbers.

     The square root transformation is appropriate when the dependent variable is a count variable that follows a Poisson distribution.

3   If the disturbance variance is thought to be proportional to some function of one of the x variables, the values of that variable can be used to stabilize the variance. For example, if

$$\sigma_{e_i}^2 = \sigma^2 \, x_i^2$$

is thought to express the relationship between the variance at each observation i and the associated value of the x variable, then dividing each variable in the regression by x stabilizes the variance. If the original equation is

$$y_i = \beta_0 + \beta_1 x_i + e_i$$

then after dividing through by x_i, the transformed model becomes

$$\frac{y_i}{x_i} = \beta_0 \left(\frac{1}{x_i} \right) + \beta_1 + e_i'$$

where $e_i' = e_i / x_i$ is a new disturbance with constant variance. Note that the roles played by β_0 and β_1 have been reversed in the transformed equation. The transformation is not defined when x_i is zero.

EXAMPLE 6.4   **FOC Sales (continued)**

The MINITAB regression output for the regression of the natural log of sales (LOGSALES) on TIME is shown in Figure 6.37, and the residual plots are in Figures 6.38 and 6.39. In the residual plots, the cone-shaped pattern has been greatly reduced. Using the log transformation stabilized the variance, so it is now relatively constant for all values of x. Caution should be exercised in interpreting and using the regression output, however. The output in Figure 6.37 shows results concerning the relationship of the log of sales to TIME. All information from the output must be interpreted in light of this fact. Thus, 68.7% of the variation in the log of sales has been explained. This value is not directly comparable to the R^2 from the regression of y on x in Figure 6.31

FIGURE **6.37**   **MINITAB Output for Regression of LOGSALES on TIME**

```
The regression equation is
LOGSALES = 8.74 + 0.00537 TIME


Predictor      Coef       StDev          T           P
Constant    8.73903     0.03430      254.80       0.000
TIME      0.0053746   0.0002235       24.04       0.000


S = 0.2784       R-Sq = 68.7%       R-Sq(adj) = 68.6%


Analysis of Variance


Source             DF         SS         MS          F           P
Regression          1     44.797     44.797     578.09       0.000
Residual Error    263     20.380      0.077
Total             264     65.177


Unusual Observations
Obs      TIME    LOGSALES      Fit    StDev Fit     Residual    St Resid
  1         1      7.7936    8.7444     0.0341      -0.9508      -3.44R
 48        48      7.8966    8.9970     0.0256      -1.1005      -3.97R
 53        53      8.3891    9.0239     0.0247      -0.6348      -2.29R
105       105      8.3950    9.3034     0.0182      -0.9083      -3.27R
209       209      9.2183    9.8623     0.0241      -0.6440      -2.32R
210       210      8.6253    9.8677     0.0243      -1.2424      -4.48R
257       257      9.1668   10.1203     0.0326      -0.9535      -3.45R
262       262      8.9168   10.1472     0.0335      -1.2304      -4.45R


R denotes an observation with a large standardized residual
```

(64.2%). No conclusions can be drawn concerning which regression does "better" based on the R^2 because two different measures of the dependent variable are used.

Also keep in mind that, if the equation from Figure 6.37 is used for forecasting, natural logs of the y values are forecasted, not the y values themselves. For example, what is the forecast of sales in week 300? Using the estimated regression equation

$$LOGSALES = 8.74 + 0.00537(300) = 10.351$$

The forecast value for LOGSALES is 10.351. The resulting forecast value for y must be computed as

$$SALES = e^{10.351} = 31,288$$

FIGURE **6.38** MINITAB Plot of Standardized Residuals Versus Fitted Values for Transformed Model

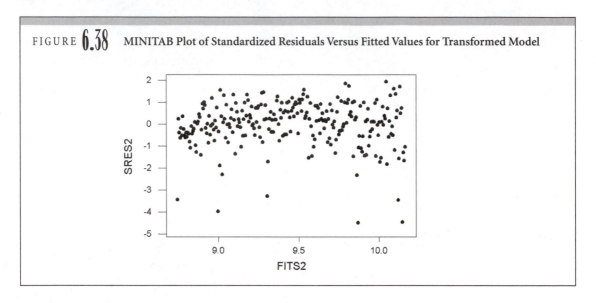

FIGURE **6.39** MINITAB Plot of Standardized Residuals Versus Explanatory Variable TIME for Transformed Model

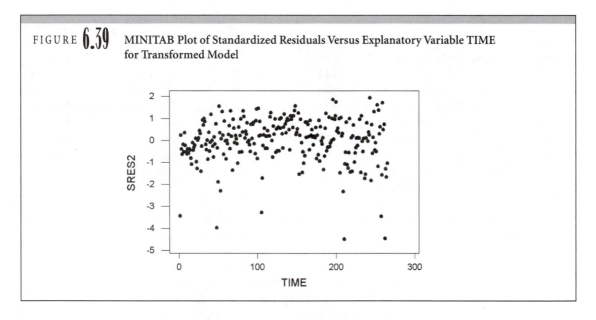

When deciding whether the transformation has improved our results, comparing the R^2 is not always dependable as noted. The residual plots can be used to help in this decision. If the pattern suggesting a violation in the original residual plots is no longer present in the plots from a transformed model, then the transformed model is preferable. If there is little or no improvement in the residual plots, then another transformation should be tried and the resulting residual plots examined to see whether they indicate an improved model. Choosing the correct transformation to produce an adequate model is thus an iterative process that may take several tries. And when all else fails, consult your neighborhood statistician!

EXERCISES

3 **S&P 500 Index Prices**   The data in Table 6.3 show the monthly prices for the S&P 500 Stock Index for the time period January 1970 through December 1998. Our objective is to build a regression model relating the current price to the price in the previous month. The regression equation can be written as

$$y_i = \beta_0 + \beta_1 y_{i-1} + e_i$$

where y_i represents the S&P 500 Index price in time period i.

Figure 6.40 is the output for the regression of current index price on the previous month's price. Figures 6.41 and 6.42 are the residual plots from this regression.

Is there evidence that the constant variance assumption has been violated? Justify your answer. Suggest a correction for the violation of the constant variance assumption for this example. Try the correction using a regression routine. Does the correction appear to have eliminated the problem of nonconstant variance? State why or why not.

These data are in a file with prefix SP5006.

TABLE **6.3**   **S&P 500 Index Prices**

Year	Month	S&P500	Year	Month	S&P500	Year	Month	S&P500	Year	Month	S&P500
1970	1	85.28	1971	1	99.82	1972	1	111.62	1973	1	128.20
1970	2	90.03	1971	2	100.98	1972	2	114.71	1973	2	123.68
1970	3	90.43	1971	3	104.96	1972	3	115.66	1973	3	123.78
1970	4	82.52	1971	4	109.04	1972	4	116.44	1973	4	119.04
1970	5	77.75	1971	5	104.78	1972	5	118.74	1973	5	117.11
1970	6	74.12	1971	6	105.13	1972	6	116.43	1973	6	116.64
1970	7	79.82	1971	7	101.06	1972	7	116.98	1973	7	121.38
1970	8	83.64	1971	8	104.98	1972	8	121.30	1973	8	117.24
1970	9	86.66	1971	9	104.51	1972	9	120.99	1973	9	122.25
1970	10	85.94	1971	10	100.42	1972	10	122.42	1973	10	122.45
1970	11	90.29	1971	11	100.44	1972	11	128.32	1973	11	108.87
1970	12	95.68	1971	12	109.37	1972	12	130.14	1973	12	111.02

Continues

TABLE **6.3**   *(continued)*

Year	Month	S&P500	Year	Month	S&P500	Year	Month	S&P500	Year	Month	S&P500
1974	1	110.23	1977	3	128.50	1980	5	171.86	1983	7	295.96
1974	2	110.15	1977	4	129.03	1980	6	177.30	1983	8	300.40
1974	3	107.89	1977	5	126.50	1980	7	189.64	1983	9	304.55
1974	4	104.02	1977	6	132.75	1980	8	191.55	1983	10	301.03
1974	5	100.88	1977	7	130.71	1980	9	197.19	1983	11	307.38
1974	6	99.73	1977	8	128.85	1980	10	201.18	1983	12	305.77
1974	7	92.34	1977	9	129.05	1980	11	222.61	1984	1	304.06
1974	8	84.36	1977	10	124.02	1980	12	215.90	1984	2	293.37
1974	9	74.64	1977	11	127.94	1981	1	206.86	1984	3	298.45
1974	10	87.19	1977	12	128.90	1981	2	210.46	1984	4	301.28
1974	11	82.93	1978	1	121.50	1981	3	218.87	1984	5	284.60
1974	12	81.64	1978	2	119.04	1981	4	214.64	1984	6	290.78
1975	1	92.02	1978	3	122.54	1981	5	215.19	1984	7	287.17
1975	2	97.89	1978	4	133.60	1981	6	213.84	1984	8	318.89
1975	3	100.38	1978	5	134.82	1981	7	214.28	1984	9	318.97
1975	4	105.49	1978	6	132.97	1981	8	201.91	1984	10	320.20
1975	5	110.52	1978	7	140.72	1981	9	191.96	1984	11	316.61
1975	6	115.80	1978	8	144.96	1981	10	202.32	1984	12	324.95
1975	7	108.34	1978	9	144.49	1981	11	210.67	1985	1	350.27
1975	8	106.43	1978	10	131.89	1981	12	205.27	1985	2	354.56
1975	9	103.11	1978	11	134.73	1982	1	202.59	1985	3	354.80
1975	10	109.85	1978	12	137.37	1982	2	191.26	1985	4	354.46
1975	11	112.95	1979	1	143.46	1982	3	190.27	1985	5	374.94
1975	12	112.03	1979	2	138.85	1982	4	198.87	1985	6	380.82
1976	1	125.67	1979	3	147.13	1982	5	192.09	1985	7	380.26
1976	2	124.61	1979	4	148.06	1982	6	189.20	1985	8	377.01
1976	3	128.81	1979	5	144.84	1982	7	185.83	1985	9	365.22
1976	4	127.81	1979	6	151.14	1982	8	208.39	1985	10	382.09
1976	5	126.39	1979	7	153.17	1982	9	210.99	1985	11	408.30
1976	6	131.99	1979	8	162.01	1982	10	235.28	1985	12	428.05
1976	7	131.36	1979	9	162.70	1982	11	244.78	1986	1	430.44
1976	8	131.12	1979	10	152.29	1982	12	249.50	1986	2	462.62
1976	9	134.50	1979	11	159.53	1983	1	258.77	1986	3	488.42
1976	10	132.00	1979	12	162.94	1983	2	264.70	1986	4	482.93
1976	11	131.46	1980	1	173.06	1983	3	274.48	1986	5	508.62
1976	12	138.84	1980	2	173.05	1983	4	296.11	1986	6	517.21
1977	1	132.27	1980	3	156.23	1983	5	293.53	1986	7	488.28
1977	2	129.86	1980	4	163.45	1983	6	304.96	1986	8	524.49

TABLE 6.3   (continued)

Year	Month	S&P500	Year	Month	S&P500	Year	Month	S&P500	Year	Month	S&P500
1986	9	481.13	1989	10	785.67	1992	11	1103.39	1995	12	1713.75
1986	10	508.88	1989	11	801.69	1992	12	1116.93	1996	1	1772.08
1986	11	521.25	1989	12	820.94	1993	1	1126.21	1996	2	1788.51
1986	12	507.95	1990	1	765.83	1993	2	1141.56	1996	3	1805.72
1987	1	576.34	1990	2	775.69	1993	3	1165.65	1996	4	1832.35
1987	2	599.12	1990	3	796.25	1993	4	1137.47	1996	5	1879.60
1987	3	616.40	1990	4	776.38	1993	5	1167.90	1996	6	1886.77
1987	4	610.93	1990	5	852.08	1993	6	1171.32	1996	7	1803.42
1987	5	616.23	1990	6	846.33	1993	7	1166.61	1996	8	1841.46
1987	6	647.35	1990	7	843.62	1993	8	1210.87	1996	9	1945.10
1987	7	680.14	1990	8	767.36	1993	9	1201.59	1996	10	1998.75
1987	8	705.52	1990	9	730.02	1993	10	1226.44	1996	11	2149.83
1987	9	690.05	1990	10	726.91	1993	11	1214.74	1996	12	2107.23
1987	10	541.44	1990	11	773.90	1993	12	1229.43	1997	1	2238.88
1987	11	496.82	1990	12	795.46	1994	1	1271.22	1997	2	2256.43
1987	12	534.62	1991	1	830.10	1994	2	1236.72	1997	3	2163.72
1988	1	557.10	1991	2	889.46	1994	3	1182.80	1997	4	2292.89
1988	2	583.07	1991	3	911.00	1994	4	1197.97	1997	5	2432.49
1988	3	565.06	1991	4	913.16	1994	5	1217.63	1997	6	2541.47
1988	4	571.31	1991	5	952.55	1994	6	1187.78	1997	7	2743.68
1988	5	576.25	1991	6	908.91	1994	7	1226.79	1997	8	2589.98
1988	6	602.70	1991	7	951.28	1994	8	1277.08	1997	9	2731.82
1988	7	600.41	1991	8	973.82	1994	9	1245.85	1997	10	2640.59
1988	8	580.03	1991	9	957.52	1994	10	1273.84	1997	11	2762.83
1988	9	604.74	1991	10	970.39	1994	11	1227.45	1997	12	2810.27
1988	10	621.58	1991	11	931.29	1994	12	1245.66	1998	1	2841.36
1988	11	612.72	1991	12	1037.80	1995	1	1277.96	1998	2	3046.29
1988	12	623.41	1992	1	1018.46	1995	2	1327.77	1998	3	3202.29
1989	1	669.06	1992	2	1031.65	1995	3	1366.95	1998	4	3234.50
1989	2	652.39	1992	3	1011.59	1995	4	1407.20	1998	5	3178.91
1989	3	667.60	1992	4	1041.34	1995	5	1463.44	1998	6	3308.03
1989	4	702.27	1992	5	1046.44	1995	6	1497.43	1998	7	3272.81
1989	5	730.68	1992	6	1030.88	1995	7	1547.09	1998	8	2799.63
1989	6	726.53	1992	7	1072.99	1995	8	1550.98	1998	9	2978.98
1989	7	792.13	1992	8	1051.03	1995	9	1616.44	1998	10	3221.3
1989	8	807.62	1992	9	1063.38	1995	10	1610.66	1998	11	3416.53
1989	9	804.34	1992	10	1067.05	1995	11	1681.36	1998	12	3613.41

Source: www.economagic.com/em-cgi/data.exe/fedst1/trsp500

FIGURE **6.40**   MINITAB Regression of Current S&P 500 Index Price on Previous Month's Price

```
The regression equation is
S&P500 = - 2.55 + 1.02 S&P LAG1

347 cases used 1 cases contain missing values

Predictor      Coef      StDev          T          P
Constant      -2.554     3.393      -0.75      0.452
S&P LAG1     1.01918    0.00339     300.74      0.000

S = 47.35        R-Sq = 99.6%      R-Sq(adj) = 99.6%

Analysis of Variance

Source             DF          SS          MS          F          P
Regression          1   202762112   202762112   90443.96      0.000
Residual Error    345      773439        2242
Total             346   203535552

Unusual Observations
Obs  S&P LAG1     S&P500        Fit     StDev Fit      Residual     St Resid
214       690     541.44     700.73        2.54       -159.29       -3.37R
319      1887    1803.42    1920.40        4.86       -116.98       -2.48R
323      1999    2149.83    2034.53        5.19        115.30        2.45R
327      2256    2163.72    2297.16        5.97       -133.44       -2.84R
329      2293    2432.49    2334.31        6.08         98.18        2.09R
330      2432    2541.47    2476.59        6.51         64.88        1.38 X
331      2541    2743.68    2587.66        6.85        156.02        3.33RX
332      2744    2589.98    2793.75        7.49       -203.77       -4.36RX
333      2590    2731.82    2637.10        7.01         94.72        2.02RX
334      2732    2640.59    2781.66        7.46       -141.07       -3.02RX
335      2641    2762.83    2688.68        7.17         74.15        1.58 X
336      2763    2810.27    2813.27        7.56         -3.00       -0.06 X
337      2810    2841.36    2861.62        7.71        -20.26       -0.43 X
338      2841    3046.29    2893.30        7.81        152.99        3.28RX
339      3046    3202.29    3102.16        8.47        100.13        2.15RX
340      3202    3234.50    3261.16        8.97        -26.66       -0.57 X
341      3235    3178.91    3293.98        9.08       -115.07       -2.48RX
342      3179    3308.03    3237.33        8.90         70.70        1.52 X
343      3308    3272.81    3368.93        9.32        -96.12       -2.07RX
344      3273    2799.63    3333.03        9.20       -533.40      -11.48RX
345      2800    2978.98    2850.77        7.67        128.21        2.74RX
346      2979    3221.30    3033.56        8.25        187.74        4.03RX
347      3221    3416.53    3280.53        9.03        136.00        2.93RX
348      3417    3613.41    3479.51        9.67        133.90        2.89RX

R denotes an observation with a large standardized residual
X denotes an observation whose X value gives it large influence.
```

FIGURE **6.41**   MINITAB Plot of Standardized Residuals Versus Fitted Values
for S&P 500 Index Exercise

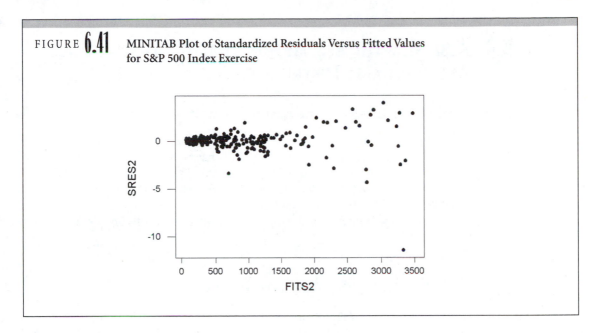

FIGURE **6.42**   MINITAB Plot of Standardized Residuals Versus Explanatory Variable
for S&P 500 Index Exercise

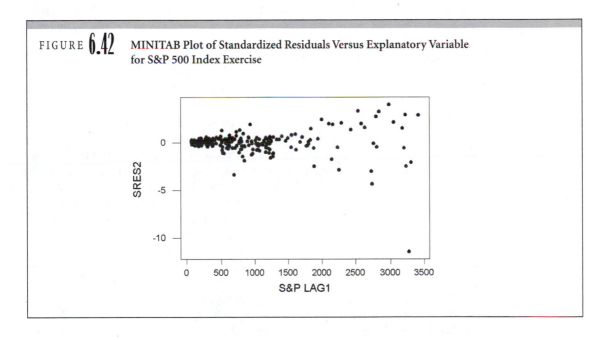

6.6 ASSESSING THE ASSUMPTION THAT THE DISTURBANCES ARE NORMALLY DISTRIBUTED

6.6.1 Using Plots to Assess the Assumption of Normality

Residual plots of the standardized residuals versus the fitted values can be used to assess graphically whether the sample residuals have come from a normally distributed population. For normally distributed data, about 68% of the standardized residuals should be between −1 and +1, about 95% should be between −2 and +2, and about 99% should be between −3 and +3.

Normal probability plots also can be a useful graphical technique in assessing normality.

EXAMPLE 6.5   Communications Nodes (continued)

Figure 6.43 shows the MINITAB regression of cost (COST) on the number of ports (NUMPORTS) and the bandwidth (BANDWIDTH) for the communications nodes data discussed in several examples in Chapters 3 and 4. The Excel regression is shown in Figure 6.44. The plots of the standardized residuals versus the fitted values are shown in Figure 6.45 for MINITAB and in Figure 6.46 for Excel. A printout of the standardized residuals is shown in Figure 6.47.

As can be seen from the plots and the printout, 13 of the 14 standardized residuals (93%) are between ±2. So there are about the number of residuals we would expect to see if they came from a normal distribution. From these plots, we conclude that the normality assumption seems reasonable.

Note that MINITAB also flags any observations with standardized residuals that are greater than or equal to 2 in absolute value. These values are shown with an R next to the value of the standardized residual in the table of Unusual Observations. Often, it is the observations with large standardized residuals with which we are concerned. This is why MINITAB takes the time to flag these observations. This does not mean that there is anything wrong with these data values or that they should be deleted. It simply means that these observations may be different from the others in our data set for some reason and may deserve special attention. When examining the normality assumption, concern should be placed on relatively large standardized residuals. Thus, an excessive number of residuals outside the ±2 limit or the ±3 limit might cause concern about this assumption. But remember to expect some values outside these limits, especially in large data sets.

Figure 6.48 shows the normal probability plot for the standardized residuals produced by MINITAB. In this plot, the observed standardized residuals (horizontal axis) are plotted against the "normal scores." The normal scores can be thought of as the values expected if a sample of the same size as the one used (14 in this case) was selected from a normal distribution. The vertical scale shows the cumulative probabilities at or below the normal scores rather than the normal scores themselves. The normal scores and the probabilities are computed by MINITAB.

FIGURE **6.43**   **MINITAB Output for Regression of COST on NUMPORTS and BANDWIDTH**

```
The regression equation is
COST = 17086 + 469 NUMPORTS + 81.1 BANDWIDTH


Predictor      Coef       StDev          T          P
Constant      17086        1865       9.16      0.000
NUMPORTS     469.03       66.98       7.00      0.000
BANDWIDT      81.07       21.65       3.74      0.003


S = 2983        R-Sq = 95.0%       R-Sq(adj) = 94.1%


Analysis of Variance

Source              DF           SS          MS          F          P
Regression           2   1876012662   938006331     105.45      0.000
Residual Error      11     97849860     8895442
Total               13   1973862521


Source      DF       Seq SS
NUMPORTS     1   1751268376
BANDWIDT     1    124744286


Unusual Observations
Obs  NUMPORTS       COST       Fit   StDev Fit   Residual    St Resid
  1      68.0      52388     53682        2532      -1294     -0.82 X
 10      24.0      23444     29153        1273      -5709     -2.12R


R denotes an observation with a large standardized residual
X denotes an observation whose X value gives it large influence.
```

When the plot of the normal scores (cumulative probabilities) and the data is approximately a straight line, the normality assumption appears reasonable. The normal scores are numbers we expect to see from a sample from a normal distribution, so for the two to plot on a straight line, the two sets of data have to be similar. Thus, we reason that the data must also have come from a normal distribution. If the data did not come from a normal distribution, the plot will show curvature. (Note that whether the normal probability plot is linear or not has nothing to do with whether the relationship between y and x is linear. We are not assessing whether the relationship between the original variables is linear, but whether the disturbances come from a normal distribution.)

FIGURE **6.44** Excel Output for Regression of COST on NUMPORTS and BANDWIDTH

SUMMARY OUTPUT

Regression Statistics
Multiple R	0.975
R Square	0.950
Adjusted R Square	0.941
Standard Error	2982.523
Observations	14.000

ANOVA

	df	SS	MS	F	Significance F
Regression	2.000	1876012661.776	938006330.888	105.448	0.000
Residual	11.000	97849859.724	8895441.793		
Total	13.000	1973862521.500			

	Coefficients	Standard Error	t Stat	P-value	Lower 95%	Upper 95%
Intercept	17085.751	1865.407	9.159	0.000	12980.016	21191.486
NUMPORTS	469.032	66.984	7.002	0.000	321.601	616.464
BANDWIDTH	81.074	21.650	3.745	0.003	33.423	128.725

FIGURE **6.45** MINITAB Plot of Standardized Residuals Versus Fitted Values

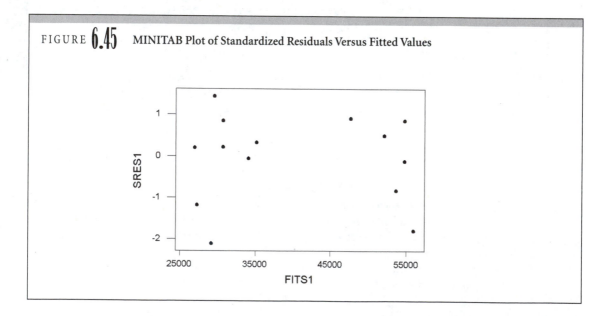

FIGURE **6.46**   Excel Plot of Standardized Residuals Versus Fitted Values

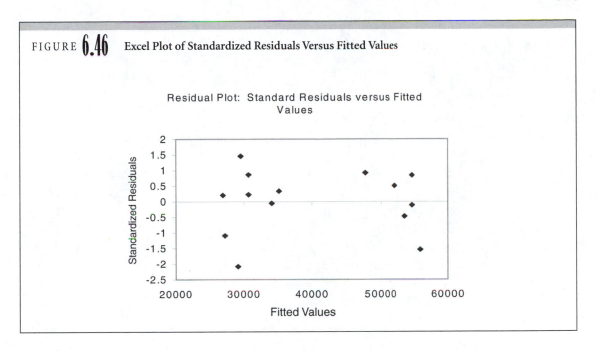

FIGURE **6.47**   Printout of Standardized Residuals for Communications Nodes Regression

Observation	Standardized Residuals
1	-0.472
2	-1.541
3	0.921
4	0.335
5	0.204
6	0.840
7	−0.112
8	−0.051
9	0.224
10	−2.081
11	−1.088
12	0.504
13	1.456
14	0.861

FIGURE **6.48** MINITAB Normal Probability Plot and Test for Normality

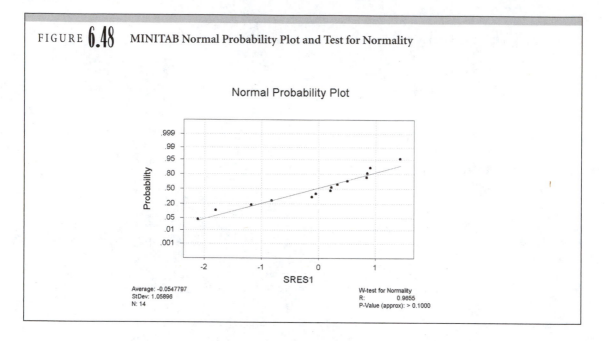

In this example, the plot of the normal scores versus the data is nearly linear (MINITAB has drawn in the line). This suggests that the standardized residuals could have come from a normal distribution. Thus, the normality assumption is supported.

6.6.2 Test for Normality

The plot of the standardized residuals versus the normal scores in the normal probability plot should be approximately linear if the disturbances are normal. The "straightness" of the line in the normal probability plot can be measured by computing the Ryan-Joiner test statistic, R (we use R to represent the test statistic since this is what MINITAB uses; note, however, that this has nothing to do with the R that MINITAB uses to flag large standardized residuals).

The hypotheses can be stated as

H_0: Disturbances are normal

H_a: Disturbances are nonnormal.

The decision rule is

Reject H_0 if $R < c_\alpha$

Accept H_0 if $R \geq c_\alpha$

Here c_α represents the critical value chosen from Table B.6 in Appendix B for level of significance α. If a p value for the test statistic is provided (as in MINITAB), this can also be used to conduct the test.

Note that the test for normality is referred to as the W-test in the MINITAB output. The test used here is essentially equivalent to a test called the Shapiro-Wilk W-test [see Shapiro and Wilk "An Analysis of Variance Test for Normality (Complete Samples)"] and takes its name from this test.

EXAMPLE **6.6**   ## Communications Nodes (continued)

The test statistic for the test for normality is given in Figure 6.48 as $R = 0.9655$. Using a 5% level of significance, the decision rule for the normality test is:

Reject H_0 if $R < 0.9383$

Accept H_0 if $R \geq 0.9383$

Since $n = 14$ in the example, we used the critical value 0.9383 ($n = 15$). Our decision is to accept the null hypothesis. The disturbances are normally distributed. Or using the p value:

Reject H_0 if p value < 0.05

Accept H_0 if p value ≥ 0.05

The output in Figure 6.48 indicates that the p value is greater than 0.10, so we accept H_0.

EXAMPLE **6.7**   ## Saving and Loan (S&L) Rate of Return

In "Return, Risk, and Cost of Equity for Stock S&L Firms: Theory and Empirical Results," Lee and Lynge discuss methods of estimating the cost of equity capital for S&L associations. One aspect of their analysis included an examination of the relationship between the rate of return of the S&L stocks (y) and two measures of the risk of the stocks: the beta coefficient (x_1), which is a measure of nondiversifiable risk, and the standard deviation of the security returns (x_2), which measures total risk. The data for their sample of 35 S&Ls is shown in Table 6.4. Scatterplots of y versus x_1 and y versus x_2 are shown in Figures 6.49 and 6.50, respectively. The MINITAB regression output is in Figure 6.51 and the Excel output is in Figure 6.52. Figures 6.53 through 6.55 show the residual plots of the standardized residuals versus the fitted values, x_1, and x_2, respectively. These plots highlight the presence of one standardized residual that falls well above the +3 limit. The normal probability plot and results of the normal probability plot test for normality are shown in Figure 6.56. To perform the test for normal disturbances at the 5% level of significance, the decision rule is

Reject H_0 if $R < .9715$

Accept H_0 if $R \geq .9715$.

(The critical value for $n = 40$ is used because $n = 35$ is not in the table.) The test statistic computed by MINITAB is $R = .8275$, so the null hypothesis is rejected. The disturbances do not appear to be normally distributed.

FIGURE 6.49 MINITAB Scatterplot of RETURN Versus BETA for S&L Rate of Return Example

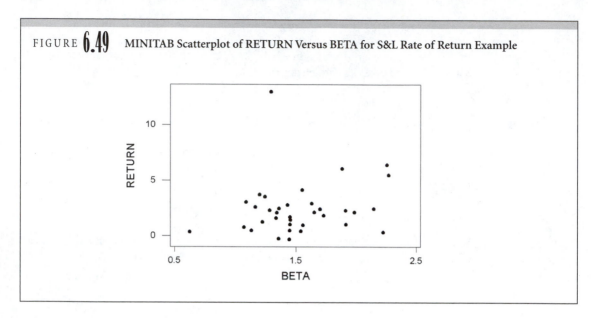

FIGURE 6.50 MINITAB Scatterplot of RETURN Versus SIGMA for S&L Rate of Return Example

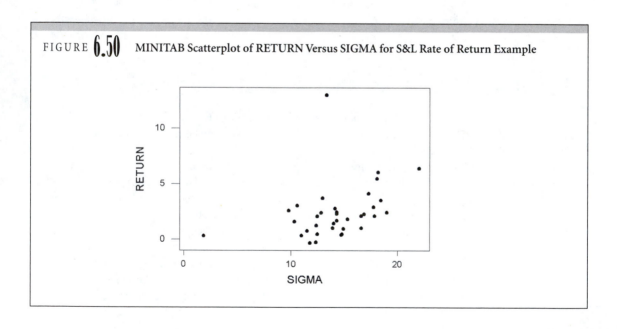

TABLE **6.4**   Data for S&L Rate of Return Example

Name	Time Period	RETURN	BETA	SIGMA
1. H.F. Ahnanson	1/78–12/82	2.29	1.2862	14.2896
2. Alamo Savings Bank	9/78–12/82	0.34	0.6254	10.9786
3. American Federal S&L	12/80–12/82	2.57	1.1706	9.7917
4. American S&L	1/78–12/82	2.91	1.6328	17.7219
5. Bell National Ind.	1/78–12/82	3.50	1.2492	18.4450
6. Beverly Hills S&L	11/78–12/82	0.47	1.1363	12.4691
7. Broadview Financial Ind.	1/78–12/82	−0.28	1.3585	12.3396
8. Buckeye Financial Ind.	10/80–12/82	0.40	1.5415	14.7000
9. Citizens Savings Financial	6/80–12/82	2.42	2.1457	18.9970
10. City Federal Bank	6/80–12/82	5.48	2.2701	18.0840
11. Danney S&L	1/78–12/82	1.67	1.4527	14.2785
12. Far West Financial	1/78–12/82	1.01	1.4532	13.8673
13. Financial Corp. of America	1/78–12/82	6.06	1.8826	18.1800
14. Financial Corp. of Santa Barbara	1/78–12/82	0.48	1.4493	14.7792
15. Financial Federation	1/78–12/82	0.96	1.5590	14.9088
16. First Charter Financial	1/78–12/82	1.24	1.2247	12.3504
17. First City Federal Ind.	5/81–12/82	6.39	2.2567	22.0455
18. First Financial S&L	1/81–12/82	2.39	1.7003	12.8343
19. First Lincoln Financial Bank	1/78–12/82	0.30	2.2226	1.8750
20. First Western Financial Bank	1/78–12/82	2.09	1.6535	16.5737
21. Freedom S&L Bank	5/80–12/82	2.46	1.3616	14.2680
22. Gibraltar Financial	1/78–12/82	2.10	1.9851	17.8500
23. Golden West Financial Corp.	1/78–12/82	2.76	1.4311	14.1036
24. Great Western Financial	1/78–12/82	2.06	1.3448	12.4630
25. Guarantee Financial Ind.	1/78–12/82	1.42	1.4560	13.9728
26. Homestead Financial Bank	1/78–12/82	4.12	1.5543	17.2628
27. Imperial Corp. of America	1/78–12/82	1.82	1.7280	15.2880
28. Land of Lincoln Ind.	12/79–12/82	1.59	1.3389	10.3032
29. Mercury Saving	1/78–12/82	13.05	1.2973	13.3110
30. Naples Federal	2/80–12/82	3.04	1.0945	10.5792
31. Palmetto Federal S&L	11/79–12/82	3.72	1.2051	12.9456
32. Prudential Federal S&L	1/78–12/82	0.75	1.0756	11.5200
33. Texas Federal Bank	7/81–12/82	1.00	1.9157	16.6000
34. Transohio Financial	1/78–12/82	−3.35	1.4456	11.7705
35. Western Financial Corp.	1/78–12/82	2.26	1.9128	16.8370

FIGURE 6.51   MINITAB Regression Output for S&L Rate of Return Example

```
The regression equation is
RETURN = - 1.33 + 0.30 BETA + 0.231 SIGMA

Predictor      Coef      StDev         T          P
Constant     -1.330      2.012      -0.66      0.513
BETA          0.300      1.198       0.25      0.804
SIGMA        0.2307     0.1255       1.84      0.075

S = 2.377        R-Sq = 12.5%       R-Sq(adj) = 7.0%

Analysis of Variance

Source          DF          SS          MS          F          P
Regression       2      25.808      12.904       2.28      0.118
Residual Error  32     180.815       5.650
Total           34     206.624

Source      DF      Seq SS
BETA         1       6.708
SIGMA        1      19.100

Unusual Observations
Obs     BETA      RETURN        Fit    StDev Fit     Residual     St Resid
 19     2.22       0.300     -0.231       2.078        0.531       0.46 X
 29     1.30      13.050      2.130       0.474       10.920       4.69R

R denotes an observation with a large standardized residual
X denotes an observation whose X value gives it large influence.
```

FIGURE **6.52**   Excel Regression Output for S&L Rate of Return Example

SUMMARY OUTPUT

Regression Statistics

Multiple R	0.353
R Square	0.125
Adjusted R Square	0.070
Standard Error	2.377
Observations	35.000

ANOVA

	df	SS	MS	F	Significance F
Regression	2.000	25.808	12.904	2.284	0.118
Residual	32.000	180.815	5.650		
Total	34.000	206.624			

	Coefficients	Standard Error	t Stat	P-value	Lower 95%	Upper 95%
Intercept	-1.330	2.012	-0.661	0.513	-5.428	2.768
BETA	0.300	1.198	0.250	0.804	-2.140	2.740
SIGMA	0.231	0.125	1.839	0.075	-0.025	0.486

FIGURE **6.53**   MINITAB Plot of the Standardized Residuals Versus the Fitted Values
for S&L Rate of Return Example

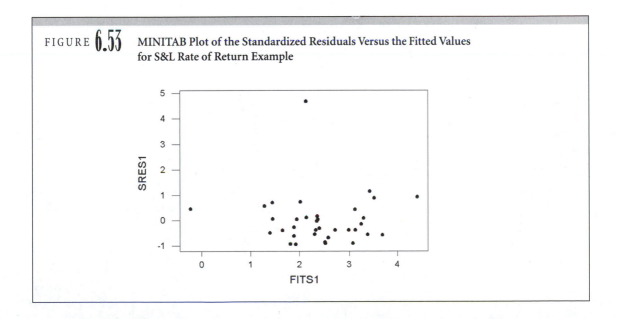

FIGURE **6.54**   MINITAB Plot of the Standardized Residuals Versus the Explanatory Variable BETA for S&L Rate of Return Example

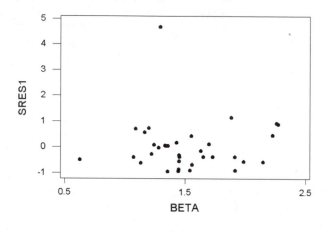

FIGURE **6.55**   MINITAB Plot of the Standardized Residuals Versus the Explanatory Variable SIGMA for S&L Rate of Return Example

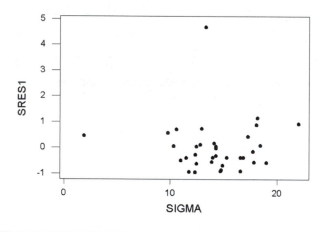

FIGURE 6.56   MINITAB Normal Probability Plot and Test for Normality for S&L Rate of Return Example

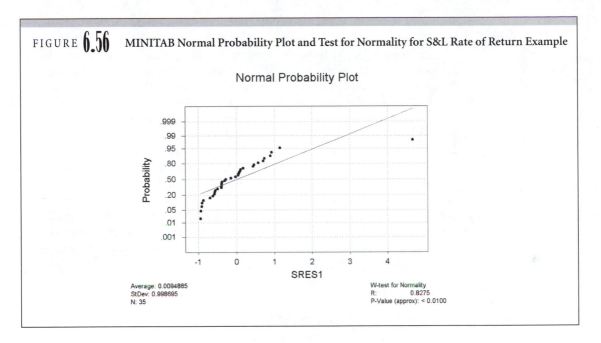

6.6.3   Corrections for Normality

The assumption of normally distributed disturbances is not necessary to use least-squares estimation to produce an estimated regression equation. However, for making inferences with small samples, it is necessary. In large samples, the assumption is not as important because the sampling distribution of the estimators of the regression coefficients is still approximately normal. Recall that when estimating a population mean, μ, the cutoff point for a large sample is $n = 30$. When $n \geq 30$, the central limit theorem guarantees that the sampling distribution of the sample mean is approximately normal. A similar theorem operates in the regression context for the sampling distribution of the regression coefficients, b_k. The cutoff for a large sample may differ, however, because several coefficients may be estimated in a multiple regression context. It is uncertain exactly how many observations ensure normality of the sampling distributions in the multiple regression context. If the assumption of normal disturbances does not hold, additional observations are necessary for each additional explanatory variable. For a simple regression, 30 observations with 10 to 20 additional observations for *each* additional explanatory variable are commonly suggested.

When the normality assumption is violated and the sample size is too small to ensure normality of the sampling distributions, there are a variety of possible corrections. Some of these corrections involve transformations of the dependent variable that are beyond the scope of this text. These transformations are called *Box-Cox transformations* and include the natural logarithm transformation as a special case. (For more on the use of Box-Cox transformations, the interested reader is referred to Neter, Wasserman, and Kutner, *Applied Linear Statistical Models*, pp. 394–400.)

When considering the normality assumption, be sure to correct for other violations before worrying about normality. A violation of the linearity or the constant variance assumption can introduce outliers (discussed in Section 6.7) into a data set that make the normality assumption appear to be violated also. Choosing the correct model by correcting for nonlinearity or nonconstant variance may eliminate the outliers, however. So check for violations of the linearity and constant variance assumptions before being too concerned with the normality assumption.

In some cases, the primary reason for the nonnormality of the disturbances may be the presence of one or a few data points that are much different from the remaining observations in the data set. Even in large samples, it is important to recognize such unusual observations because their presence may drastically alter results. In such instances, the sampling distributions of the estimated regression coefficients should not be assumed normal, even if the sample size is large. These cases, and some possible corrections, are discussed in the next section.

 INFLUENTIAL OBSERVATIONS

6.7.1 Introduction

The method of least-squares estimation chooses the regression coefficient estimates so that the error sum of squares, *SSE*, is a minimum. In doing this, the sum of squared distances from the true y values, y_i, to the points on the regression line or surface, $\hat{y}_i$, are minimized. Least squares thus tries to avoid any large distances from y_i to $\hat{y}_i$. As shown in Figure 6.57, this can have an effect on the placement of the regression line. In Figure 6.57(a), the points are all clustered near the regression line. In Figure 6.57(b), one of the points has been moved so that its y value is much different from the y values of the remaining sample points. The effect of moving this one point on the placement of the estimated regression line is also shown. Note that the regression line has been pulled toward the point that was moved to the extreme position. This is a result of the requirement of the least-squares method to minimize the error sum of squares. Squaring the residuals gives proportionally more weight to extreme points in the error sum of squares. The least-squares regression line is often drawn toward such extreme points.

When a sample data point has a y value that is much different than the y values of the other points in the sample, it is called an *outlier*. Outliers can be either good or bad. They can provide information concerning the behavior of the process being studied that would be unavailable otherwise. In this sense, the presence of the outlier could be viewed as positive. On the other hand, the presence of an outlier can at times produce confusing results and mask important information that could otherwise be obtained from the regression. In either case, it is important to recognize an outlier when it is present, and outlier detection techniques are discussed in this section.

FIGURE 6.57(A)   MINITAB Scatterplot with Regression Line for Data Shown Below

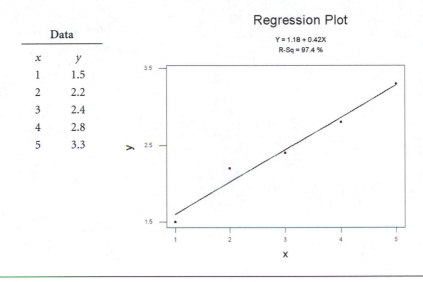

Data	
x	y
1	1.5
2	2.2
3	2.4
4	2.8
5	3.3

FIGURE 6.57(B)   MINITAB Scatterplot Showing Effect on Regression Line of Outlier

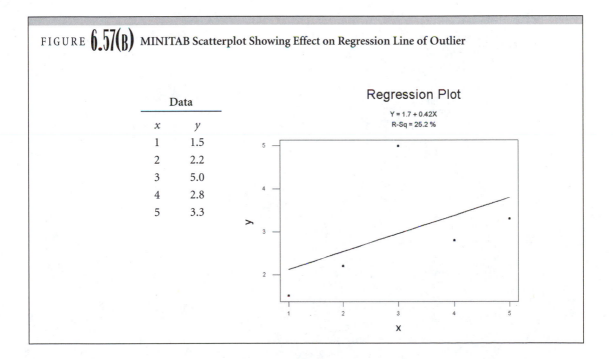

Data	
x	y
1	1.5
2	2.2
3	5.0
4	2.8
5	3.3

FIGURE 6.58(A) MINITAB Scatterplot Showing Effect of Leverage Point in Line with Other Data

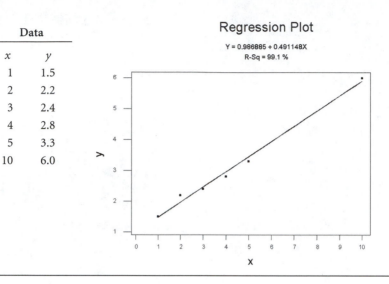

Data	
x	y
1	1.5
2	2.2
3	2.4
4	2.8
5	3.3
10	6.0

Regression Plot

Y = 0.986885 + 0.491148X
R-Sq = 99.1 %

FIGURE 6.58(B) MINITAB Scatterplot Showing Effect of Moving Leverage Point to Alternate Position

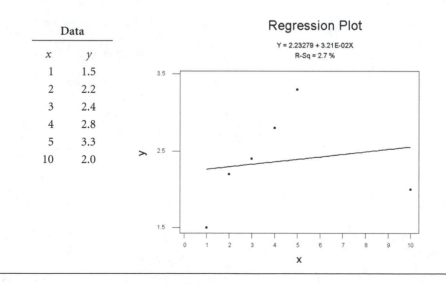

Data	
x	y
1	1.5
2	2.2
3	2.4
4	2.8
5	3.3
10	2.0

Regression Plot

Y = 2.23279 + 3.21E-02X
R-Sq = 2.7 %

Now consider Figure 6.58. In both Figure 6.58(a) and 6.58(b), the same five initial points are used as in Figure 6.57. One additional point is added to each figure but is placed in a different position. The positioning of this point is seen to have a large effect on the estimated regression line. In Figure 6.58(a), the slope of the line appears to have changed little from its value with only the five original points [see Figure 6.57(a)]. In Figure 6.58(b), the placement of the additional point has drastically changed the slope of the line.

In fact, the slope of the line appears to be determined almost entirely by this one point. This sixth observation is said to have high leverage and is referred to as a *leverage point*. The term "leverage point" means that the point is placed in such a way that it has the *potential* to affect the regression line.

In both Figure 6.58(a) and 6.58(b), the added point is a leverage point. This is due to its extreme placement on the *x* axis. The *x* value for this point is much different than the *x* values for the other sample points. The point, however, does not exert much influence in Figure 6.58(a) because it is in line with all the other points in terms of the position of its *y* value relative to its *x* value. It is important to recognize any leverage points due to their possible effect on the regression line. As with outliers, leverage points may be good or bad depending on whether they add information about the process under study or mask information that otherwise would be obtained.

Finally, it is important to note that an observation can be both a leverage point and an outlier.

6.7.2   Identifying Outliers

The use of the standardized residuals already has been discussed. The standardized residuals are computed by dividing the raw residual, $\hat{e}_i = y_i - \hat{y}_i$, by the standard deviation of $\hat{e}_i$:

$$\hat{e}_{is} = \frac{\hat{e}_i}{\text{stdev}(\hat{e}_i)}$$

where $\hat{e}_{is}$ indicates the standardized residual. The variance of the standardized residuals is 1 (note that in this chapter it necessary to distinguish between the raw residual $\hat{e}_i$ and the standardized residual $\hat{e}_{is}$).

If the residuals come from a normal distribution, then a standardized residual with an absolute value larger than 2 is expected only about 5% of the time. Thus, any observation with a standardized residual larger than 2 in absolute value might be classified as an outlier. MINITAB, for example, indicates any such observations in a table following the regression results.

Another measure sometimes used in place of the standardized residual is the standardized residual computed after deleting the *i*th observation. This measure is called the *studentized residual* or *studentized deleted residual*. To compute the studentized deleted residual, the residual, $\hat{e}_i$, is again standardized, but the divisor is different from that used to compute the standardized residual. The standard deviation of the *i*th residual is computed from the regression with the *i*th observation deleted. By doing this, the *i*th observation exerts no influence over the value of the standard deviation. If the *i*th observation's *y* value is unusual, this is reflected in the residual but not in its divisor. Thus, unusual y values should stand out. Also, because of the way they are computed, the studentized deleted residuals are known to follow a t distribution with $n - K - 1$ degrees of freedom. The studentized deleted residuals can be compared to a value chosen from the t table to determine whether they should be classified as outliers. (The standardized residuals do not follow a t distribution.) But this approach should not be used as a test of significance to determine whether the observation should be discarded. What to do about outliers once they are identified will be discussed later in this section.

6.7.3　Identifying Leverage Points

Leverage was previously defined as the potential of an observation to affect the regression line. As shown in Figure 6.58, a point can possess leverage without significantly altering the position of the regression line. On the other hand, given sufficient leverage, a single point can significantly affect the slope of the regression line.

The leverage of the ith point in a sample is denoted h_i and is computed by some regression software packages. Leverage is a measure of how extreme the point is in terms of the values of the explanatory variables. Observations with extreme x values possess greater leverage than observations with x values that are similar to the other sample points. In Figure 6.57, the observation that was changed has smaller leverage than the observation that was changed in Figure 6.58. Note that the slope of the regression line is affected more by changes in the point with greater leverage.

MINITAB indicates certain observations with very high leverage. Any data value with leverage greater than $2(K + 1)/n$ is indicated in a table following the regression results along with observations that have large standardized residuals.

6.7.4　Combining Measures to Detect Outliers and Leverage Points

The effect of an observation on the regression line is determined both by the y value of the point and the x value(s). As shown in Figures 6.57 and 6.58, an observation with an unusual y value has a much greater effect on the regression line if it also has high leverage. Several statistics have been developed which consider both extremity in the y and x dimensions in an attempt to determine which points are highly influential on the regression line. Two of these measures, the *DFITS* statistic and Cook's *D* statistic, are discussed in this section.

Both of these measures combine information from the residuals and the leverage of each observation to try to pick out observations that may have a large influence on the regression line. As with the individual measures, unusual values of the *DFITS* statistic or Cook's *D* statistic are not indications that anything is wrong with the particular data value or that it should be discarded. It does indicate that the value with the unusual statistic is somehow different from the remaining values in the data set and should be given additional consideration before accepting the regression model.

The *DFITS* statistic can be written as

$$DFITS_i = \hat{e}_i \sqrt{\frac{n - K - 2}{SSE(1 - h_i) - \hat{e}_i^2}} \sqrt{\frac{h_i}{1 - h_i}}$$

where $\hat{e}_i$ is the residual for the ith observation, h_i is the leverage value for the ith observation, and SSE is the error sum of squares for the regression.

Cook's D statistic is computed as

$$D_i = \frac{\hat{e}_i^2}{MSE(K+1)} \left(\frac{h_i}{(1-h_i)^2} \right)$$

Where $\hat{e}_i$ and h_i are as defined for the *DFITS* statistic and *MSE* is the mean square error for the regression.

As can be seen, both statistics use the residuals and the leverage of each individual point. Since they use the values in different ways, however, different information may be obtained from each of the statistics. Cook's D statistic is usually thought to represent the combined impact on all the regression coefficients of the ith observation. *DFITS* represents the combined impact on the fitted values of the ith observation.

There are two different schools of thought about how the *DFITS* statistic and Cook's D statistic should be used:

1. The values should be compared to some absolute cutoff. For example, the Cook's D value often is compared to an $F(\alpha; K+1, n-K-1)$ value. The *DFITS* value is compared to $2\sqrt{(K+1)/n}$. Values bigger than either of the numbers should be further examined. But these are not to be viewed as statistical tests to reject or throw out observations.

2. Do not use absolute cutoffs. Simply pick out those observations with Cook's D or *DFITS* values, if any, that appear to be appreciably different from most of the values.

The second approach is used in this text. Much recent research has shown that comparison to absolute cutoffs is not as effective in identifying influential observations as examining observations with unusually large *DFITS* or Cook's D values.

When specific cutoffs are not used, a method is needed to compare the different values of each statistic to determine which observations may be unusual. One way of doing this is simply to graph the *DFITS* (or Cook's D) values for each observation on the vertical axis and the number of the observation on the horizontal axis. This can also be accomplished by doing a time-series plot of the *DFITS* (or Cook's D) values, remembering that the index on the horizontal axis refers to the number of the observation and not necessarily to a time period. This method of presenting the *DFITS* and Cook's D statistics is demonstrated in Example 6.8.

6.7.5 What to Do with Unusual Observations

As noted earlier, the fact that an observation has been classified as unusual does not mean that it is useless or that it should be deleted from the analysis. It is merely a flag to indicate that the observation deserves further examination. This is true regardless of which measure of "unusualness" has been used (standardized residual, *DFITS*, Cook's D statistic, and so on).

There are many reasons an observation may appear unusual. If there is a violation of the linearity or constant variance assumptions, this can cause certain observations to appear unusual until the violation has been corrected by choosing an appropriate transformation of the data.

If a data value has been typed in incorrectly, the value may be flagged as unusual. This is useful since incorrectly coded values should not be included in our data set. If this is the case, then the true data value should be located and used to replace the incorrect value. If the true value cannot be found, then this is one case when it is almost always better to omit the incorrect data value before running the analysis.

If the unusual value is not due to the violation of an assumption or incorrect coding but is a correct value that is simply unusual with respect to most of the values in the data set, then the choice of what to do with it is more difficult. There are certain cases when deleting the observation from the data set is appropriate. These cases occur when the unusual observation is somehow very different from the observations included in the analysis. For example, if a production process is being examined, unusual observations may occur at the beginning of the process due to start-up problems. When the process reaches a steady state of performance, the data values generated may be quite different from those generated initially. The initial observations may be deleted if the process in its steady state is to be studied.

Consider another example. Suppose data on price and size of houses are obtained to develop an equation to help set prices for the houses. If interest lies in pricing houses with 1500 to 2500 square feet of space, then it is proper to exclude a house if it contains 4500 square feet. If the x values for the unusual observation fall outside the range of interest, it may be proper to discard the observation and run the regression without that value.

In any case, before deleting an observation from an analysis, the observation should be studied carefully to see whether deletion is an appropriate option. If the observation is somehow so different from the others in the data set that it is inappropriate to include it in the analysis or if the value has been coded incorrectly and the true value is unknown, then deletion is a viable option. However, this option should not be used indiscriminately.

EXAMPLE **6.8**   **S&L Rate of Return (continued)**

Example 6.8 S&L Rate of Return (continued)
Figure 6.59 shows the MINITAB plot of *DFITS* for the S&L rate of return data. Figure 6.60 shows the plot of the Cook's *D* statistic. Both of these plots were created by doing a time-series plot of the statistics. The index on the horizontal axis refers to the number of the observation from the sample. From each of these plots, the 29th observation stands out as unusual relative to the rest of the observations in the sample. In Table 6.4, the 29th observation is Mercury Saving. Note that the return for Mercury Saving is much higher than that for the other S&Ls. Mercury Saving has a very unusual *y* value. In the table of Unusual Observations in Figure 6.51, Mercury Saving has been identified by MINITAB as an outlier (note the *R* next to this entry in the table). The standardized residual is 4.69, which is far greater than would be expected if the disturbances were normally distributed.

This observation should definitely be examined further. The question at this point is what to do with it. In the case of Mercury Saving, it is unclear whether the return of 13.05% is correct. In the article from which these data were taken, however, it appears that Mercury Saving has been deleted from the analysis. Because the true return is not known, Mercury Saving is excluded from

FIGURE **6.59**   MINITAB Plot of *DFITS* for S&L Rate of Return Example

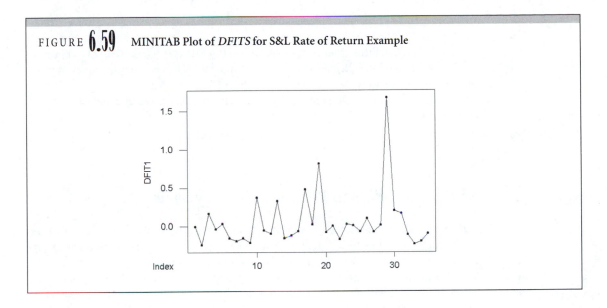

FIGURE **6.60**   MINITAB Plot of Cook's *D* Statistic for S&L Rate of Return Example

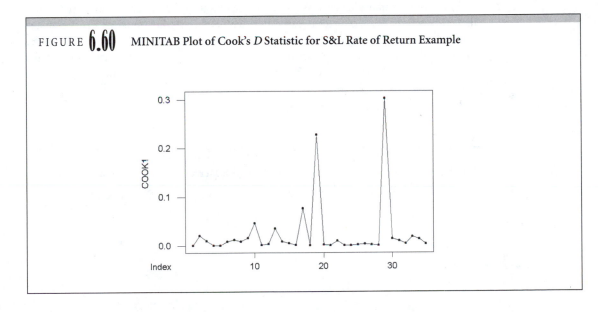

the data set and the analysis redone. It is important to emphasize that casual deletion of points from the data set is not recommended. If there is a good reason for not including a particular value, then it can be deleted. If the return for Mercury Saving is incorrect and the correct value is unknown, it is better to delete this observation than to use the incorrect information. Or if Mercury Saving is believed somehow so different from the other S&Ls that it should not be included in the analysis, this is a good reason for deletion. For example, perhaps Mercury Saving had undertaken a particularly risky line of investments, different from those of the other S&Ls,

which led to its very high return. Because the investment behavior of Mercury is extremely different from the other S&Ls in this case, there might be grounds for excluding it from the analysis. It is assumed here that there is sufficient reason for omitting Mercury Saving since that appears to be what was done in the original article. In a real application, it is beneficial to study Mercury further to see what makes it so different from the other S&Ls.

In the following example, note the difference between the analyses with and without Mercury Saving.

EXAMPLE 6.9   ## S&L Rate of Return Without Mercury Saving

Figures 6.61 and 6.62 show the scatterplots with Mercury Saving omitted. The MINITAB and Excel regression outputs are in Figures 6.63 and 6.64, respectively. The residual plots are in Figures 6.65 to 6.67, and the plots of *DFITS* and Cook's *D* are in Figures 6.68 and 6.69.

The regression results differ considerably from the regression with Mercury Saving included. Compare the Figure 6.63 or 6.64 regression (without Mercury) to the Figure 6.51 or 6.52 regression (with Mercury). In the initial regression, neither variable is significant at the 5% level. In the regression without Mercury, SIGMA is now significant. Thus, the conclusions drawn from these two regressions are completely different because of the presence (or absence) of one influential observation. This highlights the need to be careful when deleting influential observations. Knowing whether Mercury Saving belongs in our analysis is especially important because omitting it causes a reversal in our conclusion concerning the importance of the variable SIGMA.

FIGURE 6.61   **MINITAB Scatterplot of RETURN Versus BETA with Mercury Saving Omitted**

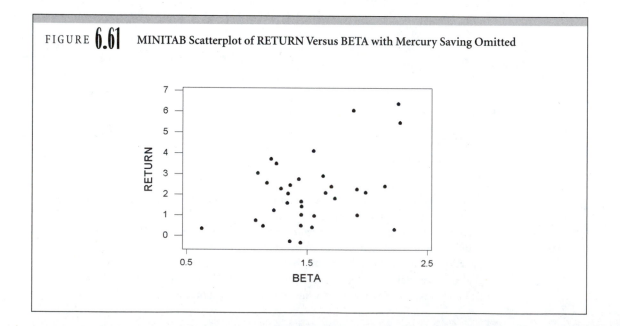

FIGURE **6.62**   MINITAB Scatterplot of RETURN Versus SIGMA with Mercury Saving Omitted

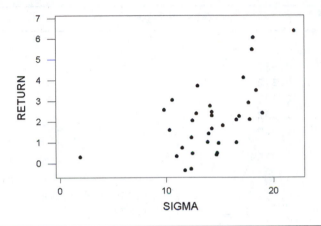

FIGURE **6.63**   MINITAB Regression for S&L Rate of Return Example with Mercury Saving Omitted

```
The regression equation is
RETURN = - 2.51 + 0.846 BETA + 0.232 SIGMA

Predictor      Coef       StDev          T          P
Constant     -2.510       1.153      -2.18      0.037
BETA          0.8463      0.6843       1.24      0.225
SIGMA         0.23220     0.07135      3.25      0.003

S = 1.352       R-Sq = 37.2%      R-Sq(adj) = 33.1%

Analysis of Variance

Source            DF          SS         MS          F          P
Regression         2      33.537     16.768       9.18      0.001
Residual Error    31      56.635      1.827
Total             33      90.172

Source      DF      Seq SS
BETA         1      14.185
SIGMA        1      19.351

Unusual Observations
Obs     BETA      RETURN       Fit    StDev Fit     Residual     St Resid
 13     1.88       6.060     3.304       0.367        2.756        2.12R
 19     2.22       0.300    -0.194       1.181        0.494        0.75 X

R denotes an observation with a large standardized residual
X denotes an observation whose X value gives it large influence.
```

FIGURE **6.64**   Excel Regression for S&L Rate of Return Example with Mercury Saving Omitted

SUMMARY OUTPUT

Regression Statistics

Multiple R	0.610
R Square	0.372
Adjusted R Square	0.331
Standard Error	1.352
Observations	34.000

ANOVA

	df	SS	MS	F	Significance F
Regression	2.000	33.537	16.768	9.178	0.001
Residual	31.000	56.635	1.827		
Total	33.000	90.172			

	Coefficients	Standard Error	t Stat	P-value	Lower 95%	Upper 95%
Intercept	-2.510	1.153	-2.177	0.037	-4.862	-0.159
BETA	0.846	0.684	1.237	0.225	-0.549	2.242
SIGMA	0.232	0.071	3.255	0.003	0.087	0.378

FIGURE **6.65**   MINITAB Plot of Standardized Residuals Versus Fitted Values for S&L Rate of Return Example with Mercury Saving Omitted

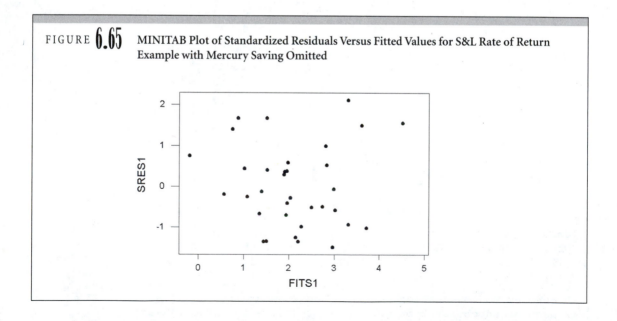

FIGURE **6.66**   MINITAB Plot of Standardized Residuals Versus BETA for S&L Rate of Return Example with Mercury Saving Omitted

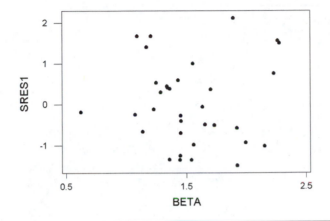

FIGURE **6.67**   MINITAB Plot of Standardized Residuals Versus SIGMA for S&L Rate of Return Example with Mercury Saving Omitted

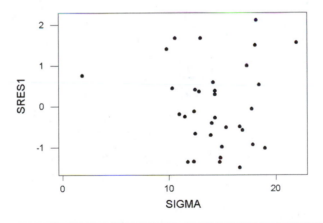

FIGURE **6.68** MINITAB Plot of *DFITS* for S&L Rate of Return Example with Mercury Saving Omitted

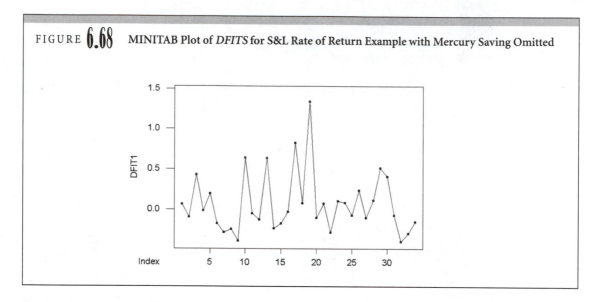

FIGURE **6.69** MINITAB Plot of Cook's *D* Statistic for S&L Rate of Return Example with Mercury Saving Omitted

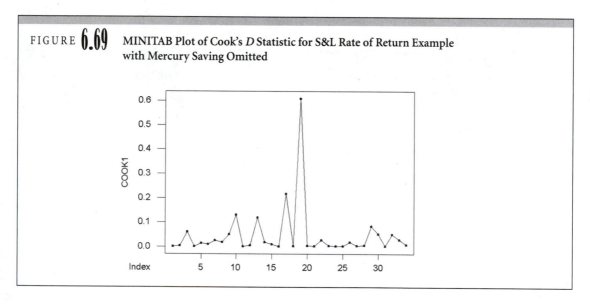

EXERCISES

4 **Petroleum Imports** The data for U.S. monthly petroleum imports from 1991 through 1997 appear in Table 6.5. Figure 6.70 shows the MINITAB regression output for the regression of monthly petroleum imports (in millions of barrels) on the one-period lagged imports. Figure 6.71 is a time-series plot of the standardized residuals

TABLE 6.5   Monthly Petroleum Imports (in millions of barrels)

Date	PETROIMP	Date	PETROIMP	Date	PETROIMP
Jan-91	180.1	May-93	211.3	Sep-95	244.9
Feb-91	163.6	Jun-93	222.5	Oct-95	226.4
Mar-91	169.2	Jul-93	229.5	Nov-95	231.6
Apr-91	177.8	Aug-93	204.1	Dec-95	235.7
May-91	215.2	Sep-93	206.7	Jan-96	239.0
Jun-91	199.2	Oct-93	223.4	Feb-96	198.1
Jul-91	201.4	Nov-93	228.3	Mar-96	201.7
Aug-91	220.2	Dec-93	203.1	Apr-96	238.2
Sep-91	190.3	Jan-94	206.0	May-96	261.6
Oct-91	189.3	Feb-94	176.9	Jun-96	253.0
Nov-91	182.9	Mar-94	219.8	Jul-96	275.2
Dec-91	182.8	Apr-94	217.2	Aug-96	251.0
Jan-92	186.7	May-94	216.6	Sep-96	260.4
Feb-92	155.0	Jun-94	248.1	Oct-96	250.7
Mar-92	172.4	Jul-94	245.6	Nov-96	217.0
Apr-92	186.0	Aug-94	242.5	Dec-96	247.8
May-92	195.5	Sep-94	260.4	Jan-97	224.1
Jun-92	193.1	Oct-94	221.0	Feb-97	211.1
Jul-92	112.7	Nov-94	229.2	Mar-97	245.6
Aug-92	201.4	Dec-94	220.9	Apr-97	250.9
Sep-92	190.0	Jan-95	212.3	May-97	278.2
Oct-92	216.5	Feb-95	195.9	Jun-97	254.2
Nov-92	193.2	Mar-95	239.7	Jul-97	266.3
Dec-92	192.0	Apr-95	212.0	Aug-97	280.9
Jan-93	212.0	May-95	240.5	Sep-97	274.6
Feb-93	175.9	Jun-95	242.0	Oct-97	280.6
Mar-93	206.1	Jul-95	245.4	Nov-97	252.8
Apr-93	220.3	Aug-95	240.8	Dec-97	250.1

Source: *Business Statistics of the United States.* Lanham, MD: Berman Press.

from this regression. Figure 6.72 shows the plot of the standardized residuals versus the fitted values. Figures 6.73 and 6.74, respectively, show plots of the *DFITS* and Cook's *D* statistics.

Are there any unusual observations that should be checked before accepting these regression results? If so, which observations? Can you determine what might be causing certain observations to appear unusual? Justify your answers.

These data are available in a file with prefix PETRO6 in one column.

FIGURE 6.70   MINITAB Output for Regression of Petroleum Imports on the Lagged Value
of Petroleum Imports

```
The regression equation is
PETROIMP = 63.1 + 0.716 PETROIMPL1

83 cases used 1 cases contain missing values

Predictor     Coef        StDev          T          P
Constant      63.09       17.04        3.70      0.000
PETROIMP    0.71605     0.07695        9.30      0.000


S = 22.22        R-Sq = 51.7%      R-Sq(adj) = 51.1%

Analysis of Variance

Source                DF         SS          MS         F           P
Regression             1       42754       42754      86.58      0.000
Residual Error        81       39999         494
Total                 82       82753

Unusual Observations
Obs    PETROIMP    PETROIMP        Fit      StDev Fit     Residual   St Resid
 19         193      112.70     201.36          3.16       -88.66     -4.03R
 20         113      201.40     143.79          8.55        57.61      2.81RX

R denotes an observation with a large standardized residual
X denotes an observation whose X value gives it large influence.
```

FIGURE **6.71**   MINITAB Time-Series Plot of Standardized Residuals for Petroleum Imports Regression

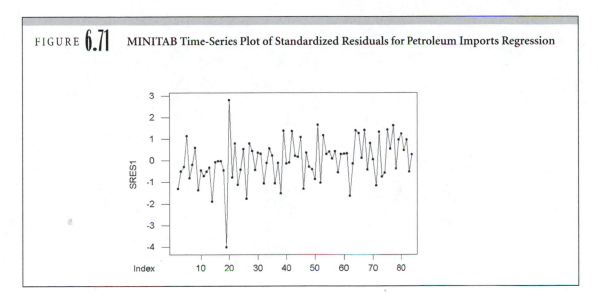

FIGURE **6.72**   MINITAB Plot of Standardized Residuals Versus Fitted Values
for Petroleum Imports Regression

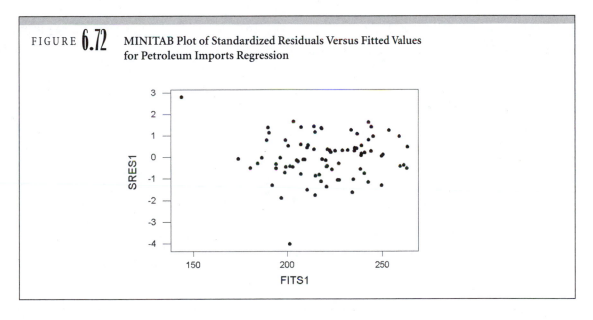

FIGURE **6.73**   MINITAB Plot of *DFITS* Statistic for Petroleum Imports Regression

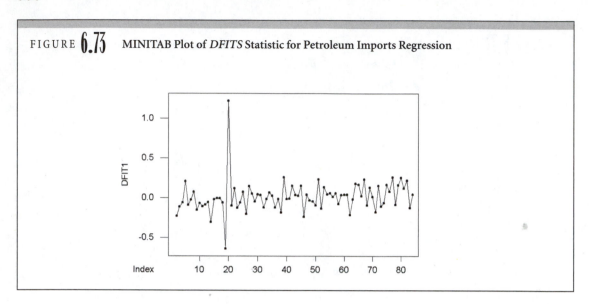

FIGURE **6.74**   MINITAB Plot of Cook's D Statistic for Petroleum Imports Regression

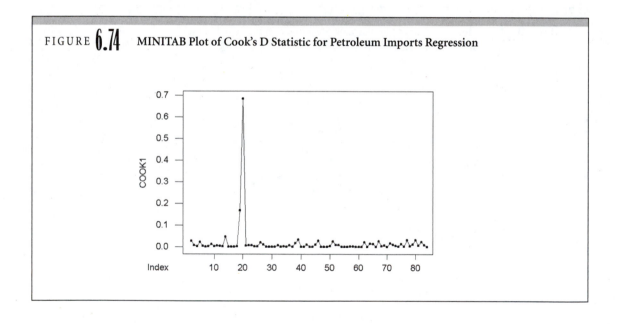

6.8 ASSESSING THE ASSUMPTION THAT THE DISTURBANCES ARE INDEPENDENT

6.8.1 Autocorrelation

One assumption that is frequently violated when using time-series data is that of independence of the disturbances, e_i. Disturbances in adjacent time periods are often correlated because an event in one time period may influence an event in the next time period. The relationship between disturbances in adjacent time periods is often represented by

$$e_i = \rho e_{i-1} + u_i$$

In this equation, e_i is the disturbance in the ith time period, e_{i-1} is the disturbance in the previous time period, ρ is called the *serial correlation coefficient* or *autocorrelation coefficient*, and u_i represents a disturbance that meets the assumption of independence. The regression relationship can be written as

$$y_i = \beta_0 + \beta_1 x_i + e_i$$

where $e_i = \rho e_{i-1} + u_i$.

When disturbances exhibit autocorrelation, least-squares estimates of the regression coefficients are unbiased, but the estimated standard errors of the coefficients are biased. As a result, confidence intervals and hypothesis tests do not perform as expected. The estimated regression coefficients also have larger sampling variance than certain other estimators that correct for autocorrelation.

The autocorrelation coefficient, ρ, determines the strength of the relationship between disturbances in successive time periods. Like any other correlation coefficient, it varies between -1 and $+1$, with values close to ± 1 indicating very strong relationships and values close to zero indicating weak relationships. Ideally, a value of $\rho = 0$ is desired since this means that the disturbances were independent and the independence assumption had not been violated.

To determine whether autocorrelation is present, the Durbin-Watson test is used. This test is discussed in the next section.

6.8.2 A Test for First-Order Autocorrelation

A well-known and widely used test for first-order autocorrelation is the *Durbin-Watson test*. When autocorrelation is present in business and economic data, it is typically positive autocorrelation ($\rho > 0$). For this reason, we test for positive autocorrelation. The hypotheses to be tested may be written as follows:

$$H_0: \quad \rho = 0$$
$$H_a: \quad \rho > 0$$

where ρ is the first-order autocorrelation coefficient. If the null hypothesis is accepted, the correlation, ρ, of adjacent disturbances is zero, and no problem of first-order autocorrelation exists. If the null hypothesis is rejected, the disturbances are correlated, and some correction for autocorrelation needs to be made.

The Durbin-Watson statistic is computed by first using least squares to estimate the regression equation and then by computing the residuals

$$\hat{e}_i = y_i - \hat{y}_i$$

where y_i represents one of the sample y values and $\hat{y}_i$ is the corresponding predicted y value. The residuals are used to compute the Durbin-Watson statistic, d:

$$d = \frac{\sum_{i=2}^{n} (\hat{e}_i - \hat{e}_{i-1})^2}{\sum_{i=1}^{n} \hat{e}_i^2}$$

When the disturbances are independent, d should be approximately equal to 2. When the disturbances are positively correlated, d tends to be smaller than 2.

The decision rule for the test is:

Reject H_0 if $d < d_L(\alpha; n, K)$

Accept H_0 if $d > d_U(\alpha; n, K)$

Here, $d_L(\alpha; n, K)$ and $d_U(\alpha; n, K)$ are the critical values which can be found in Table B.7 in Appendix B. The critical values depend on the level of significance of the test, α, the sample size, n, and the number of explanatory variables in the equation, K. For the Durbin-Watson test, there is a range of values for the test statistic where the test is said to be inconclusive. The inconclusive range of values for d is

$$d_L \leq d \leq d_U$$

If the test statistic d falls in this region, there is some question as to how to proceed. Rejection of the null hypothesis suggests that a correction for autocorrelation is necessary. Acceptance means that no correction is necessary. But what should be done when d falls in the inconclusive region? There have been some additional procedures developed to further examine these cases, but they have not been incorporated into many computer regression routines. Without easy access to the additional procedures, one possibility is to treat values of d in the inconclusive region as if they suggested autocorrelation. If the regression results after correction for autocorrelation differ from those prior to the correction, then conclude that the correction was necessary. If the results are similar, then the correction was unnecessary, and the original uncorrected results can be used.

EXAMPLE **6.10** **Sales and Advertising**

Table 6.9 shows data on sales (in thousands) and advertising (ADV) (in thousands) for the ABC Company. These are annual data covering the period from 1962 to 1997. The MINITAB regression output for the regression of SALES on ADV is shown in Figure 6.75. The Durbin-Watson

TABLE **6.6**   Sales and Advertising Data

Year	SALES	ADV	Year	SALES	ADV	Year	SALES	ADV
1962	381.0	5316.8	1974	444.2	6121.8	1986	629.3	7170.8
1963	383.9	5413.2	1975	437.2	6201.2	1987	653.9	7210.9
1964	384.4	5486.9	1976	376.1	6271.7	1988	698.6	7304.8
1965	370.5	5537.8	1977	454.6	6383.1	1989	707.8	7391.9
1966	396.4	5660.6	1978	459.2	6444.5	1990	735.9	7495.3
1967	421.8	5750.8	1979	478.2	6509.1	1991	748.3	7629.2
1968	379.2	5782.2	1980	492.8	6574.6	1992	755.4	7703.4
1969	390.9	5781.7	1981	541.2	6704.2	1993	762.0	7818.4
1970	420.9	5821.9	1982	512.0	6794.3	1994	794.3	7955.0
1971	408.8	5892.5	1983	562.0	6911.4	1995	815.5	8063.4
1972	407.2	5950.2	1984	590.1	6986.5	1996	840.9	8170.8
1973	408.4	6002.1	1985	617.7	7095.7	1997	820.8	8254.5

FIGURE **6.15**   MINITAB Regression of SALES on ADV Including Durbin-Watson Statistic

```
The regression equation is
SALES = - 633 + 0.177 ADV

Predictor      Coef      StDev         T          P
Constant    -632.69      47.28     -13.38      0.000
ADV        0.177233   0.007045      25.16      0.000

S = 36.49       R-Sq = 94.9%       R-Sq(adj) = 94.8%

Analysis of Variance

Source            DF          SS         MS         F          P
Regression         1      842685     842685    632.81      0.000
Residual Error    34       45277       1332
Total             35      887961

Unusual Observations
Obs      ADV      SALES       Fit     StDev Fit      Residual      St Resid
  1     5317     381.00    309.62        11.22         71.38         2.06R
 15     6272     376.10    478.86         6.65       -102.76        -2.86R

R denotes an observation with a large standardized residual

Durbin-Watson statistic = 0.47
```

FIGURE **6.76** MINITAB Time-Series Plot of Standardized Residuals for Sales and Advertising Example

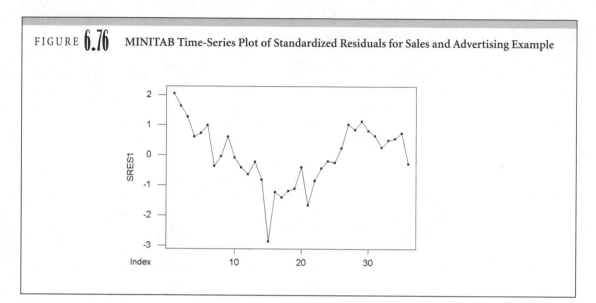

statistic is shown in the output. The MINITAB time-series plot of the standardized residuals is shown in Figure 6.76. To test for positive first-order autocorrelation, the following decision rule is used:

Reject H_0 if $d < d_L(0.05; 36, 1) = 1.41$

Accept H_0 if $d > d_U(0.05; 36, 1) = 1.52$

Inconclusive if $1.41 \leq d \leq 1.52$

Because $d = 0.47$, the null hypothesis of no autocorrelation is rejected. First-order autocorrelation is a problem and should be corrected before inferences or forecasts are made.

6.8.3 Correction for First-Order Autocorrelation

When disturbances are autocorrelated, it may be due to the omission of an important variable from the regression. If the time-ordered effects of such a missing variable are positively correlated, then the disturbances in the regression tend to be positively correlated. The remedy to this problem is to locate the missing variable and include it in the regression equation, although this is easier said than done in many cases.

Another possible correction for first-order autocorrelation transforms the original time-series variables in the regression so that a regression using the transformed variables has independent disturbances. The original regression model for the time period i can be written

$$y_i = \beta_0 + \beta_1 x_i + e_i$$

where the disturbances, e_i, have first-order autocorrelation

$$e_i = \rho e_{i-1} + u_i$$

To remove the autocorrelation, the following transformations are used. Create new dependent and explanatory variable values y_i^* and x_i^* using

$$y_i^* = y_i - \rho y_{i-1} \quad \text{and} \quad x_i^* = x_i - \rho x_{i-1}$$

for time periods $i = 2, 3, \ldots, n$.

In addition, transform the first time-period observation as

$$y_1^* = \sqrt{1-\rho^2}\, y_1 \quad \text{and} \quad x_1^* = \sqrt{1-\rho^2}\, x_1$$

The new regression can be written as

$$y_i^* = \beta_0 + \beta_1 x_i^* + u_i$$

and the disturbances u_i are independent. Now regress y_i^* on x_i^* to obtain estimates of β_0 and β_1.

In practice, there are various refinements to this process. In choosing a statistical package to perform these transformations and run the regressions, one of the most important things to keep in mind is that the transformation should include the first observation (x_1^*, y_1^*). Many statistical packages incorporated routines which simply dropped the first observation rather than transforming it as shown and including it in the new regression. Recent research shows that dropping this observation results in the loss of important information and adversely affects the results of the new regression. One common estimation procedure that drops the first observation is the Cochrane-Orcutt method. This method should be avoided. Procedures that incorporate the first observation include the Prais-Winsten method and full maximum likelihood. When using an automatic method from a statistical package to correct for autocorrelation, only those methods incorporating the initial observation should be used. Statistical packages such as SAS/ETS and SHAZAM have single commands which transform the data appropriately, rerun the regression on the transformed data, and print out the results so that correcting for autocorrelation in this case is a simple matter. MINITAB and Excel have not incorporated any of these automatic procedures, so this type of correction is difficult to perform.

When the Prais-Winsten transformation is used, forecasts are computed in a slightly different manner than shown for a regression without autocorrelation. The T-period-ahead forecast can be written in general as

$$\hat{y}_{n+T} = \hat{\beta}_0 + \hat{\beta}_1 x_{n+T} + \rho^T \hat{e}_n$$

where $\hat{\beta}_0$ and $\hat{\beta}_1$ are used to represent the estimates of β_0 and β_1 from the transformed regression model (rather than the least-squares estimates b_0 and b_1), x_{n+T} is the value of the explanatory variable in the period to be forecast, ρ is the autocorrelation coefficient, and $\hat{e}_n$ is the residual from the last sample time period. Note that only the last residual in the sample contains any information about the future. Also note that the value of this information declines as forecasts are generated further into the future. The term ρ^T can be seen to decrease (because $-1 < \rho < 1$) as T increases.

A third option to correct for autocorrelation is to add a lagged value of the dependent variable as an explanatory variable. This is a viable option especially if building an extrapolative model and if the number of observations is reasonably large (since one observation is lost because of the lagged variable).

EXAMPLE **6.11** **Sales and Advertising (again)**

A lagged value of the dependent variable will be introduced to try to correct for first-order autocorrelation in the model for sales. The new equation can be written

$$y_i = \beta_0 + \beta_1 y_{i-1} + \beta_2 x_i + e_i$$

where y_i is sales in time period i, y_{i-1} is the lagged value of sales, and x_i is ADV. The MINITAB regression is shown in Figure 6.77. Evaluating whether this model is an improvement over the previous model is discussed in the next section.

6.8.4 *h* Test for Autocorrelation

When lagged values of the dependent variable are used as explanatory variables, the Durbin-Watson test is no longer appropriate. An alternative test typically recommended in this case is Durbin's *h*. The hypotheses to be tested are

H_0: $\rho = 0$

H_a: $\rho > 0$

The test statistic is

$$h = r \left(\frac{T}{1 - T\sigma_{b_1}^2} \right)^{1/2}$$

where r is an estimate of the first-order autocorrelation coefficient, T is the sample size, and $\sigma_{b_1}^2$ is the variance of the regression coefficient of the lagged dependent variable (y_{i-1}). If the null hypothesis is true, h has a standard normal distribution. The decision rule to conduct the test is:

Reject H_0 if $h > z_\alpha$

Accept H_0 if $h \leq z_\alpha$

Note that the test statistic h cannot be computed if $1 - T\sigma_{b_1}^2 < 0$ because this results in the need to take the square root of a negative number. (Alternative test procedures are available in this case. The reader is referred to Judge et al., *The Theory and Practice of Econometrics*, pp. 326–327, for an example.) In practice, $\sigma_{b_1}^2$ in the formula for h is replaced by its estimate $s_{b_1}^2$. A quick way to estimate the autocorrelation correlation coefficient is to use $r = 1 - \frac{d}{2}$, where d is the Durbin-Watson statistic.

FIGURE 6.77   MINITAB Regression of SALES on ADV and a Lagged Dependent Variable

```
The regression equation is
SALES = - 234 + 0.0631 ADV + 0.675 SALESL1

35 cases used 1 cases contain missing values

Predictor      Coef       StDev           T           P
Constant    -234.48       78.07       -3.00       0.005
ADV         0.06307     0.02023        3.12       0.004
SALESL1      0.6751      0.1123        6.01       0.000

S = 24.12       R-Sq = 97.8%       R-Sq(adj) = 97.7%

Analysis of Variance

Source            DF          SS          MS          F           P
Regression         2      841098      420549      722.74      0.000
Residual Error    32       18620         582
Total             34      859718

Source      DF      Seq SS
ADV          1      820069
SALESL1      1       21029

Unusual Observations
Obs      ADV       SALES        Fit    StDev Fit      Residual      St Resid
 15     6272      376.10     456.24        5.54        -80.14        -3.41R
 16     6383      454.60     422.02       12.95         32.58         1.60 X
 21     6794      512.00     559.41        4.46        -47.41        -2.00R

R denotes an observation with a large standardized residual
X denotes an observation whose X value gives it large influence.

Durbin-Watson statistic = 2.33
```

Finally, it should be noted that other procedures are available for analyzing time-series data. Certain of these procedures are designed especially for extrapolative models using lagged dependent variables, autocorrelated errors, or both. For more detail on such time-series forecasting methods, the reader is referred to Bowerman and O'Connell, *Forecasting and Time Series: An Applied Approach.*

EXAMPLE **6.12** ## Sales and Advertising (for the last time)

In Example 6.10, a regression of SALES on ADV was run. The Durbin-Watson test indicated that the disturbances from this regression were not independent. In Example 6.11, a lagged dependent variable was added to the regression to try to correct for the first-order autocorrelation. The appropriate test to determine whether the introduction of the lagged variable has eliminated the autocorrelation is the h test. The quantities necessary to compute the h statistic are available in the regression output in Figure 6.77.

Using a 5% level of significance, the decision rule to conduct the test is:

Reject H_0 if $h > 1.645$

Accept H_0 if $h \le 1.645$

The estimate of the autocorrelation coefficient can be computed as

$$r = 1 - \frac{d}{2} = 1 - \frac{2.33}{2} = -0.165$$

The sample size used in the regression is 35 (one of the original observations was lost because of the use of the lagged variable), and the standard deviation of the coefficient of the lagged variable is 0.1123, so the h statistic is

$$h = -0.165 \sqrt{\frac{35}{1 - 35(0.1123)^2}} = -1.31$$

Our decision is to reject H_0 and conclude that first-order autocorrelation is not a problem. Adding the lagged variable proved effective in correcting for autocorrelation.

EXERCISES

5 **Cost Control (reconsidered)**   Consider again the data from Exercise 1 in Chapter 4. Use COST as the dependent variable and use the variables PAPER and MACHINE as explanatory variables. The MINITAB regression output for the regression of COST on PAPER and MACHINE is shown in Figure 6.78. The Durbin-Watson statistic is included in the output. The MINITAB time-series plot of the standardized residuals is shown in Figure 6.79.

Test whether the disturbances are autocorrelated. Use a 5% level of significance. Be sure to state the hypotheses to be tested, the decision rule, the test statistic, and your decision.

These data are available in a file with prefix COST6 in three columns: COST, PAPER, and MACHINE.

FIGURE 6.78   MINITAB Output for Regression of COST on PAPER and MACHINE Including
Durbin-Watson Statistic

```
The regression equation is
COST = 59.4 + 0.949 PAPER + 2.39 MACHINE

Predictor      Coef       StDev          T          P
Constant      59.43       19.64       3.03      0.006
PAPER        0.9489      0.1101       8.62      0.000
MACHINE      2.3864      0.2101      11.36      0.000

S = 10.98       R-Sq = 99.9%      R-Sq(adj) = 99.9%

Analysis of Variance

Source            DF          SS          MS          F          P
Regression         2     2271227     1135613    9413.48      0.000
Residual Error    24        2895         121
Total             26     2274122

Source       DF      Seq SS
PAPER         1     2255666
MACHINE       1       15561

Unusual Observations
Obs     PAPER       COST        Fit    StDev Fit     Residual     St Resid
 25       647    1317.00    1293.83        2.59        23.17        2.17R

R denotes an observation with a large standardized residual

Durbin-Watson statistic = 2.14
```

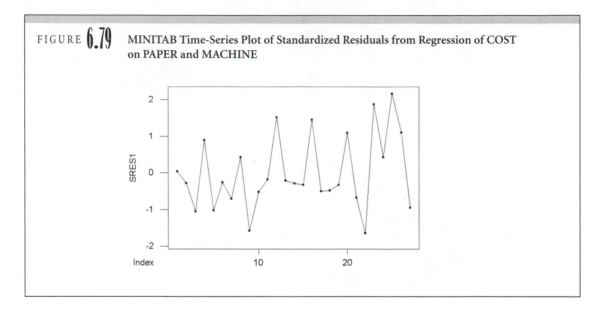

FIGURE MINITAB Time-Series Plot of Standardized Residuals from Regression of COST on PAPER and MACHINE

6.9 MULTICOLLINEARITY

6.9.1 Consequences of Multicollinearity

For a regression of y on K explanatory variables $x_1, x_2, \ldots, x_K$, it is hoped that the explanatory variables are highly correlated with the dependent variable. A relationship is sought that explains a large portion of the variation in y. At the same time, however, it is not desirable for strong relationships to exist among the explanatory variables. When explanatory variables are correlated with one another, the problem of *multicollinearity* is said to exist. How serious the problem is depends on the degree of multicollinearity. Low correlations among the explanatory variables generally do not result in serious deterioration of the quality of the least-squares estimates. But high correlations may result in highly unstable least-squares estimates of the regression coefficients.

The presence of a high degree of multicollinearity among the explanatory variables results in the following problems:

1 The standard deviations of the regression coefficients are disproprotionately large. As a result, the t values computed to test whether the population regression coefficients are zero are small. The null hypothesis that the coefficients are zero may be accepted even when the associated variable is important in explaining variation in y.

2 The regression coefficient estimates are unstable. Because of the high standard errors, reliable estimates of the regression coefficients are difficult to obtain. Signs of the coefficients may be the opposite of what is intuitively reasonable. Dropping one

variable from the regression or adding a variable causes large changes in the estimates of the coefficients of other variables.

6.9.2 Detecting Multicollinearity

Numerous ways have been suggested in the literature to help detect multicollinearity. These are listed here with some recommendations on their usefulness:

1   Compute the pairwise correlations between the explanatory variables. Because multicollinearity exists when explanatory variables are highly correlated, these correlations should help identify any highly correlated pairs of variables. One rule of thumb suggested by some researchers is that multicollinearity may be a serious problem if any pairwise correlation is bigger than 0.5.

There are two limitations to this approach. First, the correlation cutoff of 0.5 is somewhat arbitrary and not always effective in identifying serious pairwise multicollinearity problems. Second, only relationships between two explanatory variables can be investigated. For example, if there are three explanatory variables in the model, x_1, x_2, and x_3, the pairwise correlations can be computed between x_1 and x_2, x_1 and x_3, and x_2 and x_3. But the relationships resulting in the multicollinearity may be more complex than simple pairwise correlations. The variable x_1 may not be highly correlated with x_2 or x_3 individually, but may be highly correlated with some linear combination of the two variables. That is, x_1 may be highly correlated with $a_1 x_2 + a_2 x_3$.

Another suggested rule of thumb is that multicollinearity may be a serious problem if any of the pairwise correlations among the x variables is larger than the largest of the correlations between the y variable and the x variables. Although this rule does not suffer from an arbitrary cutoff point (such as 0.5), it does suffer from the same limitations concerning more complex relationships among the x variables.

2   An indication of multicollinearity is a large overall F statistic but small t statistics. As mentioned, multicollinearity results in large standard deviations of the regression coefficients and small t ratios. Thus, the test for whether the individual regression coefficients are equal to zero may result in a decision to accept the null hypotheses $H_0: \beta_k = 0$ even when the variables included in the regression are important in explaining the variation in y. The overall F statistic is typically not affected by the multicollinearity, however. If the variables are important, the F statistic should be large, indicating a good overall fit even if the t statistics appear to be saying that none of the variables are important.

This method of detecting multicollinearity is not always effective because multicollinearity may result in some, but not all, of the t values being small. The question of whether the variable is unimportant or whether it just appears so because of multicollinearity cannot be answered by looking at the output. Although this approach may be helpful in pointing out that multicollinearity exists in some instances, it does not provide any information on which of the explanatory variables are highly correlated with others.

3   Compute *variance inflation factors (VIFs)*. Let $x_1, x_2, \ldots, x_K$ be the K explanatory variables in a regression. Perform the regression of x_j on the remaining $K - 1$

explanatory variables and call the coefficient of determination from this regression R_j^2. The VIF for the variable x_j is

$$VIF_j = \frac{1}{1 - R_j^2}$$

A variance inflation factor can be computed for each explanatory variable. It is a measure of the strength of the relationship between each explanatory variable and all other explanatory variables in the regression. Thus, pairwise correlations are taken into account as well as more complex relationships with two or more of the other variables. The value R_j^2 measures the strength of the relationship between x_j and the other $K-1$ explanatory variables. If there is no relationship (an ideal case), then $R_j^2 = 0.0$ and $VIF_j = 1/(1-0) = 1$. As R_j^2 increases, VIF_j increases also. For example, if $R_j^2 = 0.9$, then $VIF_j = 1/(1-0.99) = 10$; if $R_j^2 = 0.99$, then $VIF_j = 1/(1-0.99) = 100$. Large values of VIF_j suggest that x_j may be highly related to other explanatory variables and, thus, multicollinearity may be a problem. How large the VIFs must be to suggest a serious problem with multicollinearity is not completely clear. Some suggested guidelines are as follows:

a Any individual VIF_j larger than 10 indicates that multicollinearity may be influencing the least-squares estimates of the regression coefficients.

b If the average of the VIF_j, $\overline{VIF} = \sum_{j=1}^{K} VIF_j / K$, is considerably larger than 1, then serious problems may exist. VIF indicates how many times larger the error sum of squares for the regression is due to multicollinearity than it is if the variables are uncorrelated.

c VIF's also need to be evaluated relative to the overall fit of the model. Freund and Wilson[2] note that whenever the VIF's are less than $1/(1 - R^2)$ where R^2 is the coefficient of determination for the model with all x variables included, multicollinearity is not strong enough to affect the coefficient estimates. In this case the independent variables are more strongly related to the y variable than they are to each other.

6.9.3 Correction for Multicollinearity

One obvious solution to the multicollinearity problem is to remove those variables that are highly correlated with others and thus eliminate the problem. This solution has obvious drawbacks. No information can be obtained on the omitted variables. In addition, the omission of one variable causes changes in the estimates of the regression coefficients of variables left in the equation.

In certain cases, adding more data can break the pattern of multicollinearity. But this solution is not always possible, especially in many business and economics situations. It also does not always work even when it is possible.

---

[2] Freund, R. J., and Wilson, W. J., *Regression Analysis: Statistical Modeling of a Response Variable*. San Diego: Academic Press, 1998.

When multicollinearity is present, it affects the regression coefficient estimates in the ways noted earlier. However, it does not affect the ability to obtain a good fit of the regression (high R^2). Nor does it affect the quality of forecasts or predictions from the regression (as long as the pattern of multicollinearity continues for those observations where forecasts are desired). Thus, if the regression model is to be used strictly for forecasting, corrections may be unnecessary. Even when developing a model for forecasting, however, it is often desirable to test whether individual variables are contributing significantly to the explanatory power of the model. In this case, multicollinearity remains a problem.

Finally, several other statistical procedures have been proposed as possible remedial measures with multicollinearity. These include ridge regression and principle components regression. These techniques are beyond the scope of this text. The interested reader is referred to Raymond H. Myers, *Classical and Modern Regression with Applications*, pp. 243–263.

6.10 USING THE COMPUTER

The Using the Computer section in each chapter describes how to perform the computer analyses in the chapter using MINITAB, Excel, and SAS. For further detail on MINITAB, Excel, and SAS, see Appendix C.

6.10.1 MINITAB

Note that Version 12 of MINITAB is fully menu driven. Commands can be used, however, and they are included for any interested users. The menu headings and sub-headings used to perform the procedures are listed first, followed by commands in parentheses. For example, STAT: REGRESSION: REGRESSION: STORAGE means to click on the STAT menu, then REGRESSION, then REGRESSION again, and finally, on the STORAGE button in the Regression dialog box. (REGR C_ K C_, . . . ,C_, STORE C_,C_ suggests a command to be typed in.)

Storing Standardized Residuals and Fitted Values

```
STAT: REGRESSION: REGRESSION: STORAGE
(REGR C_ K C_,...,C_, STORE C_,C_)
```

Store standardized residuals and fitted values by using the Storage button in the Regression dialog box. Then click "Fits" and "Standardized residuals" as shown in Figure 6.80. The fitted values and standardized residuals are stored in the next two free columns, respectively, in the MINITAB worksheet. (When using the REGR command to store fitted values and standardized residuals, column numbers must be assigned to the columns where you want the values stored.)

FIGURE **6.80** Regression—Storage Dialog Box for Saving Fitted Values, Standardized Residuals, and Influence Statistics

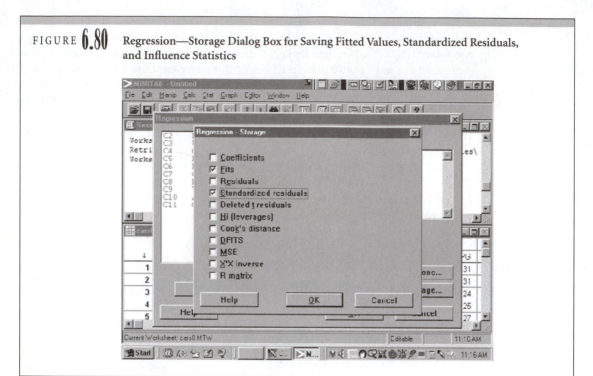

Requesting Other Influence Statistics

Refer again to Figure 6.80. Requests for other influence statistics are made by checking the appropriate boxes in the Regression—Storage dialog box. Other influence statistics available in MINITAB include leverage values (Hi), Cook's Distance, and DFITS. These values are stored in a column in the worksheet by simply clicking the box next to the desired statistic.

Requesting the Durbin-Watson Statistic

```
STAT: REGRESSION: REGRESSION: OPTIONS
(REGR C_ K C_,...,C_;
DW.)
```

To request the Durbin-Watson statistic, click the Durbin-Watson statistic box on the Regression—Options screen as shown in Figure 6.81. (If using commands, use the DW subcommand.)

FIGURE **6.81**   Regression—Options Dialog Box for Requesting Durbin-Watson Statistics and Variance Inflation Factors

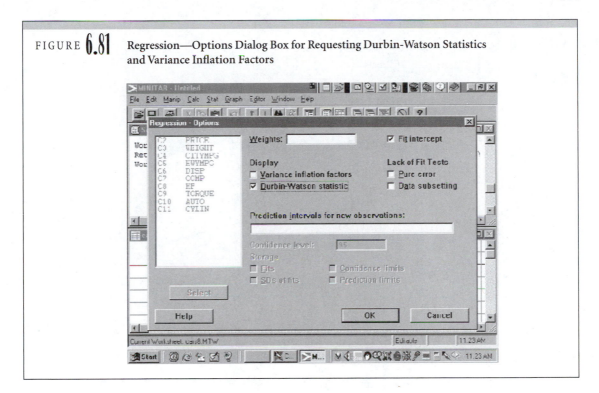

Requesting Variance Inflation Factors

```
STAT: REGRESSION: REGRESSION: OPTIONS
(REGR C_ K C_,...,C_;
VIF.)
```

To request variance inflation factors, click the Variance inflation factors box on the Regression—Options screen as shown in Figure 6.81. (If using commands, use the VIF subcommand.)

Variable Transformations

See Variable Transformations in the Using the Computer section at the end of Chapter 5.

Testing for Normality

```
STAT: BASIC STATISTICS: NORMALITY TEST
```

To request a test for normality, use the Normality Test option on the Basic Statistics menu. Fill in the variable to be tested (the standardized residuals from a regression are used in the example) and the test desired as shown in Figure 6.82. In the text, the

FIGURE **6.82**   Normality Test Dialog Box

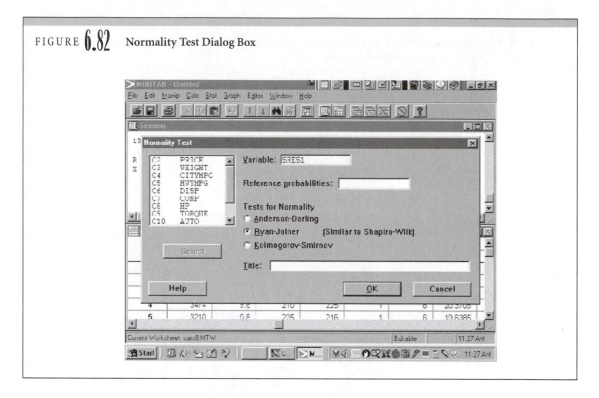

Ryan-Joiner test was discussed although there are two other tests available in MINITAB. (If commands are used, the sequence

```
NSCORES C1 C2
PLOT C1 C2
CORR C1 C2
```

produces a normal probability plot and the Ryan-Joiner test statistic, which is the correlation between the normal scores and the data being tested.)

Szroeter's Test for Nonconstant Variance

Although this test cannot be requested in MINITAB (or SAS) with a single command, it can be computed through a sequence of commands. This will be demonstrated for MINITAB. (I used commands here rather than menu items because I find it easier when there are a sequence of operations to be performed. Obviously, these same procedures could be accomplished with menus.) Assume that the dependent (y) variable is in C1 and the (one) explanatory variable (x) is in C2. First, recall that the data must be ordered according to increasing values of x. The Sort command accomplishes this. The standardized residuals from the regression of y on x are then stored in C10.

```
SORT C2, CARRY C1, PUT IN C20, C21
REGR Y IN C21 ON 1 PRED IN C20, STORE IN C10
```

A patterned Set command is used to put integers 1 through n (the sample size) in C25.

```
SET IN C25
1:n
END
```

Now compute the quantities needed to compute h in Szroeter's test statistic:

```
LET C16=C10*C10
LET C17=C16*C25
SUM C17 K2
SUM C16 K1
LET K3=K2/K1
```

The value of K3 printed will be h.

```
PRINT K3
```

Szroeter's Q statistic can then be computed using the formula

$$Q = \left(\frac{6n}{n^2 - 1} \right)^{\frac{1}{2}} \left(h - \left(\frac{n+1}{2} \right) \right)$$

6.10.2   Excel

Storing Standardized Residuals and Fitted Values

In the Regression dialog box, check Standardized Residuals as shown in Figure 6.83. Checking the box for the standardized residuals saves both the standardized residuals and the fitted values (as well as the raw residuals).

Requesting Other Influence Statistics, the Durbin-Watson Statistic, and Variance Inflation Factors

Excel does not provide options for automatically producing the other influence statistics discussed in the text, the Durbin-Watson statistic, or variance inflation factors. Although these could be computed by creating formulas, this option is not discussed in this text.

Variable Transformations

See Variable Transformations in the Using the Computer section at the end of Chapter 5.

Testing for Normality

Although there is a normal probability plot option in the Excel Regression dialog box, it does not do you much good. It provides a normal probability plot of the dependent variable, when in fact, what you really want is a normal probability plot of the standardized residuals. Plus, I find the plot difficult to interpret given the way it is produced in Excel.

FIGURE **6.83** Saving Fitted Values and Standardized Residuals with Excel

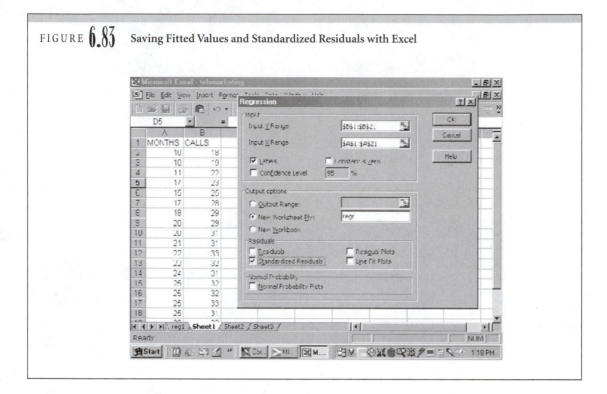

6.10.3 SAS

Storing Standardized Residuals and Fitted Value

The following command sequence produces a regression of SALES on two independent variables ADV and BONUS, saves the fitted values (variable name FITS1) and standardized residuals (variable name SRES1), and then plots the standardized residuals versus the fitted values and each of the independent variables.

```
PROC REG;
     MODEL SALES = ADV BONUS;
     OUTPUT PREDICTED = FITS1 STUDENT = SRES1;
PROC PLOT;
     PLOT SRES1*FITS1 SRES1*ADV SRES1*BONUS;
```

In the model statement, the dependent variable (SALES) is listed first; the independent variables (ADV and BONUS) follow the equal sign. In the output statement, the fitted (predicted) values are requested and labeled FITS1. The standardized residuals (STUDENT) are also requested and labeled SRES1. PROC PLOT is used to produce residual plots. As shown, residual plots of the standardized residuals versus the fitted values and each of the two explanatory variables are generated.

Requesting Other Influence Statistics

Influence statistics other than standardized residuals and fitted values can be requested in SAS as follows:

```
PROC REG;
    MODEL Y = X/INFLUENCE;
    OUTPUT COOK=COOKD;
```

The INFLUENCE option requests that SAS print out the leverage values, the studentized deleted residuals, and the *DFITS* statistics (among others not discussed in this text). The OUTPUT command requests that Cook's D statistic be computed, stored, and labeled COOKD.

Requesting the Durbin-Watson Statistic

```
PROC REG;
    MODEL SALES = ADV/DW;
```

requests that the Durbin-Watson statistic be printed. SAS also prints out an estimate of the first-order autocorrelation statistic.

Variable Transformations

See Variable Transformation in the Using the Computer section in Chapter 5.

Testing for Normality

In SAS, a normal probability plot for the variable SRES1 can be produced using the commands:

```
PROC UNIVARIATE PLOT;
VAR SRES1;
```

A variety of descriptive statistics on the variable SRES1 are printed along with a stem-and-leaf plot, a box plot, and a normal probability plot. When the sample size is 50 or fewer, the Shapiro-Wilk test statistic is computed. When $n > 50$, the Kolmogorov D statistic is used. In either case, a p value corresponding to the observed statistic is computed and printed. (Note that the Shapiro-Wilk test is essentially the same test as the Ryan-Joiner test produced in MINITAB.)

Prais-Winsten Transformation

The Prais-Winsten transformation to correct for first-order autocorrelation was discussed earlier in this chapter. Although SAS does not have a procedure to correct for autocorrelation, the associated statistical package SAS/ETS does. This procedure is outlined briefly here:

```
PROC AUTOREG;
    MODEL SALES = ADV/NLAG = 1 ITER;
```

These commands request the Prais-Winsten transformation through the PROC AUTOREG command. The dependent variable here is SALES and the explanatory variable is ADV (more than one explanatory variable can be included if necessary). The NLAG = 1 option tells the procedure that first-order autocorrelation is to be corrected (AUTOREG is a general procedure that can correct for higher-order autocorrelation not discussed in this text). The ITER option requests an iterative procedure, which has in general been shown superior in various studies.

ADDITIONAL EXERCISES

6 **Imports**   The gross domestic product (GDP) and imports (IMPORTS) for 25 countries are shown in Table 6.7. The scatterplot of IMPORTS versus GDP is shown in Figure 6.84. The MINITAB and Excel regressions are shown in Figures 6.85 and 6.86, respectively. Plots of the standardized residuals versus the fitted values and the explanatory variable are shown in Figures 6.87 and 6.88 for MINITAB and in Figures 6.89 and 6.90 for Excel. Use the outputs to help answer the following questions:

a Using the scatterplot, regression outputs, and the residual plots, do any of the assumptions of the regression model appear to be violated? If so, which one (or ones)? Justify your answers.

b Using a computer statistical package, construct the scatterplot and rerun the regression with the United States omitted. Construct the residual plots for this new regression. Do the results appear any different from the original regression results? If so, how do they differ? Do you prefer the original results or the results with the United States omitted? On what do you base your choice? Do there still appear to be problems with this regression?

c Try to develop a curvilinear model using the original data (with the United States included) that provides improved results over the linear model. Be sure to examine the residual plots from the curvilinear model to see if any regression assumptions are violated for this model.

These data are available in a file with prefix IMPORT6 in two columns: IMPORTS and GDP.

TABLE **6.7**   Data for Imports Exercise

Country	IMPORTS	GDP	Country	IMPORTS	GDP
Argentine	30.30	348.20	Israel	28.60	96.70
Australia	67.00	394.00	Jamaica	2.90	9.50
Bolivia	1.70	23.10	Japan	339.00	3080.00
Brazil	61.40	1040.00	Liberia	5.80	2.60
Canada	194.40	658.00	Malaysia	78.40	227.00
Cuba	3.20	16.90	Mauritius	2.20	11.70
Denmark	43.20	122.50	Netherlands	1791.00	343.90
Egypt	15.50	267.10	Nigeria	8.00	132.70
Finland	29.30	102.10	Panama	2.95	18.00
France	256.00	1320.00	Samoa	0.10	0.45
Greece	27.00	137.40	United Kingdom	283.50	1242.00
Haiti	0.67	7.10	United States	822.00	8083.00
India	39.70	1534.00			

Source: www.odci.gov/cia/publications/factbook/index.html

FIGURE **6.84**   MINITAB Scatterplot of IMPORTS Versus GDP

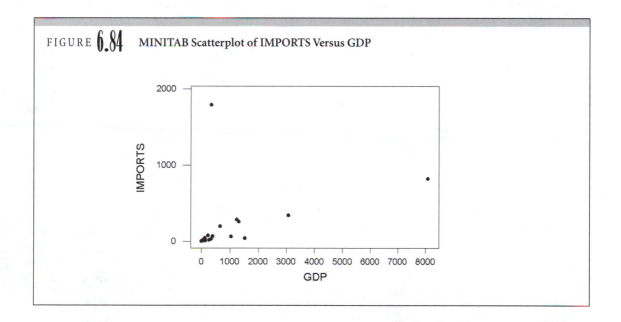

FIGURE **6.85**   MINITAB Output for Regression of IMPORTS on GDP

```
The regression equation is
IMPORTS = 95.7 + 0.0906 GDP

Predictor      Coef       StDev           T          P
Constant      95.68       79.22        1.21      0.239
GDP         0.09063     0.04359        2.08      0.049

S = 358.9       R-Sq = 15.8%      R-Sq(adj) = 12.2%

Analysis of Variance

Source           DF          SS          MS          F          P
Regression        1      556867      556867       4.32      0.049
Residual Error   23     2963126      128832
Total            24     3519993

Unusual Observations
Obs      GDP    IMPORTS        Fit    StDev Fit      Residual      St Resid
 20      344     1791.0      126.8        74.1        1664.2         4.74R
 25     8083      822.0      828.3       326.8          -6.3        -0.04 X

R denotes an observation with a large standardized residual
X denotes an observation whose X value gives it large influence.
```

FIGURE **6.86**   Excel Output for Regression of IMPORTS on GDP

```
                        SUMMARY OUTPUT

Regression Statistics
Multiple R           0.3977
R Square             0.1582
Adjusted R Square    0.1216
Standard Error     358.9311
Observations        25.000

ANOVA
                    df            SS            MS          F      Significance F
Regression       1.000    556866.7294    556866.7294    4.3224          0.0490
Residual        23.000   2963124.9903    128831.5213
Total           24.000   3519991.7197

                               Standard
                Coefficients      Error    t Stat    P-value    Lower 95%    Upper 95%
Intercept          95.6811     79.2229    1.2077     0.2394     -68.2038     259.5660
GDP                 0.0906      0.0436    2.0790     0.0490       0.0005       0.1808
```

FIGURE **6.87** MINITAB Plot of Standardized Residuals Versus Fitted Values for Imports Exercise

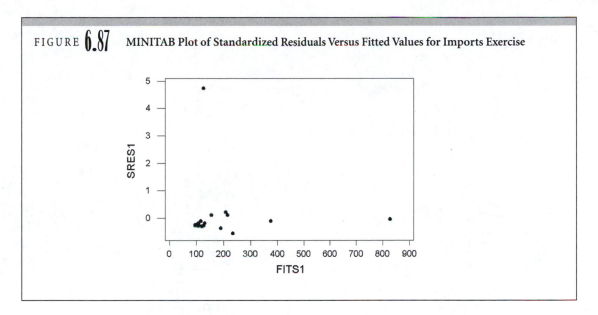

FIGURE **6.88** MINITAB Plot of Standardized Residuals Versus GDP for Imports Exercise

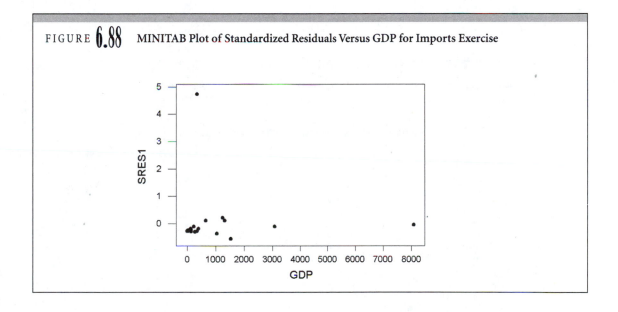

FIGURE **6.89** Excel Plot of Standardized Residuals Versus Fitted Values for Imports Exercise

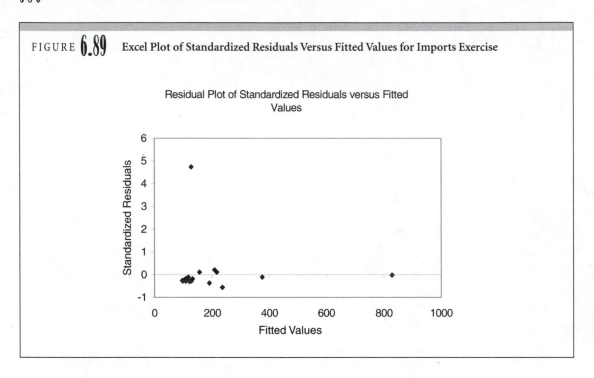

FIGURE **6.90** Excel Plot of Standardized Residuals Versus GDP for Imports Exercise

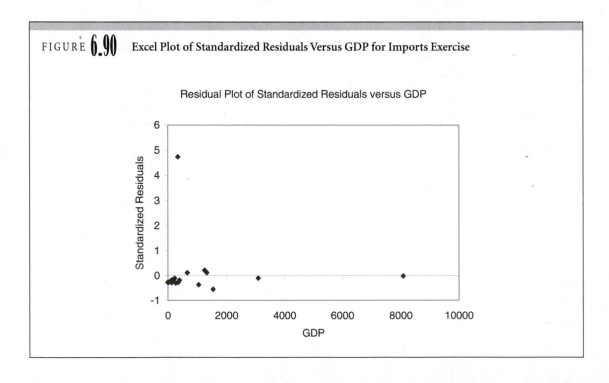

7   **ABX Company**   Consider again the data used in Exercise 11 of Chapter 4. The dependent variable is absenteeism among employees at the ABX Company. In this exercise, the explanatory variable to be considered is seniority (SENIOR). The data were shown in Table 4.15. Our goal is to express the relationship between absenteeism and seniority in the form of an equation. Start with the linear regression using absenteeism as the dependent variable and seniority as the independent variable. Based on an examination of scatterplots and residual plots, do any assumptions of the linear regression model appear to be violated? If so, which one (or ones)? If any violations are detected, suggest possible corrections. Rerun the regression with the suggested corrections and compare your results to the original results. Be sure to do residual plots for the model using the suggested correction. Which model do you prefer and why?

These data are in a file with prefix ABSENT6 in two columns: ABSENT and SE-NIOR.

8   **Coal Mining Fatalities**   The data in Table 6.8 show the annual number of fatalities from gas and dust explosions in coal mines for the years 1915 to 1978 and the number of cutting machines in use.[3] Run the regression using fatalities as the dependent variable and number of cutting machines in use as the independent variable. Based on an examination of scatterplots and residual plots, do any assumptions of the linear regression model appear to be violated? If so, which one (or ones)? If any violations are detected, suggest possible corrections. Rerun the regression with the suggested corrections and compare your results to the original results. Be sure to do residual plots for the model using the suggested correction. Which model do you prefer and why?

These data are available in a file with prefix CUTTING6 in two columns: FATALS and CUTTING.

9   **Piston Corporation (reconsidered)**   Reexamine the data from the PISTON exercise from Exercise 3 in Chapter 5. Use the variables 1/PROD and INDEX as explanatory variables. (These were the variables chosen in the exercise.) Test to see whether the disturbances are positively autocorrelated. State the hypotheses to be tested, the decision rule, the test statistic, and your decision. On the basis of the test result, what action should be taken? Use a 0.05 level of significance. The data are in a file with prefix PISTON6 in three columns: COST, PROD, and INDEX.

10   **Computer Repair**   A computer repair service is examining the time taken on service calls. The data obtained for 30 service calls are shown in Table 6.9. Information obtained includes:

x_1 = number of machines to be repaired (NUMBER)

x_2 = years of experience of service person (EXPER)

y = time taken (in minutes) to provide service (TIME)

---

[3] Data were obtained from K. D. Lawrence and L. C. Marsh, "Robust Ridge Estimation Methods for Predicting U.S. Coal Mining Fatalities." *Communications in Statistics* 13 (1984): 139–149.

TABLE **6.8**   Data for Coal Mining Fatalities Exercise

Year	FATALS	CUTTING	Year	FATALS	CUTTING	Year	FATALS	CUTTING
1915	270	15692	1937	116	11892	1959	10	6907
1916	183	16198	1938	84	11810	1960	3	6440
1917	319	17235	1939	43	12076	1961	26	6021
1918	103	18463	1940	292	12342	1962	52	5561
1919	149	18959	1941	89	12608	1963	31	5309
1920	124	19103	1942	148	13049	1964	3	5320
1921	62	19618	1943	166	11656	1965	19	4784
1922	298	20436	1944	32	13305	1966	10	4311
1923	330	21229	1945	72	13390	1967	12	3663
1924	486	18660	1946	27	13625	1968	88	3060
1925	302	17551	1947	154	13865	1969	0	2779
1926	373	17466	1948	44	14445	1970	41	2623
1927	187	17388	1949	3	14424	1971	2	2058
1928	347	15261	1950	3	14315	1972	5	1890
1929	168	14731	1951	153	13761	1973	2	1535
1930	234	14237	1952	11	12471	1974	0	1515
1931	68	13216	1953	9	10960	1975	0	1595
1932	162	12017	1954	17	9218	1976	23	1803
1933	27	11845	1955	2	9054	1977	4	1495
1934	40	11905	1956	5	9218	1978	0	1432
1935	26	11881	1957	63	8817			
1936	41	11974	1958	41	7744			

TABLE **6.9**   Data for Computer Repair Exercise

NUMBER	EXPER	TIME	NUMBER	EXPER	TIME	NUMBER	EXPER	TIME
1	9	66	11	10	225	22	9	628
1	11	74	12	7	270	22	9	636
3	11	88	13	9	265	23	10	660
4	8	99	14	9	301	24	10	731
6	9	134	15	10	343	25	11	752
6	9	120	16	11	383	26	8	800
7	10	178	17	10	383	27	10	863
8	9	139	20	9	515	28	9	918
9	8	187	19	9	474	29	9	976
11	10	227	20	9	495	30	10	1027

Develop a model to predict average time on the service calls using EXPER and NUMBER as explanatory variables. Use scatterplots and residual plots to determine whether any of the assumptions of the linear regression model have been violated. If any of the assumptions have been violated, state which one or ones and suggest possible corrections. Try the new model to see if it is an improvement over the original one. Be sure to examine residual plots from the corrected model (or models) that you try. Indicate your choice for the best model.

These data are available in a file with prefix COMPREP6 in three columns: NUMBER, EXPER, and TIME.

11 **Estimating Residential Real Estate Values**   The Tarrant County Appraisal District must appraise properties for all of the county. The appraisal district uses data such as square footage of the individual houses as well as location, depreciation, and physical condition of an entire neighborhood to derive individual appraisal values on each house. This avoids labor-intensive reinspection each year.

Regression can be used to establish the weight assigned to various factors used in assessing values. For example, Table 6.10 shows the value, size in square feet, a physical condition index, and a depreciation factor for a sample of 100 Tarrant County houses (in 1990). Using these data, develop an equation that might be useful to the appraisal district in evaluating houses.

Discuss how the equation developed here could be used to value houses. What would be the value assigned to a 1400-square-foot house with physical condition index 0.70 and depreciation factor 0.02?

The data are available in a file with prefix REALEST6 in four columns: VALUE, SIZE, DEPRECIATION, and CONDITION.

TABLE **6.10**   Data for Real Estate Valuation Exercise

VALUE	SIZE	DEPRECIATION	CONDITION	VALUE	SIZE	DEPRECIATION	CONDITION
23974	1442	0.4	0	29046	1032	0.5	0
24087	1426	0.4	0	20715	720	0.55	0
16781	1632	0.5	0	19461	734	0.5	0
29061	910	0.5	0.18	21377	720	0.5	0
37982	972	0.55	0.18	52881	1635	0.6	0.02
29433	912	0.55	0.18	43889	1381	0.55	0.02
33624	1400	0.45	0.05	45134	1372	0.55	0.02
27032	1087	0.45	0.18	47655	1349	0.6	0.02
28653	1139	0.45	0.18	53088	1599	0.6	0.02
33075	1386	0.55	0.05	38923	1171	0.5	0.02
17474	756	0.5	0.05	57870	1966	0.55	0.02
33852	1044	0.5	0.07	30489	1504	0.45	0

Continues

TABLE **6.10** *(continued)*

VALUE	SIZE	DEPRECIATION	CONDITION	VALUE	SIZE	DEPRECIATION	CONDITION
29207	1296	0.35	0	35904	960	0.5	0
44919	1356	0.55	0.12	21799	1052	0.5	0
48090	1553	0.55	0.1	28212	1296	0.55	0
40521	1142	0.55	0.1	27553	1282	0.55	0
43403	1268	0.55	0.1	15826	916	0.35	0
38112	1008	0.55	0.1	18660	864	0.5	0
27710	1120	0.5	0	21536	1404	0.4	0
27621	960	0.6	0	24147	1676	0.4	0
22258	920	0.35	0	17867	1131	0.4	0
29064	1259	0.5	0	21583	1397	0.4	0
12001	783	0.4	0	15482	888	0.4	0
37650	1874	0.35	0.02	24857	1448	0.45	0
27930	1242	0.5	0	17716	1022	0.45	0
16066	772	0.4	0	224182	2251	0.75	0.04
20411	908	0.45	0	182012	1126	0.55	0.04
23672	1155	0.45	0	201597	2617	0.9	0.03
24215	1004	0.5	0	49683	966	0.6	0.05
22020	958	0.45	0	60647	1469	0.65	0.05
52863	1828	0.6	0.02	49024	1322	0.7	0.02
41822	1146	0.6	0.02	52092	1509	0.65	0.02
45104	1368	0.6	0.02	55645	1724	0.65	0.04
28154	1392	0.65	0.24	51919	1559	0.65	0.02
20943	1058	0.65	0.24	55174	2133	0.55	0
17851	1375	0.55	0.26	48760	1233	0.55	0
16616	648	0.4	0.06	45906	1323	0.55	0
38752	1313	0.5	0	52013	1733	0.55	0
44377	1780	0.55	0	56612	1357	0.6	0
43566	1148	0.55	0.32	69197	1234	0.6	0.17
38950	1363	0.55	0.32	84416	1434	0.6	0.15
44633	1262	0.55	0.32	60962	1384	0.55	0.17
12372	840	0.35	0	47359	995	0.55	0.05
12148	840	0.4	0	56302	1372	0.65	0.14
19852	839	0.5	0	88285	1774	0.7	0.06
20012	852	0.55	0	91862	1903	0.7	0.08
20314	852	0.55	0	242690	3581	0.8	0.07
22814	974	0.55	0	296251	4343	0.8	0.04
24696	1135	0.5	0	107132	1861	0.75	0.08
23443	1170	0.7	0.02	77797	1542	0.65	0.3

TABLE **6.11**   Data for Criminal Justice Expenditures Exercise

State	EXPEND	POLICE	POP	PRISONER	State	EXPEND	POLICE	POP	PRISONER
Alabama	561	10312	2780	12357	Montana	104	1799	195	1272
Alaska	283	1928	223	1862	Nebraska	216	3696	767	2066
Arizona	962	10315	2718	11578	Nevada	332	3379	918	4881
Arkansas	233	4875	955	5519	New Hampshire	170	2978	591	1019
California	8940	75043	27808	73780	New Jersey	2118	29049	7736	16936
Colorado	701	9141	2703	5765	New Mexico	290	4520	746	2723
Connecticut	692	9282	2969	4723	New York	7145	77571	16378	44560
Delaware	158	1841	444	2207	North Carolina	1042	16259	3641	16251
Florida	2810	39853	11496	34681	North Dakota	71	1280	253	414
Georgia	1187	18118	4175	18018	Ohio	1809	23780	8594	26462
Hawaii	271	3122	849	1510	Oklahoma	442	7593	1894	10448
Idaho	133	2305	203	1581	Oregon	593	6221	1909	5991
Illinois	2340	36925	9590	21081	Pennsylvania	1919	26199	10203	17883
Indiana	688	12072	3809	11271	Rhode Island	194	2838	936	1179
Iowa	354	5631	1233	3034	South Carolina	553	8641	2127	12902
Kansas	404	6506	1344	5817	South Dakota	83	1569	208	1020
Kentucky	496	7234	1719	7119	Tennessee	756	12205	3286	7732
Louisiana	748	13349	3033	16242	Texas	2939	43745	13807	40437
Maine	169	2914	452	1214	Utah	282	3793	1321	1944
Maryland	1091	13351	4363	13572	Vermont	84	1254	108	553
Massachusetts	1449	18475	5388	6455	Virginia	1195	15500	4401	13928
Michigan	2132	22873	7416	27612	Washington	887	10398	3886	5816
Minnesota	735	8798	2900	27499	West Virginia	168	3352	677	1455
Mississippi	263	5616	800	7251	Wisconsin	864	12905	3247	6325
Missouri	829	14037	3408	12176	Wyoming	98	1598	139	945

Source: These data were obtained from the 1990 *Sourcebook of Criminal Justice Statistics*.

12 Criminal Justice Expenditures   Table 6.11 shows the following data for each of the 50 states:

total expenditures on a state's criminal justice system (in millions of dollars) (EXPEND)

total number of police employed in the state (POLICE)

population of the state (in thousands) (POP)

total number of incarcerated prisoners in the state (PRISONER)

State governments must try to project spending in many areas. Expenditure on the criminal justice system is one area of continually rising cost. Your job is to build a model that can be used to forecast spending on a state's criminal justice system. Any of the three possible explanatory variables can be used. Be sure to consider violations

TABLE **6.12**   Data for Intersections Exercise

ACCIDENT	VOLUME	ACCIDENT	VOLUME	ACCIDENT	VOLUME	ACCIDENT	VOLUME
2	2025	4	3453	0	632	7	2498
7	4526	4	3731	10	1620	5	1699
3	2028	3	1972	2	1315	5	2769
2	3723	2	2357	10	2860	10	3353
2	1337	2	2049	2	1723	4	2252
1	1985	9	3014	0	1147	6	3837
4	2673	2	3190	0	1917	1	1763
7	1958	0	1122	3	2035	5	2294
7	5811	4	1341	6	3257	10	3910
8	2870	2	3473	10	2841	2	2922
4	2239	2	2297	8	2790	6	1760
1	1909	3	3944	6	1940	5	1521
1	2372	6	2173	8	1733	11	3778
7	3485	28	4250	4	1881	3	2200
5	2768	21	2109	11	1932		
6	2068	14	4168	3	1554		

Source: City of Fort Worth

of any assumptions in building your model and correct for any violations. Once your model is complete, predict expenditures for a state that plans to hire 10,000 police personnel, has a population of 3 million, and expects 600 prisoners. Find a point prediction and a 95% prediction interval.

The data are available in a file with prefix CRIMSPN6 in four columns: EXPEND, POLICE, POP, and PRISONER.

13 **Intersections**   One factor related to the number of accidents at an intersection is the peak-hour volume of traffic. Data on both the volume of traffic during the peak hour and the total number of accidents are available for 62 intersections in Fort Worth, Texas. These data are shown in Table 6.12. The city wants to identify intersections that have an unusual number of accidents. Their definition of unusual involves first establishing some type of base-level forecast of the number of accidents, taking account of the peak-hour volume of traffic, and then judging which intersections still have an unusual number of accidents. As a consultant to the city, your job is to determine which, if any, of these 62 intersections appear to have an unusually high number of accidents given the volume of traffic.

These data are available in a file with prefix TRAFFIC6 in two columns: ACCIDENT (number of accidents) and VOLUME (peak-hour traffic volume).

14 **Mortgage Rates**   The regression in Figure 6.91 is an attempt to develop an equation to forecast mortgage rates. The explanatory variables include prime rate and the one

FIGURE 6.91   Mortgage Rate and Prime Rate Regression

```
The regression equation is
mortgrt = 5.32 + 0.627 primert - 0.115 primem1 - 0.229 primem2 - 0.314
primem3 - 0.247 primem4 - 0.037 primem5 + 0.684 primem6


90 cases used 6 cases contain missing values


Predictor      Coef       StDev          T           P
Constant     5.3188      0.5203       10.22       0.000
primert      0.6266      0.5047        1.24       0.218
primem1     -0.1148      0.8281       -0.14       0.890
primem2     -0.2286      0.8286       -0.28       0.783
primem3     -0.3137      0.8295       -0.38       0.706
primem4     -0.2468      0.8286       -0.30       0.767
primem5     -0.0368      0.8262       -0.04       0.965
primem6      0.6845      0.4947        1.38       0.170


S = 0.7587      R-Sq = 29.7%      R-Sq(adj) = 23.7%


Analysis of Variance


Source              DF           SS          MS          F           P
Regression           7      19.9288      2.8470       4.95       0.000
Residual Error      82      47.1977      0.5756
Total               89      67.1265


Source      DF       Seq SS
primert      1      14.7401
primem1      1       0.0325
primem2      1       0.2693
primem3      1       0.6507
primem4      1       1.3098
primem5      1       1.8245
primem6      1       1.1017
```

through six period lagged values of prime rate. The forecaster initially believed that prime rate in some of the past time periods and possibly the current time period may have an effect on mortgage rates. After examining the regression, the forecaster notes the small t statistics (large p values) for all the variables included in the regression and concludes that the regression is basically worthless: None of the variables included— current or lagged—are helpful in predicting mortgage rates. Do you agree or disagree? Justify your position. Either way what would you do next?

FIGURE 6.92   MINITAB Regression Output for Consumer Credit Model 1

```
The regression equation is
credit = 738 + 9.76 trend

Predictor      Coef      StDev         T         P
Constant    737.933      4.650    158.71     0.000
trend        9.7630     0.1652     59.10     0.000

S = 15.86      R-Sq = 98.7%      R-Sq(adj) = 98.7%

Analysis of Variance

Source            DF         SS         MS         F         P
Regression         1     878056     878056   3492.70     0.000
Error             46      11564        251
Total             47     889621

Unusual Observations
Obs     trend     credit       Fit    StDev Fit     Residual    St Resid
  1      1.0     795.10     747.70        4.51        47.40       3.12R
  2      2.0     790.60     757.46        4.36        33.14       2.17R
 36     36.0    1128.60    1089.40        2.97        39.20       2.52R

R denotes an observation with a large standardized residual
```

15 **Outlier**   Consider the following time-series regression model: $y_i = \beta_0 + \beta_1 x_i + e_i$. Suppose that the y value in one time period can be regarded as an outlier.

a   Indicate how you might be able to detect the presence of the outlier from any computer output you request or receive while analyzing the data.

b   Suppose the outlier is detected and the person in charge of the analysis decides to delete the point from the analysis and to rerun the regression without this observation. Are there alternate suggestions you would have prior to taking this course of action, or do you believe deletion of the observation is the best course of action?

16 **Consumer Credit**   Consider the time series of consumer installment credit (U.S.) in billions of dollars. These data are monthly and cover the time period January 1993 through December 1996.

FIGURE 6.93   MINITAB Regression Output for Consumer Credit Model 2

```
The regression equation is
logcredit = 6.63 + 0.0100 trend


Predictor      Coef      StDev          T          P
Constant    6.62890    0.00441    1504.82      0.000
trend      0.0100391  0.0001565     64.14      0.000


S = 0.01502      R-Sq = 98.9%       R-Sq(adj) = 98.9%


Analysis of Variance

Source            DF         SS         MS          F          P
Regression         1    0.92843    0.92843    4114.28      0.000
Error             46    0.01038    0.00023
Total             47    0.93881


Unusual Observations
Obs    trend    logcredi       Fit    StDev Fit     Residual    St Resid
 1      1.0     6.67847    6.63894      0.00427      0.03952       2.74R
36     36.0     7.02873    6.99031      0.00282      0.03842       2.60R


R denotes an observation with a large standardized residual
```

Two different models are being considered:

MODEL 1: $credit = \beta_0 + \beta_1 trend + e$

and

MODEL 2: $\log(credit) = \beta_0 + \beta_1 trend + e$

where *credit* is billions of dollars of consumer installment credit at the end of each month, *trend* is a linear trend component, and log(*credit*) is the natural logarithm of consumer installment credit. The regression output for these two models is shown in Figures 6.92 and 6.93, respectively. The researcher wishes to compare these two models and choose the best one. Can the choice be made on the basis of the two outputs shown? If yes, state how and state which model you would choose. If no, state why not and state what you would need to make the comparison.

CHAPTER 7

Using Indicator and Interaction Variables

7.1 USING AND INTERPRETING INDICATOR VARIABLES

Indicator variables or *dummy variables* are a special type of variable used in a variety of ways in regression analysis. Indicator variables take on only two values, either 0 or 1. They can be used to indicate whether a sample unit either does (1) or does not (0) belong in a certain category. For example, a dummy variable could be used to indicate when an individual in the sample was employed by constructing the variable as

$$D_{1i} = 1 \text{ if individual } i \text{ is employed}$$

$$= 0 \text{ if individual } i \text{ is not employed}$$

To indicate when an individual is unemployed, the variable could be constructed as

$$D_{2i} = 1 \text{ if individual } i \text{ is unemployed}$$

$$= 0 \text{ if individual } i \text{ is not unemployed}$$

Obviously, any type of split into two groups can be easily represented by indicator variables.

If there are more than two groups into which individuals may be classified, this simply requires the use of additional indicator variables. Suppose firms in a sample are to be categorized according to the exchange on which they are listed: NYSE, AMEX or NASDAQ. This could be accomplished by constructing the following variables:

$$D_{1i} = 1 \text{ if firm } i \text{ is listed on the NYSE}$$
$$= 0 \text{ if firm } i \text{ is not listed on the NYSE}$$

$$D_{2i} = 1 \text{ if firm } i \text{ is listed on the AMEX}$$
$$= 0 \text{ if firm } i \text{ is not listed on the AMEX}$$

$$D_{3i} = 1 \text{ if firm } i \text{ is listed on the NASDAQ}$$
$$= 0 \text{ if firm } i \text{ is not listed on the NASDAQ}$$

Thus far, when sample individuals could belong to one of m different groups, m indicator variables were constructed, one for each group. When indicator variables are used in a regression analysis, however, only $m - 1$ of the indicator variables are included in the regression because only $m - 1$ indicator variables are needed to indicate m groups. The one group whose indicator is omitted serves as what might be called a *base level* group. Consider the following example to clarify this point.

EXAMPLE 7.1 **Employment Discrimination**

Regression analysis has been used increasingly in employment discrimination cases. The desire in such cases is typically to compare mean salaries of two groups of employees (say, male and female employees) to determine whether one group has significantly lower salaries than the other group. Evidence of lower average salaries can provide some support for a discrimination suit against the employer. It is recognized that a simple two-sample comparison of mean salaries is not sufficient to conclude that one group has been discriminated against. Obviously, there are many factors other than discrimination that affect salary to which differences in average salary might be attributed. Regression is used to adjust for the effects of these other factors before the two groups are compared. An indicator variable is added to the regression to separate the employees into two groups: male and female.

Table 7.1 presents a portion of the data from the case of *United States Department of the Treasury* v. *Harris Trust and Savings Bank* (1981). The data include the salary of 93 employees of the bank, their educational level, and an indicator variable in the third column signifying whether the employee is male (1) or female (0). Figure 7.1 shows a MINITAB scatterplot of salary versus education for all 93 employees. Figure 7.2 shows the same plot but with the two groups indicated by different symbols (male = + and female = ○). There is some indication from the plot in Figure 7.2 that male salaries are higher than female salaries, even when differing education levels have been taken into account. To obtain a better sense of the magnitude of these differences and to provide a test for whether the differences are significant or whether they are small enough that they could have occurred by chance, the regression of SALARY on the two explanatory variables EDUCAT and MALES is shown in Figure 7.3 for MINITAB and in Figure 7.4 for Excel.

The resulting equation is:

$$\text{SALARY} = 4173 + 80.7\text{EDUCAT} + 692\text{MALES}$$

The next question is: How do we interpret this equation?

TABLE 7.1 Data for Employment Discrimination Example

SALARY	EDUCAT	MALES	SALARY	EDUCAT	MALES	SALARY	EDUCAT	MALES
3900	12	0	5220	12	0	5040	15	1
4020	10	0	5280	8	0	5100	12	1
4290	12	0	5280	8	0	5100	12	1
4380	8	0	5280	12	0	5220	12	1
4380	8	0	5400	8	0	5400	12	1
4380	12	0	5400	8	0	5400	12	1
4380	12	0	5400	12	0	5400	12	1
4380	12	0	5400	12	0	5400	15	1
4440	15	0	5400	12	0	5400	15	1
4500	8	0	5400	12	0	5700	15	1
4500	12	0	5400	12	0	6000	8	1
4620	12	0	5400	12	0	6000	12	1
4800	8	0	5400	15	0	6000	12	1
4800	12	0	5400	15	0	6000	12	1
4800	12	0	5400	15	0	6000	12	1
4800	12	0	5520	12	0	6000	12	1
4800	12	0	5520	12	0	6000	15	1
4800	12	0	5580	12	0	6000	15	1
4800	12	0	5640	12	0	6000	15	1
4800	12	0	5700	12	0	6000	15	1
4800	16	0	5700	12	0	6000	15	1
4980	8	0	5700	15	0	6000	16	1
5100	8	0	5700	15	0	6300	15	1
5100	12	0	5700	15	0	6600	15	1
5100	12	0	6000	12	0	6600	15	1
5100	15	0	6000	15	0	6600	15	1
5100	15	0	6120	12	0	6840	15	1
5100	16	0	6300	12	0	6900	12	1
5160	12	0	6300	15	0	6900	15	1
5220	8	0	4620	12	1	8100	16	1

Source: These data were obtained from D. Schafer, "Measurement-Error Diagnostics and the Sex Discrimination Problem," *Journal of Business and Economic Statistics* 5 (1987): 529–537. Copyright © 1987 American Statistical Assn.

FIGURE **7.1** MINITAB Scatterplot of Salary Versus Education for Employment Discrimination Example

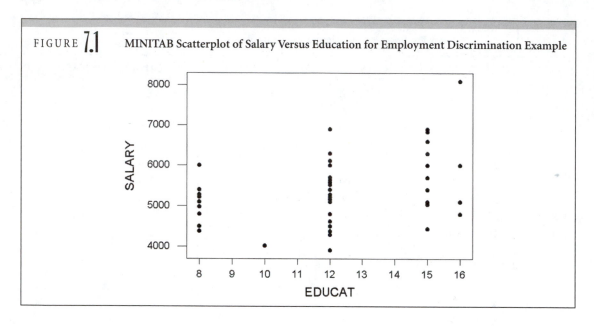

FIGURE **7.2** MINITAB Scatterplot of Salary Versus Education with Males (+) and Females (○)

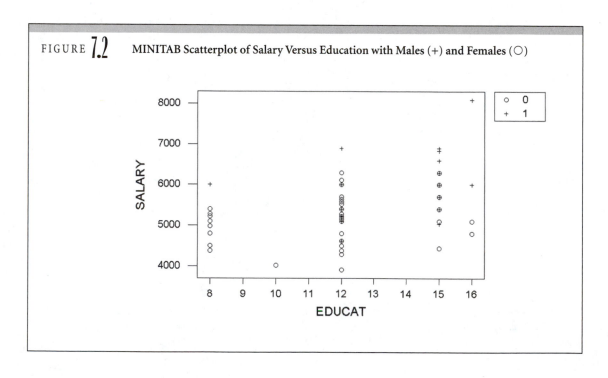

FIGURE 7.3 MINITAB Output for Regression of SALARY on EDUCAT and MALES for Employment Discrimination Example

```
The regression equation is
SALARY = 4173 + 80.7 EDUCAT + 692 MALES

Predictor        Coef       StDev         T          P
Constant       4173.1       339.2      12.30      0.000
EDUCAT          80.70       27.67       2.92      0.004
MALES           691.8       132.2       5.23      0.000

S = 572.4       R-Sq = 36.3%       R-Sq(adj) = 34.9%

Analysis of Variance

Source           DF          SS         MS         F         P
Regression        2    16831744    8415872     25.68     0.000
Residual Error   90    29491546     327684
Total            92    46323290

Source      DF      Seq SS
EDUCAT       1     7862534
MALES        1     8969210

Unusual Observations
Obs    EDUCAT   SALARY       Fit    StDev Fit    Residual    St Resid
  1     12.0    3900.0    5141.5        73.3     -1241.5       -2.19R
 60     12.0    6300.0    5141.5        73.3      1158.5        2.04R
 62     12.0    4620.0    5833.3       109.7     -1213.3       -2.16R
 73      8.0    6000.0    5510.5       183.5       489.5        0.90 X
 93     16.0    8100.0    6156.1       122.1      1943.9        3.48R

R denotes an observation with a large standardized residual
X denotes an observation whose X value gives it large influence.
```

Consider a regression such as the one in Example 7.1 with one quantitative explanatory variable (x_1) and one indicator variable (D)

$$y = \beta_0 + \beta_1 x_1 + \beta_2 D$$

The indicator variable D is coded as 1 if an item in the sample belongs to a certain group and as 0 if the item does not belong to the group. The equation can be separated into two parts as follows:

FIGURE 7.4   **Excel Output for Regression of SALARY on EDUCAT and MALES for Employment Discrimination Example**

SUMMARY OUTPUT

Regression Statistics

Multiple R	0.6028
R Square	0.3634
Adjusted R Square	0.3492
Standard Error	572.4368
Observations	93

ANOVA

	df	SS	MS	F	Significance F
Regression	2	16831743.9452	8415871.9726	25.6829	0.0000
Residual	90	29491546.3774	327683.8486		
Total	92	46323290.3226			

	Coefficients	Standard Error	t Stat	P-value	Lower 95%	Upper 95%
Intercept	4173.1251	339.1811	12.3035	0.0000	3499.2832	4846.9670
EDUCAT	80.6978	27.6729	2.9161	0.0045	25.7208	135.6748
MALES	691.8083	132.2319	5.2318	0.0000	429.1068	954.5098

If the sample item is in the indicated group ($D = 1$):

$$y = \beta_0 + \beta_1 x_1 + \beta_2(1) = (\beta_0 + \beta_2) + \beta_1 x_1$$

If the sample item is not in the indicated group ($D = 0$):

$$y = \beta_0 + \beta_1 x_1 + \beta_2(0) = \beta_0 + \beta_1 x_1$$

Using the indicator variable results in one equation for the indicated group and another for the other group. Note that the equation for the indicated group has been rewritten with two components making up the intercept term: the original intercept, β_0, and the coefficient of the indicator variable, β_2. Two lines have been fit with the same slope but different intercepts, even though only one regression has been run. Figure 7.5 shows an example of how we might draw the two estimated lines. The difference in the intercepts is given by β_2 (which is assumed to be positive in the graph). This process allows us to answer the question of whether there is a difference in the average value of the y variable for the two groups after adjusting for the effect of the quantitative variable (or variables if there are more than one)

FIGURE 7.5   Graph Showing Relative Placement of Regression Lines If β_2 Is Assumed to Be Positive

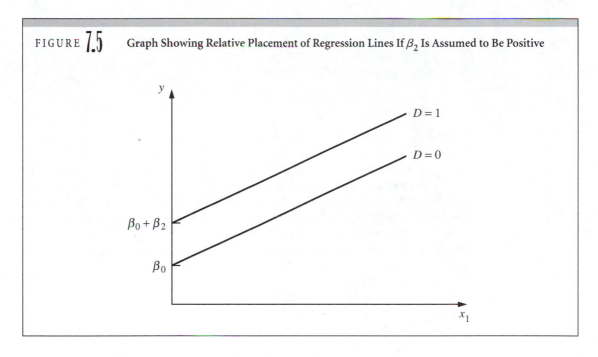

and how much the average difference is. The adjusted difference in the averages is represented by the difference in the intercepts (that is, by the coefficient of the indicator variable). A t test on this coefficient will help decide whether the difference is large enough to be considered statistically significant.

EXAMPLE 7.2   **Employment Discrimination (continued)**

The equation in the employment discrimination example can be interpreted as follows: Salary increases by $80.70 for each year of education. Males earn, on average, $692 more per year than females (this was in 1977, so $692 a year was more than it sounds like now).

The next question is whether $692 is large enough to be considered statistically significant. Or could this difference have occurred purely by chance? To determine this, the coefficient of the indicator variable can be tested to see if it is equal to zero.

$$H_0: \quad \beta_2 = 0$$
$$H_a: \quad \beta_2 \neq 0$$

If the null hypothesis is accepted, we conclude that there is no significant difference in average salaries (after taking into account education). If the null hypothesis is rejected, we conclude that the difference observed is too large to have occurred by chance.

Decision rule:

Reject H_0 if p value < 0.05

Accept H_0 if p value ≥ 0.05

Test Statistic: p value $= 0.000$
Decision: Reject H_0

Of course, the t ratio could also have been used to conduct the test.

Our conclusion is that males, on average, appear to be earning significantly more than females, even after we take into account education. There is evidence of employment discrimination. Legal counsel for Harris Trust and Savings Bank in this case would point out that education is not the only factor that could cause a difference in salary. Factors like previous experience and time on the job might also have an effect. These factors, if measurable, could be included in the regression as well (and typically are in such applications).[1]

One question that arises is whether the way the two groups were coded matters. Would the results be the same in our example if males were coded 0 and females were coded 1? Yes, they would. Figure 7.6 shows the MINITAB regression of SALARY on EDUCAT and a new variable called FEMALES. This new variable is coded 0 for males and 1 for females. Note that the coefficient of EDUCAT is exactly the same as it was for the regression in Figures 7.3 and 7.4. The coefficient of the indicator variable is the same except for the sign. In the original regression, it was positive and now it is negative. The intercept of the new equation is larger by $692. However, the interpretation of the results is exactly the same. When the variable MALES was used, our interpretation was that males earned, on average, $692 per year *more* than females. Using the FEMALES variable, our interpretation is that females earned, on average, $692 per year *less* than males. Also, the t test again tells us that the difference is statistically significant.

In the employment discrimination example, an indicator variable was used to indicate when sample observations fell into one of two groups. The groups represented qualitative variables (that is, variables that could not be quantified in a meaningful way). For example, there is no meaningful way to quantify the difference between males and females. An indicator variable was used to separate the two groups for separate analyses, but no numeric values were assigned to express the difference between being male or female. Indicator variables can be used in this manner to incorporate qualitative information into the regression equation. The next example illustrates the use of indicator variables to represent qualitative information when there are more than two categories.

---

[1] For a more detailed examination of the use of regression in employment discrimination cases, see D. A. Conway and H. V. Roberts, "Regression Analyses in Employment Discrimination Cases," in *Statistics and the Law*, New York: Wiley, 1986.

FIGURE **7.6**   **MINITAB Output for Regression of SALARY on EDUCAT and FEMALES for Employment Discrimination Example**

```
The regression equation is
SALARY = 4865 + 80.7 EDUCAT - 692 FEMALES


Predictor       Coef       StDev            T          P
Constant      4864.9       387.9        12.54      0.000
EDUCAT         80.70       27.67         2.92      0.004
FEMALES       -691.8       132.2        -5.23      0.000


S = 572.4        R-Sq = 36.3%       R-Sq(adj) = 34.9%

Analysis of Variance

Source            DF          SS          MS          F          P
Regression         2    16831744     8415872      25.68      0.000
Residual Error    90    29491546      327684
Total             92    46323290


Source        DF      Seq SS
EDUCAT         1     7862534
FEMALES        1     8969210

Unusual Observations
Obs     EDUCAT       SALARY         Fit     StDev Fit      Residual     St Resid
  1       12.0       3900.0      5141.5          73.3       -1241.5        -2.19R
 60       12.0       6300.0      5141.5          73.3        1158.5         2.04R
 62       12.0       4620.0      5833.3         109.7       -1213.3        -2.16R
 73        8.0       6000.0      5510.5         183.5         489.5         0.90 X
 93       16.0       8100.0      6156.1         122.1        1943.9         3.48R


R denotes an observation with a large standardized residual
X denotes an observation whose X value gives it large influence.
```

EXAMPLE **7.3**   Meddicorp

In the Meddicorp example in Chapter 4, the relationship between sales and several other variables was investigated. The data for the dependent variable SALES and two explanatory variables, ADV and BONUS, were shown in Table 4.1.

FIGURE 7.7   **MINITAB Regression of SALES on ADV, BONUS, and REGION**

```
The regression equation is
SALES = - 84 + 1.55 ADV + 1.11 BONUS + 119 REGION

Predictor         Coef        StDev           T           P
Constant         -84.2        177.9       -0.47       0.641
ADV             1.5460       0.3061        5.05       0.000
BONUS           1.1062       0.5727        1.93       0.067
REGION          118.90        28.69        4.14       0.000

S = 68.89      R-Sq = 92.0%      R-Sq(adj) = 90.9%

Analysis of Variance

Source               DF          SS          MS          F           P
Regression            3     1149317      383106       80.73       0.000
Residual Error       21       99657        4746
Total                24     1248974

Source    DF    Seq SS
ADV        1    1012408
BONUS      1      55389
REGION     1      81519
```

It also was noted in the example that Meddicorp sold in three different regions of the country: South, West, and Midwest. A variable has been added to the data set to indicate each of these three regions. The variable is called REGION and is coded as follows:

REGION   = 1 if South

          = 2 if West

          = 3 if Midwest

The new variable and the original variables are shown in Table 7.2. The new variable is included in a regression along with the ADV and BONUS variables. The results are shown in Figures 7.7 and 7.8 for MINITAB and Excel, respectively.

The estimated regression equation is

$$\hat{y} = -84 + 1.55\text{ADV} + 1.11\text{BONUS} + 119\text{REGION}$$

The coefficient of REGION indicates that, as the value assigned to the region increases, so does the amount of sales. On average, there is a difference of 119 units between sales in the

TABLE 7.2   Meddicorp Data Including the Variable REGION and Three
Resulting Indicator Variables SOUTH, WEST, and MIDWEST

SALES	ADV	BONUS	REGION	SOUTH	WEST	MIDWEST
963.50	374.27	230.98	1	1	0	0
893.00	408.50	236.28	1	1	0	0
1057.25	414.31	271.57	1	1	0	0
1183.25	448.42	291.20	2	0	1	0
1419.50	517.88	282.17	3	0	0	1
1547.75	637.60	321.16	3	0	0	1
1580.00	635.72	294.32	3	0	0	1
1071.50	446.86	305.69	1	1	0	0
1078.25	489.59	238.41	1	1	0	0
1122.50	500.56	271.38	2	0	1	0
1304.75	484.18	332.64	3	0	0	1
1552.25	618.07	261.80	3	0	0	1
1040.00	453.39	235.63	1	1	0	0
1045.25	440.86	249.68	2	0	1	0
1102.25	487.79	232.99	2	0	1	0
1225.25	537.67	272.20	2	0	1	0
1508.00	612.21	266.64	3	0	0	1
1564.25	601.46	277.44	3	0	0	1
1634.75	585.10	312.35	3	0	0	1
1159.25	524.56	292.87	1	1	0	0
1202.75	535.17	268.27	2	0	1	0
1294.25	486.03	309.85	2	0	1	0
1467.50	540.17	291.03	3	0	0	1
1583.75	583.85	289.29	3	0	0	1
1124.75	499.15	272.55	2	0	1	0

territories of the three regions. Each unit is $1000. Sales in territories of Region 2 (West) would be $119,000 more (on average) than sales in territories of Region 1 (South), and sales in territories of Region 3 (Midwest) would be $119,000 more than sales in Region 2. Note that the difference in territorial sales between regions is forced to be $119,000. Although this situation may not be realistic, it is required by the direct use of the variable REGION in the regression equation. A more flexible representation of the changes in average sales between regions is allowed by using indicator variables.

Note also that the coding of the variable REGION is arbitrary. The coding could be done as follows: Midwest = 1, West = 2, and South = 3. The numbers assigned to the regions are merely naming devices. They represent qualitative categories rather than quantitative data. Changing the order of the number of the categories does change the results, however, when using the REGION variable as shown. This does not happen if indicator variables are used.

FIGURE 7.8   Excel Regression of SALES on ADV, BONUS, and REGION

```
                        SUMMARY OUTPUT

Regression Statistics
Multiple R              0.959
R Square                0.920
Adjusted R Square       0.909
Standard Error         68.888
Observations           25.000

ANOVA
                  df            SS            MS           F      Significance F
Regression      3.000    1149316.739    383105.580     80.729         0.000
Residual       21.000      99657.001      4745.571
Total          24.000    1248973.740

                        Standard
            Coefficients    Error    t Stat   P-value   Lower 95%   Upper 95%
Intercept      -84.219    177.907   -0.473    0.641    -454.197     285.758
ADV              1.546      0.306    5.050    0.000       0.909       2.183
BONUS            1.106      0.573    1.932    0.067      -0.085       2.297
REGION         118.899     28.687    4.145    0.000      59.240     178.558
```

The REGION variable can be transformed into three indicator variables. An indicator variable SOUTH can be developed that indicates whether or not a territory is in the South. SOUTH is made to take on the value 1 whenever the REGION variable is 1, and SOUTH is given the value 0 if REGION is 2 or 3. An indicator variable WEST can be developed that indicates whether or not a territory is in the West. WEST takes on the value 1 whenever the REGION variable is 2 (that is, when the territory is in the West) and is given the value 0 if REGION is 1 or 3. Similarly, an indicator variable for the Midwest can be developed. The three indicator variables are as follows:

SOUTH   = 1 if the territory is in the South
          = 0 otherwise

WEST   = 1 if the territory is in the West
          = 0 otherwise

MIDWEST   = 1 if the territory is in the Midwest
          = 0 otherwise

These three indicator variables—SOUTH, WEST, and MIDWEST—indicate into which of the three mutually exclusive regions each territory falls. Table 7.2 shows the SALES, ADV, BONUS,

FIGURE 7.9   MINITAB Regression of SALES on ADV, BONUS, and the Indicator Variables WEST and SOUTH

```
The regression equation is
SALES = 435 + 1.37 ADV + 0.975 BONUS - 258 SOUTH - 210 WEST

Predictor      Coef       StDev         T          P
Constant      435.1       206.2       2.11      0.048
ADV          1.3678      0.2622       5.22      0.000
BONUS        0.9752      0.4808       2.03      0.056
SOUTH       -257.89       48.41      -5.33      0.000
WEST        -209.75       37.42      -5.61      0.000

S = 57.63        R-Sq = 94.7%       R-Sq(adj) = 93.6%

Analysis of Variance

Source              DF          SS          MS          F          P
Regression           4     1182560      295640      89.03      0.000
Residual Error      20       66414        3321
Total               24     1248974

Source        DF      Seq SS
ADV            1     1012408
BONUS          1       55389
SOUTH          1       10435
WEST           1      104328

Unusual Observations
Obs     ADV      SALES        Fit    StDev Fit     Residual    St Resid
 11     484     1304.7     1421.7        37.0       -117.0       -2.65R
 22     486     1294.2     1192.3        27.7        102.0        2.02R

R denotes an observation with a large standardized residual
```

and REGION variables and the resulting indicators. As stated previously, only two of the three indicators need to be used in the regression. The territories indicated by the third indicator serve as a base level group.

If the MIDWEST is used as the base level group, the MINITAB and Excel regressions shown in Figures 7.9 and 7.10 are obtained. The regression equation is

$$\hat{y} = 435 + 1.37ADV + 0.975BONUS - 258SOUTH - 210WEST$$

FIGURE **7.10**   Excel Regression of SALES on ADV, BONUS, and the Indicator Variables WEST and SOUTH

SUMMARY OUTPUT

Regression Statistics

Multiple R	0.973
R Square	0.947
Adjusted R Square	0.936
Standard Error	57.625
Observations	25.000

ANOVA

	df	SS	MS	F	Significance F
Regression	4.000	1182559.896	295639.974	89.030	0.000
Residual	20.000	66413.844	3320.692		
Total	24.000	1248973.740			

	Coefficients	Standard Error	t Stat	P-value	Lower 95%	Upper 95%
Intercept	435.099	206.234	2.110	0.048	4.902	865.296
ADV	1.368	0.262	5.216	0.000	0.821	1.915
BONUS	0.975	0.481	2.028	0.056	-0.028	1.978
SOUTH	-257.892	48.413	-5.327	0.000	-358.879	-156.904
WEST	-209.746	37.420	-5.605	0.000	-287.803	-131.688

The interpretation of this equation is similar to that of the equation developed in the employment discrimination example. Here, however, the territories have been separated into three groups through the use of the indicator variables. The coefficient of each dummy variable represents the difference in the intercept between the indicated group and the base level (MID-WEST) group. This can be expressed through the use of three separate equations:

$$\text{SOUTH} \quad \hat{y} = 435 + 1.37\text{ADV} + 0.975\text{BONUS} - 258$$
$$= 177 + 1.37\text{ADV} + 0.975\text{BONUS}$$

$$\text{WEST} \quad \hat{y} = 435 + 1.37\text{ADV} + 0.975\text{BONUS} - 210$$
$$= 225 + 1.37\text{ADV} + 0.975\text{BONUS}$$

$$\text{MIDWEST} \quad \hat{y} = 435 + 1.37\text{ADV} + 0.975\text{BONUS}$$

The slopes of the equations are constrained to be the same, but the intercepts are allowed to differ. As a further interpretation, consider the values of $\hat{y}$ for a given level of ADV and BONUS—say, ADV = 500 and BONUS = 250. These values are

SOUTH $\hat{y} = 177 + 1.37(500) + 0.975(250) = 1105.8$

WEST $\hat{y} = 225 + 1.37(500) + 0.975(250) = 1153.8$

MIDWEST $\hat{y} = 435 + 1.37(500) + 0.975(250) = 1363.8$

The conditional mean sales for advertising equal to 500 and bonus payment equal to 250 are shown by these computations. The sales figures differ according to the coefficients of the indicator variables: $1,105,800 for SOUTH, $1,153,800 for WEST, and $1,363,800 for MIDWEST.

To determine whether there is a significant difference in sales for territories in different regions, the following hypotheses should be tested:

H_0: $\beta_3 = \beta_4 = 0$

H_a: At least one of β_3 and β_4 is not equal to zero

The model hypothesized is

$$y = \beta_0 + \beta_1 \text{ADV} + \beta_2 \text{BONUS} + \beta_3 \text{SOUTH} + \beta_4 \text{WEST}$$

so the null hypothesis states that the coefficients of the dummy variables are both zero. If this hypothesis is accepted, then no difference between the various regions exists, and the indicator variables can be dropped from the model. The simpler model

$$y = \beta_0 + \beta_1 \text{ADV} + \beta_2 \text{BONUS}$$

explains just as much variation in sales. This hypothesis can be tested using the partial F test discussed in Chapter 4. The full model contains the indicator variables; the reduced model does not. The test statistic to be used is computed exactly as discussed in Chapter 4:

$$F = \frac{(SSE_R - SSE_F) / (K - L)}{MSE_F} = \frac{(181,176 - 66,414) / 2}{3321} = 17.3$$

using the reduced model output in Figures 7.11 or 7.12 to get SSE_R and the full model output in Figures 7.9 or 7.10 to get SSE_F.

The decision rule is

Reject H_0 if $F > 3.49$

Accept H_0 if $F \leq 3.49$

where 3.49 is the 5% F critical value with 2 numerator and 20 denominator degrees of freedom.

The null hypothesis is rejected since $17.3 > 3.49$. Thus, at least one of the coefficients of the indicator variables is not zero. This means that there are differences in average sales levels between the three regions in which Meddicorp does business.

When using indicator variables, the partial F statistic is used to test whether the variables are important as a group. The t test on individual coefficients should not be used to decide whether individual indicator variables should be retained or dropped from the equation (except when there are two groups represented and therefore only one indicator variable). The indicator variables are designed to have a particular

FIGURE **7.11**   MINITAB Regression of SALES on ADV and BONUS

```
The regression equation is
SALES = - 516 + 2.47 ADV + 1.86 BONUS

Predictor        Coef       StDev           T           P
Constant       -516.4       189.9       -2.72       0.013
ADV            2.4732      0.2753        8.98       0.000
BONUS          1.8562      0.7157        2.59       0.017


S = 90.75       R-Sq = 85.5%       R-Sq(adj) = 84.2%

Analysis of Variance

Source             DF          SS          MS          F           P
Regression          2     1067797      533899      64.83       0.000
Residual Error     22      181176        8235
Total              24     1248974


Source       DF        Seq SS
ADV           1       1012408
BONUS         1         55389
```

meaning as a group. They are either all retained in the equation or all dropped from the equation as a group. Dropping individual indicators changes the meaning of the coefficients of the remaining indicators. In the Meddicorp example, each indicator coefficient represents the difference in sales between the indicated group and the base level group (MIDWEST). If one of the other indicators is dropped (say, WEST), the remaining coefficients then represent the difference in sales between the indicated group and the new base level group, which now becomes the MIDWEST and WEST regions combined. The interpretation of the coefficients is totally different due to the change in the base level group. To answer the question of whether there is a difference in the intercepts for the groups involved, the indicators must be retained and tested as a group (although there is not universal acceptance of this point of view).

Recall that in the discrimination example, a t test was used to determine whether the intercepts for the males and females differed. Because there were only two groups and therefore only one indicator, the partial F test and the t test were equivalent. If more than two indicators are used, the partial F test is required.

FIGURE 7.12   **Excel Regression of SALES on ADV and BONUS**

```
                         SUMMARY OUTPUT

Regression Statistics
Multiple R              0.925
R Square                0.855
Adjusted R Square       0.842
Standard Error         90.749
Observations           25.000


ANOVA
                 df          SS           MS         F      Significance F
Regression    2.000   1067797.321   533898.660   64.831        0.000
Residual     22.000    181176.419     8235.292
Total        24.000   1248973.740


                            Standard
             Coefficients     Error    t Stat   P-value   Lower 95%   Upper 95%
Intercept      -516.444     189.876   -2.720    0.0125    -910.223    -122.666
ADV               2.473       0.275    8.983    0.0000       1.902       3.044
BONUS             1.856       0.716    2.593    0.0166       0.372       3.341
```

Figures 7.13 and 7.14 show the MINITAB and Excel regressions of SALES on ADV, BONUS, and the indicators WEST and MIDWEST. The base level group is now the SOUTH region. The coefficients of the indicator variables measure the difference in sales between the base level group and the indicated group. Although the regression coefficient estimates have different values from the previous regression (see Figures 7.9 and 7.10), the results are the same. For example, consider the value of $\hat{y}$ for ADV = 500 and BONUS = 250 for the SOUTH region:

$$\hat{y} = 177 + 1.37(500) + 0.975(250) = 1105.8$$

This is the same value determined from the regression using the WEST and SOUTH indicator variables. Comparisons for the other regions also show the same values regardless of which set of indicators is used. Any one of the three indicators can be omitted, and the omitted group simply serves as the base level group. The remaining indicator coefficients equal the difference between the indicated group and the chosen base level group.

FIGURE **7.13** MINITAB Regression of SALES on ADV, BONUS, and the Indicator Variables WEST and MIDWEST

```
The regression equation is
SALES = 177 + 1.37 ADV + 0.975 BONUS + 48.1 WEST + 258 MIDWEST

Predictor      Coef       StDev          T          P
Constant      177.2       170.1       1.04      0.310
ADV          1.3678      0.2622       5.22      0.000
BONUS        0.9752      0.4808       2.03      0.056
WEST          48.15       32.80       1.47      0.158
MIDWEST      257.89       48.41       5.33      0.000

S = 57.63       R-Sq = 94.7%       R-Sq(adj) = 93.6%

Analysis of Variance

Source            DF          SS          MS          F          P
Regression         4     1182560      295640      89.03      0.000
Residual Error    20       66414        3321
Total             24     1248974

Source      DF      Seq SS
ADV          1     1012408
BONUS        1       55389
WEST         1       20535
MIDWEST      1       94228

Unusual Observations
Obs      ADV       SALES        Fit     StDev Fit     Residual     St Resid
 11      484      1304.7     1421.7         37.0       -117.0       -2.65R
 22      486      1294.2     1192.3         27.7        102.0        2.02R

R denotes an observation with a large standardized residual
```

FIGURE 7.14   Excel Regression of SALES on ADV, BONUS, and the Indicator Variables WEST and MIDWEST

```
                          SUMMARY OUTPUT

Regression Statistics
Multiple R              0.973
R Square                0.947
Adjusted R Square       0.936
Standard Error         57.625
Observations           25.000
```

```
ANOVA
                  df           SS           MS          F      Significance F
Regression     4.000    1182559.896    295639.974    89.030        0.000
Residual      20.000      66413.844      3320.692
Total         24.000    1248973.740
```

```
                              Standard
              Coefficients      Error    t Stat  P-value   Lower 95%   Upper 95%
Intercept        177.207      170.116    1.042    0.310    -177.648     532.063
ADV                1.368        0.262    5.216    0.000       0.821       1.915
BONUS              0.975        0.481    2.028    0.056      -0.028       1.978
WEST              48.146       32.801    1.468    0.158     -20.276     116.568
MIDWEST          257.892       48.413    5.327    0.000     156.904     358.879
```

EXERCISES

1   **Discrimination**   The data in Table 7.3 show the values of the following variables for 93 employees of Harris Bank Chicago in 1977:

y = beginning salaries in dollars (SALARY)

x_1 = years of schooling at the time of hire (EDUCAT)

x_2 = number of months of previous work experience (EXPER)

x_3 = number of months after January 1, 1969, that the individual was hired (MONTHS)

x_4 = indicator variable coded 1 for males and 0 for females (MALES)

The MINITAB and Excel outputs for the regression of y on all four explanatory variables are shown in Figures 7.15 and 7.16, respectively. In this example, we are still concerned with whether there is evidence of discrimination, but we are now taking

TABLE 7.3   Data for Discrimination Exercise

MALES	SALARY	EDUCAT	EXPER	MONTHS	MALES	SALARY	EDUCAT	EXPER	MONTHS	MALES	SALARY	EDUCAT	EXPER	MONTHS
0	3900	12	0.0	1	0	5220	12	127.0	29	1	5040	15	14.0	3
0	4020	10	44.0	7	0	5280	8	90.0	11	1	5100	12	180.0	15
0	4290	12	5.0	30	0	5280	8	190.0	1	1	5100	12	315.0	2
0	4380	8	6.2	7	0	5280	12	107.0	11	1	5220	12	29.0	14
0	4380	8	7.5	6	0	5400	8	173.0	34	1	5400	12	7.0	21
0	4380	12	0.0	7	0	5400	8	228.0	33	1	5400	12	38.0	11
0	4380	12	0.0	10	0	5400	12	26.0	11	1	5400	12	113.0	3
0	4380	12	4.5	6	0	5400	12	36.0	33	1	5400	15	17.5	8
0	4440	15	75.0	2	0	5400	12	38.0	22	1	5400	15	359.0	11
0	4500	8	52.0	3	0	5400	12	82.0	29	1	5700	15	36.0	5
0	4500	12	8.0	19	0	5400	12	169.0	27	1	6000	8	320.0	21
0	4620	12	52.0	3	0	5400	12	244.0	1	1	6000	12	24.0	2
0	4800	8	70.0	20	0	5400	15	24.0	13	1	6000	12	32.0	17
0	4800	12	6.0	23	0	5400	15	49.0	27	1	6000	12	49.0	8
0	4800	12	11.0	12	0	5400	15	51.0	21	1	6000	12	56.0	33
0	4800	12	11.0	17	0	5400	15	122.0	33	1	6000	12	252.0	11
0	4800	12	63.0	22	0	5520	12	97.0	17	1	6000	12	272.0	19
0	4800	12	144.0	24	0	5520	12	196.0	32	1	6000	15	25.0	13
0	4800	12	163.0	12	0	5580	12	132.5	30	1	6000	15	35.5	32
0	4800	12	228.0	26	0	5640	12	55.0	9	1	6000	15	56.0	12
0	4800	12	381.0	1	0	5700	12	90.0	23	1	6000	15	64.0	33
0	4800	16	214.0	15	0	5700	12	116.5	25	1	6000	15	108.0	16
0	4980	8	318.0	25	0	5700	15	51.0	17	1	6000	16	45.5	3
0	5100	8	96.0	33	0	5700	15	61.0	11	1	6300	15	72.0	17
0	5100	12	36.0	15	0	5700	15	241.0	34	1	6600	15	64.0	16
0	5100	12	59.0	14	0	6000	12	121.0	30	1	6600	15	84.0	33
0	5100	15	115.0	1	0	6000	15	78.5	13	1	6600	15	215.5	16
0	5100	15	165.0	4	0	6120	12	208.5	21	1	6840	15	41.5	7
0	5100	16	123.0	12	0	6300	12	86.5	33	1	6900	12	175.0	10
0	5160	12	18.0	12	0	6300	15	231.0	15	1	6900	15	132.0	24
0	5220	8	102.0	29	1	4620	12	11.5	22	1	8100	16	54.5	33

Source: These data were obtained from D. Schafer, "Measurement-Error Diagnostics and the Sex Discrimination Problem," *Journal of Business and Economic Statistics* 5 (1987): 529–537. Copyright © 1987 American Statistical Assn.

into account two other potentially important variables besides education. Use the outputs to answer the following questions:

a   Conduct the *F* test for the overall fit of the regression. State the hypotheses to be tested, the decision rule, the test statistic, and your decision. Use a 5% level of significance.

FIGURE 7.15   MINITAB Regression Output for Discrimination Exercise

```
The regression equation is
SALARY = 3526 + 90.0 EDUCAT + 1.27 EXPER + 23.4 MONTHS + 722 MALES

Predictor       Coef        StDev           T           P
Constant       3526.4       327.7        10.76       0.000
EDUCAT          90.02       24.69         3.65       0.000
EXPER          1.2690      0.5877         2.16       0.034
MONTHS         23.406       5.201         4.50       0.000
MALES           722.5       117.8         6.13       0.000

S = 507.4        R-Sq = 51.1%        R-Sq(adj) = 48.9%

Analysis of Variance

Source            DF         SS          MS          F          P
Regression         4     23665351     5916338      22.98      0.000
Residual Error    88     22657939      257477
Total             92     46323290

Source      DF      Seq SS
EDUCAT       1     7862534
EXPER        1     2038491
MONTHS       1     4083411
MALES        1     9680915

Unusual Observations
Obs    EDUCAT     SALARY       Fit    StDev Fit     Residual     St Resid
  3     12.0     4290.0     5315.2      110.2       -1025.2        -2.07R
 62     12.0     4620.0     5858.7      119.4       -1238.7        -2.51R
 90     15.0     6840.0     5815.7      109.4        1024.3         2.07R
 91     12.0     6900.0     5785.3      109.1        1114.7         2.25R
 93     16.0     8100.0     6530.8      145.8        1569.2         3.23R

R denotes an observation with a large standardized residual
```

b What conclusion can be drawn from the test result in part a?

c Is there a difference in salaries, on average, for male and female workers after accounting for the effects of the three other explanatory variables? Use a 5% level of significance to answer this question. State the hypotheses to be tested, the decision rule, the test statistic, and your decision.

d Is there evidence that Harris Bank discriminated against female employees?

FIGURE 7.16 Excel Regression Output for Discrimination Exercise

SUMMARY OUTPUT

Regression Statistics
Multiple R	0.715
R Square	0.511
Adjusted R Square	0.489
Standard Error	507.422
Observations	93.000

ANOVA

	df	SS	MS	F	Significance F
Regression	4.000	23665351.393	5916337.848	22.978	0.000
Residual	88.000	22657938.930	257476.579		
Total	92.000	46323290.323			

	Coefficients	Standard Error	t Stat	P-value	Lower 95%	Upper 95%
Intercept	3526.422	327.725	10.760	0.000	2875.136	4177.708
EDUCAT	90.020	24.694	3.645	0.000	40.947	139.094
EXPER	1.269	0.588	2.159	0.034	0.101	2.437
MONTHS	23.406	5.201	4.500	0.000	13.071	33.742
MALES	722.461	117.822	6.132	0.000	488.315	956.607

e What salary would you forecast, on average, for males with 12 years education, 10 years of experience, and with time hired equal to 15? A point forecast is sufficient. What salary would you forecast, on average, for females if all other factors are equal?

These data are available in a file with prefix HARRIS7 in five columns: SALARY, EDUCAT, EXPER, MONTHS, and MALES.

2 **Automobile Transmissions** Data for 138 cars were obtained from *Road and Track's The Complete '99 Car Buyer's Guide*. The full data set is listed in Table 8.3. The following variables are considered here:

y = mileage in city driving (CITYMPG)

x_1 = weight in pounds (WEIGHT)

x_2 = indicator variable coded as 1 for cars with automatic transmissions and 0 for cars with standard transmissions (TRANS)

FIGURE 7.17   **MINITAB Regression Output for Automobile Transmission Exercise**

```
The regression equation is
CITYMPG = - 5.16 + 78741 WTINV + 1.66 TRANS


Predictor      Coef       StDev          T          P
Constant     -5.162       1.542      -3.35      0.001
WTINV         78741        4177      18.85      0.000
TRANS        1.6588      0.5272       3.15      0.002


S = 2.327         R-Sq = 78.8%       R-Sq(adj) = 78.5%

Analysis of Variance

Source            DF          SS          MS          F          P
Regression         2      2722.0      1361.0     251.35      0.000
Residual Error   135       731.0         5.4
Total            137      3453.0


Source      DF      Seq SS
WTINV        1      2668.4
TRANS        1        53.6


Unusual Observations
Obs      WTINV     CITYMPG         Fit     StDev Fit      Residual     St Resid
 30   0.000528      41.000      36.390        0.734         4.610       2.09RX
 45   0.000342      27.000      21.795        0.280         5.205       2.25R
 46   0.000301      12.000      18.562        0.372        -6.562      -2.86R
 47   0.000304      26.000      18.771        0.364         7.229       3.15R
 49   0.000268      10.000      15.976        0.478        -5.976      -2.62R
 69   0.000280       9.000      16.863        0.440        -7.863      -3.44R
 77   0.000329      15.000      20.714        0.303        -5.714      -2.48R
109   0.000352      17.000      24.242        0.421        -7.242      -3.16R
115   0.000344      17.000      21.897        0.278        -4.897      -2.12R
125   0.000532      39.000      36.766        0.753         2.234       1.01 X

R denotes an observation with a large standardized residual
X denotes an observation whose X value gives it large influence.
```

MINITAB and Excel outputs for the regressions of y on $1/x_1$ (WTINV) and x_2 are shown in Figures 7.17 and 7.18, respectively. The decision to use the variable WTINV rather than WEIGHT was based on examination of residual plots and scatterplots. Use the outputs to answer the following questions:

FIGURE 7.18 Excel Regression Output for Automobile Transmission Exercise

SUMMARY OUTPUT

Regression Statistics

Multiple R	0.888
R Square	0.788
Adjusted R Square	0.785
Standard Error	2.327
Observations	138.000

ANOVA

	df	SS	MS	F	Significance F
Regression	2.000	2722.010	1361.005	251.355	0.000
Residual	135.000	730.982	5.415		
Total	137.000	3452.993			

	Coefficients	Standard Error	t Stat	P-value	Lower 95%	Upper 95%
Intercept	-5.162	1.542	-3.347	0.001	-8.212	-2.112
WTINV	78741.316	4176.884	18.852	0.000	70480.728	87001.904
TRANS	1.659	0.527	3.146	0.002	0.616	2.701

a Conduct the F test for the overall fit of the regression. State the hypotheses to be tested, the decision rule, the test statistic, and your decision. Use a 5% level of significance.

b What conclusion can be drawn from the test result in part a?

c Is there a difference in mileage, on average, for cars with manual and automatic transmissions after the effect of weight is taken into account? State the hypotheses to be tested, the decision rule, the test statistic, and your decision. Use a 5% level of significance to answer this question.

d What mileage would you forecast, on average, for cars weighing 3500 pounds with automatic transmissions? A point forecast is sufficient. What mileage would you forecast, on average, for cars weighing 3500 pounds with manual transmissions?

These data are available in a file with prefix MPG7 in three columns: WEIGHT, CITYMPG, and TRANS.

7.2 ▪ INTERACTION VARIABLES

Another type of variable that is used in regression is called an interaction variable. An interaction variable is formed as the product of two (or more) variables. To illustrate the effect of using an interaction variable, consider a regression equation with dependent variable y and independent variables x_1 and x_2. Construct the interaction variable $x_1 x_2$ which is the product of the two explanatory variables. Now consider two possible regression models, one with the interaction term and one without it:

$$y = \beta_0 + \beta_1 x_1 + \beta_2 x_2 + e$$

and

$$y = \beta_0 + \beta_1 x_1 + \beta_2 x_2 + \beta_3 x_1 x_2 + e$$

Now determine the change in y given a one-unit change in x_1 with each of these models. For the model without the interaction term, a one-unit change in x_1 produces a change in y of β_1 units. For the model with the interaction term, rewrite the equation as

$$y = \beta_0 + (\beta_1 + \beta_3 x_2)x_1 + \beta_2 x_2 + e$$

Then a one-unit change in x_1 produces a change of $\beta_1 + \beta_3 x_2$ units in y. As shown, the change in y resulting from a one-unit change in x_1 also depends on the value of the variable x_2. If x_2 is small, smaller changes result; if x_2 is large, larger changes result. Thus, the effect of movements in x_1 cannot be judged independently of the value of x_2 (and the effect of movements in x_2 cannot be judged independently of movements in x_1).

An important application of interaction variables is in testing for differences in the slopes of two regression lines. This is done in a manner similar to the procedure to test for differences in the intercepts. Consider a regression with one quantitative explanatory variable (x_1) and one indicator variable (D):

$$y = \beta_0 + \beta_1 x_1 + \beta_2 D$$

The indicator variable D is coded as 1 if an item in the sample belongs to a certain group and as 0 if the item does not belong to the group. Now add the variable representing the interaction between x_1 and D, $x_1 D$:

$$y = \beta_0 + \beta_1 x_1 + \beta_2 D + \beta_3 x_1 D$$

This equation can be separated into two parts as follows. If the sample item is in the indicated group ($D = 1$):

$$y = \beta_0 + \beta_1 x_1 + \beta_2(1) + \beta_3 x_1 = (\beta_0 + \beta_2) + (\beta_1 + \beta_3)x_1$$

If the sample item is not in the indicated group ($D = 0$):

$$y = \beta_0 + \beta_1 x_1 + \beta_2(0) + \beta_3 x_1(0) = \beta_0 + \beta_1 x_1$$

Using the indicator variable allows us to examine differences in the intercepts for the two groups. Using the interaction variable allows us to examine differences in the slopes. Note that the equation for the indicated group has been rewritten with two components making up the intercept term (the original intercept β_0 and the coefficient of the indicator variable β_2), and two components making up the slope term (the original slope β_1 and the coefficient of the interaction term, β_3). Two lines have been fit with different slopes and different intercepts, even though only one regression has been run. The difference in the intercepts is given by β_2; the difference in the slopes by β_3.

Not only can we determine whether there is a difference in the average value of the y variable for the two groups after adjusting for the effect of the quantitative variable, but we can also tell whether there is a difference in the slopes for the two groups. A t test for whether β_3 is equal to zero helps to determine whether the slopes differ. Also, a partial F test of the hypotheses

$$H_0: \quad \beta_2 = \beta_3 = 0$$

$$H_a: \quad \text{At least one of } \beta_2 \text{ and } \beta_3 \text{ is different from zero}$$

can be used to tell us whether there is any difference in the regression lines for the two groups (intercept or slope). The following example illustrates.

EXAMPLE 7.4 Employment Discrimination (again)

In Examples 7.1 and 7.2, we concluded that there is evidence of employment discrimination at Harris Bank even after taking into account education. Now suppose the following question is considered: Does the difference in average salaries increase between the two groups as education increases? This is one question an interaction term allows us to investigate. The equation can be written as

$$\text{SALARY} = \beta_0 + \beta_1 \text{ EDUCAT} + \beta_2 \text{ MALES} + \beta_3 \text{ MSLOPE}$$

where MSLOPE represents the interaction between EDUCAT and MALES. Thus,

$$\text{MSLOPE} = \text{EDUCAT} * \text{MALES}$$

The MINITAB regression output for this equation is shown in Figure 7.19 and the Excel output is in Figure 7.20.

We ask the question: Is there *any* difference between the two groups (males and females)? To answer this, the following hypotheses can be tested:

$$H_0: \quad \beta_2 = \beta_3 = 0$$

$$H_a: \quad \text{At least one of } \beta_2 \text{ and } \beta_3 \text{ is different from zero}$$

FIGURE **7.19** **MINITAB Regression Output for Discrimination Example with Interaction Variable to Represent Different Slopes**

```
The regression equation is
SALARY = 4395 + 62.1 EDUCAT - 275 MALES + 73.6 MSLOPE

Predictor      Coef      StDev        T          P
Constant     4395.3      389.2     11.29      0.000
EDUCAT        62.13      31.94      1.95      0.055
MALES        -274.9      845.7     -0.32      0.746
MSLOPE        73.59      63.59      1.16      0.250

S = 571.4      R-Sq = 37.3%      R-Sq(adj) = 35.2%

Analysis of Variance

Source           DF         SS         MS          F          P
Regression        3   17268865    5756288      17.63      0.000
Residual Error   89   29054426     326454
Total            92   46323290

Source      DF      Seq SS
EDUCAT       1     7862534
MALES        1     8969210
MSLOPE       1      437121

Unusual Observations
Obs    EDUCAT      SALARY       Fit    StDev Fit      Residual    St Resid
  1      12.0      3900.0    5140.9        73.2       -1240.9      -2.19R
 60      12.0      6300.0    5140.9        73.2        1159.1       2.05R
 62      12.0      4620.0    5749.1       131.5       -1129.1      -2.03R
 63      15.0      5040.0    6156.2       129.3       -1116.2      -2.01R
 73       8.0      6000.0    5206.2       320.5         793.8       1.68 X
 91      12.0      6900.0    5749.1       131.5        1150.9       2.07R
 93      16.0      8100.0    6291.9       169.2        1808.1       3.31R

R denotes an observation with a large standardized residual
X denotes an observation whose X value gives it large influence.
```

FIGURE 7.20   Excel Regression Output for Discrimination Example with Interaction Variable to Represent Different Slopes

SUMMARY OUTPUT

Regression Statistics
Multiple R	0.611
R Square	0.373
Adjusted R Square	0.352
Standard Error	571.362
Observations	93.000

ANOVA

	df	SS	MS	F	Significance F
Regression	3.000	17268864.766	5756288.255	17.633	0.000
Residual	89.000	29054425.556	326454.220		
Total	92.000	46323290.323			

	Coefficients	Standard Error	t Stat	P-value	Lower 95%	Upper 95%
Intercept	4395.323	389.210	11.293	0.000	3621.971	5168.674
EDUCAT	62.131	31.943	1.945	0.055	-1.340	125.601
MALES	-274.860	845.749	-0.325	0.746	-1955.344	1405.624
MSLOPE	73.586	63.592	1.157	0.250	-52.771	199.942

To test these hypotheses, a partial F test should be used. The reduced model has only the variable EDUCAT. This regression is shown in Figure 7.21 for MINITAB and in Figure 7.22 for Excel. The F statistic is

$$F = \frac{(38,460,756 - 29,054,426)/2}{326,454} = 14.41$$

Using a 5% level of significance, the decision rule is:

Reject H_0 if $F > 3.15$

Accept H_0 if $F \leq 3.15$

The critical value used is the $F(0.05;2,60)$ value since the value for $F(0.05;2,89)$ is not in the tables. The decision is to reject H_0. We should already have guessed that this would be the decision since the test in Example 7.2 showed that the coefficient of the indicator variable was not zero.

FIGURE **7.21**   **MINITAB Regression Output for Reduced Model in Discrimination Example with Interaction Variable**

```
The regression equation is
SALARY = 3819 + 128 EDUCAT


Predictor      Coef       StDev           T           P
Constant      3818.6      377.4        10.12       0.000
EDUCAT        128.09       29.70        4.31       0.000


S = 650.1       R-Sq = 17.0%       R-Sq(adj) = 16.1%


Analysis of Variance


Source          DF          SS          MS          F           P
Regression       1       7862534     7862534      18.60       0.000
Residual Error  91      38460756      422646
Total           92      46323290


Unusual Observations
Obs    EDUCAT     SALARY       Fit     StDev Fit      Residual     St Resid
  1     12.0      3900.0     5355.6        69.1        -1455.6        -2.25R
  9     15.0      4440.0     5739.8       100.2        -1299.8        -2.02R
 91     12.0      6900.0     5355.6        69.1         1544.4         2.39R
 93     16.0      8100.0     5867.9       123.8         2232.1         3.50R


R denotes an observation with a large standardized residual
```

The coefficients can be tested individually to see whether one or both are different from zero. Note the conflicting results when we do this. The p values (or t ratios) on each of the individual coefficients for MALES and MSLOPE suggest that the coefficients are equal to zero. But the F test just told us that at least one of the coefficients is different from zero. The reason for these conflicting results is the high correlation between MALES and MSLOPE (0.986). This is an example of the multicollinearity problem discussed in Chapter 6. Since we already have concluded that the indicator variable is important in the regression and the addition of the interaction variable does not add much (R^2 only increases by 1%), it might be best in this example to stick to the simpler model in Example 7.2.

FIGURE 7.22 Excel Regression Output for Reduced Model in Discrimination Example
with Interaction Variable

SUMMARY OUTPUT

Regression Statistics

Multiple R	0.412
R Square	0.170
Adjusted R Square	0.161
Standard Error	650.112
Observations	93.000

ANOVA

	df	SS	MS	F	Significance F
Regression	1.000	7862534.292	7862534.292	18.603	0.000
Residual	91.000	38460756.031	422645.671		
Total	92.000	46323290.323			

	Coefficients	Standard Error	t Stat	P-value	Lower 95%	Upper 95%
Intercept	3818.560	377.438	10.117	0.000	3068.826	4568.293
EDUCAT	128.086	29.697	4.313	0.000	69.097	187.075

Example 7.4 illustrates one caution in using interaction variables. If the correlation is high between interaction variables and the original variables in the regression, multicollinearity problems can result. In a regression with several variables, the number of interaction variables that could be created is very large and the likelihood of multicollinearity problems is high. Therefore, it is wise not to use interaction variables indiscriminately. There should be some good reason to suspect that two variables might be related or some specific question that can be answered by an interaction variable before this type of explanatory variable is used.

EXERCISES

3 **More on Possible Discrimination**   Suppose that legal counsel representing Harris Bank suggests that an interaction exists between education and experience and that the introduction of this term into the regression may account for the difference in average salaries. The interaction term

$$EDUCEXPR = EDUCAT * EXPER$$

FIGURE 7.23   MINITAB Regression Output for Discrimination Exercise Using Interaction Term
Between Education and Experience

```
The regression equation is
SALARY = 3006 + 134 EDUCAT + 5.68 EXPER + 22.4 MONTHS + 688 MALES
   - 0.364 EDUCEXPR


Predictor       Coef       StDev          T          P
Constant      3006.2       490.7       6.13      0.000
EDUCAT        134.47       39.81       3.38      0.001
EXPER          5.679       3.164       1.79      0.076
MONTHS        22.421       5.218       4.30      0.000
MALES          687.6       119.7       5.74      0.000
EDUCEXPR     -0.3643      0.2569      -1.42      0.160


S = 504.5        R-Sq = 52.2%      R-Sq(adj) = 49.4%

Analysis of Variance


Source             DF           SS          MS          F          P
Regression          5     24177362     4835472      19.00      0.000
Residual Error     87     22145928      254551
Total              92     46323290


Source        DF       Seq SS
EDUCAT         1      7862534
EXPER          1      2038491
MONTHS         1      4083411
MALES          1      9680915
EDUCEXPR       1       512011


Unusual Observations
Obs     EDUCAT      SALARY         Fit    StDev Fit     Residual     St Resid
  3       12.0      4290.0      5299.0        110.2      -1009.0       -2.05R
 23        8.0      4980.0      5521.6        261.7       -541.6       -1.26 X
 62       12.0      4620.0      5815.7        122.5      -1195.7       -2.44R
 71       15.0      5400.0      6034.4        268.7       -634.4       -1.49 X
 73        8.0      6000.0      6125.1        268.3       -125.1       -0.29 X
 91       12.0      6900.0      5760.4        109.9       1139.6        2.31R
 93       16.0      8100.0      6577.0        148.6       1523.0        3.16R


R denotes an observation with a large standardized residual
X denotes an observation whose X value gives it large influence.
```

FIGURE 7.24 Excel Regression Output for Discrimination Exercise Using Interaction Term
Between Education and Experience

SUMMARY OUTPUT

Regression Statistics

Multiple R	0.722
R Square	0.522
Adjusted R Square	0.494
Standard Error	504.530
Observations	93.000

ANOVA

	df	SS	MS	F	Significance F
Regression	5.000	24177362.322	4835472.464	18.996	0.000
Residual	87.000	22145928.001	254550.897		
Total	92.000	46323290.323			

	Coefficients	Standard Error	t Stat	P-value	Lower 95%	Upper 95%
Intercept	3006.167	490.660	6.127	0.000	2030.927	3981.408
EDUCAT	134.470	39.814	3.377	0.001	55.336	213.605
EXPER	5.679	3.164	1.795	0.076	-0.610	11.968
MONTHS	22.421	5.218	4.297	0.000	12.050	32.791
MALES	687.630	119.697	5.745	0.000	449.719	925.540
EDUCEXPR	-0.364	0.257	-1.418	0.160	-0.875	0.146

is created and introduced into the regression. The MINITAB regression output is in
Figure 7.23 and the Excel output is in Figure 7.24. Use the outputs to help answer the
following questions:

a What is the adjusted R^2 for this regression? Compare this value to the adjusted R^2
for the regression without the interaction variable (see Figure 7.15 or 7.16). Which
model appears to be the best choice based on the adjusted R^2?

b Test to see whether the interaction term is important in this regression model. Use
a 5% level of significance. State the hypotheses to be tested, the decision rule, the
test statistic, and your decision.

c Does the interaction variable seem to be important in explaining SALARY?

d How would you respond to the suggestion that introduction of the interaction
term into the regression may account for the difference in average salaries?

(See Exercise 7.1 for instructions on accessing the data.)

4   Automobile Transmissions (continued)   Consider again the data from Exercise 7.2:

y =   mileage in city driving (CITYMPG)

x_1 =   weight in pounds (WEIGHT)

x_2 =   indicator variable coded as 1 for cars with automatic transmissions and 0 for cars with standard transmissions (TRANS)

Instead of x_1 (WEIGHT), the variable $1/x_1$ (WTINV) is used as before. We define the interaction variable

$$WTSLOPE = WTINV * TRANS$$

When WTSLOPE is included in the regression, it allows the slopes of the regression lines for cars with manual and automatic transmissions to differ. The regression model can be written

$$CITYMPG = \beta_0 + \beta_1 WTINV + \beta_2 TRANS + \beta_3 WTSLOPE + e$$

The MINITAB and Excel regression outputs for this model are shown in Figures 7.25 and 7.26, respectively. Figures 7.27 and 7.28 contain the outputs for the following model:

$$CITYMPG = \beta_0 + \beta_1 WTINV + e$$

Use the outputs to help answer the following questions:

a   Is there *any* difference between the regression lines for cars with manual and automatic transmissions? State the hypotheses to be tested, the decision rule, the test statistic, and your decision. Use a 5% level of significance.

b   Is there a difference, on average, in mileages for cars with manual and automatic transmissions? State the hypotheses to be tested, the decision rule, the test statistic, and your decision. Use a 5% level of significance.

c   Is there a difference between the slopes of the regression lines representing the relationship between CITYMPG and WTINV for cars with manual and automatic transmissions? State the hypotheses to be tested, the decision rule, the test statistic, and your decision. Use a 5% level of significance.

d   Write out the estimated equation as it would appear for cars with manual transmissions.

e   Write out the estimated equation as it would appear for cars with automatic transmissions.

(See Exercise 7.2 for instructions on how to access the data.)

FIGURE **7.25**   MINITAB Regression Output for Automobile Transmission Interaction Variable Exercise

```
The regression equation is
CITYMPG = - 7.70 + 85712 WTINV + 11.8 TRANS - 34143 WTSLOPE

Predictor      Coef       StDev          T          P
Constant     -7.698       1.659      -4.64      0.000
WTINV         85712        4507       19.02      0.000
TRANS        11.836       3.016        3.92      0.000
WTSLOPE      -34143        9974       -3.42      0.001

S = 2.240      R-Sq = 80.5%      R-Sq(adj) = 80.1%

Analysis of Variance

Source            DF         SS         MS          F          P
Regression         3    2780.80     926.93     184.78      0.000
Residual Error   134     672.19       5.02
Total            137    3452.99

Source      DF      Seq SS
WTINV        1     2668.41
TRANS        1       53.60
WTSLOPE      1       58.79

Unusual Observations
Obs     WTINV    CITYMPG        Fit    StDevFit      Residual     St Resid
  1  0.000327     25.000     20.294       0.305         4.706        2.12R
 10  0.000197     12.000     14.309       0.800        -2.309       -1.10 X
 30  0.000528     41.000     37.533       0.782         3.467        1.65 X
 45  0.000342     27.000     21.646       0.273         5.354        2.41R
 46  0.000301     12.000     18.127       0.380        -6.127       -2.78R
 47  0.000304     26.000     18.354       0.371         7.646        3.46R
 49  0.000268     10.000     15.312       0.500        -5.312       -2.43R
 59  0.000476     28.000     33.098       0.566        -5.098       -2.35R
 69  0.000280      9.000     16.278       0.457        -7.278       -3.32R
 77  0.000329     15.000     20.469       0.300        -5.469       -2.46R
 78  0.000435     25.000     29.585       0.410        -4.585       -2.08R
 83  0.000210     15.000     14.972       0.695         0.028        0.01 X
 96  0.000353     23.000     22.328       0.698         0.672        0.32 X
109  0.000352     17.000     22.309       0.695        -5.309       -2.49RX
115  0.000344     17.000     21.756       0.271        -4.756       -2.14R
117  0.000197     12.000     14.299       0.802        -2.299       -1.10 X
125  0.000532     39.000     37.942       0.802         1.058        0.51 X

R denotes an observation with a large standardized residual
X denotes an observation whose X value gives it large influence.
```

FIGURE 7.26   **Excel Regression Output for Automobile Transmission Interaction Variable Exercise**

SUMMARY OUTPUT

Regression Statistics
Multiple R	0.897
R Square	0.805
Adjusted R Square	0.801
Standard Error	2.240
Observations	138.000

ANOVA

	df	SS	MS	F	Significance F
Regression	3.000	2780.799	926.933	184.782	0.000
Residual	134.000	672.193	5.016		
Total	137.000	3452.993			

	Coefficients	Standard Error	t Stat	P-value	Lower 95%	Upper 95%
Intercept	−7.698	1.659	−4.640	0.000	−10.979	−4.417
WTINV	85712.383	4506.613	19.019	0.000	76799.097	94625.669
TRANS	11.836	3.016	3.925	0.000	5.871	17.800
WTSLOPE	−34143.493	9973.662	−3.423	0.001	−53869.637	−14417.349

FIGURE 7.27   **MINITAB Regression Output for Reduced Model for Automobile Transmission Interaction Variable Exercise**

```
The regression equation is
CITYMPG = - 1.62 + 70147 WTINV


Predictor      Coef       StDev         T         P
Constant     -1.616       1.087      -1.49     0.139
WTINV         70147        3262      21.51     0.000


S = 2.402        R-Sq = 77.3%       R-Sq(adj) = 77.1%

Analysis of Variance

Source           DF         SS         MS        F          P
Regression        1      2668.4     2668.4    462.55     0.000
Residual Error  136       784.6        5.8
Total           137      3453.0

Unusual Observations
Obs      WTINV     CITYMPG       Fit   StDev Fit    Residual     St Resid
 30    0.000528     41.000    35.401      0.685       5.599       2.43RX
 46    0.000301     12.000    19.519      0.221      -7.519      -3.14R
 47    0.000304     26.000    19.705      0.218       6.295       2.63R
 48    0.000256     11.000    16.370      0.309      -5.370      -2.25R
 49    0.000268     10.000    17.215      0.280      -7.215      -3.02R
 59    0.000476     28.000    31.771      0.526      -3.771      -1.61 X
 69    0.000280      9.000    18.005      0.257      -9.005      -3.77R
 77    0.000329     15.000    21.436      0.205      -6.436      -2.69R
 97    0.000470     33.000    31.363      0.509       1.637       0.70 X
109    0.000352     17.000    23.101      0.220      -6.101      -2.55R
115    0.000344     17.000    22.489      0.211      -5.489      -2.29R
125    0.000532     39.000    35.736      0.700       3.264       1.42 X
131    0.000478     32.000    31.947      0.534       0.053       0.02 X


R denotes an observation with a large standardized residual
X denotes an observation whose X value gives it large influence.
```

FIGURE 7.28   Excel Regression Output for Reduced Model for Automobile Transmission Interaction Variable Exercise

```
                           SUMMARY OUTPUT

Regression Statistics
Multiple R              0.879
R Square                0.773
Adjusted R Square       0.771
Standard Error          2.402
Observations          138.000
```

ANOVA

	df	SS	MS	F	Significance F
Regression	1.000	2668.413	2668.413	462.546	0.000
Residual	136.000	784.580	5.769		
Total	137.000	3452.993			

	Coefficients	Standard Error	t Stat	P-value	Lower 95%	Upper 95%
Intercept	−1.616	1.087	−1.487	0.139	−3.766	0.533
WTINV	70147.237	3261.619	21.507	0.000	63697.191	76597.282

7.3   SEASONAL EFFECTS IN TIME-SERIES REGRESSION

Seasonal effects are fairly regular patterns of movement in a time series, repeating within a 1-year period. For example, sales of swimsuits are expected to be higher in spring and summer months and lower in fall and winter. Although the influence of seasonal effects is not expected to be exactly the same every year, the same general pattern is expected to persist.

Seasonal patterns can be modeled in a regression equation by using indicator variables, which can be created to indicate the time period to which each observation belongs. For example, if quarterly data are being analyzed, the following indicator variables could be created:

$Q1$ = 1   if the observation is from the first quarter of any year
   = 0   otherwise

$Q2$ = 1   if the observation is from the second quarter of any year
   = 0   otherwise

$Q3$ = 1   if the observation is from the third quarter of any year
   = 0   otherwise

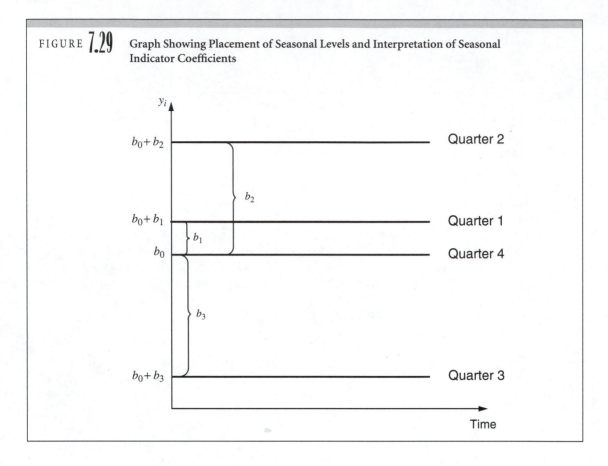

FIGURE 7.29
Graph Showing Placement of Seasonal Levels and Interpretation of Seasonal Indicator Coefficients

$$Q4 = 1 \quad \text{if the observation is from the fourth quarter of any year}$$
$$= 0 \quad \text{otherwise}$$

Four indicator variables have been created to denote the quarter to which each observation belongs, but only three of the variables should be included in the regression equation. The excluded quarter simply serves as a base level quarter from which changes in the seasonal levels are measured. The interpretation of the coefficients of the indicator variables is the same as for any set of indicator variables. To illustrate, consider the following estimated regression equation with only quarterly indicator variables:

$$\hat{y} = b_0 + b_1 Q1 + b_2 Q2 + b_3 Q3$$

Note that the fourth quarter serves as the base level quarter. Observations in the fourth quarter are represented by the equation

$$\hat{y} = b_0$$

because $Q1 = Q2 = Q3 = 0$. This point has been located on the graph in Figure 7.29.

Observations in the first quarter are represented by

$$\hat{y} = b_0 + b_1$$

because $Q1 = 1$ and $Q2 = Q3 = 0$.

Similarly, observations in the second quarter are represented by

$$\hat{y} = b_0 + b_2$$

and in the third quarter by

$$\hat{y} = b_0 + b_3$$

The coefficients b_1, b_2, and b_3 represent the differences between the fitted values for the indicated quarter (first, second, and third, respectively) and the base level quarter. The graph in Figure 7.29 has been constructed with the assumption that b_1 and b_2 are positive and b_3 is negative. The lines shown for each quarter have a zero slope because no term has been included in the regression except the indicator variables. Differences in the overall level of the series in different quarters are shown by the quarterly indicators. The regression coefficients are estimating the differences in the mean levels of y in the indicated quarters. Obviously, variables could be used in the regression in addition to the seasonal indicator variables. This is illustrated in the following example.

EXAMPLE 7.5   **ABX Company Sales**

Consider again the ABX Company from Example 3.11. The ABX Company sells winter sports merchandise including skis, ice skates, sleds, and so on. Quarterly sales in thousands of dollars for the ABX Company are shown in Table 7.4. The time period represented starts in the first quarter of 1990 and ends in the fourth quarter of 1999.

A MINITAB time-series plot of sales is shown in Figure 7.30. In Chapter 3, it was decided that a strong linear trend in sales appeared in this plot. The regression with the linear trend variable was estimated, and the resulting output is shown again in Figure 7.31 for MINITAB and in Figure 7.32 for Excel. The MINITAB residual plot of the standardized residuals versus the fitted values is shown in Figure 7.33. From this plot, no obvious violations of assumptions can be observed.

A time-series plot of the standardized residuals is shown in Figure 7.34. Here a clear pattern emerges. The residuals tend to be higher in the first and fourth quarters and lower in the second and third quarters. This is not unexpected because the ABX Company sells winter sports merchandise. This pattern is the result of seasonal variation in the data that has not been accounted for in the regression. Note that the pattern can also be seen in the time-series plot of the original data in Figure 7.30. Again, the residual plot emphasizes the pattern and points out some systematic variation in the data that we should try to model with our regression.

Figure 7.35 shows the MINITAB regression of sales on the linear trend variable and indicator variables designed to indicate the first, second, and third quarters. The Excel regression is in Figure 7.36. The original sales data, the trend variable, a variable representing the number of the quarter (1 through 4) labeled QUARTER, and four indicator variables, labeled Q1, Q2, Q3, and Q4 are shown in Table 7.4. Remember that only three of the four indicator variables should be

TABLE 7.4 Data for ABX Company Sales Example Showing Seasonal Indicator Variables

SALES	TREND	QUARTER	Q1	Q2	Q3	Q4	SALES	TREND	QUARTER	Q1	Q2	Q3	Q4
221.0	1	1	1	0	0	0	260.5	21	1	1	0	0	0
203.5	2	2	0	1	0	0	244.0	22	2	0	1	0	0
190.0	3	3	0	0	1	0	256.0	23	3	0	0	1	0
225.5	4	4	0	0	0	1	276.5	24	4	0	0	0	1
223.0	5	1	1	0	0	0	291.0	25	1	1	0	0	0
190.0	6	2	0	1	0	0	255.5	26	2	0	1	0	0
206.0	7	3	0	0	1	0	244.0	27	3	0	0	1	0
226.5	8	4	0	0	0	1	291.0	28	4	0	0	0	1
236.0	9	1	1	0	0	0	296.0	29	1	1	0	0	0
214.0	10	2	0	1	0	0	260.0	30	2	0	1	0	0
210.5	11	3	0	0	1	0	271.5	31	3	0	0	1	0
237.0	12	4	0	0	0	1	299.5	32	4	0	0	0	1
245.5	13	1	1	0	0	0	297.0	33	1	1	0	0	0
201.0	14	2	0	1	0	0	271.0	34	2	0	1	0	0
230.0	15	3	0	0	1	0	270.0	35	3	0	0	1	0
254.5	16	4	0	0	0	1	300.0	36	4	0	0	0	1
257.0	17	1	1	0	0	0	306.5	37	1	1	0	0	0
238.0	18	2	0	1	0	0	283.5	38	2	0	1	0	0
228.0	19	3	0	0	1	0	283.5	39	3	0	0	1	0
255.0	20	4	0	0	0	1	307.5	40	4	0	0	0	1

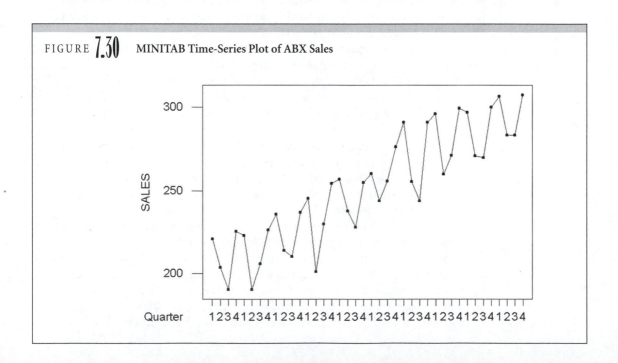

FIGURE 7.30 MINITAB Time-Series Plot of ABX Sales

FIGURE 7.31   MINITAB Output for Regression of Sales on Linear Trend Variable for ABX Sales Example

```
The regression equation is
SALES = 199 + 2.56 TREND

Predictor      Coef       StDev          T            P
Constant    199.017       5.128      38.81        0.000
TREND        2.5559      0.2180      11.73        0.000

S = 15.91        R-Sq = 78.3%       R-Sq(adj) = 77.8%

Analysis of Variance

Source            DF          SS          MS          F          P
Regression         1       34818       34818     137.50      0.000
Residual Error    38        9622         253
Total             39       44440

Unusual Observations
Obs    TREND       SALES        Fit    StDev Fit      Residual     St Resid
 14     14.0      201.00     234.80        2.89        -33.80       -2.16R

R denotes an observation with a large standardized residual
```

FIGURE 7.32   Excel Output for Regression of Sales on Linear Trend Variable
for ABX Sales Example

```
                           SUMMARY OUTPUT

Regression Statistics
Multiple R              0.885
R Square                0.783
Adjusted R Square       0.778
Standard Error         15.913
Observations           40.000

ANOVA
                 df          SS          MS          F      Significance F
Regression    1.000    34817.883   34817.883   137.505           0.000
Residual     38.000     9622.061     253.212
Total        39.000    44439.944

                       Standard
          Coefficients    Error   t Stat   P-value  Lower 95%  Upper 95%
Intercept      199.017    5.128   38.811     0.000    188.636    209.398
TREND            2.556    0.218   11.726     0.000      2.115      2.997
```

FIGURE 7.33   MINITAB Plot of Standardized Residuals Versus Fitted Values for ABX Sales Example

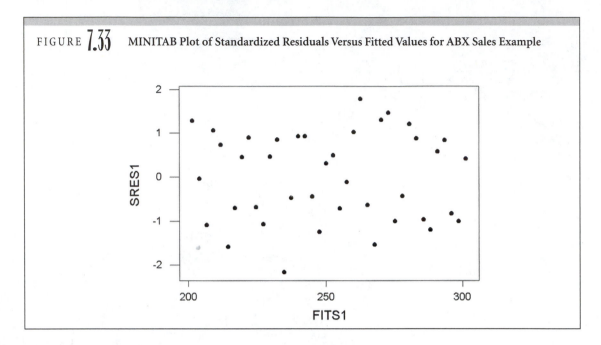

FIGURE 7.34   MINITAB Time-Series Plot of Standardized Residuals for ABX Sales Example

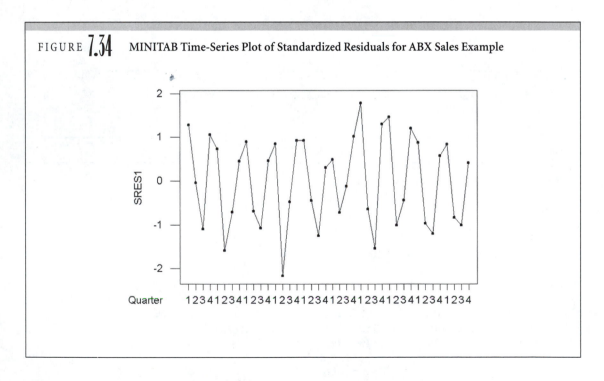

FIGURE 7.35   MINITAB Output for Regression of Sales on Linear Trend Variable and Quarterly Indicator Variables for ABX Sales Example

```
The regression equation is
SALES = 211 + 2.57 TREND + 3.75 Q1 - 26.1 Q2 - 25.8 Q3


Predictor      Coef       StDev           T          P
Constant    210.846       3.148       66.98      0.000
TREND       2.56610     0.09895       25.93      0.000
Q1            3.748       3.229        1.16      0.254
Q2          -26.118       3.222       -8.11      0.000
Q3          -25.784       3.217       -8.01      0.000


S = 7.190       R-Sq = 95.9%      R-Sq(adj) = 95.5%


Analysis of Variance


Source              DF          SS          MS          F          P
Regression           4       42630       10658     206.14      0.000
Residual Error      35        1810          52
Total               39       44440


Source      DF      Seq SS
TREND        1       34818
Q1           1        3335
Q2           1        1156
Q3           1        3321


Unusual Observations
Obs     TREND      SALES         Fit    StDev Fit      Residual     St Resid
  2       2.0     203.50      189.86        2.89         13.64         2.07R
 14      14.0     201.00      220.65        2.35        -19.65        -2.89R


R denotes an observation with a large standardized residual
```

used in the regression. (Also, note that the variable QUARTER is not used in the regression. It is merely in the table to indicate the number of each quarter.)

The residual plot of the standardized residuals versus the fitted values for the regression with the quarterly indicators is shown in Figure 7.37. A time-series plot of the standardized residuals is shown in Figure 7.38. No further violations of any assumptions appear in either of these plots.

FIGURE 7.36 Excel Output for Regression of Sales on Linear Trend Variable and Quarterly Indicator Variables for ABX Sales Example

SUMMARY OUTPUT

Regression Statistics

Multiple R	0.979
R Square	0.959
Adjusted R Square	0.955
Standard Error	7.190
Observations	40.000

ANOVA

	df	SS	MS	F	Significance F
Regression	4.000	42630.437	10657.609	206.143	0.000
Residual	35.000	1809.507	51.700		
Total	39.000	44439.944			

	Coefficients	Standard Error	t Stat	P-value	Lower 95%	Upper 95%
Intercept	210.846	3.148	66.980	0.000	204.455	217.236
TREND	2.566	0.099	25.932	0.000	2.365	2.767
Q1	3.748	3.229	1.161	0.254	-2.807	10.304
Q2	-26.118	3.222	-8.107	0.000	-32.658	-19.577
Q3	-25.784	3.217	-8.015	0.000	-32.315	-19.253

FIGURE 7.37 MINITAB Plot of Standardized Residuals Versus Fitted Values for ABX Sales Example with Quarterly Indicator Variables

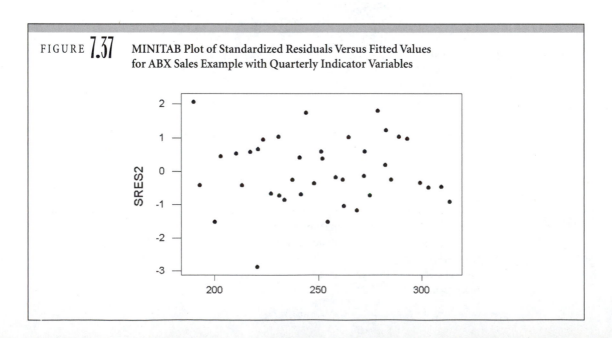

FIGURE 7.38 MINITAB Time-Series Plot of Standardized Residuals for ABX Sales Example with Quarterly Indicator Variables

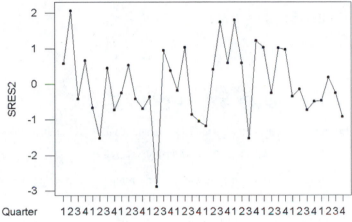

An important question to be asked in seasonal time-series models is, "Are there seasonal differences in the level of the dependent variable?" Another way of asking this question is, "Are the seasonal indicator variables necessary in the model?" The partial F test discussed in Chapter 4 can be used to answer the questions.

Consider the following model with explanatory variable x and quarterly seasonal indicators Q1, Q2, and Q3:

$$y = \beta_0 + \beta_1 x + \beta_2 Q1 + \beta_3 Q2 + \beta_4 Q3 + e$$

This is referred to as the full model. The hypotheses to be tested are

H_0: $\beta_2 = \beta_3 = \beta_4 = 0$

H_a: At least one of the coefficients β_2, β_3, and β_4 is not zero

If the null hypothesis is accepted, the seasonal indicator variables add nothing to the model and can be removed. In other words, there are no seasonal differences. In this case, the following reduced model is adopted:

$$y = \beta_0 + \beta_1 x + e$$

If the null hypothesis is rejected, then there are seasonal differences, and the quarterly indicators should remain in the model.

To conduct the test, the partial F test statistic is computed as

$$F = \frac{(SSE_R - SSE_F) / (K - L)}{MSE_F}$$

where SSE_R is the error sum of squares from the reduced model, SSE_F is the error sum of squares from the full model, and MSE_F is the mean square error from the full model. Because the hypothesis test determines whether three coefficients are equal to zero, a divisor of 3 is used in the numerator in place of $K - L$ ($K = 4, L = 1$). The decision rule for the test is:

Reject H_0 if $F > F(\alpha; K - L, n - K - 1)$

Accept H_0 if $F \le F(\alpha; K - L, n - K - 1)$

EXAMPLE **7.6** **ABX Company Sales (continued)**

In Example 7.5, the following model was examined for ABX Company sales:

$$\text{SALES} = \beta_0 + \beta_1 \text{TREND} + \beta_2 Q1 + \beta_3 Q2 + \beta_4 Q3 + e$$

To determine whether there are seasonal components affecting sales, the following hypotheses should be tested:

H_0: $\beta_2 = \beta_3 = \beta_4 = 0$

H_a: At least one of the coefficients $\beta_2, \beta_3,$ and β_4 is not zero

To test this hypothesis, the partial F test is used. The test statistic is

$$F = \frac{(9622 - 1810)/3}{52} = 50.1$$

Note that the reduced model output is in Figure 7.31 or 7.32, and the full model output is in Figure 7.35 or 7.36. Using a 5% level of significance, the decision rule for the test is:

Reject H_0 if $F > F(0.05; 3,35) = 2.92$ (approximately)

Accept H_0 if $F \le 2.92$

The null hypothesis should be rejected. Thus, the conclusion is that seasonal components do affect sales and should be taken into account, as was done in Example 7.5.

When computing forecasts with seasonal models, the coefficients of the seasonal indicators are used to adjust the level of the forecast in the appropriate time periods. The quarterly forecasts for the year 2000 are as follows, using the seasonal model with trend:

Time Period	Point Forecast
2000 Q1	$211 + 2.57(41) + 3.75 = 320.12$
2000 Q2	$211 + 2.57(42) - 26.1 = 292.84$
2000 Q3	$211 + 2.57(43) - 25.8 = 295.71$
2000 Q4	$211 + 2.57(44) = 324.08$

Throughout this section, the use of quarterly indicator variables has been discussed. If monthly instead of quarterly data are used, the applications are similar. Instead of four quarterly indicators, twelve monthly indicators are created. Eleven of the twelve monthly indicators are used in the regression with the estimated coefficients interpreted in a manner similar to those of the quarterly coefficients. Tests for seasonal variation involve the set of eleven indicator variable coefficients. Since the use of monthly indicators is so similar to quarterly indicators, the demonstration of their use is reserved for the exercises.

EXERCISES

5 Furniture Sales   Table 7.5 shows monthly furniture sales (in millions of dollars) for the United States from January 1986 through December 1998. Figure 7.39 shows the time-series plot of the data. An extrapolative model to forecast furniture sales for each month in 1999 was developed. Figures 7.40 and 7.41 show the MINITAB and Excel regression outputs for the model. The model can be written as follows:

$$SALES = \beta_0 + \beta_1 TREND + \beta_2 LAGSALES + \beta_3 JAN + \beta_4 FEB$$
$$+ \beta_5 MARCH + \beta_6 APRIL + \beta_7 MAY + \beta_8 JUNE$$
$$+ \beta_9 JULY + \beta_{10} AUG + \beta_{11} SEPT + \beta_{12} OCT$$
$$+ \beta_{13} NOV + e$$

FIGURE 7.39   **MINITAB Time-Series Plot of Furniture Sales**

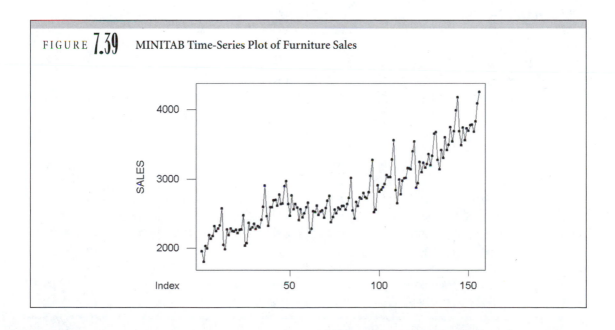

TABLE 7.5   Data for Furniture Sales Exercise

YEAR	MONTH	SALES	YEAR	MONTH	SALES	YEAR	MONTH	SALES	YEAR	MONTH	SALES
1986	1	1952	1989	4	2596	1992	7	2614	1995	10	3141
1986	2	1796	1989	5	2693	1992	8	2613	1995	11	3400
1986	3	2031	1989	6	2699	1992	9	2557	1995	12	3540
1986	4	1992	1989	7	2618	1992	10	2639	1996	1	2876
1986	5	2188	1989	8	2777	1992	11	2731	1996	2	2943
1986	6	2133	1989	9	2641	1992	12	3020	1996	3	3246
1986	7	2173	1989	10	2646	1993	1	2544	1996	4	3101
1986	8	2315	1989	11	2897	1993	2	2428	1996	5	3237
1986	9	2247	1989	12	2973	1993	3	2673	1996	6	3165
1986	10	2280	1990	1	2639	1993	4	2610	1996	7	3215
1986	11	2328	1990	2	2468	1993	5	2733	1996	8	3362
1986	12	2577	1990	3	2765	1993	6	2715	1996	9	3201
1987	1	2046	1990	4	2563	1993	7	2798	1996	10	3334
1987	2	1979	1990	5	2641	1993	8	2742	1996	11	3656
1987	3	2272	1990	6	2585	1993	9	2725	1996	12	3675
1987	4	2187	1990	7	2403	1993	10	2810	1997	1	3275
1987	5	2281	1990	8	2563	1993	11	3047	1997	2	3141
1987	6	2249	1990	9	2445	1993	12	3274	1997	3	3419
1987	7	2241	1990	10	2503	1994	1	2525	1997	4	3304
1987	8	2265	1990	11	2595	1994	2	2556	1997	5	3599
1987	9	2215	1990	12	2659	1994	3	2909	1997	6	3421
1987	10	2264	1991	1	2221	1994	4	2820	1997	7	3494
1987	11	2268	1991	2	2283	1994	5	2844	1997	8	3745
1987	12	2473	1991	3	2534	1994	6	2883	1997	9	3540
1988	1	2035	1991	4	2525	1994	7	2931	1997	10	3688
1988	2	2068	1991	5	2615	1994	8	3060	1997	11	3989
1988	3	2363	1991	6	2481	1994	9	3031	1997	12	4180
1988	4	2268	1991	7	2526	1994	10	3027	1998	1	3687
1988	5	2302	1991	8	2549	1994	11	3280	1998	2	3486
1988	6	2350	1991	9	2443	1994	12	3557	1998	3	3741
1988	7	2278	1991	10	2584	1995	1	2841	1998	4	3558
1988	8	2315	1991	11	2687	1995	2	2650	1998	5	3732
1988	9	2299	1991	12	2757	1995	3	2996	1998	6	3692
1988	10	2411	1992	1	2378	1995	4	2784	1998	7	3775
1988	11	2602	1992	2	2450	1995	5	2979	1998	8	3781
1988	12	2906	1992	3	2560	1995	6	3009	1998	9	3685
1989	1	2464	1992	4	2504	1995	7	3017	1998	10	3832
1989	2	2320	1992	5	2586	1995	8	3158	1998	11	4089
1989	3	2592	1992	6	2564	1995	9	3153	1998	12	4257

Source: www.economagic.com/em-cgi/data.exe/cenret/rt15

FIGURE **7.40**   **MINITAB Regression Output with Seasonal Indicators for Furniture Sales Exercise**

```
The regression equation is
SALES = 413 + 1.23 TREND + 0.888 LAGSALES - 664 JAN - 286 FEB + 47.3 MARCH
       - 294 APRIL - 83.2 MAY - 232 JUNE - 190 JULY - 111 AUG - 273 SEPT
       - 127 OCT - 9.4 NOV

155 cases used 1 cases contain missing values

Predictor        Coef       StDev           T           P
Constant       412.65       93.22        4.43       0.000
TREND          1.2308      0.4359        2.82       0.005
LAGSALES      0.88806     0.04065       21.85       0.000
JAN           -664.21       34.10      -19.48       0.000
FEB           -285.79       36.20       -7.89       0.000
MARCH           47.25       37.66        1.25       0.212
APRIL         -294.48       33.82       -8.71       0.000
MAY            -83.19       35.08       -2.37       0.019
JUNE          -232.18       33.76       -6.88       0.000
JULY          -189.81       34.23       -5.55       0.000
AUG           -111.02       34.22       -3.24       0.001
SEPT          -273.40       33.49       -8.16       0.000
OCT           -126.86       34.36       -3.69       0.000
NOV             -9.44       33.70       -0.28       0.780

S = 83.98         R-Sq = 97.6%          R-Sq(adj) = 97.4%

Analysis of Variance

Source              DF           SS           MS           F           P
Regression          13     40134092      3087238      437.76       0.000
Residual Error     141       994374         7052
Total              154     41128467

Source         DF       Seq SS
TREND           1     33158631
LAGSALES        1      2658878
JAN             1      2371813
FEB             1       320105
MARCH           1       423966
APRIL           1       318651
MAY             1        38048
JUNE            1       142313
JULY            1        73131
AUG             1          248
SEPT            1       504823
OCT             1       122932
NOV             1          554

Unusual Observations
Obs      TREND        SALES         Fit     StDev Fit      Residual     St Resid
 23         23      2268.00     2442.08        25.00       -174.08        -2.17R
 49         49      2639.00     2448.94        25.33        190.06         2.37R
 55         55      2403.00     2586.16        23.70       -183.16        -2.27R
 75         75      2560.00     2727.95        23.40       -167.95        -2.08R
 97         97      2525.00     2775.32        24.45       -250.32        -3.12R
109        109      2841.00     3041.41        25.16       -200.41        -2.50R
121        121      2876.00     3041.08        25.07       -165.08        -2.06R
137        137      3599.00     3432.21        25.01        166.79         2.08R
140        140      3745.00     3576.81        25.43        168.19         2.10R

R denotes an observation with a large standardized residual
```

FIGURE **7.41**   Excel Regression Output with Seasonal Indicators for Furniture Sales Exercise

```
                          SUMMARY OUTPUT
```

Regression Statistics
Multiple R   0.9878
R Square   0.9758
Adjusted R Square   0.9736
Standard Error   83.9780
Observations   155.0000

ANOVA

	df	SS	MS	F	Significance F
Regression	13.0000	40134092.2407	3087237.8647	437.7632	0.0000
Residual	141.0000	994374.4948	7052.3014		
Total	154.0000	41128466.7355			

	Coefficients	Standard Error	t Stat	P-value	Lower 95%	Upper 95%
Intercept	412.6548	93.2246	4.4265	0.0000	228.3562	596.9535
TREND	1.2308	0.4359	2.8233	0.0054	0.3690	2.0926
LAGSALES	0.8881	0.0406	21.8482	0.0000	0.8007	0.9684
JAN	-664.2117	34.0987	-19.4791	0.0000	-731.6225	-596.8009
FEB	-285.7916	36.2002	-7.8948	0.0000	-357.3569	-214.2263
MARCH	47.2524	37.6618	1.2546	0.2117	-27.2025	121.7072
APRIL	-294.4786	33.8196	-8.7073	0.0000	-361.3377	-227.6195
MAY	-83.1936	35.0765	-2.3718	0.0191	-152.5374	-13.8499
JUNE	-232.1840	33.7636	-6.8768	0.0000	-298.9323	-165.4357
JULY	-189.8133	34.2304	-5.5452	0.0000	-257.4845	-122.1421
AUG	-111.0182	34.2221	-3.2440	0.0015	-178.6731	-43.3633
SEPT	-273.3967	33.4911	-8.1633	0.0000	-339.6063	-207.1871
OCT	-126.8580	34.3592	-3.6921	0.0003	-194.7839	-58.9321
NOV	-9.4450	33.7013	-0.2803	0.7797	-76.0701	57.1802

TREND is a linear trend variable, LAGSALES is SALES lagged one period, and JAN through NOV are 11 monthly seasonal indicators. Note that December has been used as the base level month.

Figures 7.42 and 7.43 show the MINITAB and Excel regressions, respectively, for the model without the seasonal indicators.

FIGURE 7.42   MINITAB Regression Output Without Seasonal Indicators for Furniture Sales Exercise

```
The regression equation is
SALES = 811 + 4.29 TREND + 0.594 LAGSALES


155 cases used 1 cases contain missing values


Predictor      Coef      StDev         T          P
Constant      811.0      138.9       5.84      0.000
TREND        4.2874     0.7704       5.56      0.000
LAGSALES    0.59392    0.06808       8.72      0.000


S = 186.9       R-Sq = 87.1%       R-Sq(adj) = 86.9%


Analysis of Variance

Source            DF         SS          MS          F          P
Regression         2   35817509    17908754     512.55      0.000
Residual Error   152    5310958       34941
Total            154   41128467


Source       DF      Seq SS
TREND         1    33158631
LAGSALES      1     2658878


Unusual Observations
Obs    TREND     SALES       Fit    StDev Fit     Residual    St Resid
 36       36    2906.0    2510.7       26.7        395.3        2.14R
 61       61    2221.0    2651.8       16.5       -430.8       -2.31R
 73       73    2378.0    2761.4       15.2       -383.4       -2.06R
 85       85    2544.0    2969.1       18.8       -425.1       -2.29R
 97       97    2525.0    3171.4       25.8       -646.4       -3.49R
109      109    2841.0    3390.9       36.0       -549.9       -3.00R
121      121    2876.0    3432.3       29.9       -556.3       -3.01R
143      143    3989.0    3614.5       30.9        374.5        2.03R
144      144    4180.0    3797.5       44.9        382.5        2.11R
145      145    3687.0    3915.3       55.4       -228.3       -1.28 X
156      156    4257.0    3908.4       45.8        348.6        1.92 X


R denotes an observation with a large standardized residual
X denotes an observation whose X value gives it large influence.
```

FIGURE 7.43 Excel Regression Output Without Seasonal Indicators for Furniture Sales Exercise

SUMMARY OUTPUT

Regression Statistics
Multiple R	0.9332
R Square	0.8709
Adjusted R Square	0.8692
Standard Error	186.9238
Observations	155.0000

ANOVA

	df	SS	MS	F	Significance F
Regression	2.0000	35817508.8955	17908754.4478	512.5499	0.0000
Residual	152.0000	5310957.8400	34940.1521		
Total	154.0000	41128466.7355			

	Coefficients	Standard Error	t Stat	P-value	Lower 95%	Upper 95%
Intercept	811.0063	138.8661	5.8402	0.0000	536.6491	1085.3634
TREND	4.2874	0.7704	5.5650	0.0000	2.7653	5.8095
LAGSALES	0.5939	0.0681	8.7234	0.0000	0.4594	0.7284

Use the computer outputs to help answer the following questions. For any hypothesis tests, use a 5% level of significance. Be sure to state the hypotheses to be tested, the decision rule, the test statistic, and your decision.

a Is there seasonal variation in furniture sales?

b Are the TREND and LAGSALES variables important to the equation explaining furniture sales?

c Using the better of the two equations (with or without seasonal indicators) as determined by you, develop a forecast of furniture sales for each month in 1999.

These data are available in a file with prefix FURNSAL7 in three columns: YEAR, MONTH, and SALES.

7.4   USING THE COMPUTER

The Using the Computer section in each chapter describes how to perform the computer analyses in the chapter using MINITAB, Excel, and SAS. For further detail on MINITAB, Excel, and SAS, see Appendix C.

7.4.1   MINITAB

Note that Version 12 of MINITAB is fully menu driven. Commands can be used, however, and they are included for any interested users. The menu headings and subheadings used to perform the procedures are listed first, followed by commands in parentheses. For example CALC: MAKE INDICATOR VARIABLES means to click on the CALC menu and then MAKE INDICATOR VARIABLES.

Creating and Using Indicator Variables

CALC: MAKE INDICATOR VARIABLES

Indicator variables have values of either 0 or 1. Obviously, one way to create an indicator variable (or variables) is simply to type it into a data set. Make Indicator Variables on the CALC menu can be useful in creating indicator variables more quickly in some cases.

Consider the data in Table 7.2 for the Meddicorp example. The variable REGION was typed into the original data set. This variable numbers the three regions as 1, 2, or 3. It can be used to create the indicator variables for the three regions after they are defined as follows:

SOUTH   =   1 whenever REGION is 1 and 0 otherwise

WEST   =   1 whenever REGION is 2 and 0 otherwise

MIDWEST   =   1 whenever REGION is 3 and 0 otherwise

To create the indicator variables SOUTH, WEST, and MIDWEST click on CALC and then Make Indicator Variables. The Make Indicator Variables dialog box is shown in Figure 7.44. Fill in the "Indicator variables for" box with the name of the variables to be transformed into indicators (REGION in this case). Then list the locations of the indicator variables in the "Store results in" box. Be sure to list locations for all m indicators (m being the number of categories) even though only $m - 1$ indicators are used in the regression. (The following command creates these three variables: INDICATOR C6 PUT IN C7,C8,C9, where C6 is the variable REGION and C7, C8, and C9 contain the three indicator variables defined as SOUTH, WEST, and MIDWEST, respectively.)

FIGURE 7.44 Make Indicator Variables Dialog Box

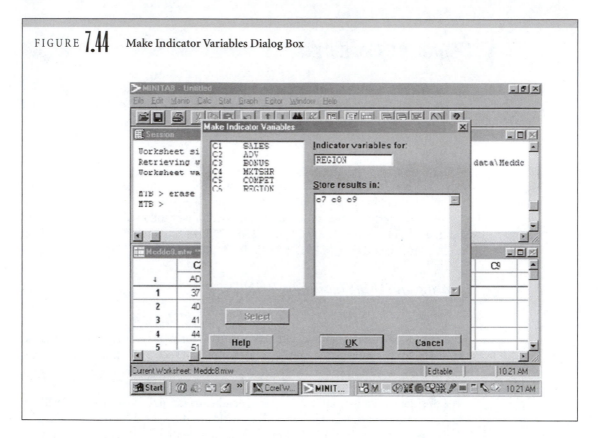

Creating and Using Interaction Variables

CALC: CALCULATOR

Interaction variables are created by multiplying one variable by another. This can be done in MINITAB by using the CALCULATOR on the CALC menu. Put the interaction variable column number in the "Store result in variable" box and put the action to be taken in the "Expression" box (see Figure 7.45). For example, put C6 in the "Store result in variable" box and C2*C3 in the "Expression" box and MINITAB multiplies C2 by C3 and stores the resulting interaction variable in C6. The interaction variable can then be used just like other variables. (The LET command can be used to create interaction variables. For example, LET C6=C2*C3 multiplies C2 by C3 and stores the result in C6.)

Creating and Using Seasonal Indicators for Time-Series Regression

To create quarterly seasonal indicators, follow this sequence: First, create a variable that numbers each quarter 1 through 4: CALC: MAKE PATTERNED DATA: SIMPLE SET OF NUMBERS. In the Simple Set of Numbers dialog box, fill in a column number in the "Store patterned data in" box, put 1 in the "From first value" box, 4 in the

FIGURE 7.45   Using the Calculator to Create Interaction Variables

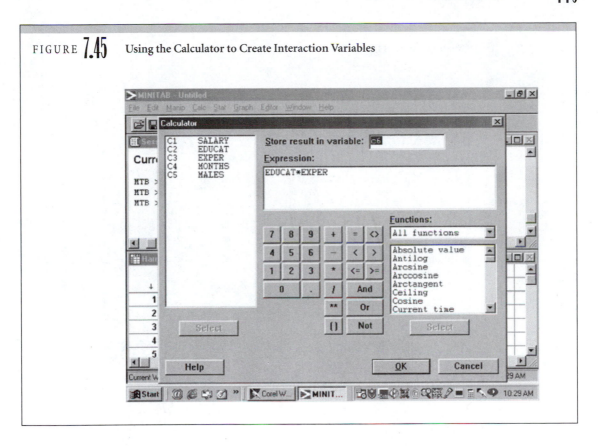

"To last value" box, and 1s in the "In steps of" and "List each value" boxes. In the "List the whole sequence" box, put the number of years of data you have available. This creates a variable with the sequence of numbers 1,2,3,4 for each year of data, thus numbering the quarters in each year 1 through 4 (see Figure 7.46). Now click on CALC: MAKE INDICATOR VARIABLES. Put the column number of the variable you just created in the "Indicator variables for" box and list four columns in the "Store results in" box. Click OK and the seasonal indicators are created. You can alter this process for monthly data by numbering the months from 1 to 12 and then creating 12 monthly indicators.

7.4.2   Excel

Creating and Using Indicator Variables

Indicator variables have values of either 0 or 1. Obviously, one way to create an indicator variable (or variables) is simply to type it into a data set. Logical if statements can be used to simplify the creation of indicators in some cases.

Consider the data in Table 7.2 for the Meddicorp example. The variable REGION was typed into the original data set. This variable numbers the three regions as 1, 2, or

FIGURE **7.46** Creating Seasonal Indicators

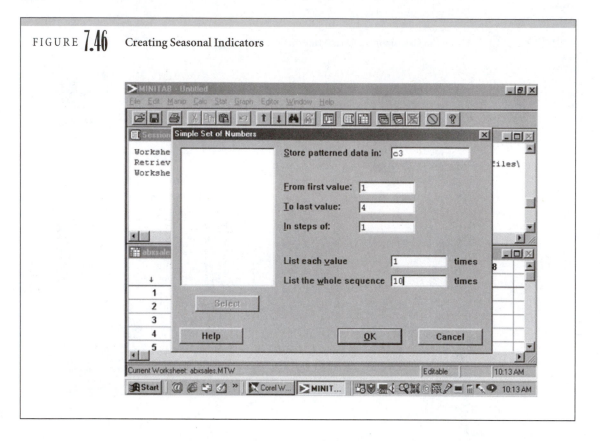

3. It can be used to create the indicator variables for the three regions after they are defined as follows:

SOUTH = 1 whenever REGION is 1 and 0 otherwise

WEST = 1 whenever REGION is 2 and 0 otherwise

MIDWEST = 1 whenever REGION is 3 and 0 otherwise

Suppose the REGION variable is in column D, as shown in Figure 7.47. The indicator SOUTH can be created as follows. In the first cell of the column where the SOUTH indicator is desired, type in the formula =if(d2=1,1,0). This formula puts 1 in the SOUTH column if the entry in cell d2 is 1; it puts 0 in the SOUTH column otherwise. Copy this formula down the SOUTH column. Now type the formula =if(d2=2,1,0) in the first cell of the WEST column. This formula puts 1 in the WEST column if the entry in cell d2 is 2; it puts 0 in the WEST column otherwise. Copy this formula down the WEST column. Now type the formula =if(d2=3,1,0) in the first cell of the MIDWEST column. This formula puts 1 in the MIDWEST column if the entry in cell d2 is a 3; it puts 0 in the MIDWEST column otherwise. Copy this formula down the MIDWEST column. This creates the three indicator variables.

FIGURE **7.47**   Creating Indicator Variables in Excel

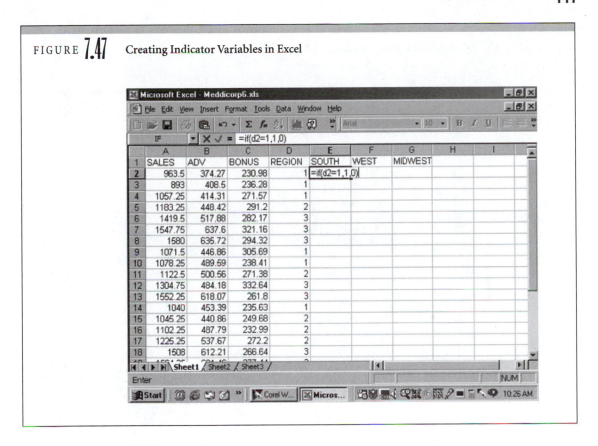

Creating and Using Interaction Variables

Interaction variables are created by multiplying one variable by another. This can be done in Excel by using formulas. Consider the example shown in Figure 7.48. To create an interaction variable between ADV and BONUS, type the formula =b2*c2 into the first cell of the interaction variable column. Then copy this formula down the column.

Creating and Using Seasonal Indicators for Time-Series Regression

To create quarterly seasonal indicators, follow this sequence: First, type in a variable that numbers the quarters 1 through 4 for each year. Then use the logical if statement to create the indicators. Consider the example shown in Figure 7.49. The column labeled "quarter" numbers the quarters of each year. In the column labeled Q1, type in the formula =if(c2=1,1,0). If cell c2 is 1, this results in 1 in the column for Q1. Otherwise, 0 is entered. Copy this formula down the column for Q1. In the column labeled Q2, type in the formula =if(c2=2,1,0). If cell c2 is 2, this results in 1 in the column for Q2. Otherwise, 0 is entered. Copy this formula down the column for Q2. Continue this process for each indicator variable. You can alter this process for monthly data by numbering the months from 1 to12 and then creating 12 monthly indicators.

FIGURE 7.48   Creating Interaction Variables in Excel

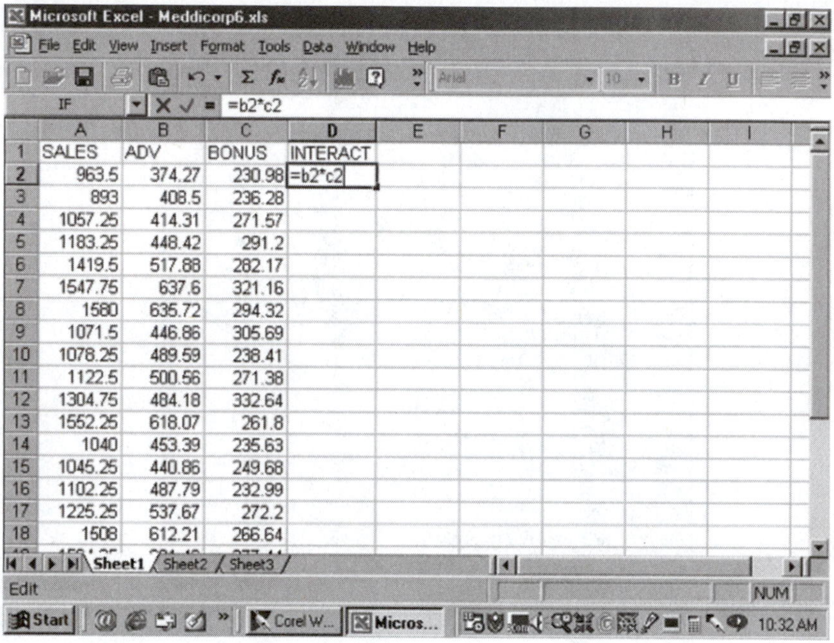

7.4.3 SAS

Creating and Using Indicator Variables

Indicator variables have values of either 0 or 1. Obviously, one way to create an indicator variable (or variables) is simply to type it into a data set. IF/THEN statements can be used to simplify the creation of indicator variables in some cases.

Consider the data in Table 7.2 for the Meddicorp example. The variable REGION was typed into the original data set. This variable numbers the three regions as 1, 2, or 3. It can be used to create the indicator variables for the three regions after they are defined as follows:

SOUTH   =   1 whenever REGION is 1 and 0 otherwise

WEST   =   1 whenever REGION is 2 and 0 otherwise

MIDWEST   =   1 whenever REGION is 3 and 0 otherwise

The three indicators can be created during the Input phase in SAS as follows:

INPUT SALES ADV BONUS REGION;
IF REGION = 1 THEN SOUTH = 1;

FIGURE **7.49**   Creating Quarterly Seasonal Indicator Variables in Excel

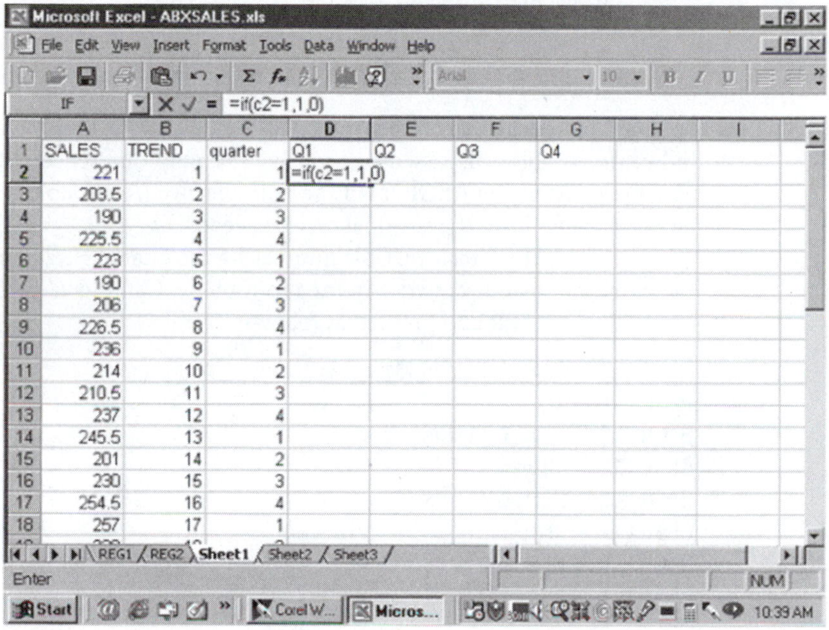

ELSE SOUTH = 0;
IF REGION = 2 THEN WEST = 1;
ELSE WEST = 0;
IF REGION = 3 THEN MIDWEST = 1;
ELSE MIDWEST = 0;

After creating the three indicator variables, any two of them can be used in PROC REG. For example,

PROC REG;
    MODEL SALES = ADV BONUS SOUTH WEST;

runs a regression with SALES as the dependent variable and ADV, BONUS, SOUTH, and WEST as independent variables.

Creating and Using Interaction Variables

Interaction variables are created by multiplying one variable by another. In SAS, such variable transformations are performed during the data input phase. For example, the following commands create the interaction variable called EDUCEXPR, which is the product of EDUCAT and EXPER:

```
INPUT SALARY EDUCAT EXPER MONTHS MALES;
EDUCEXPR = EDUCAT*EXPER;
```

The interaction variable, EDUCEXPR, can then be used in PROC REG, PROC PLOT, and so on, just like other variables.

Creating and Using Seasonal Indicators for Time-Series Regression

Seasonal indicators are simply indicator variables, and their creation is like that of indicator variables discussed previously. The only difference is that, instead of the variable representing REGION in the example given, a variable numbering the quarters or the months in the seasonal cycle is needed.

For quarterly data, a variable numbering the quarters 1,2,3, or 4 is used with the following command sequence in the input phase. Call the variable that numbers the quarters QUARTER and proceed as follows:

```
IF QUARTER = 1 THEN Q1 = 1;
ELSE Q1 = 0;
IF QUARTER = 2 THEN Q2 = 1;
ELSE Q2 = 0;
IF QUARTER = 3 THEN Q3 = 1;
ELSE Q3 = 0;
IF QUARTER = 4 THEN Q4 = 1;
ELSE Q4 = 0;
```

Q1, Q2, Q3, and Q4 are the four quarterly indicator variables. Three of these four can then be used in Proc Reg.

ADDITIONAL EXERCISES

6 Absenteeism In Exercise 11 in Chapter 4, data on 77 employees of the ABX Company were introduced. The dependent variable was absenteeism. The possible explanatory variables were defined in Table 4.14 and shown in Table 4.15.

In this exercise, use the following explanatory variables:

COMPLX = job complexity
SENINV = 1/SENIOR = the reciprocal of the seniority variable

Indicator variables are created from the variable SATIS. These variables are as follows:

FS1 = 1 if SATIS = 1 (very dissatisfied)
    = 0 otherwise

FS2 = 1 if SATIS = 2 (somewhat dissatisfied)
    = 0 otherwise

FS3 = 1 if SATIS = 3 (neither satisfied nor dissatisfied)
    = 0 otherwise

$$FS4 = \quad 1 \text{ if SATIS} = 4 \text{ (somewhat satisfied)}$$
$$= \quad 0 \text{ otherwise}$$

$$FS5 = \quad 1 \text{ if SATIS} = 5 \text{ (very satisfied)}$$
$$= \quad 0 \text{ otherwise}$$

Five indicator variables are created to represent all five supervisor satisfaction categories. Recall that only four need to be used in the regression. Run the regression with the explanatory variables shown here. Answer the following questions:

a Is there a difference in average absenteeism for employees in different supervisor satisfaction groups? Perform a hypothesis test to answer this question. State the hypotheses to be tested, the decision rule, the test statistic, and your decision. Use a 5% level of significance.

b Using the model chosen in part a (and keeping the variables COMPLX and SENINV in the model), what would be your estimate of the average absenteeism rate for all employees with COMPLX = 60 and SENIOR = 30 who were very dissatisfied with their supervisor? What if they were very satisfied with their supervisor, but COMPLX and SENIOR were the same values?

c How do you account for the differences in the estimates in part b?

d How could this equation be used to help identify employees who might be prone to absenteeism?

These data are available in a file with prefix ABSENT7 in four columns: ABSENT, COMPLX, SATIS, and SENIOR.

7 **Work-Order Closing** Management at the Texas Christian University (TCU) Physical Plant Department is interested in reducing the average time to completion of routine work orders. The time to completion is defined as the difference between the date of receipt of a work order and the date closing information is entered. The number of labor hours charged to each work order and the cost of materials are two variables believed to be related to the time to completion of the work order. Management wants to know if there is any difference in the time to completion of work orders, on average, for different types of buildings. Buildings are classified into four types on the TCU campus: residence halls, athletic, academic, and administrative. In answering the question, take into account the possible effect of labor hours charged and materials cost. The data for a random sample of 72 work orders (chosen from a population of 11,720) are shown in Table 7.6. The variables are labeled as follows:

$$y \quad = \text{DAYS} \quad = \quad \text{number of days to complete each work order}$$
$$x_1 \quad = \text{HOURS} \quad = \quad \text{number of hours of labor charged to each work order}$$
$$x_2 \quad = \text{MATERIAL} = \quad \text{cost of materials charged to each work order}$$
$$x_3 \quad = \text{BUILDING} = \quad \begin{array}{l} 1 \text{ for residence halls} \\ 2 \text{ for athletic buildings} \\ 3 \text{ for academic buildings} \\ 4 \text{ for administrative buildings} \end{array}$$

TABLE **7.6** Data for Work-Order Closing Exercise

DAYS	HOURS	MATERIAL	BUILDING	DAYS	HOURS	MATERIAL	BUILDING	DAYS	HOURS	MATERIAL	BUILDING
7	0.50	0	1	3	2.50	93	1	50	11.00	33	3
9	6.50	117	3	13	0.50	1	1	4	0.50	4	4
3	1.00	6	1	1	0.50	8	1	3	0.50	0	1
4	0.50	0	1	4	0.25	0	2	5	1.00	0	3
1	1.00	4	1	3	0.50	0	1	6	0.25	0	1
1	1.50	27	1	12	0.25	2	1	1	0.45	4	1
1	0.50	0	3	14	2.00	4	1	21	0.50	0	1
1	0.25	0	3	4	4.00	0	1	5	0.50	0	1
13	0.50	87	4	4	1.00	2	1	8	2.00	0	3
19	30.00	131	3	29	2.00	25	1	12	1.00	0	1
3	0.25	0	3	1	0.50	0	1	3	0.50	0	1
6	7.00	18	4	3	0.50	0	1	2	0.25	44	1
0	0.50	0	1	3	0.50	0	1	1	0.25	2	4
1	0.25	0	1	5	1.00	28	3	4	0.50	8	3
2	0.50	0	4	25	0.50	1350	2	3	0.75	6	1
2	1.00	6	1	1	0.50	4	1	1	0.50	0	2
1	3.50	6	1	30	0.50	3	1	1	0.50	0	4
1	0.50	0	1	1	0.75	13	1	1	0.50	0	1
1	0.50	0	3	5	0.50	0	3	1	0.50	4	1
1	0.25	0	1	7	0.25	0	3	3	1.00	10	3
1	0.25	10	4	10	0.50	0	3	1	0.50	0	1
29	2.75	4	1	1	1.00	139	4	2	1.00	13	3
7	1.00	242	4	2	0.25	0	1	17	1.50	0	3
5	0.25	2	4	1	2.00	14	3	3	0.50	1	3

These data are available in a file with prefix WORKORD7 in four columns: DAYS, HOURS, MATERIAL, and BUILDING.

8 Beer Production Table 7.7 shows monthly U.S. beer production in millions of barrels for January 1982 through December 1991.[2] Develop an extrapolative model for these data and use it to examine whether there is seasonal variation in beer production and whether beer production seems to be increasing, decreasing, or staying fairly constant over this time period. Use the model you select as best for beer production to forecast monthly production for each month in 1992.

The beer production data are available in a file with prefix BEER7 in one column.

[2] Data were obtained from *Business Statistics 1963–91* and *Survey of Current Business*.

TABLE 7.7   Data for Beer Production Exercise

Mo/Yr	Barrels (millions)	Mo/Yr	Barrels (millions)	Mo/Yr	Barrels (millions)	Mo/Yr	Barrels (millions)
1/82	15.19	7/84	18.64	1/87	15.60	7/89	18.28
2/82	15.00	8/84	17.59	2/87	15.63	8/89	18.88
3/82	17.65	9/84	14.58	3/87	17.66	9/89	15.28
4/82	17.62	10/84	15.14	4/87	17.42	10/89	15.82
5/82	18.22	11/84	13.06	5/87	17.44	11/89	14.78
6/82	18.19	12/84	12.89	6/87	18.59	12/89	13.45
7/82	17.17	1/85	15.50	7/87	18.09	1/90	16.46
8/82	19.50	2/85	14.46	8/87	16.81	2/90	15.74
9/82	15.64	3/85	16.76	9/87	15.82	3/90	17.97
10/82	15.07	4/85	17.97	10/87	15.50	4/90	17.48
11/82	13.65	5/85	18.86	11/87	13.18	5/90	18.10
12/82	13.31	6/85	18.23	12/87	13.69	6/90	18.58
1/83	14.77	7/85	18.59	1/88	15.80	7/90	18.25
2/83	14.56	8/85	17.71	2/88	15.85	8/90	18.96
3/83	16.78	9/85	14.54	3/88	17.12	9/90	16.08
4/83	15.54	10/85	14.36	4/88	17.73	10/90	16.62
5/83	18.17	11/85	13.12	5/88	18.31	11/90	15.44
6/83	18.47	12/85	13.13	6/88	18.58	12/90	13.97
7/83	18.50	1/86	15.71	7/88	18.17	1/91	16.27
8/83	18.27	2/86	15.21	8/88	17.72	2/91	15.17
9/83	15.71	3/86	16.50	9/88	15.78	3/91	16.08
10/83	15.30	4/86	17.99	10/88	15.61	4/91	17.23
11/83	13.62	5/86	18.67	11/88	14.02	5/91	18.90
12/83	12.46	6/86	18.65	12/88	13.32	6/91	19.16
1/84	14.15	7/86	18.33	1/89	15.88	7/91	19.88
2/84	14.75	8/86	17.06	2/89	15.29	8/91	18.63
3/84	17.72	9/86	15.26	3/89	17.57	9/91	16.11
4/84	16.81	10/86	15.62	4/89	17.30	10/91	16.65
5/84	18.59	11/86	13.53	5/89	18.41	11/91	14.47
6/84	18.47	12/86	13.97	6/89	18.82	12/91	13.64

TABLE 7.8   Average Monthly Temperatures for Dallas-Fort Worth

Mo/Yr	Temp (°F)	Mo/Yr	Temp (°F)	Mo/Yr	Temp (°F)	Mo/Yr	Temp (°F)
1/78	33.8	9/80	80.3	5/83	69.5	1/86	48.8
2/78	36.7	10/80	65.4	6/83	77.3	2/86	51.2
3/78	54.1	11/80	54.9	7/83	83.6	3/86	60.2
4/78	67.1	12/80	49.4	8/83	84.9	4/86	67.2
5/78	73.1	1/81	44.6	9/83	77.1	5/86	71.5
6/78	82.3	2/81	48.9	10/83	67.8	6/86	80.8
7/78	88.4	3/81	55.7	11/83	57.3	7/86	86.4
8/78	84.6	4/81	69.2	12/83	34.8	8/86	83.4
9/78	80.2	5/81	70.5	1/84	39.3	9/86	80.2
10/78	68.9	6/81	80.3	2/84	50.9	10/86	65.7
11/78	57.7	7/81	85.9	3/84	56.3	11/86	52.4
12/78	46.1	8/81	83.4	4/84	63.7	12/86	46.1
1/79	35.4	9/81	76.2	5/84	73.7	1/87	44.5
2/79	42.2	10/81	66.1	6/84	82.5	2/87	50.8
3/79	56.7	11/81	57.5	7/84	85.5	3/87	53.9
4/79	64.4	12/81	47.3	8/84	85.8	4/87	65.0
5/79	69.7	1/82	44.6	9/84	76.1	5/87	75.1
6/79	81.0	2/82	44.5	10/84	67.0	6/87	79.6
7/79	84.5	3/82	59.8	11/84	54.6	7/87	83.4
8/79	82.5	4/82	62.5	12/84	52.6	8/87	86.5
9/79	77.0	5/82	72.5	1/85	37.8	9/87	77.1
10/79	70.8	6/82	79.2	2/85	45.0	10/87	66.5
11/79	52.9	7/82	84.6	3/85	60.8	11/87	55.7
12/79	49.4	8/82	86.7	4/85	67.2	12/87	47.3
1/80	45.5	9/82	78.1	5/85	74.0	1/88	42.2
2/80	46.6	10/82	67.0	6/85	80.2	2/88	47.1
3/80	54.2	11/82	55.6	7/85	84.4	3/88	56.0
4/80	63.1	12/82	49.2	8/85	87.6	4/88	64.5
5/80	75.0	1/83	43.4	9/85	77.7	5/88	72.8
6/80	87.0	2/83	48.5	10/85	67.6	6/88	80.4
7/80	92.0	3/83	54.5	11/85	56.3	7/88	85.3
8/80	88.5	4/83	60.6	12/85	42.3	8/88	87.9

9   Monthly Temperatures   Lone Star Gas recognizes that one of the simplest and most effective ways to forecast natural gas use is with average monthly temperatures. A model can be developed that relates gas usage to average temperature, and then forecasts can be made based on forecasts of average temperatures in the area of interest. Lone Star first needs a model to forecast average temperatures in the Dallas-Fort

TABLE 7.8   (*continued*)

Mo/Yr	Temp (°F)	Mo/Yr	Temp (°F)	Mo/Yr	Temp (°F)	Mo/Yr	Temp (°F)
9/88	79.2	4/91	67.4	11/93	51.6	6/96	82.5
10/88	65.7	5/91	75.4	12/93	49.5	7/96	86.1
11/88	58.1	6/91	81.0	1/94	45.7	8/96	82.5
12/88	49.1	7/91	85.0	2/94	48.6	9/96	74.5
1/89	50.0	8/91	82.5	3/94	59.0	10/96	66.9
2/89	42.2	9/91	75.2	4/94	65.9	11/96	54.9
3/89	56.7	10/91	68.1	5/94	71.5	12/96	49.2
4/89	66.4	11/91	51.7	6/94	84.1	1/97	44.0
5/89	74.3	12/91	50.3	7/94	83.9	2/97	49.5
6/89	77.9	1/92	46.9	8/94	84.0	3/97	58.3
7/89	82.8	2/92	54.4	9/94	76.3	4/97	60.4
8/89	82.3	3/92	59.1	10/94	67.3	5/97	70.1
9/89	74.7	4/92	66.0	11/94	57.9	6/97	78.8
10/89	69.0	5/92	71.1	12/94	49.0	7/97	84.9
11/89	58.2	6/92	79.4	1/95	48.2	8/97	83.1
12/89	39.0	7/92	84.3	2/95	52.5	9/97	80.2
1/90	51.8	8/92	80.2	3/95	56.9	10/97	67.2
2/90	53.9	9/92	77.7	4/95	64.2	11/97	52.1
3/90	57.7	10/92	69.5	5/95	73.2	12/97	45.6
4/90	64.0	11/92	52.7	6/95	79.9	1/98	48.4
5/90	73.4	12/92	49.9	7/95	85.5	2/98	51.1
6/90	84.0	1/93	45.1	8/95	85.5	3/98	54.9
7/90	82.5	2/93	49.0	9/95	76.6	4/98	63.8
8/90	84.6	3/93	56.1	10/95	67.8	5/98	78.5
9/90	80.0	4/93	63.3	11/95	54.8	6/98	85.5
10/90	66.4	5/93	71.9	12/95	47.4	7/98	91.6
11/90	59.8	6/93	81.7	1/96	43.1	8/98	87.8
12/90	44.0	7/93	87.3	2/96	52.1	9/98	83.6
1/91	42.8	8/93	87.5	3/96	53.3	10/98	69.5
2/91	53.7	9/93	78.2	4/96	64.2	11/98	57.6
3/91	59.8	10/93	63.8	5/96	80.8	12/98	47.0

Worth area. Table 7.8 shows the average monthly temperatures for January 1978 to December 1998 for the Dallas-Fort Worth area.[3] Develop an extrapolative model for these data and use the model to forecast average monthly temperatures for each month in the years 1999 and 2000.

The temperature data are available in a file with prefix TEMPDFW7 in one column.

[3] Data were obtained from the Website www.srh.noaa.gov/fwd/clmdfw.html.

10 **BigTex Services** BigTex Services is undergoing scrutiny for a possible wage discrimination suit. As consulting statistician hired by the corporate lawyer, you are to examine data on BigTex employees to further investigate the charges. The data are shown in Table 7.9 and are as follows:

monthly salary for each employee (SALARY)

years with the company (YEARS)

position with the company (POSITION) coded as
    1 = manual labor
    2 = secretary
    3 = lab technician
    4 = chemist
    5 = management

amount of education completed (EDUCAT) coded as
    1 = high school degree
    2 = some college
    3 = college degree
    4 = graduate degree

gender (GENDER) coded as
    0 = female
    1 = male

What would you conclude from the data? Should BigTex Services be worried about possible wage discrimination charges? Why or why not?

These data are available in a file with prefix BIGTEX7 in five columns: SALARY, YEARS, POSITION, EDUCAT, and GENDER.

11 **FOC Sales** Techcore is a high-tech company located in Fort Worth, Texas. The company produces a part called a fibre-optic connector (FOC) and wants to generate reasonably accurate but simple forecasts of the sales of FOC's over time. They have weekly sales data for 265 weeks starting in January of 1995. These data are shown in Table 6.1. (The data have been disguised to provide confidentiality.) The time-series plot of FOC sales is shown in Figure 6.30. You are to build an extrapolative regression model to forecast FOC sales. You can refer to the analyses shown in Examples 6.3 and 6.4 for help. Do you detect any "seasonal" patterns where the use of indicator variables might be useful?

The weekly sales data are in a file with prefix FOC7.

12 **Fort Worth Crime** In the early 1990s, a concerted effort was put into place to revitalize downtown Fort Worth, Texas. This was a combined effort involving both the city and private investors. The city police and private security coordinated their communications networks. New entertainment and dining establishments were located in the area. Buildings were refurbished and remodeled. Prior to this time, the downtown area had experienced high crime rates. Because of police and private security efforts

TABLE 7.9   Data for BigTex Services Exercise

SALARY	YEARS	POSITION	EDUCAT	GENDER	SALARY	YEARS	POSITION	EDUCAT	GENDER
1720	6.0	3	2	0	1650	2.2	1	1	1
2400	4.9	1	1	1	2200	2.0	4	3	1
1600	4.2	2	2	0	900	0.5	3	1	0
2900	3.7	4	3	0	1000	0.5	3	2	0
1200	1.6	3	1	0	1220	2.0	3	1	0
1000	0.3	3	1	0	2100	0.5	4	3	1
2900	1.0	4	3	1	900	0.5	3	1	0
2400	1.8	4	3	1	900	0.2	3	1	0
1900	6.8	3	1	0	2000	0.5	4	3	1
2200	1.2	4	3	1	2330	0.6	4	3	1
1000	0.3	3	1	0	2400	0.3	4	3	1
900	0.2	3	1	0	900	1.0	1	1	1
1250	0.6	3	1	0	1069	0.5	3	1	0
950	0.5	3	1	0	1400	0.5	1	1	1
2000	0.7	4	3	1	1650	1.0	1	1	1
2000	1.9	4	3	1	1200	0.3	1	1	1
1900	1.6	1	1	1	3500	13.5	5	4	1
1000	1.4	3	1	0	1750	11.0	5	3	0
1000	1.4	3	1	0	4000	6.4	5	3	1
2800	3.4	4	3	0	1800	7.2	2	1	0
2900	3.5	4	3	1	4000	6.1	5	3	1
1550	3.1	3	1	0	4600	5.8	5	4	1
1550	3.0	2	1	0	1350	5.1	4	5	1
2200	2.5	4	3	1					

beginning in the summer of 1992, there is interest in determining whether these interventions had a significant effect in decreasing crime in downtown Fort Worth. You are to use an extrapolative regression model to examine the data and to produce a report for the city of Fort Worth outlining your findings regarding any changes in the downtown crime rate. The report should be written in two parts: an executive summary outlining your findings and a technical report to support those findings.

There are eight columns of data as shown in Table 7.10. The variables included are YR/MONTH, which gives the year and month of the observation and the number of monthly occurrences of crimes in the categories shown: MURDER, RAPE, ROBBERY, ASSAULT, BURGLARY, LARCENY and AUTO THEFT. These data are in a file with prefix FWCRIME7.

TABLE 7.10   Data for Fort Worth Crime Exercise

YR/MONTH	MURDER	RAPE	ROBBERY	ASSAULT	BURGLARY	LARCENY	AUTO THEFT
8801	0	2	6	6	25	93	37
8802	0	5	5	5	23	113	44
8803	0	1	5	12	29	132	26
8804	0	2	12	8	34	108	38
8805	0	3	9	18	39	113	29
8806	1	3	9	11	44	127	40
8807	0	1	14	15	40	102	39
8808	0	3	16	18	43	117	32
8809	0	2	11	22	38	111	33
8810	1	1	9	13	21	115	35
8811	0	1	6	10	27	137	20
8812	1	0	8	5	24	119	35
8901	0	0	12	13	33	120	46
8902	0	2	4	18	20	69	29
8903	0	0	4	10	21	85	32
8904	0	0	6	12	23	108	30
8905	0	1	6	14	34	111	18
8906	0	1	10	8	22	101	36
8907	0	5	9	22	31	113	33
8908	3	2	13	7	28	107	17
8909	0	3	13	11	37	144	25
8910	0	1	7	11	21	137	49
8911	0	1	6	14	24	92	32
8912	1	1	7	11	16	100	34
9001	0	1	5	9	30	126	22
9002	0	1	4	9	25	104	45
9003	2	1	9	16	31	101	44
9004	0	1	13	17	13	103	31
9005	0	2	10	21	19	119	24
9006	1	1	7	27	19	86	31
9007	0	5	7	32	16	89	40
9008	0	3	8	24	15	120	54
9009	1	2	12	18	20	105	43
9010	0	0	8	20	21	100	30
9011	0	2	10	10	25	116	30
9012	0	1	11	6	16	89	37
9101	0	2	5	9	20	105	24
9102	0	0	4	11	15	76	17
9103	0	0	10	27	27	124	25

TABLE 7.10   (*continued*)

YR/MONTH	MURDER	RAPE	ROBBERY	ASSAULT	BURGLARY	LARCENY	AUTO THEFT
9104	0	2	7	16	18	112	35
9105	0	5	12	17	24	104	49
9106	0	2	14	19	26	110	65
9107	0	3	11	23	33	133	66
9108	0	1	14	28	33	123	63
9109	0	1	14	11	14	103	51
9110	1	1	13	14	17	90	49
9111	0	0	8	24	18	84	51
9112	1	1	8	14	26	106	70
9201	0	4	9	10	28	121	58
9202	0	1	17	15	41	123	31
9203	1	2	12	19	27	114	75
9204	0	2	13	16	15	103	34
9205	1	0	10	23	20	97	30
9206	1	1	7	15	23	118	37
9207	4	1	15	29	38	132	49
9208	0	1	9	11	25	108	36
9209	0	0	9	17	25	82	34
9210	1	2	8	18	23	86	34
9211	0	1	6	7	21	74	33
9212	0	0	9	9	14	76	25
9301	0	1	3	2	13	81	18
9302	0	1	9	8	15	61	17
9303	0	0	7	7	17	57	18
9304	0	3	2	9	17	89	18
9305	0	0	7	9	7	89	19
9306	0	1	5	9	18	66	10
9307	0	2	6	4	12	77	15
9308	0	1	4	12	15	72	12
9309	0	0	7	14	13	64	13
9310	0	4	8	5	29	94	13
9311	0	1	2	4	21	65	24
9312	0	1	5	8	16	69	14
9401	0	2	9	6	16	50	9
9402	1	0	10	11	8	70	12
9403	0	1	3	10	15	65	9
9404	0	0	11	4	14	76	6

Continues

TABLE **7.10** (*continued*)

YR/MONTH	MURDER	RAPE	ROBBERY	ASSAULT	BURGLARY	LARCENY	AUTO THEFT
9405	1	0	3	11	8	62	19
9406	0	2	7	15	21	66	11
9407	0	0	3	5	15	71	16
9408	0	0	10	14	10	43	8
9409	0	0	2	9	11	50	12
9410	0	0	8	5	13	77	9
9411	0	1	14	9	13	74	10
9412	0	0	4	7	13	76	7
9501	0	1	1	9	12	71	11
9502	0	0	4	5	7	42	10
9503	0	0	4	9	7	48	8
9504	0	0	5	3	15	56	14
9505	1	1	4	1	19	68	10
9506	0	3	2	6	11	50	3
9507	0	0	3	7	12	47	13
9508	0	2	2	8	7	64	16
9509	0	1	3	7	12	57	5
9510	0	0	7	9	11	44	9

13 Rangers' Attendance The Texas Rangers major league baseball team needs your help. They are interested in determining key identifiable variables that affect attendance at games played at the Ballpark in Arlington. They have provided you with an extensive data set including the following variables:

Date: The date of the game played

Weekday: The day of the week, coded as 1 = Monday, 2 = Tuesday, ... , 7 = Sunday

Promotion: Equal to 1 if there was a special promotion (Dollar Decker Dog Night, Half Price Group Night, and so on); equal to 0 if there was no special promotion

Wins: The cumulative number of wins for the Rangers prior to playing the game

Ahead: Equal to 1 if the Rangers were ahead in their division when the game was played; equal to zero otherwise

Attendance: The attendance at all home games for the years 1994 through 1998; this provides a total of 375 observations

School: Equal to 1 if public schools were in session; equal to zero otherwise

Opponent: Coded as

1   =   New York

2   =   Baltimore

3   =   Cleveland

4   =   Chicago

5   =   Anaheim

6   =   Minnesota

7   =   Any National League team (coded this way since the teams played vary from year to year)

8   =   Oakland

9   =   Detroit

10   =   Seattle

11   =   Toronto

12   =   Milwaukee

13   =   Kansas City

14   =   Boston

NightGame: Equal to 1 for a night game; 0 for a day game

The data are presented in Table 7.11. The variables are in a file with prefix RANGERS7 in the order shown above.

TABLE 7.11   Data for Rangers' Attendance Exercise

Date	Weekday	Promotion	Wins	Ahead	Attendance	School	Opponent	NightGame
4/11/1994	1	1	1	0	46056	1	12	0
4/13/1994	3	1	2	0	45455	1	12	1
4/14/1994	4	0	2	0	34427	1	12	1
4/15/1994	5	1	3	0	37760	1	2	1
4/16/1994	6	1	3	0	46607	1	2	1
4/17/1994	7	0	3	0	29228	1	2	1
4/22/1994	5	1	4	0	31346	1	3	1
4/23/1994	6	1	4	0	44926	1	3	1
4/24/1994	7	1	4	0	33924	1	3	0
4/26/1994	2	0	5	0	22995	1	9	1
4/27/1994	3	0	6	1	38055	1	11	1
4/28/1994	4	0	7	1	27287	1	11	1
5/6/1994	5	1	11	0	38370	1	6	1
5/7/1994	6	1	11	0	42519	1	6	1
5/8/1994	7	1	11	0	32663	1	6	0

Continues

TABLE 7.11 (*continued*)

Date	Weekday	Promotion	Wins	Ahead	Attendance	School	Opponent	NightGame
5/9/1994	1	0	12	0	35407	1	5	1
5/10/1994	2	0	12	0	24054	1	5	1
5/11/1994	3	0	12	1	33647	1	5	1
5/13/1994	5	1	13	1	39420	1	4	1
5/14/1994	6	1	14	0	46490	1	4	1
5/15/1994	7	1	14	0	46419	1	4	0
5/27/1994	5	1	19	0	43761	1	14	1
5/28/1994	6	0	19	0	46396	0	14	1
5/29/1994	7	1	20	1	46354	0	14	0
6/6/1994	1	1	25	0	36733	0	1	1
6/7/1994	2	0	26	0	42461	0	1	1
6/8/1994	3	0	27	0	32574	0	1	1
6/9/1994	4	0	28	0	46433	0	13	1
6/10/1994	5	1	29	0	46379	0	13	1
6/11/1994	6	0	29	0	46582	0	13	1
6/12/1994	7	0	29	0	39844	0	13	1
6/13/1994	1	1	30	0	38363	0	10	1
6/14/1994	2	0	30	0	37483	0	10	1
6/15/1994	3	0	30	0	35450	0	10	0
6/16/1994	4	1	30	0	39599	0	8	1
6/17/1994	5	0	30	0	44936	0	8	1
6/18/1994	6	0	30	0	46422	0	8	1
6/19/1994	7	1	30	0	46153	0	8	1
7/1/1994	5	0	35	1	40852	0	9	1
7/2/1994	6	0	36	0	46665	0	9	1
7/3/1994	7	0	37	0	46164	0	9	1
7/4/1994	1	1	38	0	46265	0	9	1
7/5/1994	2	0	39	0	33012	0	3	1
7/6/1994	3	1	39	0	46490	0	3	1
7/7/1994	4	1	40	0	38904	0	3	1
7/14/1994	4	0	42	0	42621	0	11	1
7/15/1994	5	0	42	0	46511	0	11	1
7/16/1994	6	0	43	0	46510	0	11	1
7/17/1994	7	1	43	0	46394	0	11	1
7/25/1994	1	0	46	0	46506	0	6	1
7/26/1994	2	0	47	0	37412	0	6	1
7/27/1994	3	0	47	0	35364	0	6	1
7/28/1994	4	1	48	0	46580	0	5	1
7/29/1994	5	0	49	0	44011	0	5	1

TABLE **7.11**   (*continued*)

Date	Weekday	Promotion	Wins	Ahead	Attendance	School	Opponent	NightGame
7/30/1994	6	0	49	0	46679	0	5	1
7/31/1994	7	0	49	0	34910	0	5	1
8/2/1994	2	0	49	0	45152	0	4	1
8/3/1994	3	0	50	0	38319	0	4	1
8/4/1994	4	1	51	0	46362	0	4	1
8/8/1994	1	0	51	0	32708	0	10	1
8/9/1994	2	0	51	0	36937	0	10	1
8/10/1994	3	0	51	0	38892	0	10	1
4/27/1995	4	1	0	0	32161	1	3	1
4/28/1995	5	1	0	0	22179	1	3	1
4/29/1995	6	1	1	0	28048	1	3	1
4/30/1995	7	1	1	0	26026	1	3	0
5/1/1995	1	1	1	0	19104	1	10	1
5/2/1995	2	1	1	0	17983	1	10	1
5/3/1995	3	1	1	0	17375	1	10	1
5/12/1995	5	0	5	0	21393	1	9	1
5/13/1995	6	1	6	0	31160	1	9	1
5/14/1995	7	1	6	0	21182	1	9	0
5/15/1995	1	0	7	0	17982	1	11	1
5/16/1995	2	0	8	0	19014	1	11	1
5/17/1995	3	0	9	0	18910	1	11	1
5/18/1995	4	0	10	0	22776	1	12	1
5/19/1995	5	0	10	0	23393	1	12	1
5/20/1995	6	0	11	0	30161	1	12	1
5/21/1995	7	1	12	0	27521	1	12	0
6/1/1995	4	0	18	0	23934	1	6	1
6/2/1995	5	0	19	0	24306	1	6	1
6/3/1995	6	1	19	0	35236	1	6	1
6/4/1995	7	1	20	0	24402	1	6	0
6/5/1995	1	0	20	0	22448	1	13	1
6/6/1995	2	0	21	0	25135	0	13	1
6/7/1995	3	1	22	0	28175	0	13	1
6/8/1995	4	0	23	0	20425	0	13	1
6/9/1995	5	1	24	0	36354	0	4	1
6/11/1995	7	0	25	0	32045	0	4	1
6/23/1995	5	0	30	0	33625	0	8	1
6/24/1995	6	0	31	1	40204	0	8	1
6/25/1995	7	1	31	0	32758	0	8	1

Continues

TABLE 7.11 *(continued)*

Date	Weekday	Promotion	Wins	Ahead	Attendance	School	Opponent	NightGame
6/26/1995	1	0	31	0	22497	0	8	1
6/27/1995	2	0	32	1	26246	0	5	1
6/28/1995	3	0	33	0	38053	0	5	1
6/29/1995	4	1	33	1	38280	0	5	1
7/6/1995	4	1	36	0	33934	0	1	1
7/7/1995	5	0	37	1	35435	0	1	1
7/8/1995	6	0	37	0	45645	0	1	1
7/9/1995	7	1	38	1	31893	0	1	0
7/17/1995	1	0	41	0	26410	0	2	1
7/18/1995	2	0	41	0	31837	0	2	1
7/19/1995	3	1	41	0	42928	0	3	1
7/20/1995	4	0	41	0	28160	0	3	0
7/28/1995	5	0	42	0	39199	0	14	1
7/29/1995	6	1	42	0	46717	0	14	1
7/30/1995	7	1	43	0	37219	0	14	1
8/8/1995	2	0	47	0	27760	0	9	1
8/9/1995	3	0	48	0	22680	0	9	1
8/10/1995	4	1	49	0	32084	0	9	1
8/11/1995	5	0	49	0	31269	0	11	1
8/12/1995	6	0	50	0	40040	0	11	1
8/13/1995	7	1	51	0	25308	0	11	1
8/15/1995	2	0	52	0	21591	0	12	1
8/16/1995	3	0	52	0	29617	0	12	1
8/21/1995	1	0	56	0	26213	0	6	1
8/22/1995	2	0	56	0	21065	0	6	1
8/23/1995	3	0	57	0	23435	0	6	1
9/1/1995	5	0	58	0	21864	0	13	1
9/2/1995	6	1	59	0	32888	0	13	1
9/3/1995	7	0	59	0	32811	0	13	1
9/4/1995	1	0	59	0	18036	0	4	1
9/5/1995	2	0	59	0	18001	0	4	1
9/6/1995	3	0	59	0	22415	0	4	1
9/7/1995	4	0	60	0	9046	0	4	1
9/22/1995	5	0	68	0	25081	0	5	1
9/23/1995	6	0	69	0	36675	0	5	1
9/24/1995	7	0	69	0	24202	0	5	0
9/26/1995	2	0	70	0	19257	0	8	1
9/27/1995	3	0	71	0	18369	0	8	1
9/28/1995	4	0	71	0	21502	0	10	1

TABLE 7.11   (*continued*)

Date	Weekday	Promotion	Wins	Ahead	Attendance	School	Opponent	NightGame
9/29/1995	5	0	71	0	25336	0	10	1
9/30/1995	6	0	72	0	33792	1	10	1
10/1/1995	7	0	73	0	25714	1	10	0
4/1/1996	1	1	0	1	40484	1	14	0
4/3/1996	3	1	1	1	24483	1	14	1
4/4/1996	4	0	2	1	18086	1	14	1
4/6/1996	6	1	3	1	35510	1	1	1
4/7/1996	7	1	4	1	36248	1	1	1
4/15/1996	1	0	5	0	19312	1	8	1
4/16/1996	2	0	7	0	20948	1	8	1
4/17/1996	3	1	8	0	24120	1	8	1
4/19/1996	5	1	9	1	41184	1	2	1
4/20/1996	6	1	10	1	45358	1	2	1
4/21/1996	7	1	11	1	39456	1	2	0
4/22/1996	1	1	12	1	22348	1	4	1
4/23/1996	2	0	12	1	29123	1	4	1
4/30/1996	2	0	15	1	27272	1	10	1
5/1/1996	3	1	16	1	31775	1	10	1
5/7/1996	2	0	20	1	23005	1	11	1
5/8/1996	3	0	21	1	20694	1	11	1
5/9/1996	4	1	21	1	34451	1	11	1
5/10/1996	5	0	22	1	31426	1	9	1
5/11/1996	6	1	23	1	42732	1	9	1
5/12/1996	7	1	23	1	35677	1	9	1
5/13/1996	1	1	24	1	22981	1	13	1
5/14/1996	2	0	25	1	28999	0	13	1
5/15/1996	3	0	25	1	26881	0	13	1
5/27/1996	1	1	30	1	46521	0	3	1
5/28/1996	2	0	31	1	35727	0	3	1
5/29/1996	3	0	32	1	35893	0	3	1
5/31/1996	5	0	33	1	32861	0	6	1
6/1/1996	6	1	33	1	43413	0	6	1
6/2/1996	7	0	33	1	33809	0	6	0
6/7/1996	5	1	35	1	40046	0	11	1
6/8/1996	6	0	36	1	43439	0	11	1
6/9/1996	7	1	37	1	41605	0	11	0
6/10/1996	1	1	38	1	43275	0	12	1
6/11/1996	2	0	38	1	33519	0	12	1

Continues

TABLE 7.11 (*continued*)

Date	Weekday	Promotion	Wins	Ahead	Attendance	School	Opponent	NightGame
6/12/1996	3	0	39	1	34842	0	12	0
6/21/1996	5	0	43	1	40726	0	14	1
6/22/1996	6	0	44	1	46414	0	14	1
6/23/1996	7	0	44	1	39399	0	14	1
6/24/1996	1	1	44	1	39701	0	2	1
6/25/1996	2	0	45	1	41685	0	2	1
6/26/1996	3	0	46	1	38984	0	2	1
7/4/1996	4	1	49	1	46668	0	10	1
7/5/1996	5	1	49	1	46397	0	10	1
7/6/1996	6	1	49	1	46458	0	10	1
7/7/1996	7	1	50	1	36933	0	10	1
7/15/1996	1	1	52	1	45655	0	5	1
7/16/1996	2	0	53	1	34680	0	5	1
7/17/1996	3	1	54	1	44220	0	5	1
7/18/1996	4	0	54	1	28585	0	8	1
7/19/1996	5	0	54	1	37455	0	8	1
7/20/1996	6	0	55	1	46062	0	8	1
7/21/1996	7	1	55	1	36039	0	8	1
7/30/1996	2	0	59	1	39637	0	1	1
7/31/1996	3	0	60	1	30645	0	1	1
8/1/1996	4	0	60	1	34855	0	1	1
8/2/1996	5	0	60	1	36299	0	4	1
8/3/1996	6	0	60	1	46481	0	4	0
8/4/1996	7	1	61	1	32854	0	4	1
8/5/1996	1	0	61	1	29973	0	4	1
8/12/1996	1	1	66	1	25210	0	9	1
8/13/1996	2	0	67	1	31331	0	9	1
8/14/1996	3	1	68	1	33942	0	9	1
8/16/1996	5	0	69	1	32053	0	13	1
8/17/1996	6	0	69	1	41855	0	13	0
8/18/1996	7	1	70	1	30480	0	13	1
8/30/1996	5	1	75	1	40383	1	3	1
8/31/1996	6	0	76	1	46319	1	3	1
9/1/1996	7	1	76	1	46084	1	3	0
9/2/1996	1	1	76	1	24786	1	6	0
9/3/1996	2	1	77	1	28401	1	6	1
9/4/1996	3	1	77	1	29744	1	6	1
9/12/1996	4	1	82	1	41303	1	12	1
9/13/1996	5	1	82	1	39235	1	12	1

TABLE **7.11**   (*continued*)

Date	Weekday	Promotion	Wins	Ahead	Attendance	School	Opponent	NightGame
9/14/1996	6	1	82	1	45901	1	12	1
9/15/1996	7	1	83	1	45941	1	12	0
9/26/1996	4	1	87	1	33895	1	5	1
9/27/1996	5	1	87	1	46764	1	5	1
9/28/1996	6	1	88	1	45651	1	5	1
9/29/1996	7	1	89	1	45434	1	5	0
4/1/1997	2	1	0	1	45098	1	12	0
4/4/1997	5	1	0	0	26058	1	2	1
4/5/1997	6	1	0	0	39073	1	2	1
4/6/1997	7	1	1	0	36156	1	2	0
4/14/1997	1	1	3	0	27891	1	4	1
4/15/1997	2	1	4	0	27990	1	4	1
4/18/1997	5	1	6	0	30452	1	11	1
4/19/1997	6	1	6	0	44206	1	11	1
4/20/1997	7	1	7	0	34333	1	11	0
4/21/1997	1	1	7	0	21562	1	9	1
4/23/1997	3	1	8	0	35230	1	9	1
4/24/1997	4	1	9	0	31902	1	9	0
5/2/1997	5	1	13	0	35338	1	14	1
5/3/1997	6	0	14	0	43557	1	14	1
5/4/1997	7	1	15	0	37294	1	14	0
5/12/1997	1	1	19	1	25327	1	3	1
5/13/1997	2	1	19	0	31798	1	3	1
5/14/1997	3	1	20	0	30268	1	3	1
5/15/1997	4	0	20	0	35488	1	1	1
5/16/1997	5	0	21	1	42420	1	1	1
5/17/1997	6	0	21	1	46625	1	1	1
5/18/1997	7	1	22	1	46850	1	1	0
5/20/1997	2	1	23	1	29745	1	8	1
5/21/1997	3	1	23	1	42312	0	8	1
5/22/1997	4	1	24	1	36204	0	8	0
5/30/1997	5	1	27	1	35606	0	13	1
5/31/1997	6	0	28	1	43769	0	13	1
6/1/1997	7	1	28	1	45831	0	13	0
6/2/1997	1	1	29	1	32347	0	6	1
6/3/1997	2	0	29	1	28620	0	6	1
6/12/1997	4	1	31	0	46507	0	7	1
6/13/1997	5	1	32	0	44168	0	7	1

Continues

TABLE 7.11   (*continued*)

Date	Weekday	Promotion	Wins	Ahead	Attendance	School	Opponent	NightGame
6/14/1997	6	0	33	0	44288	0	7	1
6/15/1997	7	0	34	0	34765	0	7	1
6/19/1997	4	1	35	0	45572	0	10	1
6/20/1997	5	0	35	0	46013	0	10	1
6/21/1997	6	0	35	0	46193	0	10	1
6/22/1997	7	0	35	0	40814	0	10	1
6/23/1997	1	1	35	0	41984	0	5	1
6/24/1997	2	1	35	0	36914	0	5	1
6/25/1997	3	1	36	0	42863	0	5	0
7/2/1997	3	1	39	0	38569	0	7	1
7/3/1997	4	0	40	0	38907	0	7	1
7/4/1997	5	1	41	0	46934	0	8	1
7/5/1997	6	0	42	0	43612	0	8	1
7/6/1997	7	1	42	0	38361	0	8	1
7/16/1997	3	1	45	0	45313	0	11	1
7/17/1997	4	1	45	0	46239	0	11	1
7/18/1997	5	0	45	0	35074	0	9	1
7/19/1997	6	0	45	0	45025	0	9	1
7/20/1997	7	0	46	0	33655	0	9	1
7/21/1997	1	1	46	0	35842	0	2	1
7/22/1997	2	1	46	0	43421	0	2	1
7/23/1997	3	1	46	0	40834	0	2	1
8/1/1997	5	0	49	0	44859	0	3	1
8/2/1997	6	0	49	0	44920	0	3	1
8/3/1997	7	1	50	0	42303	0	3	1
8/4/1997	1	1	50	0	29601	0	14	1
8/5/1997	2	1	50	0	36289	0	14	1
8/6/1997	3	1	51	0	34067	0	1	1
8/7/1997	4	1	51	0	39918	0	1	1
8/18/1997	1	1	59	0	28637	1	12	1
8/19/1997	2	1	59	0	28982	1	12	1
8/20/1997	3	1	59	0	33531	1	12	1
8/22/1997	5	0	60	0	33353	1	4	1
8/23/1997	6	0	61	0	46090	1	4	1
8/24/1997	7	1	61	0	27441	1	4	1
9/2/1997	2	0	64	0	31506	1	7	1
9/3/1997	3	1	65	0	33116	1	7	1
9/11/1997	4	1	67	0	33996	1	6	1
9/12/1997	5	1	68	0	29461	1	6	1

TABLE **7.11**   (*continued*)

Date	Weekday	Promotion	Wins	Ahead	Attendance	School	Opponent	NightGame
9/13/1997	6	0	69	0	34760	1	6	1
9/14/1997	7	0	69	0	25923	1	6	0
9/15/1997	1	1	69	0	25377	1	13	1
9/16/1997	2	1	70	0	22714	1	13	1
9/17/1997	3	1	71	0	30467	1	10	1
9/18/1997	4	0	71	0	30697	1	10	1
9/19/1997	5	1	71	0	31809	1	5	1
9/20/1997	6	1	71	0	38902	1	5	1
9/21/1997	7	1	71	0	35308	1	5	0
3/31/1998	2	1	0	0	45909	1	4	0
4/2/1998	4	1	0	0	32662	1	4	1
4/10/1998	5	1	4	1	32314	1	11	1
4/11/1998	6	1	4	1	37520	1	11	1
4/12/1998	7	1	5	1	28435	1	11	0
4/13/1998	1	1	6	1	28671	1	9	1
4/14/1998	2	1	7	1	24409	1	9	1
4/15/1998	3	1	8	1	24085	1	9	1
4/17/1998	5	1	9	1	37415	1	2	1
4/18/1998	6	0	9	1	43883	1	2	1
4/19/1998	7	1	10	1	43037	1	2	0
4/21/1998	2	0	11	1	26776	1	7	1
4/22/1998	3	1	12	1	30770	1	7	1
4/23/1998	4	1	12	1	33319	1	7	0
5/5/1998	2	1	18	1	31693	1	1	1
5/6/1998	3	1	18	1	33274	1	1	1
5/7/1998	4	1	18	1	28504	1	3	1
5/8/1998	5	0	19	1	38067	1	3	1
5/9/1998	6	0	20	1	46355	1	3	1
5/10/1998	7	1	21	1	31232	1	3	1
5/11/1998	1	1	22	1	40275	1	14	1
5/12/1998	2	1	23	1	39614	1	14	0
5/19/1998	2	0	26	1	37258	0	10	1
5/20/1998	3	0	27	1	29454	0	10	1
5/21/1998	4	0	28	1	34613	0	10	1
5/22/1998	5	1	29	1	38411	0	13	1
5/23/1998	6	0	30	1	46372	0	13	1
5/24/1998	7	1	30	1	46243	0	13	0
5/25/1998	1	1	30	1	30887	0	6	1

Continues

TABLE 7.11 (*continued*)

Date	Weekday	Promotion	Wins	Ahead	Attendance	School	Opponent	NightGame
5/27/1998	3	1	30	1	32657	0	6	0
6/5/1998	5	1	35	1	37903	0	7	1
6/6/1998	6	0	36	1	46022	0	7	1
6/7/1998	7	1	36	1	46372	0	7	0
6/12/1998	5	0	38	1	35505	0	5	1
6/13/1998	6	0	38	1	46289	0	5	1
6/14/1998	7	1	39	1	36648	0	5	1
6/15/1998	1	1	39	1	43380	0	5	1
6/16/1998	2	1	39	0	34066	0	8	1
6/17/1998	3	1	39	0	31052	0	8	1
6/18/1998	4	1	40	0	35930	0	8	0
6/22/1998	1	1	41	0	37840	0	7	1
6/23/1998	2	0	42	0	31904	0	7	1
6/30/1998	2	0	45	0	37873	0	7	1
7/1/1998	3	1	45	0	28928	0	7	1
7/2/1998	4	1	45	0	38514	0	7	1
7/3/1998	5	0	45	0	45233	0	10	1
7/4/1998	6	1	46	0	46067	0	10	1
7/5/1998	7	0	47	0	38053	0	10	1
7/15/1998	3	1	50	0	46682	0	2	1
7/16/1998	4	1	50	0	45171	0	2	1
7/17/1998	5	0	51	0	33876	0	7	1
7/18/1998	6	0	52	0	44356	0	7	1
7/19/1998	7	1	53	1	34700	0	7	1
7/31/1998	5	0	56	1	38846	0	4	1
8/1/1998	6	0	57	1	42425	0	4	1
8/2/1998	7	1	58	1	28175	0	4	1
8/4/1998	2	1	59	1	45213	0	11	1
8/5/1998	3	1	60	1	27766	0	11	1
8/6/1998	4	1	61	1	32132	0	14	1
8/7/1998	5	0	62	1	34906	0	14	1
8/8/1998	6	0	62	1	44242	0	14	1
8/9/1998	7	1	62	1	31127	0	14	1
8/19/1998	3	1	65	0	26146	0	3	1
8/20/1998	4	1	66	0	37094	0	3	1
8/21/1998	5	0	66	0	45841	0	1	1
8/22/1998	6	0	66	0	46483	0	1	1
8/23/1998	7	0	67	0	37284	0	1	1
8/24/1998	1	1	68	0	24544	0	9	1

TABLE 7.11   (*continued*)

Date	Weekday	Promotion	Wins	Ahead	Attendance	School	Opponent	NightGame
8/25/1998	2	1	68	0	23378	0	9	1
8/26/1998	3	1	69	0	22618	0	9	1
9/4/1998	5	1	74	0	25580	1	6	1
9/5/1998	6	1	74	0	38581	1	6	1
9/6/1998	7	1	74	0	35328	1	6	1
9/7/1998	1	1	75	0	24519	1	6	0
9/8/1998	2	1	76	0	22336	1	13	1
9/9/1998	3	1	77	0	28441	1	13	1
9/16/1998	3	1	80	0	37481	1	5	1
9/17/1998	4	0	81	1	45928	1	5	1
9/18/1998	5	1	82	1	40874	1	8	1
9/19/1998	6	1	82	1	46036	1	8	1
9/20/1998	7	1	82	1	37606	1	8	0

Reprinted courtesy of the Texas Rangers organization and Major League Baseball.

CHAPTER 8

Variable Selection

8.1 INTRODUCTION

One of the primary tasks discussed in this text has been choosing which variables to include in the regression equation. Several hypothesis tests have been suggested to aid in this task. The F test for overall fit of the regression, the partial F test, and the t test are all designed to help decide whether certain variables should be included in the regression.

Several additional procedures, usually called *variable selection techniques*, also can be used to help choose which variables are important. These procedures are discussed in this chapter. The importance of choosing the correct variables is highlighted by examining what happens when either (a) important variables are omitted from the regression equation or (b) unimportant variables are included in the equation.

If an important variable is omitted from the regression, the effect of this variable is not taken into account. The estimates of the other regression coefficients become biased (either systematically too high or too low). Forecasts generated by the regression are also biased.

If an unimportant variable is included in the regression equation, the standard errors of the coefficients and forecasts become inflated. Thus, forecasts and coefficient estimates are more variable than they would be with a proper choice of variables. The larger standard errors may also make results from inferences less dependable.

Whether identifying important variables to be included or unimportant variables to be deleted, variable choice is an important aspect of regression analysis. As a result, considerable work has been done in developing methods to help choose the "best" group of variables to include in the regression equation. A word of caution is in order before these techniques are introduced, however. None of these methods is guaranteed to automatically pick the best of all regression models. Otherwise, this text could have started with these procedures and stopped after one chapter.

Any regression analysis requires considerable input from the researcher performing the analysis. This person must define the problem to be solved, determine what variables might be useful in the regression equation, obtain data on these variables, and set up the data to be analyzed in a data file. During the analysis itself, the researcher must check the regression assumptions to ensure that none have been violated. The automatic methods do not do that. For example, if $\ln(y)$ rather than y is the appropriate dependent variable for analysis, the variable selection procedures cannot determine this. The functional form of the relationship must be determined separately from the use of these procedures. In fact, any correction for a violation of one of the assumptions of regression must be determined by the researcher. These methods also cannot suggest explanatory variables to add to the regression unless they have been initially determined by the researcher and included in the data set.

Finally, none of these automatic procedures has the ability to use the researcher's knowledge of the business or economic situation being analyzed. This knowledge should be used to help establish what form the regression model takes, what variables should be included, and so on. This knowledge of the theory associated with the subject being analyzed is important. In many cases in business and economics, theoretical results are available that suggest what variables should be included in a relationship or what functional form the relationship should have. This theory will be provided throughout other courses in your business or economics major. Be sure to examine the theory in that field for suggestions that may help in building a model for your data.

The variable selection techniques discussed here are tools to aid the researcher in sifting through a number of explanatory variables to determine which one(s) he or she feels should be included in the regression equation. With the knowledge that the techniques cannot be reliably applied without the judgment of the person researching the problem and the use of subject matter theory, the following variable selection procedures are discussed in this chapter:

1   all possible regressions (along with several criteria to choose which is the best regression)

2   backward elimination

3   forward selection

4   stepwise regression

8.2   ALL POSSIBLE REGRESSIONS

One of the possible variable selection techniques suggested to aid in choosing the best regression model is called *all possible regressions*. As the name suggests, the procedure is designed to run all possible regressions between the dependent variable and all possible subsets of explanatory variables. For example, if the three possible explanatory variables identified for consideration in the problem are denoted x_1, x_2, and x_3, then a total of eight possible regressions may be best. The possible regressions include the following subsets of the three explanatory variables:

1   no variables
2   x_1
3   x_2
4   x_3
5   x_1 and x_2
6   x_1 and x_3
7   x_2 and x_3
8   all three variables

The all possible regressions procedure evaluates each of these regressions and prints out summary statistics to aid in choosing which of the eight possibilities is best. The choice of the criterion to use and the final choice of a model are then up to the researcher. Two commonly used criteria to help in choosing between the alternative regressions are:

1   R^2 (adjusted or unadjusted, as the researcher prefers)
2   C_p

The coefficient of determination, R^2, has been discussed extensively in previous chapters, but the statistic C_p has not. C_p measures the total mean square error of the fitted values of the regression. The total mean square error involves two components: one resulting from random error and one resulting from bias. When there is no bias in the estimated regression model, the expected value of C_p is equal to p, which, in the notation of this text, is equal to $K + 1$, the number of coefficients to be estimated. When evaluating which regression is best, it is recommended that regressions with small C_p values and those with values near $K + 1$ be considered. If the value of C_p is large, then the mean square error of the fitted values is large, indicating either a poor fit, substantial bias in the fit, or both. If the value of C_p is much greater than $K + 1$, then there is a large bias component in the regression, usually indicating omission of an important variable.

The formula for computing C_p is

$$C_p = \frac{SSE_p}{MSE_F} - (n - 2p)$$

where SSE_p is the error sum of squares for the regression with p ($p = K + 1$) coefficients to be estimated and MSE_F is the mean square error for the model with all possible explanatory variables included.

Although the C_p measure is highly recommended as a useful criterion in choosing between alternate regressions, keep in mind that the bias is measured with respect to the total group of variables provided by the researcher. This criterion cannot determine when the researcher has forgotten about some variable not included in the total group. In other words, the input of the researcher is still important. The all possible regressions procedure is illustrated in the following example.

EXAMPLE 8.1 ## Meddicorp Revisited

Consider again Example 4.1, the study of sales in the Meddicorp Company. The complete data set for this example is shown in Table 8.1 with descriptions of each variable as follows:

y, Meddicorp's sales (in thousands of dollars) in each territory for 1999 (SALES)

x_1, the amount (in hundreds of dollars) that Meddicorp spent on advertising in each territory in 1999 (ADV)

x_2, the total amount of bonuses paid (in hundreds of dollars) in each territory in 1999 (BONUS)

x_3, the market share currently held by Meddicorp in each territory (MKTSHR)

x_4, the largest competitor's sales (in thousands of dollars) in each territory (COMPET)

x_5, a variable coded to indicate the region in which each territory is located: 1 = SOUTH, 2 = WEST, and 3 = MIDWEST (REGION)

The REGION variable was transformed to a set of three possible indicator variables—SOUTH, WEST, and MIDWEST—in Chapter 7. The interpretation of the coefficients of these variables was preferred to the single REGION variable. Recall from Chapter 7, however, that indicator variables should be treated as a group rather than individually. The all possible regressions technique combines each indicator variable with each other possible combination of variables. To keep the indicator variables grouped together, they are not included as possible explanatory variables in the all possible regressions procedure. Instead, they are examined later as a group (this also greatly reduces the amount of computation necessary and simplifies this example).

Figure 8.1 presents a summary of results for all possible regressions. These were run in MINITAB and simply are summarized here. MINITAB and Excel do not have all possible regressions procedures. Some statistical packages (SAS, for example) do. The summary measures included are: R^2, R^2_{adj}, C_p, and the standard error of the regression, s_e. These are descriptive measures that are often used to evaluate individual regression equations and to compare different equations. The R^2 does not compensate for the number of variables in the model, but the other three measures do. For this reason, the latter three measures are often considered more reliable for comparing equations with different numbers of variables.

Note that only 15 of the 16 ($2^4 = 16$) possible regressions are shown in the summary. The missing one is the "regression" with no variables included, which would be chosen as best only if none of the possible explanatory variables were linearly related to the dependent variable.

The researcher now must use the summary measures along with subject matter knowledge to choose from among the possible regressions. Recall that small values of C_p and values close to p are of interest in choosing good sets of explanatory variables. The smallest C_p value is for a two-variable regression. This is the regression with ADV and BONUS as explanatory variables; it has a C_p value of 1.61 and explains 85.5% of the variation in sales ($R^2 = 85.5\%$). As competing models, for example, there are two three-variable models with relative small C_p values:

Variables	R^2	R^2_{adj}
ADV, BONUS, COMPET	85.7%	83.6
ADV, BONUS, MKTSHR	85.8%	83.8

TABLE **8.1**　　　**Data for Meddicorp Example**

Territory	SALES	ADV	BONUS	MKTSHR	COMPET	REGION
1	963.50	374.27	230.98	33.	202.22	1
2	893.00	408.50	236.28	29.	252.77	1
3	1057.25	414.31	271.57	34.	293.22	1
4	1183.25	448.42	291.20	24.	202.22	2
5	1419.50	517.88	282.17	32.	303.33	3
6	1547.75	637.60	321.16	29.	353.88	3
7	1580.00	635.72	294.32	28.	374.11	3
8	1071.50	446.86	305.69	31.	404.44	1
9	1078.25	489.59	238.41	20.	394.33	1
10	1122.50	500.56	271.38	30.	303.33	2
11	1304.75	484.18	332.64	25.	333.66	3
12	1552.25	618.07	261.80	34.	353.88	3
13	1040.00	453.39	235.63	42.	262.88	1
14	1045.25	440.86	249.68	28.	333.66	2
15	1102.25	487.79	232.99	28.	232.55	2
16	1225.25	537.67	272.20	30.	273.00	2
17	1508.00	612.21	266.64	29.	323.55	3
18	1564.25	601.46	277.44	32.	404.44	3
19	1634.75	585.10	312.35	36.	283.11	3
20	1159.25	524.56	292.87	34.	222.44	1
21	1202.75	535.17	268.27	31.	283.11	2
22	1294.25	486.03	309.85	32.	242.66	2
23	1467.50	540.17	291.03	28.	333.66	3
24	1583.75	583.85	289.29	27.	313.44	3
25	1124.75	499.15	272.55	26.	374.11	2

Note that only modest increases in R^2 are achieved in these models. The adjusted R^2 is highest for the two-variable model, again supporting this model as best. Other models with small C_p values could be examined, but there appears to be little bias in the two-variable model with ADV and BONUS (the small deviation of C_p from p probably results from random variation), and it has the smallest C_p value, largest adjusted R^2, and smallest standard error. Therefore, the all possible regressions procedure suggests using this model.

The number of computations involved in the all possible regressions technique is very large. This is a limiting factor in using this procedure, especially when no specific procedure is provided to do the computations. (Even in the SAS all possible regressions procedure, it is recommended that no more than 14 explanatory variables be used in a single analysis.) Because the all possible

FIGURE 8.1   Summary Results for All Possible Regressions

Variables in the Regression	R^2	R^2_{adj}	C_p	s_e
ADV	81.1%	80.2	5.90	101.42
BONUS	32.3%	29.3	75.19	191.76
COMPET	14.2%	10.5	100.85	100.80
MKTSHR	0.0%	0.0	120.97	232.97
ADV, BONUS	85.5%	84.2	1.61	90.75
ADV, MKTSHR	81.2%	79.5	7.66	103.23
ADV, COMPET	81.2%	79.5	7.74	103.38
BONUS, COMPET	38.7%	33.2	68.03	186.51
BONUS, MKTSHR	32.8%	26.7	76.46	195.33
MKTSHR, COMPET	16.1%	8.5	100.18	218.20
ADV, BONUS, MKTSHR	85.8%	83.8	3.11	91.75
ADV, BONUS, COMPET	85.7%	83.6	3.33	92.26
ADV, MKTSHR, COMPET	81.3%	78.6	9.59	105.52
BONUS, MKTSHR, COMPET	40.9%	32.5	66.95	187.48
ADV, BONUS, MKTSHR, COMPET	85.9%	83.1	5.00	93.77

FIGURE 8.2   MINITAB Best Subsets Results Using Default Number (2) of Regression Shown

```
Response is SALES

                                    M C
                                  B K O
                                  O T M
                                  A N S P
                    Adj.          D U H E
 Vars   R-Sq   R-Sq    C-p      s V S R T

   1    81.1   80.2    5.9   101.42  X
   1    32.3   29.3   75.2   191.76    X
   2    85.5   84.2    1.6   90.749  X X
   2    81.2   79.5    7.7   103.23  X   X
   3    85.8   83.8    3.1   91.751  X X X
   3    85.7   83.6    3.3   92.255  X X   X
   4    85.9   83.1    5.0   93.770  X X X X
```

FIGURE **8.3**   **MINITAB Best Subsets Results Using Maximum Number (5) of Regression Shown**

```
Response is SALES
```

Vars	R-Sq	Adj. R-Sq	C-p	s	MBOADUV	CKOTNSUSR	COMMPHRT

Vars	R-Sq	Adj. R-Sq	C-p	s	A D V	B O T N S U R	M B K O O T M S P U H E S R T
1	81.1	80.2	5.9	101.42	X		
1	32.3	29.3	75.2	191.76		X	
1	14.2	10.5	100.8	215.83			X
1	0.1	0.0	121.0	232.97		X	
2	85.5	84.2	1.6	90.749	X X		
2	81.2	79.5	7.7	103.23	X	X	
2	81.2	79.5	7.7	103.38	X		X
2	38.7	33.2	68.0	186.51		X X	
2	32.8	26.7	76.5	195.33	X X		
3	85.8	83.8	3.1	91.751	X X X		
3	85.7	83.6	3.3	92.255	X X	X	
3	81.3	78.6	9.6	105.52	X	X X	
3	40.9	32.5	66.9	187.48	X X X		
4	85.9	83.1	5.0	93.770	X X X X		

regressions procedure is so computationally intensive, several alternatives have been suggested. One that is available in MINITAB is called best subsets regression.

In MINITAB, best subsets regression first examines all one-predictor regression models and then selects the two models giving the largest R^2. MINITAB displays information on these models, examines all two-predictor models, selects the two models with the largest R^2, and displays information on these two models. This process continues until the model contains all predictors.

The best subsets procedure applied to the Meddicorp data produces the results shown in Figure 8.2. By default, MINITAB only prints out the regressions for the two subsets with the highest R^2 values for each number of explanatory variables. Requests for as many as five subsets are allowed. The results of the best subsets procedure asking for the five best subsets to be shown are given in Figure 8.3. Note that five best subsets are not available for all combinations of explanatory variables. Note also that this procedure is not the same as all possible regressions since not all regressions are shown even if the default of five subsets is used (unless there are three or fewer possible explanatory variables).

8.3 OTHER VARIABLE SELECTION TECHNIQUES

As noted in the previous section, the all possible regressions technique becomes computationally unwieldy when the number of possible explanatory variables is large. The techniques examined in this section attempt to cut down on the computational expense while still choosing variables that are important in explaining variation in the dependent variable.

Three procedures are discussed in this section:

1 backward elimination

2 forward selection

3 stepwise regression

Again, it should be stressed that none of these procedures is guaranteed to produce the best possible regression equation. The judgment of the researcher as well as careful examination of scatterplots, residual plots, and regression diagnostics are vital in choosing an appropriate model. The stepwise techniques are merely tools to help the researcher sort through a large number of possible explanatory variables. They help identify some important variables but by themselves are not sufficient to produce a good regression model.

8.3.1 Backward Elimination

The *backward elimination* procedure begins with a regression on all possible explanatory variables. After this regression is run, the explanatory variables are examined to determine which one has the smallest partial F statistic value. Calling this variable x_k, the following hypothesis test is performed:

$$H_0: \quad \beta_k = 0$$

$$H_a: \quad \beta_k \neq 0$$

The decision rule is:

Reject H_0 if $F > F_c$

Accept H_0 if $F \leq F_c$

where F_c represents some critical value chosen as a cutoff for the test. If H_0 is rejected, the coefficient is judged to be nonzero, and the variable is considered important in the relationship. Because the partial F statistics for all other coefficients are known to exceed the partial F statistic for β_k, the null hypothesis is rejected for these coefficients also. The backward elimination procedure terminates at this point and produces summary statistics of the chosen regression.

On the other hand, if the null hypothesis is accepted, then the variable is deleted from the equation, and a new regression is run with one less explanatory variable. The procedure is repeated until the null hypothesis is rejected, at which point the procedure terminates.

In this way, the backward elimination procedure sorts through the list of possible explanatory variables, eliminating those that are of little importance in explaining the variation in y and keeping those that are important. Importance is judged by the size of the partial F statistic for testing $H_0: \beta_k = 0$ relative to some critical value.

Two additional aspects of this procedure to note are:

1　Although the test was described as a partial F test, it can just as easily be thought of as a t test. Rather than the partial F statistic, the t statistic is used and the decision rule is

Reject H_0 if $t > t_c$ or $t < -t_c$

Accept H_0 if $-t_c \leq t \leq t_c$

where t_c is the chosen critical value. The t test and the partial F test for a *single* coefficient are equivalent, as was discussed in Chapter 4, as long as the same levels of significance are used for both tests.

2　Another way the test could be performed is by using p values. Whether the t or F statistic is computed, the p value could be calculated and compared to the decision rule:

Reject H_0 if p value $< \alpha$

Accept H_0 if p value $\geq \alpha$

where α is the chosen level of significance. When using p values, the critical value is α while with the t or F tests, it is a value chosen from the t or F tables. The p value form of the test is a better choice, if available, because the level of significance used to determine whether a variable stays or goes is the same regardless of the sample size or the number of variables in the equation. When a single t or F critical value is chosen, level of significance varies depending on the sample size and number of variables.

Example 8.2 demonstrates the backward elimination procedure as well as the other procedures. First, however, the remaining techniques are discussed.

8.3.2　Forward Selection

Forward selection starts by examining the list of possible explanatory variables and computing a simple regression for each one. The partial F statistic (or t statistic or the p value) is computed for the slope coefficient in each of these regressions, and the variable with the largest partial F statistic is noted. The hypothesis test

$H_0: \quad \beta_k = 0$

$H_a: \quad \beta_k \neq 0$

is conducted just as was done in the backward elimination procedure. If the null hypothesis is accepted, then the conclusion is that x_k is of no importance to the regression, and none of the other variables are important because they have smaller partial F statistics. The forward selection procedure terminates at this point.

If the null hypothesis is rejected, then x_k is judged important and is retained in the regression. Next, each remaining variable is examined to determine which one will have the largest partial F statistic if added to the regression that already contains x_k. The hypothesis test is performed for the added variable, and the decision is made either to keep the variable in the regression or to discard it. When no more variables are judged to have nonzero coefficients, the procedure terminates and summary statistics are printed.

8.3.3 Stepwise Regression

The *stepwise regression* procedure combines elements of both backward elimination and forward selection. It begins like forward selection by examining the list of all possible explanatory variables in simple regressions and choosing the one with the largest partial F statistic. The hypothesis test for significance is performed, and if the variable is judged important, this variable is added to the model. Each of the remaining variables is then examined. The variable with the largest partial F statistic is chosen, and the hypothesis test for significance is performed on the coefficient of this variable to determine whether it should be added to the model. If the variable is judged important, it is added as in the forward selection procedure.

At this point, however, the stepwise procedure begins to act like the backward elimination procedure. After adding a new variable to the model, the stepwise procedure retests the coefficients of the previously added variables, deleting these variables if the test judges them to be unnecessary and retaining them otherwise. Because the addition of one variable can result in a change in the partial F statistic associated with another variable, it is possible for the stepwise procedure to allow a variable to enter the equation at one step, delete the variable at a later step, and even allow the variable to reenter at an even later step.

Once none of the remaining out-of-equation variables test as significant and all of the variables in the equation are judged to be necessary, the stepwise regression procedure terminates.

8.4 WHICH VARIABLE SELECTION PROCEDURE IS BEST?

In an attempt to identify the best set of variables for a regression model, several techniques have been examined. This leaves the user to decide which technique is best for his or her purposes. As noted, none of the techniques examined is guaranteed to find the best possible regression model. The judgment of the researcher, including incorporation of relevant theory and subject matter knowledge, and careful examination of scatterplots, residual plots, and regression diagnostics are vital in choosing an appropriate model. With this caveat in mind, several trade-offs must be considered when choosing the variable selection technique to be used.

The all possible regressions technique is considered the best because it examines every possible model, given a certain list of variables. From the summary statistics such as R^2 and C_p, the researcher can decide which model is best. Note that even with the all possible regressions technique, a single best model might not be identifiable. There may be several competing models that have nearly identical summary statistics, leaving the researcher with the task of using judgment in choosing between these similar best models. This should not be looked upon as a drawback, however, but as a benefit. With a variety of models from which to chose, the researcher has more freedom to pick the one, say, with the most easily obtainable data or the simplest interpretation.

The remaining procedures are not as highly favored as variable selection procedures, but they do have one advantage over all possible regressions: computational cost. The all possible regressions procedure can be very expensive in terms of the computer time needed to produce a solution. If the variable list is a very large one, the researcher may be forced to avoid all possible regressions in favor of one of the computationally less expensive methods. As is shown in Example 8.2, the forward selection, backward elimination, and stepwise regression procedures can be useful in identifying important variables. Research, however, has shown that these procedures can also choose unimportant variables for inclusion in the regressions by chance and may miss important variables. Thus, some caution must be exercised in their use. Among the three procedures, the stepwise regression and backward elimination procedures are very similar. The forward selection procedure is generally considered the least reliable of the techniques.

EXAMPLE **8.2**   ## Meddicorp Once Again

Figure 8.4 shows the MINITAB backward elimination output when applied to the Meddicorp data. The forward selection output is shown in Figure 8.5, and the stepwise output is in Figure 8.6. The indicator variables have not been included in these analyses because these variables are treated as a group rather than individually.

The MINITAB outputs summarize the results of each step of these variable selection procedures in a column. For example, in the backward elimination output shown in Figure 8.4, the variables included in the model are in the left-hand column. In the column numbered Step 1, a summary of the regression equation at the first step is given. The estimated equation is

$$\text{SALES} = -593.5 + 2.51\text{ADV} + 1.91\text{BONUS} + 2.70\text{MKTSHR} - 0.12\text{COMPET}$$

Below the estimated coefficients in the columns are the t ratios for testing $H_0: \beta_k = 0$. At the bottom of the column are the standard error of the regression and the R^2 (unadjusted). The variable with the smallest partial F statistic (or t ratio) is chosen: COMPET. The hypothesis test

$$H_0: \quad \beta_k = 0$$

$$H_a: \quad \beta_k \neq 0$$

is performed, and the null hypothesis is accepted. COMPET is removed from the regression, and a new equation is estimated. This regression is summarized in the Step 2 column. This process continues until the null hypothesis $H_0: \beta_k = 0$ is rejected for all remaining variables. The last column (Step 3 in this example) shows the result of the final regression.

FIGURE 8.4   MINITAB Output for Backward Elimination

```
F-to-Enter: 100000.00  F-to-Remove:    4.00

Response is SALES  on 4 predictors, with N = 25

        Step          1          2          3
    Constant     -593.5     -620.6     -516.4

    ADV             2.51       2.47       2.47
    T-Value         8.00       8.87       8.98

    BONUS           1.91       1.90       1.86
    T-Value         2.57       2.62       2.59

    MKTSHR          2.7        3.1
    T-Value         0.57       0.72

    COMPET         -0.12
    T-Value        -0.32

    S              93.8       91.8       90.7
    R-Sq          85.92      85.85      85.49
```

For the three procedures available in MINITAB (backward elimination, forward selection, and stepwise regression), a value of 4 is used as the critical value for all partial F tests. This is the default critical value—that is, the value chosen by MINITAB if no other value is provided. The researcher can enter his or her own choice for a critical value. The procedure for doing this is discussed in Section 8.5, Using the Computer.

The justification for the partial F test cutoff value of 4 is that this results in a test with a 5% level of significance (approximately) if a large number of observations are available. When using any of these three procedures, it is often recommended that a smaller cutoff value be used, say, $F_c = 2$ or $F_c = 1$. After examining the variables chosen by the procedure(s) at this critical value, the researcher is left to make the final choice about which variables should remain in the model.

Combining all information gathered from the all possible regressions procedure and the various stepwise procedures, the best model appears to be

$$SALES = -516.4 + 2.47ADV + 1.86BONUS$$

Before concluding, recall that the indicator variables for the region have not been included in any of this analysis. They could be added to the regression at this point to see whether they

FIGURE **8.5**   MINITAB Output for Forward Selection

```
F-to-Enter:   4.00  F-to-Remove:   0.00

Response is SALES on 4 predictors, with N = 25

      Step        1       2
   Constant   -157.3   -516.4

   ADV          2.77     2.47
   T-Value      9.92     8.98

   BONUS                 1.86
   T-Value               2.59

   S             101     90.7
   R-Sq        81.06    85.49
```

FIGURE **8.6**   MINITAB Output for Stepwise Regression

```
F-to-Enter:   4.00  F-to-Remove:   4.00

Response is SALES on 4 predictors, with N = 25

      Step        1       2
   Constant   -157.3   -516.4

   ADV          2.77     2.47
   T-Value      9.92     8.98

   BONUS                 1.86
   T-Value               2.59

   S             101     90.7
   R-Sq        81.06    85.49
```

FIGURE 8.7   MINITAB Output for Model Including Indicator Variables

```
The regression equation is
SALES = 435 + 1.37 ADV + 0.975 BONUS - 258 SOUTH - 210 WEST

Predictor        Coef        StDev          T           P
Constant        435.1       206.2        2.11        0.048
ADV            1.3678       0.2622        5.22        0.000
BONUS          0.9752       0.4808        2.03        0.056
SOUTH         -257.89       48.41        -5.33        0.000
WEST          -209.75       37.42        -5.61        0.000

S = 57.63       R-Sq = 94.7%       R-Sq(adj) = 93.6%

Analysis of Variance

Source               DF         SS          MS           F           P
Regression            4    1182560      295640       89.03       0.000
Residual Error       20      66414        3321
Total                24    1248974

Source        DF       Seq SS
ADV            1      1012408
BONUS          1        55389
SOUTH          1        10435
WEST           1       104328

Unusual Observations
Obs       ADV       SALES        Fit     StDev Fit      Residual      St Resid
 11       484      1304.7     1421.7         37.0        -117.0        -2.65R
 22       486      1294.2     1192.3         27.7         102.0         2.02R

R denotes an observation with a large standardized residual
```

improve the model. The MINITAB regression output with the indicators included is shown in Figure 8.7. The partial F test to test the hypotheses

$$H_0: \quad \beta_3 = \beta_4 = 0$$

$$H_a: \quad \text{At least one of } \beta_3 \text{ and } \beta_4 \text{ is not equal to zero}$$

can be used to determine whether the indicator variables improve the model. The null hypothesis is rejected, and the conclusion is to retain the indicator variables as well.

8.5   USING THE COMPUTER

The Using the Computer section in each chapter describes how to perform the computer analyses in the chapter using MINITAB, Excel, and SAS. For further detail on MINITAB, Excel, and SAS, see Appendix C.

8.5.1   MINITAB

Note that Version 12 of MINITAB is fully menu driven. Commands can be used, however, and they are included for any interested users. The menu headings and subheadings used to perform the procedures are listed first, followed by commands in parentheses. For example, STAT: REGRESSION: BEST SUBSETS means to click on the STAT menu, then on REGRESSION, and then on BEST SUBSETS. (Breg C_, C_, ...,C_ is a command to be typed in.)

Best Subsets Regression

```
STAT: REGRESSION: BEST SUBSETS (BREG C_, C_,...,C_)
```

MINITAB has a procedure that is similar to the all possible regressions approach discussed in this chapter. To use the best subsets procedure, click on STAT, then on REGRESSION from the STAT menu, and then on BEST SUBSETS. The Best Subsets dialog box is shown in Figure 8.8. Fill in the "Response" variable (y) and the "Free predictors (x variables) and click OK. Use "Predictors in all models" if you want certain x variables to be included in all regressions. Options allows, among other things, the choice of from one to five subsets to be shown in the results. (The command BREG C_, C_, ...,C_ performs best subsets regression. The first column listed is the y variable. All other columns are used as x variables. The BEST K subcommand determines how many subset regressions are shown.)

Backward elimination, forward selection, and stepwise regression are all run from the STEPWISE option on the REGRESSION menu. Figure 8.9 shows the stepwise regression dialog box.

Stepwise Regression

```
STAT: REGRESSION: STEPWISE
```

For stepwise regression, fill in the "Response" variable (y) and the names of the x variables in the "Predictors" box (Figure 8.9). Then click OK. Default critical values of 4.0 are used in MINITAB (see Figure 8.10) for entry and removal of variables. These critical values can be altered as desired (as shown under Backward Elimination and Forward Selection, changing the critical values is how these methods are produced). It is often suggested that critical values of 1.0 be used on a first pass through the data. This smaller critical value allows the inclusion of more variables in the regression initially.

FIGURE **8.8**   MINITAB Best Subsets Dialog Box

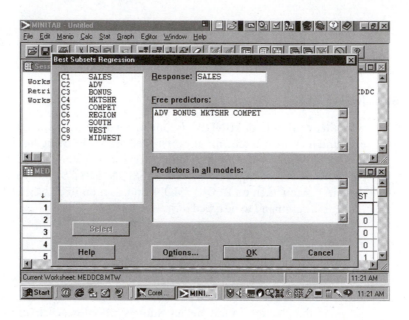

FIGURE **8.9**   MINITAB Stepwise Regression Dialog Box

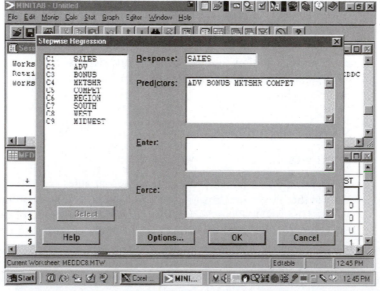

FIGURE 8.10   MINITAB Stepwise—Options Dialog Box

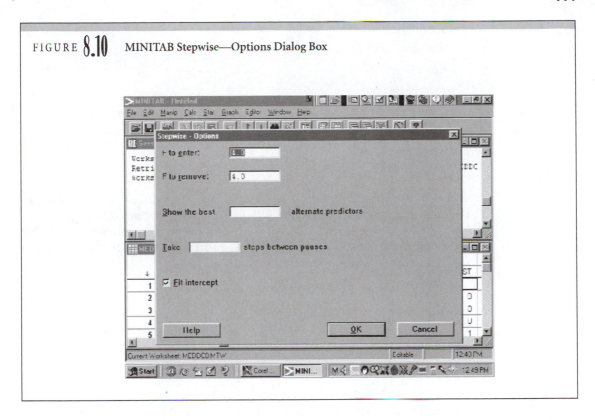

The researcher can then use theory or judgment to decide whether the inclusion of weaker variables is justified. (The stepwise command is STEPWISE C_, C_, . . . C_, where the first column listed is *y* and the remaining columns are *x* variables. The FENTER= and FREMOVE= subcommands can be used to change the critical values.)

Backward Elimination

STAT: REGRESSION: STEPWISE

For backward elimination, fill in the "Response" variable (*y*) and the names of the *x* variables in the "Predictors" box and again in the "Enter" box (Figure 8.9). (The Enter box is left empty for forward selection and stepwise regression.) Now click on Options, and the dialog box shown in Figure 8.10 opens. The backward elimination option is requested by making sure that, once a variable leaves the regression, it never reenters. This is accomplished by making the "F to enter" a very large number. I use 100000. No variable can ever produce a coefficient with a partial *F* statistic this large, so no variable can ever be a candidate to reenter the regression. Since variables leave the regression but never reenter, this is the backward elimination procedure. Note that you have to fill in the *x* variables in the "Enter" box. This tells MINITAB what variables to start with in the equation. If you do not do this, it starts with no variables, and because the "F to enter" value is set so high, no variables enter. This produces a pretty boring regression.

(For backward elimination, use the commands

>Stepwise C_, C_, ... C_ ;
>
>Enter C_, ... ,C_;
>
>Fenter=100000.

where the first column listed is *y* and the remaining columns are *x* variables.)

Forward Selection

STAT: REGRESSION: STEPWISE

For forward selection, fill in the "Response" variable (*y*) and the names of the *x* variables in the "Predictors" box (Figure 8.9). In the stepwise options dialog box (Figure 8.10), leave the "F to enter" value at 4.0, but change the "F to remove" value to 0.0. Once a variable enters the regression, it never leaves because the "F to remove" value is set at 0.0. (For forward selection, use the commands

>STEPWISE C_, C_, ... C_ ;
>
>ENTER=0.

where the first column listed is *y* and the remaining columns are *x* variables.)

8.5.2 SAS

In SAS, the PROC REG command can be used to request all possible regressions, backward elimination, forward selection, and stepwise. The choice of variable selection procedure is made using the SELECTION option in the MODEL statement. Each of the choices is demonstrated here.

All Possible Regressions

```
PROC REG CP;
    MODEL SALES = ADV BONUS MKTSHR COMPET/SELECTION = RSQUARE;
```

This command sequence produces all possible regressions output for the dependent variable SALES and independent variables ADV, BONUS, MKTSHR, and COMPET. The CP option requests that the C_p value associated with each regression be printed. In addition, the R^2 value (unadjusted) is printed. The MODEL statement works just like it does for PROC REG. The dependent variable is listed to the left of the equal sign, and the possible explanatory variables are listed to the right. The SELECTION = RSQUARE option requests all possible regressions.

Stepwise Regression

```
PROC REG;
    MODEL SALES = ADV BONUS MKTSHR COMPET/SELECTION = STEPWISE;
```

Control of the variables to enter or leave the regression is through the *p* values for the partial *F* test (rather than the *F* critical values as in MINITAB). SLENTRY represents the maximum p value the coefficient of a variable can have and still have the variable enter the model. SLSTAY represents the maximum p value the coefficient of a variable can have for the variable to remain in the model. For stepwise regression, these values are set at SLENTRY = 0.15 and SLSTAY = 0.15. These default values can be changed. For example, to change SLENTRY and SLSTAY each to 0.2, the following sequence could be used:

```
PROC REG;
   MODEL SALES = ADV BONUS MKTSHR COMPET/SELECTION =
      STEPWISE/SLENTRY = 0.2 SLSTAY = 0.2;
```

Backward Elimination

```
PROC REG;
   MODEL SALES = ADV BONUS MKTSHR COMPET/SELECTION = BACKWARD;
```

Backward elimination uses SLSTAY = 0.1 in SAS. SLENTRY is automatically set so that once a variable leaves the regression it does not reenter.

Forward Selection

```
PROC REG;
   MODEL SALES = ADV BONUS MKTSHR COMPET/SELECTION = FORWARD;
```

Forward selection uses SLENTRY = 0.5 in SAS. SLSTAY is automatically set so that once a variable enters the regression it does not leave.

EXERCISES

1 **Cost Control**   Exercise 1 in Chapter 4 discussed data available for a firm that produces corrugated paper for use in making boxes and other packing materials. The variables discussed were

   y, total manufacturing cost per month in thousands of dollars (COST)

   x_1, total production of paper per month in tons (PAPER)

   x_2, total machine hours used per month (MACHINE)

   x_3, total variable overhead costs per month in thousands of dollars (OVERHEAD)

   x_4, total direct labor hours used each month (LABOR)

The data, shown in Table 4.2, are monthly and refer to the time period from January 1998 to March 2000. The MINITAB backward elimination output is in Figure 8.11. Use the MINITAB backward elimination output to answer the following questions:

a What is the regression equation chosen by the backward elimination procedure?

FIGURE 8.11   MINITAB Backward Elimination Output for Cost Control Exercise

```
F-to-Enter: 100000.00   F-to-Remove:    4.00

Response is   COST  on 4 predictors, with N =   27

        Step          1         2         3
Constant          51.72     51.17     59.43

PAPER              0.95      0.94      0.95
T-Value            7.90      8.69      8.62

MACHINE            2.47      2.51      2.39
T-Value            5.31     11.01     11.36

OVERHEAD           0.05
T-Value            0.09

LABOR            -0.051    -0.051
T-Value          -1.26     -1.29

S                  11.1      10.8      11.0
R-Sq              99.88     99.88     99.87
```

b What is the R^2 for the chosen equation?

c What is the adjusted R^2 for the chosen equation?

d What is the standard error of the chosen equation?

e What variables were omitted? Do you feel these variables are unrelated to $y = $ COST? Why or why not? Do you feel the omitted variables are necessary in the regression equation? Why or why not?

These data are available in a file with prefix COST8 and are arranged in five columns: COST, PAPER, MACHINE, OVERHEAD, and LABOR.

2 **Sales Force Performance**   Data on the following variables were obtained for a random sample of 25 sales territories for a company (the data have been transformed to preserve confidentiality).

y, sales in units for the territory (SALES)

x_1, length of time territory salesperson has been with the company (TIME)

x_2, industry sales in units for the territory (POTENT)

x_3, dollar expenditures on advertising (ADV)

x_4, weighted average of past market share for 4 previous years (SHARE)

TABLE 8.2   Data for Sales Force Performance Exercise

SALES	TIME	POTENT	ADV	SHARE	SHARECHG	ACCTS	WORKLOAD	RATING
3669.88	43.10	74065.11	4582.88	2.51	0.34	74.86	15.05	4.9
3473.95	108.13	58117.30	5539.78	5.51	0.15	107.32	19.97	5.1
2295.10	13.82	21118.49	2950.38	10.91	−0.72	96.75	17.34	2.9
4675.56	186.18	68521.27	2243.07	8.27	0.17	195.12	13.40	3.4
6125.96	161.79	57805.11	7747.08	9.15	0.50	180.44	17.64	4.6
2134.94	8.94	37806.94	402.44	5.51	0.15	104.88	16.22	4.5
5031.66	365.04	50935.26	3140.62	8.54	0.55	256.10	18.80	4.6
3367.45	220.32	35602.08	2086.16	7.07	−0.49	126.83	19.86	2.3
6519.45	127.64	46176.77	8846.25	12.54	1.24	203.25	17.42	4.9
4876.37	105.69	42053.24	5673.11	8.85	0.31	119.51	21.41	2.8
2468.27	57.72	36829.71	2761.76	5.38	0.37	116.26	16.32	3.1
2533.31	23.58	33612.67	1991.85	5.43	−0.65	142.28	14.51	4.2
2408.11	13.82	21412.79	1971.52	8.48	0.64	89.43	19.35	4.3
2337.38	13.82	20416.87	1737.38	7.80	1.01	84.55	20.02	4.2
4586.95	86.99	36272.00	10694.20	10.34	0.11	119.51	15.26	5.5
2729.24	165.85	23093.26	8618.61	5.15	0.04	80.49	15.87	3.6
3289.40	116.26	26878.59	7747.89	6.64	0.68	136.58	7.81	3.4
2800.78	42.28	39571.96	4565.96	5.45	0.66	78.86	16.00	4.2
3264.20	52.84	51866.15	6022.70	6.31	−0.10	136.58	17.44	3.6
3453.62	165.04	58749.82	3721.10	6.35	−0.03	138.21	17.98	3.1
1741.45	10.57	23990.82	860.97	7.37	−1.63	75.61	20.99	1.6
2035.75	13.82	25694.86	3571.51	8.39	−0.43	102.44	21.66	3.4
1578.00	8.13	23736.35	2845.50	5.15	0.04	76.42	21.46	2.7
4167.44	58.54	34314.29	5060.11	12.88	0.22	136.58	24.78	2.8
2799.97	21.14	22809.53	3552.00	9.14	−0.74	88.62	24.96	3.9

These data were analyzed in D. W. Cravens, R. B. Woodruff, and J. C. Stamper, "An Analytical Approach for Evaluating Sales Territory Performance," *Journal of Marketing* 36 (1972): 31–37.

x_5, change in market share over the 4 years before the time period analyzed (SHARECHG)

x_6, total number of accounts assigned to salesperson (ACCTS)

x_7, average workload per account using a weighted index based on annual purchases of accounts and concentration of accounts (WORKLOAD)

x_8, an aggregate rating on a 1–7 scale on eight dimensions of performance by applicable field sales manager (RATING).

The data are shown in Table 8.2.

The goal of the study is to identify factors that influence territory sales (y). The equation to be developed will be used to assess whether salespersons in respective territories are performing up to standard.

Develop an appropriate model to explain sales territory performance. Use any of the techniques discussed to select appropriate variables. Be sure to examine scatterplots and residual plots for violations of assumptions and to correct for any such violations.

a For the model you select, report the estimated regression equation. Be sure to define the variables used.

b For the model you select, report any corrections for violations of assumptions.

c For the model you select, report the R^2, R^2_{adj}, standard error, and C_p value.

d Discuss how this equation could be used to set a performance standard for sales territories. How would average performance be determined? Below-average performance? What limitations would this approach have for setting performance standards?

These data are available in a file with prefix TERRITR8 in nine columns: SALES, TIME, POTENT, ADV, SHARE, SHARECHG, ACCTS, WORKLOAD, and RATING.

3 **1999 Cars**   Data on 138 cars were obtained from *Road and Track's The Complete '99 Car Buyer's Guide*. The data shown in Table 8.3 are as follows:

name of car

price, in dollars (PRICE)

weight, in pounds (WEIGHT)

mileage in city driving (CITYMPG)

mileage in highway driving (HWYMPG)

displacement, in cubic centimeters (DISP)

compression ratio, measured as #:1 (COMP)

horsepower, @ 6300 rpm (HP)

torque, @ 5200 rpm (TORQUE)

type of transmission: 1 = automatic, 0 = manual (TRANS)

number of cylinders (CYLIN)

Using the available data, try to determine what factors involved in the construction of a car affect either mileage in city driving or mileage in highway driving. (Choose either CITYMPG or HWYMPG as your dependent variable. If you choose CITYMPG, do not use HWYMPG as a possible explanatory variable, and vice versa.) Use any of the techniques discussed to select appropriate variables. Be sure to examine scatterplots and residual plots for violations of assumptions and to correct for any such violations.

a For the model you select, report the estimated regression. Be sure to define the variables used.

TABLE **8.3**   Data for 1999 Cars Exercise

Car	PRICE	WEIGHT	CITYMPG	HWYMPG	DISP	COMP	HP	TORQUE	TRANS	CYLIN
Acura 2.3 CL	22745	3062	25	31	2254	9.3	150	152	0	4
Acura Integra LS Coupe	19635	2640	25	31	1834	9.2	140	127	0	4
Acura NSX	84725	3066	17	24	3179	10.2	290	224	0	6
Acura 3.5RL	41635	3660	19	25	3474	9.6	210	225	1	6
Acura TL	28385	3447	19	27	3210	9.8	225	216	1	6
Aston Martin DB7Coupe	130000	3890	14	21	3239	8.3	335	361	0	6
Audi A4 1.8T	24290	2877	23	32	1781	9.5	150	155	0	4
Audi A6	34250	3473	17	28	2771	10.3	200	207	1	6
Audi A8 3.7	57900	3682	17	26	3697	10.8	230	235	1	8
Bentley Arnage	203800	5070	12	18	4398	8.5	350	413	1	8
BMW 318ti Coupe	24440	2778	23	31	1895	10.0	138	133	0	4
BMW 3 323i Sedan	26970	3153	20	29	2494	10.5	170	181	0	6
BMW 528i	40040	3450	20	29	2793	10.2	193	206	0	6
BMW 740i	63540	4255	17	24	4398	10.0	282	310	1	8
BMW Z3 2.3 Roadster	30520	2899	20	30	2494	10.5	170	181	0	6
Buick Century Custom	19335	3335	20	29	3130	9.6	160	185	1	6
Buick LeSabre Custom	23340	3443	19	30	3794	9.4	205	230	1	6
Buick Park Avenue	31800	3778	19	28	3794	9.4	205	230	1	6
Buick Regal LS	22255	3439	19	30	3794	9.4	200	225	1	6
Buick Riviera	34490	3713	18	27	3794	8.5	240	280	1	6
Cadillac Catera	30635	3770	18	24	2962	10.0	200	192	1	6
Cadillac DeVille	39300	4012	17	26	4565	10.3	275	300	1	8
Cadillac Eldorado	39905	3843	17	26	4565	10.3	275	300	1	8
Cadillac Seville SLS	44025	3970	17	26	4565	10.3	275	300	1	8
Chevrolet Camaro Coupe	17160	3306	19	30	3785	9.4	200	225	0	6
Chevrolet Cavalier Coupe	12381	2617	24	34	2196	9.0	115	135	0	4
Chevrolet Corvette Coupe	39171	3245	17	25	5670	10.1	345	350	1	8
Chevrolet Lumina	17300	3330	20	29	3139	9.6	160	185	1	6
Chevrolet Malibu Sedan	16485	3051	23	32	2392	9.5	150	155	1	4
Chevrolet Metro Coupe	8655	1895	41	44	993	9.5	55	58	0	3
Chevrolet Monte Carlo LS	17795	3306	20	29	3130	9.6	160	185	1	6
Chevrolet Prizm Sedan	13800	2403	31	37	1794	10.1	120	122	0	4
Chrysler Cirrus Lxi	19995	3146	20	29	2497	9.4	168	170	1	6
Chrysler Concorde LX	22060	3446	21	30	2736	9.7	200	190	1	6
Chrysler LHS	28995	3579	18	27	3518	10.1	253	255	1	6
Chrysler Sebring LX	24405	2959	22	31	1996	9.6	140	130	0	4
Chrysler Sebring Convertible JX	24405	3331	21	30	2429	9.4	150	167	1	4

Continues

TABLE **8.3**   *(continued)*

Car	PRICE	WEIGHT	CITYMPG	HWYMPG	DISP	COMP	HP	TORQUE	TRANS	CYLIN
Chrysler 300M	28895	3567	18	27	3518	10.1	253	255	1	6
Daewoo Lanos S 3-door	8999	2447	26	36	1598	9.5	105	106	0	4
Daewoo Leganza SE	15590	3086	20	29	2198	9.6	131	148	0	4
Daewoo Nubira SX 4-door	12500	2566	22	31	1998	9.5	129	136	0	4
Dodge Avenger	15905	2897	22	32	1996	9.6	140	130	0	4
Dodge Intrepid	20440	3422	21	30	2736	9.7	200	190	1	6
Dodge Neon Highline Coupe	12020	2470	27	40	1996	9.8	132	129	0	4
Dodge Stratus	15675	2921	27	37	1996	9.8	132	128	0	4
Dodge Viper RT/10	67000	3319	12	21	7990	9.6	450	490	0	10
Ferrari F355 Berlinetta	122825	3290	26	31	3496	11.0	375	268	0	8
Ferrari 456M GT	219400	3900	11	14	5474	10.6	436	398	0	12
Ferrari 550 Maranello	201600	3725	10	15	5474	10.8	485	419	0	12
Ford Contour LX	14995	2769	24	34	1983	9.6	125	130	0	4
Ford Crown Victoria	22510	3917	17	24	4605	9.9	200	275	1	8
Ford Escort LX Sedan	11870	2468	25	34	1988	9.2	110	125	0	4
Ford Mustang Coupe	16000	3069	20	30	3802	9.4	190	220	0	6
Ford Taurus LX Sedan	17995	3329	19	28	2982	9.3	145	170	1	6
Ford Escort ZX2 Cool	12025	2478	26	33	1983	9.6	130	127	0	4
Honda Accord DX Sedan	15690	2888	25	31	2254	8.8	135	145	0	4
Honda Civic CX Hatchback	11095	2295	32	37	1590	9.4	106	103	0	4
Honda Prelude	23400	2954	23	27	2157	10.0	200	156	0	4
Hyundai Accent L Coupe	8850	2101	28	36	1495	10.0	92	97	0	4
Hyundai Elantra Sedan	11550	2458	24	32	1975	10.3	138	131	0	4
Hyundai Sonata	15500	3020	21	28	2384	10.0	150	155	0	4
Hyundai Tiburon	14000	2566	24	32	1975	10.3	140	133	0	4
Infiniti G20	21490	2913	23	31	1998	9.5	140	132	0	4
Infiniti I30	29395	3150	21	28	2988	10.0	190	205	1	6
Infiniti Q45	48695	3879	18	23	4130	10.5	266	278	1	8
Jaguar XJ8	55780	3996	17	24	3996	10.8	290	290	1	8
Jaguar XK8 Coupe	66330	3673	17	25	3996	10.8	290	290	1	8
KIA Sephia	9995	2478	24	31	1793	9.5	125	108	0	4
Lamborghini Diablo Roadster VT	279400	3575	9	13	5707	10.0	530	445	0	12
Lexus ES 300	31400	3378	19	22	2995	10.5	210	220	1	6
Lexus GS 300	37800	3635	20	25	2997	10.5	225	220	1	6
Lexus LS 400	54100	3890	19	25	3969	10.5	290	300	1	8

TABLE **8.3**   *(continued)*

Car	PRICE	WEIGHT	CITYMPG	HWYMPG	DISP	COMP	HP	TORQUE	TRANS	CYLIN
Lexus SC 300	43400	3560	19	24	2995	10.5	225	220	1	6
Lincoln Continental	38995	3868	17	24	4605	9.9	275	275	1	8
Lincoln LS V6	32000	3500	17	25	2985	10.0	220	220	0	6
Lincoln Town Car Executive	38995	4015	17	25	4605	9.0	205	280	1	8
Lotus Esprit V8	85675	3043	15	23	3506	8.0	350	295	0	8
Mazda Miata MX-5	20220	2299	25	29	1839	9.5	140	119	0	4
Mazda Millenia	26995	3216	20	27	2497	9.2	170	160	1	6
Mazda Protégé DX	12420	2449	29	34	1597	9.0	105	107	0	4
Mazda 626 LX	18115	2798	26	33	1991	9.0	125	127	0	4
Mercedes-Benz C230 Kompressor	31795	3250	21	29	2295	8.8	185	200	1	4
Mercedes-Benz CL500	92495	4760	15	22	4973	11.0	315	347	1	8
Mercedes-Benz CLK320	41195	3316	21	29	3199	10.0	215	229	1	6
Mercedes-Benz E300 Sedan	42995	3525	21	30	3199	10.0	221	232	1	6
Mercedes-Benz S320	65345	4506	17	24	3199	10.0	228	232	1	6
Mercedes-Benz SL500	81695	4121	16	23	4966	10.0	302	339	1	8
Mercedes-Benz SLK320	40595	3036	22	30	2295	8.8	185	200	0	4
Mercury Cougar	16595	2892	24	34	1989	9.6	125	130	0	4
Mercury Grand Marquis GS	22825	3917	17	24	4605	9.0	200	275	1	8
Mercury Mystique GS	16925	2805	24	34	1989	9.6	125	130	0	4
Mercury Sable GS Sedan	18995	3302	19	28	2985	9.3	145	170	1	6
Mercury Tracer GS Sedan	11945	2469	28	38	1988	9.2	110	125	0	4
Mitsubishi Diamante	28000	3363	18	26	3497	9.0	210	231	1	6
Mitsubishi Eclipse RS	16180	2767	22	33	1996	9.6	140	130	0	4
Mitsubishi Galant DE	17410	2835	23	31	2351	9.0	145	155	1	4
Mitsubishi Mirage DE Sedan	12880	2127	33	40	1468	9.0	92	93	0	4
Mitsubishi 3000GT	25880	3131	19	24	2972	8.9	161	185	0	6
Nissan Altima XE	15480	2859	24	31	2389	9.2	150	154	0	4
Nissan Maxima GXE	21989	3012	22	27	2988	10.0	190	205	0	6
Nissan Sentra XE	14189	2315	30	40	1597	9.9	115	108	0	4
Oldsmobile Alero GX Sedan	16850	3026	21	29	2392	9.5	150	155	1	4
Oldsmobile Aurora	36900	3967	17	26	3994	10.3	250	260	1	8
Oldsmobile Cutlass GL	18325	3102	20	29	3136	9.6	150	185	1	6
Oldsmobile Eighty Eight	23400	3455	19	29	3791	9.4	205	220	1	6

Continues

TABLE 8.3 *(continued)*

Car	PRICE	WEIGHT	CITYMPG	HWYMPG	DISP	COMP	HP	TORQUE	TRANS	CYLIN
Oldsmobile Intrigue GX	21735	3467	19	30	3791	9.4	195	220	1	6
Plymouth Breeze	15510	2929	26	37	1996	9.8	132	129	0	4
Plymouth Neon Coupe	12220	2470	29	38	1996	9.8	132	129	0	4
Plymouth Prowler	40000	2838	17	23	3518	10.1	253	255	1	4
Pontiac Bonneville SE	23495	3446	19	29	3792	9.4	205	230	1	6
Pontiac Firebird Coupe	18700	3340	19	28	3791	9.4	200	225	0	6
Pontiac Grand Am SE Coupe	16595	3066	21	29	2392	9.5	150	155	1	4
Pontiac Grand Prix SE Sedan	19975	3396	20	29	3137	9.6	160	185	1	6
Pontiac Sunfire SE Coupe	13255	2630	24	34	2189	9.0	115	135	0	4
Porsche 911 Carrera Coupe	65815	2910	17	25	3400	11.3	296	258	0	6
Porsche Boxster	41785	2822	19	26	2480	11.0	201	181	0	6
Rolls-Royce Silver Seraph	216400	5075	12	18	5379	10.0	322	361	1	12
Saab 9-3 3-door	26225	2990	21	27	1985	9.2	185	194	0	4
Saab 9-5	30570	3280	21	28	2290	9.3	170	207	0	4
Saturn Coupe SC1	12385	2320	29	40	1901	9.3	100	114	0	4
Saturn SL Sedan	11035	2327	29	40	1901	9.3	100	114	0	4
Subaru Impreza L Coupe	16390	2730	22	29	2212	9.7	142	149	0	4
Subaru Legacy Brighton Wagon	17390	2885	22	29	2212	9.7	142	149	0	4
Suzuki Esteem GL Sedan	12629	2183	31	37	1590	9.5	98	94	0	4
Suzuki Swift	9479	1878	39	43	1295	9.5	79	75	0	4
Toyota Avalon XL	24998	3340	21	31	2995	10.5	200	214	1	6
Toyota Camry CE	17458	2998	23	31	2164	9.5	133	147	0	4
Toyota Camry Solara SE	19058	3120	23	32	2164	9.5	135	147	0	4
Toyota Celica GT Liftback	20238	2755	22	28	2156	9.5	135	145	0	4
Toyota Corolla VE	12638	2414	31	38	1794	10.0	120	122	0	4
Toyota Tercel CE 2-door	10698	2090	32	39	1497	9.4	93	100	0	4
Volkswagen Golf GL	13630	2600	24	31	1984	10.0	115	122	0	4
Volkswagen Jetta GL	15000	2700	24	31	1984	10.0	115	122	0	4
Volkswagen New Beetle GL	16425	2712	23	29	1984	10.0	115	122	0	4
Volkswagen Passat GLS	21700	3243	23	32	1751	9.5	150	155	0	4
Volvo C70 Coupe LPT	37570	3601	20	27	2345	9.0	190	199	1	5
Volvo S70	27960	3148	20	28	2435	10.3	162	162	0	5
Volvo S80 2.9	36395	3560	19	27	2922	10.7	201	243	1	6

Source: From *Road & Track '99 Car Buyer's Guide.* Copyright 1999 by Hachette Filipacchi Magazines, Inc. Reprinted with permission.

b For the model you select, report any corrections for violations of assumptions. Explain why the correction was needed and justify the correction you used.

c Justify your choice of variables from both a statistical and a practical standpoint.

d State any limitations of the model.

These data are available in a file with prefix CARS8 in ten columns: the name of the car, PRICE, WEIGHT, CITYMPG, HWYMPG, DISP, COMP, HP, TORQUE, TRANS, and CYLIN.

4 **1998 American League Pitchers**   Data on 44 American League pitchers were obtained for the 1998 season. The pitchers included in the data set must have pitched in at least 40 innings to be listed here. Also, these pitchers were used only as starting pitchers (pitchers with even one appearance in relief were not included). The data shown in Table 8.4 are as follows:

name of pitcher

team: coded as

  1 = Baltimore
  2 = Boston
  3 = Cleveland
  4 = Detroit
  5 = Anaheim
  6 = Chicago
  7 = Kansas City
  8 = Milwaukee
  9 = Minnesota
  10 = Seattle
  11 = New York
  12 = Oakland
  13 = Texas
  14 = Toronto
  15 = Tampa Bay

number of wins (W)

number of losses (L)

earned run average (ERA)

innings pitched (IP)

hits allowed (H)

home runs allowed (HR)

bases on balls (BB)

strikeouts (SO)

As a consultant to the Texas Rangers' coaching staff, you have been hired to determine what makes a starting pitcher successful. The Rangers are painfully aware of the need for good starting pitchers. Although they won their division of the American League in the 1999 season, many of their wins were due to their offensive output

TABLE 8.4   Data for 1998 American League Pitchers Exercise

Pitcher	TEAM	W	L	ERA	IP	H	HR	BB	SO
Mussina, Mike	1	13	10	3.49	206.1	189	22	41	175
Clemens, Roger	14	20	6	2.65	234.2	169	11	88	271
Alvarez, Wilson	15	6	14	4.73	142.2	130	18	68	107
Wells, David	11	18	4	3.49	214.1	195	29	29	163
Erickson, Scott	1	16	13	4.01	251.1	284	23	69	186
Guzman, Juan	1	10	16	4.35	211	193	23	98	168
Hentgen, Pat	14	12	11	5.17	177.2	208	28	69	94
Williams, Woody	14	10	9	4.46	209.2	196	36	81	151
Cone, David	11	20	7	3.55	207.2	186	20	59	209
Martinez, Pedro	2	19	7	2.89	233.2	188	26	67	251
Saberhagen, Bret	2	15	8	3.96	175	181	22	29	100
Saunders, Tony	15	6	15	4.12	192.1	191	15	111	172
Johnson, Jason	15	2	5	5.7	60	74	9	27	36
Arrojo, Rolando	15	14	12	3.56	202	195	21	65	152
Hernandez, Orlando	11	12	4	3.13	141	113	11	52	131
Sirotka, Mike	6	14	15	5.06	211.2	255	30	47	128
Moehler, Brian	4	14	13	3.9	221.1	220	30	56	123
Thompson, Justin	4	11	15	4.05	222	227	20	79	149
Ogea, Chad	3	5	4	5.61	69	74	9	25	43
Hawkins, Latroy	9	7	14	5.25	190.1	227	27	61	105
Radke, Brad	9	12	14	4.3	213.2	238	23	43	146
Rapp, Pat	7	12	13	5.3	188.1	208	24	107	132
Barber, Brian	7	2	4	6	42	45	5	13	24
Belcher, Tim	7	14	14	4.27	234	247	37	73	130
Gooden, Dwight	3	8	6	3.76	134	135	13	51	83
Colon, Bartolo	3	14	9	3.71	204	205	15	79	158
Wright, Jaret	3	12	10	4.72	192.2	207	22	87	140
Greisinger, Seth	4	6	9	5.12	130	142	17	48	66
Parque, Jim	6	7	5	5.1	113	135	14	49	77
Milton, Eric	9	8	14	5.64	172.1	195	25	70	107
Haynes, Jimmy	12	11	9	5.09	194.1	229	25	88	134
Moyer, Jamie	10	15	9	3.53	234.1	234	23	42	158
Sele, Aaron	13	19	11	4.23	212.2	239	14	84	167
Finley, Chuck	5	11	9	3.39	223.1	210	20	109	212
McDowell, Jack	5	5	3	5.09	76	96	11	19	45
Stottlemyre, Todd	13	5	4	4.33	60.1	68	5	30	57
Helling, Rick	13	20	7	4.41	216.1	209	27	78	164
Rogers, Kenny	12	16	8	3.17	238.2	215	19	67	138

TABLE **8.4**   *(continued)*

Pitcher	TEAM	W	L	ERA	IP	H	HR	BB	SO
Burkett, John	13	9	13	5.68	195	230	19	46	131
Candiotti, Tom	12	11	16	4.84	201	222	30	63	98
Fassero, Jeff	10	13	12	3.97	224.2	223	33	66	176
Loaiza, Esteban	13	3	6	5.9	79.1	103	15	22	55
Hill, Ken	5	9	6	4.98	103	123	6	47	57
Cloude, Ken	10	8	10	6.37	155.1	187	29	80	114

Source: Reprinted courtesy of the *Fort Worth Star-Telegram*.

rather than quality starting pitching. They would like to improve their starting pitching before the next season. You have data available for American League starting pitchers in the 1998 season. Your goal is to determine what factors might be important in the success of a starting pitcher during a particular season. First, you must define success (the dependent variable). Then decide which of the variables available might make sense in evaluating a pitcher's success.

Write up a report to the Rangers' with your recommendations. Your report should consist of two parts: (a) an executive summary with a brief nontechnical discussion of your recommendations and (b) a technical report to support your suggestions. The technical report should include a discussion of the analysis that led to your conclusions. This should include regression results, model validation, corrections for violations of assumptions, justification of your choice of variables, and an explanation of how this choice will help the Rangers in their decision making.

These data are available in a file with prefix ALPITCH8 in ten columns: name of the pitcher, TEAM, W, L, ERA, IP, H, HR, BB, and SO.

5 FOC Sales   Techcore is a high-tech company located in Fort Worth, Texas. The company produces a part called a fibre-optic connector (FOC) and wants to generate reasonably accurate but simple forecasts of the sales of FOC's over time. They have weekly sales data for the past 265 weeks. These data are shown in Table 8.5. (The data have been disguised to provide confidentiality.) The time-series plot of FOC sales is shown in Figure 6.30. Data on a number of additional variables have been gathered to help build a forecasting model for FOC sales. The additional variables are as follows:

FOV: Sales of a complementary product; sales of FOV are much easier to forecast than FOC sales

COMPOSITE: Friday close of the NYSE Composite Index

INDUSTRIAL: Friday close of the NYSE Industrial Stocks

TRANS: Friday close of the NYSE Transportation Stocks

UTILITY: Friday close of the NYSE Utility Stocks

FINANCE: Friday close of the NYSE Financials

PROD: Industrial Production—computers, communications equipment, and semiconductors, not seasonally adjusted

HOUSE: Monthly housing permits in thousands, seasonally adjusted rates

You have been hired as a consultant to Techcore to help build the forecasting model. Create a two-part report for Techcore that includes an executive summary with the essential nontechnical results of your study and a technical report that contains the details of your model building process.

The data are in a file in the following columns: SALES, MONTH (numbers the month in which the observations were taken), FOV, COMPOSITE, INDUSTRIAL, TRANS, UTILITY, FINANCE, PROD, and HOUSE. The filename prefix is FOC8.

TABLE 8.5 Data for FOC Sales Exercise

SALES	MONTH	FOV	COMPOSITE	INDUSTRIAL	TRANS	UTILITY	FINANCE	PROD	HOUSE
2425	1	476908	260.34	318.63	276.57	224.42	217.01	30.13	347.5
6742	1	712435	262.9	321.97	281.27	223.81	220.52	30.13	347.5
5708	1	859298	263.12	322.76	278.8	224.78	218.83	30.13	347.5
5354	1	793448	265.42	324.05	280.64	229.36	223.32	30.13	347.5
6099	2	695173	261.21	320.6	277.97	222.63	216.93	31.48	317.25
5574	2	710936	261.31	321.32	275.34	221.5	216.54	31.48	317.25
7148	2	673710	259.87	320.85	275.15	215.98	214.73	31.48	317.25
6112	2	817447	258.57	318.94	269.64	216.69	213.64	31.48	317.25
5682	3	573598	257.7	318.4	267.09	218.14	209.79	27.39	268.4
5545	3	634943	258.53	319.82	266.24	217.13	210.8	27.39	268.4
5957	3	758737	261.35	323.83	270.67	215.56	214.5	27.39	268.4
5664	3	593575	256.29	316.79	264.59	213.12	211.39	27.39	268.4
6011	3	810500	247.06	304.56	252.48	208.35	204.19	27.39	268.4
5954	4	651178	248.29	306.08	253.94	206	207.8	32.54	348
5415	4	822677	247.66	303.64	251.04	208.66	210	32.54	348
5048	4	855307	247.95	303.37	248.32	214.36	208.21	32.54	348
6650	4	742558	250.36	307.61	253.74	213.53	208.32	32.54	348
6082	5	553554	248.47	306.26	245.5	206.44	208.89	34	349
6348	5	653608	245.76	303.56	237.5	201.1	207.69	34	349
6566	5	624761	251.58	309.94	245.16	206.49	214.27	34	349
7159	5	821066	252.79	311.22	249.14	207.56	215.56	34	349
5374	6	646506	254.34	312.38	248.6	208.84	219.3	29.74	271.4
4967	6	565764	253.59	310.66	245.63	210.59	219.43	29.74	271.4

TABLE **8.5** *(continued)*

SALES	MONTH	FOV	COMPOSITE	INDUSTRIAL	TRANS	UTILITY	FINANCE	PROD	HOUSE
7122	6	829549	253.29	311.49	250.84	207.21	217.41	29.74	271.4
7359	6	709434	244.55	301.13	241.17	200.13	208.86	29.74	271.4
8126	6	1201495	246.34	303.04	243.4	203.11	210	29.74	271.4
7868	7	774569	248.11	305.73	244.92	204.37	210.22	35.41	333.75
4917	7	714570	251.06	309.64	247.13	206.46	212.27	35.41	333.75
6791	7	1069777	250.24	308.74	244.59	206.39	211	35.41	333.75
9494	7	870334	252.62	311.42	244.38	209.95	212.81	35.41	333.75
8959	8	907760	252.5	310.83	245.14	211.82	212.37	37.28	344.25
9767	8	997735	254.77	314.34	244.22	212.05	213.85	37.28	344.25
9471	8	1187932	255.81	316.84	240.19	209.75	214.16	37.28	344.25
7142	8	905684	260.82	323.95	246.05	210.59	218.11	37.28	344.25
6702	9	772546	259.93	323.18	248.2	208.05	217.4	32.67	353
7611	9	739137	258.38	322.52	243.66	204.18	214.81	32.67	353
6012	9	659046	259.77	325.31	241.47	204.16	214.09	32.67	353
8463	9	886722	253.81	318.02	231.45	202.52	206.84	32.67	353
6717	9	1183395	255.52	320.63	231.66	205.26	205.94	32.67	353
7575	10	771186	251.33	315.76	225.12	201.81	201.8	39.21	349.25
10818	10	1004144	257.99	324.71	233.67	206.96	205.33	39.21	349.25
7802	10	997993	255.59	322.3	230.66	203.39	203.01	39.21	349.25
7322	10	999014	259.43	327.56	236.17	204.94	205.76	39.21	349.25
6407	11	705619	254.21	320.87	231.44	200.78	201.93	41	335
8325	11	855388	253.25	320.62	226.99	198.96	199.56	41	335
7631	11	742146	252.3	320.6	226.94	197.31	195.99	41	335
9892	11	1020701	247.6	312.04	221.42	200.66	194.49	41	335
2688	12	469336	248.01	312.91	222.47	199.34	194.99	35.34	279.2
7394	12	867281	244.17	307.65	213.38	199.61	191.21	35.34	279.2
4836	12	880260	250.54	316.08	219.06	201.86	197.29	35.34	279.2
12655	12	1371880	250.95	317.83	221.02	199.08	196.29	35.34	279.2
9114	12	1160032	250.94	318.1	222.46	198.41	195.8	35.34	279.2
4399	1	570653	251.59	317.8	229.78	198.97	198.8	33.46	256.4
8529	1	641795	253.95	320.83	230.72	198.97	202.08	33.46	256.4
12080	1	717435	253.38	320.26	230.62	200.31	199.79	33.46	256.4
9011	1	1080775	255.89	321.28	231.02	206.8	204.67	33.46	256.4
7127	1	1515479	260.44	326.24	232.7	209.84	211.24	33.46	256.4
10917	2	1006447	261.8	328.88	235.99	208.63	211.18	44.55	313.5
8525	2	966578	261.83	329.4	240.25	205.58	211.7	44.55	313.5
6834	2	1010739	264.86	332.87	244.38	207.61	215.24	44.55	313.5
8660	2	1584940	263.29	331.99	240.82	203.12	213.57	44.55	313.5

Continues

TABLE 8.5 (*continued*)

SALES	MONTH	FOV	COMPOSITE	INDUSTRIAL	TRANS	UTILITY	FINANCE	PROD	HOUSE
8377	3	1038053	264.83	335.08	241.81	204.03	211.78	39.15	245.2
9435	3	1138929	267.84	339.45	246.16	205.18	213.33	39.15	245.2
10633	3	1515522	270.5	343.39	245.9	206.46	214.72	39.15	245.2
7965	3	972753	271.04	344.26	252.43	205.07	215.33	39.15	245.2
12965	3	1504820	273.73	346.13	253.19	210.26	219.66	39.15	245.2
9443	4	1019817	275	348.27	256.24	210.11	219.81	46.01	314.75
6185	4	976311	274.76	348.5	255.14	208.2	219.49	46.01	314.75
11846	4	1582479	277.31	351.85	257.2	210.32	221.12	46.01	314.75
10620	4	894690	279.9	354.58	251.66	212.02	225.8	46.01	314.75
8906	5	1005088	282.9	358.19	256.01	213.03	229.5	48.07	317.75
9787	5	1129520	279.49	354.2	252.55	208.54	227.3	48.07	317.75
9446	5	1243076	281.58	356.31	250.1	210.63	230.58	48.07	317.75
8901	5	1393553	286.53	361.2	250.13	215.74	237.89	48.07	317.75
7025	6	819271	284.05	360.24	250.34	211.67	231.16	42.37	261
11133	6	1050369	289.96	368.24	256.13	216.71	233.99	42.37	261
8122	6	1148554	294.17	372.97	262.81	218.69	239.72	42.37	261
10113	6	1070152	291.84	370.63	262.99	216.94	235.86	42.37	261
12531	6	1286232	297.71	377.86	277.03	219.55	241.66	42.37	261
8302	7	755322	298.9	380.19	280.55	217.2	242.54	51.29	338.5
10725	7	1154205	296.67	377.7	280.62	219.44	236.6	51.29	338.5
14100	7	1164874	301.38	383.18	287.52	221.38	242.7	51.29	338.5
13198	7	1224516	299.91	380.41	288.3	222.12	242.49	51.29	338.5
10097	8	995425	297.77	377.66	281.78	220.15	241.61	53.64	346.5
11046	8	991932	299.79	379.38	286.27	221.79	245.24	53.64	346.5
10756	8	1205758	300.85	379.59	286.66	223.86	248.34	53.64	346.5
12432	8	1165905	303.23	381.4	289.83	224.99	254.1	53.64	346.5
9813	9	922378	307.39	387.06	299.26	226.51	256.97	47.05	284.2
10058	9	775399	313	393.1	298.1	231.23	264.77	47.05	284.2
9577	9	995967	311.88	392.64	293.34	231.1	261.01	47.05	284.2
8871	9	958737	313.26	392.66	294.59	234.9	264.89	47.05	284.2
12558	9	1059229	312.38	390.59	291.6	234.4	266.92	47.05	284.2
10570	10	826226	313.65	391.05	295.03	235.39	270.95	56.61	350
12688	10	993989	313.83	392.21	292.25	238.95	266.15	56.61	350
13078	10	993827	308.63	386.2	287.18	236.62	259.18	56.61	350
10032	10	1116915	314.27	393.24	298.08	239.74	264.31	56.61	350
8893	11	910654	315.78	395.82	300.83	236.7	266.72	58.46	357.5
13590	11	989349	320.12	402.63	300.02	239.8	267.2	58.46	357.5
15818	11	987107	320.4	402.96	303.1	239.21	267.8	58.46	357.5
8480	11	515841	324.43	407.11	309.18	242.31	273.43	58.46	357.5

TABLE 8.5 (*continued*)

SALES	MONTH	FOV	COMPOSITE	INDUSTRIAL	TRANS	UTILITY	FINANCE	PROD	HOUSE
16157	12	925576	329.02	414.23	308.33	243.3	275.85	49.96	288.4
11433	12	797008	328.66	413.94	302.54	248.15	271.74	49.96	288.4
13828	12	1156746	326.35	409.95	296.63	249.72	270.72	49.96	288.4
11664	12	1176444	327.64	411.44	296.87	251.01	272	49.96	288.4
4425	12	428707	329.51	413.29	301.96	252.9	274.25	49.96	288.4
6856	1	706538	330.18	414.4	304.12	256.63	271.48	57.81	346.75
10422	1	888047	322.95	404.59	297.48	250.91	267.63	57.81	346.75
11959	1	1077199	327.86	409.97	296.93	253.52	275.3	57.81	346.75
13098	1	933072	332.84	417.96	299.94	254	277.28	57.81	346.75
10228	2	754140	340.09	427.49	306.85	257.06	284.01	62.58	284
11967	2	824444	349.44	438.87	316.45	264.23	292.67	62.58	284
10337	2	904941	346.19	435.37	314.94	256.65	292.04	62.58	284
12970	2	937389	350.94	442.6	322.54	255.69	295.64	62.58	284
12186	3	926853	345.18	434.73	317.52	249.8	293.75	54.97	287.4
12283	3	843925	339.74	430.35	314.51	242.55	284.63	54.97	287.4
15702	3	855443	343.39	437.57	325.88	238.52	284.74	54.97	287.4
16675	3	1106900	348.77	442.22	330.25	247.07	291.68	54.97	287.4
11764	3	998123	346.92	439.26	323.4	245.68	292.39	54.97	287.4
9566	4	762076	351.92	446.71	325.15	246.17	296.11	62.89	365.75
14276	4	1119870	342.41	435.92	316.02	240.23	283.94	62.89	365.75
12954	4	829565	346.4	440.49	331.8	245.11	285.77	62.89	365.75
15769	4	1008962	350.82	446.42	333.47	248.48	288.62	62.89	365.75
10427	5	1005804	345.4	440.7	329.83	243.57	281.57	65.98	364.25
14089	5	1209745	350.02	444.64	330.97	249.99	288.6	65.98	364.25
10723	5	1345921	358.78	457.98	338.26	251.84	293.3	65.98	364.25
14525	5	1265638	363.74	464.47	338.79	254.6	297.89	65.98	364.25
10841	6	705125	358.83	458.93	333.93	248.75	293.8	59.6	285.8
16282	6	1057832	360.61	461.87	334.47	247.83	295.24	59.6	285.8
14603	6	777701	357.2	457.21	329.53	244.38	294.24	59.6	285.8
16673	6	1047343	357.02	457.17	330.38	247.62	290.91	59.6	285.8
13721	6	1355498	359.2	457.35	329.8	254.55	295.83	59.6	285.8
11548	7	602658	360.37	458.2	334.68	254.92	298.5	70.95	362.5
15127	7	961833	353.24	450.08	326.42	249	290.89	70.95	362.5
17947	7	1129069	346.84	440.53	320.02	249.24	285.76	70.95	362.5
15886	7	1024697	342.91	434.76	312.42	244.05	286.83	70.95	362.5
14299	8	1104244	340.87	431.97	309.86	240.44	287.37	74.82	353.25
16727	8	1174622	353.87	447.79	317.59	247.58	302.06	74.82	353.25
17251	8	1044081	353.44	447.82	320.42	244.28	302.1	74.82	353.25

Continues

TABLE 8.5 (*continued*)

SALES	MONTH	FOV	COMPOSITE	INDUSTRIAL	TRANS	UTILITY	FINANCE	PROD	HOUSE
17063	8	1357487	355.96	450.78	322.21	245.14	305.61	74.82	353.25
15195	9	1103483	357.23	452.74	323.89	245.52	306.03	66.65	278.4
11866	9	823180	350.99	445.46	320.92	240.4	299.35	66.65	278.4
18312	9	1379108	352.67	448.9	316.93	237.18	301.16	66.65	278.4
17634	9	1395841	363.7	462.43	325.09	244.85	311.94	66.65	278.4
18414	9	1601140	365.77	466.5	330.21	245.33	310.24	66.65	278.4
16071	10	842779	366.27	466.39	326.83	243.38	314.76	76.12	339.5
18727	10	1092569	374.16	474.85	330.68	249.86	325.12	76.12	339.5
20121	10	929210	372.89	473.94	329.66	248.18	322.77	76.12	339.5
21417	10	1571196	378.32	481.13	337.67	251.18	326.87	76.12	339.5
15016	11	1011957	373.26	472.58	336.64	250.64	325.66	80.1	353
15511	11	1261415	373.68	470.85	337.51	252.64	330.7	80.1	353
16290	11	1643660	386.32	487.61	344.16	258.47	342.16	80.1	353
20031	11	1387534	390.02	493.28	347.26	259.06	344.24	80.1	353
9258	12	709279	394.66	498.36	352.76	260.93	351.19	68.45	282.2
15293	12	932189	398.43	502.17	358.51	261.67	358.18	68.45	282.2
18773	12	1314489	390.15	492.74	351.94	256.93	347.46	68.45	282.2
14069	12	1020793	384.07	485.41	345.93	252.71	341.33	68.45	282.2
9712	12	780832	394.11	497.4	353.69	256.23	354.58	68.45	282.2
12623	1	578833	398.1	500.87	355.65	265.11	357.71	78.65	349.75
11030	1	1000340	394.06	497.64	351.75	259.94	351.05	78.65	349.75
12156	1	1195200	400.76	508.41	355.01	260.81	353.87	78.65	349.75
18692	1	1403964	409.31	517.67	362	267.25	365.01	78.65	349.75
15535	2	1334402	405.51	510.76	364.37	265.09	366.4	83.97	362.5
18926	2	1259400	411.98	518.93	365.41	267.94	373.66	83.97	362.5
18529	2	1413597	413.8	518.99	363.36	268.18	382.33	83.97	362.5
15930	2	1405337	423.48	529.54	365.82	273.7	396.61	83.97	362.5
13528	3	1407910	415.51	520.34	360.51	270.09	385.79	75.09	287.6
19739	3	1225547	423.83	529.53	379.33	268.63	400.82	75.09	287.6
16451	3	1187902	417.7	524.65	373.28	264.55	387.94	75.09	287.6
17785	3	1006197	412.8	518.42	370.04	262.44	382.69	75.09	287.6
16298	3	836784	407.43	514.28	365.68	257.8	371.77	75.09	287.6
14799	4	1052722	398.02	502.15	361.81	253.74	361.96	87.19	355.75
16557	4	1266828	389.47	490.75	357.11	248.73	355.16	87.19	355.75
16391	4	1301494	402.64	510.23	369.8	251.99	363.34	87.19	355.75
18792	4	1607136	400.38	507.11	370.44	252.03	360.62	87.19	355.75
12734	5	1130299	422.97	533.43	386.68	264.55	388.69	90.67	355.5
17173	5	1114811	429.23	543.16	390.73	266.82	391.05	90.67	355.5
13516	5	1124177	432.44	548.62	394.38	268.22	390.67	90.67	355.5

TABLE 8.5   (continued)

SALES	MONTH	FOV	COMPOSITE	INDUSTRIAL	TRANS	UTILITY	FINANCE	PROD	HOUSE
20956	5	1488881	440.28	559.87	404.53	269.43	396.8	90.67	355.5
12589	6	751889	441.78	560.57	402.96	273.77	399.03	81.8	279.6
19564	6	1178997	448.13	567.35	407.23	276.4	409.24	81.8	279.6
16406	6	1202442	465.17	588.85	413.58	285.97	426.53	81.8	279.6
15861	6	1431026	467.84	591.22	420.48	285.61	432.73	81.8	279.6
17291	6	1608170	463.3	586.95	415.94	282.13	425.21	81.8	279.6
11632	7	797973	477.68	604.55	427.14	290.92	440.24	99.07	360.25
13842	7	833020	478.12	607.05	431.41	289.21	436.61	99.07	360.25
19804	7	1183523	475.97	605.81	429.18	284.12	433.62	99.07	360.25
24103	7	1460330	486.8	618.59	439.21	287.26	448.67	99.07	360.25
15016	8	1424429	490.98	621.22	443.36	290	459.4	103.6	361.25
15809	8	1424731	483.79	613.95	441.46	288.26	445.49	103.6	361.25
15879	8	1230136	469.1	591.58	430.67	284.02	438.15	103.6	361.25
23434	8	1248564	478.93	606.4	440.18	285.72	444.07	103.6	361.25
16196	9	1429342	470.48	595.59	428.83	280.15	437.26	91.89	295
17041	9	1026749	484.64	613.46	439.06	288.13	451.14	91.89	295
17658	9	1252271	483.3	610.29	446.86	289.89	451	91.89	295
23447	9	1304644	496.56	625.5	467.02	295.71	468.36	91.89	295
30010	9	1428738	495.2	623.16	456.41	295.98	468.72	91.89	295
18307	10	1256946	505.69	633.67	463.3	304.87	484.04	106.09	375.5
23636	10	1159942	506.85	636.7	467.38	304.44	481.56	106.09	375.5
24844	10	1435948	496.57	620.98	466.24	302.71	475.09	106.09	375.5
29739	10	1473563	495.76	619.3	470.9	303.13	474.97	106.09	375.5
20720	11	1014687	481.14	601.96	453.77	295.79	457.55	110.89	368.75
21575	11	1260656	487.29	609.79	454.64	297.74	464.84	110.89	368.75
20466	11	1242133	486.06	609.8	446.43	305.36	453.84	110.89	368.75
24650	11	1498115	502.85	628.54	456.94	316.63	475.54	110.89	368.75
12509	11	629133	499.1	621.61	458.68	320.77	472.53	93.26	293.4
25198	12	1118483	514.31	638.24	471.2	322.1	499.74	93.26	293.4
20084	12	1426989	500	617.87	459.89	320.09	487.26	93.26	293.4
20877	12	1327670	497.39	612.43	449.16	326.72	484.97	93.26	293.4
10080	12	538451	493.6	607.91	445	327.57	478.43	93.26	293.4
5571	1	440102	512.15	632.13	463.17	334.95	496.37	108.58	388.25
14443	1	1103473	487.47	602.68	446.21	322.49	466.41	108.58	388.25
16831	1	1122475	503.67	624.09	457.22	330.57	480.6	108.58	388.25
24679	1	1331786	500.68	621.51	451.49	334.77	470.18	108.58	388.25
14537	2	1150152	510.63	633.54	462.52	337.12	483.55	113.46	408.75
13951	2	892942	526.31	653.51	481.34	339.79	502.43	113.46	408.75

Continues

TABLE 8.5 *(continued)*

SALES	MONTH	FOV	COMPOSITE	INDUSTRIAL	TRANS	UTILITY	FINANCE	PROD	HOUSE
17114	2	1003187	531.28	660.79	491.92	339.12	506.63	113.46	408.75
26375	2	1283626	537.49	667.84	490.18	344.21	514.15	113.46	408.75
13525	3	962464	544.26	675.99	481.12	349.12	522.27	97.82	313.8
20938	3	1107031	549.64	681.95	495.22	355.26	526.41	97.82	313.8
13773	3	1128171	557.17	689.51	503.53	363.23	535.74	97.82	313.8
21644	3	1025321	572.61	704.41	524	380.36	555.52	97.82	313.8
25054	3	1275577	569.8	703.12	518.79	377.83	547.94	97.82	313.8
15754	4	1079301	583.08	719.41	537.19	388.87	558.74	115.18	379.25
17766	4	912784	578.35	709.99	519.85	380.16	568.83	115.18	379.25
19075	4	1169489	584.11	717.21	533.93	381.92	574.8	115.18	379.25
21718	4	1289690	574.47	709.38	515.93	374.43	556.71	115.18	379.25
19815	5	963358	581.91	718.77	512.77	380.04	563.75	119.23	385.75
21979	5	1235982	575.72	714.11	510.24	377.15	548.83	119.23	385.75
22063	5	1484762	574.4	712.93	507.46	369.98	551.35	119.23	385.75
28064	5	1435067	574.78	711.8	502.12	371.19	555.69	119.23	385.75
14462	6	1055106	565.28	700.37	490.65	367.94	543.77	105.49	303.4
29676	6	1317249	575.37	712.05	490.39	379.61	552.57	105.49	303.4
21617	6	1521460	566.67	699.67	494.84	376.78	545.17	105.49	303.4
19068	6	1665332	563.92	697.04	489.82	374.25	541.37	105.49	303.4
22706	6	1707089	577.53	714.3	496.64	379.03	556.89	105.49	303.4
13779	7	1083356	585.8	721.04	504.77	384.32	573.75	126.02	395.25
14576	7	1124674	592.18	724.44	516.65	385.81	592.77	126.02	395.25
23166	7	1401763	600.75	736.35	511.7	393.15	597.54	126.02	395.25
28113	7	1434062	576.32	705.13	486.21	392.38	565.72	126.02	395.25
22449	8	1184824	565.27	691.24	477.17	382.9	557.24	133.23	404.5
25389	8	1325002	549.5	675.86	459.08	372.89	531.69	133.23	404.5
24570	8	1358543	535.71	661.37	435.12	369.45	508.76	133.23	404.5
39514	8	1651727	540.82	670.9	438.67	374	504.73	133.23	404.5
14004	9	1223008	512.12	636.17	413.69	369.46	464.55	117.06	308.8
28502	9	1926624	486.31	607.34	384.64	355.23	430.63	117.06	308.8
19945	9	1243068	500.03	624.05	394.62	366.78	442.89	117.06	308.8
24518	9	1327628	507.54	629.21	418.49	376.25	456.12	117.06	308.8
34138	9	1832609	515.68	640.12	419.35	381.42	462.44	117.06	308.8
21071	10	1046013	498.16	614.97	386.9	392.32	440.39	137.94	422.5
23312	10	1073198	486.7	605.58	365.29	383.7	418.75	137.94	422.5
20894	10	993859	522.24	649.71	414.12	388.69	464.84	137.94	422.5
37976	10	1306378	529.82	661.21	412.3	389.94	469.98	137.94	422.5
17546	11	1188695	543.35	676.99	433.23	400.55	483.54	142.97	414
35900	11	1541946	565.1	705.19	447.83	412.67	503.15	142.97	414

TABLE 8.5 *(continued)*

SALES	MONTH	FOV	COMPOSITE	INDUSTRIAL	TRANS	UTILITY	FINANCE	PROD	HOUSE
26701	11	1235015	556.17	696.79	433.05	404.36	489.53	142.97	414
29392	11	1160202	572.08	714.1	446.15	417.69	509.41	142.97	414
9574	12	811251	571.5	712.82	450.45	414.81	511.99	119.32	345.8
16205	12	1339325	573.49	711.58	456.3	427.08	515.51	119.32	345.8
40481	12	1784334	564.82	705.28	443.81	423.92	493.81	119.32	345.8
28947	12	1149021	572.07	709.29	452.81	430.8	512.31	119.32	345.8
31091	12	1487185	589.07	732.77	465.49	443.05	521.66	119.32	345.8
7456	1	255971	595.81	743.65	482.38	445.94	521.42	138.82	444.5
17953	1	994794	611.06	758.46	506.94	455.94	545.91	138.82	444.5
16302	1	1139978	593.39	738.54	477.12	446.09	523.91	138.82	444.5
19521	1	1235139	583.75	724.44	461.94	454.59	510.34	138.82	444.5

CHAPTER 9

An Introduction to Analysis of Variance

 ## 9.1 ONE-WAY ANALYSIS OF VARIANCE

Analysis of variance (ANOVA) is a term used with regression to describe the decomposition of the total sum of squares into two parts: the regression ("explained") sum of squares and the error ("unexplained") sum of squares. ANOVA also describes a statistical technique used to test whether there is a difference between means of several populations. The procedure is very similar to regression analysis. In fact, for one-way analysis of variance, the procedure is the same as if a regression were performed using only indicator variables as explanatory variables. The actual analyses are usually performed with ANOVA routines rather than regression routines because the analysis of variance routines are more efficient computationally for this specific type of problem.

To describe the ANOVA procedure, consider a problem with K populations. One way that the ANOVA model can be written is

$$y_{ij} = \mu_i + e_{ij}$$

where

y_{ij} is the jth observation from population i

μ_i is the population mean for population i

e_{ij} is a random disturbance for the jth observation from population i

Because there are K populations, i ranges from 1 to K. Assuming that there are n_i observations from each population, j ranges from 1 to n_i. The use of the subscript on

n_i implies that the number of sample observations from each population can differ. The total number of observations combining all samples is denoted

$$n = \sum_{i=1}^{K} n_i$$

The following assumptions are made concerning the disturbances e_{ij}:

1 The e_{ij} have mean zero

2 The e_{ij} have constant variance, σ^2

3 The e_{ij} are normally distributed

ANOVA has its own special terminology. As in regression, y_{ij} is called the *dependent variable*. The explanatory variables are called *factors*. A *level* of the factor is a particular value of the explanatory variable. The μ_i are called *factor-level means*. The ANOVA model allows for a different mean for each factor level. Factor levels are also referred to as *treatments* in one-way ANOVA.

An alternative way of writing the ANOVA model is

$$y_{ij} = \mu + \gamma_i + e_{ij}$$

where μ is a constant component common to all observations and γ_i is the effect of the *i*th treatment (or factor level). Here the treatment means are

$$\mu_1 = \mu + \gamma_1$$
$$\mu_2 = \mu + \gamma_2$$

$$.$$
$$.$$
$$.$$

$$\mu_K = \mu + \gamma_K$$

The question to be answered is, "Are the means of all *K* populations equal?" The hypotheses to be tested to answer this question can be stated as

H_0: $\mu_1 = \mu_2 = \ldots = \mu_K$

H_a: Not all means are equal

or as

H_0: $\gamma_1 = \gamma_2 = \cdots = \gamma_K$

H_a: Not all treatment effects are equal

depending on the form of the model used. The test procedure is the same regardless of the way the model is written.

The test statistic used to conduct the test is

$$F = \frac{MSTR}{MSE}$$

where *MSTR* is the *mean square due to treatments* and *MSE* is the *mean square error.* This statistic is similar to the F statistic used to test the overall fit of a regression. The ANOVA F statistic has an F distribution with $K-1$ numerator and $n-K$ denominator degrees of freedom. K is the number of populations and n is the total sample size. The decision rule for the test is

Reject H_0 if $F > F(\alpha; K - 1, n - K)$

Accept H_0 if $F \le F(\alpha; K - 1, n - K)$

The reasoning behind the name *analysis of variance* can be seen by further examination of the test statistic. The F statistic is the ratio of two mean squares, and each mean square is an estimate of the common population variance. One of the assumptions necessary for using ANOVA is that the variances of all populations are equal. This common variance is called σ^2.

MSE provides an unbiased estimate of the variance σ^2. Furthermore, if the means (μ_i) are all equal, *MSTR* also provides an unbiased estimate of σ^2. But when some of the means are not equal, *MSTR* is biased. Thus, if H_0 is false, *MSTR* tends to be bigger than *MSE*, and the null hypothesis is likely to be rejected. If H_0 is true, *MSTR* and *MSE* provide similar estimates, and the F statistic is close to 1, leading to acceptance of the null hypothesis.

The formulas for *MSTR* and *MSE* are as follows:

$$MSTR = \frac{SSTR}{K - 1}$$

The treatment sum of squares, *SSTR*, is

$$SSTR = \sum_{i=1}^{K} n_i (\bar{y}_{i.} - \bar{y}_{..})^2$$

and has $K - 1$ degrees of freedom

$$MSE = \frac{SSE}{n - K}$$

The error sum of squares, *SSE*, is

$$\sum_{i=1}^{K} \sum_{j=1}^{n_i} (y_{ij} - \bar{y}_{i.})^2$$

The notation in these formulas is as follows:

y_{ij} is the jth sample observation from population i,

$\bar{y}_{i.}$ is the mean of all the sample observations for the ith population:

$$\bar{y}_{i.} = \frac{\sum_{j=1}^{n_i} y_{ij}}{n_i}$$

$\bar{y}_{..}$ is the overall mean of all n observations:

$$\bar{y}_{..} = \frac{\sum\limits_{i=1}^{K} \sum\limits_{j=1}^{n_i} y_{ij}}{n}$$

As mentioned, the one-factor ANOVA model is equivalent to a regression model in which all the explanatory variables are indicator variables. The equivalent regression model can be written in two ways, just as the ANOVA model can be written in two ways. For example, the following regression equation is equivalent to the first form of the ANOVA model:

$$y_{ij} = \mu_1 x_{ij1} + \mu_2 x_{ij2} + \cdots + \mu_K x_{ijK} + e_{ij}$$

In this equation, the x_{ijk}s are defined as

x_{ij1} = 1 if the observation corresponds to factor-level one

= 0 otherwise

x_{ij2} = 1 if the observation corresponds to factor-level two

= 0 otherwise,

and so on.

Note that no constant term is included in the regression equation. The constant is unnecessary (and would result in a perfect multicollinearity problem if included). There is an alternate form of the regression model equivalent to the second ANOVA model, but it is not discussed here because regression is typically not used for ANOVA-type problems.

EXAMPLE 9.1   **Automobile Injuries**

U.S. News & World Report, September 28, 1987, listed injury claims for 1984–1986 cars. The claims are listed for cars in the following categories:

small two-door

midsized two-door

large two-door

small four-door

midsized four-door

large four-door

small station wagons and vans

midsized station wagons and vans

large station wagons and vans

The variable CARCLAS is used to indicate into which category each car falls. The categories are coded from 1 to 9 in the order shown. Table 9.1 shows the name of each car, the CARCLAS variable, and a variable INJURY that indicates the number of injury claims for each car.

TABLE **9.1**   Data for Automobile Injuries Example

CAR	CARCLAS	INJURIES	CAR	CARCLAS	INJURIES
Saab 900	1	70	Volkswagen Jetta	4	102
Honda Prelude	1	97	Nissan Stanza	4	103
Mazda 626	1	103	Honda Civic	4	112
Toyota Celica	1	109	Toyota Corolla	4	115
Subaru Hatchback	1	115	Chevrolet Nova	4	115
Volkswagen Scirocco	1	115	Plymouth Horizon	4	116
Mitsubishi Starion	1	119	Toyota Tercel	4	121
Dodge Daytona	1	120	Ford Escort	4	121
Plymouth Colt	1	124	Renault Alliance	4	131
Ford Escort	1	125	Subaru Dl/Gl Sedan	4	132
Mercury Lynx	1	137	Mazda 323	4	137
Mitsubishi Cordia	1	137	Dodge Colt	4	140
Dodge Colt	1	139	Nissan Sentra	4	142
Renault Alliance	1	139	Mitsubishi Tredia	4	149
Nissan Sentra	1	139	Hyundai Excel	4	161
Plymouth Turismo	1	140	Chevrolet Spectrum	4	177
Nissan Pulsar	1	151	Ford Taurus	5	73
Chevrolet Sprint	1	152	Volvo 240	5	78
Chevrolet Spectrum	1	153	Toyota Camry	5	80
Mitsubishi Mirage	1	158	Pontiac Bonneville	5	81
Oldsmobile Cutlass Ciera	2	80	Plymouth Caravelle	5	84
Pontiac 6000	2	85	Pontiac 6000	5	84
Chrysler Lebaron	2	91	Mercury Marquis	5	86
Honda Accord	2	93	Honda Accord	5	87
Chevrolet Monte Carlo	2	95	Chrysler Lebaron Gts	5	87
Buick Regal	2	97	Ford Ltd	5	90
Ford Thunderbird	2	102	Dodge Lancer	5	90
Mercury Cougar	2	111	Chevrolet Celebrity	5	91
Plymouth Reliant	2	117	Nissan Maxima	5	91
Pontiac Grand Am	2	117	Dodge 600	5	94
Ford Tempo	2	123	Audi 4000	5	95
Buick Skyhawk	2	123	Buick Skyhawk	5	102
Chevrolet Cavalier	2	131	Mitsubishi Galant	5	106
Mercury Grand Marquis	3	55	Plymouth Reliant	5	107
Ford Crown Victoria	3	70	Mercury Topaz	5	107
Oldsmobile Ninety-Eight	3	73	Ford Tempo	5	110
Chevrolet Caprice	3	75	Oldsmobile Firenza	5	113
Saab 900	4	66	Chevrolet Cavalier	5	118
Mazda 626	4	96	Pontiac Sunbird	5	121

Continues

TABLE **9.1** *(continued)*

CAR	CARCLAS	INJURIES	CAR	CARCLAS	INJURIES
Dodge Diplomat	6	61	Oldsmobile Cutlass Ciera	8	75
Mercury Grand Marquis	6	63	Nissan Maxima	8	81
Plymouth Gran Fury	6	66	Ford Celebrity	8	82
Buick Electra	6	68	Pontiac Sunbird	8	89
Pontiac Parisienne	6	70	Plymouth Reliant	8	91
Oldsmobile Ninety-Eight	6	70	Dodge Colt Vista	8	93
Toyota Van	7	75	Plymouth Colt Vista	8	97
Volkswagen Vanagon	7	78	Chevrolet Cavalier	8	98
Subaru Dl/Gl 4-Wh. Dr.	7	84	Buick Skyhawk	8	103
Toyota Tercel 4-Wh. Dr.	7	90	Pontiac Parisienne	9	52
Nissan Stanza	7	93	Mercury Grand Marquis	9	53
Subaru Dl/Gl	7	98	Oldsmobile Custom Cruiser	9	54
Honda Civic	7	100	Chevrolet Caprice	9	60
Volvo 240	8	58	Plymouth Voyager	9	63
Mercury Marquis	8	60	Dodge Caravan	9	65
Buick Century	8	73	Ford Aerostar	9	65
Chrysler Lebaron	8	74	Chevrolet Astro Van	9	68

Figure 9.1 shows the MINITAB ANOVA output for this problem. Figure 9.2(a) shows the ANOVA table for MINITAB in general form. The sums of squares due to the treatment variable, error, and the total sum of squares are printed along with their degrees of freedom. *MSTR, MSE,* the *F* statistic, and a *p* value associated with the observed *F* statistic are computed. Below the ANOVA table, MINITAB also lists summary information for the factor levels. The sample size, mean, and standard deviation for the observations in each factor-level are given. Individual confidence intervals for each factor-level (population) mean are shown graphically. (Note that these intervals should be used with caution for comparing two factor-level means. A better approach is discussed later.)

The description of a general ANOVA table for Excel is given in Figure 9.2(b). Figure 9.3 shows the Excel ANOVA output for the example. Information similar to that shown in the MINITAB ANOVA table is represented in the Excel ANOVA table. One difference is that the Excel table also provides a critical value for the *F* statistic. Above the ANOVA table, Excel also lists summary information for the factor levels. The sample size, the sum of the observations, the mean, and the variance for the observations in each factor level are given. Excel refers to the treatment sum of squares as the between groups sum of squares and the error sum of squares as the within groups sum of squares.

The decision rule for the test using a 5% level of significance is

Reject H_0 if $F > 2.10$

Accept H_0 if $F \leq 2.10$

FIGURE 9.1   MINITAB ANOVA Output for Automobile Injuries Example

```
Analysis of Variance for INJURY
Source               DF          SS          MS          F          P
CARCLAS               8       54762        6845      22.80      0.000
Error               103       30917         300
Total               111       85679

                                          Individual 95% CIs For Mean
                                          Based on Pooled StDev
Level      N       Mean      StDev    -+---------+---------+---------+-----
1         20     127.10      21.89                                 (--*--)
2         13     105.00      16.29                         (---*---)
3          4      68.25       9.07    (------*------)
4         18     124.22      25.58                             (---*--)
5         23      94.57      13.38                      (--*--)
6          6      66.33       3.72      (-----*----)
7          7      88.29       9.64             (----*-----)
8         13      82.62      14.21            (---*---)
9          8      60.00       6.23      (----*----)
                                       -+---------+---------+---------+-----
Pooled StDev =    17.33              50          75        100        125
```

FIGURE 9.2   Structure of the MINITAB and Excel ANOVA Tables

(a) MINITAB   Analysis of Variance for (dependent variable name)

Source	DF	SS	MS	F	p
Treatment var	$K - 1$	SSTR	MSTR	$\dfrac{MSTR}{MSE}$	p value
Error	$n - K$	SSE	MSE		
Total	$n - 1$	SST			

(b) Excel   ANOVA

Source of Variation	SS	df	MS	F	P-value	F crit
Between Groups	SSTR	$K - 1$	MSTR	$\dfrac{MSTR}{MSE}$	p value	$F(\alpha; K - 1, n - K)$
Within Groups	SSE	$n - K$	MSE			
Total	SST	$n - 1$				

FIGURE 9.3   Excel ANOVA Output for Automobile Injuries Example

```
Anova: Single Factor
```

SUMMARY OUTPUT

Groups	Count	Sum	Average	Variance
class1	20	2542	127.100	479.042
class2	13	1365	105.000	265.500
class3	4	273	68.250	82.250
class4	18	2236	124.222	654.418
class5	23	2175	94.565	178.893
class6	6	398	66.333	13.867
class7	7	618	88.286	92.905
class8	13	1074	82.615	201.923
class9	8	480	60.000	38.857

ANOVA

Source of Variation	SS	df	MS	F	P-value	F crit
Between Groups	54762.268	8	6845.283	22.805	0.000	2.030
Within Groups	30917.152	103	300.167			
Total	85679.420	111				

The critical value is chosen from the $\alpha = 0.05$ level F table with 8 numerator and 103 (approximately) denominator degrees of freedom. (Using Excel, the critical value provided is 2.03. Excel computes the exact critical value rather than approximating the value from a table.) The test statistic value, 22.80, exceeds the critical value, so the null hypothesis is rejected. There is a difference in the factor-level means. The average level of injuries differs depending on the type of car.

Analysis of variance is often used in an experimental design situation. The term *experiment* refers to the data collection process. The term *design* refers to the plan for conducting the experiment. In many situations, the researcher can assign objects upon which measurements are to be made (called *experimental units*) to the factor levels or treatments. This was not done in the previous example. Once a car was chosen for the example—say, a Ford Thunderbird—the researcher had no control over which factor level this case was assigned. A Ford Thunderbird is a midsized two-door, so it automatically is assigned to factor level two.

EXAMPLE 9.2   **Computer Sales**

Consider a situation where experimental design can be used. The effect of different selling approaches on sales of computers is to be studied. Three different selling approaches are to be compared. The object is to determine whether there is a difference in the effectiveness of the selling approaches. We will judge differences in effectiveness by looking at the average sales of the three approaches. An approach with significantly higher average sales will be judged more effective. Fifteen salespeople are chosen to participate in the study. Five salespeople each are randomly assigned to use one of the three approaches for the next month. At the end of the month, sales figures will be computed for each salesperson. These data will be analyzed to determine whether the sales approaches produce the same or different average sales.

In this situation, the salespeople were randomly assigned to the factor levels or treatments. This random assignment is possible when an experiment is designed to help answer a particular question. The type of experimental design used in this case is called a *completely randomized design*. Analysis of variance can be used in this situation to analyze the data just as in the automobile-injuries example.

Suppose the following sales figures (in $1000) resulted from the experiment just described:

	Selling Approaches		
Salesperson	A	B	C
1	15	19	28
2	17	17	25
3	21	17	22
4	13	25	31
5	12	30	34

The hypotheses to be tested are

$$H_0: \quad \mu_A = \mu_B = \mu_C$$

$$H_a: \quad \text{All three means are not equal}$$

where μ_i is the population average sales for selling approach i. The MINITAB output for this analysis is shown in Figure 9.4 and the Excel output is in Figure 9.5. To test the hypotheses, either the F statistic or its associated p value could be used. If the F statistic is used, the decision rule is (with a 5% level of significance):

Reject H_0 if $F > 3.89$

Accept H_0 if $F \leq 3.89$

where the critical value is chosen with 2 numerator and 12 denominator degrees of freedom. The test statistic is $F = 8.47$, so the decision is to reject the null hypothesis.

Rejection of the null hypotheses leads to the conclusion that the population average sales differ depending on what selling approach is used.

FIGURE 9.4 MINITAB ANOVA Output for Computer Sales Example

```
Analysis of Variance for SALES
Source            DF          SS          MS          F          P
CARCLAS            2       384.5       192.3       8.47      0.005
Error             12       272.4        22.7
Total             14       656.9
                                        Individual 95% CIs For Mean
                                        Based on Pooled StDev
Level      N       Mean      StDev    --+---------+---------+---------+----
1          5     15.600      3.578    (-------*-------)
2          5     21.600      5.727              (-------*-------)
3          5     28.000      4.743                        (-------*-------)
                                      --+---------+---------+---------+----
Pooled StDev =   4.764               12.0      18.0      24.0      30.0
```

FIGURE 9.5 Excel ANOVA Output for Computer Sales Example

```
Anova: Single Factor
```

SUMMARY OUTPUT

Groups	Count	Sum	Average	Variance
APPROACH A	5	78	15.6	12.8
APPROACH B	5	108	21.6	32.8
APPROACH C	5	140	28	22.5

ANOVA

Source of Variation	SS	df	MS	F	P-value	F crit
Between Groups	384.533	2.000	192.267	8.470	0.005	3.885
Within Groups	272.400	12.000	22.700			
Total	656.933	14.000				

Note that rejection of the null hypothesis simply says that the population means are not all equal. It does not say they are all different or tell which ones are different from the others. In a case such as this, the researcher probably wants to know which population averages are different or whether two particular ones differ. A $(1 - \alpha)100\%$ confidence interval estimate of the difference between two means, μ_i and μ_j, can be constructed as follows:

$$\bar{y}_{i.} - \bar{y}_{j.} \pm t_{\alpha/2} s \sqrt{\left(\frac{1}{n_i}\right) + \left(\frac{1}{n_j}\right)}$$

where $t_{\alpha/2}$ is the value chosen to put $\alpha/2$ probability in the upper tail of the t distribution using $n - K$ degrees of freedom, s is the square root of MSE, and $\bar{y}_{i.}$ and $\bar{y}_{j.}$ are the sample means for samples i and j (or factors i and j).

EXAMPLE 9.3   ## Computer Sales (continued)

In the computer sales example, the following is the 95% confidence interval estimate of the difference between selling approaches A and C:

$$(15.6 - 28.0) \pm (2.179)(4.76) \sqrt{\left(\frac{1}{5}\right) + \left(\frac{1}{5}\right)}$$

or $(-18.96, -5.84)$

Because the 95% confidence interval estimate of the difference between these two population means does not contain zero, this suggests that the population means for methods A and C are not equal.

This type of comparison works when only two means are compared. If this type of interval estimate is used for a series of comparisons, the level of significance will no longer be appropriate. Three procedures can be used when such multiple comparisons are desired: the Tukey method, the Scheffé method, and the Bonferroni method. Only the Bonferroni method is discussed here. The *Bonferroni approach* is a method of comparing multiple quantities (means in this case) that assumes the user can specify in advance which quantities are to be compared.[1] The Bonferroni intervals used to compare pairs of means are constructed as

$$\bar{y}_{i.} - \bar{y}_{j.} \pm Bs \sqrt{\left(\frac{1}{n_i}\right) + \left(\frac{1}{n_j}\right)}$$

---

[1] See Neter, Wasserman, and Kutner, *Applied Linear Statistical Models*, p. 584, for a discussion of when the Tukey and Scheffé methods may be preferred to the Bonferroni. See References for complete publication information.

where B is a t value chosen to put $\dfrac{\alpha}{2g}$ probability in the upper tail of the t distribution using $n - K$ degrees of freedom. Here g is the number of comparisons to be made.

EXAMPLE 9.4 **Computer Sales (continued)**

Suppose all possible pairs of means are to be compared in the computer sales example with a 95% confidence level. Intervals are to be constructed to estimate $\mu_A - \mu_B$, $\mu_B - \mu_C$, and $\mu_A - \mu_C$. Because there are three comparisons to be made ($g = 3$), the Bonferroni confidence coefficient, B, is the t value that puts $0.05/(2)(3) = 0.008$ probability in the upper tail of the t distribution. In this example, the 0.005 column is used in order to insure at least a 95% confidence level. The interval estimates are

$$\mu_A - \mu_B: \qquad (15.6 - 21.6) \pm (3.055)(4.76)\sqrt{\left(\frac{1}{5}\right) + \left(\frac{1}{5}\right)}$$

$$\text{or} \qquad (-15.20, 3.20)$$

$$\mu_B - \mu_C: \qquad (21.6 - 28.0) \pm (3.055)(4.76)\sqrt{\left(\frac{1}{5}\right) + \left(\frac{1}{5}\right)}$$

$$\text{or} \qquad (-15.6, 2.80)$$

$$\mu_A - \mu_C: \qquad (15.6 - 28.0) \pm (3.055)(4.76)\sqrt{\left(\frac{1}{5}\right) + \left(\frac{1}{5}\right)}$$

$$\text{or} \qquad (-21.60, -3.20)$$

The three estimates are said to have a *familywise* confidence level of 95%. This means that the estimates can be viewed simultaneously rather than one at a time and that the 95% confidence level applies.

EXERCISES

1 **Automobile Collisions**   The *U.S. News & World Report*, September 28, 1987, issue lists numbers of collision claims (COLLISION) reported for 1984–1986 cars. The claims are listed in the same categories as described for Example 9.1 and are shown in Table 9.2. Using the classification variable (CARCLAS) described in that example, an ANOVA was run on the number of collisions. Figures 9.6 and 9.7 provide the MINITAB and Excel ANOVA outputs, respectively. Use the outputs to determine whether there is a difference in the average number of collisions for different types of

TABLE **9.2**   Data for Automobile Collisions Exercise

Car	CARCLAS	COLLISION	Car	CARCLAS	COLLISION
Saab 900	1	155	Honda Civic	4	100
Honda Prelude	1	119	Toyota Corolla	4	88
Mazda 626	1	137	Chevrolet Nova	4	91
Toyota Celica	1	137	Plymouth Horizon	4	87
Subaru Hatchback	1	103	Toyota Tercel	4	81
Volkswagen Scirocco	1	232	Ford Escort	4	82
Mitsubishi Starion	1	254	Renault Alliance	4	102
Dodge Daytona	1	160	Subaru Dl/Gl Sedan	4	113
Plymouth Colt	1	122	Mazda 323	4	112
Ford Escort	1	98	Dodge Colt	4	124
Mercury Lynx	1	98	Nissan Sentra	4	111
Mitsubishi Cordia	1	186	Mitsubishi Tredia	4	145
Dodge Colt	1	111	Hyundai Excel	4	123
Renault Alliance	1	118	Chevrolet Spectrum	4	103
Nissan Sentra	1	118	Ford Taurus	5	75
Plymouth Turismo	1	135	Volvo 240	5	95
Nissan Pulsar	1	142	Toyota Camry	5	70
Chevrolet Sprint	1	106	Pontiac Bonneville	5	67
Chevrolet Spectrum	1	103	Plymouth Caravelle	5	78
Mitsubishi Mirage	1	147	Pontiac 6000	5	83
Oldsmobile Cutlass Ciera	2	80	Mercury Marquis	5	76
Pontiac 6000	2	70	Honda Accord	5	92
Chrysler Lebaron	2	98	Chrysler Lebaron Gts	5	93
Honda Accord	2	103	Ford Ltd	5	75
Chevrolet Monte Carlo	2	108	Dodge Lancer	5	97
Buick Regal	2	91	Chevrolet Celebrity	5	73
Ford Thunderbird	2	114	Nissan Maxima	5	121
Mercury Cougar	2	119	Dodge 600	5	79
Plymouth Reliant	2	88	Audi 4000	5	158
Pontiac Grand Am	2	104	Buick Skyhawk	5	87
Ford Tempo	2	93	Mitsubishi Galant	5	130
Buick Skyhawk	2	110	Plymouth Reliant	5	83
Chevrolet Cavalier	2	121	Mercury Topaz	5	85
Mercury Grand Marquis	3	52	Ford Tempo	5	84
Ford Crown Victoria	3	68	Oldsmobile Firenza	5	83
Oldsmobile Ninety-Eight	3	72	Chevrolet Cavalier	5	91
Chevrolet Caprice	3	67	Pontiac Sunbird	5	101
Saab 900	4	122	Dodge Diplomat	6	65
Mazda 626	4	108	Mercury Grand Marquis	6	55
Volkswagen Jetta	4	110	Plymouth Gran Fury	6	65
Nissan Stanza	4	109	Buick Electra	6	79

Continues

TABLE 9.2 *(continued)*

Car	CARCLAS	COLLISION	Car	CARCLAS	COLLISION
Pontiac Parisienne	6	59	Ford Celebrity	8	64
Oldsmobile Ninety-Eight	6	76	Pontiac Sunbird	8	80
Toyota Van	7	77	Plymouth Reliant	8	69
Volkswagen Vanagon	7	76	Dodge Colt Vista	8	91
Subaru Dl/Gl 4-Wh. Dr.	7	94	Plymouth Colt Vista	8	89
Toyota Tercel 4-Wh. Dr.	7	70	Chevrolet Cavalier	8	75
Nissan Stanza	7	79	Buick Skyhawk	8	65
Subaru Dl/Gl	7	87	Pontiac Parisienne	9	59
Honda Civic	7	76	Mercury Grand Marquis	9	82
Volvo 240	8	84	Oldsmobile Custom Cruiser	9	59
Mercury Marquis	8	74	Chevrolet Caprice	9	63
Buick Century	8	80	Plymouth Voyager	9	58
Chrysler Lebaron	8	90	Dodge Caravan	9	57
Oldsmobile Cutlass Ciera	8	66	Ford Aerostar	9	63
Nissan Maxima	8	113	Chevrolet Astro Van	9	49

FIGURE 9.6 MINITAB ANOVA Output for Automobile Collisions Example

```
Analysis of Variance for COLLISIO
Source      DF        SS        MS        F        P
CARCLAS      8     63790      7974    14.82    0.000
Error      103     55427       538
Total      111    119218

                               Individual 95% CIs For Mean
                               Based on Pooled StDev
Level       N      Mean     StDev  -------+---------+---------+---------
1          20    139.05     42.47                               (--*---)
2          13     99.92     15.18                  (---*----)
3           4     64.75      8.77   (-------*------)
4          18    106.17     16.63                    (--*---)
5          23     90.26     21.04              (--*--)
6           6     66.50      9.38    (-----*-----)
7           7     79.86      8.03        (-----*----)
8          13     80.00     13.74        (----*---)
9           8     61.25      9.45   (----*-----)
                                     -------+---------+---------+---------
Pooled StDev =     23.20                  60        90       120
```

FIGURE **9.7**   Excel ANOVA Output for Automobile Collisions Exercise

Anova: Single Factor

SUMMARY OUTPUT

Groups	Count	Sum	Average	Variance
CLASS1	20	2781	139.050	1803.945
CLASS2	13	1299	99.923	230.410
CLASS3	4	259	64.750	76.917
CLASS4	18	1911	106.167	276.500
CLASS5	23	2076	90.261	442.656
CLASS6	6	399	66.500	87.900
CLASS7	7	559	79.857	64.476
CLASS8	13	1040	80.000	188.833
CLASS9	8	490	61.250	89.357

ANOVA

Source of Variation	SS	df	MS	F	P-value	F crit
Between Groups	63790.264	8.000	7973.783	14.818	0.000	2.030
Within Groups	55427.415	103.000	538.130			
Total	119217.679	111.000				

cars. Use a 5% level of significance. State the hypotheses to be tested, the decision rule, the test statistic, and your decision.

These data are available in a file with prefix CRASH9 in two columns: CARCLAS and COLLISION.

9.2   ANALYSIS OF VARIANCE USING A RANDOMIZED BLOCK DESIGN

In some situations, designs other than the completely randomized design discussed in the previous section can be beneficial. Another type of experimental design is called a *randomized block design*. Only randomized block designs with one value per treatment-block combination are considered in this text. (Randomized block designs with

TABLE 9.3 The Assignment of Treatments to Experimental Units for Computer Sales Example

Blocks	Treatment Order		
1	T_1	T_3	T_2
2	T_2	T_1	T_3
3	T_3	T_1	T_2
4	T_3	T_2	T_1
5	T_1	T_2	T_3

more than one value per treatment-block combination can be used, but there are adjustments that are needed such as different equations for various degrees of freedom.) Consider again the problem in Example 9.2 involving the study of the three different selling approaches. In the completely randomized design, fifteen salespeople were used. Five people each were randomly assigned to each selling approach (treatment). One-way ANOVA was then used to determine whether the average sales for each group were significantly different. Two types of variation affect the sample averages computed in this case: (a) the variation that results from the differences in selling approaches and (b) the variation from the individuals involved in the study. Certain individuals simply may be better salespeople than others regardless of the sales approach used.

The goal of the study is to determine whether the difference in the sample means that results from differences in selling approaches is significant. The second type of variation is a hindrance to this goal because the additional variation may make it difficult to determine what is actually causing the differences in the means. Is it the selling approaches themselves or the individuals assigned to the three groups? To eliminate this second source of variation, a randomized block design can be used. The idea of the randomized block design is to compare the means of treatments within fairly homogeneous blocks of experimental units.

In the example given, instead of choosing fifteen people and randomly assigning them to use a particular selling approach, it might be better to choose five people and let each person use all three of the selling approaches. The treatments in this study are still the three selling approaches. The blocks are the salespeople themselves. The experimental units within a block are instances when the different treatments can be "applied" to the salespeople. Table 9.3 illustrates this situation. The treatments (selling approaches) are denoted T_1, T_2, and T_3. The three treatments have been applied to each block (salesperson) in a randomized order. Thus, during the first month, salespersons 1 and 5 use approach 1, salespersons 3 and 4 use approach 3, and salesperson 2 uses approach 2. The order of the treatments within each block is determined by using a random number table.

When the blocks are the subjects to be used in the experiment, the design is often referred to as a *repeated measures design*. One advantage of this type of randomized block design is that all sources of variability between subjects are removed. Another

TABLE **9.4**   The Assignment of Treatments to Experimental Units for Cereal Package Design Example

Blocks	Treatment Order			
1	T_2	T_1	T_3	T_4
2	T_1	T_2	T_4	T_3
3	T_4	T_3	T_1	T_2
4	T_3	T_1	T_2	T_4
5	T_1	T_4	T_3	T_2

advantage is that fewer subjects are needed. In this example, five subjects were needed rather than the fifteen needed when the completely randomized design was used.

One serious potential disadvantage of the repeated measures design is the effect of time order in the application of the treatments. In this example, sales may vary somewhat by month—that is, those treatments applied in month 1 may produce higher sales than in month 2 simply because of some type of monthly seasonal variation. An attempt has been made to minimize this variation by randomizing the treatment order independently for each subject.

Another example of a randomized block design that is not a repeated measures design follows.

EXAMPLE **9.5**   ## Cereal Package Design

A company wishes to evaluate the effect of package design on one of its products, a certain brand of cereal. The four package designs (treatments) are to be tested in different stores throughout a large city. There are twenty stores available for the study. Cereal sales is known to vary depending on the size of the stores, so size is used as a blocking variable. The twenty stores are divided into five groups of four stores each by size. Table 9.4 illustrates the design. The treatments are randomized within each block. The randomization is performed independently between blocks.

The model for a randomized block design can be written

$$y_{ij} = \mu + \gamma_i + B_j + e_{ij}$$

where

μ is an overall mean

γ_i is the ith treatment effect

B_j is the jth block effect

e_{ij} is the random disturbance for treatment i and block j

There are K treatments and b blocks, so $i = 1, \ldots, K$ and $j = 1, \ldots, b$.

FIGURE 9.8   ANOVA Table for Randomized Block Design

Source	DF	SS	MS	F	p
Blocks	$b-1$	SSBL	MSBL	MSBL/MSE	p value
Treatments	$K-1$	SSTR	MSTR	MSTR/MSE	p value
Error	$(b-1)(K-1)$	SSE	MSE		
Total	$bK-1$	SST			

An example of the type of ANOVA table used to analyze this model is shown in Figure 9.8. Three sources of variation are identified: blocks, treatments, and error. The sums of squares, the mean squares, and the degrees of freedom associated with each of these sources are shown, along with F statistics and p values. Note that the degrees of freedom from the three sources sum to the total degrees of freedom: $(b-1) + (K-1) + (b-1)(K-1) = bK-1$. This is also true for the sums of squares: $SSBL + SSTR + SSE = SST$.

The goal of the analysis is to determine whether the treatment effects differ:

$H_0: \quad \gamma_1 = \gamma_2 = \cdots = \gamma_K$

$H_a: \quad$ All treatment effects are not equal

The decision rule to perform the test is:

Reject H_0 if $F > F(\alpha; K-1, (b-1)(K-1))$

Accept H_0 if $F \leq F(\alpha; K-1, (b-1)(K-1))$

The test statistic is

$$F = \frac{MSTR}{MSE}$$

If the null hypothesis is rejected, then the conclusion is that the treatment effects differ.

A test can also be conducted to determine whether the block effects differ:

$H_0: \quad B_1 = B_2 = \cdots = B_b$

$H_a: \quad$ All block effects are not equal

The decision rule to perform the test is

Reject H_0 if $F > F(\alpha; b-1, (b-1)(K-1))$

Accept H_0 if $F \leq F(\alpha; b-1, (b-1)(K-1))$

The test statistic is

$$F = \frac{MSBL}{MSE}$$

where $MSBL$ is the mean square due to blocks.

If the null hypothesis is rejected, then the conclusion is that the block effects differ. In this case, the use of blocking has helped and should continue. But if the null hypothesis is accepted, then the conclusion is that the block effects are equal. The use of blocks appears unnecessary, and information may actually be lost by blocking. In many cases, however, the use of blocking continues regardless of the outcome of this test if it is felt that blocking truly produces more homogeneous groups and therefore reduces variation. As a result, the test for block effects is often not used.

A $(1 - \alpha)100\%$ confidence interval estimate for the difference between two treatment means is given by

$$(\bar{y}_i - \bar{y}_{i'}) \pm t_{\alpha/2} s \sqrt{\frac{2}{b}}$$

where $\bar{y}_i$ and $\bar{y}_{i'}$ are sample means for treatments i and i', $t_{\alpha/2}$ is chosen with $(b - 1)$ $(K - 1)$ degrees of freedom, s is the square root of MSE, and b is the number of blocks.

If more than one pair of treatment means is to be compared, a familywise $(1 - \alpha)$ 100% level of confidence can be achieved by using the Bonferroni confidence coefficient described in the previous section.

EXAMPLE **9.6**   ## Cereal Package Design (continued)

Consider again the design of cereal packages. Four package designs (treatments) are to be tested in twenty stores. The twenty stores are divided into five groups (blocks) of four stores each by size. The treatments are randomized within each block and independently between blocks. The data obtained are shown in Table 9.5. This is the way the data would be entered in Excel (discussed further in the Using the Computer section). Table 9.6 shows the data in an alternate form. This is the way the data would be entered for analysis in MINITAB.

The MINITAB output for this example is shown in Figure 9.9 and the Excel output is in Figure 9.10. In the output, the blocks are denoted SIZE and the treatments are denoted DESIGN. The MINITAB and Excel ANOVA tables contain the information in the general ANOVA table of Figure 9.8. The general structure of the MINITAB and Excel ANOVA tables is shown in Figure 9.11. The Excel output shows some additional information above the ANOVA table. Included are the number of observations, the sum, average, and variance of the observations in each block and at each treatment level.

To determine whether there is a difference in sales because of package design, the following hypotheses should be tested:

H_0: $\gamma_1 = \gamma_2 = \gamma_3 = \gamma_4$

H_a: All treatment effects are not equal

TABLE **9.5**   Data for Cereal Package Design Example as It Would Be Entered for Excel Analysis

Sales (in $1000)

Blocks	Treatments			
1	40	23	17	33
2	32	45	40	25
3	43	31	38	47
4	44	41	56	45
5	43	60	47	64

TABLE **9.6**   Data for Cereal Package Design Example as It Would Be Entered for MINITAB Analysis

SALES	SIZE	DESIGN
40	1	1
23	1	2
17	1	3
33	1	4
32	2	1
45	2	2
40	2	3
25	2	4
43	3	1
31	3	2
38	3	3
47	3	4
44	4	1
41	4	2
56	4	3
45	4	4
43	5	1
60	5	2
47	5	3
64	5	4

FIGURE **9.9**   MINITAB ANOVA Output for Cereal Package Design Example

```
Analysis of Variance for SALES
Source          DF          SS          MS          F          P
SIZE             4      1521.7       380.4       4.17      0.024
DESIGN           3        31.0        10.3       0.11      0.951
Error           12      1093.5        91.1
Total           19      2646.2
```

FIGURE **9.10**   Excel ANOVA Output for Cereal Package Design Example

```
Anova: Two-Factor Without Replication
```

SUMMARY OUTPUT

Summary	Count	Sum	Average	Variance
SIZE1	4	113	28.250	104.917
SIZE2	4	142	35.500	77.667
SIZE3	4	159	39.750	47.583
SIZE4	4	186	46.500	43.000
SIZE5	4	214	53.500	101.667
DESIGN1	5	202	40.400	24.300
DESIGN2	5	200	40.000	199.000
DESIGN3	5	198	39.600	209.300
DESIGN4	5	214	42.800	221.200

ANOVA

Source of Variation	SS	df	MS	F	P-value	F crit
Rows	1521.700	4.000	380.425	4.175	0.024	3.259
Columns	31.000	3.000	10.333	0.113	0.951	3.490
Error	1093.500	12.000	91.125			
Total	2646.200	19.000				

FIGURE 9.11   Structure of the MINITAB and Excel ANOVA Tables for a Randomized Block Design

(a) MINITAB

Analysis of Variance for (dependent variable name)

Source	DF	SS	MS	F	p
Blocks	$b - 1$	SSBL	MSBL	MSBL/MSE	p value
Treatments	$K - 1$	SSTR	MSTR	MSTR/MSE	p value
Error	$(b - 1)(K - 1)$	SSE	MSE		
Total	$bK - 1$	SST			

(b) Excel

ANOVA

Source of Variation	SS	df	MS	F	P value	F crit
Rows	SSBL	$b - 1$	MSBL	MSBL/MSE	p value	$F(\alpha; b - 1, (b - 1)(K - 1))$
Columns	SSTR	$K - 1$	MSTR	MSTR/MSE	p value	$F(\alpha; K - 1, (b - 1)(K - 1))$
Error	SSE	$(b - 1)(K - 1)$	MSE			
Total	SST	$bK - 1$				

The decision rule for the test is

Reject H_0 if $F > F(0.05; 3,12) = 3.49$

Accept H_0 if $F \leq F(0.05; 3,12) = 3.49$

The test statistic is

$$F = \frac{MSTR}{MSE} = 0.11$$

The null hypothesis cannot be rejected. There is no evidence of a difference in sales because of package design.

EXERCISES

2 **Advertising**   A study was undertaken by a company that markets iced tea to determine the effectiveness of three types of advertising: (a) price discounts, (b) manufacturer's coupons, and (c) rebates. Three cities of nearly equal size are selected for the experiment. Each of the advertising strategies is to be used for a period of 2 months in each city, and the sales of the company's iced tea recorded for the 2-month period. It is known, however, that iced tea sales are highly seasonal. Thus, the months selected for a particular ad strategy could highly influence the level of sales. A randomized block design is used to eliminate the seasonal effects.

For each time period (block), the advertising strategies (treatments) are randomly assigned to the three cities. The results are shown in Table 9.7. The variable ADV is coded as 1 = price discounts, 2 = manufacturer's coupons, and 3 = rebates. The variable BLOCK is coded as 1 = first 2-month period, 2 = second 2-month period, and 3 = third 2-month period.

Treating the experiment as a randomized block design, the MINITAB and Excel outputs in Figures 9.12 and 9.13, respectively, were obtained. Use the outputs to determine whether the effects of the advertising strategies differ. Use a 5% level of significance. State any hypotheses to be tested, the decision rule, the test statistic, and your decision.

These data are available in a file with prefix ADVERT9 in three columns: SALES, ADV, and BLOCK.

TABLE **9.7**   Data for Advertising Exercise

SALES (in $1000)	BLOCK	ADV
30	1	1
21	2	1
14	3	1
33	1	2
25	2	2
19	3	2
41	1	3
32	2	3
24	3	3

FIGURE 9.12 MINITAB Output for Advertising Exercise

```
Analysis of Variance for SALES
Source      DF         SS          MS         F           P
BLOCK        2    369.556     184.778    302.36       0.000
ADV          2    174.222      87.111    142.55       0.000
Error        4      2.444       0.611
Total        8    546.222
```

FIGURE 9.13 Excel Output for Advertising Exercise

```
Anova: Two-Factor Without Replication
```

SUMMARY OUTPUT

SUMMARY	Count	Sum	Average	Variance
BLOCK1	3	104	34.667	32.333
BLOCK2	3	78	26.000	31.000
BLOCK3	3	57	19.000	25.000
ADV1	3	65	21.667	64.333
ADV2	3	77	25.667	49.333
ADV3	3	97	32.333	72.333

ANOVA

Source of Variation	SS	df	MS	F	P-value	F crit
Rows	369.556	2.000	184.778	302.364	0.000	6.944
Columns	174.222	2.000	87.111	142.545	0.000	6.944
Error	2.444	4.000	0.611			
Total	546.222	8.000				

9.3 TWO-WAY ANALYSIS OF VARIANCE

Two-way ANOVA refers to a situation where there are two factors or explanatory variables. For example, suppose a company wants to investigate the effect of selling price and type of advertising on sales of its top-of-the-line printer. The two possible prices investigated are $600 and $700. There are three types of advertising: television, radio, and newspaper.

In general, denote the two factors in the study as A and B and the number of levels of each factor as n_1 and n_2, respectively. Each combination of a factor level of A and a factor level of B is called a *treatment*. The total number of possible treatments in a two-factor study is $n_1 n_2$. In the example given, there are $2 \times 3 = 6$ possible treatments:

1   $600 price and television advertising
2   $600 price and radio advertising
3   $600 price and newspaper advertising
4   $700 price and television advertising
5   $700 price and radio advertising
6   $700 price and newspaper advertising

This type of design is called a *factorial design*. When all treatment combinations (or factor-level combinations) are used, the experiment is termed a *complete factorial experiment*. This is the design considered in this section.

Equal sample sizes are assumed for each treatment. (Unequal sample sizes are not considered in this text.) The number of observations for each treatment is denoted r. The total number of observations is $n = n_1 n_2 r$. The number of observations for each treatment must be at least two ($r \geq 2$).

The two-way ANOVA model is written

$$y_{ijk} = \mu + \alpha_i + \beta_j + (\alpha\beta)_{ij} + e_{ijk}$$

where

y_{ijk} is the kth observation for factor level i of factor A and factor level j of factor B

μ is a common component for all treatments

α_i is the effect of factor A at level i

β_j is the effect of factor B at level j

$(\alpha\beta)_{ij}$ is called the interaction effect for factors A and B

e_{ijk} is a random disturbance

Here, $i = 1, 2, \ldots, n_1$; $j = 1, 2, \ldots, n_2$; and $k = 1, 2, \ldots, r$ with $r \geq 2$.

In the two-way ANOVA setting, hypotheses can be tested to determine whether the effects due to either factor A or factor B are equal or different. The factor effects

FIGURE **9.14** Sample ANOVA Table for Two-Way Design

Source	df	SS	MS	F	P
Factor A	$n_1 - 1$	SSA	$MSA = SSA/(n_1 - 1)$	MSA/MSE	p value
Factor B	$n_2 - 1$	SSB	$MSB = SSB/(n_2 - 1)$	MSB/MSE	p value
Interaction	$(n_1 - 1)(n_2 - 1)$	SSINT	$MSINT = SSINT/[(n_1 - 1)(n_2 - 1)]$	MSINT/MSE	p value
Error	$n_1 n_2 (r - 1)$	SSE	$MSE = SSE/[n_1 n_2 (r - 1)]$		
Total	$n_1 n_1 r - 1$	SST			

due to A and B are called *main effects*. Hypotheses also can be tested to determine whether the interaction effects are equal. *Interaction effects* are used to represent situations when differences in mean levels of factor A may depend on the levels of factor B. The model has no interaction effects if the difference in mean levels of factor A is independent of the levels of B.

The first test that should be conducted is the test for interaction effects. The tests for main effects are relevant only if no interaction exists. If interaction exists, then the tests for factor-level means are inappropriate. In this case, individual treatment means must be examined, as is demonstrated in Example 9.7.

An example of the type of ANOVA table used in two-way analysis of variance problems is shown in Figure 9.14. Total variation in the dependent variable is attributed to four sources: the two factors A and B, the interaction between the two factors, and random error. The degrees of freedom, sum of squares, and mean square for each source are shown, along with F statistics and p values. The tests that can be performed using the ANOVA table are outlined next.

Test for Interaction Effects

H_0: No interaction between factors A and B exists—All $(\alpha\beta)_{ij} = 0$

H_a: Factors A and B interact—At least one $(\alpha\beta)_{ij}$ is not equal to zero

The decision rule for the test is:

Reject H_0 if $F > F(\alpha; (n_1 - 1)(n_2 - 1), n_1 n_2(r-1))$

Accept H_0 if $F \leq F(\alpha; (n_1 - 1)(n_2 - 1), n_1 n_2(r-1))$

The test statistic is

$$F = \frac{MSINT}{MSE}$$

where *MSINT* is the mean square due to interaction. If the null hypothesis is accepted, then conclude that there is no interaction between the factors A and B. To determine whether the factor-level means are equal, the following tests can be performed.

Test for Factor A Effects

H_0: $\alpha_1 = \alpha_2 = \cdots = \alpha_{n_1}$

H_a: The α_i are not all equal

The decision rule for the test is

Reject H_0 if $F > F(\alpha; n_1 - 1, n_1 n_2(r-1))$

Accept H_0 if $F \leq F(\alpha; n_1 - 1, n_1 n_2(r-1))$

The test statistic is

$$F = \frac{MSA}{MSE}$$

Test for Factor B Effects

H_0: $\beta_1 = \beta_2 = \cdots \beta_{n_2}$

H_a: The β_j are not all equal

The decision rule for the test is

Reject H_0 if $F > F(\alpha; n_2 - 1, n_1 n_2(r-1))$

Accept H_0 if $F \leq F(\alpha; n_2 - 1, n_1 n_2(r-1))$

The test statistic is

$$F = \frac{MSB}{MSE}$$

To construct a $(1 - \alpha)100\%$ confidence interval estimate of the difference between two treatment means, use the following formula

$$\bar{y}_i - \bar{y}_{i'} \pm t_{\alpha/2} s \sqrt{\frac{2}{r}}$$

where s is the square root of *MSE*, $t_{\alpha/2}$ is chosen with $n_1 n_2 (r-1)$ degrees of freedom, and y_i and $y_{i'}$ are sample means using the r observations of the appropriate treatments (factor-level combinations).

If more than one pair of treatment means is compared, a familywise $(1 - \alpha)100\%$ level of confidence can be achieved by using the Bonferroni confidence coefficient described in the one-way ANOVA section.

EXAMPLE **9.7**   **Printer Sales**

Consider again the company investigating sales of its top-of-the-line printer. An experiment was conducted to determine the effects of type of advertising and selling price on sales. The two levels of selling price considered were $600 and $700. The three types of advertising were television, radio, and newspaper.

Table 9.8 shows the data obtained from the experiment. The first column of the table (SALES) shows total sales for a period of 1 month (in $1000). The second column (PRICE) indicates the level of price (1 = $600 and 2 = $700), and the third column (ADV) indicates the type of advertising (1 = television, 2 = radio, and 3 = newspaper).

The MINITAB output is shown in Figure 9.15 and the Excel output is in Figure 9.16. The MINITAB and Excel ANOVA tables contain the information in the general ANOVA table in Figure 9.14. The general structure of the MINITAB and Excel ANOVA tables is shown in Figure 9.17.

First, we test to see if interaction effects are present. The decision rule is:

Reject H_0 if $F > F(0.05; 2,6) = 5.14$

Accept H_0 if $F \leq 5.14$

The test statistic is $F = 5.87$. The decision is to reject H_0.

We conclude that there are interaction effects. The F tests for main effects discussed in this section cannot be used to determine whether price effects differ or advertising effects differ because the two factors interact. In this case, it may be helpful to examine the individual treatment means. The treatment means are computed by averaging the r observations for each treatment (or factor-level combination). For example, for the treatment when price was $600 and television advertising was used, the treatment mean is $(18.0 + 16.8)/2 = 17.4$. These means can be computed by hand, but some computer routines allow simple procedures that compute them. Figure 9.18 shows the output from MINITAB that results from using the TABLE procedure (see Section 9.5, Using the Computer). Each of the treatment means is shown in this table.

TABLE **9.8**   **Data for Printer Sales Example**

SALES (in $1000)	PRICE	ADV
18.0	1	1
16.8	1	1
12.0	1	2
13.2	1	2
7.8	1	3
9.0	1	3
14.0	2	1
14.7	2	1
10.8	2	2
9.6	2	2
9.8	2	3
8.4	2	3

FIGURE **9.15**   MINITAB ANOVA Output for Printer Sales Example

```
Analysis of Variance for SALES
Source         DF         SS         MS         F          P
PRICE          1       7.521      7.521      10.99      0.016
ADV            2     103.752     51.876      75.82      0.000
Interaction    2       8.032      4.016       5.87      0.039
Error          6       4.105      0.684
Total         11     123.409
```

FIGURE **9.16**   Excel ANOVA Output for Printer Sales Example

```
Anova: Two-Factor With Replication
```

SUMMARY OUTPUT

Summary	ADV1	ADV2	ADV3	Total
PRICE1				
Count	2.000	2.000	2.000	6.000
Sum	34.800	25.200	16.800	76.800
Average	17.400	12.600	8.400	12.800
Variance	0.720	0.720	0.720	16.656
PRICE2				
Count	2.000	2.000	2.000	6.000
Sum	28.700	20.400	18.200	67.300
Average	14.350	10.200	9.100	11.217
Variance	0.245	0.720	0.980	6.522
Total				
Count	4.000	4.000	4.000	
Sum	63.500	45.600	35.000	
Average	15.875	11.400	8.750	
Variance	3.422	2.400	0.730	

ANOVA						
Source of Variation	SS	df	MS	F	P-value	F crit
Sample	7.521	1.000	7.521	10.993	0.016	5.987
Columns	103.752	2.000	51.876	75.823	0.000	5.143
Interaction	8.032	2.000	4.016	5.870	0.039	5.143
Within	4.105	6.000	0.684			
Total	123.409	11.000				

FIGURE 9.17 Structure of the MINITAB and Excel ANOVA Tables for a Two-Way Design

(a) MINITAB

Analysis of Variance on (dependent variable name)

Source	DF	SS	MS	F	p
Factor A	$n_1 - 1$	SSA	MSA	MSA/MSE	p value
Factor B	$n_2 - 1$	SSB	MSB	MSB/MSE	p value
Interaction	$(n_1 - 1)(n_2 - 1)$	SSINT	MSINT	MSINT/MSE	p value
Error	$n_1 n_2 (r - 1)$	SSE	MSE		
Total	$n_1 n_2 r - 1$	SST			

(b) Excel

ANOVA

Source of Variation	SS	df	MS	F	P value	F crit
Sample	SSA	$n_1 - 1$	MSA	MSA/MSE	p value	$F(\alpha; n_1 - 1, n_1 n_2 (r - 1))$
Columns	SSB	$n_2 - 1$	MSB	MSB/MSE	p value	$F(\alpha; n_2 - 1, n_1 n_2 (r - 1))$
Interaction	SSINT	$(n_1 - 1)(n_2 - 1)$	MSINT	MSINT/MSE	p-value	$F(\alpha; (n_1 - 1)(n_2 - 1), n_1 n_2 (r - 1))$
Within	SSE	$n_1 n_2 (r - 1)$	MSE			
Total	SST	$n_1 n_2 r - 1$				

FIGURE 9.18 MINITAB Output Showing Treatment Means for Printer Sales Example

```
Rows: PRICE   Columns: ADV

               1          2          3         All

1          17.400     12.600     8.400      12.800
2          14.350     10.200     9.100      11.217
All        15.875     11.400     8.750      12.008

Cell Contents --
    SALES:Mean
```

FIGURE 9.19   MINITAB Plot of Treatment Means for Printer Sales Example

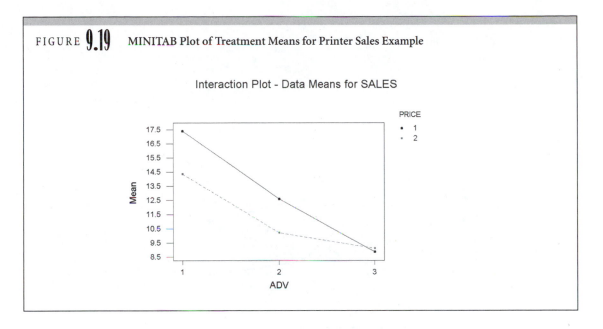

Excel provides the treatment means as part of the ANOVA output. Above the ANOVA table are the number of observations, sum, average, and variance of the observations for each factor-level combination. The treatment means are found in the cell labeled Average.

Figure 9.19 shows a plot of the treatment means. It appears from the plot that the highest level of sales is associated with television advertising in combination with a $600 price. Sales are higher for the $600 price when either television or radio advertising is used. When newspaper advertising is used, however, the $700 price is associated with slightly higher sales. This crossover of the lines illustrates the interaction effect. If there were no interaction, the effects of factors A and B might appear as illustrated in Figure 9.20. The two lines are almost parallel, which indicates a complete absence of interaction. Figure 9.21 illustrates another possible situation. Here the two lines are not parallel, but they do not cross. In this case, the interaction does not appear to be serious, and the model could be treated as one without interaction. Thus, the F tests for main factor effects are appropriate.

If there were no differences in the factor A effects, the two lines drawn would nearly coincide (see Figure 9.22, for example). If there were no differences in the factor B effects, the two lines drawn would be nearly horizontal (see Figure 9.23, for example).

A 95% confidence interval estimate for the difference between the treatment means for $700 price and television advertising and $700 price and radio advertising is given by

$$(14.35 - 10.2) \pm 2.447(0.887)\sqrt{\frac{2}{2}}$$

or $(2.13, 6.17)$.

Note that the interval does not contain zero. If we were interested just in a comparison of these two means, we would conclude that the two means differ.

FIGURE **9.20** Example of Treatment Mean Plot Showing No Interaction Effects

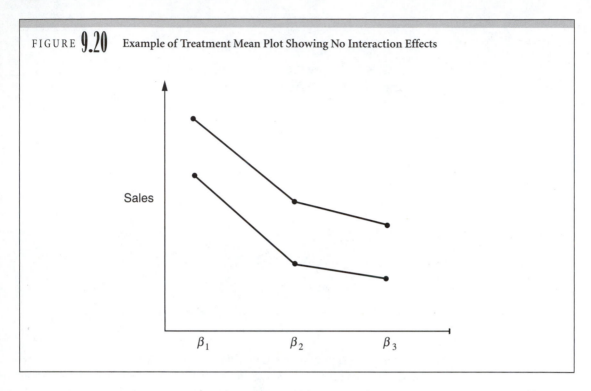

FIGURE **9.21** Example of Treatment Mean Plot Showing Weak Interaction Effects

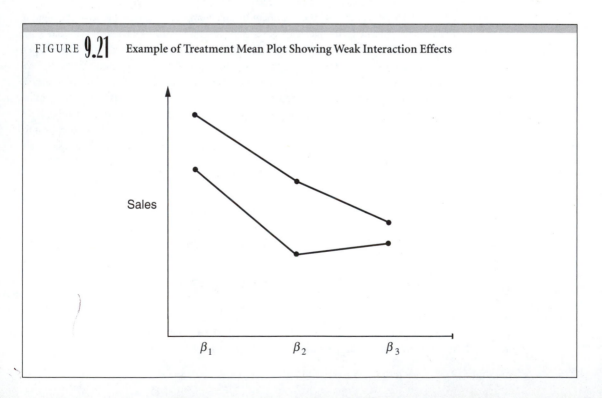

FIGURE 9.22   **Example of Treatment Mean Plot Showing No Interaction Effects and No Factor *A* Main Effects**

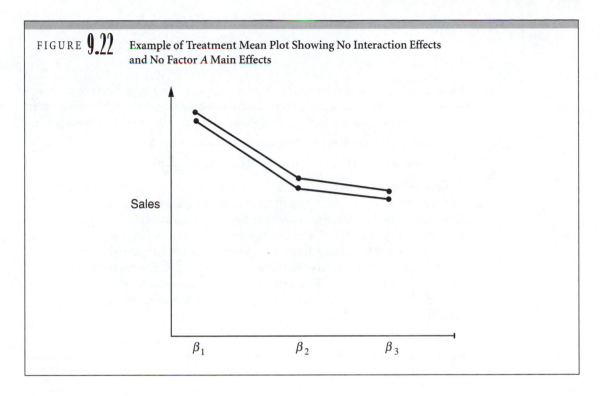

FIGURE 9.23   **Example of Treatment Mean Plot Showing No Interaction Effects and No Factor *B* Main Effects**

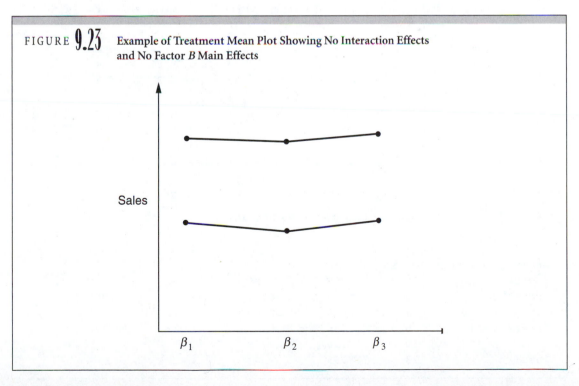

EXERCISES

3 **Satisfaction** A company designs applications software for a large number of firms. A study is conducted to assess the level of satisfaction of these firms with the software supplied. The effects of two factors on the level of satisfaction are to be investigated:

1 the industry of the firm that receives the software and

2 the contact person from whom the software was purchased

Four industries are served and there are three contact people. For each combination of industries and contacts, two firms are randomly selected and surveyed. A satisfaction score is obtained from the questionnaire administered. The results are shown in Table 9.9. MINITAB and Excel outputs for this two-factor study are shown in Figures 9.24 and 9.25, respectively. Use the outputs to determine whether industry or contact person affects satisfaction. Use a 5% level of significance. State any hypotheses to be tested, the decision rule, the test statistic, and your decision.

These data are available in a file with prefix SATIS9 in three columns: SATIS, INDUSTRY and CONTACT.

TABLE **9.9** Data for Satisfaction Exercise

SATIS	INDUSTRY	CONTACT	SATIS	INDUSTRY	CONTACT	SATIS	INDUSTRY	CONTACT
74	1	1	75	2	2	85	3	3
72	1	1	70	2	2	82	3	3
73	1	2	71	2	3	84	4	1
71	1	2	72	2	3	81	4	1
75	1	3	81	3	1	85	4	2
69	1	3	84	3	1	83	4	2
73	2	1	83	3	2	82	4	3
71	2	1	82	3	2	85	4	3

FIGURE **9.24** MINITAB ANOVA Output for Satisfaction Exercise

```
Analysis of Variance for SATIS
Source           DF        SS        MS        F         P
INDUSTRY          3    716.12    238.71     49.82     0.000
CONTACT           2      0.25      0.13      0.03     0.974
Interaction       6      5.75      0.96      0.20     0.970
Error            12     57.50      4.79
Total            23    779.63
```

FIGURE 9.25   Excel ANOVA Output for Satisfaction Exercise

Anova: Two-Factor With Replication

SUMMARY OUTPUT

Summary	CONTACT1	CONTACT2	CONTACT3	Total
INDUST1				
Count	2.000	2.000	2.000	6.000
Sum	146.000	144.000	144.000	434.000
Average	73.000	72.000	72.000	72.333
Variance	2.000	2.000	18.000	4.667
INDUST2				
Count	2.000	2.000	2.000	6.000
Sum	144.000	145.000	143.000	432.000
Average	72.000	72.500	71.500	72.000
Variance	2.000	12.500	0.500	3.200
INDUST3				
Count	2.000	2.000	2.000	6.000
Sum	165.000	165.000	167.000	497.000
Average	82.500	82.500	83.500	82.833
Variance	4.500	0.500	4.500	2.167
INDUST4				
Count	2.000	2.000	2.000	6.000
Sum	165.000	168.000	167.000	500.000
Average	82.500	84.000	83.500	83.333
Variance	4.500	2.000	4.500	2.667
Total				
Count	8.000	8.000	8.000	
Sum	620.000	622.000	621.000	
Average	77.500	77.750	77.625	
Variance	30.571	37.357	43.411	

ANOVA

Source of Variation	SS	df	MS	F	P-value	F crit
Sample	716.125	3.000	238.708	49.817	0.000	3.490
Columns	0.250	2.000	0.125	0.026	0.974	3.885
Interaction	5.750	6.000	0.958	0.200	0.970	2.996
Within	57.500	12.000	4.792			
Total	779.625	23.000				

9.4 ANALYSIS OF COVARIANCE

Analysis of covariance (ANCOVA) is a procedure sometimes used with models containing some quantitative and some qualitative independent variables. In ANCOVA, however, the main interest is in the qualitative variables. In this respect, ANCOVA might be viewed as a modification of ANOVA procedures rather than as a special case of regression analysis (it is, in fact, both). The term ANCOVA is used when the quantitative independent variables are added to the ANOVA model to reduce the variance of the error terms and thus provide more precise measurement of the treatment effects. These quantitative variables should be constructed in such a way that they are not influenced by the treatments.

Although some statistical programs do provide specific routines for performing ANCOVA, these are not discussed in this text. ANCOVA can be performed using regression routines with appropriately constructed indicator variables.

9.5 USING THE COMPUTER

The Using the Computer section in each chapter describes how to perform the computer analyses in the chapter using MINITAB, Excel, and SAS. For further detail on MINITAB, Excel, and SAS, see Appendix C.

9.5.1 MINITAB

Note that Version 12 of MINITAB is fully menu driven. Commands can be used, however, and they are included for any interested users. The menu headings and subheadings used to perform the procedures are listed first, followed by commands in parentheses. For example, STAT: ANOVA: ONE-WAY means to click on the STAT menu, then on ANOVA, and then on ONE-WAY.

One-Way Analysis of Variance

```
STAT: ANOVA: ONE-WAY  or  STAT: ANOVA: ONE-WAY(UNSTACKED)
```

The ANOVA: ONE-WAY procedure is used when all data on the dependent variable are in a single column. A second column is used to specify the factor level assigned to each value of the dependent variable. Data would be arranged as in Table 9.1, for example, with one column containing the car classification and the other the number of injuries. The dialog box for this procedure is shown in Figure 9.26. Fill in the Response (dependent) variable and the Factor and click OK.

Another way of arranging the data is to separate (unstack) the values for each different factor level and put these values into separate columns. If this arrangement is used, the STAT: ANOVA: ONE-WAY (UNSTACKED) procedure is appropriate. Figure 9.27 shows the dialog box. Fill in the columns containing the observations for

FIGURE **9.26**   MINITAB One-Way Analysis of Variance (Stacked Data) Dialog Box

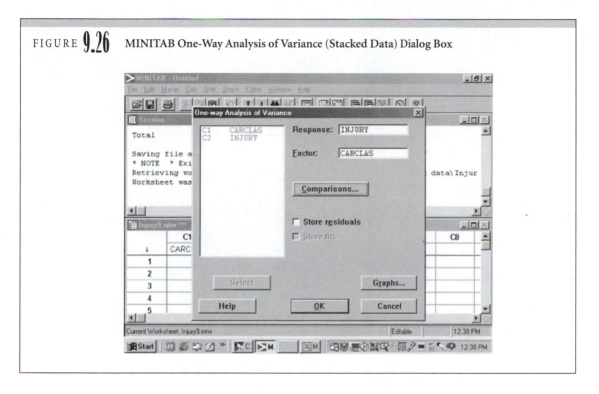

each factor level. Remember that these must be in separate columns to use this ANOVA procedure. Then click OK. (If you are using commands, ONEWAY C2, C1 should be used if the data are in column 2 and the variable specifying the factor levels is in column 1. AOVONEWAY C1,C2, . . . CK is the command if the data for each factor level are in a separate column, in this case, C1,C2, . . . ,CK.)

Analysis of Variance Using a Randomized Block Design

STAT: ANOVA: TWO-WAY

To do a randomized block design in MINITAB, use the two-way analysis of variance option on the ANOVA menu. The dialog box is shown in Figure 9.28. Fill in the response (dependent) variable, the row factor (blocking variable), and the column factor (treatment). Click the "Fit additive model" box. This is important! Otherwise, MINITAB does a two-way analysis of variance which is not appropriate if you really have a randomized block design.

(The appropriate command sequence is

```
TWOWAY C1, C2, C3;
ADDITIVE.
```

where C1 contains the data, C2 the blocking variable, and C3 the treatment variable.)

FIGURE **9.27**   MINITAB One-Way Analysis of Variance (Unstacked Data) Dialog Box

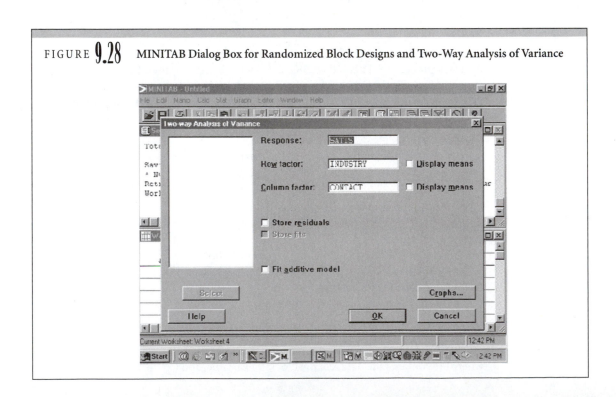

FIGURE **9.28**   MINITAB Dialog Box for Randomized Block Designs and Two-Way Analysis of Variance

FIGURE **9.29**   **MINITAB Interactions Plot Dialog Box**

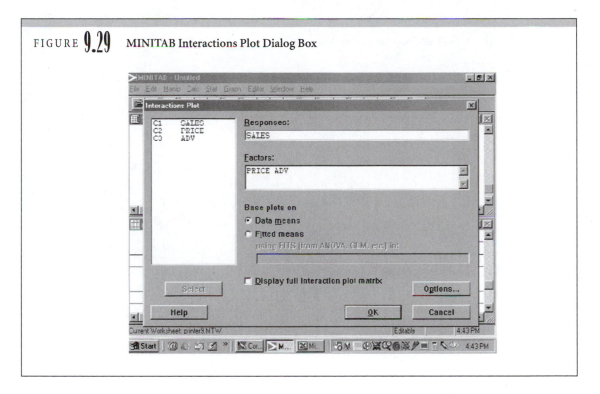

Two-Way Analysis of Variance

STAT: ANOVA: TWO-WAY

The dialog box for a two-way ANOVA is shown in Figure 9.28. Fill in the response (dependent) variable, the Row factor (Factor *A*) and the Column factor (Factor *B*), and click OK.

To do an interactions plot such as the one in Figure 9.19, use STAT: ANOVA: INTERACTIONS PLOT. Fill in the Responses and the Factors and click OK. See the dialog box in Figure 9.29.

To produce a table of treatment means such as the one in Figure 9.18 use STAT: TABLES: CROSS TABULATION. In the Cross Tabulation dialog box (Figure 9.30), fill in the "Classification variables." The classification variables are the two factors of the two-way ANOVA. Click "Summaries..." and fill in the response variable in "Associated variables" in the Cross Tabulation—Summaries dialog box (Figure 9.31). Click the box for Means to display the treatment means.

(The command for a two-way ANOVA is TWOWAY C1, C2, C3 where C1 contains the data, C2 contains factor *A*, and C3 contains factor *B*. The command sequence for an interaction plot is

```
%INTERACT C2 C3;
RESPONSE C1.
```

FIGURE **9.30** MINITAB Cross Tabulation Dialog Box

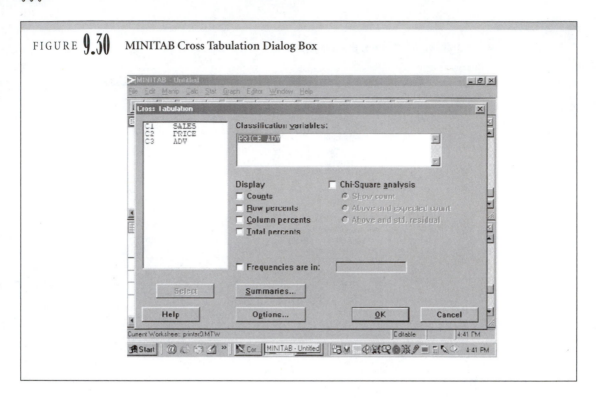

FIGURE **9.31** MINITAB Cross Tabulation—Summaries Dialog Box

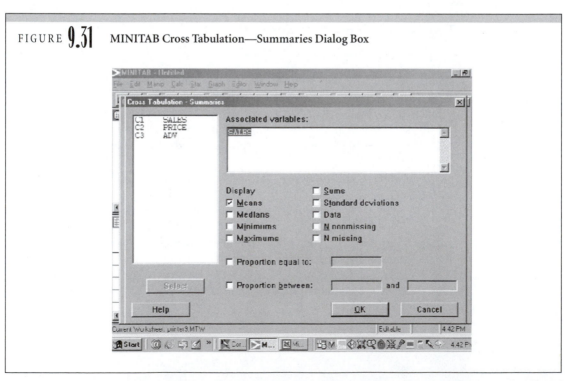

FIGURE **9.32**   Data for One-Way ANOVA in Excel

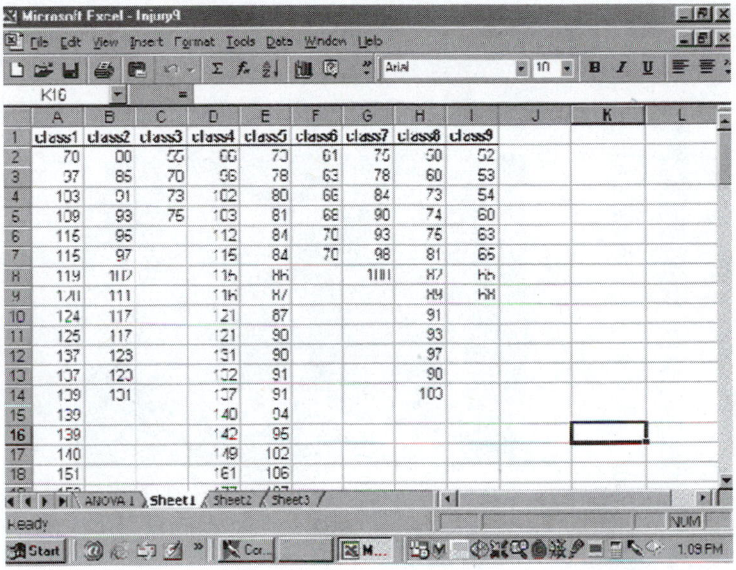

where C1, C2, and C3 are as previously defined, and the % indicates that you are requesting a MINITAB macro. To construct a table of treatment means, use

```
TABLE C2 C3;
MEANS C1.)
```

9.5.2 Excel

One-Way Analysis of Variance

Figure 9.32 shows the data arrangement for a one-way ANOVA in Excel. The data for each factor level must be in a separate column. In the example shown, there are nine factor levels, so there are nine columns of data. The columns do not have to be of equal length. For a one-way ANOVA, choose Anova: Single Factor from the Data Analysis menu. The dialog box is shown in Figure 9.33. Fill in the Input Range. For the example shown, the factor level labeled class5 has 23 observations, so the column ends at row 24. To select the input range, use A1:I24. The fact that some columns do not have 24 rows of data is not a problem. Click Labels in First Row because the columns are labeled and specify the desired output option. (Note that data can be in columns or rows. Indicate which using the Grouped By option.) The default level of significance is 0.05, but this can be changed as desired. The level of significance is used to look up the critical value for the F test. Then click OK.

FIGURE **9.33** Excel Dialog Box for One-Way ANOVA

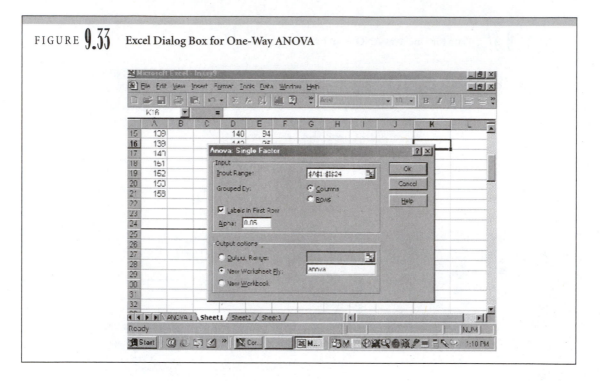

Analysis of Variance Using a Randomized Block Design

Figure 9.34 shows the data arrangement for a randomized block ANOVA in Excel. The names of the levels for the blocking variable are listed in the left-hand column. The names of the factor levels are listed in the first row. The columns of data represent the observations for each factor level. There is one observation for each level of the blocking variable. For a randomized block ANOVA, choose Anova: Two-Factor Without Replication from the Data Analysis menu. The dialog box is shown in Figure 9.35. Fill in the Input Range. For the example shown, use A1:E6 as the input range. Click Labels because the rows and columns are labeled and specify the desired output option. The default level of significance is 0.05, but this can be changed as desired. The level of significance is used to look up the critical values for the F tests. Then click OK.

Two-Way Analysis of Variance

Figure 9.36 shows the data arrangement for a two-way ANOVA in Excel. The names of the levels for factor A are listed in the left-hand column. The names of the factor B levels are listed in the first row. The columns of data represent the observations for each level of factor B. There are at least two observations for each treatment. A treatment represents a factor A and factor B combination. For example, for the first level of factor A (INDUST1) and factor B (CONTACT1), the two observations are 74 and 72.

FIGURE 9.34   Data for Randomized Block ANOVA in Excel

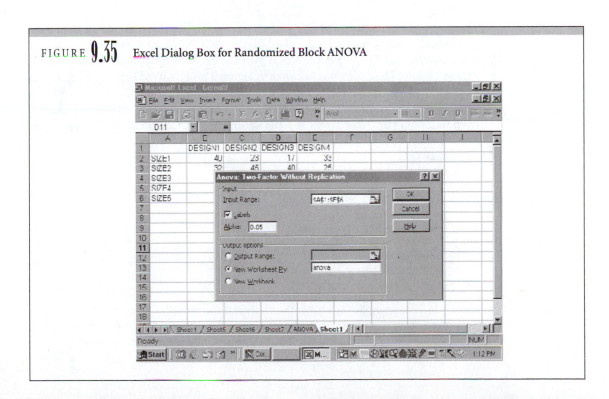

FIGURE 9.35   Excel Dialog Box for Randomized Block ANOVA

FIGURE **9.36** Data for Two-Way ANOVA in Excel

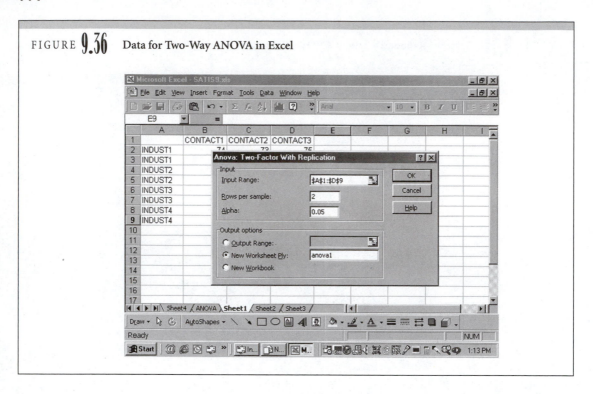

These two values must be the first two entries in the CONTACT1 column. The next two values in that column are for the INDUST2/CONTACT1 treatment and so on. For a two-way ANOVA, choose Anova: Two-Factor With Replication from the Data Analysis menu. The dialog box is shown in Figure 9.37. Fill in the Input Range. For the example shown, use A1:D9 as the input range. Fill in "Rows per sample" with the number of replications at each treatment ($r = 2$, in this example). Specify the desired output option. The default level of significance is 0.05, but this can be changed as desired. The level of significance is used to look up the critical values for the F tests. Then click OK.

9.5.3 SAS

One-Way Analysis of Variance

```
PROC ANOVA;
    CLASS CARTYPE;
    MODEL INJURY = CARTYPE;
```

CLASS indicates which variable is the classification variable—that is, which variable denotes the factor levels for each observation in the data set. The variable on the left-hand side of the equality in the MODEL statement is the dependent variable.

FIGURE **9.37**   Excel Dialog Box for Two-Way ANOVA

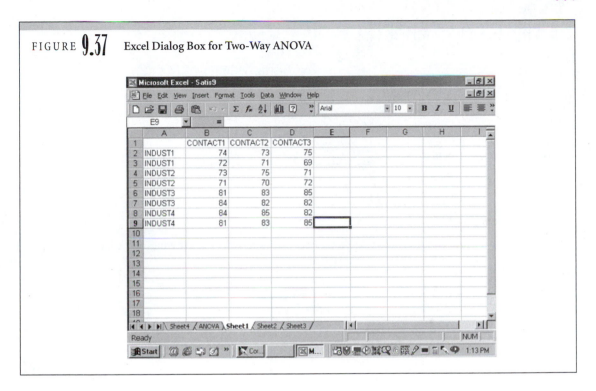

Analysis of Variance Using a Randomized Block Design

```
PROC ANOVA;
   CLASS SIZE DESIGN;
   MODEL SALES = SIZE DESIGN;
```

The PROC ANOVA statement is the same as the statement used for a one-way analysis of variance. The CLASS statement now specifies both the blocking and treatment variables. The MODEL statement lists the dependent variable on the left-hand side of the equality and the blocking and treatment variables on the right-hand side.

Two-Way Analysis of Variance

```
PROC ANOVA;
   CLASS PRICE ADV;
   MODEL SALES = PRICE ADV PRICE*ADV;
```

The SAS command sequence for two-way analysis of variance requires that the interaction term be explicitly included in the MODEL statement as shown: PRICE*ADV. Otherwise, the interaction term is omitted (as in the randomized block design). The MODEL statement lists the dependent variable on the left-hand side of the equality and the main effects and interaction variables on the right-hand side.

ADDITIONAL EXERCISES

4 **ANOVA Tables**

a Assume that one-way analysis of variance is to be performed. Complete the ANOVA table for this analysis:

Source	DF	SS	MS	F
Treatment	3			
Error		20		
Total	23	170		

b Assume that a randomized block experiment is to be performed. Complete the ANOVA table for this analysis:

Source	DF	SS	MS	F
Blocks	4			
Treatment		80	40	
Error	39		2	
Total	45	198		

5 **Assembly Line** Three assembly lines are used to produce a certain component for a computer. To examine the production rate of the assembly lines, a random sample of six hourly periods is chosen for each assembly line, and the number of components produced during these periods for each line is recorded. The data are shown in Table 9.10.

Is there a difference in the average production rates for the three assembly lines? Use a 5% level of significance in answering this question. State any hypotheses to be tested, the decision rule, the test statistic, and your decision.

These data are available in a file with prefix ASSEMBL9 in two columns: NUMBER and LINE.

6 **Salaries** A large state university is interested in comparing salaries of its graduates (BA or BS) in the following areas: business, education, engineering, and liberal arts. Five graduates in each major are randomly selected and their starting salaries recorded. The data are shown in Table 9.11.

a The university wants to know if there is a difference in the population average salaries for the four majors. Use a 5% level of significance in making the decision. State any hypotheses to be tested, the decision rule, the test statistic, and your decision.

b Find a 95% interval estimate for the difference between the business and engineering mean salaries.

TABLE **9.10**   Data for Assembly Line Exercise

NUMBER	LINE	NUMBER	LINE	NUMBER	LINE	NUMBER	LINE
37	1	38	1	52	2	37	3
35	1	50	2	53	2	39	3
34	1	57	2	31	3	34	3
37	1	56	2	36	3		
36	1	58	2	37	3		

TABLE **9.11**   Data for Salaries Exercise

SALARY (in $1000)	MAJOR[a]	SALARY (in $1000)	MAJOR	SALARY (in $1000)	MAJOR
14.5	1	12.8	2	28.7	3
22.4	1	11.7	2	10.6	4
24.1	1	12.5	2	14.7	4
21.7	1	24.7	3	15.2	4
17.9	1	25.6	3	12.1	4
12.2	2	26.7	3	16.4	4
13.4	2	24.9	3		

[a] 1 = business, 2 = education, 3 = engineering, 4 = liberal arts

c   Use the Bonferroni method to compare all possible pairs of means with a family-wise confidence level of 90%. Use the familywise comparisons to determine if there is a significant difference in the population mean salaries for

(1) business and education majors

(2) business and engineering majors

(3) education and liberal arts majors

If so, which major has a higher mean salary in each comparison?

These data are available in a file with prefix SALMAJ9 in two columns: SALARIES and MAJOR. The variable MAJOR is coded as 1 = business, 2 = education, 3 = engineering, and 4 = liberal arts.

7   **Test Scores**   A large financial planning firm wants to compare the results of three training programs for its staff. Twenty-seven employees are selected for the study. These employees are grouped into three blocks of nine for the comparison. The blocks are based on number of years since college graduation, with block 1 being the

TABLE **9.12**   Data for Test Scores Exercise

SCORE	PROGRAM	BLOCK	SCORE	PROGRAM	BLOCK
82	1	1	93	2	2
85	1	1	82	3	2
91	1	1	79	3	2
95	2	1	81	3	2
97	2	1	82	1	3
94	2	1	86	1	3
81	3	1	89	1	3
80	3	1	97	2	3
78	3	1	92	2	3
83	1	2	98	2	3
85	1	2	78	3	3
90	1	2	82	3	3
96	2	2	83	3	3
96	2	2			

most recent graduates and block three the most distant graduates. After the training programs are completed, the employees are tested and the test scores recorded. These data are shown in Table 9.12 and are denoted SCORE for the test score, PROGRAM for the training program used (1, 2, or 3), and BLOCK for the block in which the employee was placed (1, 2, or 3).

a   Determine whether there is a difference in average test scores because of the training programs. Use a 5% level of significance. State any hypotheses to be tested, the decision rule, the test statistic, and your decision.

b   Construct a 95% confidence interval estimate of the difference between the means for program 1 and program 2.

These data are available in a file with prefix TESTSCR9 in three columns: SCORE, PROGRAM and BLOCK.

8   **Employee Productivity**   A study of employee productivity is to be conducted with employees who enter data at computers. The amount of data entered is the dependent variable. Two factors that may influence the dependent variable are examined. One factor is the type of keyboard used (three types are available in the company). The second factor is the time of day (morning or afternoon). Four employees are randomly assigned to each type of keyboard. Two employees' production levels are recorded for a period of 1 hour in the morning. The other two are recorded in the afternoon. The production level is the number of forms completely entered by each employee. The data are shown in Table 9.13. In the table, NUMBER is the number of forms processed by each employee, KEYBOARD is the keyboard type (1, 2, or 3), and TIME is coded as 1 for morning and 2 for afternoon.

TABLE **9.13**   Data for Employee Productivity Exercise

NUMBER	KEYBOARD	TIME	NUMBER	KEYBOARD	TIME
14	1	1	12	2	2
15	1	1	13	2	2
10	1	2	20	3	1
8	1	2	18	3	1
17	2	1	14	3	2
19	2	1	12	3	2

Do the two factors, KEYBOARD and TIME, appear to influence production rate (NUMBER)? Use a 5% level of significance for any hypothesis tests used. State any hypotheses to be tested, the decision rule, the test statistic, and your decision. How would you describe the influence you observed in words?

These data are available in a file with prefix PRODRAT9 in three columns: NUMBER, KEYBOARD, and TIME.

9   **Bill's Sales**   Bill's is a popular restaurant/bar in southwest Fort Worth, Texas. Table 9.14 shows daily sales data for Bill's for the period from October 14 through December 8. Also shown is the day of the week, coded as 1 = Monday, 2 = Tuesday, 3 = Wednesday, 4 = Thursday, 5 = Friday, 6 = Saturday, and 7 = Sunday. Determine

TABLE **9.14**   Data for Bill's Sales Exercise

SALES	DAY	SALES	DAY	SALES	DAY	SALES	DAY
2,573.5	1	1,749.7	1	1,845.2	1	2,195.1	1
3,509.1	2	3,245.0	2	2,412.3	2	2,451.0	2
2,979.0	3	2,454.0	3	2,700.7	3	4,045.6	3
4,037.1	4	2,779.8	4	3,371.1	4	1,569.0	4
9,521.4	5	6,048.2	5	6,826.7	5	5,574.1	5
7,015.5	6	6,397.3	6	6,611.4	6	5,194.8	6
3,516.8	7	2,865.1	7	2,768.2	7	2,494.2	7
2,309.9	1	2,068.9	1	2,145.0	1	1,970.6	1
3,673.0	2	2,141.0	2	2,021.9	2	2,511.6	2
3,329.2	3	2,782.6	3	2,341.7	3	2,481.3	3
4,818.0	4	3,590.8	4	3,259.3	4	2,318.2	4
7,078.0	5	6,396.7	5	5,816.0	5	4,460.8	5
5,570.6	6	10,154.9	6	6,697.3	6	5,330.4	6
3,722.8	7	2,595.1	7	2,465.2	7	2,424.0	7

whether there is a difference in Bill's average sales on different days of the week. If there is a difference, on which day (or days) do sales appear to be highest? What does this suggest to the owner of Bill's about staffing?

These data are available in a file with prefix BILLS9 in two columns: SALES and DAY.

CHAPTER 10

Qualitative Dependent Variables: An Introduction to Discriminant Analysis and Logistic Regression

10.1 INTRODUCTION

A bank is interested in determining whether certain large borrowers are creditworthy. Should loans be made to these potential customers or not? The bank has a variety of quantitative information about each potential borrower and would like some way of classifying them into groups of qualifying and nonqualifying candidates.

An investment company is trying to determine the likelihood that certain firms will end up in bankruptcy. The investment company has quantitative information on the firms it is considering and wants to classify them into two groups: those that will go bankrupt and those that will not.

The director of personnel for a large corporation would like to know which of a group of new trainees will be successful in a certain position at the company. Using demographic information and the results of certain aptitude tests, the director wants to classify trainees into two groups: those who will succeed and those who will not.

The marketing department of a retail firm is interested in predicting whether people will buy a new product within the next year. The marketing department will have the results from surveys given to a sample of potential buyers and a quantitative score representing propensity to buy as a summary measure from these surveys. The department wants to use this score to divide the people into groups of potential buyers and nonbuyers so it can better target future advertising.

Each of these examples represents a case in which certain observations (people, firms, and so on) are to be divided into two groups: firms that do and do not qualify for credit; firms that will and will not go bankrupt; people that will and will not be successful in new positions; people who will and will not purchase a new product. The goal is to try to pick which of the two groups each observation will fall into based on available information. This type of problem can be placed in a regression setting. Write the regression model as

$$y = \beta_0 + \beta_1 x_1 + \cdots + \beta_K x_K + e$$

where

$y = 1$ if the observation falls into the group of interest

$y = 0$ if the observation does not fall into the group of interest

In Chapter 7, methods were discussed for dealing with explanatory variables representing qualitative information. Examples used were employed/unemployed, male/female, and so on. The way this information was incorporated into the regression was with indicator variables. These variables took on values of either 0 or 1 to indicate whether an item was or was not in a certain group (male = 1, female = 0, for example). In this chapter, we adopt a similar approach for situations where the dependent variable of interest is qualitative in nature. Situations are examined where the task is to try and determine whether items do or do not fall into a certain group. The dependent variable used to represent this situation will be a variable that has either the value 1 if the item is in the group or the value 0 if the item is not in the group.

Standard linear regression analysis is not designed for directly analyzing this situation. In the regression applications examined so far in this text, the dependent variable was a variable that could be effectively modeled as a continuous variable. The assumptions of the regression model are designed for such a situation. When a 0/1 dependent variable is used, several problems occur. To discuss the first problem, it is important to note that the conditional mean of y given x has a different interpretation when the dependent variable is a 0/1 variable than it did in the previous case when the dependent variable was modeled as continuous. It can be shown that $\mu_{y|x}$ is equal to the probability that the observation belongs to the indicated group: $\mu_{y|x} = p$, where $p = P(Y = 1)$. Probabilities must be between 0 and 1, of course, but when the regression is estimated, there is nothing to guarantee that the predictions from the estimated regression equation fall between 0 and 1. The actual predictions can vary considerably, with values above 1 or even negative values occurring.

Second, certain assumptions of the regression model will be violated. For example, the disturbances are not normally distributed and the variance around the regression line is not constant.

As a result of the problems that occur with applying standard regression techniques to situations with 0/1 dependent variables, several alternative methods of analysis have been proposed. Two of these methods are discussed in this chapter: discriminant analysis and logistic regression. Both techniques have characteristics similar to the regression models that have been presented thus far in this text. Even though linear regression, discriminant analysis, and logistic regression differ, their similarities will help the reader understand the use of these procedures.

10.2 DISCRIMINANT ANALYSIS

EXAMPLE 10.1   Employee Classification

The personnel director for a firm that manufactures computers has classified the performance of each of the employees in a certain position as either satisfactory or unsatisfactory. The director has two tests that she would like to use to help determine which future employees will perform in a satisfactory manner and which will not before they are assigned to the position. With this knowledge, she will be better able to suggest jobs within the firm at which each employee will have a greater chance of success. To help determine whether the tests will be useful, she administers them to the current employees and records their scores. The resulting data are shown in Table 10.1. The first column notes whether the employee is currently classified as satisfactory (1) or unsatisfactory (0). The next two columns show the test score results on each of the two tests. Her task is now to determine how to use the test scores to predict the correct classification of each employee.

Figure 10.1 shows a scatterplot of each employee's scores on the two tests. The employees classified as successful are denoted with + and those classified as unsuccessful as ○. From the plot, it does appear that knowledge of the test score may provide information useful in classifying the employees. There is no exact cutoff to separate the two groups precisely, but there is enough separation of the members to indicate that the information provided on the tests may be useful.

FIGURE 10.1   Scatterplot of TEST1 Versus TEST2 for Satisfactory (+) and Unsatisfactory (○)

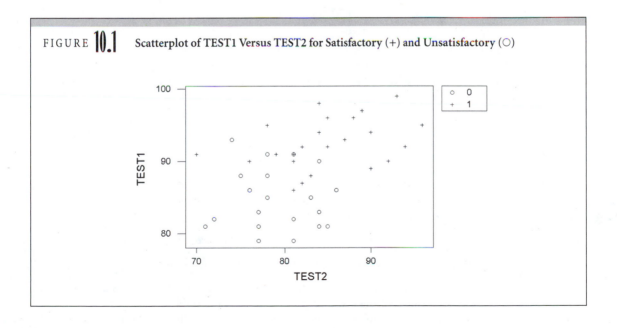

TABLE 10.1   Data and Discriminant Analysis Results for Employee Classification Example

Group	Test1	Test2	Predicted Group	Discriminant Score	Group	Test1	Test2	Predicted Group	Discriminant Score
1	96	85	1	0.99694	1	87	82	0*	0.42376
1	96	88	1	1.04291	0	93	74	1*	0.65266
1	91	81	1	0.64276	0	90	84	1*	0.63014
1	95	78	1	0.83111	0	91	81	1*	0.64276
1	92	85	1	0.76262	0	91	78	1*	0.59679
1	93	87	1	0.85185	0	88	78	0	0.42105
1	98	84	1	1.09878	0	86	86	0	0.42647
1	92	82	1	0.71666	0	79	81	0	−0.06020
1	97	89	1	1.11681	0	83	84	0	0.22009
1	95	96	1	1.10691	0	79	77	0	−0.12149
1	99	93	1	1.29526	0	88	75	0	0.37508
1	89	90	1	0.66350	0	81	85	0	0.11825
1	94	90	1	0.95639	0	85	83	0	0.32192
1	92	94	1	0.90052	0	82	72	0	−0.02236
1	94	84	1	0.86446	0	82	81	0	0.11554
1	90	92	1	0.75272	0	81	77	0	−0.00433
1	91	70	0*	0.47421	0	86	76	0	0.27325
1	90	81	1	0.58418	0	81	84	0	0.10293
1	86	81	0*	0.34986	0	85	78	0	0.24531
1	90	76	0*	0.50757	0	83	77	0	0.11283
1	91	79	1	0.61211	0	81	71	0	−0.09626
1	88	83	0*	0.49766					

* Next to a value in the Predicted Group column indicated a misclassification

Discriminant analysis can be used to help solve the type of problem posed in Example 10.1. Discriminant analysis can be described as follows: Let y represent the dependent variable, defined as

$y = 1$ if the observation falls into the group of interest

$y = 0$ if the observation does not fall into the group of interest

Let $x_1, \ldots x_K$ be explanatory variables that are used to help predict into which of the two groups each of the observations in the sample should be classified. The explanatory variables are assumed to be approximately normally distributed. Although discriminant analysis can be used when the explanatory variables are not normally distributed, it is not guaranteed to be optimal in such cases and may not provide good results. This is one of the more serious limitations of this technique because it limits the kinds of variables that can be used as explanatory variables in the equation. It should be noted, however, that a study by Amemiya and Powell[1] showed that discriminant analysis does well in prediction and estimation even when the explanatory variables are nonnormal if sample sizes are large. Discriminant analysis also assumes that the variation of the explanatory variables is the same for each group. Write the equation representing the relationship between y and the explanatory variables as

$$y = \beta_0 + \beta_1 x_1 + \cdots + \beta_K x_K + e$$

Apply linear regression to the data and estimate the previous equation. The estimated equation is written

$$d = b_0 + b_1 x_1 + \cdots + b_K x_K$$

where d is called the discriminant score. The *discriminant score* is just the predicted value from the estimated regression equation. These discriminant scores are used to classify each of the observations in the sample. A cutoff value is chosen, call it c, and the following classification rule is used:

If $d \leq c$, assign the observation to group 0

If $d > c$, assign the observation to group 1

How is the cutoff value in the classification rule chosen? Our real goal in such a situation is not to classify the items in the sample correctly; we know what group these items are in. The goal is to classify future observations correctly. In the employee classification example, this means being able to correctly classify future employees as satisfactory or unsatisfactory in a particular position on the basis of their test scores. So ideally, the estimates $b_0, b_1, \ldots, b_K$ should be chosen so that the number of misclassified future observations is minimized.

In the problem considered here, this can be done as follows: Estimate the equation for the discriminant score with least-squares regression using the 0/1 dependent variable. Record the predicted or fitted values from this estimated equation. These are the discriminant scores, d. Choose a value, c, as a cutoff in such a way that the probability of misclassification for future observations is minimized. This is done by choosing d halfway between the average discriminant scores for the two groups if the sample sizes are equal. If we write

$\bar{d}_1$ = average discriminant score for the 1 group

$\bar{d}_0$ = average discriminant score for the 0 group

then

$$c = \frac{\bar{d}_0 + \bar{d}_1}{2}$$

---

[1] See T. Amemiya and J. Powell, "A Comparison of the Logit Model and Normal Discriminant Analysis When Independent Variables Are Binary." See References for complete publication information.

If the sample sizes are not equal, then a weighted average of the two average discriminant scores can be used:

$$c = \frac{n_0 \bar{d}_0 + n_1 \bar{d}_1}{n_0 + n_1}$$

where n_0 is the sample size for the group labeled 0 and n_1 is the sample size for the group labeled 1.

EXAMPLE 10.2 **Employee Classification (Continued)**

Continuing with Example 10.1, the discriminant scores for the employees in the sample in Table 10.1 have been computed and are shown in the fifth column of the table. Column 4 shows the results of a classification rule applied to the discriminant scores. The employees who were incorrectly classified have been denoted with an *. Note that five employees who were in group 1 have been classified as being in group 0, and four employees who were in group 0 have been classified as being in group 1. These errors are termed misclassifications. The percentage of correct classifications in this example is 79.1%.

FIGURE 10.2 **MINITAB Regression Output to Perform Discriminant Analysis for Employee Classification Example**

```
The regression equation is
Group = - 5.93 + 0.0586 TEST1 + 0.0153 TEST2

Predictor       Coef        StDev          T          P
Constant     -5.9291       0.9633      -6.15      0.000
TEST1         0.05858      0.01119      5.23      0.000
TEST2         0.015322     0.009954     1.54      0.132

S = 0.3518      R-Sq = 53.7%      R-Sq(adj) = 51.4%


Analysis of Variance

Source              DF           SS          MS          F          P
Regression           2       5.7472      2.8736      23.22      0.000
Residual Error      40       4.9505      0.1238
Total               42      10.6977


Source      DF       Seq SS
TEST1        1       5.4540
TEST2        1       0.2932
```

The average discriminant score computed from the linear regression for the satisfactory (1) group can be found from the data in column 5. This average is 0.7848. The average for the unsatisfactory (0) group is 0.2475. The weighted average of these two values is given by

$$\frac{20(0.2475) + 23(0.7848)}{20 + 23} = 0.5349$$

This number can be used to classify each of the observations in Table 10.1 and to check the classifications in column 4. Whenever the d score in column 5 is less than or equal to 0.5349, the observation should be classified as belonging to group 0. When the d score in column 5 is greater than 0.5349, the observation should be classified as belonging to group 1. This is how the classifications in the table were determined.

The MINITAB regression used to determine the d scores is shown in Figure 10.2. For future employees, this regression can be used to determine the d scores for classification.

Even though linear regression was used to perform the discriminant analysis, this is not typically the method of choice. There are specific computer routines available for discriminant analysis. Figure 10.3 shows the MINITAB output for the employee classification problem when a procedure designed specifically for discriminant analysis is used. The results of the classification are identical to those from the regression approach, but the method used is somewhat different and the output differs considerably.

The primary reason that specific discriminant analysis routines are used rather than the regression approach is that discriminant analysis can be extended to more than two groups. When more than two groups are included in the analysis, the regression approach is not as straightforward. The case for more than two groups can be handled easily by specific discriminant analysis routines, however. Each group is given a different number. The numbers assigned do not have to include 0 and 1. (In fact, in the two-group case, the numbers that identify the two groups can be any integers, not necessarily 0 and 1. The values 0 and 1 were used here for convenience in extending the discussion to the topic of logistic regression.)

Discriminant analysis routines proceed by computing the means of each of the different groups for each explanatory variable. Then a measure of the distance from each observation to each set of means is computed. The observation is classified into the group whose set of means is closest. Example 10.3 illustrates a discriminant analysis routine applied to the employee classification data.

EXAMPLE **10.3**   ## Employee Classification (continued)

Figure 10.3 shows the MINITAB discriminant analysis output applied to the employee classification data. In this example, the group counts are noted. There are 20 in the group denoted 0 and 23 in the group denoted 1. A Summary of Classification table is provided next. For example, for those employees who were actually unsatisfactory (True Group 0), 16 were classified as unsatisfactory (Put into Group 0) and 4 were classified as satisfactory (Put into Group 1) out of the total of 20. The 16 correct classifications for this group yield a proportion correct of 0.800 (80.0%). The

FIGURE **10.3** MINITAB Discriminant Analysis Output for Employee Classification Example

```
Linear Method for Response:  Group
Predictors: TEST1 TEST2

Group      0     1
Count     20    23

Summary of Classification

Put into     ....True Group....
Group            0         1
0               16         5
1                4        18
Total N         20        23
N Correct       16        18
Proportion    0.800     0.783

N =  43    N Correct =  34    Proportion Correct = 0.791

Squared Distance Between Groups
                 0         1
0           0.00000   4.44946
1           4.44946   0.00000

Linear Discriminant Function for Group
                 0         1
Constant    -298.27   -351.65
TEST1          5.20      5.68
TEST2          1.97      2.10

Summary of Misclassified Observations
```

Observation	True Group	Pred Group	Group	Squared Distance	Probability
17 **	1	0	0	6.657	0.586
			1	7.352	0.414
19 **	1	0	0	0.1911	0.799
			1	2.9454	0.201
20 **	1	0	0	2.561	0.518
			1	2.703	0.482
22 **	1	0	0	1.034	0.538
			1	1.340	0.462
23 **	1	0	0	0.5264	0.682
			1	2.0567	0.318
24 **	0	1	0	6.438	0.244
			1	4.177	0.756
25 **	0	1	0	2.2891	0.280
			1	0.4008	0.720
26 **	0	1	0	2.6389	0.259
			1	0.5416	0.741
27 **	0	1	0	2.900	0.339
			1	1.564	0.661

same information is given for each group. Overall, there were 43 employees, 34 were correctly categorized, and the overall proportion correct was 0.791 (79.1%).

The Squared Distance Between Groups table is not discussed in this text.

The next item in the output is the Linear Discriminant Function for Group. When a discriminant analysis procedure is used, a separate equation is computed for each group. Note that these equations are not the same as the discriminant function computed using the regression approach. The two equations can be combined in a certain way to produce the overall discriminant function, however. The way this combination is achieved is not discussed here, but the use of the equations for the separate groups is demonstrated:

Group 0: $-298.27 + 5.20\text{TEST1} + 1.97\text{TEST2}$

Group 1: $-351.65 + 5.68\text{TEST1} + 2.10\text{TEST2}$

These equations are applied to each employee. The employee is then classified into the group for which his or her score is the highest. These equations can also be used to classify any future applicants. Administer the tests, record the test scores, and compute the values for each equation. The applicant is then assigned to the group for which the value from the equations is the highest. Although this method differs from the way the linear regression approach classified the employees, the results are the same as can be seen from the Summary of Misclassified Observations. This is always true in the two-group case. For three or more groups, however, discriminant analysis procedures should be used.

In the Summary of Misclassified Observations, the number of each employee misclassified is shown along with the True Group and the Pred (predicted) Group. The Squared Distance column shows a measure of the distance computed from each observation to the means of each group. Each employee has been classified into the group with the smaller distance. In the last column, a Probability has been computed that can be thought of as the predicted probability that the employee belongs to a particular group. The employee has been classified into the group that has the highest probability.

In linear regression, an equation was developed using a certain set of observations. It is typically not these observations for which predictions are desired, however. The quality of predictions is important for observations not included in the original sample. This situation is the same in discriminant analysis. What really matters in discriminant analysis is how well the discriminant equations classify future observations. The percentage of correctly classified observations given in the discriminant analysis output can be used as a guide for this, but this percentage will likely overstate the quality of future classifications. The same is true of the R^2 for a linear regression. The R^2 represents a measure of fit of the sample data, but may not reflect how well the equation will do in classifying future data.

There are other methods to assess the quality of future classifications when using discriminant analysis. One method is to split the original sample into two parts (if sample size is large enough) called an *estimation sample* and a *validation sample*. Use the estimation sample to determine the discriminant equations. Then use the discriminant equations to classify the items in the validation sample. The percentage of correct classifications in the validation sample should provide a better indication of how discriminant analysis will perform on future observations. After this has been done, the two samples can then be combined to compute the discriminant function for future use.[2]

10.3 LOGISTIC REGRESSION

Discriminant analysis is known to be statistically valid when we can assume that the independent variable in the regression equation is normally distributed. When the equation has more than one independent variable, the assumption is that the x variables have a multivariate normal distribution, a strong assumption that is not discussed in detail here. Suffice it to say that this normality assumption excludes many possible variables as explanatory variables in the discriminant function equation. *Logistic regression* is another procedure for modeling a 0/1 dependent variable that does not depend on the assumption that the independent variables are normally distributed. As a result, many other types of variables, including indicator variables, are in the possible set of explanatory variables.

The logistic regression approach does have its own set of assumptions, however. To briefly describe logistic regression, the notion presented earlier that the conditional mean of y given x has a different interpretation when the dependent variable is a 0/1 variable must be reconsidered. When the dependent variable is either 0 or 1, it can be shown that the conditional mean of y given x, $\mu_{y|x}$, is equal to the probability that the observation belongs to the indicated group:

$$\mu_{y|x} = p = P(Y = 1)$$

Probabilities must be between 0 and 1; thus, to model the conditional mean of y, a function that is restricted to lie between 0 and 1 must be used. The function considered in logistic regression is called the *logistic function* (what a coincidence!) and can be written as follows:

$$\mu_{y|x} = \frac{1}{1 + e^{-\left(\beta_0 + \sum_{j=1}^{K} \beta_j x_j\right)}}$$

where the x_j are explanatory variables, K is the number of explanatory variables, and β_0 and β_j the are coefficients to be estimated.

This function works well for modeling probabilities because it is restricted to be between 0 and 1. The function forms an S-shaped curve such as the one in Figure 10.4. The logistic function is a nonlinear function of the regression coefficients and must be solved by a nonlinear regression routine. This makes the description of the solution process more complicated than that for linear least squares. However, logistic regression routines are available in certain statistical software packages and usually use a procedure called *maximum likelihood estimation* to estimate the regression coefficients in the logistic regression function. The following example illustrates.

---

[2] For more detail on discriminant analysis including a discussion of discriminant analysis with more than two groups, see C. T. Ragsdale and A. Stam, "Introducing Discriminant Analysis to the Business Statistics Curriculum." See References for complete publication information.

FIGURE 10.4   The S-Shaped Curve of the Logistic Function

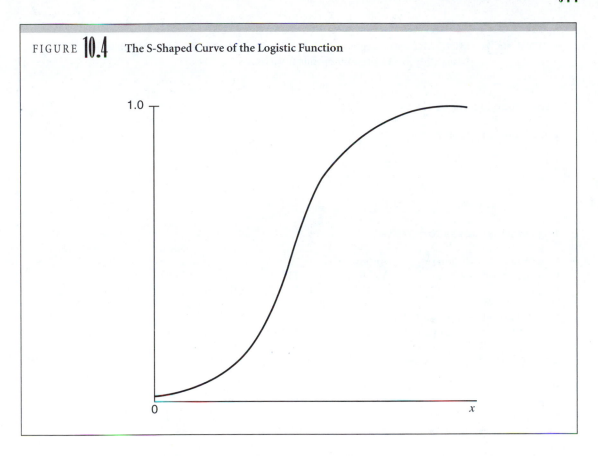

Logistic Regression and Employee Classification

EXAMPLE 10.4

Consider again the employee classification problem discussed in Example 10.1. Consider trying to estimate the probability that each employee belongs to the satisfactory group (the group coded 1). A possible nonlinear model to estimate this probability using only the result from TEST1 can be written

$$\mu_{y|x} = \frac{1}{1 + e^{-(\beta_0 + \beta_1 x_1)}}$$

where x_1 is the TEST1 result.

The MINITAB logistic regression output used to estimate this equation is shown in Figure 10.5. The Response Information table shows the number of observations in each group (satisfactory = 1, unsatisfactory = 0). The Logistic Regression Table shows information pertinent to the estimation of β_0 (Constant row) and β_1 (TEST1 row). Estimates of the coefficients are in the Coef column, and standard errors of these estimates are in the StDev column. A Z statistic and the associated p value are shown. These are used just as in simple linear regression to test whether β_0 or β_1 are equal to zero as follows, using β_1 to illustrate:

FIGURE 10.5 MINITAB Logistic Regression Output for Employee Classification Example Using Only TEST1 as an Independent Variable

```
Link Function: Logit

Response Information

Variable   Value    Count
Group        1        23 (Event)
             0        20
           Total      43

Logistic Regression Table
                                                   Odds        95% CI
Predictor    Coef      StDev       Z       P      Ratio    Lower   Upper
Constant    -43.37     12.92     -3.36   0.001
TEST1        0.4897    0.1450     3.38   0.001    1.63     1.23    2.17

Log-Likelihood = -15.585
Test that all slopes are zero: G = 28.232, DF = 1, P-Value = 0.000

Goodness-of-Fit Tests

Method              Chi-Square      DF          P
Pearson                9.195        17        0.934
Deviance               9.530        17        0.922
Hosmer-Lemeshow        2.282         8        0.971

Table of Observed and Expected Frequencies:
(See Hosmer-Lemeshow Test for the Pearson Chi-Square Statistic)

                                  Group
Value    1     2     3     4     5     6     7     8     9    10    Total
1
  Obs    0     0     1     2     4     3     4     4     4     1     23
  Exp   0.1   0.2   1.0   1.6   3.2   3.8   4.3   3.8   3.9   1.0
0
  Obs    6     4     4     2     1     2     1     0     0     0     20
  Exp   5.9   3.8   4.0   2.4   1.8   1.2   0.7   0.2   0.1   0.0

 Total   6     4     5     4     5     5     5     4     4     1     43

Measures of Association:
(Between the Response Variable and Predicted Probabilities)

Pairs           Number    Percent    Summary Measures
Concordant        411      89.3%     Somers' D                 0.82
Discordant         35       7.6%     Goodman-Kruskal Gamma     0.84
Ties               14       3.0%     Kendall's Tau-a           0.42
Total             460     100.0%
```

Hypotheses: $H_0: \beta_1 = 0$
$H_a: \beta_1 \neq 0$

Decision rule: Reject H_0 if $Z > 1.96$ or $Z < -1.96$ (using a 5% level of significance)
Accept H_0 if $-1.96 \leq Z \leq 1.96$

Test statistic: $Z = 3.38$

Decision: Reject H_0

Conclusion: TEST1 is useful in this model.

The p value can also be used to conduct the test in the usual manner:

Decision rule: Reject H_0 if p value < 0.05
Accept H_0 if p value ≥ 0.05

Test statistic: p value $= 0.001$

The same decision and conclusion are reached whether the Z statistic or its p value is used.[3]

Information in the first row of the table can be used to test hypotheses about β_0, although interest is generally centered on the coefficients of the explanatory variables, as in linear regression.

Below this table is a statistic to test whether all slopes are zero. This is similar to the overall-fit F test in linear regression. The p value provided can be used in the usual way to conduct this test. The remainder of the output is not discussed in this text.

When using logistic regression, the goal of the analysis may be to classify the observations into a particular group (as in discriminant analysis). In this case, some rule must be designed to help decide into which group each observation should be classified. Predicted values of the probability of group membership in the indicated group can be computed from the logistic regression. A rule using these predicted probabilities can then be designed. The form of such a rule is:

Classify observations into the

$y = 0$ group if the predicted value is below the cutoff

$y = 1$ group otherwise

---

[3]Some statistical software use a chi-square statistic to test whether coefficients are equal to zero rather than a z statistic. The distribution of the test statistic is called a chi-square distribution. To test the hypotheses

$H_0: \beta_k = 0$

$H_a: \beta_k \neq 0$

the decision rule is:

Reject H_0 if $\chi^2 > \chi^2(\alpha, 1)$

Accept H_0 if $\chi^2 \leq \chi^2(\alpha, 1)$

where χ^2 is the test statistic and $\chi^2(\alpha, 1)$ is a chi-square critical value chosen from the chi-square table in Appendix B. One degree of freedom is used in selecting the proper critical value for the α level of significance.

A cutoff value of 0.5 is reasonable when the 0 and 1 outcomes are equally likely and the costs of misclassification into each group are about equal. In other cases, a different cutoff may be considered superior.[4]

10.4 USING THE COMPUTER

The Using the Computer section in each chapter describes how to perform the computer analyses in the chapter using MINITAB, Excel, and SAS. For further detail on MINITAB, Excel, and SAS, see Appendix C.

10.4.1 MINITAB

Note that Version 12 of MINITAB is fully menu driven. Commands can be used, however, and they are included for any interested users. The menu headings and subheadings used to perform the procedures are listed first, followed by commands in parentheses. For example, STAT: MULTIVARIATE: DISCRIMINANT ANALYSIS means to click on the STAT menu, then on MULTIVARIATE, and then on DISCRIMINANT ANALYSIS. (DISC C_, C_ is a command to be typed in.)

Discriminant Analysis

`STAT: MULTIVARIATE: DISCRIMINANT ANALYSIS (DISC C_, C_)`

Performs a discriminant analysis. The "Groups:" (dependent) variable, which designates the two (or more) groups into which the observations are classified, and the explanatory or predictor variables are requested in the dialog box. See Figure 10.6.

Logistic Regression

`STAT: REGRESSION: BINARY LOGISTIC REGRESSION (BLOG C1=C2 C3)`

Performs a logistic regression. Binary logistic regression assumes the sample observations come from two groups. More than two groups can be considered by using ORDINAL LOGISTIC REGRESSION (categories are ordinal in nature) or NOMINAL LOGISTIC REGRESSION (categories have no natural ordering). Figure 10.7 shows the dialog box for a binary logistic regression.

---

[4]For a more complete presentation of logistic regression, see C. E. Lunneborg, *Modeling Experimental and Observational Data*, Chapters 16, 17, and 18, or J. Neter, W. Wasserman, and M. Kutner, *Applied Linear Regression Models*, Chapter 16.

FIGURE **10.6**   MINITAB Dialog Box for Discriminant Analysis

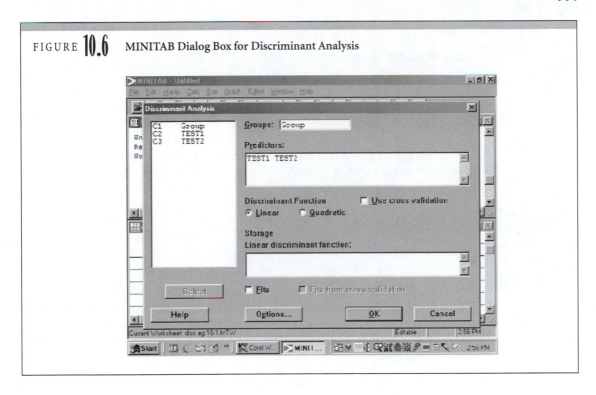

FIGURE **10.7**   MINITAB Dialog Box for Binary Logistic Regression

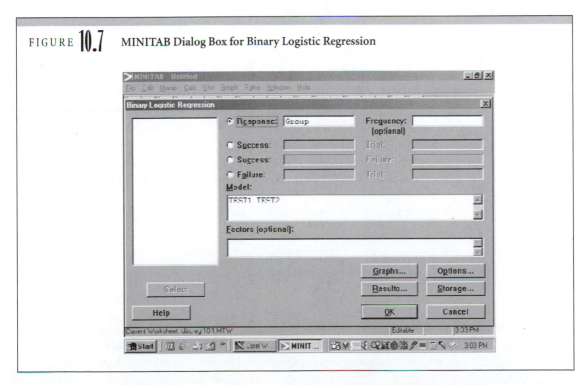

10.4.2 SAS

Discriminant Analysis

```
PROC DISCRIM;
    CLASS VAR1;
    VAR VAR2;
```

Performs a discriminant analysis. The dependent variable, which designates the two (or more) groups into which the observations are classified, is denoted here as VAR1 and is listed on the CLASS statement. The explanatory or predictor variables are listed on the VAR statement. In this example, only one predictor variable, VAR2, is used.

Logistic Regression

```
PROC LOGISTIC;
    MODEL VAR1=VAR2;
```

Performs a logistic regression. VAR1 is assumed to be the dependent variable. This variable is a 0/1 variable (as discussed in this chapter). The explanatory variables are listed on the right-hand side of the equality in the MODEL statement. In this example, the only variable listed is VAR2. The MODEL statement setup is similar to PROC REG.

EXERCISES

1 **Employee Classification** Figure 10.8 shows the logistic regression output for the employee classification data from Example 10.4 using both test results as explanatory variables. Use the output shown to answer the following questions.

a Which variable or variables appear to be useful in the logistic regression function? Justify your answer. Use a 5% level of significance for any hypotheses tests.

b Using the logistic output in either Figure 10.8 or 10.5 (whichever you feel is the best model) and a cutoff probability of 0.5, classify potential employees whose test scores were as follows:

  1. TEST1 = 94   TEST2 = 88

  2. TEST1 = 80   TEST2 = 87

  3. TEST1 = 82   TEST2 = 74

  4. TEST1 = 90   TEST2 = 80

2 **Harris Salaries** In Exercise 1 in Chapter 7, data from Harris Bank were examined to test for possible discrimination. In that exercise, the dependent variable was salary and one of the explanatory variables was an indicator variable to separate the employees into male and female groups. The coefficient of the indicator variable served as a measure of whether males earned more (or less), on average, than females.

FIGURE **10.8** MINITAB Logistic Regression Output for Employee Classification Example Using TEST1 and TEST2 as Independent Variables

```
Link Function: Logit

Response Information

Variable   Value    Count
Group          1       23 (Event)
               0       20
           Total       43

Logistic Regression Table
                                                 Odds        95% CI
Predictor     Coef      StDev       Z       P    Ratio   Lower   Upper
Constant     -56.17     17.45    -3.22   0.001
TEST1         0.4833    0.1578    3.06   0.002    1.62    1.19    2.21
TEST2         0.1652    0.1021    1.62   0.106    1.18    0.97    1.44


Log-Likelihood = -13.959
Test that all slopes are zero: G = 31.483, DF = 2, P-Value = 0.000

Goodness-of-Fit Tests

Method              Chi-Square       DF        P
Pearson                 21.884       39    0.988
Deviance                25.145       39    0.958
Hosmer-Lemeshow          5.034        8    0.754

Table of Observed and Expected Frequencies:
(See Hosmer-Lemeshow Test for the Pearson Chi-Square Statistic)

                                     Group
Value   1     2     3     4     5     6     7     8     9    10    Total
1
 Obs    0     0     0     2     3     2     3     4     4     5      23
 Exp   0.0   0.1   0.4   1.3   1.8   2.8   4.0   3.7   3.9   5.0
0
 Obs    4     4     4     3     1     2     2     0     0     0      20
 Exp   4.0   3.9   3.6   3.7   2.2   1.2   1.0   0.3   0.1   0.0

Total   4     4     4     5     4     4     5     4     4     5      43

Measures of Association:
(Between the Response Variable and Predicted Probabilities)

Pairs           Number    Percent     Summary Measures
Concordant         428      93.0%     Somers' D                0.86
Discordant          31       6.7%     Goodman-Kruskal Gamma    0.86
Ties                 1       0.2%     Kendall's Tau-a          0.44
Total              460     100.0%
```

Another way of examining this problem might be to use the male/female indicator variable as the dependent variable and see if group membership can be predicted from knowledge of salary. This can be done with either discriminant analysis or logistic regression. Try discriminant analysis and/or logistic regression and see how well these methods do in predicting whether employees are male or female based only on knowledge of their salary. Does your result support the claim that Harris Bank discriminated by underpaying female employees?[5]

The data are the same as in Table 7.3, but only two variables are used: SALARY and MALE. MALE has been coded as 1 for a male employee and 0 for a female employee. These data are in the file with SALARY in column 1 and MALE in column two. The filename prefix is HARRIS10.

3   **Automatic Versus Standard Transmissions**   The mileage in city driving (CITYMPG) and the type of transmission of the car (TRANS) are available in a file with prefix TRANS10. CITYMPG is in column 1 and TRANS is in column 2 (TRANS is coded as 1 = AUTO and 0 = MANUAL). Use these data to see whether the type of transmission can be predicted by knowing the mileage of the car in city driving. This can be investigated using either discriminant analysis or logistic regression. From the result, does it appear that there may be differences in city mileage due to the type of transmission?

4   **Loan Performance**   The National Bank of Fort Worth, Texas wants to examine methods for predicting subpar payment performance on loans. They have data on unsecured consumer loans made over a 3-day period in October 1994 with a final maturity of 2 years. There are a total of 348 observations in the sample. The data, which have been transformed to provide confidentiality, include the following:

PAST DUE:	Coded as 1 if the loan payment is past due and zero otherwise.
CBSCORE:	Score generated by the CSC Credit Reporting Agency. Values range from 400 to 8390, with higher values indicating a better credit rating.
DEBT:	This is a debt ratio calculated by taking required monthly payments on all debt and dividing it by the gross monthly income of the applicant and coapplicant. This ratio represents the amount of the applicant's income which will go toward repayment of debt.
GROSS INC:	Gross monthly income of the applicant and coapplicant.
LOAN AMT:	Loan amount.

You have been asked to examine the feasibility of predicting past-due loan payment. Report your results to the bank in a two-part report. The report should include an executive summary with a brief nontechnical description of your results and an accompanying technical report with the details of your analysis. The data are in a file in the order shown above. The filename prefix is LOAN10.

---

[5] Note: Using discriminant analysis or logistic regression in this manner would probably not be the preferred method of examining this question in a legal proceeding. The regression approach discussed in Chapter 7 would be preferred, but this makes an interesting exercise.

Summation Notation

A sample of n items chosen from a population can be denoted as $X_1, X_2, \ldots, X_n$. To represent the sum of these n items, the notation

$$\sum_{i=1}^{n} X_i$$

is used. This is simply shorthand notation for writing $X_1 + X_2 + \cdots + X_n$.

As an example, suppose a sample of four items is drawn, and the four sample values are 2, 3, 4, and 11. The sum of these four items can be represented by

$$\sum_{i=1}^{4} X_i = 2 + 3 + 4 + 11 = 20$$

Some other useful examples are

1 $\quad \sum_{i=1}^{4} X_i^2 = 4 + 9 + 16 + 121 = 150$

2 $\quad \sum_{i=1}^{4} (X_i - 5) = (2-5) + (3-5) + (4-5) + (11-5) = 0$

3 $\quad \sum_{i=1}^{4} (X_i - 5)^2 = (2-5)^2 + (3-5)^2 + (4-5)^2 + (11-5)^2 = 50$

4 $\quad \sum_{i=1}^{4} 4X_i = 8 + 12 + 16 + 44 = 80 = 4\sum_{i=1}^{4} X_i$

EXERCISES

Use the following information to complete each exercise. A sample of six items is chosen with the following result values: 5, 8, 10, 11, 12, 20.

a $\displaystyle\sum_{i=1}^{6} X_i =$

b $\displaystyle\sum_{i=1}^{6} X_i^2 =$

c $\displaystyle\sum_{i=1}^{6} (X_i - 11) =$

d $\displaystyle\sum_{i=1}^{6} (X_i - 11)^2 =$

e $\displaystyle\sum_{i=1}^{6} 2X_i =$

Statistical Tables

TABLE B.1   Standard Normal Distribution

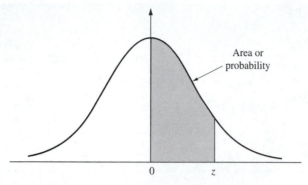

Area or probability

0   z

Entries in the table give the area under the curve between the mean and z standard deviations above the mean. For example, for z = 1.25 the area under the curve between the mean and z is .3944.

z	.00	.01	.02	.03	.04	.05	.06	.07	.08	.09
.0	.0000	.0040	.0080	.0120	.0160	.0199	.0239	.0279	.0319	.0359
.1	.0398	.0438	.0478	.0517	.0557	.0596	.0636	.0675	.0714	.0753
.2	.0793	.0832	.0871	.0910	.0948	.0987	.1026	.1064	.1103	.1141
.3	.1179	.1217	.1255	.1293	.1331	.1368	.1406	.1443	.1480	.1517
.4	.1554	.1591	.1628	.1664	.1700	.1736	.1772	.1808	.1844	.1879
.5	.1915	.1950	.1985	.2019	.2054	.2088	.2123	.2157	.2190	.2224
.6	.2257	.2291	.2324	.2357	.2389	.2422	.2454	.2486	.2518	.2549
.7	.2580	.2612	.2642	.2673	.2704	.2734	.2764	.2794	.2823	.2852
.8	.2881	.2910	.2939	.2967	.2995	.3023	.3051	.3078	.3106	.3133
.9	.3159	.3186	.3212	.3238	.3264	.3289	.3315	.3340	.3365	.3389
1.0	.3413	.3438	.3461	.3485	.3508	.3531	.3554	.3577	.3599	.3621
1.1	.3643	.3665	.3686	.3708	.3729	.3749	.3770	.3790	.3810	.3830
1.2	.3849	.3869	.3888	.3907	.3925	.3944	.3962	.3980	.3997	.4015
1.3	.4032	.4049	.4066	.4082	.4099	.4115	.4131	.4147	.4162	.4177
1.4	.4192	.4207	.4222	.4236	.4251	.4265	.4279	.4292	.4306	.4319
1.5	.4332	.4345	.4357	.4370	.4382	.4394	.4406	.4418	.4429	.4441
1.6	.4452	.4463	.4474	.4484	.4495	.4505	.4515	.4525	.4535	.4545
1.7	.4554	.4564	.4573	.4582	.4591	.4599	.4608	.4616	.4625	.4633
1.8	.4641	.4649	.4656	.4664	.4671	.4678	.4686	.4693	.4699	.4706
1.9	.4713	.4719	.4726	.4732	.4738	.4744	.4750	.4756	.4761	.4767
2.0	.4772	.4778	.4783	.4788	.4793	.4798	.4803	.4808	.4812	.4817
2.1	.4821	.4826	.4830	.4834	.4838	.4842	.4846	.4850	.4854	.4857
2.2	.4861	.4864	.4868	.4871	.4875	.4878	.4881	.4884	.4887	.4890
2.3	.4893	.4896	.4898	.4901	.4904	.4906	.4909	.4911	.4913	.4916
2.4	.4918	.4920	.4922	.4925	.4927	.4929	.4931	.4932	.4934	.4936
2.5	.4938	.4940	.4941	.4943	.4945	.4946	.4948	.4949	.4951	.4952
2.6	.4953	.4955	.4956	.4957	.4959	.4960	.4961	.4962	.4963	.4964
2.7	.4965	.4966	.4967	.4968	.4969	.4970	.4971	.4972	.4973	.4974
2.8	.4974	.4975	.4976	.4977	.4977	.4978	.4979	.4979	.4980	.4981
2.9	.4981	.4982	.4982	.4983	.4984	.4984	.4985	.4985	.4986	.4986
3.0	.4986	.4987	.4987	.4988	.4988	.4989	.4989	.4989	.4990	.4990

Abridged from Table I of A. Hald, *Statistical Tables and Formulas* (New York: John Wiley and Sons, 1952). Reproduced by permission of the publisher.

TABLE **B.2**   *t* Distribution

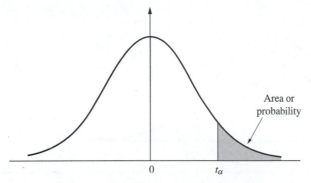

Area or
probability

0 t_α

Entries in the table give t_α values, where α is the area or probability in the upper tail of the *t* distribution. For example, with 10 degrees of freedom and a .05 area in the upper tail, $t_{.05} = 1.812$

Degrees	Area in Upper Tail				
of Freedom	.10	.05	.025	.01	.005
1	3.078	6.314	12.706	31.821	63.657
2	1.886	2.920	4.303	6.965	9.925
3	1.638	2.353	3.182	4.541	5.841
4	1.533	2.132	2.776	3.747	4.604
5	1.476	2.015	2.571	3.365	4.032
6	1.440	1.943	2.447	3.143	3.707
7	1.415	1.895	2.365	2.998	3.499
8	1.397	1.860	2.306	2.896	3.355
9	1.383	1.833	2.262	2.821	3.250
10	1.372	1.812	2.228	2.764	3.169
11	1.363	1.796	2.201	2.718	3.106
12	1.356	1.782	2.179	2.681	3.055
13	1.350	1.771	2.160	2.650	3.012
14	1.345	1.761	2.145	2.624	2.977
15	1.341	1.753	2.131	2.602	2.947
16	1.337	1.746	2.120	2.583	2.921
17	1.333	1.740	2.110	2.567	2.898
18	1.330	1.734	2.101	2.552	2.878
19	1.328	1.729	2.093	2.539	2.861
20	1.325	1.725	2.086	2.528	2.845
21	1.323	1.721	2.080	2.518	2.831
22	1.321	1.717	2.074	2.508	2.819
23	1.319	1.714	2.069	2.500	2.807
24	1.318	1.711	2.064	2.492	2.797
25	1.316	1.708	2.060	2.485	2.787
26	1.315	1.706	2.056	2.479	2.779
27	1.314	1.703	2.052	2.473	2.771
28	1.313	1.701	2.048	2.467	2.763
29	1.311	1.699	2.045	2.462	2.756
30	1.310	1.697	2.042	2.457	2.750
40	1.303	1.684	2.021	2.423	2.704
60	1.296	1.671	2.000	2.390	2.660
120	1.289	1.658	1.980	2.358	2.617
∞	1.282	1.645	1.960	2.326	2.576

TABLE **B.3**   Critical Values for the *F* Statistic ($\alpha = .10$)

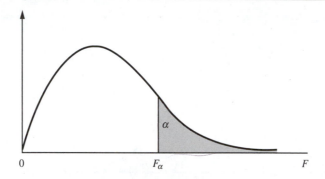

$v2$	$v1$								
	Numerator Degrees of Freedom								
	1	2	3	4	5	6	7	8	9
1	39.86	49.50	53.59	55.83	57.24	58.20	58.91	59.44	59.86
2	8.53	9.00	9.16	9.24	9.29	9.33	9.35	9.37	9.38
3	5.54	5.46	5.39	5.34	5.31	5.28	5.27	5.25	5.24
4	4.54	4.32	4.19	4.11	4.05	4.01	3.98	3.95	3.94
5	4.06	3.78	3.62	3.52	3.45	3.40	3.37	3.34	3.32
6	3.78	3.46	3.29	3.18	3.11	3.05	3.01	2.98	2.96
7	3.59	3.26	3.07	2.96	2.88	2.83	2.78	2.75	2.72
8	3.46	3.11	2.92	2.81	2.73	2.67	2.62	2.59	2.56
9	3.36	3.01	2.81	2.69	2.61	2.55	2.51	2.47	2.44
10	3.39	2.92	2.73	2.61	2.52	2.46	2.41	2.38	2.35
11	3.23	2.86	2.66	2.54	2.45	2.39	2.34	2.30	2.27
12	3.18	2.81	2.61	2.48	2.39	2.33	2.28	2.24	2.21
13	3.14	2.76	2.56	2.43	2.35	2.28	2.23	2.20	2.16
14	3.10	2.73	2.52	2.39	2.31	2.24	2.19	2.15	2.12
15	3.07	2.70	2.49	2.36	2.27	2.21	2.16	2.12	2.09
16	3.05	2.67	2.46	2.33	2.24	2.18	2.13	2.09	2.06
17	3.03	2.64	2.44	2.31	2.22	2.15	2.10	2.06	2.03
18	3.01	2.62	2.42	2.29	2.20	2.13	2.08	2.04	2.00
19	2.99	2.61	2.40	2.27	2.18	2.11	2.06	2.02	1.98
20	2.97	2.59	2.38	2.25	2.16	2.09	2.04	2.00	1.96
21	2.96	2.57	2.36	2.23	2.14	2.08	2.02	1.98	1.95
22	2.95	2.56	2.35	2.22	2.13	2.06	2.01	1.97	1.93
23	2.94	2.55	2.34	2.21	2.11	2.05	1.99	1.95	1.92
24	2.93	2.54	2.33	2.19	2.10	2.04	1.98	1.94	1.91
25	2.92	2.53	2.32	2.18	2.09	2.02	1.97	1.93	1.89
26	2.91	2.52	2.31	2.17	2.08	2.01	1.96	1.92	1.88
27	2.90	2.51	2.30	2.17	2.07	2.00	1.95	1.91	1.87
28	2.89	2.50	2.29	2.16	2.06	2.00	1.94	1.90	1.87
29	2.89	2.50	2.28	2.15	2.06	1.99	1.93	1.89	1.86
30	2.88	2.49	2.28	2.14	2.05	1.98	1.93	1.88	1.85
40	2.84	2.44	2.23	2.09	2.00	1.93	1.87	1.83	1.79
60	2.79	2.39	2.18	2.04	1.95	1.87	1.82	1.77	1.74
120	2.75	2.35	2.13	1.99	1.90	1.82	1.77	1.72	1.68
∞	2.71	2.30	2.08	1.94	1.85	1.77	1.72	1.67	1.63

Denominator Degrees of Freedom

TABLE **B.3**   *(continued)*

$v2$	$v1$ Numerator Degrees of Freedom									
	10	12	15	20	24	30	40	60	120	∞
1	60.19	60.71	61.22	61.74	62.00	62.26	62.53	62.79	63.06	63.33
2	9.39	9.41	9.42	9.44	9.45	9.46	9.47	9.47	9.48	9.49
3	5.23	5.22	5.20	5.18	5.18	5.17	5.16	5.15	5.14	5.13
4	3.92	3.90	3.87	3.84	3.83	3.82	3.80	3.79	3.78	3.76
5	3.30	3.27	3.24	3.21	3.19	3.17	3.16	3.14	3.12	3.10
6	2.94	2.90	2.87	2.84	2.82	2.80	2.78	2.76	2.74	2.72
7	2.70	2.67	2.63	2.59	2.58	2.56	2.54	2.51	2.49	2.47
8	2.54	2.50	2.46	2.42	2.40	2.38	2.36	2.34	2.32	2.29
9	2.42	2.38	2.34	2.30	2.28	2.25	2.23	2.21	2.18	2.16
10	2.32	2.28	2.24	2.20	2.18	2.16	2.13	2.11	2.08	2.06
11	2.25	2.21	2.17	2.12	2.10	2.08	2.05	2.03	2.00	1.97
12	2.19	2.15	2.10	2.06	2.04	2.01	1.99	1.96	1.93	1.90
13	2.14	2.10	2.05	2.01	1.98	1.96	1.93	1.90	1.88	1.85
14	2.10	2.05	2.01	1.96	1.94	1.91	1.89	1.86	1.83	1.80
15	2.06	2.02	1.97	1.92	1.90	1.87	1.85	1.82	1.79	1.76
16	2.03	1.99	1.94	1.89	1.87	1.84	1.81	1.78	1.75	1.72
17	2.00	1.96	1.91	1.86	1.84	1.81	1.78	1.75	1.72	1.69
18	1.98	1.93	1.89	1.84	1.81	1.78	1.75	1.72	1.69	1.66
19	1.96	1.91	1.86	1.81	1.79	1.76	1.73	1.70	1.67	1.63
20	1.94	1.89	1.84	1.79	1.77	1.74	1.71	1.68	1.64	1.61
21	1.92	1.87	1.83	1.78	1.75	1.72	1.69	1.66	1.62	1.59
22	1.90	1.86	1.81	1.76	1.73	1.70	1.67	1.64	1.60	1.57
23	1.89	1.84	1.80	1.74	1.72	1.69	1.66	1.62	1.59	1.55
24	1.88	1.83	1.78	1.73	1.70	1.67	1.64	1.61	1.57	1.53
25	1.87	1.82	1.77	1.72	1.69	1.66	1.63	1.59	1.56	1.52
26	1.86	1.81	1.76	1.71	1.68	1.65	1.61	1.58	1.54	1.50
27	1.85	1.80	1.75	1.70	1.67	1.64	1.60	1.57	1.53	1.49
28	1.84	1.79	1.74	1.69	1.66	1.63	1.59	1.56	1.52	1.48
29	1.83	1.78	1.73	1.68	1.65	1.62	1.58	1.55	1.51	1.47
30	1.82	1.77	1.72	1.67	1.64	1.61	1.57	1.54	1.50	1.46
40	1.76	1.71	1.66	1.61	1.57	1.54	1.51	1.47	1.42	1.38
60	1.71	1.66	1.60	1.54	1.51	1.48	1.44	1.40	1.35	1.29
120	1.65	1.60	1.55	1.48	1.45	1.41	1.37	1.32	1.26	1.19
∞	1.60	1.55	1.49	1.42	1.38	1.34	1.30	1.24	1.17	1.00

Denominator Degrees of Freedom

TABLE B.4   Critical Values for the F Statistic ($\alpha = .05$)

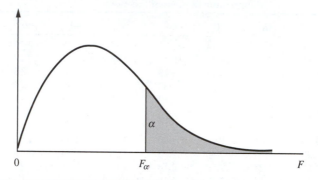

$v2$ ╲ $v1$	Numerator Degrees of Freedom								
	1	2	3	4	5	6	7	8	9
1	161.40	199.50	215.70	224.60	230.20	234.00	236.80	238.90	240.50
2	18.51	19.00	19.16	19.25	19.30	19.33	19.35	19.37	19.38
3	10.13	9.55	9.28	9.12	9.01	8.94	8.89	8.85	8.81
4	7.71	6.94	6.59	6.39	6.26	6.16	6.09	6.04	6.00
5	6.61	5.79	5.41	5.19	5.05	4.95	4.88	4.82	4.77
6	5.99	5.14	4.76	4.53	4.39	4.28	4.21	4.15	4.10
7	5.59	4.74	4.35	4.12	3.97	3.87	3.79	3.73	3.68
8	5.32	4.46	4.07	3.84	3.69	3.58	3.50	3.44	3.39
9	5.12	4.26	3.86	3.63	3.48	3.37	3.29	3.23	3.18
10	4.96	4.10	3.71	3.48	3.33	3.22	3.14	3.07	3.02
11	4.84	3.98	3.59	3.36	3.20	3.09	3.01	2.95	2.90
12	4.75	3.89	3.49	3.26	3.11	3.00	2.91	2.85	2.80
13	4.67	3.81	3.41	3.18	3.03	2.92	2.83	2.77	2.71
14	4.60	3.74	3.34	3.11	2.96	2.85	2.76	2.70	2.65
15	4.54	3.68	3.29	3.06	2.90	2.79	2.71	2.64	2.59
16	4.49	3.63	3.24	3.01	2.85	2.74	2.66	2.59	2.54
17	4.45	3.59	3.20	2.96	2.81	2.70	2.61	2.55	2.49
18	4.41	3.55	3.16	2.93	2.77	2.66	2.58	2.51	2.46
19	4.38	3.52	3.13	2.90	2.74	2.63	2.54	2.48	2.42
20	4.35	3.49	3.10	2.87	2.71	2.60	2.51	2.45	2.39
21	4.32	3.47	3.07	2.84	2.68	2.57	2.49	2.42	2.37
22	4.30	3.44	3.05	2.82	2.66	2.55	2.46	2.40	2.34
23	4.28	3.42	3.03	2.80	2.64	2.53	2.44	2.37	2.32
24	4.26	3.40	3.01	2.78	2.62	2.51	2.42	2.36	2.30
25	4.24	3.39	2.99	2.76	2.60	2.49	2.40	2.34	2.28
26	4.23	3.37	2.98	2.74	2.59	2.47	2.39	2.32	2.27
27	4.21	3.35	2.96	2.73	2.57	2.46	2.37	2.31	2.25
28	4.20	3.34	2.95	2.71	2.56	2.45	2.36	2.29	2.24
29	4.18	3.33	2.93	2.70	2.55	2.43	2.35	2.28	2.22
30	4.17	3.32	2.92	2.69	2.53	2.42	2.33	2.27	2.21
40	4.08	3.23	2.84	2.61	2.45	2.34	2.25	2.18	2.12
60	4.00	3.15	2.76	2.53	2.37	2.25	2.17	2.10	2.04
120	3.92	3.07	2.68	2.45	2.29	2.17	2.09	2.02	1.96
∞	3.84	3.00	2.60	2.37	2.21	2.10	2.01	1.94	1.88

Denominator Degrees of Freedom

TABLE **B.4**   (*continued*)

v2 \ v1	Numerator Degrees of Freedom									
	10	12	15	20	24	30	40	60	120	∞
1	241.90	243.90	245.90	248.00	249.10	250.10	251.10	252.20	253.30	254.30
2	19.40	19.41	19.43	19.45	19.45	19.46	19.47	19.48	19.49	19.50
3	8.79	8.74	8.70	8.66	8.64	8.62	8.59	8.57	8.55	8.53
4	5.96	5.91	5.86	5.80	5.77	5.75	5.72	5.69	5.66	5.63
5	4.74	4.68	4.62	4.56	4.53	4.50	4.46	4.43	4.40	4.36
6	4.06	4.00	3.94	3.87	3.84	3.81	3.77	3.74	3.70	3.67
7	3.64	3.57	3.51	3.44	3.41	3.38	3.34	3.30	3.27	3.23
8	3.35	3.28	3.22	3.15	3.12	3.08	3.04	3.01	2.97	2.93
9	3.14	3.07	3.01	2.94	2.90	2.86	2.83	2.79	2.75	2.71
10	2.98	2.91	2.85	2.77	2.74	2.70	2.66	2.62	2.58	2.54
11	2.85	2.79	2.72	2.65	2.61	2.57	2.53	2.49	2.45	2.40
12	2.75	2.69	2.62	2.54	2.51	2.47	2.43	2.38	2.34	2.30
13	2.67	2.60	2.53	2.46	2.42	2.38	2.34	2.30	2.25	2.21
14	2.60	2.53	2.46	2.39	2.35	2.31	2.27	2.22	2.18	2.13
15	2.54	2.48	2.40	2.33	2.29	2.25	2.20	2.16	2.11	2.07
16	2.49	2.42	2.35	2.28	2.24	2.19	2.15	2.11	2.06	2.01
17	2.45	2.38	2.31	2.23	2.19	2.15	2.10	2.06	2.01	1.96
18	2.41	2.34	2.27	2.19	2.15	2.11	2.06	2.02	1.97	1.92
19	2.38	2.31	2.23	2.16	2.11	2.07	2.03	1.98	1.93	1.88
20	2.35	2.28	2.20	2.12	2.08	2.04	1.99	1.95	1.90	1.84
21	2.32	2.25	2.18	2.10	2.05	2.01	1.96	1.92	1.87	1.81
22	2.30	2.23	2.15	2.07	2.03	1.98	1.94	1.89	1.84	1.78
23	2.27	2.20	2.13	2.05	2.01	1.96	1.91	1.86	1.81	1.76
24	2.25	2.18	2.11	2.03	1.98	1.94	1.89	1.84	1.79	1.73
25	2.24	2.16	2.09	2.01	1.96	1.92	1.87	1.82	1.77	1.71
26	2.22	2.15	2.07	1.99	1.95	1.90	1.85	1.80	1.75	1.69
27	2.20	2.13	2.06	1.97	1.93	1.88	1.84	1.79	1.73	1.67
28	2.19	2.12	2.04	1.96	1.91	1.87	1.82	1.77	1.71	1.65
29	2.18	2.10	2.03	1.94	1.90	1.85	1.81	1.75	1.70	1.64
30	2.16	2.09	2.01	1.93	1.89	1.84	1.79	1.74	1.68	1.62
40	2.08	2.00	1.92	1.84	1.79	1.74	1.69	1.64	1.58	1.51
60	1.99	1.92	1.84	1.75	1.70	1.65	1.59	1.53	1.47	1.39
120	1.91	1.83	1.75	1.66	1.61	1.55	1.50	1.43	1.35	1.25
∞	1.83	1.75	1.67	1.57	1.52	1.46	1.39	1.32	1.22	1.00

Denominator Degrees of Freedom

TABLE **B.5**   Critical Values for the F Statistic ($\alpha = .01$)

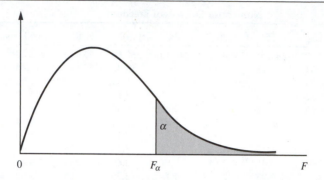

$v1$	Numerator Degrees of Freedom								
$v2$	1	2	3	4	5	6	7	8	9
1	4,052.00	4,999.50	5,403.00	5,625.00	5,764.00	5,859.00	5,928.00	5,982.00	6,022.00
2	98.50	99.00	99.17	99.25	99.30	99.33	99.36	99.37	99.39
3	34.12	30.82	29.46	28.71	28.24	27.91	27.67	27.49	27.35
4	21.20	18.00	16.69	15.98	15.52	15.21	14.98	14.80	14.66
5	16.26	13.27	12.06	11.39	10.97	10.67	10.46	10.29	10.16
6	13.75	10.92	9.78	9.15	8.75	8.47	8.26	8.10	7.98
7	12.25	9.55	8.45	7.85	7.46	7.19	6.99	6.84	6.72
8	11.26	8.65	7.59	7.01	6.63	6.37	6.18	6.03	5.91
9	10.56	8.02	6.99	6.42	6.06	5.80	5.61	5.47	5.35
10	10.04	7.56	6.55	5.99	5.64	5.39	5.20	5.06	4.94
11	9.65	7.21	6.22	5.67	5.32	5.07	4.89	4.74	4.63
12	9.33	6.93	5.95	5.41	5.06	4.82	4.64	4.50	4.39
13	9.07	6.70	5.74	5.21	4.86	4.62	4.44	4.30	4.19
14	8.86	6.51	5.56	5.04	4.69	4.46	4.28	4.14	4.03
15	8.68	6.36	5.42	4.89	4.56	4.32	4.14	4.00	3.89
16	8.53	6.23	5.29	4.77	4.44	4.20	4.03	3.89	3.78
17	8.40	6.11	5.18	4.67	4.34	4.10	3.93	3.79	3.68
18	8.29	6.01	5.09	4.58	4.25	4.01	3.84	3.71	3.60
19	8.18	5.93	5.01	4.50	4.17	3.94	3.77	3.63	3.52
20	8.10	5.85	4.94	4.43	4.10	3.87	3.70	3.56	3.46
21	8.02	5.78	4.87	4.37	4.04	3.81	3.64	3.51	3.40
22	7.95	5.72	4.82	4.31	3.99	3.76	3.59	3.45	3.35
23	7.88	5.66	4.76	4.26	3.94	3.71	3.54	3.41	3.30
24	7.82	5.61	4.72	4.22	3.90	3.67	3.50	3.36	3.26
25	7.77	5.57	4.68	4.18	3.85	3.63	3.46	3.32	3.22
26	7.72	5.53	4.64	4.14	3.82	3.59	3.42	3.29	3.18
27	7.68	5.49	4.60	4.11	3.78	3.56	3.39	3.26	3.15
28	7.64	5.45	4.57	4.07	3.75	3.53	3.36	3.23	3.12
29	7.60	5.42	4.54	4.04	3.73	3.50	3.33	3.20	3.09
30	7.56	5.39	4.51	4.02	3.70	3.47	3.30	3.17	3.07
40	7.31	5.18	4.31	3.83	3.51	3.29	3.12	2.99	2.89
60	7.08	4.98	4.13	3.65	3.34	3.12	2.95	2.82	2.72
120	6.85	4.79	3.95	3.48	3.17	2.96	2.79	2.66	2.56
∞	6.63	4.61	3.78	3.32	3.02	2.80	2.64	2.51	2.41

Denominator Degrees of Freedom

Source: From M. Merrington and C. M. Thompson, "Tables of Percentage Points of the Inverted Beta (F)-Distribution," *Biometrika* 33 (1943): 73–88. Reproduced by permission of the *Biometrika* Trustees.

TABLE **B.5**   *(continued)*

v2	Numerator Degrees of Freedom									
v1	10	12	15	20	24	30	40	60	120	∞
1	6,056.00	6,106.00	6,157.00	6,209.00	6,235.00	6,261.00	6,287.00	6,313.00	6,339.00	6,366.00
2	99.40	99.42	99.43	99.45	99.46	99.47	99.47	99.48	99.49	99.50
3	27.23	27.05	26.87	26.69	26.60	26.50	26.41	26.32	26.22	26.13
4	14.55	14.37	14.20	14.02	13.93	13.84	13.75	13.65	13.56	13.46
5	10.05	9.89	9.72	9.55	9.47	9.38	9.29	9.20	9.11	9.02
6	7.87	7.72	7.56	7.40	7.31	7.23	7.14	7.06	6.97	6.88
7	6.62	6.47	6.31	6.16	6.07	5.99	5.91	5.82	5.74	5.65
8	5.81	5.67	5.52	5.36	5.28	5.20	5.12	5.03	4.95	4.86
9	5.26	5.11	4.96	4.81	4.73	4.65	4.57	4.48	4.40	4.31
10	4.85	4.71	4.56	4.41	4.33	4.25	4.17	4.08	4.00	3.91
11	4.54	4.40	4.25	4.10	4.02	3.94	3.86	3.78	3.69	3.60
12	4.30	4.16	4.01	3.86	3.78	3.70	3.62	3.54	3.45	3.36
13	4.10	3.96	3.82	3.66	3.59	3.51	3.43	3.34	3.25	3.17
14	3.94	3.80	3.66	3.51	3.43	3.35	3.27	3.18	3.09	3.00
15	3.80	3.67	3.52	3.37	3.29	3.21	3.13	3.05	2.96	2.87
16	3.69	3.55	3.41	3.26	3.18	3.10	3.02	2.93	2.84	2.75
17	3.59	3.46	3.31	3.16	3.08	3.00	2.92	2.83	2.75	2.65
18	3.51	3.37	3.23	3.08	3.00	2.92	2.84	2.75	2.66	2.57
19	3.43	3.30	3.15	3.00	2.92	2.84	2.76	2.67	2.58	2.49
20	3.37	3.23	3.09	2.94	2.86	2.78	2.69	2.61	2.52	2.42
21	3.31	3.17	3.03	2.88	2.80	2.72	2.64	2.55	2.46	2.36
22	3.26	3.12	2.98	2.83	2.75	2.67	2.58	2.50	2.40	2.31
23	3.21	3.07	2.93	2.78	2.70	2.62	2.54	2.45	2.35	2.26
24	3.17	3.03	2.89	2.74	2.66	2.58	2.49	2.40	2.31	2.21
25	3.13	2.99	2.85	2.70	2.62	2.54	2.45	2.36	2.27	2.17
26	3.09	2.96	2.81	2.66	2.58	2.50	2.42	2.33	2.23	2.13
27	3.06	2.93	2.78	2.63	2.55	2.47	2.38	2.29	2.20	2.10
28	3.03	2.90	2.75	2.60	2.52	2.44	2.35	2.26	2.17	2.06
29	3.00	2.87	2.73	2.57	2.49	2.41	2.33	2.23	2.14	2.03
30	2.98	2.84	2.70	2.55	2.47	2.39	2.30	2.21	2.11	2.01
40	2.80	2.66	2.52	2.37	2.29	2.20	2.11	2.02	1.92	1.80
60	2.63	2.50	2.35	2.20	2.12	2.03	1.94	1.84	1.73	1.60
120	2.47	2.34	2.19	2.03	1.95	1.86	1.76	1.66	1.53	1.38
∞	2.32	2.18	2.04	1.88	1.79	1.70	1.59	1.47	1.32	1.00

Denominator Degrees of Freedom (row label for v2)

TABLE B.6   Critical Values for the Ryan-Joiner Test for Normality

		α	
n	0.01	0.05	0.10
4	.8951	.8734	.8318
5	.9033	.8804	.8320
10	.9347	.9180	.8804
15	.9506	.9383	.9110
20	.9600	.9503	.9290
25	.9662	.9582	.9408
30	.9707	.9639	.9490
40	.9767	.9715	.9597
50	.9807	.9764	.9664
60	.9835	.9799	.9710
75	.9865	.9835	.9757

Source: *MINITAB Statistical Software Reference Manual—Release 6.1,* 1988, p. 63. Reproduced by permission of MINITAB, Inc.

TABLE **B.7**   Critical Values for the Durbin-Watson Statistic ($\alpha = .05$)

n	K=1		K=2		K=3		K=4		K=5	
	d_L	d_U	d_L	d_U	d_L	d_U	d_L	d_U	d_L	d_U
15	1.08	1.36	0.95	1.54	0.82	1.75	0.69	1.97	0.56	2.21
16	1.10	1.37	0.98	1.54	0.86	1.73	0.74	1.93	0.62	2.15
17	1.13	1.38	1.02	1.54	0.90	1.71	0.78	1.90	0.67	2.10
18	1.16	1.39	1.05	1.53	0.93	1.69	0.82	1.87	0.71	2.06
19	1.18	1.40	1.08	1.53	0.97	1.68	0.86	1.85	0.75	2.02
20	1.20	1.41	1.10	1.54	1.00	1.68	0.90	1.83	0.79	1.99
21	1.22	1.42	1.13	1.54	1.03	1.67	0.93	1.81	0.83	1.96
22	1.24	1.43	1.15	1.54	1.05	1.66	0.96	1.80	0.86	1.94
23	1.26	1.44	1.17	1.54	1.08	1.66	0.99	1.79	0.90	1.92
24	1.27	1.45	1.19	1.55	1.10	1.66	1.01	1.78	0.93	1.90
25	1.29	1.45	1.21	1.55	1.12	1.66	1.04	1.77	0.95	1.89
26	1.30	1.46	1.22	1.55	1.14	1.65	1.06	1.76	0.98	1.88
27	1.32	1.47	1.24	1.56	1.16	1.65	1.08	1.76	1.01	1.86
28	1.33	1.48	1.26	1.56	1.18	1.65	1.10	1.75	1.03	1.85
29	1.34	1.48	1.27	1.56	1.20	1.65	1.12	1.74	1.05	1.84
30	1.35	1.49	1.28	1.57	1.21	1.65	1.14	1.74	1.07	1.83
31	1.36	1.50	1.30	1.57	1.23	1.65	1.16	1.74	1.09	1.83
32	1.37	1.50	1.31	1.57	1.24	1.65	1.18	1.73	1.11	1.82
33	1.38	1.51	1.32	1.58	1.26	1.65	1.19	1.73	1.13	1.81
34	1.39	1.51	1.33	1.58	1.27	1.65	1.21	1.73	1.15	1.81
35	1.40	1.52	1.34	1.58	1.28	1.65	1.22	1.73	1.16	1.80
36	1.41	1.52	1.35	1.59	1.29	1.65	1.24	1.73	1.18	1.80
37	1.42	1.53	1.36	1.59	1.31	1.66	1.25	1.72	1.19	1.80
38	1.43	1.54	1.37	1.59	1.32	1.66	1.26	1.72	1.21	1.79
39	1.43	1.54	1.38	1.60	1.33	1.66	1.27	1.72	1.22	1.79
40	1.44	1.54	1.39	1.60	1.34	1.66	1.29	1.72	1.23	1.79
45	1.48	1.57	1.43	1.62	1.38	1.67	1.34	1.72	1.29	1.78
50	1.50	1.59	1.46	1.63	1.42	1.67	1.38	1.72	1.34	1.77
55	1.53	1.60	1.49	1.64	1.45	1.68	1.41	1.72	1.38	1.77
60	1.55	1.62	1.51	1.65	1.48	1.69	1.44	1.73	1.41	1.77
65	1.57	1.63	1.54	1.66	1.50	1.70	1.47	1.73	1.44	1.77
70	1.58	1.64	1.55	1.67	1.52	1.70	1.49	1.74	1.46	1.77
75	1.60	1.65	1.57	1.68	1.54	1.71	1.51	1.74	1.49	1.77
80	1.61	1.66	1.59	1.69	1.56	1.72	1.53	1.74	1.51	1.77
85	1.62	1.67	1.60	1.70	1.57	1.72	1.55	1.75	1.52	1.77
90	1.63	1.68	1.61	1.70	1.59	1.73	1.57	1.75	1.54	1.78
95	1.64	1.69	1.62	1.71	1.60	1.73	1.58	1.75	1.56	1.78
100	1.65	1.69	1.63	1.72	1.61	1.74	1.59	1.76	1.57	1.78

Source: From J. Durbin and G. S. Watson, "Testing for Serial Correlation in Least Squares Regression, II." *Biometrika* 38 (1951): 159–178. Reproduced by permission of the *Biometrika* trustees.

TABLE **B.8**   Critical Values for the Chi-Square Statistic

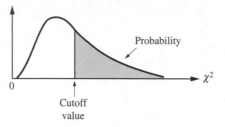

Probability

χ^2

0

Cutoff
value

Note: Entries on this page are cutoff values to place a specified probability amount in the right tail. For example, to have probability = .10 in the right tail when $df = 4$, the table value is $\chi^2 = 7.779$.

Degrees of Freedom, df	Probability in Right Tail				
	.10	.05	.025	.01	.005
1	2.706	3.841	5.024	6.635	7.879
2	4.605	5.991	7.378	9.210	10.597
3	6.251	7.815	9.348	11.345	12.838
4	7.779	9.488	11.143	13.277	14.860
5	9.236	11.070	12.833	15.086	16.750
6	10.645	12.592	14.449	16.812	18.548
7	12.017	14.067	16.013	18.475	20.278
8	13.362	15.507	17.535	20.090	21.955
9	14.684	16.919	19.023	21.666	23.589
10	15.987	18.307	20.483	23.209	25.188
11	17.275	19.675	21.920	24.725	26.757
12	18.549	21.026	23.337	26.217	28.300
13	19.812	22.362	24.736	27.688	29.819
14	21.064	23.685	26.119	29.141	31.319
15	22.307	24.996	27.488	30.578	32.801
16	23.542	26.296	28.845	32.000	34.267
17	24.769	27.587	30.191	33.409	35.718
18	25.989	28.869	31.526	34.805	37.156
19	27.204	30.144	32.852	36.191	38.582
20	28.412	31.410	34.170	37.566	39.997
21	29.615	32.671	35.479	38.932	41.401
22	30.813	33.924	36.781	40.289	42.796
23	32.007	35.172	38.076	41.638	44.181
24	33.196	36.415	39.364	42.980	45.558
25	34.382	37.652	40.647	44.314	46.928
26	35.563	38.885	41.923	45.642	48.290
27	36.741	40.113	43.194	46.963	49.645
28	37.916	41.337	44.461	48.278	50.993
29	39.087	42.557	45.722	49.588	52.336
30	40.256	43.773	46.979	50.892	53.672
50	63.167	67.505	71.420	76.154	79.490
60	74.397	79.082	83.298	88.379	91.952
80	96.578	101.879	106.629	112.329	116.321
100	118.498	124.342	129.561	135.807	140.169

Source: Computed by R. E. Shiffler and A. J. Adams.

APPENDIX C

A Brief Introduction to MINITAB™, Microsoft® Excel, and SAS®

C.1 INTRODUCTION

This appendix presents a brief summary of procedures in MINITAB, Excel, and SAS. MINITAB Version 12, Excel 2000, and Version 6 of SAS are used. Depending on the version of MINITAB, Excel, or SAS, the available procedures and output may differ slightly from what is presented in this text (but should be fairly similar). Only a general description of the use of these software packages is given here. Further details on statistical procedures are provided in the Using the Computer sections at the end of various chapters.

C.2 MINITAB

C.2.1 Data Input

Storage of data during a MINITAB session is accomplished through the use of columns. (Note: There are two other storage modes in MINITAB: constants, which represent single numbers and are denoted K1, K2, . . . , and matrices, which represent arrays of numbers and are denoted M1, M2, . . . These storage modes are not discussed.)

Data stored in a MINITAB file (MTB suffix) can be accessed through the File menu. Figure C.1 shows the contents of the File menu. Click on Open Worksheet and a dialog box opens requesting the name of the worksheet you want to open, as shown

FIGURE **C.1**   **MINITAB File Menu**

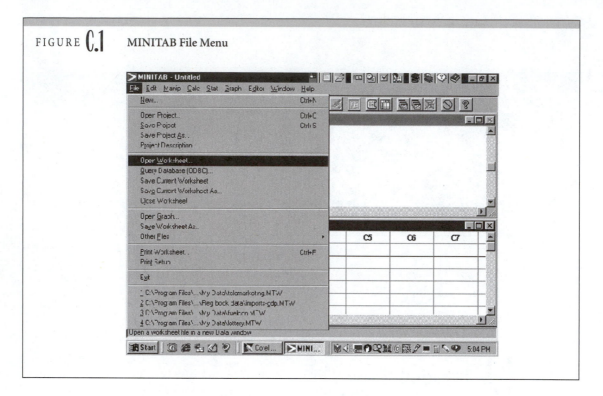

in Figure C.2. If you highlight cars8 and click on Open, the data from cars8 open into the current worksheet, as shown in Figure C.3. Once you have data in the worksheet columns, you can begin to analyze the data.

If you have data of your own to analyze and you want to put the data into a MINITAB worksheet, you can just begin typing. In MINITAB, it is best to start typing data in the first row of each column and to leave no empty rows. These columns serve as variables, so you can assign a name to each of the variables (columns) used.

Certain MINITAB procedures that may be useful for data manipulation and analysis are discussed next.

C.2.2 The Stat Menu

Statistical procedures are accessed in MINITAB through the Stat menu. The Stat menu is shown in Figure C.4. In this text, the Basic Statistics, ANOVA, Regression, Multivariate, and Time Series categories from this menu were used.

Figure C.5 shows the Basic Statistics menu. Display Descriptive Statistics computes a number of descriptive statistics for specified columns. The statistics requested are the count of the number of observations in the column, the mean, median, the trimmed mean, the standard deviation, the standard error of the mean, the minimum and maximum, and the first and third quartiles. 1-Sample Z provides confidence

FIGURE **C.2**   **MINITAB Open Worksheet Dialog Box**

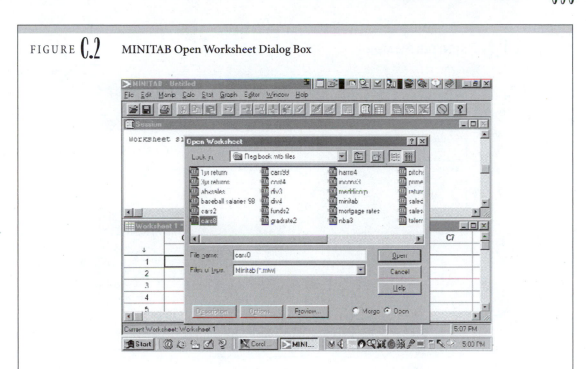

FIGURE **C.3**   **MINITAB Worksheet**

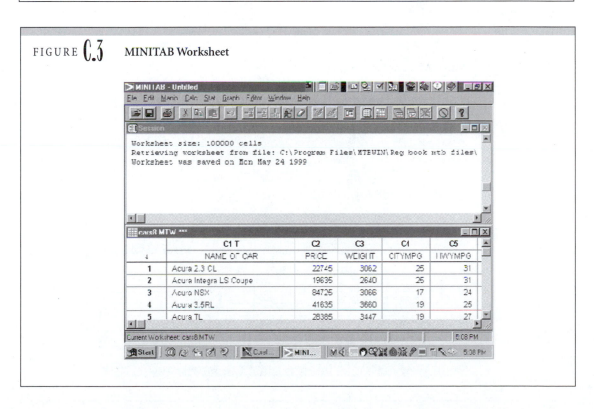

FIGURE **C.4**   **MINITAB Stat Menu**

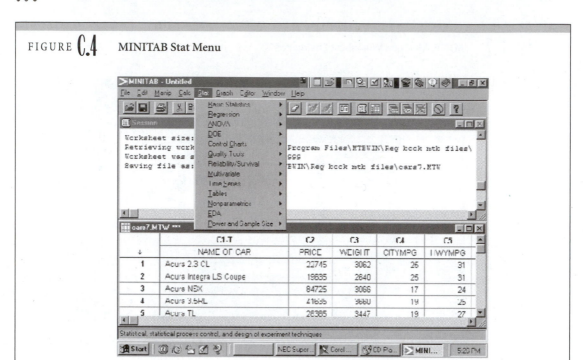

FIGURE **C.5**   **MINITAB Basic Statistics Menu**

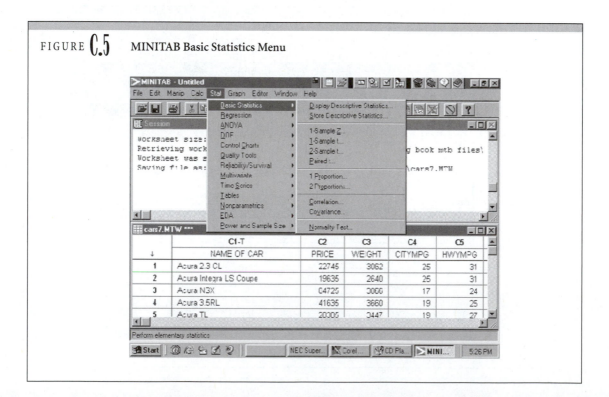

FIGURE **C.6**   **MINITAB Regression Menu**

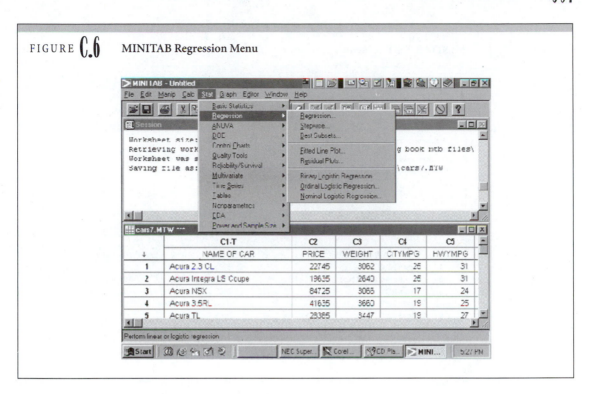

intervals and hypothesis tests for a population mean when the population standard deviation is known. 1-Sample *t* provides confidence intervals and hypothesis tests for a population mean when the population standard deviation is unknown. 2-Sample *t* provides confidence intervals and hypothesis tests about the difference between two population means. Correlation provides pairwise correlations between two or more variables. Covariance provides pairwise covariances between two or more variables. Normality Test provides a choice of three different tests for normality. The other items on this menu were not discussed in this text.

The Regression menu is shown in Figure C.6. Regression allows simple or multiple regressions to be computed and a variety of optional statistical measures to be computed. Stepwise provides for computation of stepwise regression with several options. Best Subsets provides for computation of a selection of the "best" regressions for a given group of variables along with summary statistics. The regressions computed as best subset regressions are those with the highest R^2 values for various subsets of variables. Fitted Line Plot can be used to perform a simple regression and to plot the regression line on a scatterplot. Residual Plots provide a variety of residual plots to be used for diagnostic purposes for a regression. Binary Logistic Regression performs a logistic regression for a dependent variable with two possible values. Ordinal and Nominal Logistic Regression perform logistic regressions when there are more than two groups for classification.

FIGURE C.7   **MINITAB ANOVA Menu**

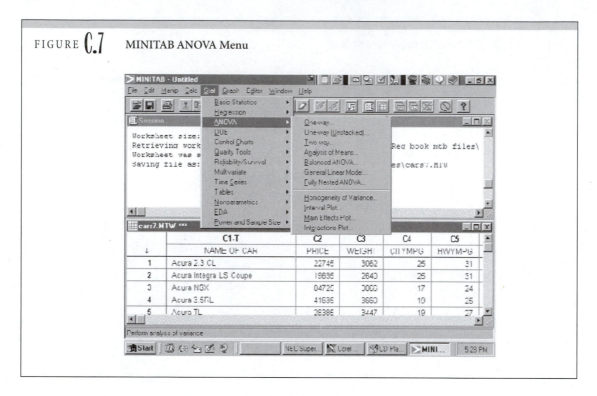

The ANOVA menu is shown in Figure C.7. One-way performs a one-way analysis of variance (ANOVA). This form of the command assumes that the data are in one column, and a second column is used to designate which group or sample each observation belongs to. One-way (Unstacked) also performs a one-way ANOVA but assumes the items in each sample are in separate columns. Two-way performs a two-way ANOVA. Main Effects Plot and Interactions Plot provide useful graphs for two-way analysis of variance. The other items on this menu were not discussed in this text.

The Multivariate menu is shown in Figure C.8. Discriminant Analysis provides a way of examining the relationship between a qualitative dependent variable and one or more quantitative independent variables. The other items on this menu were not discussed in this text.

The Time Series menu is shown in Figure C.9. Time Series Plot produces a graph of a variable or variables over time (also available on the Plot menu). Trend Analysis provides for the fitting of a variety of trends to data. As shown in this text, the fitting of these trends to data can also be accomplished through the use of Regression. Lag allows for the creation of lagged variables. The other items on this menu were not discussed in this text.

FIGURE **C.8**   **MINITAB Multivariate Menu**

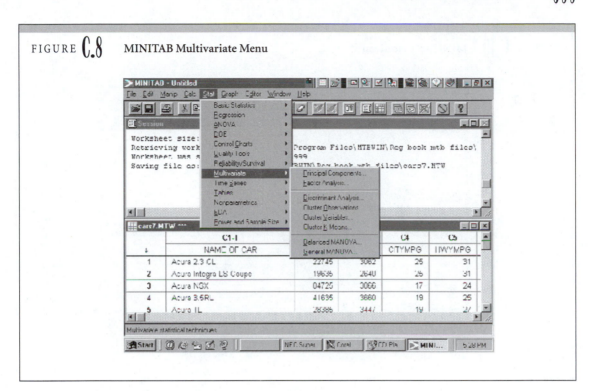

FIGURE **C.9**   **MINITAB Time Series Menu**

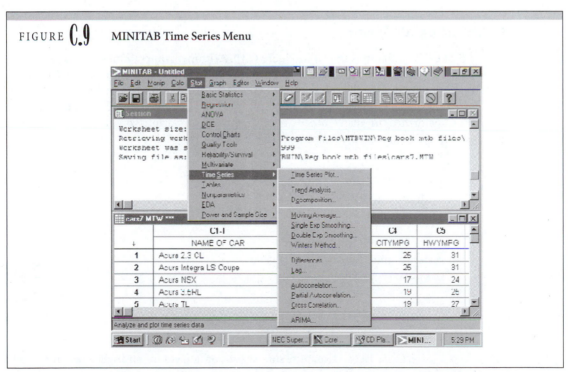

FIGURE **C.10** MINITAB Calc Menu

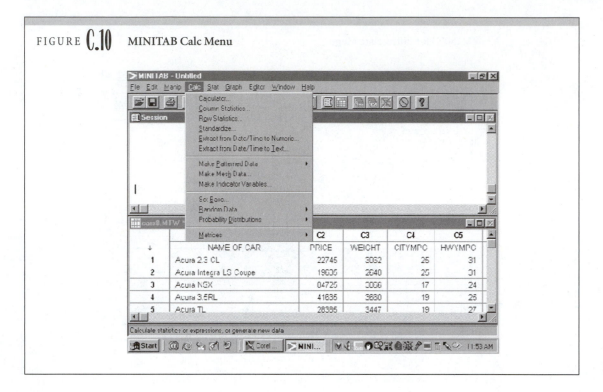

C.2.3 The Calc Menu

The CALC menu is shown in Figure C.10. Arithmetic operations may be performed on the columns. This is accomplished through the use of the Calculator (see figure C.11). By placing the column for the result in "Store result in variable" and a mathematical expression in "Expression," columns can be added, subtracted, divided, and transformed in many other ways. Examples of various operations available in MINITAB and the symbols used to denote them are:

Addition	+
Subtraction	−
Multiplication	*
Division	/
Exponentiation	**

A variety of functions are also available:

ABSOLUTE	Compute absolute value
SQRT	Compute square root
LOGE	Compute logarithm to base e
LOGTEN	Compute logarithm to base 10
SIN, COS, TAN	Compute sine, cosine, or tangent for an angle given in radians

FIGURE **C.11**   MINITAB Calculator

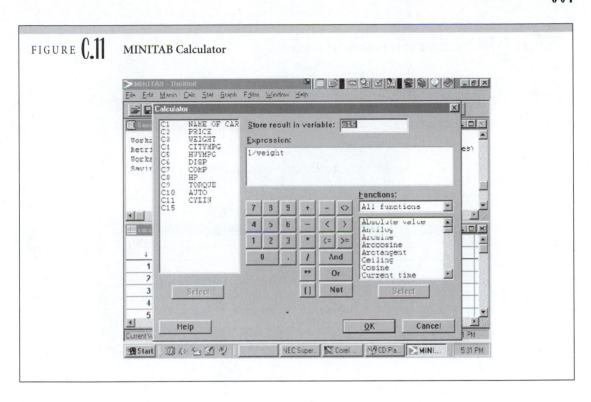

Figure C.11 shows the operation that finds the inverse of the variable weight and stores the result in c15.

Make Patterned Data (see Figure C.12) is useful when creating variables where the data take on certain regular patterns. The creation of a time trend variable (see Figure C.13) and other patterned variables is explained more fully in Using the Computer sections throughout the text. Make Indicator Variables is another useful procedure that is explained more fully in the text. The remaining procedures on the Calc menu are not used in this text.

FIGURE **C.12**   **MINITAB Make Patterned Data Menu**

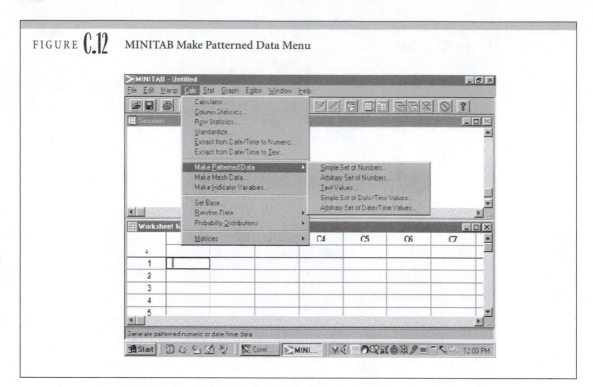

FIGURE **C.13**   **Creating a MINITAB Time Trend Variable**

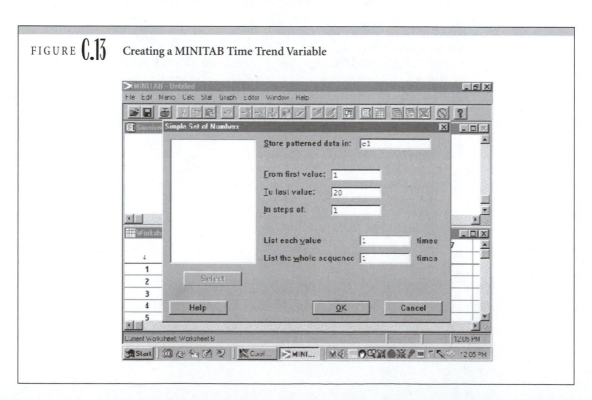

FIGURE  **C.14** Excel File Menu

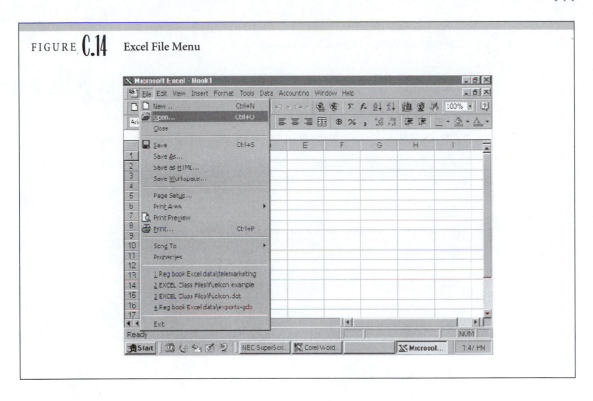

C.3 EXCEL

C.3.1 Data Input

Data that have been stored in an Excel spreadsheet can be accessed through the File menu. Figure C.14 shows the contents of the File menu. Click on Open and a dialog box opens requesting the name of the spreadsheet you want to open, as shown in Figure C.15. If you highlight cars8 and click on Open, the cars8 spreadsheet opens, as shown in Figure C.16. Once you open the spreadsheet, you can begin to analyze the data.

If you have data of your own to analyze and you want to put the data into an Excel spreadsheet, you can just begin typing. For statistical analysis, columns typically serve as variables, so you can assign a name to each of the variables (columns) used (although the use of columns as variables is not required in Excel).

Certain Excel procedures that may be useful for data manipulation and analysis are discussed next.

FIGURE **C.15**   Excel Request for Spreadsheet to Be Opened

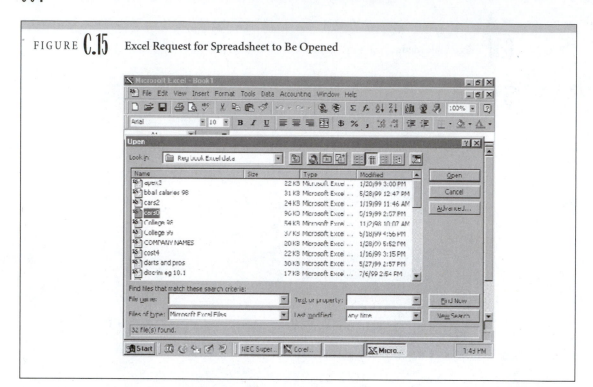

FIGURE **C.16**   Data File cars8 Opened As Excel Spreadsheet

FIGURE **C.17**   Excel's Chart Wizard

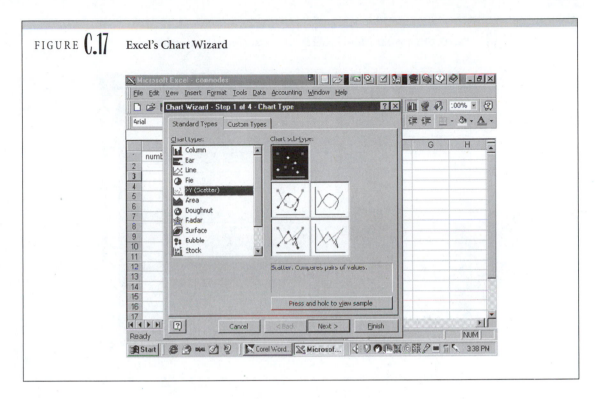

C.3.2 Excel's Chart Wizard

Scatterplots, time-series plots, pie charts, and bar charts are all constructed using the Chart Wizard. As an example, consider constructing a scatterplot. Click on Excel's Chart Wizard button and the Chart Wizard appears, as in Figure C.17. You have a variety of chart types from which to choose. In Figure C.17, the scatterplot (or XY plot) option has been chosen. The chart subtypes show you the different variations on the basic scatterplot. Choose the subtype that works best for your application. I like the plain old vanilla-flavored scatterplot, so that's the one I've highlighted. Click the Next button. Excel leads you through a series of screens that allow you to set up the scatterplot as you want it to appear. In Figure C.18, Excel is asking you to specify the data range and to indicate whether the data are arranged in rows or columns.

Note: To create a scatterplot in Excel, the variable you want to appear on the horizontal axis (the x axis) must be in a column directly to the left of the variable you want to appear on the vertical axis (the y axis).

In Figure C.19, the titles for the chart and the axis labels can be specified. (You can do this later if you want.) In Figure C.20, Excel allows you to place the chart on a separate sheet in the workbook or to put it on the current worksheet ply. Finally, Figure C.21 shows the completed scatterplot. You can size the chart and make changes to its appearance as you like.

FIGURE **C.18** Excel's Chart Wizard: Specifying the Data Range for a Scatterplot

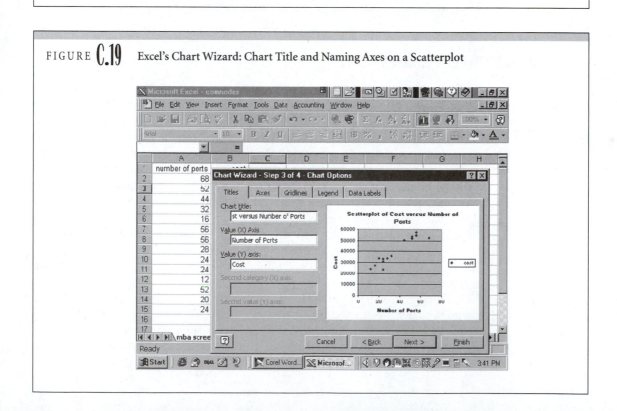

FIGURE **C.19** Excel's Chart Wizard: Chart Title and Naming Axes on a Scatterplot

FIGURE **C.20**   Excel's Chart Wizard: Choosing a Location for the Chart

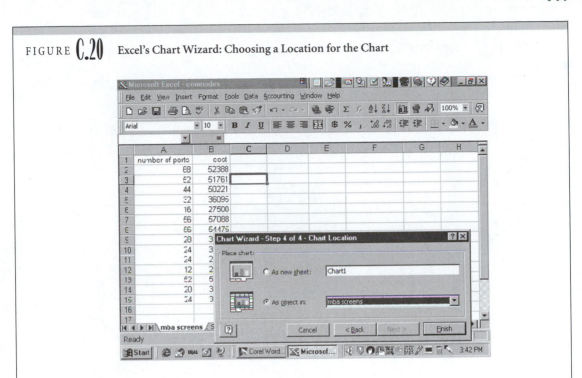

FIGURE **C.21**   Excel's Chart Wizard: The Completed Scatterplot

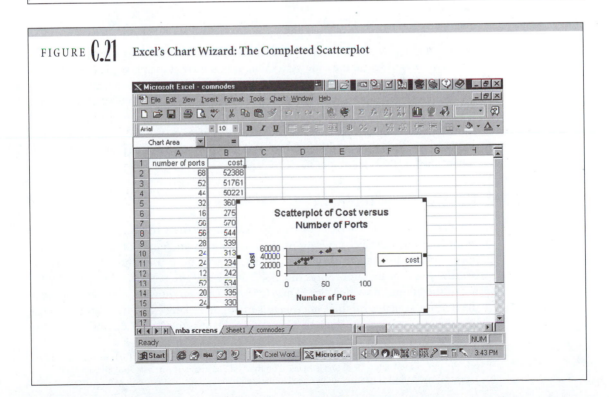

FIGURE **C.22**   Excel Data Analysis Option on Tools Menu

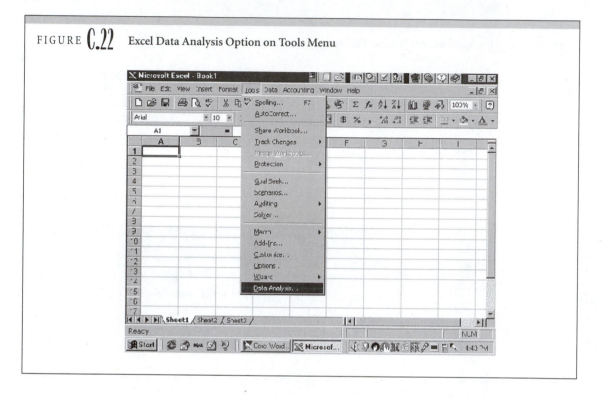

To construct a time-series plot with Excel, click on Excel's Chart Wizard button and highlight Line. Click the Next button. Excel leads you through a series of screens that allow you to set up the time-series plot as you want it to appear. The sequence of screens is similar to the sequence used in illustrating the creation of a scatterplot.

To construct a pie chart with Excel, click on Excel's Chart Wizard button and highlight Pie. Click the Next button. Excel leads you through a series of screens that allow you to set up the pie chart as you want it to appear. The sequence of screens is similar to the sequence used in illustrating the creation of a scatterplot. Bar charts are constructed in a similar manner.

C.3.3 Data Analysis Toolpack

The data analysis toolpack can be used to perform a variety of statistical analyses. Go to the Tools menu. Click on Data Analysis,[1] as shown in Figure C.22. You then see a list of options for statistical analysis of data. This menu is used throughout this text because many of the procedures discussed in the text are performed in Excel by the use of the options provided. See Figure C.23 for a screen showing a listing of some of the options available on the Data Analysis menu. Both single and two-factor ANOVA options are explained in the text. Correlation, Descriptive Statistics, and Histogram

---

[1] If Data Analysis does not appear on your Tools menu, click Add-Ins (also on the Tools menu) and make sure the square for Analysis Tool Box is checked on the Add-Ins menu. If Analysis Tool Box does not appear on your Add-Ins menu, you may need to reinstall Excel.

FIGURE **C.23**   **Excel Screen Showing Part of Data Analysis Menu**

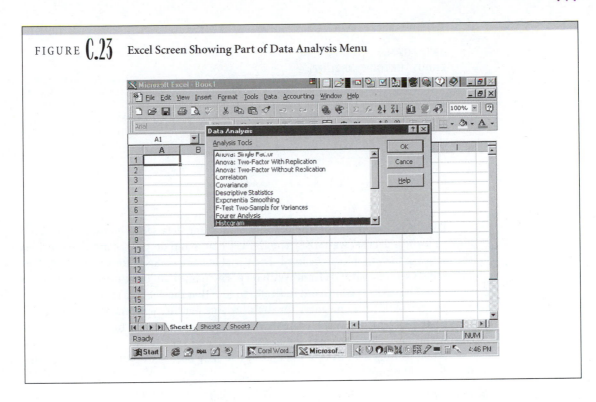

are all used. On the part of the menu that you cannot see in Figure C.23, there are options for Regression and Two-sample *t* tests that are used as well. To use any of these procedures, click on the desired option, click OK, and follow the instructions in the dialog box that appears.

C.4 SAS

C.4.1 Data Input

SAS analyses consist of at least two steps: (a) a DATA step to input the data set and create any new variables and (b) a PROC step to conduct any analyses.

Consider the following measurements of height and weight made on five people:

Height (in inches)	Weight (in pounds)
60	140
66	195
70	185
71	190
73	210

To input these data in SAS, the following lines are used:

```
DATA SIZE;
INPUT HEIGHT WEIGHT;
CARDS;

60    140

66    195

70    185

71    190

73    210
```

The DATA command on the first line names the data set to be used. The name chosen for this data set was SIZE. The INPUT command on the second line specifies the names of the variables to be used. The variable names chosen for the two variables in this data set were HEIGHT and WEIGHT. The names can be at most eight characters long. The CARDS command indicates to SAS that the data are to follow. The data are then typed in with one entry for each variable per line with each entry on a line separated by at least one space. Note that each command in SAS is followed by a semicolon. The data values, however, are not.

When reading data from a file that has already been set up, the following commands might be used:

```
DATA DIV;
INFILE DIV3.DAT;
INPUT DIVYIELD EPS;
```

The DATA line indicates the name assigned to the data set in SAS. The INFILE command indicates the file name from which the data are to be read. The INPUT line names the variables to be read. This form of the DATA step assumes the data are arranged in the file DIV3.DAT in two columns with the entries in each column separated by at least one space. These data were presented in Table 3.9 of the text. They represent the dividend yield and earnings per share for a sample of 46 firms.

C.4.2   Arithmetic with SAS Variables

During the DATA step in SAS, other variables can also be created. The following example illustrates some of the possible variables that might be of use in a SAS analysis:

```
DATA EXAMPLE;
INFILE EXAMPLE.DAT;
INPUT Y X1 X2 X3 X4;
X1SQR=X1**2;
X2INV=1/X2;
X3X4=X3*X4;
```

In this example, data on five variables were read in from a file called EXAMPLE.DAT. The variables were named Y, X1, X2, X3, and X4. Several new variables were then created during the data input. The variable X1SQR is the square of X1, the variable X2INV is the inverse of X2, and the variable X3X4 is the product of the two variables X3 and X4.

Examples of various arithmetic operations available in SAS and the symbols used to denote them are:

Addition	+
Subtraction	−
Multiplication	*
Division	/
Exponentiation	**

SAS can also be used to produce certain functions of variables. For example, to create a variable equal to the natural logarithm of X1, the following command could be used:

```
LOGX1 = LOG(X1)
```

A variable named LOGX1 has been created by finding the natural logarithm of the values of the original variable.

Other functions available in SAS include

ABS	Compute absolute value
SQRT	Compute square root
LOG10	Compute logarithm to base 10
SIN, COS, TAN	Compute sine, cosine, or tangent for an angle given in radians

These are used in the same manner as the LOG function.

C.4.3 Statistical Procedures in SAS

Statistical analyses of all types in SAS are performed in the PROC steps. PROC stands for "procedure," and each PROC statement in SAS specifies a certain procedure to be performed with the data. The following PROCS may be useful in data analysis.

```
PROC ANOVA;
CLASSES X1;
MODEL Y = X1;
```

performs a one-way analysis of variance. The dependent variable is listed first on the MODEL statement, and the variable used to specify the factor levels is indicated in the CLASSES statement and listed second on the MODEL statement.

```
PROC ANOVA;
CLASSES X1 X2;
MODEL Y = X1 X2 X1*X2;
```

performs a two-way analysis of variance. The dependent variable is listed first on the MODEL statement, and the variables used to specify the factor levels are indicated in the CLASSES statement and listed second on the MODEL statement. If an interaction term is desired, it is listed on the model statement as shown: X1*X2.

```
PROC CHART;
VBAR Y;
```

produces a bar chart for the variable named Y. PROC CHART should be used with discrete data.

```
PROC CORR;
VAR Y X1;
```

produces pairwise correlations for the variables Y and X1.

```
PROC FREQ;
TABLES Y;
```

produces a frequency distribution for the variable named Y. PROC FREQ should be used with discrete data.

```
PROC MEANS;
VAR Y;
```

produces the following summary statistics for the variable named Y: a count of the number of observations, the mean, standard deviation, minimum, maximum, and standard error of the mean.

```
PROC PLOT;
PLOT Y*X1 Y*X2 Y*X3 Y*X4;
```

produces a scatterplot of each indicated pair of variables with the first variable of each pair plotted on the vertical axis and the second variable on the horizontal axis.

```
PROC REG
MODEL Y = X1 X2 X3 X4/OPTIONS;
OUTPUT PREDICTED=FITS STUDENT=STRES;
```

performs a regression analysis. The MODEL statement specifies the Y variable (listed first) and the explanatory variables (X1, X2, X3, and X4 in this example). In place of OPTIONS on the MODEL statement, there a variety of choices. These include

DW to request the Durbin-Watson statistic.

VIF to request variance inflation factors.

INFLUENCE to request a variety of influence diagnostics.

P to request that predicted values be printed.

R to request that residuals be printed.

CLM prints 95% upper and lower confidence interval limits for the estimate of the point on the regression line (the estimate of the conditional mean) for each observation.

CLI prints 95% upper and lower prediction interval limits for the prediction of an individual point for each observation.

The OUTPUT statement can be used to create a variety of new variables. As shown earlier, the predicted or fitted values are saved in a variable named FITS, and the standardized residuals are saved in a variable named STRES.

```
PROC STEPWISE;
MODEL Y = X1 X2 X3 X4/OPTIONS;
```

performs a stepwise regression. In place of OPTIONS, there are a variety of choices. These include

FORWARD if forward selection is to be used.

BACKWARD if backward elimination is to be used.

STEPWISE if stepwise regression is to be used.

MAXR if the maximum R-squared improvement technique is to be used.

SLE= desired level of significance for entering a variable when using STEPWISE or FORWARD.

SLS= desired level of significance for deleting a variable when using STEPWISE or BACKWARD.

INCLUDE= variables to be included in all models.

```
PROC TTEST;
CLASS X1;
VAR X2;
```

produces a test for whether the difference between two population means is zero or not. The data from the two samples are in the variable X2. The variable X1 is used to indicate from which population the sample value was chosen.

```
PROC UNIVARIATE PLOT NORMAL;
VAR Y;
```

produces a variety of descriptive statistics for the variable named Y: the count of the number of observations, the mean, standard deviation, variance, standard error of the mean, coefficient of variation, measures of skewness and kurtosis, a t value for testing whether the population mean is zero, the minimum, maximum, quartiles, median, range, interquartile range, mode, 1st, 5th, 10th, 90th, 95th, and 99th percentiles, and the five largest and smallest values.

PLOT and NORMAL are options. If PLOT is specified, a stem and leaf plot, box plot, and a normal probability plot are produced. If NORMAL is specified, a test for whether the data came from a normal distribution is conducted.

APPENDIX D

Matrices and Their Application to Regression Analysis

D.1 INTRODUCTION

In Chapter 3, the equations were provided to compute b_0 and b_1, the least-squares estimates of the simple regression coefficients. When multiple regression was discussed in Chapter 4, no equations were shown for the coefficient estimates because of the complexity involved. Instead, the computer was used to solve for the estimates of the multiple regression coefficients. There is, however, a very general way to represent the equations for the estimates of the regression coefficients (either simple or multiple). This involves the use of matrices.

A *matrix* is a rectangular array of numbers. For example, the following are matrices:

$$\mathbf{A} = \begin{bmatrix} 5 & 7 & 3 \\ 4 & 2 & 6 \end{bmatrix} \quad \mathbf{B} = \begin{bmatrix} 2 & 4 \\ 1 & 5 \end{bmatrix} \quad \mathbf{C} = \begin{bmatrix} 7 \\ 4 \\ 6 \end{bmatrix}$$

The *dimensions* of a matrix are the number of its rows and columns. The matrix $\mathbf{A}$ has two rows and three columns, so $\mathbf{A}$ is referred to as a 2×3 matrix. Similarly, $\mathbf{B}$ is a 2×2 matrix and $\mathbf{C}$ is a 3×1 matrix. $\mathbf{B}$ is called a *square matrix* because it has equal numbers of rows and columns. The *diagonal elements* of a square matrix are the elements that are located on the diagonal that runs from the upper left-hand corner of the matrix to the lower right-hand corner. In the case of the matrix $\mathbf{B}$, the diagonal elements are 2 and 5. A matrix with only one column is usually referred to as a *vector*. In the previous example, the matrix $\mathbf{C}$ is a vector.

Certain arithmetic operations can be performed with matrices—addition, subtraction, and multiplication. Another operation of importance in working with matrices is determining the *transpose* of the matrix. Square matrices can also be inverted. In this appendix, each of these matrix operations is defined, and then the use of matrices to represent a regression equation and the computations necessary to produce the estimates of the regression coefficients are shown. This treatment is not intended to be complete by any means, but it may serve as a brief introduction to the matrix approach to regression analysis. For a more complete treatment using the matrix approach, see, for example, A. Hadi, *Matrix Algebra as a Tool*, or R. Myers, *Classical and Modern Regression with Applications*.[1]

D.2 MATRIX OPERATIONS

D.2.1 Matrix Addition

Two matrices can be added together if their dimensions are the same. Consider the following matrices denoted **A** and **B**:

$$\mathbf{A} = \begin{bmatrix} 3 & 6 & 1 \\ 3 & 4 & 6 \end{bmatrix} \quad \mathbf{B} = \begin{bmatrix} 2 & 4 & 2 \\ 4 & 5 & 4 \end{bmatrix}$$

The sum of these two matrices is **A** + **B**:

$$\mathbf{A} + \mathbf{B} = \begin{bmatrix} 3+2 & 6+4 & 1+2 \\ 3+4 & 4+5 & 6+4 \end{bmatrix} = \begin{bmatrix} 5 & 10 & 3 \\ 7 & 9 & 10 \end{bmatrix}$$

Note that the corresponding elements of the original matrices **A** and **B** have simply been added together to obtain the sum of the two matrices.

D.2.2 Transpose of a Matrix

The *transpose* of a matrix is formed by exchanging its rows and columns. For example, consider the matrix

$$\mathbf{A} = \begin{bmatrix} 3 & 6 & 1 \\ 3 & 4 & 6 \end{bmatrix}$$

The transpose of **A** (denoted $\mathbf{A}^T$) is

$$\mathbf{A}^T = \begin{bmatrix} 3 & 3 \\ 6 & 4 \\ 1 & 6 \end{bmatrix}$$

The rows of the matrix **A** have now become the columns of $\mathbf{A}^T$, and the columns of **A** have become the rows of $\mathbf{A}^T$.

---

[1] See References for complete publication information.

D.2.3 Matrix Multiplication

Consider the following two matrices:

$$A = \begin{bmatrix} 4 & 1 \\ 2 & 6 \end{bmatrix} \quad B = \begin{bmatrix} 3 & 2 & 4 \\ 1 & 4 & 5 \end{bmatrix}$$

The product, **AB**, of the two matrices is found by multiplying the elements of each row of **A** by the corresponding elements of each column of **B** and then summing the individual products. In this example,

$$AB = \begin{bmatrix} (4\times3+1\times1) & (4\times2+1\times4) & (4\times4+1\times5) \\ (2\times3+6\times1) & (2\times2+6\times4) & (2\times4+6\times5) \end{bmatrix}$$

$$= \begin{bmatrix} 13 & 12 & 21 \\ 12 & 28 & 38 \end{bmatrix}$$

To obtain the product matrix, **AB**, the first element in row 1 of **A** is multiplied by the first element in column 1 of **B**. Then the second element in row 1 of **A** is multiplied by the second element in column 1 of **B**. These two products are then added together to obtain the element in the first row and first column of **AB**. To obtain the element in the first row and second column of **AB**, the first element in row 1 of **A** is multiplied by the first element in column 2 of **B**. Then the second element in row 1 of **A** is multiplied by the second element in column 2 of **B**. This row-by-column multiplication process continues until all elements of the product matrix **AB** have been computed. For this process to work, the number of columns in **A** must equal the number of rows in **B**. In terms of the dimensions of the matrices, if **A** is an $m \times n$ matrix and **B** is a $p \times q$ matrix, n and p must be equal before the product matrix can be computed. The product matrix, **AB**, will be an $m \times q$ matrix. In this example, **A** is a 2×2 matrix, **B** is a 2×3 matrix, and the product matrix, **AB**, is a 2×3 matrix.

Consider another example. If

$$A = \begin{bmatrix} 5 & 7 & 3 \\ 4 & 2 & 6 \end{bmatrix} \quad \text{and} \quad B = \begin{bmatrix} 7 \\ 4 \\ 6 \end{bmatrix}$$

then

$$AB = \begin{bmatrix} 5\times7+7\times4+3\times6 \\ 4\times7+2\times4+6\times6 \end{bmatrix} = \begin{bmatrix} 81 \\ 72 \end{bmatrix}$$

D.2.4 Matrix Inversion

A familiar property of multiplication is that any number multiplied by its multiplicative inverse results in the answer 1. For example, $2 \times \frac{1}{2} = 1$, $3 \times \frac{1}{3} = 1$, and so on. Thus, $\frac{1}{2}$ is the multiplicative inverse of the number 2 and $\frac{1}{3}$ is the multiplicative inverse of 3. The inverse of a matrix A, denoted A^{-1}, is defined as the matrix that produces an identity matrix when multiplied by the original matrix:

$$AA^{-1} = I$$

where **I** is the identity matrix. An *identity matrix* is a matrix with 1s as diagonal elements and 0s everywhere else. For example, consider the matrix

$$\mathbf{A} = \begin{bmatrix} 4 & 2 \\ 5 & 3 \end{bmatrix}$$

The inverse of **A** is

$$\mathbf{A}^{-1} = \begin{bmatrix} 1.5 & -1 \\ -2.5 & 2 \end{bmatrix}$$

Multiplying **A** by **A**$^{-1}$ verifies that these two matrices are inverses:

$$\mathbf{AA}^{-1} = \begin{bmatrix} (4\times1.5+2\times(-2.5)) & (4\times(-1)+2\times2) \\ (5\times1.5+3\times(-2.5)) & (5\times(-1)+3\times2) \end{bmatrix}$$

$$= \begin{bmatrix} 1 & 0 \\ 0 & 1 \end{bmatrix}$$

The resulting product is an identity matrix, denoted **I**. It has the property that any square matrix of appropriate dimension multiplied by an identity matrix results in the original matrix. For example, it is easy to verify that **AI** = **A**. When working with numbers rather than matrices, the number 1 serves as the multiplicative identity. Thus, in matrix multiplication, the identity matrix serves the same purpose as the number 1.

Note that inverses can only be computed for square matrices. Any identity matrix **I** also must be a square matrix.

One method of finding the inverse of a matrix is demonstrated through the following example. Consider the matrix **A**:

$$\mathbf{A} = \begin{bmatrix} 4 & 2 \\ 5 & 3 \end{bmatrix} \qquad \mathbf{I} = \begin{bmatrix} 1 & 0 \\ 0 & 1 \end{bmatrix}$$

The identity matrix of the same dimension has been written next to **A**. A series of identical computations can now be performed on **A** and **I**. The intent of these computations is to transform **A** to an identity matrix. The same operations applied to **I** transform this identity matrix to the inverse of **A**, **A**$^{-1}$. There are two types of computations that are allowed:

1   Any row of **A** can be multiplied or divided by a number.
2   One row of **A** can be added to or subtracted from another row of **A**.

The computations to produce **A**$^{-1}$ are as follows:

Step 1: Because the goal is to transform **A** to an identity matrix, start by dividing the first row of **A** by the value of the element in the first row and first column (4). This results in 1 as the first diagonal element. Perform the identical computation on **I**; that is, divide the elements in the first row by 4.

$$\mathbf{A} = \begin{bmatrix} 1 & 0.5 \\ 5 & 3 \end{bmatrix} \qquad \mathbf{I} = \begin{bmatrix} 0.25 & 0 \\ 0 & 1 \end{bmatrix}$$

Step 2: Subtract 5 times row 1 from row 2; the result is 0 in the first element of this row. As always, do the same to **I**. Also note that row 1 is not actually changed in this computation. A multiple of row 1 is subtracted from row 2, producing a new row 2, but row 1 remains as it was originally:

$$\mathbf{A} = \begin{bmatrix} 1 & 0.5 \\ 0 & 0.5 \end{bmatrix} \quad \mathbf{I} = \begin{bmatrix} 0.25 & 0 \\ -1.25 & 1 \end{bmatrix}$$

Step 3: Multiply row 2 by 2. The result is 1 for the diagonal element in that row.

$$\mathbf{A} = \begin{bmatrix} 1 & 0.5 \\ 0 & 1 \end{bmatrix} \quad \mathbf{I} = \begin{bmatrix} 0.25 & 0 \\ -2.5 & 2 \end{bmatrix}$$

Step 4: Subtract 0.5 times row 2 from row 1 to eliminate the nondiagonal element.

$$\mathbf{A} = \begin{bmatrix} 1 & 0 \\ 0 & 1 \end{bmatrix} \quad \mathbf{I} = \begin{bmatrix} 1.5 & -1 \\ -2.5 & 2 \end{bmatrix}$$

The matrix **A** has now been transformed into an identity matrix. The inverse of **A** is

$$\mathbf{A}^{-1} = \begin{bmatrix} 1.5 & -1 \\ -2.5 & 2 \end{bmatrix}$$

D.3 MATRICES AND REGRESSION ANALYSIS

In Chapter 4, the multiple regression model was written as follows:

$$y_i = \beta_0 + \beta_1 x_{1i} + \beta_2 x_{2i} + \ldots + \beta_K x_{Ki} + e_i \qquad (D.1)$$

In matrix notation, the multiple regression model can be written:

$$\mathbf{Y} = \mathbf{X}\beta + \mathbf{e} \qquad (D.2)$$

where $\mathbf{Y}, \mathbf{X}, \beta$, and e are matrices defined as follows:

$$\mathbf{Y} = \begin{bmatrix} y_1 \\ y_2 \\ \vdots \\ y_n \end{bmatrix} \quad \mathbf{X} = \begin{bmatrix} 1 & x_{11} & x_{12} & \cdots & x_{1K} \\ 1 & x_{21} & x_{22} & \cdots & x_{2K} \\ \vdots & \vdots & \vdots & & \vdots \\ 1 & x_{n1} & x_{n2} & \cdots & x_{nK} \end{bmatrix}$$

$$\beta = \begin{bmatrix} \beta_0 \\ \beta_1 \\ \vdots \\ \beta_K \end{bmatrix} \quad \mathbf{e} = \begin{bmatrix} e_1 \\ e_2 \\ \vdots \\ e_n \end{bmatrix}$$

The matrix **Y** is an $n \times 1$ matrix containing all n observations on the dependent variable. These observations are denoted y_1, y_2, and so on, as in Chapter 4.

The matrix **X** is an $n \times (K + 1)$ matrix. The first column of the matrix **X** is a column of 1s. The second column of **X** consists of all n values of the first explanatory variable ($k = 1$) denoted $x_{11}, x_{21}, \ldots x_{n1}$. The third column of **X** consists of all n values of the second explanatory variable ($k = 2$) denoted, $x_{12}, x_{22}, \ldots x_{n2}$ and so on. The initial column of 1s in the **X** matrix is necessary because there is a constant (or intercept) in the equation. These 1s can be thought of as multipliers of β_0 just as the appropriate x values can be thought of as multipliers of β_k (k not equal to zero).

The matrix β is a $(K + 1) \times 1$ matrix containing all of the population regression coefficients to be estimated. These are denoted $\beta_0, \beta_1, \ldots, \beta_K$.

The matrix e is an $n \times 1$ matrix containing the disturbances $e_1, e_2, \ldots, e_n$.

Equation (D.2) represents the same relationship as equation (D.1) except in matrix form. This can be verified by actually performing the multiplication and addition of the matrices shown in equation (D.2).

Equation (D.2) is the general representation of any multiple regression model. As a specific example, consider again the data from Example 3.1:

x	1	2	3	4	5	6
y	3	2	8	8	11	13

The **X** and **Y** matrices for this example are as follows:

$$\mathbf{Y} = \begin{bmatrix} 3 \\ 2 \\ 8 \\ 8 \\ 11 \\ 13 \end{bmatrix} \quad \mathbf{X} = \begin{bmatrix} 1 & 1 \\ 1 & 2 \\ 1 & 3 \\ 1 & 4 \\ 1 & 5 \\ 1 & 6 \end{bmatrix}$$

The matrix β is

$$\beta = \begin{bmatrix} \beta_0 \\ \beta_1 \end{bmatrix}$$

and the matrix e is

$$\mathbf{e} = \begin{bmatrix} e_1 \\ e_2 \\ e_3 \\ e_4 \\ e_5 \\ e_6 \end{bmatrix}$$

(There are no actual numbers in e because the disturbances are not observable.)

As least-squares estimates of β_0 and β_1 in Chapter 3, those values b_0 and b_1 that minimized the error sum of squares (SSE) were used. SSE was written as

$$\sum_{i=1}^{n} (y_i - \hat{y}_i)^2$$

where the $\hat{y}_i$ were the points on the regression line determined by b_0 and b_1. In matrix notation, the equation for the error sum of squares can be written as

$$(\mathbf{Y} - \mathbf{Xb})^T (\mathbf{Y} - \mathbf{Xb})$$

where b is the matrix of estimated regression coefficients:

$$\mathbf{b} = \begin{bmatrix} b_0 \\ b_1 \end{bmatrix}$$

The equations representing the least-squares estimates of the regression coefficients is

$$\mathbf{b} = (\mathbf{X}^T\mathbf{X})^{-1}\mathbf{X}^T\mathbf{Y} \tag{D.3}$$

This equation represents the least-squares estimates of the regression coefficients in any simple or multiple regression. The matrices $\mathbf{b}$, $\mathbf{X}$, and $\mathbf{Y}$ just need to be defined appropriately. In the example used in this section, the least-squares estimates are found as follows:

$$\mathbf{X}^T = \begin{bmatrix} 1 & 1 & 1 & 1 & 1 & 1 \\ 1 & 2 & 3 & 4 & 5 & 6 \end{bmatrix}$$

$$\mathbf{X}^T\mathbf{X} = \begin{bmatrix} 1 & 1 & 1 & 1 & 1 & 1 \\ 1 & 2 & 3 & 4 & 5 & 6 \end{bmatrix} \begin{bmatrix} 1 & 1 \\ 1 & 2 \\ 1 & 3 \\ 1 & 4 \\ 1 & 5 \\ 1 & 6 \end{bmatrix} = \begin{bmatrix} 6 & 21 \\ 21 & 91 \end{bmatrix}$$

$$(\mathbf{X}^T\mathbf{X})^{-1} = \begin{bmatrix} \dfrac{91}{105} & \dfrac{-21}{105} \\ \dfrac{-21}{105} & \dfrac{6}{105} \end{bmatrix}$$

$$\mathbf{X}^T\mathbf{Y} = \begin{bmatrix} 1 & 1 & 1 & 1 & 1 & 1 \\ 1 & 2 & 3 & 4 & 5 & 6 \end{bmatrix} \begin{bmatrix} 3 \\ 2 \\ 8 \\ 8 \\ 11 \\ 13 \end{bmatrix} = \begin{bmatrix} 45 \\ 196 \end{bmatrix}$$

$$(\mathbf{X}^T\mathbf{X})^{-1}(\mathbf{X}^T\mathbf{Y}) = \begin{bmatrix} \dfrac{91}{105} & \dfrac{-21}{105} \\ \dfrac{-21}{105} & \dfrac{6}{105} \end{bmatrix} \begin{bmatrix} 45 \\ 196 \end{bmatrix} = \begin{bmatrix} 39 - 39.2 \\ -9 + 11.2 \end{bmatrix} = \begin{bmatrix} -0.2 \\ 2.2 \end{bmatrix}$$

The least-squares estimate of β is

$$\mathbf{b} = \begin{bmatrix} -0.2 \\ 2.2 \end{bmatrix}$$

Because

$$\mathbf{b} = \begin{bmatrix} b_0 \\ b_1 \end{bmatrix}$$

it is clear that the regression equation can be written

$$\hat{y} = -0.2 + 2.2x$$

as in Chapter 3.

Many of the other relationships discussed throughout this text also can be expressed in matrix form. Some of these are listed but not discussed in detail.

1 $\hat{\mathbf{Y}} = \mathbf{Xb}$ is the vector of predicted or fitted values.

2 $\mathbf{Y} - \hat{\mathbf{Y}}$ is the vector of residuals.

3 $(\mathbf{Y} - \hat{\mathbf{Y}})^T (\mathbf{Y} - \hat{\mathbf{Y}})$ is the error sum of squares (SSE). SSE can also be written as $\mathbf{Y}^T\mathbf{Y} - \mathbf{b}^T\mathbf{X}^T\mathbf{Y}$.

4 $\mathbf{b}^T \mathbf{X}^T \mathbf{Y} - n\bar{\mathbf{Y}}^2$ is the regression sum of squares.

5 The variances of the regression coefficients are the diagonal elements of the matrix $s_e^2 (\mathbf{X}^T \mathbf{X})^{-1}$.

6 The estimate of s_e^2 is $SSE/(n-K-1)$ with SSE as given in list item 3.

7 The variance of the estimate of a point on the regression line, denoted in Chapters 3 and 4 as s_m^2, is given by $s_m^2 = s_e^2 (x(\mathbf{X}^T\mathbf{X})^{-1}x^T)$, and the variance of the prediction for a single individual is $s_p^2 = s_e^2(1 + x(\mathbf{X}^T\mathbf{X})^{-1}x^T)$. The xs in these formulas represent the vectors of the values of the explanatory variables used to generate estimates or predictions.

EXERCISES

In Exercises 1 through 3, find the sum of the following matrices.

1 $\mathbf{A} = \begin{bmatrix} 1 & 3 & 4 \\ 2 & 1 & 2 \\ 3 & 1 & 5 \end{bmatrix}$ $\mathbf{B} = \begin{bmatrix} 4 & 1 & 6 \\ 2 & 1 & 5 \\ 1 & 4 & 3 \end{bmatrix}$

2 $\mathbf{A} = \begin{bmatrix} 1 & 2 \\ 7 & 6 \end{bmatrix}$ $\mathbf{B} = \begin{bmatrix} 4 & 5 \\ 1 & 9 \end{bmatrix}$

3 $\mathbf{A} = \begin{bmatrix} 1 \\ 3 \\ 2 \end{bmatrix}$ $\mathbf{B} = \begin{bmatrix} 6 \\ 1 \\ 5 \end{bmatrix}$

In Exercises 4 through 6, find the transpose of the following matrices.

4 $\mathbf{A} = \begin{bmatrix} 1 & 3 & 4 \\ 2 & 1 & 2 \\ 3 & 1 & 5 \end{bmatrix}$

5 $\mathbf{B} = \begin{bmatrix} 1 & 7 & 5 \\ 3 & 4 & 6 \end{bmatrix}$

6 $\mathbf{C} = \begin{bmatrix} 1 \\ 3 \\ 2 \end{bmatrix}$

In Exercises 7 through 10, find the product of the following matrices.

7 $\mathbf{A} = \begin{bmatrix} 1 & 2 \\ 7 & 6 \end{bmatrix}$ $\mathbf{B} = \begin{bmatrix} 4 & 5 \\ 1 & 9 \end{bmatrix}$

8. $\quad \mathbf{A} = \begin{bmatrix} 1 & 3 & 4 \\ 2 & 1 & 2 \\ 3 & 1 & 5 \end{bmatrix} \quad \mathbf{B} = \begin{bmatrix} 4 & 1 & 6 \\ 2 & 1 & 5 \\ 1 & 4 & 3 \end{bmatrix}$

9. $\quad \mathbf{A} = \begin{bmatrix} 1 & 7 & 5 \\ 3 & 4 & 6 \end{bmatrix}$ and $\mathbf{A}^T$

10. $\quad \mathbf{A} = \begin{bmatrix} 1 & 3 & 4 \\ 2 & 1 & 2 \\ 3 & 1 & 5 \end{bmatrix} \quad \mathbf{B} = \begin{bmatrix} 1 & 0 & 0 \\ 0 & 1 & 0 \\ 0 & 0 & 1 \end{bmatrix}$

In Exercises 11 and 12, compute the inverse of the following matrices.

11. $\quad \mathbf{A} = \begin{bmatrix} 1 & 2 \\ 4 & 6 \end{bmatrix}$

12. $\quad \mathbf{A} = \begin{bmatrix} 4 & 1 \\ 2 & 3 \end{bmatrix}$

In Exercises 13 through 16, use the following data:

x	y
1	5
2	6
4	9
5	10
6	14

13. Define the **X** and **Y** matrices that will be used to determine the least-squares estimates.

14. Find the least-squares estimate $\mathbf{b} = (\mathbf{X}^T\mathbf{X})^{-1}\mathbf{X}^T\mathbf{Y}$.

15. Find the standard error of the regression, s_e.

16. Find a 95% confidence interval estimate of β_1.

Solutions to Selected Odd-Numbered Exercises

E.1 CHAPTER 2

1   Mean of HWYMPG = 29.304
    Standard deviation of HWYMPG = 5.4727
    Median of HWYMPG = 29.000

3   $\mu = 3.5$ $\quad\quad\quad\quad$ $\sigma = 1.71$

    If the die was tossed a large number of times and the outcome recorded on each toss, the average of the numbers representing those outcomes would be close to 3.5.

5   $\mu = 7$ $\quad\quad\quad\quad$ $\sigma = 2.415$

7   a $\mu = 1.10$
    b $110.
    c 0.2

9   a 0.8413
    b 0.0228
    c 2103.25 (approximately 2103)

11 a $z = 2.0$
    b $z = 1.65$
    c $z = 2.33$
    d $z = 2.58$

13 $k = 84 - 2.06(7) = 69.58$

15 a 0.0228

b $1 - 0.6826 = 0.3174$

17 a 0.0228

b 0.0

19 0.5762

21 One way to approach this problem would be as follows. Suppose the average lifetime of the new hard drives has not changed so it is still 3250 hours. Are the data obtained consistent with this stated average lifetime? If so, then a sample mean of 3575 hours in a random sample of 50 hard drives should not be unusual. To measure how unusual this value is, find the probability of obtaining a sample mean of 3575 or more if the true average lifetime of the hard drives is 3250. If the mean lifetime of the hard drives has not changed, then the probability of finding a sample mean lifetime of 3575 hours or more in a random sample of 50 hard drives is 0.0. That is, there is virtually no chance that this should happen. But this is what we found. Therefore, we conclude that the mean lifetime of the hard drives must have changed and it must be larger than the previous mean of 3250 hours. This type of reasoning will be placed in a more structured setting in the section on hypothesis testing.

23 $(5.66, 6.34)$

25 $(28.383, 30.226)$

27 If a null hypothesis is rejected at the 5% level of significance, it would also be rejected at the 10% level of significance since the 10% level requires less "evidence" to reject the hypothesis than does the 5% level. In other words, a test statistic that is more extreme than the 5% critical value is also more extreme than the 10% critical value.

29 Critical value: $t(0.05,15) = 1.753$

Test Statistic: $t = 0.5$

Decision: Accept H_0; standards are being met.

31 Critical Value $t(0.05,59) = 1.645$ (z value)

Test Statistic: $t = -5.58$

Decision: Accept H_0; there is no evidence that the population average return is greater than that of the S&P 500 index (19.9%).

33 $(2.55, 5.45)$

35 $(-14.7, 0.7)$

37 Critical value: $z(.025) = 1.96$ is used since df is large.

Test Statistic: $z = 1.76$

Decision: Accept H_0; there is no difference in the population average test scores.

39 Critical value: $t(0.025,28) = 2.048$

Test Statistic: $t = 3.97$

Decision: Reject H_0; there is a difference in mean rating scores for the two divisions.

41 Critical value: $t(0.05,101) \approx 1.645$ (z value)

Test Statistic: $t = 6.98$

Decision: Reject H_0; average city mileage for cars with manual transmissions is higher than average city mileage for cars with automatic transmissions ($\mu_0 > \mu_1$)

43 a Critical value: $t(.025,21) = 2.080$

Test Statistic: $t = -0.09$

Decision: Accept H_0

b Conclusion: The population mean starting salaries for marketing and finance majors do not differ.

45 a Critical value: $t(0.05,51) \approx 1.645$ (z value)

Test Statistic: $t = -5.83$

Decision: Reject H_0

Based on the result of the test, the average starting salary for females appears to be less than the average for males.

b Statistical evidence alone may not be sufficient to prove discrimination. Often, it must also be shown that there was an intent to discriminate. However, when Harris Bank recognizes that a possible discriminatory situation exists, it should be concerned about correcting that situation.

c Later in the book, certain other variables are introduced into this problem; for example, education of the employee and years of experience. Variables such as these might have some sort of moderating effect on the result of the test reported in this problem and should be considered.

47 a 18.2%

b 25.0%

c No, since 130,000 is not a limit of one of the classes. You could only approximate this percentage.

d Between 80,000 and 89,999 (since the median represents the 50th percentile).

49 Based on the time series plot, management may want to reconsider their decision. The time series plot shows a pattern of increasing errors over time which may indicate that machine is experiencing wear and needs some type of maintenance. If the pattern continues, the subsequently drilled holes will not be of the correct diameter. Exercises 2.48 and 2.49 indicate the importance of using more than one type of graph, if appropriate, to examine data.

E.2 CHAPTER 3

1 b $b_1 = 0.9107$ $\qquad$ $b_0 = 7.1001$

3 a VALUE $= -50035 + 72.8$SIZE

b COST $= 16594 + 650$NUMPORTS

c STARTS $= 1688 - 18.2$RATES

5 a Critical value: $\qquad$ $t(0.025,8) = 2.306$

Test Statistic: $\qquad$ $t = 41.92$

Decision: $\qquad$ Reject H_0

b Yes. Hours of labor and number of items produced appear to be linearly related.

c Critical value: $\qquad$ $t(0.025,8) = 2.306$

Test Statistic: $\qquad$ $t = -0.61$

Decision: $\qquad$ Accept H_0

d The intercept of the line representing the relationship between number of items and labor is not significantly different from 0 (note: This test does not suggest anything about whether there is or is not a relationship between number of items and labor).

7 a Critical value: $\qquad$ $t(0.025,18) = 2.101$

Test Statistic: $\qquad$ $t = 10.70$

Decision: $\qquad$ Reject H_0

b Sales and advertising appear to be linearly related. (Caution: See section 3.7 in text. There may not be a *causal* relationship here.)

c SALES $= -57 + 17.6$ADV

d $(-941.29, 826.69)$

e $(14.12, 21.02)$

f Critical value: $\qquad$ $t(0.025, 18) = 2.101$

Test Statistic: $\qquad$ $t = -1.48$

Decision: $\qquad$ Accept H_0

g The slope of the regression line is not significantly different from 20.

9 a 0.9955

b 99.55%

c Critical value: $\qquad$ $F(0.05; 1,8) = 5.32$

Test Statistic: $\qquad$ $F = 1763.88$

Decision: $\qquad$ Reject H_0

d Yes. Hours of labor and number of items produced appear to be linearly related.

11   a   86.4%

     b $F(0.05; 1,18) = 4.41$

        Test Statistic: $F = 114.54$

        Decision: Reject H_0

13   a   119.4007

     b   (117.36, 121.45)

     c   119.4007

     d   (112.62, 126.18)

15   a   (4007,4663)   (in $100)

     b

x	Point Est.	95% Prediction Interval
20000	3457	2131, 4783
25000	4335	3043, 5627
30000	5214	3933, 6494
35000	6092	4800, 7384

        Note: Both point estimates and interval limits are in $100.

17   a   10503   ($1,050,300)

        Yes. The regression equation was developed using a range of values for the x variable (ADV) of 160 to 415. The value 600 is well outside this range. Caution should be exercised if this estimate is used, because the relationship between SALES and ADV has been observed only over the range 160 to 415. It is not known whether the same relationship will serve as well outside this range.

     b   Disagree. The model was developed over the range of 160 to 415 for the x variable (ADV). Because ADV = 0 is outside this range, the resulting forecasts cannot be depended upon to make sense. Still, the least squares method must choose a value as a y intercept. In this case, the intercept value that minimized the error sum of squares was –5700.

19   a   Critical value: $t(0.025,22) = 2.074$

        Test Statistic: $t = 8$

        Decision: Reject H_0

     b   Critical value: $F(0.10; 1,22) = 2.95$

        Test Statistic: $F = 64$

        Decision: Reject H_0

     c   0.744 or 74.4%

21   a   Critical value: $t(0.05, 91) \approx 1.645$ (z value)

        Test Statistic: $t = 4.31$

        Decision: Reject H_0

        Conclusion: There is a linear relationship between salary and education.

     b   17%

    c 5355

    d 5355

    e As will be seen when this problem is continued later in this text, other factors might include experience and, unfortunately in this case, whether the employee is male or female. You can probably think of other factors that might be useful.

23 a COST = 207 + 4.18MACHINE

    b 99.5%

    c Critical value: $t(0.025, 25) = 2.06$

       Test Statistic: $t = 69.05$

       Decision: Reject H_0; total cost and machine hours are linearly related.

    d Point estimate of the conditional mean of y given $x = 350$: 1669.44

    e Point estimate of the conditional mean of y given $x = 550$: 2505.20

E.3 CHAPTER 4

1 a COST = 51.7 + 0.948PAPER + 2.47MACHINE + 0.048OVERHEAD − 0.0506 LABOR

    b Critical value: $F(0.05; 4,22) = 2.82$

       Test Statistic: $F = 4629.17$

       Decision: Reject H_0

       Conclusion: At least one of the coefficients is not equal to 0. In other words, at least one of the variables is explaining a significant amount of the variation in y.

    c 2.47   2.47 ± (2.074)(0.4656)

    d Critical value: $t(0.025,22) = 2.074$

       Test Statistic: $t = -0.43$

       Decision: Accept H_0

       Conclusion: The true marginal cost of output associated with total production of paper is 1.

    e 99.9%

    f 99.9%

    g The regression equation can be used to identify factors that are related to cost. After doing this, these factors might be useful in reducing cost. For example, machine hours are related to cost. Obviously we cannot just start reducing machine hours, since these hours are part of the manufacturing process. But there may be a way to use the hours more efficiently, resulting in a reduction of overall hours without sacrificing production and a decrease in cost. The regression equation shows the influence of a one-unit reduction of the variables included on cost.

3 Critical value: $F(0.05; 2,22) = 3.44$

Test Statistic: $F = 0.8$

Decision: Accept H_0

Conclusion: Both coefficients are equal to 0. Neither OVERHEAD nor LABOR adds
significantly to the model's ability to explain the variation in COST.
Choose the REDUCED model.

5 a $RATES_i = 0.0342 + 0.993\ RATES_{i-1}$

b   Critical value: $t(0.025, 213) \approx 1.96$ (z value)

Test Statistic: $t = 144.45$

Decision: Reject H_0

c   99.0%

d   Forecasts for 1999 (using MINITAB):

Date	Fit	Stdev.Fit	95% C.I.	95% P.I.
1/99	6.7076	0.0323	(6.6439, 6.7713)	(6.1253, 7.2898)
2/99	6.6953	0.0324	(6.6314, 6.7591)	(6.1130, 7.2775)
3/99	6.6830	0.0324	(6.6191, 6.7470)	(6.1008, 7.2653)
4/99	6.6708	0.0325	(6.6067, 6.7349)	(6.0885, 7.2531)
5/99	6.6587	0.0326	(6.5945, 6.7229)	(6.0764, 7.2410)
6/99	6.6467	0.0326	(6.5824, 6.7110)	(6.0644, 7.2290)
7/99	6.6348	0.0327	(6.5703, 6.6992)	(6.0524, 7.2171)
8/99	6.6230	0.0328	(6.5584, 6.6876)	(6.0406, 7.2053)
9/99	6.6112	0.0328	(6.5465, 6.6760)	(6.0289, 7.1936)
10/99	6.5995	0.0329	(6.5347, 6.6644)	(6.0171, 7.1819)
11/99	6.5879	0.0330	(6.5229, 6.6529)	(6.0055, 7.1703)
12/99	6.5764	0.0330	(6.5113, 6.6415)	(5.9940, 7.1588)

Forecasts versus Actual Values:

Date	Forecast	Actual Value
1/99	6.7076	6.79
2/99	6.6953	6.81
3/99	6.6830	7.04
4/99	6.6708	6.92
5/99	6.6587	7.15
6/99	6.6467	7.55
7/99	6.6348	7.63
8/99	6.6230	7.94
9/99	6.6112	7.82
10/99	6.5995	7.85
11/99	6.5879	7.74
12/99	6.5764	7.91

One of the problems encountered when trying to produce forecasts for February or subsequent months is that the actual value in the previous month is not available at the end of 1998. One way around this problem is to use the forecast value for the previous month to generate the next month's forecast. To develop the 2/99 forecast, use 6.7076 as the value of the lagged variable. Then use the forecast for 2/99 as the value of the lagged variable to generate the forecast for 3/99, and so on. As forecasts are generated farther into the future, we expect them to be less accurate in part because we are using previous month's forecasts to develop forecasts for future months. But, until we know the true values, there is not much alternative.

e Critical value: $t(0.025, 213) \approx 1.96$ (z value)

   Test Statistic: $t = 0.46$

   Decision: Accept

f Critical value: $t(0.025, 213) \approx 1.96$ (z value)

   Test Statistic: $t = -1.01$

   Decision: Accept H_0

g From parts e and f, we cannot reject the hypotheses that the intercept of the equation is 0.0 and the slope is 1.0. This suggests that using the current mortgage rate to predict next month's rate might produce accurate forecasts. This is a simple forecasting model called the naive model that often produces forecasts that are as good (or better) than a more complicated model. The naive model is often used as a benchmark for more complex models. If the more complex model cannot do better (according to some criterion) than the naive model, then stick with the simpler model. The naive model often seems to do well with certain business and economic quantities such as interest rates and stock returns.

7 a $\text{DIVYIELD} = 0.157 + 0.216\text{EPS} + 0.00501\text{PRICE}$

  b 32.6%

  c Critical value: $F(0.10; 2,43) \approx 2.44$ (approximate)

    Test Statistic: $F = 10.40$

    Decision: Reject H_0

  d The coefficients are not both equal to 0. In other words, at least one of the variables is explaining a significant amount of the variation in y.

E.4 CHAPTER 5

1 Model Summaries:

	R^2	R^2 adjusted	s_e
Linear Model	99.2	99.0	14.34
Second-Order Model	100.0	99.9	3.538

The second-order model appears better than the first order model. The p value on the second-order term is 0.000, so the second-order term is significant at any reasonable level of significance. The adjusted R-square is higher and the standard error is lower. The R-square on the second-order model is stated as 100%. Note that not all of the variance in the y variable is explained, but the R-square rounds off to 100%.

3 Model Summaries:

	R^2	R^2 adjusted	s_e
Linear Model	91.9	91.0	0.2280
Inverse Production	95.5	95.0	0.1694

The Inverse Production model appears to be an improvement.

5 Model Summaries:

	R^2	R^2 adjusted	s_e
Linear Model	95.1	94.8	68.41
Second-Order Model	99.8	99.7	15.14

The second-order model appears better than the first-order model. The p value on the second-order term (NUMBER is squared) is 0.000, so the second-order term is significant at any reasonable level of significance. The adjusted R-square is higher and the standard error is lower. Note that the experience variable appears to be unnecessary in the model and could be omitted.

E.5 CHAPTER 6

1 a Yes. It is not, however, a linear relationship.

b $\hat{y} = 10.0$

c Critical value: $t(0.005,9) = 3.25$

   Test Statistic: $t = 0.0$

   Decision: Accept H_0

   Conclusion: There is no *linear* relationship between y and x.

d There is a "strong" association. In fact, this is an exact relationship, but not a linear one. The equation expressing the relationship is $y = x^2$

3 There is evidence that the constant variance assumption has been violated. The cone-shaped pattern that is typical of instances when this assumption is violated is evident in the residual plots. One possible correction would be to use the log of the monthly prices as the dependent variable.

5 Critical values for DW test: 1.24 and 1.56

   Test Statistic: $d = 2.14$

   Decision: Accept H_0

   Conclusion: The disturbances are NOT autocorrelated.

7 The linearity assumption appears to be violated. From the pattern in the residual plots, it appears that the variable SENIOR should enter in a curvilinear manner. Examining the scatterplot of ABSENT versus SENIOR suggests that a curvilinear inverse relationship might provide an improved model.

9 Critical values for DW test: 1.10 and 1.54

Test Statistic: $d = 1.69$

Decision: Accept H_0

Conclusion: The disturbances are not autocorrelated. No correction is necessary.

11 From the residual plots, it is clear that an assumption has been violated. In this case it is the linearity assumption. To correct for the violation, logs of the dependent variable, VALUE, and two of the independent variables, CONDITION and SIZE are used. In the revised regression, the variable DEPRECIATION is not significant. The final model is obtained by deleting this variable.

13 *VOLUME* is important in explaining the number of accidents, although it explains only 16.4% of the variance. From the residual plots, two observations stand out as unusual in the *y* direction. These are observations 30 and 31. Both of these intersections have more accidents than would be expected given their volume of traffic. The city may want to investigate whether measures could be taken to make these intersections safer (install lights, remove obstructions, etc).

15 a Outliers will be indicated by the presence of large standardized residuals. The cutoff for large is somewhat arbitrary, but typically a cutoff of ± 2 is used.

   b Deletion of an outlier should be the last course of action, unless the observation can be shown to differ in some way that makes its inclusion in the analysis unnecessary or unwanted. The first course of action should always be to check the outlier to be sure data values have been coded correctly.

E.6 CHAPTER 7

1 a Critical value: $F(0.05; 4, 88) \approx 2.53$ (approximate)

   Test Statistic: $F = 22.98$

   Decision: Reject H_0

   b At least one of the coefficients is not equal to 0. At least one of the four explanatory variables is important in explaining the variation in SALARY.

   c Critical value: $t(0.025, 88) \approx 1.96$ (z value)

   Test Statistic: $t = 6.13$

   Decision: Reject H_0

   d YES. There is a difference in salaries, on average, for male and female workers after accounting for the effects of the EDUC, EXPER, and MONTHS variables. Males' salaries are, on average, $722 higher, a statistically significant difference.

e Forecast of average salary for males with 12 years education, 10 years of experience and with time equal to 15: SALARY = 3526 + 722 + 90(12) + 1.27(10) + 23.4(15) = 5691.7

Forecast of average salary for females with 12 years education, 10 years of experience and with time equal to 15: SALARY = 3526 + 90(12) + 1.27(10) + 23.4(15) = 4969.7

3 a R-square adjusted = 49.4% with interaction variable.

R-square adjusted = 48.9% without interaction variable.

Although the full model has a higher adjusted R-square value, the difference is very small. It is unclear from the adjusted R-square alone whether the interaction variable is necessary. The hypothesis test in part b results in the conclusion that it is not.

b Critical value: $t(0.025,87) \approx 1.96$ (z value)

Test Statistic: $t = -1.42$

Decision: Accept H_0

c The interaction term is not important in this regression model. Choose the REDUCED model.

d From the test results, it appears that the interaction term is not useful in explaining the difference in average salaries.

5 a Critical value: $F(0.05;11,141) \approx 1.91$ (approximate)

Test Statistic: $F = 55.65$

Decision: Reject H_0; there is seasonal variation in furniture sales.

b Critical value: $t(0.025,141) \approx 1.96$ (z value)

Test Statistic: $t = 2.82$ for the trend coefficient

Decision: Reject H_0 ; the trend variable is important.

Test Statistic: $t = 21.85$ for the coefficient of the lagged variable

Decision: Reject H_0 ; the lagged variable is important.

c Month   Forecast

Month	Forecast
January	413 + 1.23(156) + 0.888(4257) − 664 = 3721.1
February	413 + 1.23(157) + 0.888(3721.1) − 286 = 3624.4
March	413 + 1.23(158) + 0.888(3624.4) + 47.3 = 3873.1
April	413 + 1.23(159) + 0.888(3873.1) − 294 = 3743.9
May	413 + 1.23(160) + 0.888(3743.9) − 83.2 = 3851.2
June	413 + 1.23(161) + 0.888(3851.2) − 232 = 3798.9
July	413 + 1.23(162) + 0.888(3798.9) − 190 = 3795.7
August	413 + 1.23(163) + 0.888(3795.7) − 111 = 3873.1
September	413 + 1.23(164) + 0.888(3873.1) − 273 = 3781.0
October	413 + 1.23(165) + 0.888(3781.0) − 127 = 3846.5
November	413 + 1.23(166) + 0.888(3846.5) − 9.4 = 4023.5
December	413 + 1.23(167) + 0.888(4023.5) = 4191.3

E.7 CHAPTER 8

1   a   COST = 59.43 + 0.95 PAPER + 2.39 MACHINE

b   99.87%

c   R-square adjusted = 99.86%

d $s_e = 11.0$

e   OVERHEAD and LABOR

Overhead and labor are related to COST (when examined individually). However, they add little to the ability of the equation to explain the variation in COST. The variables PAPER and MACHINE explain over 99% of the variation in COST. Due to the high correlation between these two variables and OVERHEAD and LABOR, the problem of multicollinearity discussed in Chapter 6 is present. The variables OVERHEAD and LABOR appear unrelated to COST in the equation since they are highly correlated with PAPER and MACHINE. OVERHEAD and LABOR are probably unnecessary since most of the variation in COST is explained by the other two variables.

E.8 CHAPTER 9

1   Critical value: $F(0.05;8,103) \approx 2.02$ (approximate)

Test Statistic: $F = 14.82$

Decision: Reject H_0

Conclusion: There is a difference in the average number of collisions for different types of cars.

3   *First test for interaction effects.*

Critical value: $F(0.05;6,12) = 3.00$

Test Statistic: $F = 0.20$

Decision: Accept H_0

Conclusion: There are no interaction effects. Note that this means that the F-tests for main effects can be used.

Test for main effects due to industry.

Critical value: $F(0.05;3,12) = 3.49$

Test Statistic: $F = 49.82$

Decision: Reject H_0

Conclusion: There are differences in treatment means associated with different industries.

Test for main effects due to contact.

Critical value: $F(0.05;2,12) = 3.89$

Test Statistic: $F = 0.03$

Decision: Accept H_0

Conclusion: There are no differences in treatment means associated with different contacts.

5 Critical value: $F(0.05;2,15) = 3.68$

Test Statistic: $F = 102.32$

Decision: Reject H_0

Conclusion: There is a difference in the average production rates.

7 Critical value: $F(0.05;2,4) = 6.94$

Test Statistic: $F = 103.32$

Decision: Reject H_0

Conclusion: There is a difference in the average test scores due to training program.

95% confidence interval estimate of the difference between program 1 and program 2 means:

$$(-16.96, -10.38)$$

9 Critical value: $F(0.05;6,49) \approx 2.34$ (approximate)

Test Statistic: $F = 29.21$

Decision: Reject H_0

Conclusion: There is a difference in the average sales on different days of the week.

 # CHAPTER 10

1 a   The TEST1 variable appears to be useful, while the TEST2 variable does not. This can be confirmed through testing whether the coefficients of these variables are equal to zero, just as in linear regression.

Critical value: $z(0.025) = 1.96$

Test Statistic: $Z = 3.06$ for TEST 1

Decision: Reject H_0

Conclusion: TEST 1 is useful.

Test Statistic: $Z = 1.62$ for TEST2

Decision: Accept H_0

Conclusion: TEST2 is NOT useful.

b Using only the equation with TEST1

1. $-43.37 + 0.4897(94) = 2.6618$ probability $= 0.93$

2. $-43.37 + 0.4897(80) = -4.194$ probability $= 0.01$

3. $-43.37 + 0.4897(82) = -3.2146$ probability $= 0.04$

4. $-43.37 + 0.4897(90) = 0.703$ probability $= 0.67$

Potential employees 1 and 4 would be classified in the "success" group, while numbers 2 and 3 would not.

References

Albright, S., Winston, W., and Zappe, C. *Data Analysis and Decision Making with Microsoft® Excel*. Pacific Grove, CA: Duxbury Press, 1999.

Amemiya, T. and Powell, J. "A Comparison of the Logit Model and Normal Discriminant Analysis When Independent Variables are Binary." Technical Report No. 320, Institute for Mathematical Studies in the Social Sciences, Encina Hall, Stanford University, Stanford, CA.

Berk, K. and Carey, P. *Data Analysis with Microsoft® Excel*. Pacific Grove, CA: Duxbury Press, 2000.

Bessler, D. and Babubla, R. "Forecasting Wheat Exports: Do Exchange Rates Really Matter?" *Journal of Business and Economic Statistics* 5(1987): 397–406.

Bowerman, B. and O,Connell, R. *Forecasting and Time Series: An Applied Approach.* (3rd ed.) Pacific Grove, CA: Duxbury Press, 1993.

Brightman, H. *Data Analysis in Plain English with Excel*. Pacific Grove, CA: Duxbury Press, 1999.

Carver, R. *Doing Data Analysis with MINITAB 12*. Pacific Grove, CA: Duxbury Press, 1999.

Conway, D. and Roberts, H. "Regression Analyses in Employment Discrimination Cases". *Statistics and the Law*. New York, NY: Wiley, 1986.

Cravens, D., Woodruff, R., and Stamper, J. "An Analytical Approach for Evaluating Sales Territory Performance.. *Journal of Marketing* 36(1972): 31–37.

Freund, R. and Littell, R. *SAS® System for Regression* (2nd ed.). Cary, NC: SAS Institute, 1991.

Graybill, F. and Iyer, H. *Regression Analysis: Concepts and Applications*. Pacific Grove, CA: Duxbury Press, 1994.

Griffiths, W. and Surekha, K. "A Monte Carlo evaluation of the power of some tests for heteroscedasticity." *Journal of Econometrics* 31(1986): 219–231.

Hadi, A. *Matrix Algebra as a Tool*. Pacific Grove, CA: Duxbury Press, 1996.

Hildebrand, D. and Ott, R. *Statistical Thinking for Managers* (4th ed.). Pacific Grove, CA: Duxbury Press, 1998.

Judge, G., Griffiths, W., Hill, R., Lutkepohl, H., and Lee, T. *The Theory and Practice of Econometrics* (2nd ed.). New York, NY: Wiley, 1985.

Keller, G. and Warrack, B. *Statistics for Management and Economics* (5th ed.). Pacific Grove, CA: Duxbury Press, 2000.

Kleinbaum, D., Kupper, L., Muller, K., and Nizam, A. *Applied Regression Analysis and Other Multivariable Methods* (3rd ed.). Pacific Grove, CA: Duxbury Press, 1998.

Lawrence, K. and Marsh, L. "Robust Ridge Estimation Methods for Predicting U.S. Coal Mining Fatalities. *Communications in Statistics* 13 (1984): 139–149.

Lee, C. and Lynge, M. "Return, risk, and cost of equity for stock S&L firms: Theory and empirical results". *Journal of the American Real Estate and Urban Economics Association* 13(1985): 167–180.

Lehmann, M. and Zeitz, P. *Statistical Explorations with Microsoft® Excel.* Pacific Grove, CA: Duxbury Press, 1998.

Lunneborg, C. *Modeling Experimental and Observational Data.* Pacific Grove, CA: Duxbury Press, 1994.

Mendenhall, W., Reinmuth, J., and Beaver, R. *Statistics for Management and Economics.* (7th ed.) Pacific Grove, CA: Duxbury Press, 1993.

Meyers, R. *Classical and Modern Regression with Applications* (2nd ed.). Boston, MA: PWS-Kent Publishing Co., 1990.

MINITAB™ User's Guide, Release 12 for Windows. State College, PA: Minitab, Inc., February 1998.

Moser, B. and Stevens, G. "Homogeneity of Variance in the Two-Sample Means Test." *The American Statistician* 46 (1992): 19–21.

Neter, J., Wasserman, W., and Kutner, M. *Applied Linear Statistical Models* (2nd ed.). Homewood, IL: Richard D. Irwin, Inc., 1985.

Neufeld, J. *Learning Business Statistics with Microsoft®639 Excel.* Upper Saddle River, NJ: Prentice Hall, 1997.

Peixoto, J. "A Property of Well Formulated Polynomial Regression Models." *The American Statistician* 44 (1990): 26–30.

Ragsdale, C. and Stam, A. "Introducing Discriminant Analysis to the Business Statistics Curriculum." *Decision Sciences* 23 (1992): 724–745.

Schafer, D. "Measurement-Error Diagnostics and the Sex Discrimination Problem." *Journal of Business and Economic Statistics* 5 (1987): 529–537.

Shapiro, S. and Wilk, M. "An analysis of variance test for normality (complete samples)." *Biometrika* 52 (1965): 591–611.

Shiffler, R. and Adams, A. *Introductory Business Statistics with Computer Applications.* (2nd ed.). Pacific Grove, CA: Duxbury Press, 1995.

Index